GREENLAND

NOVAYA
ZEMLYA

ICELAND

MURMANSK

NORWAY

SWEDEN

MOSCOW

BRITISH
IS

NEWFOUNDLAND

BERLIN

PLOESTI

NORTH ATLANTIC

OCEAN

AZORES
IS

SPAIN

ITALY

TUNIS

CANARY
IS

CAIRO

EGYPT

INDIA
KARACHI

RTO
CO

C VERDE
IS

DAKAR

AFRICA

AMERICA

ASCENSIÓN

INDIAN OCEAN

BRAZIL

N
W E
S

Volume Seven

SERVICES AROUND THE WORLD

THE ARMY AIR FORCES

In World War II

PREPARED UNDER THE EDITORSHIP OF

WESLEY FRANK CRAVEN
Princeton University

JAMES LEA CATE
University of Chicago

New Imprint by the
Office of Air Force History
Washington, D.C., 1983

For sale by the Superintendent of Documents, U.S. Government Printing Office
Washington, D.C. 20402

Library of Congress Number: 48–3657

THE UNIVERSITY OF CHICAGO PRESS, CHICAGO 37

Cambridge University Press, London, N.W. 1, England
The University of Toronto Press, Toronto 5, Canada

Library of Congress Cataloging in Publication Data
Main entry under title:

The Army Air Forces in World War II.

Vol. 1 originally prepared by the Office of Air Force
History; v. 2, by the Air Historical Group; and v. 3–7,
by the USAF Historical Division.

Reprint. Originally published: Chicago: University
of Chicago Press, 1948–1958.

Includes bibliographical references and indexes.

Contents: v. 1. Plans and early operations, January
1939 to August 1942—v. 2. Europe, torch to point-
blank, August 1942 to December 1943—[etc.]—v. 7.
Services around the world.

1. World War, 1939–1945—Aerial operations,
American. 2. United States. Army Air Forces—
History—World War, 1939–1945. I. Craven, Wesley
Frank, 1905–   . II. Cate, James Lea, 1899–   .
III. United States. Air Force. Office of Air Force
History. IV. United States. Air Force. Air Historical
Group. V. United States. USAF Historical Division.
D790.A89 1983   940.54′4973   83–17288
ISBN O–912799–03–X (v. 1)

FOREWORD
to the New
Imprint

I N March 1942, President Franklin D. Roosevelt wrote to the Director of the Bureau of the Budget ordering each war agency to prepare "an accurate and objective account" of that agency's war experience. Soon after, the Army Air Forces began hiring professional historians so that its history could, in the words of Brigadier General Laurence Kuter, "be recorded while it is hot and that personnel be selected and an agency set up for a clear historian's job without axe to grind or defense to prepare." An Historical Division was established in Headquarters Army Air Forces under Air Intelligence, in September 1942, and the modern Air Force historical program began.

With the end of the war, Headquarters approved a plan for writing and publishing a seven-volume history. In December 1945, Lieutenant General Ira C. Eaker, Deputy Commander of Army Air Forces, asked the Chancellor of the University of Chicago to "assume the responsibility for the publication" of the history, stressing that it must "meet the highest academic standards." Lieutenant Colonel Wesley Frank Craven of New York University and Major James Lea Cate of the University of Chicago, both of whom had been assigned to the historical program, were selected to be editors of the volumes. Between 1948 and 1958 seven were published. With publication of the last, the editors wrote that the Air Force had "fulfilled in letter and spirit" the promise of access to documents and complete freedom of historical interpretation. Like all history, *The Army Air Forces in World War II* reflects the era when it was conceived, researched, and written. The strategic bombing campaigns received the primary emphasis, not only because of a widely-shared belief in bombardment's contribution to victory, but also because of its importance in establishing the United States Air Force as a military service independent of the Army. The huge investment of men and machines and the effectiveness of the combined Anglo-American bomber offensive against Germany had not been subjected to the critical scrutiny they have since received. Nor, given the personalities involved and the immediacy of the events, did the authors question some of the command arrangements. In the tactical area, to give another example, the authors did not doubt the effect of aerial interdiction on both the German withdrawal from Sicily and the allied landings at Anzio.

Editors Craven and Cate insisted that the volumes present the war through the eyes of the major commanders, and be based on information available to them as important decisions were made. At the time, secrecy still shrouded the Allied code-breaking effort. While the link between decoded message traffic and combat action occasionally emerges from these pages, the authors lacked the knowledge to portray adequately the intelligence aspects of many operations, such as the interdiction in 1943 of Axis supply lines to Tunisia and the systematic bombardment, beginning in 1944, of the German oil industry.

All historical works a generation old suffer such limitations. New information and altered perspective inevitably change the emphasis of an historical account. Some accounts in these volumes have been superseded by subsequent research and other portions will be superseded in the future. However, these books met the highest of contemporary professional standards of quality and comprehensiveness. They contain information and experience that are of great value to the Air Force today and to the public. Together they are the only comprehensive discussion of Army Air Forces activity in the largest air war this nation has ever waged. Until we summon the resources to take a fresh, comprehensive look at the Army Air Forces' experience in World War II, these seven volumes will continue to serve us as well for the next quarter century as they have for the last.

RICHARD H. KOHN
Chief, Office of Air Force History

FOREWORD

THIS is the seventh and final volume of *The Army Air Forces in World War II*. The first five volumes told the story of combat operations in the several theaters; the sixth described the means by which men were recruited and trained and machines were provided to insure victory in those operations. The present volume deals with certain services which were common to the whole of the Army Air Forces. In part, these were the non–Air Corps organizations which in the AAF were subsumed under the ambiguous designation of "Arms and Services," but the Table of Contents will show both additions and deletions from that AGO listing. There is, inevitably, some repetition, for the services herein described were so inextricably a part of air combat that they have received, it is hoped, due attention in the account of each air campaign. There, however, the focus was on the activities of the tactical units comprising the theater air force; here it is upon the services as each in its unique way contributed to the fulfilment of the AAF mission. But there is some merit in telling the story from the point of view of the various service organizations, not only to give a unified account of the accomplishments of each, but because in sum these narratives provide a most useful guide for those who would understand the nature of the air war.

These services encountered, as did the tactical air forces, problems at two different levels. First, and perhaps more simple of solution if more pressing, were those of devising and securing the equipment necessary for a war in which technology and production counted heavily and of training men whose skills were even more important than the machines—though this latter need may easily be slighted now that we have crossed the horizon toward the push-button age. The other problems were organizational in form, but in essence they hinged on intricate points of command and control which were fundamental to the American concept of war. World War II was unique not only in that it was the *first* war truly world wide in geographical scope but in that for the first time combat operations were divided in fairly equal proportions among our ground, sea, and air forces. To a remarkably satisfactory degree the strategic problems of the universal, three-dimensional war were worked out by the Joint Chiefs of Staff and the Combined Chiefs of Staff, but within the theaters (or areas, as they were called in the U.S. Navy–controlled Pacific) the standard doctrine was maintained of an unfettered control of all land, sea, and air forces by the theater commander-in-chief, acting under directives of JCS and CCS. In detail, commanders might differ in their interpretation of prerogative, but, in general, their views were antagonistic to those thought essential by the new AAF services.

The basic argument for these services was to some extent rooted in the fundamental concept of an autonomous or independent air force that achieved some recognition in the reorganizations of 20 June 1941 and 9 March 1942. But, beyond that, there were important areas in which the new ideas conflicted with standard AAF doctrines, to a lesser degree than when opposed to the theater doctrine but still to a degree that was hard to resolve. From any point of view—theater, AAF, or AAF service—the argument was always the same whatever the immediate issue: unity of command. Because the interpretation of this issue has continued to be of national interest—indeed, has grown as a matter of prime public concern—the editors have thought that the organizational struggles described in the following chapters go far beyond their immediate purpose by illustrating the complexity of modern warfare.

It is not without reason that the Air Transport Command occupies the first and most prominent place in this book. In terms of size ATC was by far the greatest of the organizations under consideration; it was an important user, along with the tactical air forces, of most of the other services; its struggle for a separate and corporate existence exerted some influence within the other organizations; and it was ATC that set a pattern for close collaboration with the civilian world that was necessary during the rapid expansion of the Air Corps after 1939. Originally, ATC had to depend heavily upon the commercial airlines, but so vast were its operations and so varied its experiences that in the end there was much that the civilian lines could learn from the command.

Early experiments with air transport within the Air Corps were born of the necessity for economy and were limited to intraservice delivery of airplane parts. The tremendous expansion of this function was accompanied by the assumption of two other major responsibilities: the delivery—or ferrying, to use the term borrowed from the British—of military aircraft to the using agency and the movement of passengers. When cargo and passenger services were extended to other Army forces and ATC became a common carrier for the War Department, its growth beyond the most sanguine dreams of 1939 was assured.

Dependence upon the commercial airlines began with the expansion of the Air Corps in 1939 and was most pronounced in the early days of the war, but it continued in some degree until V-J Day, by which time ATC's size and accumulated experience overshadowed that of the combined civilian carriers. The most important forms of aid may be classified roughly in terms of planes and personnel borrowed, techniques adapted to military use, and direct transport service performed under contract.

Early Air Corps attempts to develop transport planes had produced no satisfactory model, and, in spite of redoubled efforts, no successful design was produced during the war years. So, inevitably, the AAF turned to civilian models already in production and to various modifications of heavy bombers. The early standby, and indeed the most dependable plane within its capacities throughout the war, was the Douglas DC-3, known alternately, according to its special modifications, as the C-47 and the C-53. Long successful in civilian passenger service but already obsolescent at Pearl Harbor time, the twin-engine DC-3 had many features ill suited to the convenient handling of bulky freight, and its pay load was too light for the new tasks. But it was flyable under almost any conditions, was easily maintained, and, above all, was in production. Similarly, the AAF adopted the Douglas DC-4, a newer four-engine airliner just coming into production in 1941, and, as the C-54, this plane became the workhorse where long range and a heavy load were important considerations. Much was expected of the Curtiss C-46, designed in 1940 as a twin-engine competitor of the DC-4 and Boeing Stratoliner; it was easy to load and had great lift, reasonable speed, and a comfortable range. Eventually, it came to do yeoman service in certain areas, but until 1944 the C-46 was subject to various mechanical ailments calling for numerous modifications and was a hard plane to fly and to maintain.

Of the converted bombers, the most important were the variants of the B-24—the C-87 and a tanker model, the C-109. In spite of the obvious disadvantages of a made-over tactical plane, the C-87 had speed and range and proved a lifesaver until the C-54 came into full production.

In view of the AAF's later stress on air transport, it may seem strange in retrospect that its development program for the necessary planes lagged so far behind that for tactical aircraft. But it must be remembered that the transport doctrine, though beginning to crystallize by the time of Pearl Harbor, was profoundly affected by the additional responsibilities (welcome enough to ATC) delegated by the War Department. In this respect the original air war plan, AWPD/1 of August 1941, is instructive. Though remarkably accurate in its forecast of requirements in general and in most individual types, and though written under the direction of ATC's later commander, the plan fell far short in its estimate of the number of four-engine planes needed for victory. However, the fairest test is to compare the American transport aircraft, in quality and quantity, with those of our enemies and Allies; in such a comparison the AAF, with a fleet which was largely improvised, was without a rival.

ATC borrowed actual planes as well as plane models and production potential from the airlines, and it borrowed men as well. These included top-ranking executives, pilots and crewmen, and mechanics and technicians of all sorts. The terms of the loan varied from individual to individual and often with the same man—induction, temporary military service, civilian employment by ATC, or contract service.

Contract service, which began before the United States entered the war, enlisted the aid of an airline to do a specific job of ferrying, or of hauling cargo and passengers, or of operating air bases. The experience of these companies, their aircraft and equipment, and their installations were of enormous help. There was often friction between their civilian employees and military personnel doing the same job under less favorable circumstances, and there were instances when it seemed to the latter that the airlines were more interested in present profits and future status than in winning the war. But, indeed, victory would have come harder without the very real aid of the airlines.

If the AAF depended heavily upon an existing civilian structure for men and planes in its transport service, its doctrine and organization were born of its own experience and imagination. The Air Transport Command grew out of the Air Corps Ferrying Command, established in May 1941 to direct the delivery of lend-lease planes to our Allies. This duty continued at an accelerating pace, and to it was added that of ferrying U.S. replacement planes and of supervising the overseas flight of combat units bound for a theater of operations. For the ACFC there was some guidance in RAF ferrying experience but not for the broader concept of mass transport of passengers and freight which became eventually a larger operation. The new designation of Air Transport Command came on 20 June 1942 along with the expanded responsibilities. The reorganization included a new headquarters in Washington and, in various strategic locations overseas, a wing organization with control over local troops and installations but not over aircraft or crews passing through. This was in accord with the new idea of a strategic transport service, directed from Washington, with local transport being provided by theater carrier units. This design ran counter to accepted ideas of unified command of all forces within a theater, and it was only after many controversies and after theater commanders came to understand its over-all advantages that the new concept won general acceptance. The theater commander reserved the right to levy on ATC forces in an emergency, a proviso subject to varying interpretations, but, as transport facilities became more plentiful, this clause was invoked less frequently. This revolutionary idea of a strategic command for air transport was an important factor in ATC's enormous accomplishment; attempts to extend the principle to include Navy air transport services failed to materialize until after the war when MATS proved to be the first practical form of unification between the services and demonstrated in the Berlin airlift the mobility and power of concentration inherent in its strategic concept.

The magnitude of the ATC effort can be read in the statistics plentifully supplied in the pages which follow. With a peak force of 200,-000 officers and men and 3,700 planes, ATC in the single month of July 1945 carried 275,000 passengers and 100,000 tons of cargo, mostly in overseas flights; in all, the command ferried more than a quarter of a million planes. To secure the requisite transport planes was an arduous task, but far mort difficult was the job of recruiting and training pilots and crews in direct competition with combat forces enjoying always a higher priority. Pilots were drawn from several sources: originally from the pool of airline pilots trained by the Air Corps and

holding reserve commissions; then from veteran civilian pilots of varying types of experience; later from pilots rotated home after a combat
tour; in greatest numbers from Training Command graduates; and
from women pilots, both experienced (WAFS) and newly trained
(WASP). Except for the first group, most of the pilots needed additional instruction—transitional training in the many aircraft types ferried by ATC and training for long overwater flights, novel to most of
the recruits. A contract program provided by the civilian Airlines
War Training Institute proved unequal to the demand, and in the long
run most of the instruction was given by ATC's operational training
unit program which trained crews for the several types of transport
planes and in the techniques needed for transport flying.

The over-all command pattern and the common strategic mission
gave some unity to ATC operations in all theaters, however competitive the simultaneous demands of the theaters might be. This unity did
not exclude variety, for each theater had its special problems and its
own tempo. Essentially, the ATC story is that of building and operating a half-dozen major airways, some with branch or feeder lines. The
story is told in some detail in the following chapters, and here it is
necessary only to indicate the main lines of development in those airways.

Oldest in service was the South Atlantic route (comprising by 1943
the Caribbean, South Atlantic, North Africa, and Central Africa
Wings), which was born of the need to ferry lend-lease aircraft to the
British in the Near East and to the Russians via Tehran. The opening
in July 1942 of a staging base on Ascension Island midway across the
South Atlantic made the route practicable for twin-engine planes. Fear
of an Axis victory in Egypt sent ATC south of the Equator to set up
a possible alternate to the Accra-Khartoum-Cairo (or -Aden) route to
the Middle East, but, fortunately, need for its use never materialized.
Early plans to reinforce Australia via a trans-African airway also
faded early in the war. But great impetus was given to ATC's operations over the South Atlantic by the Allied invasion of French Africa
in November 1942. This called for a branch line from Accra up to
Dakar and eventually for a direct route from Natal to Dakar suitable
for four-engine planes. There was also a line from Northwest Africa
to the United Kingdom, and, after the invasion of Italy, a branch was
fed into that peninsula, Corsica, and southern France. The extension
of intratheater services had come only with the absorption of duties

previously handled by Mediterranean Air Transport Service against the wishes of the British.

Another and more direct line—the Middle Atlantic—from Newfoundland to Marrakech (or to Great Britain) via the Azores was pioneered in 1943 and was regularly used from the beginning of 1944.

The North Atlantic route, began as an airway for ferrying lend-lease planes to the United Kingdom, was given a greater load when the build-up for the Combined Bomber Offensive began in 1942. Alternate routes—staging through either Newfoundland or Labrador, either eastern or western Greenland, and Iceland—were developed, though four-engine planes could fly directly from North America. In the beginning there was much trouble with weather on this route, but losses dwindled as installations and instruments were improved and as personnel became more experienced. The invasion of France in 1944 increased the flow of traffic over this airway and led to the establishment of feeder lines and of new transport services for the Continent.

No airway attracted public attention as did the "Hump," the route from Bengal to Assam, then over the rugged mountain chains that provided the route's familiar name, to Kunming in China. The difficulty of the flight over high mountains through notoriously bad weather was publicized as no other non-combat flight was. Beyond that, the airway became early in the war the sole means by which supplies and personnel could be carried into or out of China, and it hence took on a prime strategic and diplomatic importance. This line was the last link in an airway that came from the United States via Africa to Karachi and across India to Calcutta, but much of the materiel hauled over the Hump had come out by surface ship or a combination of ship and aircraft.

In flying the Hump, ATC long had to face the formidable weather and terrain conditions with inadequate installations and too little in the way of aircraft assigned. What added to the command's difficulties were the recurrent promises made to China by top authorities of ever heavier delivery schedules, made often without full consideration of the means by which the schedules could be met. The India-China Wing's history, then, is one of long and often frustrating effort to meet quotas made by others than their own leaders. Eventually, they received enough planes and crews for the task, and their leadership improved with experience. By mid-1944 monthly totals began to top earlier estimates, then in 1945 climbed to a fantastic sum of 71,042 tons in July; the wartime grand total was 650,000 tons. The strategic importance of this accomplishment may be open to debate, but in terms of the development of air-transport concepts and techniques the airlift to China was of first importance.

The Northwest air route stretched out some 2,210 miles from Great Falls, Montana, to Anchorage in Alaska. The apparent strategic importance of Alaska in the early days of the war made this route seem vital to national defense as a means of reinforcing rapidly our meager forces there. After the Japanese feint in that direction in 1942 the danger subsided until Alaska ceased to figure as an active theater. From September 1942 to V-J Day the chief function of the airway was the delivery of lend-lease planes to Russia via Siberia. This was as difficult in personal relations as other tasks involving Russian co-operation, but it was a mission of great scope and importance, resulting, all told, in the transfer at Fairbanks of more than 7,800 aircraft.

In the Pacific, ATC developed slowly, since before Pearl Harbor in its vast areas there was no considerable lend-lease traffic such as had given impetus to ferrying across the Atlantic. Most areas in the Pacific were under command of the U.S. Navy, which provided its own air transport; in the one exception—the Southwest Pacific—General MacArthur's views on command prerogative left little opportunity for the development of a Washington-controlled transport system. However, early in 1942 a Pacific Sector of ACFC began to direct the westward movement of U.S. bombers flown out by their own crews to the Fifth and other air forces fighting Japan. In March a transport service was begun, Hawaii to Australia; and, with the creation of ATC, this and the ferrying service were continued by its South Pacific Wing. Contract transports carried the freight and passengers, and the build-up of ATC forces was slow. By summer 1943 the Pacific Wing, with headquarters in Hawaii, had provided a needed unity of control in traffic from California to Australia, and eventually some order was established in what had been a confused service.

Early in the war the airway to Australia had gone far south of the direct line as a matter of precaution, but by 1944 the route had been swung northward following the advance of Allied forces. In April 1944, by special agreement between the theater and ATC, the latter's Southwest Pacific wing took over part of the intratheater transport job, which, with the increasing distance of the front from Australia, had become a heavy one.

Early in 1945 the Central Pacific Wing moved to Guam, where it contributed heavily to the establishment and nourishment of XXI Bomber Command, whose B-29's were attacking Japan's cities. The last important job of ATC in the Pacific war was the spectacular airlift of occupying forces into Japan after the surrender. But there was still a vaster and more welcome job—that of bringing home such forces as would be released from service.

From its earliest days ATC had carried in its homeward-bound planes some high-priority passengers and some rare strategic materials. More important were the sick and wounded personnel of whatever service evacuated either to theater hospitals or back to the United States. In all they numbered about one-third of a million passengers, and certainly there was no accomplishment of ATC that rated so high in human values. But an even larger task (and one not without its appeal to the individual serviceman) was the aid provided by ATC in the return of AAF units to the United States in the redeployment program and of personnel of all sorts when the Japanese surrender turned redeployment into an overwhelming torrent of men bound for home and separation.

In June 1940 the Corps of Engineers, at the request of the Air Corps, activated a regiment of engineers whose special duty was the preparation or repair of airfields and other air installations. This was the beginning of an organization that eventually included 117,851 officers and men. Breaking with the practice of European air forces that left construction in the hands of army engineers, the Air Corps conceived of a unit trained specifically for aviation needs. With the full co-operation of the Corps of Engineers, the Air Corps designed a self-contained battalion of 27 officers and 761 men, equipped with a lavish array of heavy machines typical of American civilian construction practices. Machines and men skilled in their use were then plentiful, and, when war came, engineer aviation battalions were already overseas, where they took part in the initial operations. Although designed on a purely theoretical basis with no model to imitate or experience to guide its planners, the self-contained battalion remained the standard unit, with relatively little need to modify its table of organization and equipment.

Early in 1942 the Air Engineer developed an engineer aviation battalion (airborne) for mobile use in an invasion. Its complement of 28 officers and 500 men was light, its equipment lighter still by normal standards. The unit was designed to be parachuted into enemy territory, to hack out an emergency strip, and, with light equipment landed by gliders, to improve the runway until it could accommodate transports and tactical planes. The idea was appropriate to certain phases of the war, but the services rendered never justified the effort and resources spent on this specialized type of unit. Whether the fault lay entirely in the concept or in part with the use of the airborne battalions is not entirely clear. On three spectacular occasions—at Tebessa in Algeria, in Burma, and at Tsili Tsili in New Guinea—the airborne engineers functioned as smoothly and as efficiently as in a textbook exercise under conditions impossible for a standard battalion. But, in general, their equipment was too light and the whole concept of their purpose was too specialized for general usage. Theater commanders greatly preferred the standard battalion, and the airborne units sometimes sat idle or were used in routine small jobs; eventually, many of them were merged with other units. The rare successes showed that there was some need for the airborne unit but certainly not for so many as were provided, and this criticism was valid as well for such other specialized units as the petroleum-distribution company, the camouflage battalion, etc.

Over-all planning was a responsibility of the Air Engineer in AAF Headquarters in Washington, but he had little command responsibility. Officers and men were trained by the Corps of Engineers, allocated by the Operations Division, War Department General Staff, and assigned to a theater commander when reaching a combat zone. There they might be merged indiscriminately with other engineers—Army, Navy, and civilian—to perform any and all types of construction whether of interest to air operations or not. Hence there was a constant struggle on the part of AAF Headquarters to secure for them some sort of separate existence. The success of aviation engineers working at their own proper tasks in Northwest Africa resulted in the establishment of an engineer command within the theater organization. Here this pattern worked so well that it was later adopted for the invasion forces in the ETO in 1944, and, indeed, AAF Headquarters urged this as a model for other theaters. But throughout the Pacific theaters and in CBI, commanders were unanimously opposed, and so the aviation engineers remained a part of a pool, performing such tasks as were assigned, whether connected with the air war or not. Often the aviation engineers complained of preferential treatment accorded their colleagues in the other services, but, unlike their officers in

Washington, they were not generally enthusiastic about a separate existence; their chief loyalty as professionals was toward the crenelated towers of the Corps of Engineers rather than toward the younger crossed propellers of the Air Corps.

Certain problems of command, of personnel, and of supply were fundamentally similar in all theaters, but the nature of the aviation engineer's task differed with the nature of the air war in each and with the terrain, transportation, and equipment and labor locally avaliable. Most of the unit equipment had been proved in grueling civilian use, and usually it was sturdy enough and plentiful enough for the task at hand, but transportation remained throughout the war a limiting factor. Too often men arrived long before their equipment, and in many of the amphibious invasions inept loading of machinery slowed down the initial construction of airstrips.

In England control of the aviation engineers fell to the Army's SOS. Their chief task was to build the many airfields in East Anglia and Huntingdon required for the Combined Bomber Offensive. They worked with British civilian help, and, if there were inconveniences, shortages, discomforts, and monotony, conditions were not notably more rugged than in a boom community in the United States.

The invasion of North Africa offered a greater variety of experiences. Landing with the invasion troops in several places, the aviation engineers began their never ending task of repairing old fields and creating new ones. Heavy rains hampered their efforts to provide all-weather landing strips, and it was only by ingenious use of plateau and desert locations that the engineers were able to keep up with the early advances of the troops. After Kasserine, better weather and a larger and more experienced force enabled the engineers to catch up with the heavy demands. By the end of the campaign they had built or rehabilitated (with British aid) 129 airfields at the rate of one every two days and had won the respect of all combat forces.

In the Sicilian campaign the task of the AAF engineers was to provide airstrips in support of the U.S. Seventh Army, and, though their officers had little advance knowledge of conditions on the island, the assigned battalions were able to keep up with the whirlwind campaign. As it ended, the long-sought separate organization came with the formation of the AAF Engineer Command (MTO), which was to serve as a model for the larger structure used later in the invasion of northern Europe.

The invasion of Italy called first for the familiar procedure of laying down emergency fighter strips, in Calabria and then for Anzio. Later came the less spectacular but more lasting task of building all-weather fields for strategic bombers in Apulia and around Foggia; in both areas the heavy rains of "sunny" Italy caused serious but not insurmountable difficulties. By comparison, the assignments in Corsica and southern France in connection with the DRAGOON operation were routine.

For the OVERLORD invasion of France the Ninth Air Force had at its disposal sixteen regular and three airborne aviation engineer battalions, most of whose members were veterans with much experience in the construction of airdromes in England, topped off with a casual training for their new and more mobile duties. Not without long debate, the Ninth Air Force secured for this corps separate status as a provisional IX Engineer Command, numbering more than 17,000 personnel. From D Day until V-E Day the activities of this command were intimately entwined with those of the tactical air forces and, indeed, with those of the ground troops. Along with other invading forces, the engineers were hampered by the rugged resistance of the Germans at the beaches and in Normandy; their schedules were disrupted by the slow breakout from the Cotentin and equally by the unexpectedly rapid advance thereafter; and important changes in plans were required by the need for more fighter-bomber fields than had been predicted and by the tardy decision to base medium bombers on the Continent. As the First and Third Armies moved across France, supported, respectively, by the IX and XIX Tactical Air Commands, the Engineer Command was split into the 1st and 2d Engineer Aviation Brigades, each with the duty of providing in the wake of the advancing armies a series of clutches of airfields in immediate support. Supply and transportation were never adequate, and the engineers were hard put to keep up with the breakneck pace of the ground troops; but throughout their performance was remarkable enough to win the unqualified praise of all.

In the war against Japan the experiences of the engineers were more varied than in Europe and Africa. In part the variety resulted from the wide range in climate and topography, in part from the command structures encountered. In few instances were the aviation engineers in the Pacific areas or in CBI able to call on the resources of an industrial society, and their supply problems were made prodigious by distances and low priorities.

In the Southwest Pacific Area, aviation engineers began their operations at Darwin in Australia early in 1942 and finished, as a part of FEAF, far to the north as war ended. From the first they worked side by side with Army and Navy engineers, under the Chief Engineer of GHQ, SWPA. Attempts to secure a separate aviation engineer command were made periodically by AAF Headquarters and (though apparently with less zeal) by the Fifth Air Force, but to no avail. Problems of manpower and supply were of more immediate concern to engineers in the theater than were those of command, and indeed it is hard to say from the record whether the air forces there would have profited greatly by the proposed change.

As SWPA forces held at Port Moresby and then began the slow movement northward, each jump in the hopscotch pattern of advance depended upon the previous development of new air bases. The terrain often was rugged, living conditions were primitive, and the climate was debilitating and unhealthy. Sites for airfields had to be chosen on the basis of inadequate information, and land transportation was incredibly difficult. These factors made for unorthodox methods, and in many cases the standards accepted for airstrips were far different from those demanded at home or in the ETO. But, whatever the book may have said, the strips laboriously hewed out of jungles or laid on coral beaches still under enemy fire usually stood up under the pragmatic test of hard use. Road-building frequently became, as between Lae and Nadzab, a necessary adjunct to airfield construction, and more often than they liked aviation engineers were employed in miscellaneous tasks bearing little relation to the air war.

Occasionally, advance intelligence was so faulty as to require a radical revision of plans, as at Hollandia, where designs for a huge complex of bases to be built by 25,000 engineers were scaled down to a minimum, with most of the force moving on to develop Wadke instead. Sometimes, too, as at Biak and Noemfoor, unheralded local difficulties interfered with construction schedules. In regard both to construction supplies and to provisions for their own existence aviation engineers felt that they suffered unduly while the Seabees lived a life of plenty; they felt, too, some resentment when the highly publicized Seabees received wide acclaim for accomplishments no whit different from those of the unsung aviation engineers.

With the return to the Philippines the engineers passed a crucial test under fire in the mud of Leyte, then moved northward to Mindoro and Luzon, where a variety of tasks necessary for the restoration of those islands competed with airfield construction for the attention of the engineers.

In the North Pacific the Japanese threat of June 1942 seemed to reinforce ideas about the strategic importance of Alaska and to demand the immediate extension of air facilities in the area. As a point of attack against Japanese-held Kiska and Attu, two companies of aviation engineers built a usable airfield on Adak, working under most formidable circumstances. Later fields were built on Amchitka and Attu, but eventually, as operations practically ceased in that area, construction forces were moved to a more active theater.

In the South Pacific, a Navy command, construction policies were largely determined by Navy officers. In 1943, however, the Thirteenth Air Force gained immediate control of the aviation engineer battalions through its XIII Air Service Command. Much of their work was in support of Navy Seabees, who outnumbered them and who enjoyed their usual advantages in supply and in living accommodations. While performing their tasks creditably, the aviation engineers in this theater had a somewhat less important role than in the SWPA.

In China-Burma-India the activities of the aviation engineers were as far from normal as were most operations in that vast and confusing theater. In China there were no U.S. engineer units but only a handful of officers to advise General Chennault and to some extent the Chinese who built his fields. In India the Tenth Air Force used fields prepared by native labor under British supervision. Until 1944 all five aviation engineer battalions (all Negro units) in CBI were assigned to work on the Ledo Road, where they were joined later by three other such units. Their fine work was finished only with the completion of the road early in 1945, and, though some units moved then into China, they arrived too late to accomplish much before V-J Day. Perhaps the most nearly normal project in the theater was when aviation engineers under AAF control supported the campaign in Burma and developed the important complex of bases around Myitkyna.

The MATTERHORN project provided the theater's greatest single challenge to air engineers, but it was handled in a typically complex CBI fashion. Because the project called for B-29 bases in both China and India, some over-all direction was provided by the establishment of an Air Engineer, Air Forces, CBI. In China the fields were built, somewhat tardily, by hundreds of thousands of peasants working with primitive hand tools under direction of local contractors. In

Bengal the task was divided among the British, Indian, and U.S. armies, using some civilian help and throttled by enough red tape to choke off any threat of initiative. Four aviation engineer battalions sent out in the hope of making MATTERHORN self-sufficient arrived late but still well ahead of their equipment. From start to finish the job lagged far behind schedule, so that by comparison the China side of the task was a model of dispatch and efficiency.

Even larger was the job of preparing bases for the B-29's of XXI Bomber Command in the Marianas, but it went more smoothly. Fifteen battalions were available for developing the islands. Plans based on insufficient data had to be modified frequently, and the command set-up, while not so impractical as that in CBI, was cumbersome enough to make the requisition of supplies a major operation. Nevertheless, the B-29 fields with their generous specifications were built in time to accommodate the constantly expanding force of VHB's. An even greater construction project involving the use of ninety-three battalions was planned for Okinawa but was canceled by the cessation of hostilities.

Accurate forecasting of weather conditions, useful to all modern military services, is of especial significance to air forces. It was not without reason then that on the eve of World War II the Air Corps was given primary responsibility for the Army's weather service. Using techniques developed by Scandinavian meteorologists, the U.S. Weather Bureau had built and maintained an excellent reporting system within the continental United States. The more difficult task that war brought was to extend a similar service to combat areas where local data would not be so easily available. In terms of the general movement of weather and of the help available from allies, the war against Germany in this one respect presented perhaps a less formidable problem than did the war against Japan, although it was axiomatic among fliers in any area that their own particular brand of weather was the worst to be found anywhere.

Early plans for expanding the Air Corps weather services were entirely too modest, but they were sharply revised late in 1940, when the estimated need for weather officers was jumped from 40 to 1,550. Contracts were made with five leading universities and technical institutes to conduct a training program in meteorology, and recruits were sought from washed-out pilot trainees and among college students with the educational qualifications. As estimated requirements soared to a fantastic figure of 10,000 weather officers by 1945, the AAF made further arrangements with twenty other institutions to offer premeteorological programs for college students in an enlisted-reserve status. By 1943 a more realistic appraisal of requirements could be made; the estimate was slashed in two, but, even so, of 6,200 weather officers trained, 1,800 served in other capacities.

The organizational pattern in the United States divided the country into several weather regions, each operated by a meteorological squadron through detachments of varying sizes at the many air bases. This system was extended overseas, with the squadron normally taking its numerical designation from the theater air force and with its commanding officer becoming the regional control officer. Before the war ended, the AAF had nine hundred weather stations, two-thirds of them outside the United States.

Liaison with other services and with Britain was provided through a number of joint and combined committees, but co-operation with the U.S.S.R. was difficult and never satisfactory. Difficult, too, was the problem of control within the AAF and in overseas theaters, where the desire of AAF Headquarters to exercise some supervision over men operating a world-wide weather service ran counter to the prerogatives of the theater commander.

Within the AAF, direction of the Weather Service changed frequently with the periodic reorganizations in the Pentagon. In 1943 control fell to the new Flight Control Command, which exercised its responsibilities through a Weather Wing located at Asheville, North Carolina. It was only at the very end of the war, in July 1945, that further administrative changes concentrated authority in the hands of the Chief of the AAF Weather Service, with Headquarters, AAFWS, succeeding the Weather Wing at Asheville.

Overseas, weather personnel operated both along the air routes leading to the theaters and in the combat zones. Even before the United States entered the war weather stations were functioning along the South Atlantic and North Atlantic routes, and thereafter the number of stations was rapidly increased; by 1943 a station in the Azores was serving the Middle Atlantic route as well. Weather stations in the North Atlantic, some of them well within the Arctic Circle, were isolated by the winter weather they observed, and mere physical existence was a problem. But the hand-picked men stood up well to the hardships and loneliness, and morale generally was good. From 1942 on increasing use was made of weather reconnaissance flights in the North Atlantic, eventually with especially qualified observers and planes equipped for the purpose, and later this practice was extended to the South Atlantic. Eventually, a system of area reconnaissance was perfected that almost eliminated weather as an important factor in plane losses along those airways.

In CBI there was much weather to observe and, through most of the war, too few qualified observers. There the crucial area was the Hump, "the turbulent meeting place of three major Eurasian air masses." ATC, by far the principal user, tried without success to take over the weather service. By 1944 forecasting for XX Bomber Command's B-29's was moderately successful, partly because of information furnished by the Russians and by U.S. personnel on the Asiatic mainland.

During the invasion of North Africa the AAF worked out a pattern, subsequently followed elsewhere, by which the 12th Weather Squadron was assigned to the Twelfth Air Force, where its commander served simultaneously as regional control officer, weather officer for the ranking AAF commander, and chief source of weather information for the theater commander. As personnel became available, officers were assigned to echelons down to the combat group level, allowing a modification of early concepts of fixed stations by the frequent use of mobile units. With weather as with other services, the experience gained in the MTO was of great value in the invasion of northern Europe.

In the Pacific, weather stations fanned out from Hawaii along the air routes and into the combat areas occupied by the Fifth and Thirteenth Air Forces. Co-operation with the weather services of New Zealand and Australia was close. From Alaska, AAF weather detachments moved westward along the Aleutian chain with the American advance in 1943, but their efforts, combined with those of the Navy, CAA, and U.S. Weather Bureau, never made possible any sustained combat operations in the area. But weather squadrons in the northwestern reaches of the continent helped keep open the lend-lease route to the U.S.S.R. and collected information invaluable to their colleagues at home and abroad.

In the Pacific, as in Europe, regular forecasting had to be supplemented with special weather reconnaissance flights to secure spot data on target areas or on flight paths. This practice went counter to earlier plans for area reconnaissance—which proved highly successful along the Atlantic routes—but in support of B-29 strikes against Honshu it was only from data collected *ad hoc* by VLR planes that reasonably accurate forecasts could be made.

Although the AAF Weather Service participated in the significant advances made in the science of meteorology during the war years, its unique contribution cannot be isolated from those of the Navy, the civilian agencies, and the universities, all working toward a common goal and often in close collaboration. New equipment was designed by the Signal Corps at AAF request, and, though the AAF engaged in some research programs of its own, its more important work was the vast extension of reporting over a large portion of the earth's surface. Among its most troublesome problems was that of security of communications, where the desire to make available to friendly aircraft all pertinent weather information was balanced by the need of withholding such data from the enemy. This conflict of interests resulted inevitably in compromise, weighted somewhat more heavily in favor of the friendly plane than was common with our British allies, whose proximity to German bomber bases made them somewhat more cautious about the dissemination of information; but, in general, policies became less strict as the Allies gained air supremacy.

This was only one of the many instances in which rapid but safe means of communications were necessary for victory in the air. Actually, the whole concept of a global war was dependent upon a world-wide communications system of unprecedented complexity, and not least important for the AAF was that part of the system that guided, aided, and controlled its planes in flight. The development of this system in the 1930's had been slow, but under pressure of war a combination of new techniques and new administrative procedures met the new needs successfully. Long a branch of the Signal Corps, the air arm left to its parent organization the development of communications equipment even after it assumed equal status as the Air Corps and long depended upon the civilian airways for navigational aids within the continental United States. Recognizing the growing need for a unified traffic control system of its own, the Air Corps established late in 1938 the Army Airways Communications System under direction of the Chief of the Air Corps, which comprised three regions, each served by a communications squadron. The technological improvements of the war years and the increase in traffic added vastly to the equipment and the responsibilities of the AACS, but its organizational pattern and its name were maintained with a stability unusual in that era.

With the approach and the arrival of war AACS extended its services along the airways developed eastward and westward from the United States. Instruction in the new and ever newer instruments and techniques was provided by the Training Command for military personnel and by the Air Service Command for the many civilians employed.

Inevitably, the effort to establish a world-wide communications system with personnel stationed in every area where AAF planes flew, but all controlled centrally by a stateside headquarters, ran afoul the standard pattern of unified theater command; and in the struggle for its own centralized control AACS enjoyed the support of ATC, a principal user of its facilities and an ardent suitor in the same cause. Some gains were achieved in 1943 in AACS's relation to theater commands, and subsequently its internal structure underwent several modifications, so that before V-J Day it had come to represent a truly world-wide airways system.

Beyond the organizational issue AACS had as a prime task adapting the available equipment and personnel to the needs of the several theaters and the airways connecting them with the homeland. The problems differed somewhat in kind and in intensity from area to area, but the very universality of AACS tended to iron out some of the differences, and in the total picture its efforts did much to quicken the pace of air traffic and to cut down on avoidable losses.

For writing the chapter on aviation medicine the editors, rank laymen in the field on two scores, were happy to secure the services of a distinguished physician and administrator whose wartime experience with another military medical service should qualify him as an expert and non-partisan author. His essay, departing from the narrative organized along geographical lines which has been followed in most chapters, consists of an analysis of those factors that differentiated aviation medicine from medicine as conceived and practiced by the forces of the War Department's Surgeon General and that led—not without reason if this interpretation be correct—to a long struggle for an independent medical service for the air arm.

The chief distinguishing feature of aviation medicine was its recognition of the importance of the individual flier and its consequent emphasis on what was known technically as the "Care of the Flier"; this, with the dispensing of normal clinical services, the selection of candidates for flight training, and research in the medical problems of flight, constituted the duties of the flight surgeon. In his general clinical work the air surgeon made important contributions to the more rapid healing of sick and wounded and their consequent return to duty; his researches helped adapt fliers to the new stresses of new machines; his tests controlled entrance to candidacy for coveted flight careers. But the essence of his job was maintaining, with equity toward the individual and with conscience toward the demands of the war, an optimum percentage of fliers available for combat. This involved a delicate set of relations between the air surgeon, the commanding officer (himself always a flier), and the individual flier; and the surgeon's success in this, the art of aviation medicine, was measured by his skill in satisfying at the same time the military needs of the one and the personal needs of the other.

Aviation medicine as it developed from the time of World War I studied the various types of stresses involved in flight—physical, gravitational, physiological, psychological, and emotional—with emphases that varied according to current medical views and the prepossessions of air surgeons. From 1934, air surgeons at the laboratory of the Aero Medical Research Unit studied the effect of new equipment on men in flight with a view toward its improvement. And, since World War I, flight surgeons had operated, under several names and in several localities, their own School of Aviation Medicine. But underlying all their functions lay an administrative issue of prime concern.

Since 1917, flight surgeons had insisted that an effective air force must have full control over its own medical service. Air force needs could be satisfied only by physicians in sympathy with the revolutionary ideas of airpower, including an acceptance of the parity of the man and the machine. Sympathy with the airman's unconventional views was not only an incentive toward research for the mutual adaptation of man and machine but, more important, also an absolute prerequisite for the understanding and treatment of the individual flier. Such a medical service would demand two administrative changes. First, it was necessary that the chief medical officer be directly responsible to the commander of the air arm without the necessity of reporting through some non-medical staff officer, as was customary in other military organizations. Second, it was necessary to win freedom from control by the Surgeon General, and this was difficult, since the latter officer maintained a professional control over Army physicians even after they had been assigned to a major command such as a corps area or a combat theater. Neither of these objectives was obtained en bloc during World War II; but by gradual stages aviation medicine won a degree of independence comparable to that of the air arm itself, and, as in the case of the AAF, the realities of power often ran far ahead of its formal acknowledgment. Freedom of action in some areas, particularly those involving research and teaching, came by default though use of Air Corps funds when the Army medical establishment was unwilling to provide them. But the central issue of administrative control was fought out in a long and acrimonious paper conflict that ended only with the establishment of the U.S. Air Force in 1947. Functionally, aviation medicine performed three types of service: physical examination, field medical, and hospitalization. Control over the first was easily gained, but it was only under the exigencies of war that the Air Surgeon sharply modified the field services and encroached upon the general hospital system.

In the selection and classification of fliers, air surgeons of World War II had behind them a long tradition of testing but little in the way of test evaluation by biostatistical methods. Under the demand for flight crews in unprecedented numbers, the selection program was changed in two fashions: first, by emphasis on the prediction of aptitudes of aviation cadets, classification was made a positive program; second, the emphasis was divided among the several categories of aircrewmen rather than being centered on the pilot alone. In spite of changes in the nature of the testing devices and, indeed, in the concepts of what factors should be tested—physical, physiological, psychological, or psychiatric—the selection process as measured by successful completion of the training program involved was not notably more efficient than in World War I. Nevertheless, this service seems to have satisfied personnel and training officers most immediately concerned.

Of more interest to the flight surgeon was his duty to provide "Care for the Flier" for something like three-quarters of a million aircrewmen in training and in subsequent operations. Part of the program was within the normally high competence of the doctors serving with the AAF; part demanded some specialized physiological knowledge that was supposed to be furnished by the School of Aviation Medicine. But the most difficult responsibility of the air surgeon was the diagnosis of symptoms resulting from emotional reactions and the handling of cases arising from the peculiar anxieties of flight and aerial combat. The latter sort of duty lay within an area of knowledge and practice vigorously debated by physicians and psychiatrists—an area of interest in civilian practice wherever emotional factors affected health but one which became of crucial importance where the willingness or emotional ability to participate in combat flying was a military matter, subject to stringent sanctions applied through martial law. In a field of medical practice ill understood by common practitioners, the lay public, and the military, the flight surgeon at the squadron level had to act as personal adviser to the airman and as arbiter between this client, his commanding officer, and higher medical authority when their respective interests were in opposition. To keep the largest number of crewmen flying without endangering their comrades and without permanent damage to the individual—that was the peculiar task of the air surgeon, and his success, which was generally of a high order, was in direct ratio to his skill in the art of aviation medicine.

The airman's relation with the air surgeon began when the former was a trainee, continued through his tour of combat, and remained close until his separation from the service. Many of the medical problems were those common to all military personnel within any area, but those which were of special concern to aviation medicine were the ones connected with flight under combat conditions: anoxia, frostbite, aero-itis, battle wounds, and stress. The first three were materially reduced in incidence, and the seriousness of their results was ameliorated by the development of better equipment at the instance of the flight surgeons and by better indoctrination in its use. In the matter of battle wounds, too, great reduction in incidence was effected through the development of body armour by the doctors and its enforced use.

In the matter of hospitalization the AAF's interest in the individual flier and desire to keep him as a member of his individual team conflicted sharply with the Army's practice, which in reassignment after prolonged treatment was concerned less with returning a given "body" to his own unit than with filling his place with an identical (and hence interchangeable) MOS. Lacking their own system of general hospitals in the Zone of Interior or in theaters of operations, AAF physicians were unable fully to enforce their doctrines concerning hospitalization and disposition of patients, but they made substantial progress in that direction. At home air-base station hospitals became professionally, though not administratively, the equivalent of general hospitals, and by 1944 a system of regional hospitals eased without eliminating the administrative problems. Overseas no such formal adjustment was made, but it does not appear that the patients or the war effort suffered as much as the amount of correspondence on both sides might suggest.

In the matter of the disposition of the airman considered unfit for flying—whether by himself, his flight surgeon, or his commanding officer—the surgeon was the middleman between two individuals whose interests were not easily reconciled, and he had to face his problem without benefit of tradition or statistical evidence. Success in this field was perhaps the severest test of those practicing the art of aviation medicine. The commanding officer found it easier on his conscience (he was, it must be remembered, himself a flier subject to the same stresses as the patient and usually differing from him little in age and at the squadron level in rank) to dispose of a case by medical cause than by administrative action, but there was never any desire by higher authorities (again, fliers) to take from the line commander his prerogative in this respect. Attempts to apply psychiatric diagnosis to the problem of the flier unwilling to fly did little to clarify the issue. Eventually, the air surgeon lost his power to ground the flier except under certain recognized medical or psychoneurotic conditions. But, in the matter of prescribing rest leaves in the case of unusual stress, he had an important preventive and therapeutic device. Air surgeons of all ranks favored a policy of a fixed tour of duty and of a reasonable rotation plan, but these matters were determined by theater commanders in accordance with their respective missions and resources and hence differed widely among the several combat areas. Often the policy seemed severe, and never was it as comfortable as the average flier wished, but there is no evidence that most fliers suffered any permanent emotional damage.

In the realm of "human engineering" the AAF medical establishment played an important role in research dedicated to the recurrent problems of flight in standard military planes and in planes with revolutionary flight characteristics. In all such experiments doctors have served as research subjects as well as researchers, and many of the improvements that have made supersonic flight possible are a result of the courage as well as of the scientific skills of the air surgeon.

The chapter on morale was written by a veteran of World War II whose own experiences provided insight on a wide range of problems that faced the airman—from induction through the various phases of training, the move overseas, a tour of combat in an active theater that ended when his plane was shot down over enemy territory where he sweat out a term in a POW camp, and on through the return to freedom, to the United States, and to civilian life. Appreciating the hazards inherent in the treatment of a subject on which every serviceman has a certain expertness but where there is little in the way of quantitative evidence, the author has provided a disciplined approach by defining his topic in functional terms and by examining as objectively as might be the positive and negative factors involved before making what could be only a value judgment. Morale he conceives as an attitude of mind leading to the willing (and good) or to the unwilling (and bad) performance of duty under a given condition. Morale factors might differ from place to place and from unit to unit and were apt to be volatile within any unit at any place. But there were certain constants—belief in ultimate victory, realization that efforts were being made toward their well-being, and a general preference for the AAF over other services—that affected favorably most airmen of whatever status.

Allowing for wide variations among the many organizations concerned and for ups and downs within any single one, the author renders the verdict that morale within the AAF as a whole "hovered, on a rough average, between fair and good." Organizations and individuals whose attitudes transcended or lapsed below this comfortably better-than-average median—and especially the latter—have demanded usually an undue measure of attention, and even in this chapter the emphasis is perhaps on the causes of discontent. The factors that affect morale have been analyzed here, and on the whole they are fundamentally—perhaps by definition—moral rather than physical in nature. Effective leadership, proper assignment of jobs, identification of the individual with his unit, recognition of the value of that job—these were far more important in determining attitudes than weather, physical comforts, or the activities of morale agencies, though these latter factors became increasingly important as the former were lacking.

AAF leaders realized the vital importance of morale during the initial stages of the airman's career as he made the difficult transition from civilian to military life. But in the period of rapid expansion of the Air Corps it was impossible to provide proper leadership and qualified enlisted permanent party personnel in basic-training centers. In job classification the AAF is reputed to have done better on the whole than the AGF or ASF, but there were many mistakes and inequities, both among cadets and enlisted airmen. Some of the worst problems were to be found among cadets and enlisted reservists, where overzealous recruiting in an effort to stockpile talent and a constant shifting of requirements and quotas led to unwelcome reassignments or timeless idleness in manpower pools which bred discontent. At technical and flying schools morale was on average better among trainees, who could hope to move on, than among instructors and permanent party personnel, who felt doomed eternally to a task enjoying few rewards and little status. Occasionally, a training program would go sour all over, as with the glider-pilot program, and there was always the special morale problem of the washout and the combat veteran returned from overseas for additional or new training.

Generally, morale of the individual improved as he found some group identification in OTU, though here there was difficulty as certain aircraft models—the P-38, B-24, and B-26, to cite examples—became ill famed among trainees for reputedly dangerous flying characteristics. This problem was handled forthrightly by the establishment of special transitional schools and the purveyance of information more accurate than that current in latrine rumors, so that a feeling of fear was often transformed into one of pride in the plane.

Departure for overseas stations brought problems of final leaves and furloughs and of the trip over, which was relatively short and filled with novelties for those going by air but which might drag out to the edge of eternity in some of the longer voyages by surface ships, where comforts were few and boredom rampant.

Physical comforts differed from theater to theater. Generally, it might be said that in all such matters—climate, health conditions, food, housing—airmen fared better in the ETO and MTO than in the Pacific or CBI. Whatever the food situation, men tended to gripe in the time-honored fashion of soldiers, but those who had any basis of comparison were well aware of the differences between the menus in, say, Assam and Italy. In the Pacific there was little in the way of local fresh food, and the long supply lines, the lack of control over transportation facilities, and the shortage of refrigerating machinery doomed most AAF units to a perpetual diet of canned and dehydrated foods. During active periods discontent over food (and other physical matters) was overshadowed by satisfaction in accomplishment, but perennially morale was strained when airmen saw Navy personnel in the same area living a more abundant life.

Ground personnel of the AAF rarely had over any considerable period enough immediate contact with the enemy for danger to be much of a morale problem—in fact, the occasional skirmish on an airstrip was more often than not a welcome relief from monotony. Overwork, if prolonged, could strain a unit beyond endurance, while normally hard work was a powerful positive factor. But busy work, assigned to keep airmen out of mischief, was easily recognized and hated; so was work to provide amenities for officers who already lived better than the enlisted men assigned, say, to build an officers' club. Lulls in work between campaigns, the slow pace of work in rear echelons, or bypassed stations bred discontent, only occasionally allayed by information programs that related the airman's seemingly inconsequential job to the war effort. Perhaps the greatest spur to optimism in an active theater came with the recurrent advances which, whatever its compass direction, was oriented in the airman's heart toward his own home.

The flier shared with ground personnel most of the latter's morale problems, and he faced some that were peculiar to his genus. Chief of these was attrition. Heavy casualties tended to depress morale, though there were so many qualifying factors that there was certainly no precisely definable ratio between combat losses and the martial attitude of a unit. Even small losses in an inactive theater might seriously affect survivors, while in a great offensive a well-led unit could absorb severe punishment without breaking—if replacements were prompt and plentiful, if the objective of the campaign or mission seemed worth the effort expended, and if the aircrewmen believed they had succeeded in their assignment. Everywhere, but especially where losses were high, morale was improved by efforts of command to diminish casualties—as in the long struggle, eventually successful, to provide fighter escort for long-range daylight bomber missions, the complex arrangements for air-sea rescue, or the development of such safety devices as navigational aids and body armor.

Recognition of accomplishments was one of the most powerful positive factors in morale. Since recognition was not conditioned inexorably by climate or distance or logistics, its skilful manipulation might have provided a compensating value against some of the unavoidable unpleasantnesses of war. But in many cases what Herodotus called the "due meed of glory" was dispensed most liberally where needed least and even at times where it was not deserved. The "big-league" air forces tended to hog most of the newspaper publicity, and even in the award of decorations there were inequalities as among air forces and within any one. Most coveted of all forms of recognition was promotion, and in this matter inequities—caused most frequently by inflexible TO's and the habit of making replacements in grade—caused serious problems, particularly in veteran combat units overseas, where it seemed that, the farther one stayed away from the enemy, the better the chance for advancement.

Much was done to make more endurable, or less dreary, such leisure time as fell to the airman. By far the most important service of this sort was mail, and, in spite of occasional blunders and unavoidable accidents, mail was delivered with a regularity and dispatch remarkable under the circumstances. Materials for other diversions were provided by Special Services officers, Information and Education officers, chaplains, and such agencies as the American Red Cross and USO. Again the advantages lay with the ETO and MTO, where the airman at his station could readily be provided with recreational materials from the United States and the airman on leave could enjoy the pleasures (including female companionship) of a culture not radically different from his own. It was only by ingenious improvisation of local talent and facilities and by heroic endeavors on the part of visiting entertainers that airmen in outlying stations in Asia and the Pacific could be afforded some recreation. Rest areas and camps of various degrees of attractiveness were established in most theaters; but, in the Pacific, distances from the front were too great for any full use thereof, especially for ground personnel, whose leaves were few and far between.

Far more important to the airman than temporary rest leave was the matter of rotation—the return to a stateside station after a definitely prescribed tour of combat duty measured in missions, combat hours, or time spent overseas. Eventually, most combat crews were rotated before permanent exhaustion set in, but the fluctuating tactical situation in each theater and the inevitable competition for newly trained aircrews between those who wished replacements for existing units and those who were building additional units for an expanding total effort made it hard to formulate a lasting policy. Under the circumstances it was impossible to please all, and the worst blows to morale came perhaps because of well-intentioned but ill-advised declarations of policy which could not be implemented. As far as the ground personnel were concerned, there was little chance for relief until late in the war and often not even then, and it was precisely in the same areas that were most unpleasant in other respects, and to a large degree because of the same limiting factors of distance and low shipping priorities that affected adversely so many phases of his life, that the mechanic or clerk was doomed so often to finish the war in his unloved foreign station.

There can be no doubt that throughout the war the top echelons of AAF command were acutely aware of the tremendous importance of morale and that, according to their insights, their conscience, and their capabilities, they did what they could to promote a better spirit among their men. In some of the most crucial issues they were circumscribed by conditions of war that lay beyond their control, and there any action must be palliative rather than curative. Evidence provided by this chapter (and by the common-sense observation of most reflective persons who spent a fair amount of time in military service during the war) would seem to indicate that effective leadership at any level was the key to morale, but how to provide that leadership under conditions obtaining presents a problem as complex as that of morale itself. To some it has seemed that too much emphasis was placed on trying to preserve under battle conditions the American standard of living, too little on making clear to the airman the values for which he was fighting. In this latter aim, if not in the values or the method of inculcation, it may be that we have something to learn from our enemies. But this is a matter for present and future study, not for history, which must deal with the past.

Air-sea rescue service was a valuable aid to morale, and it reinforced, as did the air surgeon's doctrine, the AAF stress on the value of the individual flier. But beyond these humanitarian considerations, deep rooted in the American view of life, there was the hardheaded desire to conserve the precious supply of aircrewmen who represented a great investment in time, effort, and money and who frequently had the irreplaceable advantages of experience. Air-sea rescue was an important boon to operations in the ETO and MTO, but it was at the same time more necessary and more difficult in the Pacific areas, where long overwater flights were a common feature in most offensive campaigns.

At the beginning of the war the AAF had no organization or equipment designed for air-sea rescue. AAF responsibility included only the provision of emergency survival equipment and the indoctrination of crews in its use. Responsibility for the actual rescue of fliers down at sea was a command rather than a headquarters matter, and in the early part of the war the overseas air forces were content to rely on the facilities of Allies or of a sister service: of the RAF in the ETO, the U.S. Navy and the Royal Navy in the NATO and MTO, and the U.S. Navy and the services of the Allies in the Pacific areas. The limited AAF responsibilities were shunted around among various agencies with the frequent headquarters changes, falling in August 1943 to the Emergency Rescue Branch of OC&R. By that time it was evident that the increasing tempo of air operations would put a strain on the borrowed facilities of the Navy and our Allies, and hence it seemed expedient to give air-sea rescue the backing of that powerful office.

The economy of a greater integration of air-sea rescue facilities was recognized by all, and from the spring of 1943 this problem was studied by several agencies of the JCS. Navy representatives wished to turn top responsibility over to the Coast Guard; the AAF, to some joint liaison body which was to determine policy but exercise no command. Desiring to make its forces as nearly self-sufficient in this respect as in others, AAF Headquarters in August 1943 set up seven air-sea rescue squadrons, intending to use them chiefly in the Pacific, where contemplated B-29 operations would tax severely existing services and where the AAF preferred the assignment of rescue units to an air force as being more flexible than the Navy's practice of assigning them to a fixed area or island command. Unfortunately for the air planners, their seven squadrons came into action slowly, two in the summer of 1944, the other four during the last months of the war.

It is difficult to give any statistical estimate of the success of ASR operations because of the different methods of reporting and computing used by the various agencies concerned and because so much of the pertinent information was never reported. Such data as are available show a marked, though not always steady, improvement in every theater. By September 1944 some 90 per cent of Eighth Air Force crewmen forced down at sea were saved, and the total ran to well over two thousand men. A comparable number of Fifth Air Force men were rescued in spite of its smaller number of men assigned and the longer overwater flights. The severest test for ASR agencies was in connection with the VLR strikes against the Japanese homeland. Here about half—654 of 1,310—of Superfort crewmen reported down were saved, and at the end of the war the rate of rescues had risen to 80 per cent. This was at a tremendous cost in effort, amounting in the last strike in August 1945 to 2,400 men in airplanes, surface craft, and submarines standing guard for about three times as many in combat crews.

The chances of survival and rescue depended on many variables—weather, communications, characteristics of the ailing plane, and survival equipment at hand—but outside of luck the most important factors were the skill and discipline of the crewmen themselves. There were arguments for and against bailing out as opposed to ditching; generally, fighter pilots preferred to parachute, members of multiplace crews to ride the plane down, though the behavior of the several types of bombers varied sharply when put into open sea waters. But, in any case, it was the crew or individual who knew his equipment and followed tested procedures who had the best chance of getting back to his base.

According to AAF doctrine, its own air-sea rescue agency (whatever its designation) was responsible for developing and procuring survival equipment for the tactical plane, rescue equipment for the search-and-rescue plane, and the latter plane itself. Efforts in these duties came late and consisted of varying combinations of adoptions, adaptations, and new inventions. In life-rafts, for instance, the AAF developed its own five-man type along lines suggested by Pan American Airways experience, turned to the Navy for a one-man raft, and used an RAF dinghy until perfecting one of its own. Much care was spent on selecting the most essential items for inclusion where weight and space had to be measured carefully and in finding suitable models. Devices for attracting attention of searchers, fresh-water stills, rations, emergency kits, parachutes, and other gear were adopted as-is, modified, or built to specifications. The famed Gibson Girl portable radio transmitter, though possessing some obvious weaknesses, saved many an airman and was never wholly replaced by improved models. It was late in the war before the AAF had in operations a droppable boat of its own design.

In ASR operations almost every type of aircraft from the tiny liaison plane to the VHB Superfort was used. The bulk of the work was done by multiengine planes—Navy Catalinas (and AAF variations), British Warwicks, and AAF B-24's, B-17's, and B-29's in particular. Each plane had certain advantages, but none was ideally suited for the job, and no plane was specifically designed from scratch for this highly specialized purpose. Each plane used had a long list of notable rescues within the area it conned, but in the long reaches of the Pacific between the Marianas and Japan it was only the B-29 which had the range, stamina, and defensive power required for patrolling the flight route of the VHB's attacking the cities on Honshu. Hence the Superdumbo, as the ASR modification of the B-29 was called, came into heavy service in the last months of the war. By that time the helicopter was undergoing its first testing in ASR work under combat conditions. The AAF developed several types of surface rescue boats, but none of these—nor standard-type small craft pressed into service—possessed an ideal combination of characteristics.

In the long run it was the courage and devotion and skill of the rescue crews and the discipline and endurance of the downed flyers that counted most heavily. These human qualities made up frequently for equipment that was imperfect and command procedures that were cumbersome. In sum, ASR efforts paid off handsomely in the men actually saved and from the great lift the airman got from his knowledge that a spill into the ocean would not necessarily be fatal.

During World War II the armed services in their need sought the aid of American women for performance of the countless tasks for which they were qualified, and the editors have found this precedent both useful and pleasant as they have enlisted the help of a woman to describe the part played by women in the AAF during the war.

At Pearl Harbor time there was no general agreement as to the proper and optimum use of women under conditions of total war. The career of military nurse was a familiar one; in World War I the Army had used civilian women in some overseas jobs, and the Navy, for all its reputation for conservatism, had used enlisted women with status equivalent to that of men. There had been one prescient study, the "Hughes plan" of 1928, which recommended the full use of women in all possible capacities, but it had received little or no attention. More lively impetus came from the experiences of Great Britain and from less precise information about Russia and China during the early part of World War II, from the pressure of women's organizations, and from recent social and demographic changes which had broken down prejudices in the United States to the extent that thirteen million women were gainfully employed, while nineteen million other eligible women remained as a vast reservoir which became increasingly attractive as selective service and war industry depleted the manpower pool.

Under these conditions, but without War Department support, U.S. Representative Edith N. Rogers of Massachusetts introduced on 28 May 1941 a bill providing for a women's army auxiliary corps. Stymied for months by the Bureau of the Budget, the bill was resurrected after Pearl Harbor and became law on 15 May 1942; its provision for enlistment of 150,000 volunteers was limited temporarily to 25,000 by executive order. There was much public disapproval (as there had been for each stage in women's emancipation), and of more immediate importance there was a firm resistance on the part of Army command. Commanders were won over by the efficient service of Waacs assigned to them, but, in general, the attitude of men of all ranks was not favorable.

Negative public and military opinion made recruiting of volunteers difficult, and except during concentrated drives the rate of enlistment always lagged. Part of the trouble (and the main part in the worm's-eye view of one of the editors who spent an anxious and frustrating fortnight in 1943 trying to enlist the women of central Texas for WAC service) lay in the sales pitch, keyed somewhere between Madison Avenue and Hollywood, which tried to glamourize the WAAC job instead of appealing to patriotism and to the obvious argument that a woman's effort would help shorten, if only in an infinitesimal degree, the duration of the war and her separation from boy friend or husband or son. As Army leaders came to appreciate the wide range of services which could be rendered by women, some envisaged a tremendous expansion of the WAC (perhaps through draft) to replace more than a million men; but, as it was, the corps never secured so much as two-thirds of the 150,000 volunteers authorized. Deliberate publicity was inept, and unsought publicity was more often than not harmful. The WAAC had to face the competition of similar programs in the other services, some of which had shrewder publicity programs and all of which had—by a common opinion in which the editors concur—a sleeker uniform.

In general, the AAF's willingness to experiment proved a boon to those Waacs who were assigned to its service. The AAF was an early and staunch supporter of full military status—the issue was determined in summer 1943 when the WAAC became the WAC—and, though its effort to secure a separate women's corps was scotched, members of the Women's Army Corps became an accepted and valuable part of the air arm, receiving a popular (though wholly unofficial) distinction from their sisters in the AGF or ASF by the common designation of Air Wacs.

Used originally in the Aircraft Warning Service, Air Waacs began to move regularly into other occupations about March 1943. Contrary to prevalent views (and hopes), they were not assigned to mess and barrack and laundry duties for male units in an effort to approximate the popular conception of the traditional role of the woman as housekeeper. They were exempted from certain types of guard and MP duties and, as well, from the service as "hostesses" and "strolling minstrels" hopefully listed by Air Corps planners in 1939, but they took over an astonishing number of military specialties. In spite of discomforts and occasionally unpleasant publicity, Wacs serving with the AAF whether in ZI or overseas posts had generally the high morale of an elite corps, serving under trial but with the increasing support and confidence of top command.

The change from the semimilitary status of the WAAC to the full status of the WAC in the summer of 1943 was welcomed by the AAF. Losses in personnel at this time were few and in some individual cases not mourned, but the gap between the 15,000 Wacs remaining and the approved quota of 65,000 was wide enough to justify an enlistment policy in which the recruit chose her own branch of the Army. With an intensive campaign stressing a choice of jobs by the candidate (but still with the emphasis on self-interest and the fancy jobs) the Training Command recruited as Air Wacs more women than did the AGF and ASF combined. Still this was only half of the total desired. Part of the special attractiveness of the Air WAC program lay in its policy of opening all non-combat specialties to women, which was real even if its possibilities for most women were overplayed in the recruiting "come-ons"; part lay in the honest attempt to eliminate to the extent possible repetitive and useless military and job training.

Wacs served with overseas air forces from the summer of 1943 and in larger numbers when administrative changes of June 1944 gave the AAF greater control over the assignment of Air Wacs. Eventually, more than 7,000 Air Wacs were assigned to overseas stations; more were requested than were shipped out, and, though the number was small both actually and percentage-wise, it was sufficient to provide evidence to allay most fears concerning the practicability of combat-theater service for women. Only rarely did housing present more of a problem for women than for men, and, on the average, their health record was about as good as that of non-combat male personnel. In discipline, military courtesy, and appearance—the outward signs of morale—Air Wacs were generally superior to men, and indeed their morale on the whole was high, save when classification and job assignment were faulty. In some areas Wacs moved up into forward stations and performed admirably in spite of dangers and hardships. Studies made late in the war showed a high degree of corps loyalty among the Air Wacs, and by that time their value had become more generally recognized among outsiders.

In contrast to their enthusiastic use of women in the many specialties eventually opened to them as Air Wacs, top leaders and most pilots in the AAF were opposed to their use as fliers. There was some precedent in England, however, for the wartime use of women pilots in certain capacities, and, when women prominent in American aviation began to enlist public support, they were able to force the AAF to accept their proffered aid. Actually, two programs were proposed and adopted simultaneously. One, the Women's Auxiliary Flying Squadron, was composed of a limited number of experienced pilots who needed little additional training. The other, the Women's Flying Training Detachment, was conceived along more ambitious lines to include a much larger number of candidates for training. In August 1943 the two organizations were merged to form the Women Air Force Service Pilots, still an auxiliary body. Unlike the WAC, WASP got much favorable (if sometimes overly dramatic) publicity, and applications ran fourteen to one for each opening. Of 1,830 admitted to training, 1,074 completed the requirements (with a washout rate comparing favorably with that of aviation cadets) and were assigned to duty. Training programs varied with the experience level of the candidates, which tended to decrease progressively, but the skills taught, outside those of immediate use in combat, were comparable to those standard in Training Command schools.

The principal job for WASPs was in ferrying aircraft within the United States, and in this they took regular turns with male pilots in delivering aircraft of most models. Thus ATC was a prime user of their talents, though eventually more were assigned to Training Command for operational use and in connection with their own training programs, and they drew other assignments as well. Gradually, they won the confidence of commanding officers at every echelon and, more difficult, of many but not all of the male pilots with whom they were in direct competition.

As a civil service organization, the WASP lacked some of the advantages of military status (and, an outsider might believe, some of the disadvantages that its friends did not stress). Efforts in Congress to militarize the service began in September 1943, supported in principle by the AAF but not by the War Department. Thereafter termination of the CAA War Training Service and the AAF college-training program released many experienced civilian pilots for non-combat service at a time when it was evident that the declining attrition rate in combat would eventually provide a surplus of male pilots. So on 20 December 1944 the WASP was deactivated, before its pilots had been able to make their full contribution to the war effort. They had proved, within the opportunities opened to them, their capacity to handle tasks as efficiently as the men who were doing the same job. Whether their contribution was worth the expenditure in time, effort, and financial expenditure involved is a more difficult question to answer and one which the editors as prudent men with a high regard for the other sex and a lasting memory of the sort of national psychology that sent post-draft-age university professors into service in the AAF would not wish to pronounce on.

A more conventional type of service for women, but one which sometimes came closer to the violence of war, was rendered by the 6,500 members of the Army Nurses Corps who were assigned to the AAF. All AAF nurses underwent an additional four-week training course before being assigned to a station hospital which remained the normal duty for more than 90 per cent of their numbers. But after six months of this service such nurses as received the proper recommendations became eligible to apply for flight-nurse training. Graduates of the very rugged eight-week course became then the elite in an already elite corps. During 1943 flight nurses came into service wherever the AAF operated. Their task was to care for the wounded and sick in air evacuation, and hence their ministrations were not limited to members of the AAF. Theirs was an arduous and risky duty that carried them to evacuation points within sight of the enemy, but the rewards were rich as it became obvious how greatly air evacuation was contributing to the reduction of deaths from battle wounds, one of the most revolutionary medical gains during the war.

Women served the AAF in a civilian as well as a military capacity. By June 1943, female employees numbered 151,061 and thereafter comprised roughly 45 per cent of the AAF's civilian strength. In addition to the familiar clerical and office-management positions, these women worked in an astonishing variety of tasks, particularly in Air

Service Command depots. Other women served too in part-time jobs with the Aircraft Warning Service, the Civil Air Patrol, and other organizations, mostly on a volunteer basis.

In sum, the experience of the AAF with women tended to show that those who came in performed, within their assigned duties, about as well as men under comparable circumstances and that those who stayed out were motivated by reasons understandable in the main by men. In the minds of many this experience suggested the drafting of women in any future war, and one can only hope that there will be no occasion to test the wisdom of this judgment.

Redeployment and demobilization are quite different processes but are treated in a single chapter here. In common military usage in the United States during World War II, redeployment came to refer especially to the transfer of troops, once the war against Germany should be ended, from the European theaters to the Pacific areas. Since the move was to be made ordinarily via the United States, the early collapse of Japan made it almost inevitable that the two processes should be combined in fact as well as in speech.

The problem of disbanding armies comprised largely of civilians-in-arms was a familiar one in American history. Always before it had been accomplished in haste and without any orderly plan. Aware of this record of confusion, which would be exaggerated by the very magnitude of the forces involved in World War II, the President early in 1942 initiated planning for demobilization and transition to a civilian life of full employment. The fact that the United States was in effect fighting separate wars against Germany and Japan, each with its own timetable, added to the difficulties inherent in the numbers of personnel involved. Responsibility for the purely military phase of demobilization shifted from agency to agency in the usual fashion, but, as was so often the case, the changes were more usually in the designation of the office than in the key officers engaged in the study. The crucial part of the planning was done by the Special Planning Division of the War Department, in which a member of the Air Staff's Special Project Office represented the AAF's interests.

The War Department's SPD favored a plan of demobilization by individuals, in which priority would be determined by skills, time in service, and dependencies. The AAF, faced with a relatively heavier share in the last phases of the Japanese war than was planned for the AGF, preferred demobilization by unit as less disruptive of continuing squadrons and groups as combat teams. Here one may see a curious contrast to the AAF's stress on the individual as presented in the chapter on aviation medicine. But for the handling of extreme cases of individual need the AAF had provided some machinery in the establishment in 1943, in some resort areas of the United States, of redistribution centers and stations and rest camps, later reinforced by convalescent hospitals. Through these means it was hoped that many combat flyers rotated from a tour of duty overseas might be restored to effective duty or discharged.

It was the War Department view of individual separation in an order determined by several factors that finally prevailed, the fundamental plan being described in Readjustment Regulation 1-1 of 30 August 1944. An elaborate system of points representing length of service—total, overseas, and combat—plus other factors was established; this was acceptable to the AAF for enlisted personnel but not for officers, and in this last respect the AAF was able to modify the general rule. When the war against Germany was prolonged beyond autumn of 1944, the AAF reshaped its policies to allow for the discharge of a large proportion of the personnel in units redeploying through the United States and for their replacement by men from ZI commands.

Supervision of redeployment was the main responsibility of the Continental Air Forces, activated on 15 December 1944. An elaborate plan was devised for the return of units to the United States, the screening of personnel, the assignment of those eligible for redeployment to thirty days' "recuperation, rehabilitation, and recovery," and the replacement of all ineligible airmen before the unit shipped out for the Pacific. In the ETO, redeployment plans were held up until spring of 1945 and, once made, were changed frequently and arbitrarily. The same was true in the MTO, and in this situation AAF personnel officers found it impossible to harmonize their directives from theater headquarters with the AAF plan. Nor was the process any less capricious within the Continental Air Forces. In sum, only one bombardment and two air service groups were redeployed through the United States. Some units returned from Europe for this purpose became lost in a tangled maze of maladministration. Some units were kept in Europe as occupation forces, other melted away. It was the sudden end of the Japanese war that threw personnel procedures into complete confusion—as it had been the unexpectedly long resistance of the Germans that had begun the confusion—for this confounded the problems of demobilization with those of redeployment. Had the war lasted, it is probable that the latter process would have been improved, but in retrospect, as in 1945, redeployment appears as a classic example of military inefficiency.

By comparison demobilization was rapid and reasonably efficient. Whether this rapidity was in the best national interest was a matter that lay outside the ken of the AAF, and properly so in a democracy, though some of the pressures to get the boys home—exerted by the press, the Congress, and the men themselves—were to be repudiated later by those same forces. The AAF had reached a peak strength of 2,411,294 in March 1944, declining thereafter in total numbers, though its officer strength continued to rise for a year thereafter. This meant, then, that some enlisted personnel had been transferred or separated long before the war ended. Immediately after V-J Day the AAF was given permission to separate its own personnel in the United States, and through separation centers operated by CAF it began the task at once. This crash program was finished by the following February, though the total strength of the AAF continued to shrink both in men and in approved units as plans for the postwar air force were being reshaped. The structure of the air arm underwent a thorough reorganization in March 1946 in anticipation of the imminent establishment of the separate U.S. Air Force, the goal of most airmen since the days of Billy Mitchell. And with those plans this history of *The Army Air Forces in World War II* may close.

The contributors to this volume are identified in the Table of Contents, but it may be helpful to note here a few additional biographical facts. John D. Carter and Frank H. Heck, who have contributed the chapters on air transport, served during the war as historical officers at ATC Headquarters, as did also Jonas A. Jonasson, who is responsible for the chapters on weather, Army Airways Communications, and air-sea rescue. Mr. Carter is the author of a chapter in Volume I on "The Early Development of Air Transport and Ferrying." John E. Fagg, after service with the Far East Air Forces, became a member of the staff of the AAF Historical Division, where he undertook studies of strategic bombing operations from Britain that are represented by some of the more significant chapters published in Volume III of this history. Dr. George V. LeRoy, Associate Dean of the Division of the Biological Sciences in the University of Chicago, brings to his sympathetic discussion of the problems faced by the air surgeon an understanding gained through service as a medical officer with the

Army Ground Forces. The editors find a special satisfaction in presenting his conclusions on one of the more controversial subjects in the history of the AAF. Martin R. R. Goldman served in the war as a combat crewman with a B-24 outfit in the Eighth Air Force, was shot down over Germany, and knew finally the experience of a prisoner of war. When he wrote the chapter on morale, he was a member of the staff of the USAF Historical Division. Currently, he has a grant from the Social Science Research Council for completion of a study of German air defenses against the combined AAF-RAF attack on Germany. Kathleen Williams Boom was an especially competent member of the research staff of the AAF Historical Division during the war years and contributed so significantly to Volume I of this history as to make the editors particularly happy to have her assistance in closing the series. Chauncey E. Sanders is one of the members of the USAF Historical Division who has made the editors' visits to "headquarters" especially pleasant to remember. Dr. Sanders' willingness to accept the final responsibility for the Index to this volume has made it possible to meet a tight publication schedule.

In going to press, the editors once more have a keen sense of their indebtedness to the entire staff of the USAF Historical Division and especially to Dr. Albert F. Simpson, Air Force Historian. His professional competence and his willingness at all times to provide assistance in clearing up obscurities in the record have been most helpful. It is a special pleasure to acknowledge also the courtesies extended by Col. Garth C. Cobb, recently appointed Director of the Research Studies Institute in the Air University. The editors count it a part of their good fortune that Colonel Cobb, from the war years forward, has more than once held an assignment which put him in a position to demonstrate his friendly understanding of the historian's task. They are happy too in making here a final acknowledgment of the substantial assistance given by Colonel Cobb's predecessors, Col. Curtis D. Sluman, Brig. Gen. Clinton W. Davies, and Col. Wilfred J. Paul. A special salute belongs to Colonel Paul for the patience he showed while the editors got five of the seven volumes through the press. The number and variety of our obligations to other members of the staff, present and past, make us reluctant to single out any one of them for special mention here, but there are two who must be mentioned. From the beginning of Volume I through the completion of Volume VII, Miss Marguerite Kennedy, as custodian of the Division's archives, has been as patient as anyone could rightly expect, and Mr. David Schoem has generously lent to us his expert knowledge of the ways of government.

To specific acknowledgments made in earlier forewords, we add here our thanks to Dr. Edward C. Williamson, Mr. James Daniels, and Dr. Earle K. Stewart for assistance in the editing of the text for Volume VII; to Mr. Z. F. Shelton for the maps; to Miss Marguerite Kennedy, Mr. Frank Myers, and Miss Ethel Gaines for research assistance; and to Miss Sara Venable, Mrs. Margie McCardel, Mrs. Dorothy Turner, and Mrs. Molly Keever for typing. On the rare occasions when Dr. Simpson could not be found at his desk, Mr. Joseph W. Angell had the answer we needed.

As we come to the end of a project that has engaged much of our professional attention for the last dozen years, we would like to make two general acknowledgments. In the first place, we wish to thank the contributors to this and earlier volumes for the time and the energy they have given to the project and for the tolerance they have shown at our exercise of editorial prerogative. Few of them have had a primary interest in military history; it was the accident of war and the enterprise of Col. Clanton W. Williams, the AAF's wartime historian, that brought most of the contributors into a momentary association with the field of aviation history. Most of them have returned to other professional interests, as now the editors expect to do. In so doing, we feel inclined to say that our chief encouragement to see the project through to completion has been the willingness of respected colleagues in the profession to devote their own time and energy to the same end. For us, it has been a rewarding collaboration. In the second place, we wish to express our respect for the way in which the United States Air Force has honored its commitment, at the beginning of the project, to give its historians full access to the record and full freedom in reporting thereon. Whatever the deficiencies of this history may be, none of them can be attributed to censorship, either overt or by indirection. It is a point the editors make with some pride, as citizens of the country and former officers in its Air Force.

WESLEY FRANK CRAVEN
JAMES LEA CATE

THE QUONSET
WHISKEY CREEK
OCEANA COUNTY, MICHIGAN
12 July 1958

CONTENTS

* * * * * * * * * * *

I. AIR TRANSPORT

John D. Carter, *Headquarters, U.S. Air Force*
Frank H. Heck, *Centre College of Kentucky*

II. AVIATION ENGINEERS

John E. Fagg, *New York University*

xlv

III. WEATHER AND COMMUNICATIONS

Jonas A. Jonasson, *Linfield College*

IV. MEDICINE, MORALE, AND AIR-SEA RESCUE

Dr. George V. LeRoy, *University of Chicago*
Martin R. R. Goldman
Jonas A. Jonasson, *Linfield College*

V. WOMEN IN THE AAF

Kathleen Williams Boom, *University of Tennessee
Extension Division, Memphis Center*

VI. REDEPLOYMENT AND DEMOBILIZATION

Chauncey E. Sanders, *USAF Historical Division*

LIST OF MAPS

*   *   *   *   *   *   *   *   *   *   *

LIST OF ILLUSTRATIONS

*   *   *   *   *   *   *   *   *   *   *

   xlviii

l

United States Air Force
Historical Advisory Committee
(As of May 1, 1983)

Lt. Gen. Charles G. Cleveland, USAF
Commander, Air University, ATC

Mr. DeWitt S. Copp
The National Volunteer Agency

Dr. Warren W. Hassler, Jr.
Pennsylvania State University

Dr. Edward L. Homze
University of Nebraska

Dr. Alfred F. Hurley
Brig. Gen., USAF, Retired
North Texas State University

Maj. Gen. Robert E. Kelley, USAF
Superintendent, USAF Academy

Dr. Joan Kennedy Kinnaird
Trinity College

Mr. David E. Place,
The General Counsel, USAF

Gen. Bryce Poe II,
USAF, Retired

Dr. David A. Shannon (*Chairman*)
University of Virginia

lii

SECTION I

* * * * * * * * * * *

AIR TRANSPORT

CHAPTER 1

✳   ✳   ✳   ✳   ✳   ✳   ✳   ✳   ✳   ✳   ✳

THE AIR TRANSPORT COMMAND

B Y NO means least among the achievements of the AAF in
World War II was its development of a world-wide system of
air transport. The transport aircraft—a carrier of freight, passengers, and mail which could double as a troop carrier or as an ambulance—lacked the popular appeal belonging to the bomber or fighter
plane. Nevertheless, it added a new dimension to the art of warfare,
and around its varied capacities the AAF built an air transportation
system such as had never before been envisaged. That system, and its
functions, soon became synonymous with the organization which controlled it, the Air Transport Command.

ATC borrowed heavily from the civil airlines, which during the
1930's had grown into a large enterprise and an increasingly significant
part of the transportation services on which the country depended.
From the airlines came experienced executives who were commissioned for key posts of command in the development of a military
transport service and veteran pilots who became pioneers of distant
military air routes. From the airlines came also the two planes on
which ATC principally depended: the C-47, an adaptation of the
DC-3, workhorse of the civil airlines in the 1930's, and the C-54, military version of the DC-4 that was designed to take over from the
DC-3 along civilian air routes. But the growth of the Army's military
air transport services involved much more than an adaptation of civilian experience and equipment. The airlines had been concerned almost
exclusively with the movement of passengers and mail. Although surface carriers normally depended upon freight for as much as 80 per
cent of their earnings, air freight accounted for only 2 or 3 per cent
of the gross revenues of U.S. airlines at the beginning of the war.[1] On

the other hand, ATC was very largely engaged, as its men were wont to say, in "a trucking business."

This was a business for which the AAF was not wholly lacking in experience. As early as 1931 the Army Air Corps had experimented with the systematic use of air transport for the distribution of aviation supplies. At that time considerations of economy governed all Air Corps operations, and expensive stockpiling of supplies at Army air bases had to be avoided. Consequently, the Materiel Division in 1932 established a provisional 1st Air Transport Group with four transport squadrons, each of them intended to serve one of the four major air depots (at Sacramento; San Antonio; Fairfield, Ohio; and Middletown, Pennsylvania) in the distribution of spare parts to Army air bases. The group, no longer provisional after 1937, also transported supplies from one depot to another.[2] As the expansion of the air arm got under way in 1939, there were new uses for air transport, among them the movement to aircraft factories of government-supplied equipment and other items that became critical in an expanding production of bomber and fighter planes. By January 1941 air-cargo services had so grown, and under so many auspices, that an attempt was made to bring all such activities under a new wing organization designated as the 50th Transport Wing. During the first six months of its existence, the wing hauled more cargo than all the American civil airlines combined.[3]

Its scheduled services included deliveries to the Panama Canal Zone, and the 50th Transport Wing might well have developed into the world-wide agency that ATC later became. Instead, the Air Transport Command had its origins in the Air Corps Ferrying Command that was established in May 1941 for assistance of the British in the movement by air of American-built planes from factories in the United States to Britain and the Middle East. The Ferrying Command (its name was borrowed from the British custom of describing the delivery of aircraft under their own power to tactical units as a "ferrying" operation) had at first a very limited responsibility. It flew the planes, chiefly from California, across country to points in Canada and on the East Coast of the United States at which British pilots took charge. But the command soon acquired additional responsibilities. Oriented from the first toward the support of combat forces overseas, the Ferrying Command became a pioneer of U.S. military air routes across the Atlantic to Britain and Africa. Before Pearl Harbor it had

4

inaugurated a transatlantic courier service to facilitate the increasingly close collaboration of the British and American armed services, and to this was added, especially after the United States entered the war, a growing transport service for cargo of critical military importance. In June 1942 the Air Corps Ferrying Command became the Air Transport Command.

Prewar Plans

Not until after the fall of France in the summer of 1940 did the U.S. aircraft program include substantial orders for transport planes. The Air Corps ordered 545 C-47's in September 1940 and at the same time placed an order with Curtiss-Wright for 200 of a wholly new and much larger two-engine transport, the C-46 (Commando). An additional 256 Commandos were ordered in May 1941, and in the following June an order was placed for just under a hundred C-53's, the Army's passenger version of the DC-3. In the same month, the AAF took over the orders of civilian airlines for sixty-one of Douglas' newly designed four-engine C-54. Contracts were signed in September for fifty more C-53's and for an additional seventy C-47's.[4] Each of these planes had been designed originally for passenger service on civilian airways. A series of single-engine freighters had been developed by the Air Corps in earlier years, and after 1939 several larger cargo planes were designed by manufacturers for military use, but few of these were produced, and none of them was used to any significant extent during the war.[5] Until virtually the end of hostilities ATC continued to depend upon planes that were either converted passenger aircraft or converted bombers.

The AAF's basic strategic plan, AWPD/1 of August 1941, proposed the use of transport aircraft in two categories. First, some 1,200 airplanes, with a depot reserve of over 300, would be required as troop carriers for direct support of ground operations. Between tactical commitments the troop carriers would double as cargo planes in order to provide for each theater of operations a service comparable to that currently supplied at home by the 50th Transport Wing. Second, 160 four-engine long-range transports and 880 two-engine transports of medium range would be needed "to effect the movement of critical essential aircraft and engine spares and supplies within the United States, between the United States and distant air bases of theaters and within theaters."[6] It was assumed that short supplies of aircraft engines and other spare parts would make necessary a system of central stockage and that the effectiveness of this system would depend upon "some method of ultra-rapid transportation" for the movement of "critical items from the central stock point to the point of need." Since the ultimate source of supply would be the United States, the plan called for long-range transport services across the North Atlantic to Britain, down by way of the Caribbean to Brazil, and then across the Atlantic narrows to Africa, westward across the Pacific to Hawaii and the Philippines, and northward through western Canada to Alaska.[7]

These were the air routes along which ATC built its fame, except that a base in the Azores made it possible after 1943 to develop a middle Atlantic run connecting with both Britain and Africa, that services were extended from Africa all the way into China, and that in the Pacific the airway at first ran south of the Solomons to Australia instead of into the Philippines. And there were other assumptions on which AWPD/1 was based that stood up well enough in the final test. The heavy commitment of transport aircraft to tactical operations found no small part of its justification in the fact that troop-carrier units served admirably between paratroop drops to provide significant intratheater transport services. The proposal that 160 four-engine transports be employed for intertheater services fell far short of the more than 1,000 actually used by ATC at its peak strength, but in the summer of 1941, when a land-based four-engine transport had yet to be put into production, the estimate made was daring enough. Nor should the authors of AWPD/1 apologize for their assumption that the long-range transports would need the support of more than 800 two-engine cargo aircraft, for this figure represented a very substantial part of the some 2,000 actually employed by ATC at its top strength.[8]

That the Air War Plans Division of AAF Headquarters should have failed in August 1941 to realize the full military potential of air transport is not surprising, for there was no model to follow except that of the Air Corps' own limited experience. It is evident that the planners were still thinking very largely of providing air transport for AAF technical supplies—for engines and other spare parts necessary to keep tactical planes in operation. Actually, ATC quickly developed into an agency of the War Department serving the whole war effort. Its planes carried out from the United States almost everything—from bulldozers to blood plasma, from college professors to Hollywood entertainers, from high-explosive ammunition to the most delicate signal equipment, from eminent scientists to the most obscure technicians, from heads of state to the ordinary G.I.—and they brought back hog bristles and tungsten from China, cobalt and tin from Africa, rubber and quinine from Latin America, and from all over the globe the wounded G.I. who could not expect to find in New Guinea, Luzon, Burma, North Africa, or even western Europe the medical attention he could have in the United States. And when the war ended in Europe, ATC had the capacity to bring home as many as 50,000 veterans per month.

In still another respect the war plans embodied in AWPD/1 failed to anticipate actual developments. Despite the fact that ATC had its beginning in the Ferrying Command, there seems to have been no appreciation of the magnitude of the effort ferrying activities would require. For some time after August 1941 the Air Staff continued to assume that the ferrying job would involve little more than guidance for tactical units flying their own planes to battle stations.[9] This estimate proved to be accurate enough for overseas operations during the earlier part of the war. But ACFC soon found it necessary to develop an elaborate organization within the United States for shuttling planes about from factory to modification center to training base or to aerial port of embarkation, and time imposed on ATC a heavy obligation to provide specially trained crews for delivery of lend-lease planes to Allied countries and of replacement aircraft to AAF combat units overseas. Experience also demonstrated that this ferrying activity added greatly to other responsibilities, for ferrying crews had to be returned by air transport to their stations of departure, and incidental services along the airways had to be proportionately enlarged.

The Air Corps Ferrying Command

Meanwhile, the Air Corps Ferrying Command plotted the course.* As early as November 1940, the British had undertaken to fly American-built bombers across the Atlantic from Canada by way of Newfoundland to Scotland. When the responsible agencies in the spring of 1941 found it difficult to recruit a sufficient number of qualified pilots for the transatlantic hop, General Arnold proposed to lend the assistance of the Air Corps. The British had been accepting delivery at the factory, and thus might have to provide pilots for flights extend-

* For full discussion with documentation, see Vol. I, 310–65.

7

ing all the way from California to Scotland. By having Air Corps pilots fly planes built on British contracts from the factory to the eastern port of embarkation it would be possible to enlarge the number of pilots who would be available for employment in flights across the Atlantic. The proposal found its technical justification in the need for Air Corps pilots to secure all possible training, and President Roosevelt readily indorsed the suggestion. As a result, the Air Corps Ferrying Command was established on 29 May 1941 under the command of Col. Robert Olds.[10]

Depending upon pilots on temporary assignment from the Combat Command, the new Ferrying Command flew more than 1,300 aircraft across country from factories to points of transfer on the East Coast before the Japanese attack at Pearl Harbor in December 1941. By that time a beginning also had been made in the delivery of planes from factories and modification centers to AAF units within the United States, a service that became during the first half of 1942 the heaviest single responsibility of the Ferrying Command. In delivering a few four-engine bombers to British forces in the Middle East and in the effort after Pearl Harbor to rush replacement aircraft to our own hard-pressed units in the Southwest Pacific, the command made a natural progression from a "domestic" to a "foreign" ferrying service. For some time, however, AAF planes moving by air to overseas theaters were usually flown by their own combat crews, and lend-lease planes by civilian pilots under contracts between the government and the airlines. Not until the problem of delivering replacement aircraft to AAF units overseas assumed large proportions would the ferrying of aircraft beyond the borders of the United States become a major activity of ATC.

In the development of overseas passenger and cargo services the story is different. As early as July 1941 the Ferrying Command had inaugurated a round-trip passenger service across the North Atlantic to Britain. Using converted B-24's of bucket-seat fame, the command averaged six trips per month until the service was terminated in October because of the approaching winter. Special flights were also made, such as that delivering a part of the Harriman mission to Moscow in September 1941 or that carrying Maj. Gen. George H. Brett, Chief of the Air Corps, to the Middle East in the same month. As with the ferrying of lend-lease planes, through-transport services along the critical South Atlantic air route to Africa and the Middle East were first developed on an important scale by contract with the civil airlines, which also assumed the main responsibility for reopening the transport service to Britain early in 1942. But in a variety of ways and in response to the most diverse emergency calls, ACFC found itself engaged in a growing transport activity.

Especially important was the aid rendered by it in the development of the transatlantic air routes. The responsibility for the actual establishment of necessary bases and facilities belonged to a variety of other agencies, some of them representing Allied countries; but in the continuing effort to supplement facilities along these routes the Ferrying Command gave important, if unavoidably limited, assistance in the conduct of preliminary surveys and in the movement of men, equipment, and supplies. In the early development of the transpacific air route, ACFC had little if any part to play. As an organization that had been brought into existence for the assistance of the British, its activities continued to show a focus appropriate to its original mission. The assignment of a control officer to Hamilton Field, California, early in January 1942 for the purpose of clearing aircraft to be ferried across the Pacific seems to mark the first identification of ACFC with the Pacific air route.*

The Ferrying Command had begun its existence with only a small headquarters staff, headed by Colonel Olds and including Maj. Edward H. Alexander as executive, Maj. William H. Tunner as personnel officer, and Maj. Thomas L. Mosley as operations officer.[11] For a year thereafter the staff remained small enough for its business to be conducted quite informally, with heavy dependence upon word-of-mouth agreements and hand-carried memos, as is revealingly told by a headquarters memorandum issued in June 1942 on the occasion of the command's move from cramped quarters in Washington across the river to Gravelly Point, Virginia. "Now that we are located in a much larger building area," advised the administrative executive, "our affairs can be conducted on a more orderly basis, and much time can be saved, if, instead of walking around to see if someone you desire to see is in, you will ring his office first on the inter-phone." And to this he added: "With respect to the operation of the office of the Commanding General, the practice of just walking in when you have something to discuss will be discontinued."[12]

The field organization began with the establishment of control

* See below, p. 175; and for the early story of the Pacific air route, see Vol. I, 178–93.

9

officers at key points along the air routes used in the ferrying of planes for the British. As representatives of the Ferrying Command, these officers supervised all plane movements under its jurisdiction and had responsibility for the return of aircrews to their starting points. Control officers situated at the several aircraft plants in the southwestern area of the United States functioned under the direction of a Western Division with headquarters initially located at Santa Monica, California. At eastern terminals, where the planes were transferred to the British, Montreal and Presque Isle (from early in 1942) were the most important assignments. Developed on the initiative of ACFC, Presque Isle promptly became the chief port of embarkation for U.S. aircraft flying the North Atlantic. With the growing importance of the South Atlantic route, ACFC received jurisdiction in January 1942 over Morrison Field, near West Palm Beach, Florida, which was quickly developed into another major port of embarkation. Provision had been made in the fall of 1941 for the assignment of ACFC control officers at all key bases on the South Atlantic route as far east as Cairo, though none of these officers reached his station before the Pearl Harbor attack.

Shortly after the United States became an active belligerent, ACFC Headquarters was expanded and two subordinate divisions were established: the Foreign and the Domestic. This reorganization confirmed an informal division of labor previously worked out, whereby Major Mosley directed overseas operations while Major Tunner handled those within the United States.[13] The Domestic Division, which was soon redesignated the Domestic Wing and was charged with supervision of all ferrying activities within the United States, functioned through six subordinate sectors with headquarters geographically distributed according to need.* During the first half of 1942, ACFC acquired possession of several materiel squadrons for maintenance and repair work, assumed the responsibilities of base command at key points, and secured the activation of a number of ferrying squadrons, a new type of military unit which gave to the command for the first time its own subordinate flying units. Under the Foreign Wing, Presque Isle became the headquarters of a North Atlantic Sector,

* The original sectors and their locations were: Northwest, Seattle, Wash.; California, Long Beach, Calif.; Midwest, Grand Prairie, Tex.; Nashville, Nashville, Tenn.; Detroit, Detroit, Mich.; and Northeast, Baltimore, Md.

Bolling Field, D.C., of a Transatlantic Sector, Morrison Field of a South Atlantic Sector, and Hamilton Field of a Pacific Sector.[14]

The extension of ACFC's overseas services had seemed to its leaders a logical development. But such a development required time for its completion, if only because of the limited resources of the command itself. A wide variety of war programs had placed the highest premium on all men having any experience whatsoever with aviation, and ACFC by no means enjoyed the highest priority. It often had to depend upon men who were not only unfamiliar with aviation but who also enjoyed little acquaintance with the ways of the Army itself. Its crews were subject to recall by the Air Force Combat Command, as were even the few B-24's that had been modified for its overseas service.

The most obvious recruiting ground for the Ferrying Command was that provided by the civil airlines. But in the post–Pearl Harbor emergency the government adopted the quickest expedient for putting their experience and equipment to use by pressing them into the national service on contract.* The pattern, indeed, had been set well before Pearl Harbor. Three subsidiaries of Pan American Airways had been established by agreement with the British and American governments in the early summer of 1941: Pan American Air Ferries for the delivery of U.S.-built aircraft from Miami to Khartoum in the Sudan, Pan American Airways Co. for the operation of a transport service from the United States to western Africa, and Pan American Airways–Africa, Ltd., for a transport service across Africa.† The services of PAA Ferries and PAA–Africa were extended by contract from Khartoum to Cairo and Tehran soon after Pearl Harbor. Eastern Air Lines supplemented PAA's services south from Miami after May 1942. Northeast Airlines had contracted for transport services along the North Atlantic route in the preceding January, and Transcontinental and Western Air in April began operations along the same route. In February 1942 Northwest Airlines undertook a service to Alaska, its efforts being supplemented by later contracts with Western Air Lines and United Air Lines.‡ And there were other such contracts, including those made for transport services within the United States.

* See Vol. I, 350–51.

† See Vol. I, 322–23.

‡ See Vol. I, 350–60.

ACFC had been made the monitor of some of the contracts, but it lacked full power, and its experiences with the airlines were not always happy. ATC's historian later had this to say:

> In the day-by-day working of the relations between the contract airlines and the Ferrying Command there were numerous occasions for friction. Airline personnel were sometimes resentful of what they termed interference by Army men, and often cocksure of their own superior qualifications. The advantage of the airlines and the convenience of their employees seem on occasion to have been the controlling factors in the determination of policy and the performance of duty by airline representatives in the field, if not in the home offices. The personal behavior of some airline pilots seems to have been consistently offensive. Ferrying Command officers, for their part, were by no means blameless....[15]

Despite the many advantages in the original dependence on contracts with the civil airlines and the valiant service rendered by civilian aircrews in the pioneering of untried airways, it was soon obvious that the mixing of civil and military agencies did not make a perfect blend.

That the Ferrying Command would carry the major responsibility for the development of an increasingly militarized service was indicated by the transfer in March 1942 of Col. Harold L. George from his post as Chief of the Air War Plans Division to the command of ACFC.* George, who became a brigadier general in April, had made his mark as a bombardment expert. As early as 1925 he had served as chief of the Bombardment Section in the Office, Chief of the Air Corps, and in the 1930's he had been the chief instructor in bombardment tactics at the Air Corps Tactical School. Head of the Air War Plans Division since June 1941, he had played a major role in the drafting of AWPD/1 and of other plans fundamentally affecting the development of America's war effort. There were few other officers whose assignment to ACFC could have offered comparable proof of the growing appreciation of its importance to the war effort.

For General George's executive officer, Arnold personally chose Cyrus R. Smith, the president of American Airlines.[16] Commissioned with the rank of colonel in mid-April, he served thereafter under more than one official designation, in keeping with immemorial military custom, but under all titles he was in effect chief of staff to General George. The partnership thus formed is representative of the foundations on which ATC would build its fabulous career.[17] In all areas of ATC's activity and at all levels of command, there were to be

---

* Olds, who had been promoted to brigadier general, became commanding general of the Second Air Force and was shortly promoted to major general.

12

found those who brought to their military duties valuable experience with the civil airlines, not to mention a keen sense of the long-range interests of civil aviation.

Although the spring of 1942 brought some changes in the organization of the Domestic Wing, among them a redesignation of the geographical sectors as headquarters of numerically designated ferrying groups,* there were more important developments in the Foreign Wing. By mid-June provision had been made for five overseas wings, each embracing a broad geographical area and carrying a geographical designation, the latter a departure from standard War Department practice. Wing headquarters, for which necessary headquarters and headquarters squadrons were activated, were to be located on the East Coast at Presque Isle (North Atlantic Wing) and West Palm Beach (Caribbean Wing), on the West Coast at Hamilton Field (South Pacific Wing), and overseas at Georgetown, British Guiana (South Atlantic Wing), and at Cairo in Egypt (Africa Middle East Wing). Plans at ACFC Headquarters called for each wing commander to be responsible for the "safe and expeditious movement of aircraft" through his wing, and to have necessary control of "weather, communications, maintenance and inspection facilities throughout his wing area."[18]

It took some time, however, to translate these plans into action and to clarify all the questions they raised. To take but one example for purposes of illustration, the jurisdiction of the North Atlantic Wing presumably extended from Presque Isle in Maine to Prestwick in Scotland. It had a commander from 8 June 1942 in the person of Col. Benjamin F. Giles, theretofore commanding the Greenland Base Command, and a mission defined as the "expeditious movement of all U.S. Army aircraft destined for Great Britain."[19] But when the Eighth Air Force began the air movement of its combat units to Britain that same month, the control was vested in the commanding general of the VIII Fighter Command. Not until late July did the North Atlantic Wing take full charge.

ATC

The Air Corps Ferrying Command, meanwhile, had been redesignated as the Air Transport Command and given a greatly expanded

---

* See above, p. 10. The 1st Ferrying Group, constituted on March 3, left for India by boat on March 17. Six additional groups (2–7) gave their designations to the old sectors.

mission.* Under General Orders No. 8 of 20 June 1942, ATC was established and made responsible for (1) "ferrying all aircraft within the United States and to destinations outside the United States" as directed by the Commanding General, AAF; (2) the "transportation by air of personnel, materiel, and mail for all War Department agencies, except those served by Troop Carrier units"; and (3) the "control, operation, and maintenance of establishments and facilities on air routes outside of the United States which are, or which may be made, the responsibility of the Commanding General, Army Air Forces."[20] Strictly speaking, these orders conferred upon the command no really new function, but the command now had a clear mandate to develop its air transport activities to the fullest possible extent and to extend its control of air traffic along all routes leading from the United States to the several battle fronts.

Especially significant was the provision making ATC the agent not merely of the AAF but of the whole War Department. Important, too, was the assignment to ATC of responsibilities theretofore largely carried by the 50th Transport Wing. The activities of that wing had been drastically modified on 30 April 1942, when it was transferred, with its equipment, to a newly activated Troop Carrier Command,† an organization charged primarily with the training of troop-carrier units for combat operations. Deprived thus of its principal air transport agency, the Air Service Command promptly turned to the civil airlines for assistance and organized a Contract Air Cargo Division staffed in large part by airline executives commissioned direct from civilian life. The tendency of this division to extend its services to points outside the United States, by contract with civil carriers, helped to shape the decision to concentrate responsibility in ATC. At one time General Arnold seems to have considered a division of function that would have given the responsibility for air transport within the Western Hemisphere to the Air Cargo Division and for air transport outside the hemisphere to the Ferrying Command. But in the end Arnold decided on a single command. The Air Service Command terminated its Air Cargo Division and transferred its personnel to ATC. As a final token of the War Department's agreement with the new plan, the Services of Supply on 1 July surrendered to the AAF,

* For full discussion, see Vol. I, 349–65.

† First designated the Air Transport Command but soon renamed the Troop Carrier Command.

14

and thus to ATC, the assignment of priorities for travel on military and commercial aircraft, a function theretofore held by the Transportation Service of SOS.

Simultaneously, ATC adjusted its own organization to new requirements. The staff organization of ATC Headquarters underwent little change, but two new offices took the place of the old Domestic and Foreign Wings.* A newly established Ferrying Division, under the command of Col. William H. Tunner, who formerly had commanded the Domestic Wing, took charge of all ferrying operations. The Air Transportation Division began with a nucleus of thirty-five officers transferred from ASC's Contract Air Cargo Division, including the commander of the new division, Col. Robert J. Smith, formerly vice-president of Braniff Airlines.[21] Upon him fell the especially heavy responsibility for providing the "United States Armed Forces and those of the United Nations," to quote an official statement of the division's mission, "with swift dependable world-wide transportation by air for the movement of vital passengers, cargo, and mail wherever and whenever needed."[22] The five overseas wings previously established were continued, and to them were added an Alaskan Wing in October and an India-China Wing in December. In January 1943 the South Pacific Wing was divided to form the Pacific and West Coast Wings. A European Wing was established that same month for control of operations within ETO, especially those between Great Britain and North Africa.

When the several sectors of the Foreign Wing had been inactivated in June preparatory to the establishment of the new foreign wings, the Transatlantic Sector at Bolling Field in Washington had survived. The plan was to convert it and its operating unit, the 10th Ferrying Squadron, into a headquarters transportation squadron for special missions originating in Washington. Instead, both the sector and the squadron were transferred to the jurisdiction of the Air Transportation Division in August.[23] But this is a point chiefly of administrative significance. In effect, the 10th Squadron did become the headquarters transport unit, and as such it served chiefly to provide for official Washington rapid communication by air with many different parts of the world. It carried more Very Important Persons and very important mail than did any other unit.

---

* Actually the Foreign Wing had been disbanded with the activation of the overseas wings early in June.

The varying conditions under which the newly established wings operated make generalization difficult, but certain points, representing the ideal toward which ATC sought to move, seem to be worth the attempt. Wing commanders were responsible for the routing of all ferried and transport aircraft through their wing, for the briefing of crews, and for the servicing of the aircraft. They were expected to provide housing, ground transportation, and commissary and medical services for ATC and contract carrier personnel and for transient passengers. They had disciplinary authority over ATC crews. They were responsible for the provision of necessary communications and weather information. Where it was possible, the wing commander sought actual command, except for technical control, over the communications and weather services within his wing; elsewhere he negotiated for the necessary services with whatever authority, American or foreign, might have the right to command. The extent of his own command authority varied according to circumstances, but at no time did it include the aircraft passing through his wing.* Rather, they remained, like the ferrying and transport crews which flew them, subject to the command of the Transportation or Ferrying Divisions in Washington.[24]

This last point has particular significance. The ideal shaping the whole development of ATC was that of a strategic air transport service. To the achievement of that ideal nothing was more important than a centralized control exercised in conformity with the highest considerations of national strategy. No local or other particular interest could be allowed to interfere with the movement of planes and cargo according to requirements dictated by the top command and according to schedules that would assure the most efficient employment of planes and crews. Each theater was expected to look to its own assigned troop-carrier units for the provision of local transport services. The business of ATC was to provide long-range air transport from the home front to the battle areas of the world, and to do this on predetermined and established schedules.[25]

It was a new idea and inevitably there were conflicts with traditional notions regarding the prerogatives of a theater commander. To reach some destinations, ATC aircraft might pass through a half-dozen theater or base commands. In any one of these a hard-pressed

---

* Some of the wings, and notably the India-China Wing, later had their own assigned planes which came under the direct command of the wing commander.

commander might be tempted to levy upon the cargo for his own needs or even to divert the planes and their crews to his own uses. He usually could cite some emergency in justification of his action, especially during the difficult first year of the war, and Army tradition argued that the theater commander rightfully controlled all military forces operating within his area. As early as 6 June 1942 it had been necessary for the War Department to issue a directive to theater commanders reminding them that ACFC was a War Department agency operating under the command of General Arnold and enjoining them to limit their interference to "specific" emergencies.[26]

The difficulty, in part, was one of definition. No one could question the right of any theater commander in the case of an extreme emergency to press into service all available forces. Nor could anyone doubt that most commanders in the earlier part of the war were operating under the conditions of a general emergency. Hence the War Department's insistence that the emergency be specific. But experience soon proved that this term was not explicit enough. In August 1942 General George sought through Arnold to secure another and stronger directive specifying that the schedules of ATC planes could be "violated only when required by reason of weather, mechanical failures, security or other reasons of extreme urgency."[27] The desired directive was issued on 21 September 1942. Theater commanders were reminded that ATC was *the* "War Department agency for the transportation by air of personnel, materiel, and mail," and they were specifically directed to "take all possible action to facilitate scheduled air transport operations through the area of their commands." Aircraft and crews "engaged in the operation of air transportation and ferrying services" were not to be "diverted from such operations by commanders concerned except in cases requiring that such operations be delayed until security will permit resumption of operations."[28] In other words, the security of ATC's own operations became the only consideration which might justify interference by local commanders. This action by no means ended all difficulty, but, by the end of 1942, overseas commanders were beginning to accept the idea that ATC planes moved on orders from General George by the authority of nothing less than the War Department itself. The more intelligent of them had come also to recognize the extent to which their own self-interest was involved in the effective operation of a service designed to meet emergency needs in all theaters.

There remained a necessity for spelling out in greater detail the War Department's injunction to "facilitate" the operations of ATC. A revised directive of 26 February 1943 defined more closely the relationship of theater and ATC wing commanders.[29] The directive undertook to fix their mutual obligations, one to the other, with reference to facilities, services, and personnel—a difficult task in view of the divergence of conditions among the various theaters. At times the drafters of the new directive were reduced to dependence upon the simple injunction to co-operate.

At the time of the establishment of ATC, L. W. Pogue, chairman of the Civil Aeronautics Board, had proposed that all war air transport operations should be concentrated under a single command, independent alike of Army and Navy and made responsible to the President as the commander-in-chief.[30] Instead, the Navy continued to operate its own Naval Air Transport Service (NATS), first established on 12 December 1941. Informal meetings, intended to obviate conflict and duplication and promote agreement on questions involving the use of the civil airlines, were held during the summer of 1942 between representatives of the two services. Out of these meetings came the formal establishment in September of the Joint Army-Navy Air Transport Committee (JANATC).* Helpful agreements were reached on problems of duplication, the mutual use of certain facilities, and liaison on the assignment of cargo and passenger priorities, but the two services remained distinctly independent.[31] As ATC rapidly developed into the major air transport agency of the U.S. government, its leaders continued to consider the possibility that ATC and NATS might be consolidated into one,[32] but this was a vain hope. Even the liaison developed in 1942 through the JANATC became thereafter less effective. Indeed, between April 1943 and May 1944 the committee held only one meeting.[33] Evidence that the Navy planned to expand NATS, originally charged only with the provision of air transport services to the naval establishment, led in the winter of 1943–44 to several ATC and AAF headquarters staff studies of duplication, existing and potential. The question went before the Joint Chiefs of Staff, with the result, in general, that NATS was restricted to serving the naval establishment. ATC had to be

* The Civil Aeronautics Board had representation on JANATC after January 1943.

content with the implied recognition of its status as the chief military air transport service of the U.S. government. The Joint Army-Navy Air Transport Committee was revived in May 1944.[34]

Although a fully militarized service had been set as the ideal by ATC very early in its history, and though transport services were increasingly rendered by military personnel and equipment, the use of contract services by civil airlines continued until the end of the war. The original contracts had involved the purchase of airline equipment by the government and then payment for its operation by the airline in accordance with government directives. During the last two years of the war the government began to turn over more and more of its own military aircraft to the airlines for operation on a cost-plus-fixed-fee basis. Earlier contracts usually had been made for specified services, but from the first months of 1943 "call" contracts of a general character were substituted.[35] Under this type of contract, the airline was bound to render service to the government within general limits but on call for particular purposes. At no time did ATC become the contracting agent of the government or hold full legal power over the administration of contracts. But it necessarily had an important supervisory duty, and its responsibilities in this particular were expanding ones. Civilian pilots, employed chiefly for air transportation, flew the same routes and utilized the same services as did the military.

ATC had begun operations on 30 June 1942 with a military strength of approximately 11,000 officers and enlisted men. Nine months later, at the end of March 1943, its strength had risen to over 60,000. On 31 July 1944 the figures were close to 125,000, of which number more than 80,000 were stationed overseas. By the end of the war the grand total had passed 200,000.[36] At the end of 1943, ATC had over 1,000 transport aircraft of all types assigned to it. A year later the number had risen to over 3,000. At the end of the war assigned transports were some 3,700.[37] In July 1945, the month preceding the termination of hostilities, ATC planes carried almost 275,000 passengers on long or short hops and delivered just under 100,000 tons of mail and freight. Of these totals, less than 50,000 passengers and a little over 3,300 tons of mail and cargo were attributable to operations within the United States.[38] Deliveries of ferried aircraft rose from 30,000 in 1942 and 72,000 in 1943 to 108,000 in 1944 and then dropped in 1945 to 57,000 before V-J Day.[39]

For a military organization, and especially one that grew rapidly, ATC's structure remained remarkably stable—a fact attributable in part to the continuity of its leadership. General George remained in command until after the war, with Brig. Gen. Cyrus R. Smith in the post of Deputy Commander after July 1943. In the preceding spring the Air Transportation Division had been dissolved on the ground that no intermediate office was any longer needed between headquarters and the overseas wings. Accordingly, the functions of the division, except for those relating to transport activity within the United States, were transferred up to the appropriate offices of the headquarters staff. A new Domestic Transportation Division was established and moved from Washington to New York, where in effect it operated as a domestic wing. To its transport responsibilities were added in time important obligations for the conduct of training.* The Ferrying Division was continued, but its headquarters was transferred to Cincinnati in accordance with a plan to move operations out of Washington. Because its responsibilities had not been limited by the bounds of the United States, and because of its control over military aircrews, the Ferrying Division was soon given the task of establishing ATC's first scheduled military air transport runs to overseas destinations.[40] Heretofore, scheduled transport services to the overseas theaters had been provided by contract carriers.†

Finding the Planes

All plans for the development of wartime air supply services, and for airborne troop training as well, were dominated by the scarcity of transport aircraft. There was a shortage when war came, and thereafter the production of new transports still had to meet the competition of combat types which enjoyed, initially at least, an overriding priority. Although a substantial number of two-engine and four-engine transports had been ordered, none of these had been delivered at the time of the Pearl Harbor attack. The number of medium- and long-range transports belonging to the AAF on 7 December 1941 was so small that the eleven converted Liberator bombers on loan from the Combat Command to the Ferrying Command and the forty to fifty twin-engine planes belonging to the

* See below, p. 40.

† For discussion of the "Fireball," "Crescent," and "Snowball" runs, all flown by military crews, see below, pp. 89, 103, 129–30.

50th Transport Wing represented very nearly the full total. Only in the equipment of the civil airlines did the country possess an immediately available supply of additional transport aircraft.

A first step toward mobilizing the resources of the airlines was taken on 13 December 1941, when the President signed an executive order directing the Secretary of War to take possession of any part of any civil aviation system required for the war effort.[41] On the same day, the lend-lease administrator allocated twenty-five million dollars to the War Department for the purchase of available four-engine transports and for other action necessary to the operation of military air transport services.[42] But there were only fifteen four-engine planes to be had, not counting a Boeing 314 Clipper that already had been purchased from Pan American Airways in August 1941. In December, Pan American had eight Clippers and two Martin flying boats, and TWA owned five Boeing 307 land-based Strato-liners. All fifteen were promptly purchased and assigned to the two military services. The Navy got the two Martin flying boats and five of the Clippers. That left for the Army three Clippers and the five Stratoliners. The eleven B-24's which the Ferrying Command had been using, together with the Clipper purchased in August and the five Stratoliners, brought the Army's four-engine transports to a total of twenty aircraft.* For more than six months thereafter, only a few converted Liberators would be added to this total. In the category of two-engine planes the armed forces were more fortunate. The airlines in December 1941 were operating 289 DC-3's, and some 100 lighter two-engine types.[43] After several drafts had been made on this resource, the President, on 6 May 1942, directed the Secretary of War to commandeer all transports operated by the civil airlines in excess of 200 of the DC-3 type and to refit them "for such transport services as will most effectively serve the war purposes of the United Nations."[44] Many of the planes thus acquired from the civil airlines were turned back to them for operation under contract with the government.

As the War Department reached right and left for whatever aircraft might be immediately available, the AAF enlarged its procurement program. Fortunately, it had made a heavy commitment to the DC-3 and the DC-4 before Pearl Harbor, and fortunately the prime consideration of the speed with which the manufacturer could make

* See Vol. I, 351–53.

deliveries led to additional orders for these two planes. But neither of them was considered to be ideal for the purposes of air transport. The trouble was that both planes had been designed for passenger service. Although there had been much talk in the interval between the two world wars about the convertibility of airline equipment for military purposes, too much of this talk had ignored a point later well put by ATC's historian, who wrote: "Men, after all, can ride in freight cars, with or without improvised seats; freight cannot well be loaded in passenger cars."[45]

The DC-3 was a low-wing monoplane whose fuselage stood so high off the ground that loading from an ordinary truck platform was impractical. Also the door was narrow and the flooring lacked the strength to support heavy cargo. A larger door, reinforced flooring, special loading equipment, and other improvisations were devised for the C-47, but it was natural that ATC should have sought a plane better suited to its needs. Desired characteristics included a low-swung fuselage to facilitate loading, especially of such bulky equipment as jeeps or small tanks, a higher payload, the ability to operate from small unsurfaced airfields, and a ferrying range of at least 2,500 miles to permit delivery of the plane from factory to front under its own power. It was desirable, furthermore, that the plane be constructed as far as possible of non-critical materials, such as plywood, plastics, fabric, and tubular steel, in order not to compete with combat types at the factories.[46]

Much time and money went into the search, before and after Pearl Harbor, for a two-engine plane that would meet all these requirements. The Budd C-93, of stainless-steel construction, was developed under a joint order with the Navy, but innumerable problems of engineering and construction, plus the shortage of stainless steel, led the AAF to cancel its part of the order early in 1944.[47] The Waco C-62 project was an experiment in the construction of a wooden transport airplane. An initial order for 13 service-test models had been placed with the Waco Aircraft Company in October 1941, and early in 1942 an additional 240 were ordered. Engineering problems proved difficult, and the C-62 rated a lower priority than wooden gliders also under order at the Waco plant. By September 1943, two years after the project had been launched, the prototype of the C-62 was still incomplete. A few months later the AAF dropped the project altogether.[48] At that time, the limitations of another wooden plane, the Curtiss-Wright C-76 Caravan, whose basic design was almost identical with that of the C-62, were also well known. Production of the C-76 had proceeded somewhat further than the two models described above, but with little more success. An initial order for 200 of these was followed by two other orders for an additional 1,200 from Curtiss-Wright and 1,200 from Higgins Aircraft, Inc., of New Orleans. Curtiss-Wright built an elaborate assembly plant at Louisville and farmed out much of the fabrication work to piano and furniture manufacturers, while Higgins began a plant on "made" delta land at New Orleans that would have cost an estimated $23,-735,000 had it been completed. Engineering difficulties, similar to those encountered with the C-62, finally reduced the C-76 program to a small experimental project. In July 1943, after the first airplane produced at Louisville had crashed, the AAF canceled all orders except for 25 airplanes on the Curtiss-Wright contract. The Chief of the Materiel Command estimated an unrecoverable loss of $40,000,000.[49]

Better success was had with the Fairchild C-82 Packet. The design for the C-82 was first presented to the Materiel Command shortly after Pearl Harbor. Because the Fairchild design showed almost 100 per cent improvement in maximum load capacity and range over the C-62 and C-76, as well as greatly superior facilities for loading and unloading, a contract was awarded to the Fairchild Company for two models in August 1942. The design originally called for plywood and steel, but, as the prospects of the C-82 as the long-sought ideal cargo plane seemed to improve with study, the specifications were changed first to a greater percentage of steel and finally, early in 1943, to all-metal construction. Troop-carrier officials, especially, liked the Packet, or the "flying boxcar" as it came to be called. A small tank, a 155-mm. howitzer, or three jeeps could be quickly rolled up a rear ramp through huge tail doors, paratroopers could bail out without the risk of having their heads knocked off by the rear empennage, and the high horizontal stabilizer, fourteen feet off of the ground, made it possible for the largest trucks and trailers to back up to the rear of the fuselage without obstruction. The C-82 could carry a payload of 12,500 pounds for 500 miles, and 8,500 pounds for 1,500 miles. But the first C-82 was not delivered until June 1945, and only a few had been assigned to ATC at the end of the war.[50]

For a time it seemed that the answer to ATC's need would be found in the Curtiss-Wright C-46—the Commando. Unlike the C-47, the C-46 lacked genealogy. Its prototype, the CW-20, had been designed in 1940 at the St. Louis plant of Curtiss-Wright as a two-engine commercial competitor of the four-engine Douglas DC-4 and the Boeing Stratoliner. An original order for 200 of the C-46 military version had been placed by the Air Corps in September 1940, and 256 more were ordered in May 1941, but, because of the extensive modifications required, only two models actually existed when war came. However, the plane had been sufficiently modified and tested to cause the Air Forces to request that Curtiss-Wright proceed with its production. Two were ready for acceptance on 18 July 1942, and by the end of the month three more had been accepted. All were turned over to the airlines for use in domestic contract services until they had been more fully tested. The first reports were altogether good, with only the ordinary number of defects reported. Eastern Air Lines, after 200 hours of testing, reported that its C-46 carried 10,000 pounds of cargo (nearly double the maximum payload of the C-47) and, so loaded, could cruise at an average indicated air speed of 200 miles per hour with a consumption of 135 gallons of gasoline per hour. This was excellent performance.[51]

After the first encouraging reports, however, came discouraging ones. In heavy rain the fuselage "leaked like a sieve" because the joints had not been properly sealed, the camouflage paint began to peel off, and much more serious trouble developed with the hydraulic system and the fuel system. In late August 1942 it became necessary to ask for fifty-three immediate modifications, exclusive of winterization, and to recommend forty-six additional changes as desirable. The first thirty C-46's delivered to ATC had to be sent back to the factory. They began to return early in 1943 as the C-46A, a modified version which was flyable but still far from satisfactory.

In the meantime the Air Transport Command had made a heavy commitment to the C-46, especially because of the hope that the new plane might meet the need for an expanded airlift from India to China. The responsibility for such an expansion after December 1942 had fallen on the newly established India-China Wing of ATC, and since there was no prospect that four-engine transports could be made available for the job, ATC had little choice but to pin its hopes on the greater cargo capacity of the two-engine C-46.[52] Perhaps this helps to explain a persistent optimism at ATC Headquarters regarding the prospect that the plane's defects could be overcome. As late as April 1943, when many of these defects had become known, Brig. Gen. Cyrus R. Smith, Chief of Staff of the Air Transport Command and one of the country's ablest airline executives, declared that, for hauling cargo over distances of 1,500 miles or less, the C-46 was more efficient than the C-54. For short hauls of around 1,000 miles, he insisted that the C-46 offered "twice the value of the C-47."[53] The War Production Board, too, had gone all out for the C-46, declaring it to be the most efficient and economical cargo aircraft then in production, and the C-47 the least efficient of the short-haul carriers.

That the C-46 could be produced in quantity was amply demonstrated. By the end of 1943 acceptances reached the total of 363. An additional 1,321 were accepted during 1944, and by the end of the war the grand total stood at 3,123.[54] That the plane helped to increase ATC's airlift during a critical period of the war is also demonstrable. On the run from Miami to Natal, Eastern Air Lines' contract service used it with outstanding success, and in Africa as well as on the India-China run it carried many tons of freight, not to mention many passengers, who otherwise could not have been given a lift. But from first to last the Commando remained a headache. It could be kept flying only at the cost of thousands of extra manhours for maintenance and modification. Although Curtiss-Wright reported the accumulation by November 1943 of the astounding total of 721 required changes in production models, the plane continued to be what maintenance crews around the world aptly described as a "plumber's nightmare." Worse still, the plane was a killer. In the experienced hands of Eastern Air Lines and along a route that provided more favorable flying conditions than were confronted by military crews in Africa and on the Hump route into China, the plane did well enough. Indeed, Eastern Air Lines lost only one C-46 in more than two years of operations.[55] But among the ATC pilots the Commando was known, with good reason, as the "flying coffin." From May 1943 to March 1945, Air Transport Command received reports of thirty-one instances in which C-46's caught fire or exploded in the air. Still others were listed merely as "missing in flight," and it is a safe assumption that many of these exploded, went down in flames, or crashed as the result of vapor lock, carburetor icing, or other defects.

In the face of continuing disappointment with the C-46, ATC had no choice but to place its heaviest dependence for medium-range transport on the undervalued C-47. At the peak of operations in August 1945, well over a third of ATC's major transports—to be exact, 1,341 out of 3,090—were C-47's. In the subsequent reduction of its wartime fleet, ATC had elected by March 1946 to retain in service 402 C-47's as against only 5 C-46's.[56] While AAF storage fields filled up with C-46's retired from government service and rejected by the civil airlines, the demand for all available C-47's continued brisk.

In its attempts to develop an ideal four-engine cargo plane, the AAF came no closer to meeting the wartime need than it did in the case of the two-engine plane. In the Douglas C-74 and in Boeing's C-97, each of them capable of carrying under normal operating conditions a maximum payload of some 40,000 pounds over a distance of 1,000 miles and better than 22,000 pounds for 3,000 miles,[57] the AAF finally found the long-range transports it needed, but none of either type had been delivered at the close of the war.[58] Meantime, as with medium-range transport, it was necessary to depend upon an adaptation of a passenger-type aircraft—in this instance the DC-4, which as the C-54 proved to be as stout a plane as the C-47.

When war came, the AAF had a choice among four large land-based transports. In addition to the Douglas Skymaster (C-54), there were Lockheed's Constellation (C-69), the Boeing Stratoliner (C-75), and the converted Liberator bomber (B-24 and LB-30*). Because the Stratoliner could carry a payload of only 4,100 pounds at maximum range, there was never any thought of producing the plane in quantity.[59] Production of the Lockheed C-69, which offered great promise, was held back because of the priority given to the P-38 fighter at the Lockheed factory. Eighty Constellations had been contracted for by TWA and Pan American Airways before Pearl Harbor. These contracts were taken over by the AAF after war started, and an additional 180 of a more advanced model were also ordered. The first numbers were scheduled for delivery in 1943, but even this late date proved to be too optimistic. Only a few test C-69's were produced during the war, and none was used in regular wartime transport operations.[60]

* The LB-30 was an early model of the B-24 modified for British use.

With the elimination of the Stratoliner and the Constellation, the AAF had a choice between the Douglas C-54 and the modified Liberator bomber. The Douglas plane was a gamble, because at the time of Pearl Harbor it existed only in prototype. Had the C-54 turned out to be another C-46, the ATC would have been in a bad way indeed, but happily the gamble paid off handsomely. The original, a passenger model first delivered in June 1942, carried a payload of 9,600 pounds when fueled for a 2,500-mile flight. Its maximum range was over 3,000 miles—which gave it a safe margin for operation on the Atlantic and the Pacific air routes—with a payload at that range of 6,400 pounds. Its use for cargo was limited by both the fixed seats and the flooring, which was not designed to carry heavy loads, but these were difficulties that could be overcome. By August 1942, four C-54's were in scheduled service on the Pan American Airways' contract run from Miami to Natal, and by October C-54's flew regular schedules on the North Atlantic route into Britain.[61]

While proceeding with the production of C-54's, the Douglas Aircraft Company adapted its factory in Chicago to the manufacture of C-54A's, a cargo version with bucket seats (metal folding seats along both walls of the fuselage) and a stronger floor. Various minor improvements were embodied in this model, and the gross takeoff weight was raised to 68,000 pounds, giving it a payload of 9,000 pounds at extreme range and 10,900 for a 2,400-mile trip. The first C-54A was delivered for testing on 3 February 1943 and was in scheduled service by March. The C-54B, embodying further improvements, was ready for testing in March 1944. In this newer model, two of the four auxiliary fuel tanks in the cabin were eliminated in favor of additional wing fuel tanks, thereby increasing the cabin space and reducing the fire hazard; the passenger capacity was increased from 30 to 49, and litter capacity for air evacuation of the wounded from 24 to 36. The bucket seats were replaced by canvas folding seats with web backrests that resembled cots and were placed lengthwise along each wall. Their use meant a saving in weight of seven pounds per passenger-space, and, unlike the bucket seats, they were fairly comfortable for either sitting or sleeping. The C-54C was literally a unique aircraft, a single plane built and equipped especially for the use of President Roosevelt. The C-54D, essentially a C-54B with more powerful engines, came into use in August 1944; the others, the C-54E, a luxurious passenger model, and the C-54G, the corresponding cargo model, were not available until 1945. In August 1945, ATC had 839 C-54's of all models in service.[62]

The AAF had hedged its bet on the C-54 by a substantial investment in the modified Liberator. As early as July 1941 the Ferrying Command, in the absence of long-range transports, had begun using stripped-down B-24 bombers in its North Atlantic service. The B-24 was unusually well suited for transport work after most of its armament had been removed and its bomb-bay section rigged to accommodate passengers and cargo. With full fuel tanks, the plane was estimated to have a maximum range of 4,000 miles; two of the B-24A's in the North Atlantic service made a special 3,500-mile non-stop flight from Scotland to Moscow via Archangel without difficulty. Stripped of all combat equipment and armor plate, the Liberator could carry 7,500–8,000 pounds of payload with full fuel tanks. In addition to its long range and powerful lift, the Liberator alone among major aircraft then in production or planned for early production had one prime characteristic of true cargo aircraft—its fuselage stood low to the ground, and so it could be easily loaded.[63]

Of the eleven B-24 transports employed by the Air Corps Ferrying Command at the time of Pearl Harbor, three were lost in the Southwest Pacific during the early months of the war. Because of the more urgent need for combat models, no others were turned over to the command until June 1942, when five B-24D's were sent to the South Atlantic, at a time when the fortunes of the Allies in the Middle East were at lowest ebb and when a number of critical aircraft supply items were needed badly. In the meantime, five Liberators of the LB-30 model, repossessed from the British shortly after Pearl Harbor, had been placed in service on the Pacific run from California to Australia. The LB-30 was found to have a shorter range than the B-24, but was capable of carrying a heavier payload.

These two improvised transports served as prototypes for the Liberator Express (C-87), which came directly from the factory as a transport plane in the late summer of 1942.[64] The C-87 had an extreme range of 3,250 miles and was capable of carrying a payload of from 7,500 to 9,400 pounds, a performance not quite measuring up to that of the C-54. Lack of loading space both fore and aft of the center of gravity limited the cargo capacity and forced weight-and-balance officers to exercise the greatest care in distributing weight. By October 1942 seven C-87's had been placed in operation across

Radio Mechanics

ATC TRAINING PROGRAM

Engine Mechanics

Douglas C-47

ATC AIRCRAFT TYPES

Curtiss C-46

CONSOLIDATED C-87

DOUGLAS C-54

ATC PLANES AT ICELAND BASE

the Pacific as a badly needed addition to the small LB-30 fleet. The highest number in use by the command at one time was 308, in January 1945. By the end of hostilities the C-87 was obsolescent by comparison with the later models of the C-54 and had been largely replaced by them.[65]

Finding the Pilots

The problem of finding the pilots for ATC's varied services was in some ways more difficult than that of finding the planes. Prior to the Pearl Harbor attack there had been no difficulty. The primary mission of the Ferrying Command had then been the delivery of U.S.-built aircraft from California to British agencies on the East Coast, and for that purpose Air Force Combat Command (AFCC) placed its pilots on loan to ACFC for thirty- to ninety-day periods which served to provide them helpful experience with the latest types of combat aircraft.[66] But, after Pearl Harbor, AFCC faced the immediate need to ready all its units for overseas service, with the result that the Ferrying Command suddenly had its normal source of pilots cut off.[67] Not only did the flow of pilots from combat units cease but a reverse trend resulted from the prompt demand by AFCC that sorely needed pilots be returned. Indeed, the Ferrying Command was fortunate in being able to keep even a few of its more experienced pilots.

The problem became all the more serious because the command was required to assume by mid-January 1942 virtually full responsibility for the ferrying of AAF aircraft within the United States. It was no easy job. The ferrying of a half-dozen different types of British-owned aircraft from the West Coast to the East Coast at the rate of 200-odd planes a month—the sum of deliveries just prior to 7 December—had been simple. It was quite another matter to provide, in addition to this service, pilots who could fly practically every type of American military aircraft from factories to depots and modification centers and from these points to training bases and staging areas all over the United States—and to provide them in numbers that kept pace with an expanding combat force.[68]

Under these pressures the Ferrying Command had no recourse but to employ civilian pilots, a practice authorized in June 1941 but as yet untried. The unattached civilian pilots then available—bush fliers, small feeder-line operators, test pilots, stunt fliers, crop-dusters, barnstormers, and individuals who flew their own planes for the purposes of business or pleasure—were men, for the most part, of limited flight experience who would need a good deal of training. Accordingly, it was decided to employ civilians for a preliminary ninety-day probationary period of training. If found qualified at the end of that period, they would be commissioned as officers in the Army of the United States in ranks ranging from second lieutenant to major, depending upon age and experience, and with the aeronautical rating of service pilot, a rating established primarily for the use of ACFC with qualifications somewhat lower than those for a combat pilot. If not found qualified, they might be hired for another probationary period or released.[69]

Among the specifications laid down for the employment of civilians, the most important pertained to the hours of flying experience. The requirement at first was 500 hours, but this was soon cut to 300, and even for a brief period to 200. By September 1942 the figure had been raised again to 300 hours, and by 1944, when pilots were no longer so scarce, a prospective civilian employee had to show a total of 1,000 hours.[70]

At the end of January 1942, less than two months after recruiting began, 343 civilian pilots had been assigned to ACFC's Domestic Wing. Two months later the number had increased to nearly 800, at which time there were 315 military pilots on duty with the wing.[71] By the end of 1942, a total of 1,730 civilian pilots had been recruited, and, of these, 1,372 had been commissioned.[72] Civilians continued to be hired after 1942, but the rate sharply declined as civilian sources were dried up and more military pilots became available. Not until 1944 did recruitment of civilians become again an important factor in ATC's pilot procurement program. By that year the AAF's training program had been so cut back as to release a large number of highly qualified civilian flight instructors, each of them having at least 1,000 hours of flying time to their credit. From them came perhaps the best-qualified group of pilots ever recruited by ATC.[73]

Meanwhile, the AAF's civilian pilot recruitment program had been extended to include even women. Proposals for the use of women as pilots of military aircraft had been made well before Pearl Harbor, but all such proposals had met the stern resistance of AAF leaders on the general ground that it would be difficult to incorporate women into an organization which traditionally depended exclusively on the male.[74] It is probably true that only the extreme needs of ATC in 1942 could have broken down this resistance to the recruitment of women. In any case, the AAF adopted in the summer of 1942 a proposal of Mrs. Nancy H. Love for the recruitment of especially well-qualified women pilots for the assistance of ATC. As a result twenty-five women pilots, each having better than 1,000 hours of flying time, were recruited as members of the Women's Auxiliary Ferrying Squadron (WAFS), an organization which quickly proved its ability to fly the most advanced types of bomber and fighter aircraft.[75] At approximately the same time, Miss Jacqueline Cochran had prevailed upon General Arnold to initiate a training program for women pilots that would permit them to take over a large area of non-combat flying. The first group of graduates was ready for assignment to ATC in May 1943. By July 1944 there were 303 women pilots on duty with the Ferrying Division. In the following August the number suddenly dropped off, as the less well qualified of these pilots were transferred to the Training Command for simpler types of work. Thereafter, the number of women pilots on duty with the Ferrying Division averaged about 140 until, in December 1944, the Women's Airforce Service Pilots (WASP), the organization under which all women pilots had served since August 1943, was deactivated.* During the course of twenty-seven months women ferry pilots had completed 12,650 ferrying movements of airplanes. The aircraft ranged from the lightest liaison or trainer types to heavy bombers and the most advanced fighter types. This was an excellent record and represented a real contribution to the winning of the war.[76]

The largest single reservoir of experienced pilots in 1942 was that provided by the some 2,600 pilots employed by the civil airlines.[77] Many of these pilots had been trained originally by the Air Corps and held reserve commissions, but the AAF found itself limited in the exercise of its right to call them to active military duty by its very heavy dependence on the contract services of the civil airlines in the increasingly important area of air transport. During 1942 the airlines performed under contract with the government nearly 88 per cent of the transport work supervised by ATC. In 1943 the percentage

---

* For a fuller discussion of the subject of women pilots in the AAF, see below, pp. 528–36. The women recruited for pilot service in the AAF suffered from one marked disadvantage: they were not, as were the men, eligible for commissions.

fell to 68. By 1944 two-thirds of the transport work was being performed by military crews, and at the end of the war as much as 81 per cent.[78]

The first large group of airline reservists to be called up for active duty began arriving at Morrison Field in Florida toward the end of March 1942. Special interest is attached to this group because out of it came the pilots who were to form the nucleus of the 1st Ferrying Group, the organization that was responsible for inaugurating the airlift from India to China. In February the President had ordered General Arnold to commandeer twenty-five airplanes of the DC-3 type from the airlines and with these, and others to come from new production, to open a supply line across the Himalayas into China. Aircraft and crews brought together at Morrison Field in a temporary organization were designated the AMMISCA Project. No extensive training was necessary because the pilots had a flying experience ranging from 1,800 to over 10,000 hours in the air, much of it in DC-3's. They were not familiar, however, with long-range overwater flight and required some briefing from the veteran Ferrying Command crews at Morrison Field—a point that could be made with reference to all but a very few of the most experienced pilots at that time.[79] The AMMISCA aircraft and crews began leaving Florida for India in late April, and the movement continued on into the fall.* Upon arriving in India, the crews were assigned to the 1st Ferrying Group of the Tenth Air Force, which bore the brunt of the difficult and dangerous work over the Hump during the first year of operations.[80]

A smaller group of reservists already had been called to active duty in connection with plans for the early heavy-bomber reinforcement of the Southwest Pacific theater. Soon after Pearl Harbor, General Arnold, upon direct instructions from the President, had ordered all heavy-bomber units then ready for overseas movement and those soon to be ready—comprising a total of eighty heavy bombers and crews—into the Southwest Pacific to reinforce that area. About a month later, in anticipation of heavy losses, orders were issued for the ferrying of eighty replacement four-engine bombers to Australia. Because no replacement crews were ready or otherwise available, the Ferrying Command was given orders to furnish the crews. The plan for delivery of the replacements was tailored to the rate of flow of

* For the movement of the ground echelon, see below, p. 118.

the aircraft from the factories. An estimated sixteen heavy bombers a month would be coming from the production line for the next several months. This would require a minimum of sixteen ferrying crews to effect delivery, but, in order to meet all possible foreign ferrying commitments in the immediate future, the Ferrying Command requested and received authority to train twice that number of four-engine crews. Each crew consisted of three officers—pilot, co-pilot, and navigator; and two enlisted men—radio operator and engineer. To prepare the crew members for the job that lay ahead, a training project, designated PROJECT 32 because it was composed originally of thirty-two crews, was organized at Morrison Field in late February 1942. This was the first program undertaken by the Ferrying Command to train its own officer and enlisted personnel for overseas ferrying.[81]

PROJECT 32 drew its personnel from three sources. Forming the hard core of the project were approximately thirty officer pilots and navigators and thirty-seven enlisted radio operators and engineers who had been among the Combat Command personnel assigned temporarily to duty with the Ferrying Command before the declaration of war. In this group were some of the most experienced heavy-bomber crewmen in the Army Air Forces, men who as members of the 19th Bombardment Group had participated in the first mass bomber flight from California to Hawaii in May 1941, and who, because of this experience, had subsequently been assigned to fly B-24's in the pre–Pearl Harbor transatlantic transport services to Britain and the Middle East. These men were still on loan from their combat units when PROJECT 32 was organized, but they were soon transferred to permanent-duty status with the Ferrying Command. Many were to become key operations and briefing officers in the future organization of ATC. Some would finish out the war in B-29 units in the Pacific.[82] Airline pilots holding Air Corps Reserve commissions were the second element drawn into PROJECT 32. Their civilian experience had been on transport planes, principally two-engine, and their military experience had seldom gone beyond piloting two-engine bombers. Consequently, they required some transition training to fit them for four-engine ferrying work.[83] The third group consisted of pilots, navigators, radio operators, and flight engineers who had recently graduated from AAF flying or technical training schools. Lacking the experience of the other two groups, these men were first sent to a four-engine transition school at Albuquerque, New Mexico, for a month of seasoning prior to assignment to the project. But only about half of the student pilots were found qualified to join the project, and these only as co-pilots; the general level of efficiency of the navigators was even less encouraging.[84] When the project was finally organized into crews, all the first-pilot positions were filled with veteran Ferrying Command pilots or the more experienced airline pilots; the co-pilot positions by the remainder of the airlines men and the best of the student pilots; and the navigator positions by Ferrying Command personnel and the best of the student navigators trained at Albuquerque.[85]

A highly concentrated training program was drawn up in order to complete the course of instruction within the allotted thirty days. Most of the time at Morrison Field was taken up with ground courses in navigation, engineering, communications, and armament. At the same time the schedule was made as flexible as possible to permit the carrying-out of urgent ferrying missions during the period of training. Project crews ferried nine heavy bombers to Panama in March and six in April and moved other aircraft to points within the United States. Classes in ground school were long, running from three to five hours, and school kept seven days a week. At the end of the all-too-brief training period, the members of the project had been welded into crews, schooled on several types of equipment likely to be encountered in immediate assignments, and briefed for many parts of the world.[86]

Late in March 1942, PROJECT 32 crews began moving out to Hamilton Field, San Rafael, California. Their work over the period of the next several months, and especially the vital part they played in bringing up bomber reinforcements for the Battle of Midway, will be discussed later in connection with Pacific operations.* Here it will be sufficient to note that the command's overseas ferrying organization grew out of the project's original thirty-two crews. The project as an organized unit came to an end in June 1942, but its crews thereafter formed the initial cadres of three new foreign ferrying squadrons activated and assigned to the equally new ATC Ferrying Division. One squadron, the 28th, remained on the West Coast to provide crews for aircraft going to Pacific areas; the 26th was assigned to South Atlantic duty; and the 27th to the North Atlantic route. The activa-

* See below, pp. 175–76.

34

tion of these squadrons enabled the Ferrying Division to provide an increasing number of crews for replacement aircraft bound overseas. Newcomers to the squadrons were mixed in with the experienced PROJECT 32 crewmen to form new crews, and these, in turn, after a period of seasoning, were broken up to form the nuclei for others.[87]

New pilots and co-pilots assigned to the foreign ferrying squadrons came principally from graduates of the domestic squadrons, but airline pilots in the Air Corps Reserve continued to provide a number of unusually highly qualified overseas pilots during 1942. The men filling other crew positions—the navigators, radio operators, and engineers—came directly from the flying and technical training schools. ATC adopted for its ferrying crews an in-service type of training which progressively moved its pilots from the simpler types of aircraft to the more complex types. For a time, hard and fast lines were drawn between domestic and foreign ferry pilots, but soon this distinction was abandoned. Experience proved that short ferrying trips within the United States afforded a necessary relaxation for pilots who had just completed one or more long flights overseas. Moreover, the rotation of pilots between domestic and foreign assignments made for a more efficient utilization of available pilots.[88] The three foreign ferrying squadrons were stationed originally at aerial ports of embarkation, not under the jurisdiction of the Ferrying Division, but these squadrons were soon withdrawn to Ferrying Division bases for assignment to recently organized ferrying groups in which they tended to lose their special identity.

PROJECT 32 was followed by PROJECT 50, which brought a group of about ninety Air Corps reservists to active duty on 25 May 1942 for a period of training preparatory to manning the new C-54 and C-87 four-engine transports. They had been called up for service as transport pilots, but, because the transports were slow in coming from the factories and because of the need for overseas ferry pilots, most of them were shifted, at least for a time, to foreign ferrying. A few of them went immediately into C-54 training; others joined the 10th Ferrying Squadron at Bolling Field, then engaged in flying B-24 converted transports on special missions. Ten of the pilots were sent to Natal to fill co-pilot positions on five new B-24D transports just assigned to the South Atlantic run to Africa.[89]

One other special group of pilots who came to the command in 1942 proved to be of great assistance to ATC in building up its foreign ferrying services. These were the experienced pilots of Pan American Air Ferries who became available for military duty when that organization, engaged for the past year in lend-lease ferrying under contract, was disbanded at the end of October. Other agencies were in competition with ATC for the services of Pan American Air Ferries personnel, but the ATC Ferrying Division was able to secure the services of about 180 pilots, all of them highly qualified, in addition to a large number of navigators, enlisted crewmen, technicians, and maintenance specialists.[90]

The regular assignment to ATC of graduates of the pilot schools by the AAF Flying Training Command began in mid-1942. By the end of that year some 35 per cent of the Ferrying Division's pilots were of that category. Fresh out of school, these young men lacked the experience of other groups, but, after going through the in-service training program of the Ferrying Division, they made good pilots.[91] Many of them, however, presented special morale problems. A natural tendency to give combat units the highest claim on Training Command graduates tended to rob an assignment to ATC of prestige. The work, moreover, often seemed dull. Ferrying and transport work, where the emphasis was on safety and economy, might be satisfactory enough for the average civilian pilot turned military, who as often as not was approaching middle age. But to many of the adventurous and ambitious young men who had completed their training in a military flying school and found themselves assigned through no choice of their own to ATC, the prospect of guiding "boxcars" from here to there and back again came as a distinct disappointment. They found neither glamor nor hope for fame and advancement in the hauling of freight or in the delivery of aircraft from factory to air base. Many of them soon caught some glimpse of the larger mission they served, but in other cases the problem remained.

In 1943 ATC began to receive returnees from overseas combat theaters—"war-weary pilots" as they were generally known. By July 1944 over 1,100 returnees had been assigned to the Ferrying Division, of which about half were former combat pilots and the other half men who had been serving with ATC overseas.[92]

Training

Although ATC was fortunate in the number of experienced pilots it managed to secure, it faced an early and expanding need for development of its own training programs. Graduates of the Training Command assigned directly to ATC usually had some 200–250 hours of flying experience. Nearly all pilots brought directly from civilian life had more than 300 hours. But this experience was limited as to the number of different planes that had been flown, with the result that some instruction on the characteristics of new or more complex types of aircraft had to be provided. The methods of instruction at first were quite informal. For transition to an unfamiliar type, the pilot received perhaps a ten-minute talk and a brief flight around the field. Then he took off, to learn the rest of his lesson by ferrying the plane to its assigned station. In educational terminology this was learning by doing—a method forced upon the command originally by circumstances, but one having enough logic in it, given the primary mission of ATC, to make it the basis of the more formal programs subsequently developed. As Col. William H. Tunner, Ferrying Division commander, explained to General Arnold in September 1942, it would have been "a waste of manpower and flying hours to train these men in cross-country and navigation type courses when they could secure this training and experience while actually delivering aircraft."[93]

The scheme adopted called for the progressive "up-grading" of the pilot from the simplest to the most complex types of aircraft. Five classifications were established:

Class 1—Single-engine trainer, cargo, and utility types
Class 2—Twin-engine trainer and utility types
Class 3—Twin-engine cargo and transport types
Class 4—Twin-engine medium bomber, heavy transport, attack and pursuit types
Class 5—Four-engine bomber and transport types

To these were added others, among them Class P for pilots qualified to ferry single-engine pursuits, and Class I for those holding instrument cards. As the pilot progressed through the several classes, the ideal was that he ultimately should be qualified to fly every conventional type of American military aircraft as circumstances might require.[94]

In such a scheme the ferrying squadron or group necessarily became the chief training agency. Refinements of the plan as it developed provided for ground instruction to be offered in time units sufficiently small to give assurance that no serious interruption of operations would result. By 1944 ground schooling had been divided into seven stages, the last of which gave instruction preparatory to overseas service.* As this arrangement suggests, it was assumed that pilots graduating from the training program of their respective units would provide a continuing supply of men qualified for handling the more advanced types of planes and for the more difficult assignments to overseas runs. In actual fact, ATC managed to meet the growing demands for its services only by instituting a more advanced training program in specialized schools.

When General George in July 1942 outlined his first broad plan for the development of ATC, he recognized the critical importance of a training program designed to provide large numbers of highly qualified pilots. He proposed an immediate expansion of contract services overseas by assigning 250 additional aircraft to the civil airlines, but he anticipated a progressive militarization of all overseas services. To man the new planes, he suggested that the airlines should transfer the experienced co-pilots then employed by the contractors to first-pilot positions and that graduates of the AAF training program be substituted as co-pilots for such a period as was necessary to qualify them for a first pilot's rating. They should then be returned to the AAF, their places being taken by other graduates of the Training Command. An estimated 200–300 graduates of the AAF flying schools would be required each month from August through December, or a total of 1,388 pilots for the remainder of the year. After the initial stages of the operation had been completed, approximately 4,000 pilots would be trained by the airlines and returned to military duty each succeeding year. For other crew positions, General George estimated the need for the remainder of 1942 at 694 radio operators, 339 navigators, and 219 flight engineers. Apparently, these, too, were to be procured from the AAF schools and trained for transport duty by the airlines.[95]

The proposal showed imagination and a sense of the tremendous task that would be put on ATC, especially in the development of overseas transport services. But the plan foundered on the hard facts of aircraft production and, more particularly, on the low priority ATC then held on graduates of the Training Command. AAF Headquarters agreed that 200 additional transport planes could be assigned to ATC in 1942, but it knocked the training scheme in the hat by warning that, instead of the 1,388 pilots requested, there would be only 150 who could be made available for ATC. Headquarters suggested that

* See Vol. VI, 674–78.

General George look elsewhere for his pilot trainees—which was to say, outside the Army.[96]

General George already had consulted with representatives of the airlines on his plan, and out of further talks with them came in August an Airlines War Training Institute—a further development in the Civilian Pilot Training Program to which the airlines for some time past had looked for pilots in the expansion of their own contract operations. Prospective transport pilots were to be recruited for 150 hours of flight instruction at the CPT schools (compared with 200 hours at the AAF pilot schools), and an additional four weeks or more of transition training with the airlines before assuming the duties of a co-pilot. An allotment to the airlines of 500 CPT graduates every other month, beginning in September 1942, was made by the Air Staff. But the result of the Institute recruiting campaign was most disappointing. Instead of 500 trainees in September there were only 355, and over 200 of these washed out. The net gain was thus approximately 150 co-pilots. Of the November quota, the Institute got less than 50. By October 1943, a year after the program had started, only 234 graduates, instead of the several thousand expected, were in service as co-pilots. It had been impossible, despite energetic recruiting, to find a greater number of qualified men. The draft, the high wages paid by war industry, and the simple fact that the best-qualified men had already been recruited, either by the airlines or by the Army and Navy for regular combat programs of training, explain the disappointment. At the end of 1942 the most encouraging statistic was that provided by 378 pilots of the Ferrying Division who had qualified for special training with the airlines.[97]

A new and larger training program was drafted for 1943, but this time it was assumed that the basic supply of trainees would come from the AAF's own training schools. General George based his plans on the AAF's "273-group program,"* in accordance with instructions from General Arnold. Consequently, he asked for the assignment of 2,633 transport aircraft, twin-engine and four-engine, a stupendous total that included 51 C-69's, 641 C-46's, and 682 twin-engine aircraft of models that never came into use.[98] Early in January 1943 the Air Staff, after taking a closer look at the estimates, reduced the total to 1,450; but on 9 January it was raised to 1,800, with 3,000 more to be expected in 1944.[99] This estimate stood firm until July 1943, by which

* See Vol. VI, p. 148.

time it had become apparent that no such number of aircraft could be delivered within the year. As a matter of fact, by the end of 1943 the command had only 782 major transports assigned; 2,292 by the end of 1944; and in August 1945, at the peak of its growth, 3,090.[100]

Upon the basis of an estimated 1,800 transports to be received in 1943, and 3,000 in 1944, the Air Transport Command embarked upon a flight- and ground-crew training program, to be carried out through the agency of the airlines, that was as impossible of realization as the aircraft production program to which it was geared. Starting in late December 1942, a series of conferences was held with representatives of the airlines, and by February, when the so-called "Transport Transition Training Program" had finally crystallized, the eighteen airlines had undertaken to train 7,216 pilots, 1,380 navigators, 3,608 radio operators, 1,380 aerial engineers, 20,919 radio and line mechanics, 280 control officers, and 722 air transportation officers.[101] All the trainees were to be military personnel, graduates of the various schools of the Flying and Technical Training Commands.

The transition training program opened on schedule early in February 1943, following the apportionment of the first group of trainees among the several airlines. Curriculums drawn up in 1942 by the Airlines War Training Institute were employed in the new program, and the Institute continued to fill a liaison position between the Air Transport Command and the airlines. Within the ATC the program came under the direct supervision first of the Air Transportation Division and then of its successor, the Domestic Transportation Division, which was established on 15 March 1943 as part of a general reorganization of the command. The military trainees were assigned to Transport Transition Training Detachments at the schools and bases where the airlines' training was conducted. Twenty-four of these detachments were put on an activated basis during March and April 1943, with one or more officers assigned to each.[102]

Although the airlines training program opened on schedule, that became about the only event of major importance in the program that did occur on schedule. For some reason, probably because of the prior claims on graduates of the Flying and Technical Training Commands enjoyed by tactical units, trainees were never made available in the numbers anticipated. Extensive arrangements were made for training space and for housing and messing space, but much of the time, energy, and money expended was wasted because the space was never more than partially occupied. If the trainees came at all, they were usually late in reporting, which threw the whole training schedule out of gear. There was a chronic shortage of training planes as well as of other types of equipment; the number of instructors was inadequate for some time; and requests for bases for flight training were long in being approved.[103]

Six weeks after training had started, the officer in general charge of the program reported that about 1,000 men were undergoing instruction, although the schedule had called for over 3,000. While the pilot and control officer programs approached fulfilment, the line mechanic program was operating at only 9 per cent of schedule, and the radio operator program at only 4 per cent. No flight engineers or radio mechanics had arrived, although a total of 266 in these two categories had been planned. By the end of June 1943, the program in the five main categories was running at only 45 per cent of schedule.[104] At about this time, with no more than a fraction of the facilities being used and with no indication that trainees would become more plentiful in the months to come, the first steps were taken to discontinue the program. In August the Airlines War Training Institute was notified that its contract would not be extended and that its supervisory functions would be taken over by the military. The Domestic Transportation Division, reluctant to see the whole program disappear, proposed that the program's scope be reduced to more realistic proportions, but its recommendations were not followed. In October, orders were issued that training by the airlines be "forthwith reduced to a minimum, and as soon as practicable, completely discontinued."[105] In the same month, all training functions of the Air Transport Command were transferred to the control of the Ferrying Division.

Emphasis on the shortcomings of the airlines training program may leave the impression that it was altogether a failure. This was not true, although it never lived up to expectations or met the crew requirements of the command. The objective had no doubt been set too high in the first place, just as had the aircraft production goal, but there may have been very good reasons, especially the need for filling flight-crew requirements of combat units, that caused AAF Headquarters to depart from the original plan and reduce drastically the number of trainees assigned. By the time the airlines training had been brought to a close, nearly 7,000 students had completed the various courses in the transport transition program and over 2,000 more had been trained in certain special schools—a total of slightly more than 9,000 in all groups. A comparison with the original plan shows that the training accomplished approximated 25–30 per cent of that which was scheduled in February 1943.[106]

Meanwhile, ATC had established its own schools or, to use the more exact terminology of the Army, its own operational training units (OTU's).* The OTU was intended to meet the more advanced requirements of operational training. The earlier phases of training emphasized the instruction of the individual, as pilot, navigator, radio operator, or flight engineer. In OTU the individual became a member of a team, where the purpose was to transform three or more individuals into a crew and to give it flight experience on the type of aircraft it would fly under the conditions to be expected in actual service. When the transport training program was in the planning stage, some consideration was given to a proposal to place operational as well as transition training in the hands of the airlines, but it was finally decided to keep the operational phase under strictly military control.[107]

The Air Transport Command established its initial operational training school, later designated the 1st Operational Training Unit, at Rosecrans Field, St. Joseph, Missouri, early in July 1942. While the St. Joseph school was intended originally to train both ferrying and transport crews in transoceanic flying, with emphasis on instrument flying and those special skills peculiar to long-range operations, the existing shortage of overseas ferrying crews forced concentration for a year or more on ferrying instruction. The shortage of ferry crews had been so acute, indeed, that most of the highly experienced transport pilots of PROJECT 50, fresh from the airlines, were transferred to ferrying work immediately or were sent through the St. Joseph school. In August 1943, when the supply of ferry crews more nearly approached demand, the 1st OTU at St. Joseph began a gradual shift to C-47 crew training.[108]

In the meantime the command had established two other operational units for the training of transport crews. A school for transport pilots, to become later the 2d Operational Training Unit, opened at Homestead, Florida, in November 1942. The Homestead base, just south of Miami, had been employed by Pan American Air Ferries (PAAF) in training ferry pilots for its contract operations to the Middle East and had become available to the Air Transport Command

* See Vol. VI, pp. 675–78.

as the result of the termination of the PAAF contract at the end of October 1942. The course of instruction at Homestead was designed originally for pilots only, rather than full crews, but in March 1943 a curriculum for the operational training of crews was adopted. In the new course a standard of forty-five hours of flying instruction was set for all crews, regardless of the type of plane. By fall, after the course had been revised several times, it was decided that the same requirements for the crews of all planes were not advisable and that, in order to attain proficiency on the C-46 and four-engine types, more flying instruction was required. Flying time was then increased to 60 hours for C-47's, 75 hours for C-46's, and 100 hours for C-54's and other four-engine craft. Also at this time a new feature was introduced into transport-crew training. One object of operational training was the simulation, for crew members, of conditions which they would meet after graduation. Accordingly, whenever it was possible to carry cargo on training flights, the ships were loaded. A substantial amount of cargo was carried between air installations in this way; in fact, so much more cargo was being carried than was necessary to the training mission that the practice was later curtailed on the ground that it interfered with the attainment of other training objectives. Another type of training was given Army co-pilots at Homestead by substituting them for the civilian co-pilots on Pan American Airways' C-47 contract run from Miami to Natal or to intermediate points in the Caribbean. By June 1943, at which time operational training of transport crews was expanded and C-46 training moved from Homestead to another base, 403 transport crews had completed their courses and been assigned to duty, all but a few of them graduating from Homestead. Their distribution according to the planes in which they had qualified were as follows: C-46, 245 crews; C-47, 131 crews; C-60, 12 crews; C-54, 3 crews; and C-87, 12 crews. The large number of C-46 crews is accounted for by the decision to substitute C-46's for C-47's on the India-China operation and to raise the Hump tonnage to 10,000 tons a month. Only a few military crews had been trained for four-engine aircraft because, up to this point, nearly all the C-54's and C-87's assigned to the command were operated by the contract airlines, which were responsible for their own operational crew training.[109]

Following the decision to employ C-46's on the run to China, C-46 crew requirements became so great that the Homestead school was

43

unable to fulfil them without reducing sharply, or eliminating, all other types of training. Accordingly, it was decided to establish an additional OTU for the training of C-46 crews only. Meanwhile, in order to maintain a steady supply of crews while the new school was getting under way, two of the contract airlines—Northwest and Western—were requested to concentrate on the training of 240 C-46 crews. The Air Transport Command's 3d Operational Training Unit, established for the training of C-46 crews exclusively, was activated at St. Joseph, Missouri, on 7 June 1943 and shortly thereafter was shifted to the AAF base at Reno, Nevada, then being evacuated by the Air Service Command. The Reno site was selected for a very good reason. Since the C-46 crewmen would be flying over the rugged, mountainous country of the Himalayas—often without benefit of radio range, and at high altitudes—it was important that training should take place in an environment in which weather and terrain would be as nearly similar as possible to conditions in the CBI theater. The Sierra Nevadas near Reno provided as ideal training conditions as could be found in the United States. At Reno, as at Homestead, cargo was carried on training flights when possible.[110]

Heretofore, the OTU at St. Joseph had served the Ferrying Division, while those at Homestead and Reno had been intended primarily to meet the needs of the Transport Division. But in October 1943 the Ferrying Division was made responsible for new foreign military transport services employing military crews exclusively. The 1st Operational Training Unit at St. Joseph shifted gradually from ferrying instruction to C-47 transport-crew training, which had been started as early as August 1943, and for a time in 1944 abandoned crew training for the instruction of individual pilots in instrument flying. Later, some C-46 crews were trained at St. Joseph in order to supplement the output of the Reno school, which had not been able to meet all requirements.[111]

After C-46 training was shifted to Reno, and the St. Joseph school began turning out C-47 crews, the 2d OTU at Homestead became exclusively a four-engine school specializing in C-54 instruction but also giving operational training to a number of C-87 and B-24 crews. In November 1943 the Ferrying Division opened the "Fireball" run from Florida to India in which C-87's and later C-54's were employed, and early in 1944 started the C-54 "Crescent" and "Snowball" flights across the Middle and North Atlantic. A similar service across the

Pacific was operated by the Pacific Division. Homestead trained the crews for these military operations and later furnished four-engine crews to the India-China Division when the C-46's on the Hump were replaced with C-54's and C-87's.[112]

Three other operational training units for the training of either transport or ferry pilots were established by the Ferrying Division before the war came to an end. The 4th OTU opened at Brownsville, Texas, on 1 April 1944 to train ferry pilots on pursuit-type aircraft. Early in the next year it was shifted to Greenwood, Mississippi.[113] Advanced pursuit instruction had been carried on for some time by the Ferrying Division at Palm Springs, California, before the 4th OTU was activated at Brownsville. When the shift to Brownsville was made, a specialized school for C-47 pilots was established at Palm Springs, and thereafter the course was lengthened to five weeks and transformed into a regular C-47 transport-crew course.[114]

This provision for an increased production of C-47 crews reflects the command's new appreciation of the C-47. In 1944, ATC took over a large intratheater transport operation in the Southwest Pacific, employing chiefly C-47's and reaching from Australia up into New Guinea and the islands to the north.* The same year brought full militarization of the domestic transport services of ATC, which employed more C-47's than any other type of craft.

The 6th Operational Training Unit, for the training of C-54 pilots and co-pilots, was established by the Ferrying Division at Charleston, South Carolina, at the end of May 1945. Up to this point, four-engine training had been concentrated at Homestead; a second school was required not only to meet the normal needs of ATC's expanding foreign transport services but also to take care of the requirements of the great transatlantic air redeployment project known as the GREEN project, which was shortly to be undertaken. In the last months of the war the two four-engine OTU's were turning out between 300 and 400 pilots and co-pilots a month.[115]

* See below, pp. 189-96.

CHAPTER 2

*   *   *   *   *   *   *   *   *   *   *

AIRWAY TO THE MIDDLE EAST

THE oldest of the air routes under ATC's jurisdiction, and throughout 1942 the most important, reached from Florida across the South Atlantic to Africa and the Middle East. It had been established in the pre–Pearl Harbor days of 1941 as a lend-lease supply line to British forces fighting in the Near East. Ferrying of aircraft along the route had started as early as June of that year, when a Pan American Airways subsidiary undertook the delivery of twenty lend-lease transport planes to Lagos on the Nigerian coast of western Africa, whence the British had developed a trans-African air route to Khartoum in the Anglo-Egyptian Sudan. The success of this first operation led to contracts between the War Department and the Pan American organization for more permanent ferrying and transport services all the way into Khartoum. Just before Pearl Harbor similar services under military control were opened into Cairo.*

Direct involvement of the United States in the war brought a quick expansion of the Pan American contract services. Two-engine Douglas transports were placed on the run from Florida to Natal, a move which made it possible to concentrate the few available long-range Clipper flying boats on the overwater hop from Brazil to the African coast. Additional airplanes and pilots were sent out to Africa to build up the trans-African transport service into Cairo. From Cairo the line was extended eastward to Basra and Tehran—transfer points for delivery of lend-lease aircraft to the Russians—and to Karachi, gateway to India. Beyond Karachi the Tenth Air Force opened a trans-India service and began flying supplies over the Hump into China in April 1942. Meanwhile, two other contract carriers had inaugurated trans-

* See Vol. I, 319–42, 353–56, for discussion of the early history of the South Atlantic route.

46

port services over the route. Transcontinental and Western Air, employing two Boeing Stratoliners which had been purchased by the government, began flying between Washington and Cairo in February; and Eastern Air Lines, having opened a two-engine transport service to Trinidad in May, extended its operations to Natal in late June, paralleling the existing Miami-Natal service of Pan American Airways. Through most of 1942, lend-lease planes, with few exceptions, were delivered over the South Atlantic route by crews of Pan American Air Ferries. Aircraft deliveries by the Pan American organization had not exceeded ten a month before February 1942, and nearly all of these had gone to the British. But business picked up in March, and by early summer a steady flow of planes was moving out to British forces in Egypt, to the Russians through Iran, and, in lesser number, across India and over the Himalayas to the Chinese.[1]

By the end of June, 391 of the AAF's own planes had been ferried across the South Atlantic (250 of them by military crews) on their way to India, China, and even the Southwest Pacific. Before the Japanese captured Singapore in February 1942, thirty-six heavy bombers, intended originally for the Philippines, had been flown to India by way of Africa and thence across southeastern Asia and the East Indies to Australia.* Thereafter reinforcements for Australia went by way of the Pacific, but the Atlantic-African route continued to have the most critical importance for military operations in India and China; in Russia, where the great spring offensive of the Germans by July had opened the road to Stalingrad and the Caucasus; and in the Middle East, where Rommel threatened destruction of Britain's long-established position.

The Overseas Wings

The southeastern air route, as it existed in the critical summer months of 1942, began in southern Florida and extended down through the Caribbean and Brazil as far south as Natal. At Natal it turned eastward across the Atlantic narrows to the African coast and then reached across central Africa to Khartoum, where it divided. The main line extended north to Cairo to eastward through Habbaniya and Basra to Karachi, thence across India and Burma into China, with a branch line from Habbaniya up to Tehran in Iran. An

* Of the forty-four bombers ferried to the Southwest Pacific by late February 1942, only eight went by the Pacific route.

alternate route eastward from Khartoum passed through Aden and skirted the Arabian coast into Karachi, where it joined with the route out of Cairo.

Strung along the route were dozens of bases in various stages of construction and subject to a variety of jurisdictions. ATC had actual command over only one of the bases, the staging base for ferried aircraft at Morrison Field, West Palm Beach, Florida; two other Florida bases, at Miami and Homestead, would be placed under its jurisdiction before the year was out.[2] Beyond the continental United States the installations through which transient planes passed were controlled by overseas theater or base commands, by foreign states, or by Pan American Airways.[3] On such bases the Air Transport Command had a position somewhat analogous to that of a tenant. It depended on theater or base commands for most housekeeping services and for heavier forms of maintenance, but had its own administrative, transient-service, and ground-crew personnel. Many of the bases along the route were used only occasionally as alternate landing fields and so had no assignment of ATC personnel at all.

During the first half of 1942, the Air Corps Ferrying Command had begun to exercise a limited degree of control over transient aircraft through a loosely organized system of "control offices" located at major bases.[4] These control offices were not formally activated units; their personnel, often no more than a half-dozen men, were assigned to domestically based squadrons and sent out on detached service. Not until June 1942, when the foreign operations of the Air Transport Command were placed under the direction of five newly activated foreign wings,[5] did these overseas units find a place in an organization specifically adapted to their needs. At that time each wing received one or two ferrying groups, later redesignated transport groups, which became the operational arms of the wings. The transport groups in turn controlled flight activities at the bases through subordinate squadrons. As a rule, one squadron was assigned to each base, but at the larger bases there might be two or more squadrons and at the smaller ones only a detachment.[6]

The group and squadron system of the Air Transport Command grew out of the usual War Department and AAF practice of organizing special units, with rigid tables of organizations, for each type of military activity. But this plan soon proved to be too inflexible for ATC, whose personnel requirements varied from base to base according to the size and type of activity conducted at each station. After more than a year of experience, the group and squadron system was scrapped in favor of what came to be known, in the peculiar jargon of the military personnel people, as "exact manning tables." Under this new plan, the personnel requirements of each station were measured exactly on a functional basis, and men were assigned accordingly, not to a standard T/O unit, such as a squadron, but to the station itself. The exact requirements of all stations were then consolidated at wing headquarters to form the basis for the wing's over-all manning table. As long as the wing commander stayed within the limits of his authorized strength, he could now shift his men about from job to job or from station to station as required. The new principle provided a necessary flexibility for efficient operation and conserved manpower.[7]

Along the southeastern route, three wings were organized initially—the Caribbean Wing, with headquarters at West Palm Beach, Florida; the South Atlantic Wing, whose headquarters was located first at Atkinson Field, British Guiana, and later moved to Natal, Brazil; and the Africa–Middle East Wing, with headquarters at Accra in Britain's Gold Coast Colony.[8] Following the invasion of North Africa and the extension of ATC activities into that area, the African jurisdiction was divided on 15 December 1943 into two wings: the North African and the Central African.[9]

The Caribbean Wing had immediate direction over activities in Florida and in the Caribbean area. Its original jurisdiction embraced only the mainland bases and Borinquen Field on Puerto Rico, the most important ferrying and transport base in the Caribbean and a key defense outpost.[10] In 1943, however, the wing's limits were extended south to the boundary between French Guiana and Brazil to coincide with those of the Antilles Department of the Caribbean Defense Command, which supplied most of the base services for transient aircraft.[11] To a large degree, the Caribbean Wing job remained that of managing the aerial ports of embarkation on the mainland. Most ferried aircraft on the way overseas were given a final checking and servicing at Morrison Field, the major continental ferrying base, and here the ferrying crews had their papers put in order, were issued overseas equipment, inoculated, and briefed on route conditions.[12] A few passengers and a small amount of freight were carried on ferried aircraft when there was extra space, but, for the most part, passengers, cargo, and mail moved out of the 36th Street Airport at nearby Miami, where transport aircraft operating south from Florida were based.[13] In September 1942 a third continental base, Homestead Field near Miami, was assigned to the Caribbean Wing in order to insure adequate staging faciliites for the heavy flow of ferried aircraft anticipated after the invasion of North Africa. It was also assumed that winter conditions along the North Atlantic route would soon cause ferrying to Britain to be shifted to the South Atlantic.[14]

Aircraft leaving Florida usually landed first at Borinquen Field, about 1,000 miles to the southeast, before proceeding on to either Waller Field on Trinidad or Atkinson Field in British Guiana. Four-engine planes, however, often overflew Borinquen and landed first at Waller or Atkinson. The few fighters or trainer aircraft ferried to Latin-American countries, or on to Africa, took a short-hop route through the Greater Antilles and the Leeward Islands into the South American continent.[15]

On leaving the Caribbean Wing, aircraft and crews came under the control of the South Atlantic Wing, whose original jurisdiction extended from Trinidad down along the Brazilian coast to Natal and across the South Atlantic as far as the African coast.[16] Along this 5,000-mile segment of the route were located five major air bases and a number of secondary bases, all spaced at intervals of several hundred miles. Waller Field and Atkinson Field were built on sites obtained from the British under the destroyer-base-lease deal of 1940. These were later transferred to the jurisdiction of the Caribbean Wing, but the South Atlantic Wing continued through the war to control ferrying and transport activities at the great bases at Belém and Natal in Brazil and at Wideawake Field on Ascension Island.

Belém and Natal were built by Panair do Brasil, a Pan American subsidiary, with funds appropriated for the Airport Development Program of 1940.[17] Both fields were ready for limited use soon after Pearl Harbor, but in June 1942 they were still in a primitive state of development, inadequately manned, and barely able to support the growing volume of traffic. At Natal the Ferrying Command had only four officers and fifty-seven enlisted men as late as mid-May, and only five nondescript buildings stood on the tract of sand and scrub brush traversed by two 6,000-foot runways.[18] However, a new construction program just under way would eventually make the Natal base one of the largest and best equipped in the world.[19] Belém was in much the same shape as Natal at the time Rommel was marching upon Egypt, but here, too, a new construction program had just been inaugurated.[20] Lesser bases were spaced conveniently along the route at Amapa, São Luiz, Fortaleza, and Recife.[21]

Probably no other air base used by the Air Transport Command had such strategic importance as that on Ascension Island. This anchored airdrome of volcanic rock, covering an area of only thirty-four square miles, was located in the South Atlantic approximately midway between the Brazilian bulge and the African coast. Ferrying Command officials had turned their attention to Ascension as a potential base as early as the fall of 1941, when it became clear that American military as well as lend-lease planes would be flying the South Atlantic route to Africa.[22] Situated 1,437 statute miles from Natal, and 1,357 from Accra in the Gold Coast Colony, Ascension would make it possible for two-engine planes to cross the South Atlantic in two fairly easy jumps with a normal gas load.[23] Before the base was opened, twin-engine craft could make the approximately 1,900-mile direct flight from Natal to Africa across the narrowest part of the Atlantic only after the installation of extra gas tanks, an expensive and time-consuming modification. Four-engine bombers and transports could fly directly from Natal to Roberts or Hastings Fields in Africa without difficulty, or even to Accra, 2,500 miles away, but, by using refueling facilities on Ascension, four-engine transports could take on a much lighter load of gasoline at Natal, increasing proportionately the amount of payload carried. With a stop at Ascension, it was even possible to ferry fighter aircraft to Africa, as was done with P-38's in 1943,* an accomplishment that otherwise would have been impossible.

In peacetime, Ascension was a British cable station and had a normal population of about 165 cable-company employees, the maximum number that could be sustained on the island by its limited water supply.[24] Negotiations were opened with the British early in 1942 for use of the island for an airdome. Britain readily agreed;[25] if for no other reason, she stood to benefit tremendously in the greater ease with which lend-lease deliveries to Africa could be effected. A board of American officers, headed by Lt. Col. Philip G. Kemp of the Ferrying Command, made a preliminary survey of Ascension and selected a tentative site for the airdrome.[26] By March 1942 an American task force, made up principally of troops of the 38th Engineer

* See below, pp. 75-76.

Combat Regiment, but containing also coast artillery, quartermaster, signal corps, hospital, army airways communications, and other units, was on its way to the island to begin construction work. Unloading the supplies, machinery, and construction materials from the three freighters was no easy job. Ascension has no harbor proper, and the projecting shelf of volcanic rock prevents ocean-going vessels from making a close approach to shore. Supplies had to be unloaded by barge or lighter, but even this was impossible when heavy southwest rollers were running. Construction work got under way by 13 April, and less than three months later, on 10 July, the 6,000-foot runway was open for traffic. In the meantime, the task force had constructed underground gasoline storage tanks, roads, barracks, a hospital, a distillation unit for distilling sea water, an electrical plant, gun emplacements, and ammunition dumps, all carefully camouflaged.[27]

There was an airman's ditty, originating with some imaginative pilot on the South Atlantic run, that goes:

> If I don't hit Ascension
> My wife will get a pension. . . .

Actually, the island had a radio beam on it, and the navigators had no great trouble hitting it. The real worry of the ferry or transport pilot, in the early days at least, was taking off from the Ascension runway in the face of a great cloud of birds. It had long been the habit of the sooty tern, known locally as the "wideawake," to come to Ascension to lay and hatch its eggs. Within a few weeks after the Ascension airfield had been opened for traffic, the terns began to arrive on schedule. One large colony's usual nesting ground was located just beyond the far end of the newly constructed runway. This did not discourage the birds, however, and they settled down to lay their eggs and stay for the nesting period. They were a real menace to plane and pilot, for every time a plane started down the runway the roar of the motors brought a huge flock of birds into the air right in its path. Heavier planes, unable to climb quickly enough, were obliged to pass right through the mass of birds, running the risk of a broken windshield, a dented leading edge, or a bird wedged in engine or air scoop.[28]

Getting rid of the wideawakes was a headache that brought sleepless nights to the highest echelons of the AAF. Smoke candles were tried, and dynamite blasts, but both proved equally ineffectual. Someone got the inspired idea that cats would do the job, but when a planeload of cats was brought in to kill off the terns, the cats were themselves eaten by booby birds, a larger species with an extremely strong beak and neck. Finally, AAF Headquarters sent down a well-known ornithologist, Dr. James P. Chapin of the American Museum of Natural History, who advised that, if the eggs were destroyed, the birds would leave and not again nest in the same area. With some 40,000 of their eggs smashed, the terns began finally to move away from the runway area to join colonies on other parts of the island. AAF officials from Washington to Chungking rested easier.[29]

A unique feature of the South Atlantic Wing and the Africa-Middle East Wing was that in each case the ATC Wing commander was also the theater commander, for in both Brazil and in central Africa, air transport and ferrying were the principal military activities. Brig. Gen. Robert L. Walsh was placed in command of the South Atlantic Wing in June 1942, assuming at once some of the duties of a theater commander.[30] The following November, when a theater command under the name of the United States Army Forces in South America (USAFSA) was organized, General Walsh took over as commanding general. His theater headquarters was established at Recife, about 150 miles to the south of Natal; but South Atlantic Wing headquarters remained at Natal.[31]

Brig. Gen. Shepler W. Fitzgerald went to Africa in June 1942 as commander of both the Africa–Middle East Wing and a new theater command, United States Army Forces in Central Africa (USAFICA). His headquarters, wing and theater, were established first at Cairo, but were soon moved to Accra, on the Gold Coast, the permanent location.[32] There he began the militarization of Pan American's contract operations in Africa, an undertaking that required about six months to complete. Pan American had gone into Africa under contracts with the American and British governments made in August 1941. Starting with seven twin-engine transports in October 1941, Pan American Airways–Africa had thirty-eight planes in operation by the following June and in the meantime had extended its flights from Khartoum up to Cairo and eastward to Karachi. PAA–Africa not only operated a transport service for the benefit of the United States and its allies but also ferried aircraft across Africa, including AAF planes, lend-lease aircraft, and British planes coming down from Britain on their way to the Middle East.*

* See Vol. I, 324–25, 354.

Shortly before Pearl Harbor the Ferrying Command, in anticipation of an enlarged military traffic to the Middle East, had taken steps to station its own military personnel at major bases in Latin America and across Africa. There was no thought, initially, of supplanting the Pan American organization; but under wartime conditions it soon became clear that military control of the African segment of the route, which skirted Vichy French territory and extended into the Middle East war zone, would become necessary for security. Furthermore, the manning of the African bases with both military and Pan American civilian personnel was wasteful.[33] General Arnold and General Olds of the Ferrying Command had already reached the conclusion that the trans-African route should be manned exclusively by military personnel when the necessary authority was given in a War Department directive of 18 February 1942.[34] This order required the termination of all civil contract activities overseas except in the Western Hemisphere and Hawaii. Militarization, strongly opposed by Pan American Airways, proceeded in the face of an unco-operative attitude on the part of some Pan American officials, leading to a bitter quarrel between General Fitzgerald and the company's manager in Africa. Nevertheless, by December all transcontinental operations and facilities had been taken over by the Air Transport Command.[35]

The forced withdrawal of the Pan American organization from Africa did not affect its contract services in the Western Hemisphere or its flying-boat, and later C-54 and C-87, operations across the South Atlantic to the western coast of Africa. It even operated transports across Africa to the Middle East and India, as did other contractors, but after December 1942 all planes crossing Africa used bases and facilities completely under military control. The Pan American Air Ferries contract was also canceled, and its lend-lease ferrying activities ceased entirely at the end of October 1942.[36]

General Fitzgerald had another difficult job in bringing to completion a more southerly and safer route across central Africa, which had been decided upon earlier in 1942. In its original conception, the alternate route, running roughly parallel to and a little south of the equator, was for moving heavy bombers across Africa and the island steppingstones in the Indian Ocean to Australia; but this plan was abandoned when the Japanese advance reached the area of the Cocos

Islands in February.* The Congo route, as it became known, now took the form of an alternate airway into the Middle East. Bases were constructed at Point Noire in French Equatorial Africa, at Leopold-ville and Elisabethville in the Belgian Congo, and at Nairobi in Kenya. In the dark days of 1942 this alternate route offered insurance against loss of the central African airway, but the rising fortunes of Allied military operations soon robbed it of value. Even before the fall of Tunisia in the spring of 1943, the Congo route no longer possessed military significance.[37]

Reinforcements for the Middle East

Through the first half of 1942 most of the aircraft flown from the United States to the British in Egypt had been transport aircraft for the RAF's local air transport fleet in Egypt, but Rommel's threat brought a sudden rush of combat planes. In June, the RAF began receiving Lockheed and Martin medium bombers flown across the South Atlantic.[38] By the end of 1942, a total of 398 such aircraft—B-34's, A-28's, and A-30's—had been delivered to the British by Pan American Air Ferries or by military crews.[39] Arriving too late to be used in the last-ditch defense of Egypt, these planes were employed to great advantage by Montgomery in the Allied counteroffensive that fall.

Thanks to Britain's gallant stand at El Alamein, the Russians continued to receive B-25's by way of the South Atlantic, and, beginning in October, Douglas A-20 light attack bombers, previously shipped by water, were being delivered by air to Soviet representatives at Basra and other airports in the Persian Gulf area. Altogether, a total of 240 aircraft were flown to Russia by way of the South Atlantic air route during 1942, of which 102 were B-25's and 138 were A-20's.[40] This does not give, by any means, a complete picture of lend-lease aid to Russia in the form of aircraft during this period. As early as January 1942, A-20's had started arriving by water transport at Persian Gulf ports, where they were assembled, tested, and flown on into Russia; and in September of that year, lend-lease planes began moving to the Russian front by way of the Alaskan ferrying route and on across Siberia,[41] a route which became increasingly favored.

Originally, American efforts in the Middle East had been confined to logistical support of the British, who carried the full combat re-

* See Vol. I, 330-31.

sponsibility. But after Rommel's victories in May and June, the United States agreed to commit to that theater a total of nine combat groups, of which seven groups were to be in operation by the end of 1942.* For more immediate assistance, the AAF diverted a detachment of twenty-three B-24's then in the Middle East on the way to China, and late in June it ordered Maj. Gen. Lewis H. Brereton to fly from India to the Middle East with all the few heavy bombers then belonging to the Tenth Air Force.† While Brereton took steps to establish the Ninth Air Force, the AAF ordered the immediate movement of three of the nine groups promised for the Middle East. These were the 57th Fighter Group, equipped with P-40's; the 12th Bombardment Group (M), a B-25 unit; and the 98th Bombardment Group (H), its equipment being B-24's. The movement of the three groups to the Middle East was made a special ferrying project which took its name from the American code word for Egypt—HEATH.[42]

Both Britain and the United States had been transporting fighter aircraft by water to the western African coast and flying them from there along the trans-Africa ferry route to the Middle East and beyond.‡ The 57th Fighter Group was moved out in the same way. The pilots, who had been given previous instruction in carrier take-offs, and their seventy-two P-40F's, were taken aboard the U.S. carrier *Ranger*, which left Quonset, Rhode Island, on 1 July. When the ship was within a hundred miles or so of the western African coast, the aircraft were launched in groups of eighteen. After landing at a coastal base, the planes were then ferried across Africa to Egypt. For the skilful piloting of the P-40's across the jungles and desert wastes of Africa, the 57th Group received commendations from General Brereton and Brig. Gen. Russell L. Maxwell, the Middle East theater commander. Losses were held to a negligible figure partly through the efforts of ground crews, who followed by air transport. After landing on the same fields as the fighters, the maintenance men would spend the night checking and putting the planes in shape for the next leg of the journey. Upon arrival in Cairo, the group moved on to a temporary station in Palestine at the end of July. Within a month, some of the pilots had flown their first missions over enemy territory.[43]

* See Vol. I, 569.

† See Vol. II, 8 ff.

‡ For earlier movements, see Vol. I, 339–40.

Meanwhile, the 98th Bombardment Group, equipped with thirty-five B-24's, had moved from its training base at Lakeland, Florida, to Morrison Field to prepare for the 10,000-mile flight to Egypt. Because the supply and maintenance facilities for heavy bombers in the Middle East were limited, the B-24's carried a stock of spare parts sufficient for a sixty-day period and as many maintenance men as possible, in addition to the regular crews. The air echelon left Florida, by squadrons, between 17 and 30 July, and by 7 August had assembled in Palestine.[44]

The air echelon of the 12th Bombardment Group (M), with fifty-seven B-25's, moved through Morrison Field and down along the South Atlantic route to Africa at about the same time as the 98th Group. By way of preparation for foreign service, the organization had already gone through a period of intensive training at Esler Field, Louisiana, and as a result was well qualified and well equipped when ready for movement overseas. The B-25's of the 12th Group were among the first aircraft to make use of the new Ascension base. All arrived safely in Egypt, having covered the 10,000 miles from Florida in an average flying time of seventy-two hours.[45]

For purposes of contrast, it is worth noting that the ground echelons of the 57th, 98th, and 12th Groups sailed from New York on 16 July and reached Egypt only in mid-August.[46]

These groups were only the advance guard of reinforcements sent to General Brereton. Replacements soon were flowing, and by the end of 1942 a total of 370 aircraft had been ferried to the Ninth Air Force. While the great majority were P-40's, B-24's, and B-25's, there were also more than 50 twin-engine transports, which made it possible to build an effective local air transport service.[47] These transports belonged to the 316th Troop Carrier Group, whose air echelon with its original equipment of forty C-47's had moved out to Egypt by way of the South Atlantic route. It arrived in the Cairo area on 23 November 1942 in time to deliver Thanksgiving turkeys to American air units serving with the British Eighth Army.[48]

Although the flow of aircraft along the South Atlantic route to the Middle East continued through the summer and fall of 1942, very few of the planes got beyond the Middle East into India and China. From July through December, only 25 B-24's, 33 B-25's, 5 P-40's, and 23 twin-engine transports were ferried to American combat and air transport units in the China-Burma-India theater.[49] This uneven distribution of aircraft was only partially corrected in 1943. During that year a total of 669 planes were delivered to the Ninth Air Force in North Africa, while only 347 were ferried to the Tenth Air Force and only 168 to the Fourteenth Air Force in China.[50]

Transport Services

The movement of the planes of the HEATH project, and the large number of replacements that came later, across 10,000 miles of ocean, jungle, and desert was no easy job, but it was simple compared with that of building up an air transportation service that would keep a steady flow of aircraft parts, spare engines, maintenance equipment, replacement aircrews, and mechanics moving out to General Brereton's force. The Middle East Air Force* was dependent upon air transport to an unusual degree. Not only was the long water supply line around the Cape a formidable handicap but no sound logistical plan making maximum use of water transport and emergency use of air transport could be devised in advance because the force was thrown together so hastily. The B-24's had carried some spares, and a freighter had started out with a stock of spare parts but was sunk by a German submarine. Among the items lost were extra tires for the B-24's; as a result, General Brereton had to cannibalize about half of his small heavy-bomber force for tires to operate the remainder.[51] In an emergency of this sort, air transport was the only means of assuring a minimum stock of supplies until the next freighter arrived. A similar disaster occurred when a ship carrying a large supply of American tools and spare parts for two RAF repair depots in Egypt and the Sudan was sunk.[52] Had the RAF been forced to wait for the arrival of replacements by water, a large number of combat planes would have been immobilized another three months for want of repair.

At the time General Brereton had been ordered to the Middle East, the Air Transport Command was already overwhelmed by the volume of cargo, mail, and passengers piling up at the Miami port of embarkation and at the transshipment points of Natal and Accra. Already deployed at the end of the South Atlantic air route, before the Middle East Air Force came into being, were British units in Egypt, Soviet forces in southern Russia, the American Tenth Air Force in India, and American and Chinese air units in China—all de-

* The predecessor of the Ninth Air Force.

pendent to some degree on the air transport line out of Miami. On 17 June, General George, in urging upon General Arnold the need for more transports, reported an accumulation of over 53 tons of cargo awaiting air shipment at Miami, while over 40 tons of supplies, as well as 91 passengers, had piled up at Natal.[53] By 12 July, after the movement of supplies to Brereton had started, the backlog at Miami had increased to 138 tons and at Natal to 88 tons, exclusive of passengers.[54] At this time there were twenty-four C-47 type transports on the Miami-Natal route, with one Pan American Clipper flying a regular but infrequent schedule. These planes together were capable of moving about 11 tons of cargo a day. On the overwater jump from Natal to Africa were five new B-24D's, four Clippers, and two Stratoliners, the whole having a daily capacity of nine tons. On the trans-African route from Accra to Cairo there were then operating forty-two C-47 type planes, capable of transporting 10 tons daily.[55] Because new transports were slow in arriving, the backlogs continued to grow through the summer and into the fall. During August an officer from ATC headquarters found 250 tons of supplies awaiting shipment at Miami, 75 tons at Natal, and over 250 tons at Accra, where the backlog was increasing at the rate of $2\frac{1}{2}$ tons a day. He did not exaggerate when he warned that "grave issues" depended on a more efficient air transport service to the Middle East.[56]

A chief cause of the congestion at Miami and other points was the shortage of transports, which could be overcome only as the production of new transport aircraft made it possible. Already the South Atlantic run enjoyed the highest priority on available transports. As with the late summer and early fall the first numbers of the long-awaited C-54's and C-87's were put into operation, the South Atlantic service continued to hold its priority. Although a few C-87's had to be sent to the Pacific, Pan American Airways inaugurated a four-engine schedule in August 1942 with four C-54's flying between Miami and Natal.[57] The first C-87 was put to work on the South Atlantic run in October.[58] By the end of 1942 the fleet operating on the transatlantic jump had been increased to twenty-six planes—nine C-54's, four C-87's, four B-24D's, five Stratoliners, and four Clippers. Their daily capacity was thirty tons, which compared most favorably with the nine tons in July.[59]

Meantime, ATC had been struggling with the problem of how to assure a more efficient employment of the available capacity. The first critical point was the 36th Street Airport at Miami, where freight from all parts of the country collected and where ATC had only a small detachment, most of its members totally inexperienced in the handling of cargo. The first step was to activate on 7 July 1942 Air Intransit Depot No. 6, staffed by experienced freight handlers of the Air Service Command.[60]

As new screening procedures were established for the accumulating freight, it quickly became evident that much of it did not need to be shipped by air. For emphasis, it may be permissible to use an extreme example. In September the depot received, for shipment to B-25's grounded for lack of parts at Natal and Accra, two complete tables of replacement parts for a group, each table consisting of 250,000 parts weighing about 375,000 pounds. Actually, only a very few parts were needed to put the grounded aircraft in flying condition. Having ascertained what those parts were, the depot shipped the critical items by air and rerouted the remainder for water shipment.[61]

The depot also saved much cargo space by repackaging. A large proportion of the freight arriving at Miami at that time was packed in heavy wooden crates or other materials suitably designed for rail or water shipment but excessively heavy for air shipment. Materials were repacked for the most part in waterproof cardboard containers which were of light weight but at the same time gave sufficient protection against knocks encountered in transit, the weight of other packages, and the humidity and rain of the tropics. At one period during 1942, repacking was required on an estimated 40 per cent of the cargo arriving at Miami, with results calculated at a 30 per cent reduction in weight. The weight saved on some items was almost fantastic. A shipment of P-39 air scoops arriving at Miami weighed 128 pounds per unit, a figure reduced by repacking to 17 pounds. On another occasion, the depot received a package of four elevator assemblies having a total weight in excess of 1,000 pounds. When repacked in packages, each package weighed 108 pounds for a total saving of 588 pounds.[62]

As these experiences demonstrated, the operation of an air transport service demanded much more than the provision of a sufficient number of planes and crews or the efficient scheduling of their flights. One of the more difficult questions was that of determining priority for air shipment. Much of the backlog at Miami, exceeding at times even the airport's capacity for storage, could be attributed to the understandable practice by factories and air depots of shipping supplies demanded during these first critical months to aerial ports of embarkation before getting a necessary priority for air shipment from ATC.[63] The practice was forbidden by a War Department order of 27 November 1942, which prohibited the forwarding of cargo and personnel to ports of aerial embarkation for shipment overseas unless a priority had been previously granted by the ATC for such movement.[64] At the time the order was issued, an estimated 75 per cent of the cargo reaching the Air Intransit Depot at Miami was without priority classification. This had been cut to 25 per cent by January 1943, and by July of that year to about 5 per cent.[65]

The War Department order gave the Air Transport Command full authority to establish better control over the volume of traffic moving from the interior to aerial ports, but this by no means solved the larger problem of determining which materials should go by air and what was the relative urgency of various shipments. The War Department had said merely that the Air Service Command and other shippers should not decide such questions. It was an ATC responsibility, but the priority officers at ATC headquarters still had to depend very largely on information received from the overseas theaters, where each commander tended to demand the highest priority for his own emergency needs and even, for safety's sake, to exaggerate the emergency. The War Department and AAF Headquarters provided helpful guidance on the relative merits of mounting claims on ATC space, but many decisions had to be made on a purely arbitrary basis until ATC had enough equipment to make a reasonably satisfactory solution possible. In August 1943 it was decided to allot to each theater commander a specific tonnage for movement by air to his area each month, leaving to him within the limit set full right to determine the priorities for movement of the individual items.[66] Eight months later, in April 1944, the War Department ordered the setting-up of local priority boards within all the theaters to act as screening agencies to pass on all requests for air transportation and to set priorities for all incoming, outgoing, and intratheater traffic.[67] To aid the theater commanders in carrying out their responsibilities, a number of ATC officers experienced in priorities evaluation were transferred to the theaters, where they assisted in setting up screening procedures and, in many cases, acted as executive officers of the boards.[68]

61

But all this lay far in the future as during the critical summer of 1942 men struggled all along the South Atlantic route to get the freight through and, in doing so, to learn a new job. Whatever questions of priority might be in debate at higher headquarters, there was one priority that quite clearly remained undisputed—that of the South Atlantic route to Africa over all others. When a few weeks later word came of the Allied landing in northwestern Africa, it became evident to all that this priority would stand for some time to come.

✳ ✳ ✳ ✳ ✳ ✳ ✳ ✳ ✳ ✳ ✳

CHAPTER 3

NORTH AFRICA
AND THE MEDITERRANEAN

THE Air Transport Command became involved in planning
for the North African invasion as early as 10 October 1942,
four weeks before the launching of the attack. On that date
General George was informed by the Air Staff that plans should be
developed immediately for the extension of ATC's services into the
invasion area. Col. Harold R. Harris, chief of the command's planning section, and his assistant, Lt. Thomas M. Murphy, went to work
at once on a preliminary report on possible routes for ATC's supply
effort. Colonel Harris and Lieutenant Murphy were handicapped by
the scarcity of information on airports and other facilities in Vichy
Africa, but their report showed a sound grasp of the problem of
supplying Allied invasion troops by air. It was completed in time for
General George to take it with him when he flew south on 12 October to confer with his wing commanders in the South Atlantic
and Africa.[1]

French North Africa was by no means easy of air approach. From
British bases in the north, General Eisenhower would move down
most of the aircraft employed in the initial stages of the attack, but
for several reasons this route was unsatisfactory for maintaining continued air communications on a large scale with the Allied forces.
While it extended only 1,300 miles from southern Britain to Casablanca and Oran, aircraft had to fly dangerously close to the German-
occupied French coast and had to steer clear of the Spanish and
Portuguese coasts. Enemy interception was a constant threat, foul
weather was commonplace, and the Gibraltar air base, the only potential refueling point along the way for short-range craft, was too

vulnerable to permit heavy aircraft concentrations there over any period of time. Finally, a large proportion of the planes and aircraft supplies moving from Britain into North Africa had first to be flown across the North Atlantic, a route which would be all but closed to normal traffic during the winter of 1942–43. Obviously, the main flow must come via the South Atlantic and over one or more of three possible branches stemming from the established trans-African route.

Cairo, about 2,000 miles from the Oran beachhead, might have served as a jumping-off point, but it was quickly dropped from consideration. The airports in Egypt were already congested, and it would be necessary to move planes and materials across 3,400 miles of central Africa before doubling back to Oran.[2]

By far the best approach, and the one that eventually became the main route, was along the string of coastal bases from Accra in the Gold Coast colony up through Roberts Field (Liberia), Hastings Field (Sierra Leone), and Bathurst (Gambia). The Bathurst airport, the most northerly Allied base on the coast, was separated from Casablanca by only 1,550 miles, but it lay in the very shadow of Dakar. From the British and Free French experience in September 1940,* it seemed clear not only that Dakar would be held to the last but that it might well become a base for a counterattack by Vichy French and Axis forces, a forbidding threat to large-scale air supply operations up along the west African coast. Furthermore, aircraft taking off for Casablanca would have to curve inland over French territory or out over the water in order to avoid the Spanish colony of Rio de Oro. Along the inland route several Vichy desert air bases offered convenient points for launching air attacks on Allied planes in transit.†[3] Thus, this route, too, was discounted.

Having decided that the coastal route would be untenable until Dakar and other points had been cleared of hostile air and ground troops, Harris and Murphy recommended that North Africa–bound aircraft, after crossing the South Atlantic to Accra or other coastal bases, proceed eastward along the central African route about 780 miles to Kano in northern Nigeria, and thence northwestward across the Sahara to Casablanca or Oran, 1,800–1,900 miles away. Kano,

---

* A Free French force and a British naval squadron which attempted to seize Dakar were sharply rebuffed by stoutly resisting Vichy French.

† Once Vichy France had surrendered, these same bases, particularly Atar and Tindouf, became important links in the main airway into North Africa.

having been for some time a major base on the regular central African route into Cairo, was a satisfactory stopover; gasoline stocks and other supplies were adequate; the weather was favorable; and heavy concentrations of aircraft there prior to the invasion would not arouse suspicion, nor would they be in danger of attack from the air or ground.[4] General George accepted these recommendations, and Kano became during the initial stages of the invasion the main take-off point for both ferried and transport aircraft.

KIT Project

General George, accompanied by Brig. Gen. Thomas J. Hanley of the Air Staff and by Colonel Harris and other members of his staff, left Washington on 12 October ostensibly for an inspection trip to the Carribbean area. At Atkinson Field, British Guiana, he conferred with Brig. Gen. Robert L. Walsh of the South Atlantic Wing and Brig. Gen. Shepler W. Fitzgerald of the Africa–Middle East Wing. Without divulging the secret of the imminent invasion, George and his staff were able to obtain information that aided greatly in developing plans for ATC's part in the coming operation.[5]

The Air Transport Command was charged with two initial undertakings in connection with TORCH: the establishment of a four-engine transport service from Accra through Kano to Oran and the support of ferrying operations from Florida through Natal, Accra, and Kano into the North African area. Ferrying plans, as of 23 October, called for the movement of the following combat groups along the South Atlantic route during the sixty-day period following the invasion.

Group	Type of Aircraft	Number of Aircraft	Due to Arrive
68th	A-20	36	D + 6
320th	B-26	57	D + 22
17th	B-26	57	D + 30
27th	A-20	44	D + 45
321st	B-25	57	D + 60

All the aircraft involved were to be staged at Morrison Field, Florida, and go by way of Ascension Island to Accra, with final staging, prior to take-off across the relatively unknown Sahara route, at Kano or Maiduguri—Roberts Field in Liberia being a possible alternate. The ATC would provide adequate supplies of gasoline, oil, and rations along the route and assume responsibility for briefing the crews and monitoring the flights. The Air Service Command was to supply, at stopping points along the way, a balanced list of spare parts for the various types of aircraft. ATC commanders in South America and Africa were to be informed of the projected invasion but were to receive only the minimum information necessary for performance of their tasks.[6]

No heavy bombers were included in this first scheduled movement of ferried aircraft. Four-engine planes were still going to the United Kingdom by the North Atlantic route, and at the outset North Africa was to be supplied with B-17's and B-24's from Britain. However, as the ferrying plans were being completed, the Air Transport Command learned that heavy-bombardment groups originally scheduled to go from the United States by way of the North Atlantic and Britain would go by the southern route instead.[7] All heavy-bomber ferrying was shifted to the South Atlantic route in December.[8]

The A-20's of the 68th Observation Group, scheduled to reach North Africa six days after D Day, began arriving at Morrison Field on 30 October. They were organized as the KIT project, with Lt. Col. Louis T. Reichers, an experienced and highly qualified officer, serving as project commander.[9] Reichers, whose service with the command predated Pearl Harbor, had been the first pilot to traverse the whole of the South Atlantic route in an east-to-west direction. On this flight, after having piloted one of the two B-24's carrying the Harriman mission from Britain to Moscow in the fall of 1941, he had then brought his plane home by way of the Middle East, Africa, the South Atlantic, and Brazil. It was a hazardous, trail-blazing flight along a route still in an extremely primitive condition.*

Upon arriving at Morrison Field, Colonel Reichers organized a staff consisting of several experienced ATC officers. As no arrangements had been completed with the Air Service Command for spare parts, the staff went to work immediately on the supply problem and had Wright Field make up and ship to Morrison Field a spare parts kit not to exceed 200 pounds in weight for each airplane. An additional 7,500 pounds of operational spares were also to be shipped out on a C-87 transport to Oran to arrive about the same time as the A-20's. When the first A-20 reached Morrison Field on 30 October, it was immediately tested for weight and balance. The loading was thoroughly out of balance, so the plane was reloaded as a criterion

---

* See Vol. I, 318.

for the others. A close inspection of the planes as they came in also found many obvious malfunctions of radio equipment, instruments, generators, and other parts. These defects could be corrected, but there was one glaring mechanical deficiency that could not be, short of replacing the engines—the defective pistons and rings of the A-20B power plant. These caused the Wright 2600-11 engine to give trouble all the way into Oran. Another major problem facing Reichers was the greenness and inexperience of the crews. Had he realized this as fully at the beginning of the 9,000-mile flight as at the end, he would probably have insisted on more training in navigation and formation flying. He had been told that the pilots were "pretty good" in instrument flying, but this proved to be very much of an exaggeration. Actually only six of the thirty-six pilots held instrument cards; the others had received only Link training.[10]

The thirty-six A-20's were divided into four flights of nine ships each, each flight to be led by a heavier convoy plane flown by an ATC crew. These flights were: TIGER, led by a B-24 commanded by Colonel Reichers; SHARK, led by a B-25 under Capt. Rodney S. Lamont; PANTHER, led by Maj. Marion E. Grevemberg in a B-24; and FOX, led by a B-25 under command of Capt. John M. Tillman. It was planned that TIGER and SHARK flights would comprise the first echelon, flying each leg on the same day, and that PANTHER and FOX flights would follow a day later.[11]

Colonel Reichers' TIGER flight departed Morrison Field on 8 November, and here began a series of mishaps of varying degrees of seriousness that resulted in general from the greenness of the crews or the bad mechanical condition of the planes. Time was lost at the very start as Reichers circled Morrison Field in his B-24, trying to pull the nine A-20's together before heading out for Borinquen Field. One plane, left behind because of difficulty in starting the engine, came on later with the SHARK flight; another circled aimlessly around the field and never did join the formation but somehow reached Borinquen on its own. About an hour short of Borinquen Field, the main flight encountered a front much heavier than the forecast had indicated.[12] Reichers himself narrowly escaped disaster from the panicky maneuvers of his green pilots, who had tried to follow his B-24 instead of dispersing for instrument flying as directed. There were several near-collisions. One of the pilots came out of a low scud to find himself headed straight for the tail of Reichers' B-24 lead plane. In order to keep from cutting it off, he rolled the A-20 on its back and peeled away in a dive. This caused the baggage to shift, and a musette bag became entangled in the controls. As the plane headed for the water, doing somewhere between 370 and 400 miles an hour, the crew chief managed to disentangle the gear just in time. When the pilot pulled violently out of the dive near the water, "the wings seemed to point straight up into the air and there was a very loud crackling noise." The dive tore off the radio antenna, broke open the escape hatch, with the resulting loss of some of the baggage, and buckled both wings along the leading edge just beyond the engine nacelles. It was only by great good fortune that the plane got into Borinquen. It had to stay there for major repairs while the others moved on.[13] Two A-20's were lost: the tail plane of the formation piloted by Maj. Thomas E. Johnson, temporary commander of the 68th Group, and another by 2d Lt. James K. Parker, only five months out of flying school. Available evidence seemed to indicate that Parker, sticking too close to his commander, had collided with the other, causing both planes to go down at sea with a total loss of the crews.[14] The other flights were more fortunate on this first leg of the journey, although SHARK flight was so long delayed in assembling that it was called back by the control tower and held until the next day, the 9th. On the 10th the other two flights under the general command of Major Grevemberg departed in good order.

At Borinquen Field Reichers' TIGER flight laid over two days. The morale of the crews was good, in spite of the loss of a respected leader and the two crews, and in spite of very poor transient service at the base—so poor that the "kids," as the pilots were described in an official report, flew to Atkinson without either breakfast or lunch.[15]

Colonel Reichers reported that the 3,000-mile flight from Borinquen to Natal, with stops at Atkinson Field and Belém, was "more or less routine," although the pilots frequently lost visual contact, with some resulting confusion. Upon arriving at a landing field, Reichers would circle the strip in his B-24 while sending out homing signals on his radio; or, after getting a general description of the country from pilots who were "lost," he would tell them where they were and how to head toward the airport. Of the thirty-six A-20's that left Florida, thirty-three reached Natal. On the take-off from Natal, one of the A-20 pilots retracted his landing gear too soon, and one propeller scraped the runway for 300 yards. In spite of orders from the control tower and advice from his crew chief, he stayed with the flight into Ascension Island, a distance of 1,437 miles, where a complete engine change was necessary.[16]

All thirty-three of the planes got across the Atlantic, though not without other mishaps caused by engine failure or poor navigation. On 24 November they flew from Accra to Kano, except for one plane left behind because of engine trouble. At daybreak of the following morning, Colonel Reichers with TIGER and SHARK flights took off on the 1,800-mile jump across the Sahara to Oran. Four planes lost the leader and had to turn back to Kano. One plane was forced to land on a desert airport at In-Sala; the others ran into a heavy front in the mountains near Oran, and it was only through the skilful work of Reichers that they reached Tafaraoui Field, where the radio range and homing beacons had quit operating. Reichers remarked in his report: "Our arrival at Oran was not under very favorable circumstances due to the lack of communications, bad weather, shortage of food and lack of sleeping accommodations, resulting in our being very unhappy."[17]

The four planes which had turned back to Kano were divided between the other two flights. PANTHER flight under Major Grevemberg, leaving Kano on the 26th with ten A-20's, had better luck. At Oran Colonel Reichers used a portable Signal Corps radio set to bring seven of the planes into Tafaraoui Field; the other three landed at La Senia Airport nearby. FOX flight under Captain Tillman also got off on the 26th but turned back when four A-20's developed engine trouble. One plane was badly damaged in an emergency landing at a water hole where the crew found some Arab herdsmen.[18] All members of the flight had been briefed on the danger of being captured by Vichy forces or unfriendly Arabs, but here the natives proved hospitable. They killed a goat and roasted some of the meat for the crew, in return for which they were given candy, cigarettes, and chewing gum, and the chief was presented with several French gold pieces carried for such emergencies. The next day a C-47 was sent out from Kano to pick up the crew and strip the A-20 of removable parts. The native chief, in return for the gold coins, insisted that the pilot take one of his daughters with him. When the pilot refused, the chief was so insulted that the greatest diplomacy had to be employed to prevent an ugly incident.[19]

FOX flight took off again on the 28th, leaving five planes at Kano because of engine trouble. Two others were forced to land at Ft. Laperine; the rest of the flight made it to Oran, but not without difficulty, because the portable Signal Corps station at Oran had been commandeered by a Signal Corps officer for other work. When last seen "it was going 40 miles an hour down the road to Algiers." Other agencies were no more helpful than the Signal Corps. When Tillman tried to get assistance from the Bomber Command in removing the crews and salvaging the planes at Ft. Laperine, he "was politely told that we were running a war and not a nursery school." Fighter Command was unable to help, but a "kind colonel" in the Air Service Command promised to do all he could.[20]

Of the original thirty-six A-20's of the KIT project, only twenty-three had reached Oran by 28 November, twenty days out from Florida. The remaining ten planes that had gotten across the Atlantic came in during December. Fortunately, the experience of the 68th Group proved to be exceptional, but it serves nonetheless to emphasize the varied hazards that had to be overcome before ATC could view the ferrying of combat planes and crews to overseas theaters as a routine operation.* ATC officers stressed in their reports two obvious conclusions: that combat crews must be better trained for long-range ferrying and that the aircraft must be in better mechanical shape at departure. Colonel Reichers recommended at least a week of special crew training prior to departure in group take-off, assembly, formation flying, dispersal, reassembly, and landing procedure. He asked also for more instruction by the Training Command and the OTU's in instrument flying and formation flying.[21] Other officers were concerned with specific improvements in the A-20's Wright engine[22] and in bettering housekeeping and health conditions for transients along the route.[23] Hazards encountered because of inadequate communications, weather reporting, and navigational aids at stations along the route would be overcome gradually, but not until the AAF had suffered severe losses in the heavy movement of aircraft into North Africa during the 1942–43 winter.[24]

Opening a Transport Service

While helping to ferry combat planes, the Air Transport Command had been busy inaugurating a transport service into North

---

* Happily, the early development of a coastal route northward from Accra made further attempts to ferry aircraft across the desert from Kano unnecessary.

Africa. Since a regular transport route already extended to Accra and across central Africa, the chief problem at first was to get long-range cargo craft for the long jump of 1,800–2,100 miles from Kano or Accra across the desert to target points in the north. On 20 October, General George had asked for an early delivery of eight C-87's to provide one daily round trip across the desert by 15 November and a second by the 25th. Six new C-87's were promptly assigned to ATC, together with extra engines and other spare parts. The movement of the C-87's to Africa was intrusted to Major Edward Coates, who christened his own plane *Old Saint Nick* because she was to take Christmas mail on her first flight into North Africa. As the planes came off a Fort Worth assembly line, they were flown directly to Morrison Field. Here they were held up for two days because the base authorities wanted to give the brand-new planes a major overhaul and their crews new physical exams and a fresh set of shots. Coates could not divulge the secret mission of the flight but by some frantic telephoning to Washington finally got the planes cleared. They left Morrison Field on 11 November and arrived at Accra on the 13th.[25]

A threat to divert the C-87's to the trans-African run to Cairo as replacements for C-47's needed by the advancing British failed to materialize, and on 16 November Coates and his crew left Accra for Kano. There he waited until 2200 before beginning the flight over French West Africa, supposedly defended by Vichy French squadrons at the desert air bases of Gao and Colomb-Bechar. Coates reached the coast at daylight and worked along it until he sighted Oran. In spite of the heavy load aboard his C-87, he landed safely on Tafaraoui's runway, which was only 3,500 feet long. In addition to the Christmas mail, this pioneer transport flight into North Africa brought in spare parts for the 68th Group's A-20's and miscellaneous supplies. Because the field had only hand-operated gasoline pumps, refueling time for the C-87 was ten hours. On the night of 19/20 November, Coates returned direct to Accra, making the non-stop flight of 2,150 miles in a little over ten hours. A second plane left on the 18th and two more on the 19th, carrying aircraft parts, a 1,200-watt radio station, and gasoline pumps, the latter two items badly needed at Tafaraoui. After the fourth or fifth trip, the detour via Kano was omitted, and flights were made directly between Accra and Oran. Still far from satisfactory, however, the new trans-Sahara service was considered only a temporary expedient until the coastal route could be cleared and both the two-engine and four-engine transports could operate across shorter distances.[26]

After the Allied position in Morocco and Algiers had been made secure, negotiations were opened with Pierre Boisson, Vichy Governor-General of French West Africa, for the peaceful occupation of Dakar and the whole of that Vichy-held territory. On 7 December, General Eisenhower reached a broad understanding with Admiral Jean Darlan and Governor Boisson, and negotiations were then turned over to Boisson and Brig. Gen. Cyrus R. Smith, ATC Chief of Staff, who had gone out to Africa as chief of a special United States Army West African Mission. By terms of the Smith-Boisson agreement, the United States secured the use of airdromes, harbors, roads, and other facilities in French West Africa and the authority to construct a new airfield near Dakar for which both the United States and the colony would contribute labor and materials.[27] This base (Dakar/Yof or Mallard Field) was not completed until 1944. Meanwhile, the United States, finding the runways on the existing French bases in the area too short to accommodate heavy bombers and large transports, took over a small field near the town of Rufisque and about seventeen miles out of Dakar. Within a few months, two 6,000-foot runways were ready at Eknes Field, as it was named, which became the main ATC base in the Dakar area until June 1944, when all personnel and facilities were moved to Mallard Field.[28] Dakar's location at the most westerly point in Africa made it a natural landfall on the airway across the South Atlantic to North Africa and Europe. By taking the direct overwater route from Natal to Dakar, the distance was cut down to only 1,872 statute miles, nearly 1,400 miles less than the route by way of Ascension Island, Accra, and Roberts Field, Liberia. The limited range of some aircraft made it necessary for them to take the longer route, but four-engine planes could easily make the jump direct to Dakar.

Between Dakar and Casablanca, and to the east of Spanish Rio de Oro, were several desert airfields of which Atar in Mauritania and Tindouf in western Algeria became important ATC bases after extensive improvement of their runways and facilities. Early plans to use Casablanca as the main northern terminal point of the coastal route were changed when General Smith found that base facilities and weather conditions were better at Marrakech, about 137 miles to the south of Casablanca and 75 miles inland. Marrakech soon became the center of ATC operations in the north and remained so until the end of 1943.[29]

Air Transport Command had next to find the personnel to man the bases on the coastal route. One source of manpower was found in the 14th Ferrying Group, previously assigned to the Congo route, the alternate airway to Khartoum and the Middle East by way of bases in French Equatorial Africa, the Belgian Congo, and Kenya Colony.* The group's headquarters had been set up at Leopoldville in the Belgian Congo, and one of its three authorized squadrons had been activated when Allied successes in the north rendered the Congo route superfluous. It was decided to use the 14th Group on the new route into North Africa, leaving only a few skeleton detachments to man the equatorial bases. Group headquarters was moved to Bathurst on 12 December 1942, a few months later to Dakar, and then to Marrakech. The three subordinate squadrons were assigned to Bathurst (later to Dakar), Marrakech, and Algiers. Detachments were placed at Atar, Tindouf, Casablanca, and Oran.[30]

With the extension of ATC activities into North Africa, the jurisdiction of the Africa–Middle East Wing was broadened to encompass these new operations. The wing's authority already spanned a territory of vast distances. From Accra on the west African coast to Karachi in India, the main air route extended nearly 6,000 miles, while auxiliary lines, exclusive of the now inactive Congo route, brought the total mileage to over 10,000. Nevertheless, General George decided to maintain for the time being a unified command in this immense region, to insure flexibility in the utilization of equipment and manpower and in the routing of aircraft and supplies. As the North African operations of ATC advanced with General Eisenhower's progress along the Mediterranean shore to Tunis, a more decentralized control became necessary, but General George still held to the principle of a single unified comamnd. Accordingly, in June 1943 two sectors were established within the Africa–Middle East Wing—the North African Sector, with direct control of operations north of Dakar, and the Central African Sector, which began at Accra and extended across the older African route to Cairo and beyond to Karachi. The sector organization remained in effect for six months, with several changes in boundary lines, the most important of which was the placing of Cairo

* See above, pp. 54–55.

73

and dependent stations farther east (all the way to Karachi) under the control of the North African Sector. This shift, which occurred in October, reflected the growing predominance of the Mediterranean coastal route to Cairo and India over the older route through Nigeria and the Anglo-Egyptian Sudan. Finally, on 15 December 1943, the Africa–Middle East jurisdiction was divided into the Central African and North African Wings.[31]

Expanding Operations

For several months after the invasion of northwest Africa the ferrying of combat planes for General Doolittle's Twelfth Air Force continued to be the heaviest responsibility imposed on ATC by the invasion. Close on the heels of the 68th Group, two B-26 groups, the 17th and 320th, passed through the Morrison Field staging base during late November and December 1942, with a few stragglers departing as late as January.[32] The advance echelon of the 17th Group arrived at Accra on 26 November. Because its B-26's as then equipped and loaded lacked the necessary range for the Kano-Oran flight by about 100 miles, they were then routed up the coast through Roberts Field to Bathurst to await developments beyond that point. After a two weeks' delay, during which time Governor Boisson had surrendered Dakar and French West Africa, the B-26's took off for Marrakech.[33] The A-20's of the 27th Group started moving through the Morrison Field port of embarkation in mid-January,[34] and a month later the 321st Group, equipped with B-25's, began arriving in Florida to prepare for the overseas journey.[35] All four groups went by way of Ascension Island and Accra and then up along the coastal route to Marrakech.

Meanwhile, the approach of winter had caused the diversion of all ferrying from the North Atlantic to the South Atlantic route. Severe losses suffered by the 319th Group (B-26's) and the 47th Group (A-20's) on the North Atlantic ferry route had led to a decision in late October to send all light- and medium-bomber reinforcements to the Twelfth Air Force by way of the South Atlantic. By mid-December, heavy-bomber ferrying across the North Atlantic was also suspended.[36] Until the northern route was again opened to traffic in the spring, all ferried aircraft going either to the Twelfth Air Force in North Africa or to the Eighth Air Force in Britain were dispatched by way of the southern route. The first heavy-bomber units to reach

North Africa via the South Atlantic were the 99th Group, which passed through the Morrison Field port of embarkation early in February, and the 2d Group, which came through in March. Both were equipped with B-17's.[37] At first the heavy bombers went through Ascension and Accra, but later they were dispatched from Natal directly across the Atlantic to Eknes Field near Dakar, where one 6,000-foot steel-mat runway had been completed in February. The peak of heavy-bomber ferrying for the North African campaign was reached in April, when 117 were delivered over the coastal route through Dakar to Marrakech.[38]

The fighter aircraft employed by American forces in the early stages of the North African campaign—P-38's, P-39's, P-40's, and British Spitfires—were either ferried down from Britain by their own crews or, in the case of the P-40's, brought in by aircraft carriers and flown from their decks to airports in the vicinity of Port Lyautey and Casablanca. Thereafter, pursuit reinforcements were brought in by every possible means. Some P-38's followed the original units down from Britain, some were flown across the South Atlantic, while others were sent in as deck loads on cargo vessels. A large number of P-40's, including the air echelon of the 325th Group, was brought to Casablanca on board the carrier *Ranger* during January and February; others came on cargo vessels and were assembled at Cazes Field.* After February, however, the P-40 reinforcements were sent to ports farther south on the African coast and ferried up the coastal route to Marrakech. At the time the coastal route was opened to traffic, P-40's were being shipped by water to Lagos in southern Nigeria for assembly and flight across central Africa to the Middle East. As early as January 1943, some of the P-40's were being diverted north to the Twelfth Air Force,[39] but, in moving P-40's into Morocco, it seemed better to establish an additional assembly plant farther north in the Dakar area. By mid-April, shops had been set up at Ouakam Field, a small airport near Dakar, where the aircraft brought in by ship were assembled and then flown a few miles east to Eknes Field. Here they were organized into convoys for the flight north.[40]

During 1942, P-38 fighters had been ferried successfully to Britain over the Labrador-Greenland-Iceland route.† The transoceanic hops from Natal by way of Ascension to Liberia were somewhat longer

* See Vol. II, 57–60, 75–77, 130–31.
† See Vol. I, 639–45.

than any single leg of the northern route but not too long for the twin-engine fighter when equipped with extra gas tanks. Consequently, when early in 1943 the AAF Director of Photography asked ATC to ferry a small group of P-38's modified for photo-reconnaissance work to the Twelfth Air Force, the job was willingly accepted. Control of the flight and provision of crews were made the responsibilities of the 2d Ferrying Group (based at Wilmington, Delaware), which had participated in the P-38 movement to Britain the year before. The twelve P-38's were divided into four flights, each flight led by a B-24. They took off from Wilmington on 7 February, flew down through the Caribbean and Brazil and across the Atlantic without mishap, and landed at Roberts Field on the 23d. Here most of the planes were turned over to combat pilots, but a few were flown by ATC pilots all the way into Casablanca. A second movement of P-38's (all told, forty-one aircraft) began in March and was completed in May. At first the planes were divided into flights of six, each led by an A-20, which had a cruising speed that was ideal for the purpose. The first flight left the Ferrying Division base at Memphis on 12 March, and within ten days a total of five flights had departed. After a long delay occasioned by the shortage of qualified pilots, the remaining planes moved out on almost an individual basis. There were a few losses, resulting largely from the inexperience of the pilots and bad weather in northern Brazil.[41]

Deliveries of aircraft along the coastal route through Bathurst, Dakar, and Marrakech increased from month to month as the North African campaign grew in intensity. During December 1942, the month the route was opened, 107 aircraft were ferried to Marrakech and other delivery points. The peak of the movement coincided with the final phase of the Tunisian campaign in May 1943, when 573 deliveries were completed. By the end of June, just before the invasion of Sicily, deliveries for the seven-month period had reached a total of 1,985. About half of these (927) consisted of light and medium bombers, but there were 569 heavy bombers, 298 twin-engine transports, 182 fighters, 5 PBY's, and 4 gliders.[42] These figures included aircraft flown from North Africa to the Eighth Air Force in Britain, but by far the largest number of the planes in all categories were intended for service in North Africa and the Mediterranean.[43]

Air transportation services into North Africa developed much more slowly than did the ferrying operations, principally because of the shortage of transport aircraft and the relative speed with which supplies could be brought in by water.[44] The six C-87's which had been placed in operation between Accra and Oran soon after the invasion continued to fly the trans-Sahara route direct until February 1943.[45] Early in January 1943 a regularly scheduled service, using C-47's, began operating between Accra and Bathurst with three flights a week.[46] On the 27th this service was extended northward through Atar and Tindouf to Marrakech, with Dakar a regular stop as soon as Eknes Field was ready. At Marrakech ATC's two-engine service tied in with a theater transport operation conducted by Twelfth Air Force troop-carrier and RAF transport units, which served Casablanca and Oran, and from Oran flew on westward to Algiers.[47]

North Africa's Link with Britain

At Marrakech a link was also established with the air route joining North Africa and Britain, a route inaugurated during the initial phase of TORCH as bombers, fighters, and loaded troop transports of the Allied air forces moved down from Britain to landing fields in the target area. Replacement aircraft continued to flow south from Britain until the very end of the Tunisian campaign, by which time a total of 1,072 replacements had been dispatched from the United Kingdom to American air units in North Africa.[48] In the meantime, with the closing-down of the North Atlantic ferrying route in December 1942, a reverse flow had started from Africa north to Britain. Two-engine and four-engine bombers assigned to the Eighth were flown thereafter across the South Atlantic and up to Marrakech, and thence to fields in southern England. During the first six months of 1943 a total of 356 aircraft reached Britain by this route.[49] This traffic diminished rapidly, however, after the North Atlantic route into Britain was reopened in April. During the next winter season (1943–44) the European theater again received most of its ferried aircraft by the long southern route, although some 300 planes a month were still sent across the North Atlantic.*[50]

For several months following the North African landings, the only air transport service between North Africa and Britain was that maintained by the Eighth Air Force Ferry and Transport Service, which intermittently dispatched a B-17 to Africa, primarily for the movement of high military officials. The need for some more regular service

* See below, pp. 100–102.

had prompted ATC to propose the use of Stratoliners flown by civilians under a contract with TWA.[51] When objections were raised to using the outmoded Stratoliners on a route involving a 14,000-foot crossing of the Atlas Mountains in North Africa, it was decided to use C-54's and to keep the Stratoliners on the South Atlantic crossing.[52] An ATC survey party left Marrakech in a C-87 on 26 December with an ATC military crew, headed by Maj. Harold Skelly and Maj. Hamilton Heard, and with a TWA civilian crew aboard. Upon arriving in England, they obtained permission to use St. Eval in Cornwall as the northern terminus of the line and for the ATC to set up there its own point-to-point and air-to-ground communications system.[53] Before their return to Marrakech, the ATC men found an opportunity to observe at first hand the hazards of flying the U.K.–North Africa route. At St. Eval on 3 January a B-17 came in from Gibraltar full of holes and with one crewman dead. On the following day two B-17's of the Eighth Air Force shuttle service arrived from Africa "completely shot up." They had been flying at about 500 feet in order to avoid radar and had been caught off Brest by JU-88's. Still another hazard arose from the habit American aircraft had of flying into Britain from the south without giving warning of their approach. The ATC's C-87 had done just that on its maiden flight, after which the crew was warned by the RAF that British fighter patrols were currently manned by young and excitable Polish flyers who were under orders to shoot down all unannounced aircraft flying under 1,000 feet. When almost immediately two AAF B-24's came in from Gibraltar unannounced, the British, feeling perhaps that the honor of the Fighter Command was involved, warned again that orders had been given to shoot down all unexpected aircraft.[54]

On 11 January a detailed plan for the operation of the TWA shuttle service into Britain was sent to all ATC wing commanders along the South Atlantic route.[55] This called for the extension northward to Britain of TWA's Washington-to-Accra C-54 service. The original schedule called for two flights a week from Washington to the U.K., with Prestwick rather than St. Eval designated as the northern terminus.

Heavy demands for special mission flights in connection with the Casablanca conference in January delayed the inauguration of this service,[56] but by the end of that month the C-54's were making one flight a week from Washington to Britain via Marrakech, carrying only the highest priority cargo and passengers.[57] Effective 8 February, the Washington-Marrakech-Prestwick schedule was ordered stepped up to two flights a week, with each C-54 making an extra shuttle between Marrakech and Prestwick before returning to the United States.[58] Actually, the records show nine arrivals in the United Kingdom during February, nineteen during March, and in April thirty-two, most of these last coming over the reopened North Atlantic route.[59]

Special mission work between North Africa and Britain occasionally interfered with the regular cargo and passenger service. In March 1943 the ATC C-54's moved the personnel and equipment of the 2037th Anti-Submarine Wing from St. Eval, Cornwall, to Port Lyautey, French Morocco. Eight flights were required to carry the 175 passengers and 23,229 pounds of equipment.[60] In September the command completed the emergency movement of aircraft, personnel, and equipment of the 2d Bombardment Wing from St. Mawgan in the U.K. to North Africa. On the night of the 16th, forty-six B-24's were cleared from St. Mawgan, and, by the 21st, forty-four others were dispatched. To complete the movement of aircrew members, mechanics, and other ground personnel, as well as their equipment, all available C-54 aircraft were diverted from Prestwick to St. Mawgan to carry 307 passengers, 31,682 pounds of gear, and 7,582 pounds of tools.[61] During October there was an even larger special movement in the opposite direction, when Ninth Air Force personnel from Cairo, making a permanent shift from the Middle East to Britain, and Twelfth Air Force men from Algiers, were transported via Marrakech to Prestwick. Between the 4th and the 18th, almost 1,000 men were carried on thirty-one special flights, and an additional 71 on regular flights which were resumed on the 19th.[62]

When C-54 transports had again started flying the North Atlantic route in April 1943, the Prestwick-Marrakech shuttle became an appendage of the North Atlantic operation rather than of the South Atlantic; in other words, transports coming into Prestwick from the north made one or two shuttle trips to Marrakech before returning to the United States. Although this new arrangement increased the lift between Britain and North Africa, the arrangement was not too satisfactory, and by September 1943 plans had been developed for divorcing the U.K.–North Africa shuttle from all transatlantic operations and assigning to it exclusively a small fleet of C-87's.[63] After some

79

delay the C-87's began arriving in March 1944, and at the end of that month the first regularly scheduled flight left St. Mawgan, the new terminus in the ETO, for Casablanca, which had replaced Marrakech as the southern terminus.[64] Concurrently, in late March, a new shuttle service between St. Mawgan and Naples via North Africa was instituted. For about two months this was a single operation extending across two theaters, but in June, in order to utilize the aircraft more effectively, ATC's European Wing was ordered to fly only as far as Casablanca.*[65]

Probably the most important single project later undertaken by the St. Mawgan—Casablanca shuttle service was a special mission for USSTAF's FRANTIC project. Mission ELEVEN, as the operation was designated by ATC, consisted of the movement of USSTAF cargo and personnel from Britain to Africa, across North Africa and the Middle East, to Tehran, and thence to the Poltava region of western Russia, where three bases had been made available to American forces for the shuttle bombing of Germany.† The movement from the U.K. began on 13 March 1944, and by 10 May a total of 479 passengers and 143,700 pounds of equipment had been transported to Casablanca. From Casablanca the North African Wing carried men and materials arriving from Britain and direct from the United States on across Africa and the Middle East to Russia. The bases were first used by U.S. bombers on 2 June 1944. Fortunately, in the surprise German attack upon the Poltava airfield on the night of 21 June, an attack which destroyed thirty-nine of the seventy-one B-17's caught on the field, the three ATC transports then at Poltava escaped with only minor damage.[66]

Expansion to the East—Absorption of MATS

The Air Transport Command's two-engine transport service northward from Accra through Roberts Field, Bathurst (later Dakar), Atar, and Tindouf had reached Marrakech on 27 January 1943, and there it came temporarily to a halt except for an occasional trip to Oran.[67] At Marrakech the men and materials brought in by ATC were picked up by troop-carrier planes and distributed locally within the theater. But, when the fighting moved on east into Tunisia during

---

* Cargo and passengers moving between Casablanca and Naples were carried on the regularly scheduled aircraft of the North African Wing.

† See Vol. III, 308–19.

the spring, ATC began to expand in that direction, originally on a very small scale. On 16 April ATC assumed responsibility for a two-engine passenger service between Marrakech and Casablanca, Oran and Algiers. This arrangement, agreed on at the Casablanca conference by Brig. Gen. Cyrus R. Smith, ATC Chief of Staff, and General Spaatz's staff, was supposed to release troop-carrier aircraft for tactical operations at the front.[68] It is doubtful, however, if this purpose was accomplished to any noticeable extent. ATC employed only four aircraft in the new service, while American troop-carrier units and RAF transport units continued to operate a constantly expanding air-cargo service between the rear areas in Morocco and Algiers and the combat zone in Tunisia.[69] Supplies coming in by ship to the ports of Casablanca, Oran, and Algiers when earmarked for air shipment to the front were picked up by troop-carrier and RAF transports and moved forward.

Theater air transport activities had so grown in size and in diversity that in May 1943 it was deemed advisable to bring them all under a single controlling agency, called the Mediterranean Air Transport Service (MATS). MATS exercised control over the operations of a polyglot group of air transport organizations which included: (1) American troop-carrier squadrons of the 51st Troop Carrier Wing, some of which operated under the control of the Air Priorities Board of the Mediterranean Air Command, while others were employed by North African Air Service Command in hauling cargo and personnel for theater air forces; (2) the 216th Transport Group of the RAF and British Overseas Airways Corporation (BOAC) which flew regular schedules between the U.K. and Cairo through Gibraltar; and (3) Air France and the French military air-cargo service.[70]

This development naturally raised questions regarding the control of ATC operations within the theater. A conference early in May, held in the office of Air Chief Marshal Sir Arthur Tedder at Algiers, accomplished little more than to define the problem.[71] But ATC was represented in a second conference held late in the same month by General Smith, ATC chief of staff. At this time General Smith gave forceful presentation of the mission, jurisdiction, and operations of his organization, stressing the fact that ATC was not subject to the control of local theater authorities but was governed by appropriate directives of the War Department. He cited particularly War Department Memorandum W95-6-43 of 26 February 1943, which had stated that ATC was a War Department agency operating under the direct supervision and control of the Commanding General, Army Air Forces. In the light of this directive, there was some question whether MATS could rightfully exercise any control whatsoever over ATC's operations, but General Smith did not insist on complete freedom within the theater. Instead, he made a clear distinction between through operations which extended across theater and national boundaries and which served more than one theater and local operations which were conducted primarily for the use and benefit of a single theater. Insofar as local intratheater services were concerned, General Smith conceded the right of MATS to allocate priorities, establish schedules, and even to divert ATC aircraft temporarily from scheduled operations to perform other services in cases of emergency. But the interruption of through services could not be permitted, "except in cases of gravest emergency."[72]

MATS continued to control priorities and schedules on ATC's local Marrakech-Casablanca-Oran-Algiers passenger service, but at the same time it kept its hands off ATC's intertheater operations—that is, the service up from Accra through Dakar to Marrakech and the operations between Marrakech and Great Britain.[73] Indeed, when MATS was organized, its jurisdiction was limited to that part of the theater north of thirtieth parallel, which in effect exempted the coastal route and the operation to the U.K. from MATS control.[74]

Probably the one matter that worried ATC most at this time in its relations with the North African Theater (NATOUSA) was the latter's desire to delay the inauguration of a C-54 through operation that would extend across the whole of North Africa from Marrakech to Cairo and would provide the missing link in a shorter route from the United States to the Middle East and the CBI.[75] Already, experimental flights were being made from Newfoundland direct across the middle Atlantic to Marrakech,* and there was a good prospect that the Azores would soon be opened to full Allied war traffic. There were some in the Air Transport Command who were inclined to blame NATOUSA's attitude on the machinations of the British or, more particularly, BOAC. It was assumed that the British did not like the idea of the American contract airlines flying the North African routes because of a fear that this would give the same airlines a postwar claim to operating through the area.[76] General Eisenhower had forbidden ATC to

---

* See below, p. 88.

employ contract operators in the theater except for the TWA service up through Marrakech to Britain.[77] But ATC intended to make the Marrakech-Cairo run a purely military operation employing military crews exclusively, and on this basis the plan was finally given approval.

At the conference of ATC and theater officials held in Marshal Tedder's office early in May, the Marrakech-Cairo transport service had been ordered "held in abeyance,"[78] but at the second conference General Smith secured the authority to start the service in July.[79] It actually got under way on 7 July with two C-54's flying a twice-weekly schedule. When two other Skymasters arrived in August, the schedule was stepped up to five trips a week. The only stop made en route was at Algiers.[80] By the end of 1943 the North African airway was well on its way to becoming the main route into the Middle East and India, overshadowing the older central African route to such an extent that all the Middle East bases from Cairo to Karachi were transferred to the jurisdiction of the North African Sector and its successor, the North African Wing.[81]

It was becoming by this time a general policy of the Air Transport Command to take over from troop-carrier units or other local transport agencies significant responsibilities for intratheater operations when asked to do so by the theater.[82] Heretofore, ATC's air supply routes had generally terminated on reaching the theater, both because of ATC's limited strength and because the areas controlled by the theaters of operations were still relatively shallow (NATOUSA controlled for a time no more than a narrow strip of North Africa), with the result that local transport agencies could handle easily enough internal distribution of supplies and men. But now the problem was changing, and very rapidly at that, as may be illustrated by the experience of NATOUSA. When General Eisenhower's troops moved into Sicily and Italy, MATS was put under a heavy strain to meet the needs of a theater whose transport lines now reached back from Italy to Morocco and Algiers. The strain was attributable in part to the large forward concentration of troop-carrier planes that was demanded by tactical operations which included a succession of troop-carrier drops. In these circumstances, MATS could see the advantage of having ATC establish regular services between the rear and forward areas. ATC, for its part, was willing enough to undertake the task, for in its view the African continent was fast becoming a rear zone of communications in which the interests of *strategic* air supply outweighed those that were more closely related to the immediate needs of tactical units at the front. And strategic air supply was the business of ATC.

In the fall of 1943 theater authorities agreed that MATS should surrender its operating responsibilities in North Africa to the ATC and the RAF Transport Command, retaining only a staff or coordinating function. The decision was reached at a conference on 2 November attended by Air Marshal Sir Arthur Tedder, Lt. Gen. Carl Spaatz, Maj. Gen. C. R. Smith of ATC (on his way to India to inspect the Hump operation), Brig. Gen. Robert Kauch, the MATS commander, Air Commodore Whitney-Straight of the RAFTC, and others. It was agreed that by 1 January 1944 all North African continental transport operations would be turned over to ATC and RAFTC, the transfer to take place as promptly as new aircraft could be procured. As MATS withdrew from Africa, its resources were to be devoted for the time being to the operation of services from the Continent to Italian points (MATS had started flying into Italy in October), but by 1 March 1944 the trans-Mediterranean services from the mainland to Italy were also to be transferred to the two transport commands. Thereafter, MATS would function merely as a staff agency, determining air transport requirements, establishing priorities, co-ordinating the work of the two carriers, and acting as arbiter on behalf of the theater in cases of disagreement between the two.[83]

The conference also decided on the division of responsibility between ATC and RAFTC in Africa. The former was given primary control over transport services and facilities in the western sector of the theater from Casablanca to Tunis, while its British counterpart would have primary responsibility from Tunis west to Cairo. Either was free to operate such through services over the other's territories as were reasonably required, and each could engage freely in the ferrying of aircraft across the theater.[84]

In the final months of 1943 the two transport commands took over MATS operations in Africa and early in the following year prepared to move north. While occasional special flights had been made by ATC into Sicily, Sardinia, and southern Italy, it was not until 7 March 1944 that regular operations were inaugurated to Naples, which soon became the hub of transport services in the Mediterranean. Although Capodichino Airport was to become the main ATC base in the Naples area, the inaugural flight was made to the nearby Pomigliano base under somewhat inauspicious circumstances. As Lt. Robert L. Johnson brought his transport in over the airport, the AA batteries of Naples opened up with a barrage that fortunately failed to score a hit. It was claimed that the barrage was the result of Johnson's improper approach to the field, but there was reason to believe that the nervousness of the crews manning the antiaircraft guns was partly responsible.[85]

During March, 80 transport landings were made at the Naples base, and in April, 433.[86] The April landings included ATC C-87's flying from St. Mawgan to Naples by way of Casablanca and Algiers. By June, the Naples base had become one of the two most important in the whole North African transport network, the other being Casablanca, the point of convergence of air supply lines reaching into North Africa from Britain and the United States and from Accra and Dakar to the south. Casablanca led all other bases during June in the amount of air cargo received and sent out, but Naples handled more passengers during the month, with 11,744 passing through the base.[87]

ATC operations spread out from Naples to the islands of Sardinia, Corsica, and Sicily and to points in the southern part of the Italian peninsula, each requiring only a small ATC detachment.[88] But as Allied forces moved up the peninsula, the command began to carry a heavy traffic north into Rome. The first ATC flight into Rome, made by Lt. Henry J. Webb piloting a C-47, landed at the Littoria Airport on 20 June 1944. The initial schedule of three flights daily from Naples to Rome was increased by 1 July to five flights daily.[89]

ATC operations continued to spread in the Mediterranean area as Axis troops were driven out. In September the North African Division began flying into Marseille; the base was turned over to the European Division the following month.[90] With the entry of Allied troops into Greece, ATC was assigned Eleusis Field near Athens. An ATC base unit (the 1269th) was formally activated on 1 November, and on the 15th the first scheduled transport flight arrived at Athens from Naples.[91] With the acquisition of bases at Marseille and Athens, ATC's European and North African Divisions were soon operating an intercontinental transport service or series of services that originated in England and extended down through Paris, Marseille, Rome, Naples, and Athens to Cairo, tying together the European, Mediterranean, and Middle East theaters.[92] From Cairo an infrequent shuttle service had been operating into Adana, Turkey, since early 1944 for the convenience of the American ambassador and his staff. In order to give a civilian appearance to the flights, ATC went in disguised as the "American Transport Company," and the few ATC officers and men stationed at Adana wore civilian clothes. When the German threat to Turkey was removed, the command was permitted to throw off the disguise and to extend its flights to Ankara, Istanbul, and for a time to Poltava, in Russia, via the Turkish bases.[93] In 1945, after the Balkans had been cleared of Axis troops, the ATC made occasional flights into Belgrade, Budapest, Bucharest, and Sofia with the permission of the Russian occupying authorities.[94]

New Route to India via North Africa

While the Air Transport Command had been extending its network of airlines over the whole of the Mediterranean area, an even heavier transport traffic had developed across North Africa as part of a great air or air-sea movement of materiel and men from the United States to India and China. Some mention has already been made of the C-54 transport service across North Africa beteen Marrakech and Cairo that began on a small scale in July 1943.* At the end of the year there were still only four Skymasters on the run, making six trips weekly from Marrakech to Cairo and one weekly flight on to Karachi, India.

This trans–North African route grew in importance during 1944 as the strategic situation changed. The new developments had been anticipated by ATC, a fact which explains the eagerness of General Smith and other ATC officials to overcome NATOUSA objections and to make an early start on the Marrakech-Cairo service.[95] After an air base in the Azores was opened to American use late in 1943, it became possible to send a large volume of air traffic directly across the middle Atlantic to the North African coast and thence across Africa and the Middle East to the CBI. Earlier, aircraft and airborne supplies bound for the India-China area had been forced to go by the older South Atlantic–Central African airway, which traversed a distance of 14,000 miles from Florida to Kunming, China. Over the newer route, which passed through Newfoundland and the Azores to North Africa, or came up from Miami through Bermuda and the Azores to the North African coast, the distance from the United States to China was cut substantially.

The deployment of B-29 units of the XX Bomber Command in

* See above, pp. 82–83.

India and China in 1944 gave added importance to the newer and shorter route to the CBI. A large share of the supplies and reinforcements required to keep the B-29's in operation was sent across the middle Atlantic to North Africa by air or by water, and thence by air to the Calcutta area and over the Hump to advanced bases in China. The basing of B-29's in China made necessary a great increase in the volume of Hump tonnage, and this in turn required a heavier flow of aircraft, supplies, and men from the United States to ATC's India-China Wing. Much of this "company traffic," like that destined for the XX Bomber Command, went by the shorter route across North Africa.

American efforts to obtain a military air base in the Azores go back to the pre–Pearl Harbor days of 1941, when Colonel Olds of the Ferrying Command was looking for an alternate route into Britain for ferrying operations during the winter. Portugal refused to grant landing rights at the time, principally because of fear of reprisals on the part of Germany.* The North African landings a year later gave the Azores a greater strategic importance, since they could provide the most direct air route for support of the North Africa operations and a shorter airway to the Middle East, India, and China. Furthermore, General George of the Air Transport Command had the imagination to see that a base in the Azores would be vitally essential to the support of any future military operations on the European continent. Following the lead of Colonel Olds, General George brought pressure upon General Arnold and indirectly upon the State Department to make further efforts to secure concessions from Portugal, but Premier Salazar refused to budge for another year.[96]

Finally, in October 1943 Britain secured the right to use the Lagens airfield on the island of Terceira and the port of Horta, primarily for the purpose of antisubmarine warfare,[97] and a few weeks later the United States managed to come in through the back door by means of an arrangement with the British. On 1 December 1943, British and American military representatives signed a joint agreement, approved shortly thereafter by the Combined Chiefs of Staff, whereby ferried and transport aircraft of the United States would be permitted to make a limited number of landings at the Lagens Airport. In return, the United States agreed to assist the British in improving and extending existing facilities at Lagens to handle a maximum of 1,200 landings

* See Vol. I, 325–26.

87

a month by aircraft of both countries.[98] On the last day of the year Premier Salazar gave his oral consent to this arrangement with the understanding that operations were to be under British control.[99] Meanwhile, on 9 December the first American bomber to be ferried through the Azores landed at Lagens. By the end of that month a regularly scheduled transport operation through the Azores to North Africa had started.[100]

While waiting for Salazar to make up his mind, the Air Transport Command had proceeded on its own initiative to attempt the opening of a route direct from Newfoundland to Marrakech in North Africa, bypassing the Azores.[101] The initial survey flight over this 2,600-mile overwater route was made on 17 April 1943 by a C-54 flown under contract by American Airlines and piloted by John F. Davidson, ship's captain.[102] With a cargo load of 4,705 pounds and two passengers, the plane took off on the early morning of the 17th and fourteen hours later landed at Marrakech with only an hour-and-a-half supply of gasoline left. One of the passengers was Brig. Gen. Benjamin F. Giles, commanding the ATC North Atlantic Wing, who went along to get a close-up view of the Azores. Unfortunately, the islands were completely obscured by clouds as the transport passed over them. The C-54 returned to the United States by way of Scotland and Iceland, since prevailing winds over the North Atlantic favored an eastbound flight and made the long flight in the opposite direction impossible. Although precluding large-scale transport operations, the winds would not affect the one-way flight delivery of heavy bombers, and subsequent planning for use of the route seemed to stress ferrying rather than transport operations.[103] Eighteen hours after the C-54 departed Newfoundland, a B-24 piloted by Capt. Charles O. Galbraith of the ATC Ferrying Division took off on a fifteen-hour flight over the same route and landed at Marrakech with a five-and-a-half-hour supply of gasoline left.[104] This proved clearly enough that the ferrying of four-engine bombers with bomb-bay tanks installed was practical, but before ferrying could get started the Lagens base in the Azores became available, and the unbroken hop across the Atlantic was no longer necessary.

Within two weeks after the British-American agreement had been made, a plan for transport operations through the Azores to both the United Kingdom and North Africa had been drawn up and schedules had been published.[105] The first scheduled flight went through on

29 December, but, because of inadequate weather and communications facilities and adverse weather conditions, it was well into February 1944 before schedules were regularly met.[106] American Airlines and TWA, the two contract carriers then flying the North Atlantic into Britain, were selected to inaugurate the new central Atlantic services, since the Azores schedules were closely enmeshed with the older North Atlantic and South Atlantic schedules. Some of the "round-robin" aircraft, for example, which had been going to Britain across the North Atlantic and returning to the United States by the long South Atlantic loop in order to take advantage of prevailing winds in both areas, were now sent home by way of the shorter Azores routes.[107]

Most of the American and TWA flights through the Lagens base turned northeastward to Prestwick in Scotland.[108] The lift into North Africa began to pick up only when two other carriers, the Ferrying Division and Pan American Airways, were assigned to the route. In February the Ferrying Division inaugurated the CRESCENT service that originated at Wilmington, Delaware, extended through Newfoundland and the Azores to North Africa, and proceeded thence across Africa and the Middle East to India.[109] CRESCENT was one of the several overseas military transport services which had been decided upon in the fall of 1943 as experienced military crews became available in large numbers. Contract carriers, using their own civilian crews, had heretofore provided most of the lift from the United States to foreign areas; a trend toward militarization of transport services now began, and before the war ended about 81 per cent of the traffic was being carried by fully militarized services. Two of the new military transport services supported the Hump operation of ATC's India-China Wing: CRESCENT and FIREBALL, which originated at Miami and extended down along the old southeastern route and across central Africa to the CBI.*

In May 1944, three months after CRESCENT got under way, Pan American Airways began flying the middle Atlantic route,[110] going from Miami through Bermuda and the Azores to Casablanca. Pan American began with one round trip daily between Miami and Casablanca. This was stepped up to two round trips in June[111] and to four in August, when Pan American's C-54's were withdrawn from the

---

* See below, pp. 129–30.

South Atlantic run and the whole fleet, amounting to twenty-seven transports (C-54A's and C-54B's), was concentrated on the middle Atlantic run to Casablanca.[112]

In addition to the increased air traffic into Casablanca during 1944, a larger volume of waterborne traffic to North Africa became possible with the decline in the submarine menace. There were two streams of traffic, then, coming into Casablanca—airborne and waterborne. All of it, however, was being shipped on eastward by air transport, some to Italy, and a small proportion that was off-loaded in the Middle East, but the heaviest flow was on across the Middle East to the CBI.

As traffic from the United States to the North African coast grew in volume, it became necessary to increase the size of the transport fleet operating eastward from Casablanca. Early in 1944 ATC decided to substitute for its small C-54 fleet a much larger two-engine fleet of C-46's and C-47's.[113] C-54's were still in short supply, but the smaller craft were now plentiful and were well suited to operations on a land route where the bases were fairly close together. The North African Wing then had, in addition to the four C-54's and a few other craft, a comparatively small fleet of forty-seven C-47's flying the old MATS routes as far east as Tunis. The wing's operations into Italy had not yet started. By May C-46's began to arrive in quantity, and the size of the fleet had more than doubled. At the end of 1944, when North African transport operations were at their peak, the fleet had grown to tremendous size—185 C-46's, 84 C-47's, and 22 of other types.[114]

During 1945 the North African Wing (or Division) turned back again to the C-54's, now more plentiful, but the smaller two-engine planes carried the heavy stream of traffic on the "Rocket Run," as the North African transport operation was known, during the peak year of 1944. One exception to this general statement should be made. In April 1944, in connection with Mission TEN, the initial movement of equipment and ground personnel of XX Bomber Command to India, a fleet of twenty-five C-54's was thrown into North Africa for a period of about two months. The men and materials involved were first brought from New York to Casablanca in six surface vessels, and the entire project was then moved from Casablanca to India by air. The movement comprised 1,237 passengers, 250 B-29 spare engines, 60,000 pounds of radar equipment and gun heaters, and

61,000 pounds of other equipment. This extraordinary effort required 155 flights by the C-54's and the few C-46's that were used.[115]

There was also a great passage of ferried B-29's across North Africa on the way to the XX Bomber Command in the CBI. Out of a total of 257 of these big bombers, 146 were ferried under the code name of WOLFE project.[116] The B-29's were, of course, only a small part of the ferried traffic through North Africa, which during the peak year 1944 included a total of 9,306 aircraft en route from the United States to overseas destinations. The largest number, 4,498 went to the Twelfth and Fifteenth Air Forces in the MTO; 3,408 went to the Eighth and Ninth Air Forces in the ETO; 603 were ferried to the Tenth, Fourteenth, and Twentieth Air Forces in the CBI; the others were transports going to the North African Division or tactical craft ferried to France after D Day.[117]

No discussion of the work accomplished by the North African Division would be complete without some mention of the part it played in certain major operations or projects which were of such scope that they require more general treatment elsewhere in this volume. The Division, for example, participated in a large air evacuation program in which thousands of sick and wounded were transported by air from forward areas in the Mediterranean theater to hospitals in North Africa and thence by air across the middle or South Atlantic routes to the United States. In the great redeployment movement after V-E Day, the North African Division handled a large proportion of the personnel and aircraft moving out of Europe and across the Atlantic on the way home. The PIPELINE project of 1945, a heavy passage of C-54 transports and supplies back and forth across North Africa on the way to or returning from India, will be discussed more appropriately in connection with the Hump augmentation program in the last year of the war. Finally, the North African Division made an important contribution to the success of Mission SEVENTEEN, the transportation by air of the President and the American delegation to and from the Yalta conference, probably the most difficult single job accomplished by the Air Transport Command during the war.

CHAPTER 4

*   *   *   *   *   *   *   *   *   *   *

THE NORTH ATLANTIC ROUTE

IN ONE sense the North Atlantic route had its beginning as a major dependence of the U.S. armed forces with the BOLERO movement—the flight delivery to the United Kingdom between June 1942 and January 1943 of some 366 heavy bombers, 150 medium bombers, 183 P-38 fighters, and the same number of transport aircraft.[1] Except for a relatively small number of replacement aircraft delivered by ATC crews late in 1942, the planes were flown by their own combat crews, the men who were destined to fly them later in combat over Europe or in Africa.[2] By all existing standards, their passage across the North Atlantic represented a tremendous achievement, one for which any one of the pilots very recently could have anticipated a parade up Broadway and a complimentary speech by the mayor of New York City.

Feverish preparations had been made for the movement,[3] which carried the highest hopes of the AAF. But the pilots had, except in rare instances, no experience to equip them for a transatlantic flight. They depended upon transient facilities on northern bases that were unequal to the demand and upon weather forecasts in an area where weather constituted under the best circumstances a major hazard to flying, which depended in turn upon the reports of half-trained radio operators scarcely able to translate the dots and dashes they laboriously received.[4] Only the exigencies of war could have justified the risks assumed by the AAF.*

The development of a North Atlantic ferrying route had been undertaken first by Britain and Canada in 1940. After passage of the

---

* The story of this movement has been told in Vol. I, 639–45. In addition to the 882 aircraft which reached their destination in Britain, there were 38 planes which had been wrecked or otherwise "lost" en route.

Lend-Lease Act early in 1941, the United States assumed an active part in the joint effort to take full advantage of the "steppingstones" provided by Newfoundland, Labrador, Greenland, and Iceland and so to make possible the ferrying of short-range fighters from North America to Great Britain. As an alternate to the previously developed base at Gander Lake in southern Newfoundland, the Canadian government in September 1941 began the development of Goose Bay in Labrador. During the preceding July the United States had sent engineers to Narsarssuak in Greenland for the building of the air base that came to be known as BLUIE WEST 1 (BW-1), and in the following September work began on BW-8, a much more northerly base on the western coast of Greenland. United States forces had taken over the defense of Iceland in July 1941, where they improved airstrips previously occupied by the RAF and began in the spring of 1942 to build two new air bases (Meeks and Patterson) near Keflavik.* The eastern terminal lay at Prestwick in Scotland. When the Eighth Air Force began its movement in the summer of 1942, work was still in progress all along the route.

At that time it was hoped that some of the disadvantages of the existing route might be overcome by developing a more northerly airway extending from Great Falls, Montana, across Canada to Hudson Bay and thence by way of Baffin Island to BLUIE WEST 8 in Greenland. By thus following the great circle course, long one of the goals of airmen, the distance from southern California, where much of the U.S. aircraft industry was concentrated, to Iceland might be cut by almost 600 miles. It was expected that more favorable flying weather would be found, that valuable experience with Arctic conditions of flight would be acquired, and that the experiment might lead to the development of a shorter airway into Russia.[5]

Preliminary surveys had been made in 1941, when weather stations were also established at Fort Chimo in Quebec (CRYSTAL I), on Frobisher Bay (CRYSTAL II), and on Padloping Island (CRYSTAL III). In consequence of a directive issued by the Chief of Staff on 24 May 1942 construction of landing strips and other necessary facilities was begun in the following summer at The Pas and Churchill in Manitoba, at Southampton Island, and at CRYSTAL I and CRYSTAL II. CRYSTAL I did not lie on the line of the proposed CRIMSON route, but it was expected that the field there would make

* See Vol. I, 342–49.

possible a useful alternate route between Goose Bay and Greenland. The program received a severe setback on 27 August when an enemy submarine operating off the Labrador coast sank a ship carrying some 6,000 tons of cargo, including vital construction equipment intended for use at CRYSTAL I, CRYSTAL II, and Southampton Island. A more predictable limitation upon the project resulted from the early onset of extremely cold weather.[6]

The winter of 1942–43 presented major problems all along the North Atlantic route. An accident rate of 2.9 per cent in September rose to 5.8 per cent in October, and it continued to climb. On 22 November ATC suspended the transportation of passengers across the North Atlantic for the duration of the winter. The operation of two-engine transports beyond Iceland already had been forbidden. Some ferrying, chiefly of long-range aircraft, continued into December, as did the transport operations of C-54's and C-87's under contract with TWA and American Airlines, but by mid-December the North Atlantic route had been virtually closed down for the winter.[7] Traffic was diverted to the South Atlantic. The distance to Britain by this route was double that of the projected CRIMSON route, but operations could be maintained on a year-round basis. The prospect in 1943 that a transatlantic route through the Azores would soon be possible brought the expensive and unlucky CRIMSON project to an early end.[8]

Problems of Control

When the air movement of the Eighth Air Force began in the summer of 1942, Brig. Gen. Benjamin F. Giles had just become the commanding officer of the newly established North Atlantic Wing of the Air Transport Command. According to his instructions, he was responsible "for all operations, facilities and installations" along the North Atlantic route, including "all meteorological and communications systems and personnel pertinent to the operation of this activity."[9] But it immediately became apparent that these instructions had not been fully "co-ordinated" back in Washington. The Eighth Air Force assigned to its fighter command full responsibility for the control and direction of its planes in flight from the United States to Great Britain, and during the first phase of the movement the orders were given by VIII Fighter Command "control" officers who had been stationed along the route for that purpose. Few if any of these officers had the experience that would qualify them for this special service, and the Eighth Air Force quickly agreed that ATC should take charge. After 22 July, when the second phase of the movement began, ATC had full operational control, and ATC pilots flew the lead planes. A sharp drop in the accident rate justified the transfer.[10]

More complex were the problems involving the Canadians and the British. No serious difficulty developed with the Canadians, whose influence along the western part of the route had tended heretofore to be dominant. There it proved to be easy enough to agree that, where bases were shared, each national service would be free to become as self-sufficient as it desired to be for the assistance and direction of its own traffic. But it was not so easy to fit American plans into the requirements of British policies governing the movement of aircraft from Iceland east into Britain. All planes flying this last leg of the North Atlantic route penetrated a zone of vital importance to the immediate defense of Great Britain, and British authorities were naturally inclined to feel that they must maintain full control over all aircraft flying within that zone.

General Giles and other responsible U.S. officers, on the other hand, saw in this situation "a major obstacle to the all out effort when the U.S. ATC ferrying operations are increased to sustain the large American forces" to be deployed ultimately in the United Kingdom.[11] Especially objectionable was the existing necessity for American pilots and navigators to "change over from American flight control procedure to unfamiliar British procedure" in the very area where the most hazardous flying conditions were encountered.[12] Had the American flyers been largely veteran transport pilots, the story might have been different, but instead the AAF's planes were flown, and quite obviously would continue to be flown, very largely by inexperienced and recently trained combat crews. Giles urged the establishment of an American controlled airway all the way into Britain and the acquisition there of additional terminal fields to be staffed by American personnel.

The problem was fully discussed in a series of meetings at Montreal and Washington during November and December 1942, in which Maj. Gen. Harold L. George of ATC and Air Chief Marshal Sir Frederick Bowhill, Air Officer Commanding in Chief of the RAF Ferry Command, participated, as did other ranking officers of the AAF and the RAF.[13] At these conferences the RAF Ferry Command insisted upon its need for "over-riding control" between the final point of departure, wherever it might be along the route,* and Prestwick.[14] In reply, General George insisted upon the need for the AAF to exercise full control over its own planes throughout the entire route. More particularly, he demanded that American communications and weather services be extended into Britain, that all communication between the ground and American planes in flight pass through AAF control officers, that two major airports in the United Kingdom be set aside for the exclusive use of the AAF, and that at least four alternate airfields be specified for ATC's use, each of them to be staffed by AAF weather, communications, and control personnel.[15]

This was a large order, but George had the advantage of speaking for the organization to which belonged, as everyone present understood, most of the planes destined to fly the North Atlantic during the coming years. Consequently, most of his demands were met. It was agreed that U.S. communications services and procedures would be established throughout the route. It was also agreed that the AAF would develop its own weather service, subject to the approval of the Air Ministry. Communications between ground stations and American aircraft normally would be conducted through the agency of ATC's control officers, but no ATC officer would dispatch an aircraft for flight into the United Kingdom until clearance with the RAF Fighter Command had been secured by ATC at the terminal point of the flight. At all points close liaison between the AAF and the RAF or RCAF would be maintained. General George agreed to accept joint tenancy at four bases, Prestwick in Scotland, Nutts Corner in North Ireland, Valley in Wales, and St. Mawgan in Cornwall, in lieu of the exclusive control of two bases. Finally, the ATC was authorized to utilize four alternate fields within the United Kingdom.[16] To direct Air Transport Command operations within the European Theater and between Great Britain and North Africa, it was decided to establish a European Wing of the ATC, under the command of Col. Paul E. Burrows, commander of the Caribbean Wing since its establishment, who was known to be acceptable to Sir Frederick Bowhill.[17]

The final agreements between the RAF Ferry Command and the

---

* Long-range planes did not necessarily land at Iceland and might fly direct from Newfoundland or Greenland.

Air Transport Command were reached on 2 December 1942. On 4 February 1943 Colonel Burrows with a skeleton staff opened his headquarters at London. Meanwhile, the new control procedures agreed upon were put into effect. In April the Air Transport Command became the principal tenant at Prestwick. At the other proposed ATC bases, additional construction and personnel were required, but in June all three were opened to ATC traffic. The Air Transport Command's control of ferrying and transport activities over the North Atlantic was now virtually complete.[18]

The Re-establishment of a Northern Route

Meanwhile, the successful Allied invasion of North Africa, together with the suspension of operations in the North Atlantic because of the adverse effects of winter weather, had redirected the flow of transoceanic traffic to the South Atlantic route. Not only did combat in North Africa and the Mediterranean greatly increase the demand for ferrying and transport of key personnel and critical items of supply by the southern airway but Allied control of Morocco and Algiers had the effect of opening a new airway to Britain.* The first weeks of 1943 saw the initial flight delivery of B-17's to the Eighth Air Force in Britain by way of Marrakech.[19] And General Spaatz, chief of the U.S. airmen on Eisenhower's staff, soon asked ATC to inaugurate a regular transport service of two round trips per week between Marrakech and the United Kingdom.[20]

ATC had already placed enough C-54's, flown by TWA crews, on the South Atlantic route from the United States to the United Kingdom to supply a through service of one round trip a week, a service designed to handle only the highest priority cargo and passengers. It now proposed to step up that service to a twice-weekly schedule early in February, with each plane making an extra round-trip shuttle between Prestwick and Marrakech before returning to the United States.[21] As the winter months wore on, the need for a larger transport operation to North Africa and Great Britain became increasingly apparent. Ferrying crews piled up in the United Kingdom, as the existing military service, even when supplemented by the commercial flights of Pan American Airways' and American Export's seaplanes, proved quite incapable of handling this load alone, much less other high priority air traffic.[22] As additional C-54 aircraft

* See above, pp. 77–80.

were made available, the military contract service over the South Atlantic was stepped up to three trips a week, and an equivalent increase in the shuttle between Marrakech and the United Kingdom was made. But it was the reopening in April of the much shorter North Atlantic air route that met the ever increasing demands. The route thus reopened was never to be shut down again until after the close of hostilities.[23]

At the beginning of the 1943 season, conditions generally along the North Atlantic route were superior to those pertaining in the previous year. Personnel at the North Atlantic Wing bases were more numerous and more experienced, and communications facilities were more complete, though far from perfect. To handle the anticipated increase of traffic, the North Atlantic Wing in March secured permission to use Dow Field at Bangor, Maine, as a second staging point for the overseas movement of tactical crews and their aircraft. In March, too, Meeks Field near Keflavik in Iceland was opened as a replacement for the crowded airdrome at Reykjavik.*

The new season opened with something of a flourish. When Col. Robert M. Love, Deputy Chief of Staff of the ATC, ferried a B-17 directly across the North Atlantic from Newfoundland to Prestwick in a ten-hour flight on 16–17 April, he was one of approximately sixty ferry pilots cleared within a few hours to fly the same route.[24] Meanwhile aircraft operated by TWA from Washington and by American Airlines from New York had inaugurated a direct transport operation over the North Atlantic, averaging approximately one round trip a day. The U.K.–Marrakech shuttle now became an appendage to the North Atlantic rather than to the South Atlantic schedules. The backlog of ferry pilots was speedily reduced, and the demand for a high priority cargo and passenger service between the United States and Great Britain was met. By summer the tempo of operations was speeded up to an average of three round-trip flights daily over the North Atlantic airway.[25]

Although the North Africa operations had made serious demands on the Eighth Air Force for men and materiel, its primary mission of daylight strategic bombing, never forgotten, was reaffirmed in May at the TRIDENT conference in the Combined Bomber Offensive Plan.[26] By devoting most of its ferrying and transport operations on the North Atlantic route to the build-up for this offensive, ATC

* See above, p. 93.

contributed significantly to its success. Over three thousand aircraft, principally four-engine bombers and especially B-17's, were flown to Britain by the North Atlantic route in 1943, while less than seven hundred planes of all types went by way of the circuitous South Atlantic route. Nearly 550 ferried planes made the eastward passage in June, the best month of the year in total deliveries.[27]

The crews which flew the ferried aircraft during 1943 and subsequently were of three sorts. During 1943 approximately 27 per cent of all planes delivered were flown by members of established tactical organizations, notably heavy- and medium-bomber groups destined to see service with the VIII Bomber Command. Thirty-eight per cent of the deliveries were made by replacement crews, that is, by crews intended for combat service in some tactical organization of the Eighth Air Force. The remaining 35 per cent were delivered by ATC's Ferrying Division crews, who, after arrival in the U.K., returned to their home bases for new ferrying assignments.[28]

The original plans for 1943 provided for sending all four-engine aircraft through Dow Field, Gander, and thence directly to Prestwick; two-engine ferried planes were to go by way of Presque Isle, Goose Bay, BW-1, Meeks Field, and Prestwick. During the spring months, however, weather conditions led to the dispatching of many four-engine planes through Goose Bay rather than Gander and in some cases over the more northerly circuit provided for two-engine craft. For a time, after Harmon Field near Stephenville in Newfoundland was transferred to the Air Transport Command in August, most of the four-engine planes flew directly from that field to Prestwick. With the coming of winter the movement of two-engine planes was stopped, and most of the heavy bombers were again routed by way of Greenland and Iceland.[29]

During the BOLERO movement nearly two hundred P-38's had been ferried over the North Atlantic route, and so planning for 1943 contemplated the flight delivery of additional pursuits over the same airway. A forecast issued in March called for the movement during the months of June and July of three fighter groups, each equipped with seventy-five P-47's.[30] This program was abandoned, however, and the only fighters to attempt the run in 1943 were ten P-47's, flown by Ferrying Division pilots, which left the Republic factory for an experimental flight on 23 July 1943. Two B-24's were assigned as lead planes, and one C-87 followed to drop emergency equipment to any pilots who might be forced to bail out. The flight was delayed at Goose Bay for twelve days, as a result of a mistaken impression by the officer in command of the movement regarding the minimum weather requirements. Pushed along finally by higher authorities of the North Atlantic Wing, the flight reached Prestwick on 11 and 12 August, minus one P-47, which had ground-looped, ruining its landing gear, at BW-1.[31] The movement was pronounced successful by the North Atlantic Wing and the Ferrying Division, and both of these organizations expressed a qualified readiness to deliver large numbers of P-47's over the route. On 20 August, however, the Air Staff decided that no further flight deliveries of P-47's should be attempted that season.[32]

The safe delivery of as many aircraft as possible was of course the goal of every ferry movement. This was emphasized afresh by ranking officers of the North Atlantic Wing during the spring of 1943. Control officers were directed to clear the early ferry movements through their stations only when conditions were "most favorable." Although it was impossible for the wing to supply command pilots to fly in the lead planes of tactical convoys, as had been done in 1942 after the first phase of the BOLERO movement, ferried aircraft in 1943 moved over the route in much greater safety than was the case the previous year. In 1942, approximately 4.12 per cent of all aircraft which entered the North Atlantic Wing for overseas movement was wrecked or otherwise lost. During the first ten and a half months of 1943, the loss ratio dropped to 1.14 per cent, and the Ferrying Division was quick to point out that its own crews had made a still better record on the planes which they ferried over the North Atlantic route. They had delivered approximately a third of the B-17's which traveled that way and had to their charge only an eighth of the B-17 accidents which had occurred on the route during the year.[33]

Meanwhile, plans for the winter use of the North Atlantic route through the season of 1943–44 took shape. Even in the latter months of 1942, Col. Lawrence Fritz, Assistant Chief of Staff for Operations at ATC headquarters, had personally demonstrated the possibility of winter flights over the route, at least by a skilled and experienced pilot. But for large-scale ferrying there was urgent need for more accurate weather forecasting, particularly of conditions at the termini of the route. The means of collecting the necessary information had indeed improved notably during the course of 1943.

The 30th Weather Reconnaissance Squadron, using stripped B-25's specially equipped for weather observations, had been flying back and forth between the stations of the North Atlantic Wing. Its pilots had also undertaken numerous scheduled daily flights along routes which were planned to give the forecasters more direct information regarding doubtful weather conditions. Meanwhile, corresponding British observers had been working out to the west, north, and southwest of the United Kingdom. The improved forecasts based on these flights encouraged those who wished to keep the North Atlantic route open during the winter of 1943–44. After the decision had been reached, the Operations Division at ATC headquarters assigned three of the command's C-54's as weather planes, to fly back and forth over the North Atlantic routes for the winter, accumulating weather data and fixing standards for safe and reliable winter operations. The information accumulated by the crews of these aircraft filled the last gaps on the weather map and contributed materially to the safe use of the route through the winter months.[34]

Meanwhile, on 4 September, Maj. Gen. Barney M. Giles, then acting in General Arnold's absence as commanding general of the AAF, directed the Air Transport Command to plan for the ferrying of three hundred four-engine bombers over the North Atlantic during each winter month. Two-thirds of these aircraft were to be delivered by ATC ferrying crews, one-third by combat crews. Within the Air Transport Command and the Second Air Force, it was feared that the use of combat crews would entail excessive losses, but the objections raised were overruled by General Giles.[35]

As it proved, the general's judgment was completely vindicated. Nearly 350 four-engine bombers were delivered by way of the North Atlantic route in November, 295 in December, 280 in January, 235 in February, and 333 in March. The pilots of the ATC's Ferrying Division flew only a minor fraction of the bombers which traveled the North Atlantic route that winter. In January a little more than a third of the total were delivered by Ferrying Division crews. The unexpectedly high degree of success experienced by combat crews led to the virtual withdrawal of the Ferrying Division's pilots from the route. They made only 6 per cent of the deliveries in February, and only 3 per cent in March.[36]

Although the winter record of the North Atlantic was most creditable, still larger quantities of aircraft were ferried to the United

Kingdom by the long South Atlantic route. As late as April 1944, 742 ferried aircraft reached Britain by that airway as against 464 by the North Atlantic route. For May the proportions were almost exactly reversed, with 742 arrivals over the North Atlantic and only 469 over the southern route. In June only 9 planes trickled in from the South, while 633 passed through the North Atlantic stations of the ATC. Ferry traffic during the first five months of 1944 exceeded the total for the previous year.[37]

In spite of its large-scale winter ferrying over the North Atlantic, the Air Transport Command was still reluctant to run regular westbound flights over the route during the winter months. The chief objection lay in the tremendously strong head winds facing a westbound plane, necessitating an inordinately heavy load of gasoline to insure a proper margin of safety. Accordingly, the ATC in mid-November 1943 put into effect a round-robin schedule for the normal route of C-54 transports during the winter. Eastbound, these aircraft, still flown by TWA and American Airlines under contract with the Army, were to follow the usual course from Newfoundland to the United Kingdom. They were to proceed homeward by way of Marrakech, Dakar, and the established South Atlantic route.[38]

Almost immediately, however, the Azores became available as a way station on eastward flights from the United States to North Africa and as an alternative to the South Atlantic route for westbound planes.* The first regularly routed ferried aircraft to go that way, a B-17, landed at Lagens Field on Terceira on 9 December 1943; twenty days later a C-54 made the first regularly scheduled eastbound transport flight through Lagens. By the middle of March all transports flying between the United States and Great Britain or North Africa were returning by way of the Azores. Bermuda was used on this run as a weather alternate to Newfoundland.[39]

Through the winter of 1943–44, the Air Transport Command provided a sizable eastward lift for the movement of key personnel, mail, and critical cargoes to the European and Mediterranean theaters. In January 1944 over 350 tons, including 785 passengers, were flown from the United States to those theaters. By June the lift had been increased to 1,178 tons, of which roughly 70 per cent went to the United Kingdom and 30 per cent to North Africa and destinations farther east. In July over 1,900 tons, including 2,570 passengers,

* See above, pp. 87–89.

moved eastward over the North Atlantic routes. The basic transport schedule then in effect called for eleven C-54 flights daily each way, connecting the United States and the United Kingdom.[40]

In July the regular North Atlantic route transport operations of C-54's flown by TWA and American Airlines crews was supplemented by the establishment of SNOWBALL, the third in a series of military transport operations flown by crews belonging to the Ferrying Division.* The establishment of this new service reflected the obvious need for an increased airlift to the United Kingdom, the availability of additional numbers of C-54 aircraft, and the existence within the Ferrying Division of a reservoir of crews experienced in four-engine operation. The original routing of the flights was from Presque Isle through Stephenville in Newfoundland to Valley in Wales and back through Meeks Field in Iceland to Stephenville and Presque Isle.[41]

The routine schedule of services of ATC constituted its most important contribution to victory, but the potentialities of air transport were dramatically demonstrated by more than one of the special cargo lifts that were made, often on very short notice and with an overriding priority. In the summer of 1943, for example, two lots of incendiary-bomb fuzes required by the Eighth Air Force were picked up in the United States and started by air for the United Kingdom within twenty-four hours after the receipt of the request at ATC headquarters. In the late autumn of 1943, when the Eighth Air Force was striving to extend the range of its fighter escorts as a means of reducing the inordinately large losses incurred in its heavy-bomber missions over Germany, the solution was sought through the use of jettisonable fuel tanks. Seventy-five tons of auxiliary tanks and related fittings were hurried to Britain on ATC transports between the last week of October and the end of the year. The first regularly scheduled cargo plane under ATC control to use Lagens Field in the Azores carried five sets of pontoons, shipped at the urgent request of Lt. Gen. Mark Clark, together with other cargo for the Mediterranean theater. Within a half-month, in June and July 1944, Air Transport Command aircraft transported to Great Britain approximately 125 tons of equipment designed to combat the robot bomb.[42]

* The earlier Foreign Military Transport operations of the Ferrying Division, the FIREBALL and CRESCENT runs, are discussed above, p. 89, and below, pp. 129–30.

The Last Year of the European War

The Allied landings in Normandy in June, 1944, marked the beginning of the final offensive which was to bring an end, in another eleven months, to the European war. The daylight bombing attack against Germany grew in intensity and fury, while tactical operations reached an unprecedented pitch. The need of the attacking ground and air forces for replacement aircraft and for cargo borne by air from the United States continued to grow. Thanks to the augmentation of its fleet of four-engine transports and the improvement of its facilities along the North Atlantic route, the Air Transport Command was able to supply an increased airlift over that route to the European and Mediterranean theaters. While the weight of air cargo and passengers landed in those theaters grew generally during the last year of the war, it fluctuated considerably from month to month. The North Atlantic lift to the European theater, which had passed 950 tons in July 1944, dropped to 779 tons in the following month. In October for the first time it exceeded 1,000 tons, with nearly 600 tons carried to the United Kingdom and over 460 directly to France. This record was not broken until March, when 1,500 tons followed the North Atlantic route to Europe. During the final drive, in April 1945, the total lift passed 1,650 tons, more than half of it to destinations on the Continent.[43]

The peak of ferrying operations was reached a little earlier. During 1944 a grand total of approximately 5,900 aircraft was flown over the North Atlantic to the European theater. In the first three months of 1945 nearly 1,100 were so delivered. In April, however, as the end came in sight, only 158 ferried aircraft made the eastward run over that route. Successive cancellations stopped the delivery, first of all, of B-17 and B-24 aircraft not radar-equipped, then of all heavy bombers, and, finally, of light and medium bombers, transports, and pursuit aircraft destined for either the European or the Mediterranean theater.[44]

The tempo of ferrying operations is not adequately measured by taking the total number of arrivals within a theater, month by month, and dividing it by the number of days in the month. The bases en route and those at the ultimate destination experienced alternate periods of activity and idleness. The ferried planes were held up, especially during winter months on the North Atlantic, by bad weather and then dispatched in large numbers. Even in the summer, the flow was very erratic. In July 1944, of the 256 ferried aircraft received at Prestwick, 50 per cent arrived on three days, 57 in a single day. At St. Mawgan 120 planes arrived between 9 and 16 November 1944; the next week only 10 appeared. Then came another week in which there were over 100 landings; the next saw only 3. During the lulls maintenance personnel and others had little to do. During the surges they were overworked, and all the facilities of the receiving bases were severely taxed.[45]

The pattern of air transport service over the North Atlantic changed rapidly in response to the Allied successes in land warfare on the Continent. On 31 August 1944, only four days after the last of the German troops left Paris, the Air Transport Command landed its first aircraft at Orly Field, nine miles away. Orly began almost at once to sustain a heavy traffic between the United Kingdom and France. Hardly a month later, on 4 October, the first scheduled ATC plane on the New York–Paris run landed at Orly. By the middle of the month the ATC's C-54's were averaging three round trips daily between the homeland and France, with Stephenville and Lagens as stopping points. As the campaign continued, this route became of increasing importance. Until December the U.S.–Paris flights were handled by military aircraft flown by Ferrying Division crews, thereafter with the additional use of contract carriers. Schedules in effect on 1 April 1945 called for fifteen round-trip flights daily between the United States and the European theater, seven between the United States and Prestwick, and eight between Paris and either Washington, Presque Isle, or New York.[46]

The first C-54 to make the New York–Paris flight carried a typical cargo, which included aircraft repairs, medical supplies, G.I. mail, and other mail for Paris and Brussels. Less conventional was the service inaugurated in mid-October, with the highest priority, for transport of 3,570 pounds of whole blood daily from New York to Paris. Interservice co-operation is illustrated by the ATC's delivery to Great Britain of a 2,500-pound blade for an American naval vessel's propeller. To combat the German breakthrough in December, 1944, ATC planes delivered 35 tons of mortar propellant charges to Paris from the Edgewood Arsenal. Other cargoes included such diverse and non-military items as vegetable seed to be used by American troops in growing some of their own food, cylinder heads required to put

French locomotives back into service, and 100,000 nipples for feeding French and Dutch infants.[47]

Victory in Europe was foreshadowed by the inauguration during the late winter of 1944–45 of a guaranteed schedule passenger service on the eastbound run, three days a week, Washington to Paris, via Newfoundland and the Azores; four days a week, Washington to Prestwick via Newfoundland. This was a "plush" service, in which the passengers, having duly made their reservations as for a commercial flight, enjoyed the comfort of airline seats.[48]

ATC's Intratheater Service

Until late in 1943 the Air Transport Command's responsibility for air operations between the United States and the United Kingdom had regularly ended at the aerial ports of arrival in Britain, first Prestwick alone and subsequently Prestwick, Valley, and St. Mawgan. Usually, aircraft flown by ATC and replacement crews were there turned over to the Ferry and Transport Service of the VIII Air Service Command, which in July 1942 had established its own air transport service within the theater. This operation supplied a vital air link between the headquarters and depots of the Eighth Air Force. The personnel and aircraft used in rendering this service were organized in April 1943 into the 27th Air Transport Group.[49]

Col. Paul E. Burrows, first commanding officer of the European Wing of the Air Transport Command, had been interested, since March 1943 at least, in establishing a service within the United Kingdom whereby aircraft would be ferried all the way to the using organizations, while high priority mail and passengers would be delivered to London, and a regular shuttle maintained between the several bases utilized by ATC in the United Kingdom. This proposal was rejected by ATC headquarters at Washington in April, but the portion of it which called for an internal transport run ultimately received the approval of General George. At the request of General Eaker, such an internal shuttle was established by the European Wing in October 1943. Initially three aircraft of the DC-3 type furnished the schedules, and Hendon, near London, was added for this purpose to the bases utilized by the wing. The new service was called the Marble Arch Line, in reference to the Hyde Park Marble Arch located just across the street from wing headquarters in London. By the end of the year additional aircraft made possible two daily round trips between Prestwick and Hendon, one between St. Mawgan and Hendon, and periodic flights to other ATC stations in the British Isles. During the first half of 1944 the operations of the Marble Arch Line more than doubled both in passenger-miles and in ton-miles flown. By far the heaviest traffic was carried on the run between Prestwick and Hendon, which was in effect a continuation of the transatlantic service.[50]

The Marble Arch Line foreshadowed operations which the European Division performed after it gained a foothold on the Continent in September 1944. In planning for these operations, the echelons of the War and State Departments participated and laid down the general principles summarized in a letter to General Arnold from Under Secretary of War Robert P. Patterson on 11 September 1944:

The State Department and certain other Government agencies have recently brought to the attention of the War Department the fact that at the present stage of the war there is an increasing need for air transportation from this country to and between various parts of Europe, including areas liberated and to be liberated.

It has been pointed out that our over-all war purposes will be served, and the overseas period of duty of our troops shortened, by making foreign air transportation available as far as possible not only to individuals whose travel is necessary in connection with the military effort, but also those whose travel will contribute to relief or rehabilitation activities in war-affected areas or to a resumption of economic or other activities, disrupted by the war, that are necessary for the re-establishment of peacetime conditions.

I know that your plans provide for extending the operations of the Air Transport Command to the various important cities and areas of the European Continent, and that all appropriate steps will be taken to facilitate air transportation of our own personnel and others engaged on military missions. I believe that we should also endeavor, on a basis subordinate to all of our purely military requirements, to make air transportation available to other individuals whose travel comes within the categories described in the preceding paragraph. . . .

It is important, in my opinion, that the Air Transport Command not carry traffic other than military traffic or traffic involved in the military effort if it can be reasonably handled by a United States civil air carrier, and I believe that any transportation of such non-military passengers by the Air Transport Command should be regarded as an interim or emergency matter until such time as the civil airlines are qualified and are operating over the various routes involved.

Subject to all the foregoing, I believe that it is in our interest to expedite the initiation of suitable air transportation by the Air Transport Command to all of the European points where our interests are involved. The service should operate with economy, but it should be so organized as to demonstrate the efficiency of this country in the air transportation field and should compare favorably with the air transport service operated by any of the other nations.[51]

Especially interesting is the concern shown here for the competitive position of American civil aviation at the end of the war.

Detailed plans for carrying out the program were necessarily tentative in character and changed from time to time in response to the changing situation and the expressed desires of interested agencies. As approved at ATC headquarters on 1 November 1944, the plan called for an extensive network of trunk routes and feeder services, all in effect extensions of the transatlantic routes originating in the United States: (1) a line from Iceland into the Scandinavian countries, with Stockholm as the terminus; (2) another from the United Kingdom and Paris to Berlin, thence by one extension to Warsaw and by another to Vienna, Budapest, Belgrade, Sofia, Istanbul, Ankara, and Cairo; (3) a line from Paris via Rome and Athens to Cairo, or via Marseille to Algiers; and (4) a route from Paris via Bordeaux and Madrid to Casablanca. The key points on the trunk lines were to be linked with each other and with certain intermediate points by a series of feeder lines, with the responsibility for development divided between the Air Transport Command and the air transport groups of the VIII Air Service Command. The latter, augmented as the need arose by troop-carrier aircraft and personnel, were to fly local feeder and distribution services on the Continent for the benefit of American Air Force units, as they had been doing within the United Kingdom. The ATC, within the limits of its capacity, was to provide local services for the American ground forces and for other official and civilian agencies.[52]

All this planning in the autumn of 1944 remained dependent on the course of military operations. For the moment, the Air Transport Command had quite enough to do in its efforts simply to meet immediate military needs. Water and rail connections between Britain and Paris were re-established so slowly that in late October a contingent of 65 troops required for guard duty by the ATC in France was reduced to landing on OMAHA beach (after a two-day wait offshore), sleeping nearby on the ground without blankets, and at length cadging a ride to Paris in British trucks driven by French soldiers. The pressure on the shuttle service which the Air Transport Command inaugurated between the United Kingdom and Paris was tremendous, and a host of special calls was made upon the European Division's resources. Ten planes were supplied on 2 September, for example, to carry gasoline to General Patton's Third Army. Toward the end of the month the Division set up a 75-flight special movement of SHAEF personnel from London to Versailles.[53]

The badly bombed airfield at Orly soon became the hub of a network of shifting air routes. Through it ran the Division's main trunk line, extending from Prestwick through London to the Mediterranean terminus at Marseille. A secondary direct route ran from St. Mawgan to Marseille and on to Naples. Lesser routes served other military purposes. Passenger weight in November and December was almost equal to that of both mail and cargo combined. The passengers included military and civilian VIP's, communication specialists, war-weary troops homeward bound, cadres for new continental bases of the ATC, and combat infantrymen on their way to the front. By the end of the year sixteen flights a day were scheduled to Orly from Bovingdon, which had replaced Hendon as ATC's base in the London area.[54]

Planning for the Air Transport Command's continental operation was complicated by the requests which various organizations within the theater made for local air transport services. For a time all requests for air service had been submitted to General Spaatz's USSTAF headquarters. As the requests multiplied, an agreement was reached in November that the Division need not establish new routes within the European theater without the approval of SHAEF and the concurrence of the Commanding General, USSTAF.[55]

During the early months of 1945 the rapid advance of the Allied lines led nevertheless to the approved extension of ATC's services. Some routes, like that from St. Mawgan to Naples, were dropped, while others were added. By early June the close of hostilities had made it possible to establish a series of schedules comparable to that contemplated during the previous autumn. In addition to the regular routes flown within the United Kingdom, and to the numerous London-Paris flights, the Division's schedules called for one flight daily between London, Brussels, and Frankfurt; another between London, Paris, and Frankfurt; still another originating at Paris, with stops at Frankfurt, Munich, Rome, and Naples; and a fourth serving Paris, Rheims, and Frankfurt. In addition, there was one flight weekly between Paris, Madrid, and Lisbon. By July a daily schedule from Paris to Stockholm, with stops at Brussels, Bremen, Copenhagen, and Oslo, had been inaugurated. Naples had become the starting point for limited services through Bari to Belgrade, Bucharest, Tirana, and Sofia and for a direct run, twice weekly, to Budapest.[56]

Scandinavian Operations

A postwar ATC route from Paris to the three Scandinavian capitals had some precedent in a number of special wartime missions. The first, the SONNIE project, began early in 1944, nominally to transport from Sweden to Great Britain some 2,000 Norwegian aircrew trainees and such American aircrew internees as the Swedish government might release. Within fifteen months, aircraft attached to the project removed over 4,300 passengers from Sweden, furnished the only dependable means of communication with the American legation in Stockholm, and brought to American aircrews in Sweden the supplies and equipment which enabled them to repair and prepare for flight to the United Kingdom nearly two-thirds of the American combat planes which had force-landed in that country. This project helped to pave the way for ATC's postwar service into the Scandinavian countries and for the ultimate entry of American civil aviation into that region.[57]

The consent of both the British and the Swedish governments was required. Sweden was concerned, of course, with the protection of its status as a neutral power. The British, with good reason, feared that an American operation into Sweden might develop into a dangerous postwar rival of British aviation interests. In consequence they tried to prevent its inauguration. Unsuccessful in this, they failed, likewise, in their efforts to bring the service to an early end.[58] To save Sweden's position as a neutral, SONNIE was put on a nominally civilian basis. Its unarmed Liberators were divested of military markings; both their crews and the ground echelon which the ATC placed at Stockholm wore civilian clothes. In form they were working for a civilian organization termed the American Air Transport Service.[59] Though the SONNIE aircraft were unarmed, they operated over enemy-held Norway. Based from March until November 1944 on the RAF station at Leuchars, near Aberdeen, Scotland, and thereafter at Metfield in Suffolk, they normally made a long detour northward before crossing Norwegian territory. Although enemy interception was a constant threat, the only aircraft lost during the project crashed into a mountain near Göteborg, Sweden, in October 1944.[60]

Col. Bernt M. Balchen, veteran polar aviator and prewar operator of a Norwegian civil airline, had a major part to play in the project as an officer assigned to AC/AS, Plans in AAF Headquarters.

He helped to make the necessary arrangements with the Swedish government and eventually was placed in command of the operation. His acquaintance with numerous persons of consequence in the Scandinavian countries, his knowledge of the weather and terrain, and his outstanding personal qualities of leadership made him an admirable choice. His letters of instruction as commanding officer designated him as the personal representative of the commanding general of the ATC's European Wing (Division) and of USSTAF. The latter organization had in fact had rather more to do with plans for the project than had the European Wing and had secured from units of the Eighth Air Force the necessary aircraft and most of the subordinate personnel for SONNIE.[61]

A second enterprise which came under Colonel Balchen's command was the BALL project. This was a program for dropping weapons, ammunition, food, radios, and equipment with which to carry on sabotage into the hands of the Norwegian underground and for dropping secret agents and radio equipment behind enemy lines in northern Norway. The project, undertaken for Special Force Headquarters, Office of Strategic Services, London, lasted from July until September, 1944. Six war-weary B-24's, specially equipped for the job, and painted with black, light-absorbent paint, dropped approximately 120 tons of cargo and personnel at designated points, mostly in southern and central Norway. Enemy opposition was encountered on fifteen of the sixty-four dropping missions undertaken. Although no direct damage was suffered as a result of enemy action, operational hazards thwarted many of the missions and caused the death of twelve men and the total loss of two of the six aircraft assigned to the BALL project. Later the task of supplying the Norwegian underground by air passed to the Eighth Air Force and then to the British.[62]

The WHEN AND WHERE project was begun in January 1945 at the request of the Norwegian government-in-exile, which made the necessary diplomatic arrangements with the Swedish and Russian governments. The mission was the delivery of Norwegian military personnel and cargo to various points in northern Norway, there to carry on the fight against the occupying German forces and to counteract any tendency of the Russians to retain the small foothold which they had won there. Ten C-47's were assigned to the project and based at Luleå, a Swedish town some 450 miles north of Stockholm. WHEN

AND WHERE was a frankly military operation; the aircraft bore AAF markings, and the crews wore uniforms, which they were supposed to conceal with coveralls while on Swedish military airfields. The ten transports flew a total of 572 missions and delivered 1,418 persons and 1,223 tons of freight. Several hundred Norwegian police troops and a field hospital with all its medical supplies and personnel were included in the airlift. Most of the freight consisted of food and forage for winter-bound communities. The larger part was landed at regular, if primitive, airfields, but some use was made of improvised landing fields, one of which was cleared on the ice of a northern river. Where even improvised landing fields were not available, personnel and cargo were dropped, as in the BALL project.[63]

These three Scandinavian operations were only distantly related to the normal mission of the Air Transport Command. The three projects had little in common beyond the fact that each involved operations over the Scandinavian peninsula and that each was directed by Colonel Balchen, nominally as an officer of the Air Transport Command.

During the summer of 1944 the British opposition to the continuance of the SONNIE project took shape in a movement to deny the project the use of the Leuchars bese. So important had the operation become, however, that Colonel Balchen suggested that it be conducted by way of Iceland, if the Leuchars-Stockholm route had to be abandoned. As it turned out, the ATC was permitted to continue its operations at Leuchars until late November, when a reasonably satisfactory substitute was provided at Metfield. Although the urgent need for opening an Iceland-Stockholm route had passed, the project was not abandoned. Indeed it—with a possible extension to Moscow—formed a significant part of the long-range thinking of ATC and AAF headquarters, well indoctrinated with the idea of paving a way in the postwar world for American aviation. In October the North Atlantic Division of the ATC became responsible for the detailed planning of such a service. Diplomatic negotiations with Sweden delayed the final action, but a satisfactory agreement allowing both American and Swedish use of the route was reached in March 1945. A further obstacle lay in the inadequate communications facilities available at Stockholm, a factor which had always hampered SONNIE operations. Only after V-E Day was the needed AACS* equipment set up at

* Army Airways Communications System.

Bromma Airport. Finally, on 1 June 1945 the first scheduled flight to Stockholm from Presque Isle via Meeks Field was undertaken. Thereafter, until late August 1945, when American Export Airlines, operating as a contract carrier, took over the run, military crews of the North Atlantic Division operated one round trip a week on this route.[64]

Nearly 900 aircraft were ferried through the North Atlantic bases to active combat theaters in 1942, approximately 3,200 in 1943, over 8,400 in 1944, and approximately 2,150 in the last five months of the European conflict in 1945; in all nearly 15,000 planes. Equally important, and indeed fundamental to the fulfilment of the ferrying mission itself, was the development of a safe, dependable service for strategic air transportation between the United States and the United Kingdom. During the last five months of the war in Europe, over 10,000 tons of air cargo were moved by ATC.[65]

CHAPTER 5

*   *   *   *   *   *   *   *   *   *   *

AIRLINE TO CHINA

IN THE period of frantic planning which followed the launching of the Japanese offensive in December 1941 China's position was early recognized as vital. It was clear that China must be given enough aid to keep her in the war, if not for China's sake, then certainly that her soil might serve later as the base for a counterattack against Japan. But the outlook was gloomy. Japanese air and naval action in the China Sea left seaborne reinforcement out of the question. The fall of Rangoon in March 1942 cut off the flow of supplies by land over the Burma Road. There remained only the air.*

The possibility of establishing a useful air route into China was under serious discussion as early as January 1942, and on 25 February President Roosevelt committed himself to the view that "it is obviously of the utmost urgency . . . that the pathway to China be kept open."[1] Planning then contemplated building up the China National Aviation Corporation's[2] fleet of DC-3's to the point where twenty or twenty-five of these craft should "maintain essential communications between Calcutta and Chungking." At the same time the AAF was planning to inaugurate a service from Sadiya, a railhead at the eastern extremity of the Brahmaputra River Valley in Assam, two hundred miles over the rugged mountains of North Burma to Myitkyina in the upper reaches of the Irrawaddy River. At Myitkyina cargoes were to be loaded on barges, floated a hundred miles down the Irrawaddy to Bhamo, there to be transloaded once more for truck shipment over the Burma Road to Kunming and Chungking. Seventy-five Douglas aircraft, C-47's and C-53's, allocated to this service were to arrive at

---

* In preparing this chapter, the writer has benefited greatly from the counsel of Mr. Thomas E. Holt, MATS Historical Office, one-time assistant Historical Officer of the India-China Division, Air Transport Command.

114

Calcutta by the 15th of June, and meanwhile work was rushed on the construction of a suitable hard-surfaced airfield at Myitkyina. It was hoped that the seventy-five two-engine transports would be able to deliver 7,500 tons a month of cargo to that point.[3]

When the middle of June came, ten C-53's had been delivered at Karachi for the use of either CNAC or the Chinese government. In addition, a total of thirty-nine Douglas planes for use by U.S. military crews had been flown out, but in July only nine of these were in commission and actually available for air movement eastward from Assam.[4] Meanwhile, their task had been made more difficult when Japanese ground forces on 8 May took the Myitkyina airfield that was to have played a key part in the air supply of China.

That disaster left only one means of keeping open a pathway to China—the grim prospect of direct flight from airfields in eastern Assam across the High Himalayas to Yunnanyi, Kunming, or other points in the Yunnan Province of China. The route from Dinjan (near Sadiya) in Upper Assam to Myitkyina had been forbidding enough,[5] but not so difficult as the more northerly course to which the American airmen would now be restricted.

The Hump

The distance from Dinjan to Kunming is some 500 air miles. The Brahmaputra valley floor lies 90 feet above sea level at Chabua, a spot near Dinjan where the principal American valley base was constructed. From this level the mountain wall surrounding the valley rises quickly to 10,000 feet and higher. Flying eastward out of the valley the pilot first topped the Patkai Range, then passed over the upper Chindwin River Valley, bounded on the east by a 14,000-foot ridge, the Kumon Mountains. He then crossed a series of 14,000–16,000-foot ridges separated by the valleys of the West Irrawaddy, East Irrawaddy, Salween, and Mekong rivers. The main "Hump," which gave its name to the whole awesome mountainous mass and to the air route which crossed it, was the Santsung Range, often 15,000 feet high, between the Salween and Mekong rivers. East of the Mekong the terrain became decidedly less rugged, and the elevations more moderate as one approached the Kunming airfield, itself 6,200 feet above sea level.

At minimum altitudes on this course violent turbulence was commonly encountered. To avoid this menace, pilots had to climb to levels at which severe icing occurred during several months each year.[6] In the spring of 1943 Col. Edward H. Alexander, commanding ATC's India-China Wing, reported:

> The weather here has been pretty awful. The icing level starts at 12,000 feet. Today a C-87 went to 29,500 feet on instruments and was unable to climb any higher, and could not get on top of the overcast. It has rained about seven and a half inches in the past five days. All aircraft are grounded.[7]

This was in the last week of March. The stifling hot ground weather of mid-May ushered in the true monsoon, in which during five and a half months a rainfall of 200 inches is common. To the stark natural hazards of the route were added those of attack by the enemy, who was particularly active in the winter months of 1942–43 and 1943–44.[8] The Hump run was short in comparison with the long overwater jumps of the air route from California to Australia or even over the North Atlantic. Few, nevertheless, will challenge the claim of the men who flew the Hump that theirs was an air transport route of surpassing danger and difficulty.

Its hazards apart, the India-China route had a unique character. The other airways operated by the ATC were extremely important for the strategic supplies, key personnel, and priority mail delivered to combat zones, but no one of them was the sole means by which a combat theater was nourished. In contrast, every vehicle, every gallon of fuel, every weapon, every round of ammunition, every typewriter, and every ream of paper which found its way to Free China for either the Chinese or the American forces during nearly three years of war was flown in by air from India.[9]

The operation became the more difficult because India itself was not an important source of the military supplies required in China. Most such goods had to be brought to India by water or by air. The water haul, vastly more important here than the air routes connecting India with the trans-African and transatlantic services, was long and painfully slow, whichever of the major ports—Karachi, Calcutta, or Bombay—was the point of debarkation. One shipload of men and supplies which, like most of the 1942 shipments, debarked at Karachi, was at sea for fifty-eight days.[10] Once ashore, the cargo was still 1,500 miles by a string of primitive railroads of varying gauges and limited capacity from the jumping-off point in Assam. Calcutta was so menaced by the Japanese in 1942 that relatively few supplies and men were sent there from the United States. Before 1943 was far along its docks were indeed receiving large shipments, both of aircraft parts and of gasoline and oil. But the Calcutta water front was still nearly 600 miles from the Assam terminus of the Hump route, and the line of communication was tenuous. Slow, ancient barges on the Brahmaputra River carried much of the fuel used by the aircraft. The Assam and Bengal Railroad, built primarily to market the Assam tea crop, had to carry a large part of the load. Between Calcutta and Assam all Hump-bound freight had to be transferred into cars used on the narrower-gauge track up the valley. Though Calcutta was in population the second city of the British Empire, there was late in 1944 no direct road, however poor, by which a truck or even a jeep could carry a load from the metropolis to the ATC base at Tezgaon, 150 miles distant by air. The only possible road connection followed a roundabout route, 450 miles long.[11]

In spite of these handicaps, the airlift to China was initiated in 1942 and came eventually to prosper greatly. In July 1942 a handful of C-47's delivered a meager 85 tons of United States Army supplies, China Defense Supplies, and passengers to China. In the same month CNAC planes carried approximately 221 tons over the same route. In July 1943 ATC aircraft lifted some 2,916 tons (net) eastbound over the Hump. In 1944 the July figure came to 18,975 net tons. In July 1945 the peak was reached when aircraft of ATC and of various units flying under its operational control hauled the amazing total of 71,042 net tons from bases in India to China.[12]

Early Efforts—to May 1943

In Washington, planning for the airlift to China involved principally two problems: (1) the provision of the necessary aircraft and (2) the assignment of personnel to fly the planes and to keep them flying. Initially, the Ferrying Command was directed early in 1942 to activate a ferrying group of three squadrons, each having 350 men and 25 C-47 or C-53 aircraft.[13]

Responsibility for planning in the field fell first on Maj. Gen. Lewis H. Brereton of the Tenth Air Force and his chief of staff, Brig. Gen. Earl L. Naiden, who had to provide for defense of the air route against the Japanese, for weather reporting, for communications, and for the command control of the entire operation. Most vital of immediate needs was that for airfields with hard-surfaced runways, hardstandings, and taxiways. General Naiden, as early as 10 March 1942, asked the RAF in India to provide three fields in Upper Assam, including one which was already being built at Chabua by native labor using the most primitive tools and methods, and two more in northern Burma, preferably at Myitkyina and Bhamo. Believing that the hard-surfaced airfields in Assam would not be ready before the monsoon season, Naiden reported to Washington that until November he could operate no more than twenty-five aircraft eastward from Assam.[14]

In Washington the responsible officers in Ferrying Command head-quarters and the Air Staff, hard put to find and deliver the transports required in every theater, were tempted to accept this conservative estimate. Nevertheless, in June, under pressure from Dr. T. V. Soong, the Ferrying Command was required to push delivery of the seventy-five aircraft already assigned to the India-China airlift.[15] The Ferrying Command had activated the 1st Ferrying Group early in March and had started its ground echelon on the long sea voyage to Karachi before the month was over. To organize the necessary aircrews, the Ferrying Command established the AMMISCA project at Morrison Field, Florida. Over a hundred of the pilots assigned to the project were airline pilots, who as reserve officers were called to active duty for this specific mission. Between 19 April and 13 May 1942 a total of twenty-six planes and crews were dispatched from Morrison Field to India. Others followed after an interval.[16]

Before the first of the AMMISCA planes left Florida, control of the 1st Ferrying Group passed from General Olds to General Brereton, who also assumed responsibility for all India-China air transport operations. Brereton and Naiden thereupon proceeded to establish what were on paper two rather imposing organizations, the Trans-India Ferrying Command and the Assam-Burma-China Ferry Command. Col. Caleb V. Haynes, who had been sent out to command a bomber group, was ordered to take over the Assam-Burma-China Ferry Command. With four Douglas transports and ten Pan American–Africa planes and crews borrowed from the trans-African route, he began the delivery over the Hump of aviation gasoline intended for refueling in China the Doolittle Tokyo raiders. Before this task was completed, the transports were diverted to the assistance of General Stilwell in northern Burma. They flew out refugees, wounded soldiers, and, finally, most of General Stilwell's staff and dropped supplies to Stilwell and his party on their famous trek out of the jungle.[17] Then came the June crisis in the Middle East which caused Brereton to be ordered west for reinforcement of the hard-pressed British with most of the tactical planes of the Tenth Air Force and twelve of its transports, leaving Naiden to carry on as best he could in India.*

The weight of cargo and personnel transported from India to China increased gradually. December was the first month in which the lift exceeded a thousand tons. Not until August were airplanes and personnel of the 1st Ferrying Group moved up from Karachi to Assam, and the transfer was completed only in November.[18]

The failure of the Hump operation to attain the volume anticipated was attributable to a combination of circumstances, the relative significance of which is difficult to assess. The number of transport aircraft which reached the theater fell far below the original intentions. Of the total of sixty-two military DC-3's delivered to India by 16 December 1942, some fifteen had been destroyed or otherwise lost to the service, and four were still with Brereton in the Middle East. This left only forty-three actually on hand in the theater, many of them frequently out of commission for lack of engines and spare parts. The planes in service had to maintain the trans-India air connection between Karachi and Assam, as well as the Hump lift, and were often diverted from their regular mission to meet some combat emergency.[19]

The fearsome problems of weather, terrain, and enemy interference had not been solved. The communications system was rudimentary. As late as September the most powerful radio sets in operation in China could reach out no more than thirty to fifty miles to provide direction with the Bendix Left-Right Indicator. There was no accurate weather reporting at either Dinjan or Kunming. As one observer put it, "The present system is that if you can see the end of the runway it's safe to take off." Pilots with experience on the Hump run were reluctant to fly at all or to carry loads substantially in excess of stateside airlines standards. Neither pilots nor operations personnel had mastered the techniques required to handle overloads under Hump conditions. Food and living conditions for flight or ground personnel were poor. As late as September refueling of aircraft was accomplished largely by native laborers pumping gasoline by hand from drums.[20]

More serious than the host of genuine physical handicaps, though based, no doubt, on them, was the mental attitude of Stilwell and Naiden, as well as Brig. Gen. Clayton L. Bissell, Brereton's successor

* See Vol. I, 512–13.

in the command of the Tenth Air Force. Flatly characterized as "defeatist" by Frank D. Sinclair, Aviation Technical Adviser of China Defense Supplies, Inc., who made a study of the operation in the field, these leaders viewed the hope of sending as much as 5,000 tons a month over the Hump as quite fantastic. "Of course I agree," wrote Sinclair, "if only 18 aircraft are assigned to the job."[21] He believed, however, that if 125 aircraft with proper supporting facilities were assigned to the Hump project alone, it would be feasible to carry 10,000 tons a month from India to China by air.*

Study of his report by the Plans Division of Air Transport Command headquarters led on 9 October to a recommendation that responsibility for the India-China air supply route should be transferred to ATC.[22] Four days later ATC officially offered to do the job under certain conditions, and on 21 October that command was instructed to take it over.

ATC's offer was based on the understanding that all aircraft, maintenance facilities, spare parts, and personnel sent out for the project would be assigned to ATC and that ATC would have full control of the operation under the supervision of General Arnold, "to work in close harmony with the Theater commander but not to be under his control so far as the conduct of the operation is concerned."[23] This offer was based ostensibly on the thesis that the 1st Ferrying Group had been handicapped in its primary mission by the frequent diversions of its resources to other tasks that seemed more urgent to the theater commander. Singleness of purpose, the control of the operation by an organization whose only mission in the theater was to "get supplies to China and to bring back return loads of strategic materials," would be achieved by assigning the responsibility to the Air Transport Command. "The principal experience of the Air Transport Command is in air transportation, as contrasted with the experience of the Theater Commander being principally in combat and in preparation for combat," argued Col. Cyrus R. Smith, ATC's chief of staff, who added: "The India-China ferry operation must be conducted on the best standards of transportation if it is to have maximum effectiveness."[24] There was a caveat attached. "Even if the responsibility should be transferred to Air Transport," wrote Colonel Smith, "there would still remain the job of increasing the effectiveness of communications, bettering the weather reporting and forecasting, materially improving

* The story is recounted from the point of view of the theater in Vol. IV, 414 ff.

the maintenance of aircraft and engines, and, perhaps, the furnishing of a type of aircraft better suited to the peculiarities of the high terrain operation."[25]

The inference was clear enough. ATC was the agency best qualified to handle any task in the field of military air transportation. The Tenth Air Force had not made the best possible use of the available resources. ATC could handle the job much more successfully if given a large measure of independence of theater control. Responsible officers in the theater would have been less than human had they not opposed the transfer.[26] They could hardly be blamed for suspecting the Air Transport Command of imperialistic ambitions.

The offer thus made was quickly accepted: eight days later a message from General Marshall informed Stilwell that the India-China transport operation was to be transferred to ATC on 1 December 1942, and named Stilwell's air officer, Col. Edward H. Alexander, as commanding officer of a new India-China Wing of the Air Transport Command.[27] Colonel Alexander, who had served from May until December 1941 as executive officer of the Ferrying Command, was thus returned to a position of key importance in the development of the Army's air transport services.[28]

When ATC assumed responsibility for the India-China operation at the beginning of December, the initial plan to provide seventy-five C-47's still had to be achieved. In addition, ATC proposed to send a dozen C-87's and during the course of 1943 some fifty C-46's. Early in January 1943 the first three of the C-87's reached India, under the command of Maj. Richard T. Kight, who had recently piloted Wendell Willkie on his 28,487-mile flight around the world. By the second week of March, eleven C-87's and seventy-six DC-3 type aircraft were on hand in the wing. During March, too, the percentage of assigned DC-3's operational daily rose to the unusually high figure of 81 per cent.[29]

Still this fleet was far from meeting the commitments of General Arnold and ATC headquarters. After the Casablanca conference in January 1943, Generals Arnold and Somervell and Field Marshal Sir John Dill had gone to Chungking to consult with General Stilwell and with Generalissimo Chiang Kai-shek, who was insistent that provision be made for early offensive action in Asia. In his own initial flight over the Hump, General Arnold gained a firsthand acquaintance with some of the problems involved in the air supply of China; his B-17, flown by a picked crew, became lost, flew for some time over Japanese-occupied territory, and finally landed, four hours overdue, at Kunming.[30] Previously he had consulted with Colonel Alexander and had dispatched orders posthaste to Washington directing that ATC's India-China fleet be built up to 112 DC-3 type aircraft, plus the 12 C-87's, and that a troop-carrier squadron with the Douglas planes be assigned to Stilwell. Alexander was confident that with such a fleet he could transport 4,000 tons a month into China, which he was promptly directed to do. In a letter to Stilwell, Arnold confessed that 4,000 tons a month did "not come anywhere near meeting the demands of either the Chinese Army or the air forces operating in China." At Chungking he learned of the Generalissimo's demands* that Chennault's air strength be built up by autumn to 500 planes and the Hump lift to 10,000 tons a month—both as prerequisites to Chinese participation in Stilwell's project for the reconquest of Burma.[31]

An immediate obstacle to meeting even the 4,000-ton objective lay in a grave shortage of aircrews. The crews on hand were being worked to the limit of endurance, often flying more than 100 hours a month on the Hump run. The more experienced among them were increasingly victims of flying fatigue. On 13 February Colonel Alexander wrote urging General George "to dispatch to this Wing by the most rapid means up to 308 complete aircraft crews to keep your transports in the air." At the same time he begged one of his intimate friends in ATC headquarters: "Get me some aircraft crews if it is humanly possible. I *hate* to see good, serviceable aircraft sitting on the ground with no one to fly them. An airplane doesn't need to *sleep*."[32]

During the winter months of 1942–43 the India-China Wing operated its China-bound transports from three neighboring fields in Upper Assam—Chabua, Sookerating, and Mohanbari. With the coming of heavy rains in March, it was necessary to discontinue the use of Sookerating and Mohanbari, where neither runways, taxiways, nor hardstandings could sustain operations. Only Chabua was left as a base for the ATC operation, and for Col. Eugene H. Beebe's 308th Bomber Group, whose B-24's began in March 1943 to fly into China the aviation fuel and other supplies required for their bomber missions against Japanese targets. Dinjan, used by the India-China Ferry Command during the 1942 monsoon season, was now occupied by CNAC and by the 51st Fighter Group. By mid-April a new field at Jorhat, 87

* See Vol. IV, 437–39.

miles southwest of Chabua, was sufficiently ready to accommodate a squadron of twenty-five C-47's. The failure of the British engineers to complete the airdromes at Sookerating and Mohanbari, in spite of reminders by Bissell and Stilwell, seemed to threaten the entire mission of the India-China Wing. Alexander went so far as to suggest in a letter to General Arnold that "in view of the potential political repercussions which may result from non-delivery of promised supplies to China and possible annoyance and embarrassment to you," representations be made "to Mr. Churchill, if necessary, to build a fire under General Wavell and get some action on Air Transport Command airdromes in Assam."[33]

Given all the handicaps which existed, it is perhaps not surprising that the Hump lift fell far short of even the 4,000-ton objective during the first eight months of ATC control. There was, to be sure, a substantial though fluctuating increase in the gross tonnage* hauled to China by ATC planes, as is indicated by the following table:[34]

December 1942	1,227	April 1943	1,910
January 1943	1,263	May 1943	2,334
February 1943	2,855	June 1943	2,382
March 1943	2,278	July 1943	3,451

Meanwhile ATC headquarters and General Arnold had increased the wing's potential by substituting C-46's for the smaller DC-3 aircraft which had thus far carried most of the Hump lift. Colonel Alexander on 20 January 1943 had reported that the DC-3's inability to attain sufficient altitude rendered it "entirely unsuitable for operations on this route." He wanted either C-46 or C-87 aircraft. Earlier, ATC headquarters had planned to send the wing a total of fifty C-46's during 1943, and this program was now pushed aggressively. On 4 March Arnold wrote directly to Alexander the cheering news that the first C-46's were to start at once for India to replace an equal number of C-47's. Thirty were to move out by 15 April, then ten more each month until the total of fifty was attained. Beginning 15 June, ten C-87's were to be sent out each month until fifty of these craft, too, were in service. Thereafter, twenty-four C-54's would be dispatched.[35]

As usual, actual deliveries were behind schedule. Still the first thirty

* Net tonnage, March to July, ranged from 383 to 651 tons a month lower than gross; the difference was the weight of fuel required for return trips China to India. From November 1943 all Hump tonnage figures mentioned are net.

C-46's, carrying some 250 men—pilots, co-pilots, radio operators, navigators, maintenance personnel, and representatives of the manufacturer—left Florida in three flights on the 5th, 10th, and 14th of April. The thirty planes were piloted by experienced pilots, most of whom were borrowed from Northwest Airlines and TWA. The first of the Commandos reached Karachi on 21 April 1943 and with their pilots were speedily sent to Gaya to inaugurate the transition training of the Army pilots and co-pilots who were to fly the new craft over the Hump. For ten days school kept, but before May was far along the C-46's, based initially at Jorhat, began to fly the Hump.[36] And here, on the most difficult of ATC's runs, the plane's faults soon became all too evident.* It was an India-China Wing mechanic who took his first look at the mechanism of the new arrival and turned away remarking, "Boy! A regular plumber's nightmare!" Nicknamed "Dumbo," counted by its pilots as a menace equal to the Hump terrain and weather, and requiring hundreds of time-consuming modifications, the C-46 had but one decided advantage. When the plane got through to China, as often it did, its large cargo compartment carried four tons of gasoline or other supplies.[37]

The 10,000-Ton Objective

Needless to say, neither Brig. Gen. Claire L. Chennault, whose China Air Task Force became the Fourteenth Air Force in March 1943, nor the Generalissimo was satisfied with the flow of cargo to China. Operating always on a minimum of supplies, Chennault found himself so short of aviation fuel and other essential materiel in March and the first third of April 1943 that he was obliged to suspend all combat operations for a time. Meanwhile, in February, Madame Chiang had addressed Congress and pleaded with President Roosevelt for a more vigorous effort to deliver supplies to China. In April, Stilwell and Chennault were summoned to Washington to present to the Combined Chiefs of Staff their conflicting programs for the war in China and Burma.† Colonel Alexander followed Chennault to Washington. As he wrote General George, "Anything that happens to General Chennault or the Fourteenth Air Force is of tremendous importance to you and to myself since ATC moves everything to China that General Chennault uses except combat aircraft."[38]

* See above, pp. 24–25.
† See Vol. IV, 442–43.

PRODUCTION-LINE MAINTENANCE, TEZGAON, INDIA

ATC ON THE RAMP

REFUELING, CHINA BASE

By Native Labor

LOADING C-46'S IN INDIA

By ATC GI's

TAKE-OFF FROM ASSAM

THE HUMP ROUTE

NEARING KUNMING

TRANSPORTATION IN CHINA

In May, during the TRIDENT conference, Stilwell and Chennault presented their decidedly divergent plans for future operations in the CBI. Neither of them gained a complete indorsement from the CCS, but that made little difference to ATC, for both plans required a notable augmentation of the airlift into China. Moreover, President Roosevelt already had promised Madame Chiang an increase in deliveries. The President ordered ATC to raise its Hump airlift to at least 7,000 tons in July, 10,000 tons in September, and the same tonnage in each month thereafter. Of these totals, the Fourteenth Air Force was given first priority on 4,700 tons a month for the initial phase of a projected air offensive, while Stilwell received second priority on 2,000 tons a month, to be used in equipping Chinese armies in Yunnan for a campaign along the Salween River. Any tonnage in excess of 6,700 a month was to be split between air and ground forces at General Stilwell's discretion.[39]

There followed eight days of conferences between Colonel Alexander and officers of ATC headquarters, CCS subcommittees, and various divisions of the War Department and the Air Staff. As the first fruit of these consultations, General Marshall on 22 May directed Maj. Gen. Raymond A. Wheeler, Commanding General, SOS in the CBI theater, to complete by 1 July the airdromes at Chabua, Mohanbari, Sookerating, and Jorhat, with a minimum of twenty hardstandings and essential taxiways at each. By 1 September three additional airdromes in Assam were to be available; all seven were to have 6,000-foot paved runways, forty hardstandings each, and the appropriate taxiways. On 23 May Colonel Alexander and the ATC headquarters staff completed a detailed estimate of the requirements for meeting the July and September objectives. Supplementary planning occupied the succeeding days and nights, and on 28 May OPD issued an order directing General Arnold to carry out the basic and supplementary plans. On 1 June the essential directives were issued. Exactly thirty days remained before the beginning of the target month.[40]

The plan called for completion of scheduled airdrome construction, for delivery to India of a large number of C-46's and some 14 C-87's, and for the assignment of additional aircrews. More aircraft mechanics and other service personnel would be needed, both in the India-China Wing and in X Air Service Command, which was responsible for third- and fourth-echelon maintenance of Alexander's transports. A steady flow of spare parts, maintenance and servicing equipment, and motor vehicles must be kept moving out to India. New groups and squadrons needed to be established. British co-operation was required, not only for the completion of airports and housing facilities, but also to insure the prompt movement by rail or barge to the Assam bases of Hump cargoes, of fuel for the Hump aircraft, and of the equipment and materials required by the British engineers in the work of airdrome construction. The portion of the task which was made primarily the responsibility of the Air Transport Command generally, as distinct from that of the India-China Wing, was known as Project 7. It involved the movement by air from Florida to India of personnel, aircraft, and materiel.[41]

The airplanes and the men who were designated for air movement to India were quickly assembled in Florida, and the great majority moved out before the end of June. By the middle of July a total of 1,961 men had departed by air, 442 on ferried aircraft and 1,519 on regular ATC runs across the South Atlantic; over 118 tons of cargo had been shipped by air; all fourteen C-87's, one C-54A, and thirty-two C-46's had departed the United States, and all but two of the aircraft had cleared Accra on the eastward flight. There were difficulties en route, particularly in the Africa–Middle East Wing, but the movement, ATC's largest to date, was eminently successful.[42]

Still larger numbers of specialized personnel were shipped to India by waterborne transport. Yet by July the men, planes, and facilities which ATC had considered essential to meeting the month's 7,000-ton objective were not yet available to Alexander, who had been promoted to brigadier general on 27 June. Early in July, he forecast a total Hump lift of only 5,100 tons for that month, and on the 11th he revised his estimate downward to 3,200 tons. In the end the actual lift for the month was 3,451 gross tons, the best record to date, but less than half of the announced objective. General Chennault sent a message of congratulations expressing appreciation for "the excellent tonnage carried to China during July." Quite different was the reaction of Arnold, who in conversation with George and in a message to Alexander pointedly expressed his dissatisfaction.[43]

Reasons for the failure were not hard to find. When July began, only two of the four airfields which were to have been completed had paved runways of the required length; in all there were forty-nine usable hardstandings instead of the eighty called for. Hardly a third of the personnel included in Project 7 had reached India, and their qualifications for service there left much to be desired. ATC had been assured that the pilots transferred from the Training Command for the project would be two-engine pilots, the "cream of their classes." As a group, to be sure, they had a high average flying time, but most of those who arrived before 1 July had served as flight instructors on single-engine aircraft and had never flown a multimotored plane. The few two-engine pilots were far from ready to handle the new, complex, and heavy C-46. An attempt to check some of them out at fields in Assam was discontinued because of a sharp increase in the ground-loop accident rate. Alexander had to establish a transition training school near Karachi, with sixteen instructor pilots and eight to ten C-46 aircraft, all badly needed on the Hump, in order to qualify the newly arrived pilots for their mission. Sandstorms soon forced removal of the training program to Gaya, where it was shortly interrupted by torrential storms. Refueling units and vehicles required to transport aircrews from their quarters to their landing strips had begun to reach Calcutta, but they were still six or seven weeks away from the points where they were needed in Assam. Spare parts for C-46 aircraft were extremely scarce. Some twenty-six of the C-46's were already out of commission, many for lack of spare engines and other parts. Maintenance personnel, still too few, were so inexperienced that the wing engineering officer and his single assistant were obliged to make frequent trips to the operating squadrons "in order personally to perform maintenance work." Even the best of maintenance men worked under terrible handicaps. Their work had to be done largely at night; Alexander reported: "Except on rainy days maintenance work cannot be accomplished because shade temperatures of from 100° to 130° Fahrenheit render all metal exposed to the sun so hot that it cannot be touched by the human hand without causing second degree burns." Meanwhile X Air Service Command, taxed to capacity, could not keep up with the demand for third- and fourth-echelon maintenance and repairs. Finally, a flooding of the field at Kunming, the only important Chinese terminus of the route, caused serious damage to several transports and slowed up the turn-about time.[44]

In spite of the monsoon, the British engineers and their native workmen continued construction on the hard-surfaced facilities at the Assam air bases. As the training program for newly arrived pilots began to bear fruit, the gross tonnage hauled over the Hump crept up gradually. From August through November the lift was augmented by the services of Project 7-A, a contingent of twenty-five flight crews, supported by thirty-four maintenance and operations men, all civilians supplied by American Airlines. These experienced flight crews were handicapped by the same difficulties as the men assigned directly to the India-China Wing, but during the four months of their service in the theater they delivered approximately 2,100 tons of cargo to China. Operating from Tezpur, a newly opened ATC field seventy-one miles west of Jorhat, the airline pilots had from seven to ten C-87's available for their work.[45]

In August the total Hump tonnage, including that carried by the civilian crews, was a thousand tons greater than in July. The July goal of 7,000 tons was finally reached and passed, three months later, in October. In December all records were broken. By the 18th of the month the November record had been equaled; on the 26th the 10,000-ton objective was reached; and by the end of the month the India-China Wing reported 12,590 (net) tons delivered to China bases.[46] One can well understand the rejoicing with which Washington greeted these glad tidings from India, for General George could now relax in the confidence that General Arnold was in a position to convey to the White House news it had long insisted upon receiving.

The problem of airport construction at the Assam fields seemed to have been licked, though heavy traffic made for constant repairs. There was still urgent need for aircraft and for the wherewithal to keep them in service. The rate of attrition on C-87 and especially C-46 aircraft was very high; yet the fleet had continued to grow in size until a figure of 229 major transports assigned to the wing was reached in October 1943. November saw a drop to 207, while the delivery of C-46's was stopped to permit modifications which ATC considered essential. For over two months no additional C-46's arrived in India. The gap was filled in part by delivering more C-87 aircraft and by borrowing 25 B-24D's, retired combat aircraft, from the theater. The number of transports actually available for operations in December was materially larger, because of the arrival of large numbers of new, modified C-46's and C-87's from the United States, and of spare parts which made it possible to put back into service aircraft long idle for lack of them. For the first time the India-China Wing had a large fleet in actual operation.[47]

Meanwhile the wing had received important gains in personnel. As against a total assigned strength of 2,759 men in June, it could muster in December a total of 10,851. Even though the incoming officers, as a whole, were young and inexperienced, and the enlisted men inexperienced and in many cases malassigned, the reinforcements helped.[48]

Early in September General George inspected the India-China Wing. Accompanying him on his visit was Col. Thomas O. Hardin, commanding officer of ATC's Central African Sector, a hard-driving airlines executive of great and varied experience. On 16 September Colonel Hardin was transferred to the India-China Wing and given direct charge of the Hump operation as commanding officer of the newly created Assam-China Sector (shortly renamed the Eastern Sector) of the wing. Hardin proved to be still a hard driver. In October and November he gradually introduced a policy of night flying, though night radio communication and radio navigational facilities were decidedly inferior to those available by day and though field-lighting equipment was poor. Brig. Gen. C. R. Smith reported from the field in December:

> Hardin is steaming like an old fire engine. . . . I have never seen a man work harder. . . . He usually works in the office in the morning and spends the afternoon going from one field to another. He has probably broken by now most of the Air Force rules about operations. . . . If Tech orders were now enforced here, I doubt that there would be an airplane in the air.[49]

During his September inspection of the India-China Wing, General George concluded that nothing was more essential to the expansion of the lift than an adequate flow of airplane parts and engine accessories. A paraphrase of one of his messages puts it clearly enough: "In this Wing condition of spares for all type transport airplanes similar to gentleman who has several sets of evening clothes, shoes and top hat but has no collar or tie. In such case his evening outfit is useless."[50] He directed his Washington headquarters to set up a weekly flight to carry the parts most in demand, direct from the Air Service Command depot at Fairfield, Ohio, to India.

This was the beginning of the much publicized FIREBALL run. The C-87's assigned to the operation were flown at first by ATC's special mission organization, the 26th Transport Group. The first of the "hot-shot" ships took off on 11 September for Agra, location of the CBI Air Service Command's depot. Early in November the job, together with four C-87's with which to do it, was turned over to the Ferrying Division. The aircraft were based at Miami, and, to speed their passage, crews were staged at key points along the Southeastern route. It was the intention stateside that the flights should extend to Chabua, but by 2 December no FIREBALL trips had arrived at that base. Cargoes had been unloaded at Agra and disposed of by the Air Service Command there. However, the cargoes carried on the FIRE-BALL ships added to the number of aircraft available for service over the Hump. Further help came in December when new C-46's arrived loaded with C-46 spare parts.[51]

Still another factor which aided in the hauling of more than 12,000 tons of cargo into China in December was the utilization by the India-China Wing of aircraft sent out to carry the materiel for constructing a gasoline pipeline from Assam to China. In August General Arnold had agreed to provide the air transportation required. On his orders ATC hurriedly set up Project 8 for the mission and provided 16 C-47 and 40 C-46 aircraft, with the necessary flight and ground personnel. By the first of November the C-47's, as well as 155 of the project's officers and 779 of its enlisted men, had reached India and were assigned to a newly opened ATC base at Misamari. The C-46's delayed by the modification program began to appear in December. Meanwhile, since no pipe had yet arrived, Colonel Hardin put the C-47's to work flying the Hump to Yunnanyi laden with aviation gasoline and bombs. In December the Project 8 planes based at Misamari hauled 8.2 per cent of the total eastbound Hump tonnage. The theater command apparently lost interest in the pipeline, and Project 8 itself for all practical purposes was merged into normal Hump operations. When, subsequently, ATC planes carried pipeline materials into China, the haul was thought of as merely a part of the regular tonnage allocation for the Hump lift.[52]

General George's September visit to the India-China and Africa–Middle East Wings led to a shake-up in the command of the ATC wings. General Alexander was brought home to take command of the Caribbean Wing. Brig. Gen. Earl S. Hoag, who had commanded the Africa–Middle East Wing for barely a hundred days, moved out to India to take Alexander's place. Brig. Gen. Vincent J. Meloy, formerly in command of the Caribbean Wing, took over the Africa–Middle East Wing and, later, the new North African Wing. Maj. Gen. George E. Stratemeyer had recently been sent out as Commanding General of Army Air Forces, India-Burma Sector, of the CBI theater.* With Stilwell's concurrence, Stratemeyer and George defined

* See Vol. IV, 449–55.

the relationship between the India-China Wing and Stratemeyer's command. They agreed, among other things, on the removal of wing headquarters to New Delhi, for greater ease in consultation and co-ordination, and designated the commanding general of the wing Assistant Chief of Air Staff for Air Transport to Stratemeyer.[53]

There were disadvantages in such a move. Some officers in ATC headquarters feared that Hoag's staff and that of Stratemeyer would become too closely linked to allow conformance with Air Transport Command doctrine. This did not happen. More serious was the fact that New Delhi, 1,252 miles from Chabua, was for communications purposes practically as distant as Washington from the Hump operation. General Hoag, who felt tied to his desk by the lack of a qualified executive, thus did not enjoy close personal contact with actual operations. On the other hand, he was vigorous in his endeavors to secure for his men in the field the materiel which they required to do the job. By personal contact with AAF, Air Service Command, and theater officers at New Delhi, he was often able to settle in a few minutes' conversation matters which might have hung fire for days or weeks had he been stationed, like his predecessor, "on the line" in Assam.[54]

As weekly reports from the Hump indicated that the December record would exceed all commitments, enthusiasm mounted. On 27 December Stratemeyer recommended that the wing be cited in War Department general orders. The next day the President himself directed the citation of the wing and sent his personal thanks to every officer and man concerned. Colonel Hardin, who received chief credit from General George, was ordered back to the United States for a month's leave and was quickly promoted to brigadier general. At the Pentagon, on 29 January, he accepted the presidential citation, formally presented to him as representative of the wing by General Arnold.[55]

General Chennault, writing to General Hoag, noted some of the accomplishments of the Fourteenth Air Force during December, "using the gasoline, ammunition, bombs, and other supplies which the India-China Wing of the ATC has delivered to us." He concluded his detailed report of combat activities by saying, "I am particularly anxious that your pilots and crews know that only through their efforts can we accomplish these important missions."[56]

The operations of the India-China Wing took a grave toll of men and aircraft. Between June and December 1943 there were 155 major aircraft accidents in the wing, 135 on the Hump route. Crew fatalities totaled 168. The introduction of twenty-four-hour-a-day flying in October helped push the monthly total for November up to 38 major accidents on the Hump; in the record month of December, however, the number dropped to 28. In spite of regrets over the many casualties, ATC headquarters at Washington, New Delhi, and Chabua, felt obliged to push the job, as General Smith put it, "for all it is worth." He continued:

> We are paying for it in men and airplanes. The kids here are flying over their head—at night and in daytime and they bust them up for reasons that sometimes seem silly. They are not silly, however, for we are asking boys to do what would be most difficult for men to accomplish; with the experience level here we are going to pay dearly for the tonnage moved across the Hump. . . . With the men available, there is nothing else to do.[57]

In the hope of reducing the accident rate by improving the technical skill of the young pilots flying the route, wing headquarters sent out a series of earnest appeals to ATC for check pilots competent to conduct a program for upgrading flight personnel. The first of these reached the theater by the end of the year.[58] At the same time the wing was developing an aggressive search and rescue program intended to save the men who crashed or bailed out over mountain or jungle. The early search missions had been impromptu affairs. When a plane crashed, was abandoned, or was reported missing, the first available crew and plane that could be spared were assigned to the search. At Chabua there gradually developed a more specialized search and rescue organization, under the leadership of Capt. John L. ("Blackie") Porter. His men became known as "Blackie's Gang." Theirs was a difficult tree-skimming mission. In July 1943 they were assigned two C-47's. One of their first rescue attempts involved the crew and the passengers (twenty men in all, including Eric Sevareid, CBS commentator) who had abandoned a disabled C-46 on 2 August over the much-feared Naga country in northern Burma. Needed supplies were dropped, and Lt. Col. Don Flickinger, Wing Flight Surgeon, and two medical aides parachuted to the assistance of the survivors. A rescue party walked in, and the mission was a complete success. Late in October wing headquarters established a special search and rescue unit at Chabua with Captain Porter in command, under the control of the operations division of the Eastern Sector. After a very successful series of rescues, Porter was killed on 10 December 1943 when his B-25 and another rescue plane were lost to enemy action. The rescue craft thus destroyed were replaced, however, and the work went on.[59]

A New Program of Expansion, 1944

The success of the wing in exceeding the 10,000-ton objective naturally led responsible leaders in the field to fear that they would be asked to increase their commitments. Generals Hoag, Smith, and Stratemeyer all warned General George and General Arnold against agreeing to such requests. Arnold personally warned President Roosevelt that he must not expect the December tonnage to be maintained month by month. General Hoag held that the saturation point of the route as then constituted lay somewhere between 12,000 and 15,000 tons. Early in January 1944, he sent Admiral Mountbatten's headquarters an estimate of Hump tonnage, by month, for the year. He envisioned a drop to 10,000 tons in August, during the worst of the monsoon period, and predicted that peaks of 15,000 and 16,000 tons, respectively, might be reached in the following November and December. Substantial increases in tonnage beyond these estimates would require a protected route over Myitkyina, as well as more freight terminal fields in China, in addition to Kunming and Chengkung, where instrument letdowns could be accomplished in bad weather. He would need, too, increases in personnel and assigned aircraft, nine airfields in Assam, and sufficient supplies, fuel, and equipment.[60]

Earlier experience with supposedly reasonable commitments may have made Hoag and his superiors conservative. For the first six months of 1944, indeed, his estimates proved pretty accurate, being overly generous by about 4,000 tons. For the second half of the year, however, his advance figures were grossly in error. Instead of the 77,000 tons he predicted, deliveries to China between 1 July and 31 December were more than twice as great. For individual months the difference between actual accomplishment and his estimate was startling: for July, 19,050 against 12,000; August, 23,675 against 10,000; December, 31,935 against 16,000.[61]

The discrepancy, however, is more imaginary than real. Hoag thought of his estimates as little more than an "educated guess," subject to change on the basis of changing conditions. He could not have foreseen these in their broad pattern—the June decision of the CCS to step up the war against Japan or the sharp increase in aircraft production which would give him more than twice as many transports and more than five times as many four-engine planes in December as he had in January. Nor could he have expected, on previous experience, the relatively lavish provision for personnel and airport construction that came.[62]

The tactical situation influenced the India-China operation in a variety of ways. In February of 1944 the Japanese launched a northward drive in the Arakan Sector. The Indian 7 Division, which received this attack, soon required the air delivery of supplies. British and American troop-carrier planes undertook the task. When they were withdrawn for overhaul, ATC transports, with five British soldiers to the plane serving as pushers, dropped some 446 tons of food, ammunition, and medical supplies. A more potent threat to the India-China operation was felt in March when the Japanese moved northward across the Assam border in the area surrounding Imphal. Their advanced elements came at one time within thirty miles of the Assam-Bengal railroad, key artery for the movement of Hump cargo and fuel to the Assam bases of ATC. Aircraft of the India-China Wing helped move British Indian troops from Arakan to meet the new thrust. Brig. Gen. Thomas O. Hardin, who succeeded to the command of the wing* on 15 March 1944, feared for a time that the Japanese might succeed in cutting off the flow of supplies to the Assam airports. During April some twenty of his C-46's were employed in direct support of the Allied defense of the region. They delivered over 2,100 tons of fuel, ammunition, and other supplies to Allied troops there, with a loss which Hardin estimated at not less than 1,200 tons of Hump tonnage. But the enemy did not succeed in cutting the rail connection supporting the Hump operation.[63]

Late in April General Stilwell started his two-pronged offensive, pushing southward across the ranges from Ledo toward Myitkyina and westward from Yunnan across the Salween. In immediate preparation for this offensive the India-China Wing, at Stilwell's request, flew approximately 18,000 Chinese troops from Yunnan to Sookerating, whence ground transport and troop-carrier aircraft moved them into position in North Burma. Although these troops were carried as reverse Hump tonnage, their transportation reduced the eastbound lift, since planes returning from Kunming had to be diverted to Yunnanyi to pick up their human cargoes. Offloading them at Sookerating delayed transports based elsewhere in Assam. Hardin felt that the move-

* General Hoag was assigned to take command of ATC's European Wing.

ment reduced Hump tonnage by at least 1,500 tons. While the tendency in ATC headquarters and elsewhere was to measure the achievement of the India-China Wing in terms of Hump tonnage, it is fair to notice that a large portion of that tonnage since the autumn of 1943 had been devoted to building up General Stilwell's YOKE force in Yunnan for this offensive. The transportation of ammunition, motor fuel, and other supplies to an army preparing to take the offensive can hardly be counted a more significant contribution to military success than the movement of troops into position, even if the movement be in a reverse direction and hence not applicable to the eastbound figure which had become almost a fetish.[64]

The India-China Wing was presently called upon for still another chore for Stilwell's campaign. On 17 May 1944 his troops captured the airstrip near Myitkyina, though the city itself did not capitulate until 3 August. Meanwhile in late May and early June, Hardin's planes flew some 2,500 combat troops, including 250 airborne engineers, from southern India via Assam to the Myitkyina area. Not only men and unit equipment but also such cumbersome items as bulldozers, tractors, graders, and rollers were included in the movement. Called the GALAHAD diversion, this whole movement had a direct bearing upon the India-China Wing's primary mission. By helping to clear the Myitkyina area of the enemy and to build airdromes there, it made possible the ultimate use of a direct air route from Calcutta to China. Even more immediately it enabled planes on the Assam-China run to take a more southerly, lower altitude course over the Hump. Chennault criticized the expenditure of air supply upon Stilwell's campaign to recover Burma; Hoag and Hardin, and ATC leaders generally, felt quite otherwise about it.[65]

Meanwhile the largest Japanese forces yet employed in China had launched a series of campaigns which won for them a corridor connecting their holdings in Manchuria and North China with French Indo-China. Driving southward from the Yellow River, south and southwest from Hankow, and west up the Hungshui River from Canton, they seized control of the chief railroad lines of eastern and southern China, and one by one overran the major bases of the Fourteenth Air Force in that area. On 4 September they captured the airfield at Lingling. On 11 November they took the important air base of Kweilin and then in quick succession the fields at Liuchow and Nanning. With Chinese resistance crumbling, it looked as if the Japanese might take Chungking and Kunming. Although the Chinese defense forces and the coming of winter finally checked the drive in that direction, eastern China had been isolated, and the political prestige of the Chinese central government had received a disastrous blow.[66]

Since the function of ATC in the theater was to carry "Aid to China," its very reason for existence was threatened. The new emergencies intensified the urgency of delivering maximum cargoes, especially to the Fourteenth Air Force. At the same time the India-China Division* was called upon for a series of special missions in aid to China. Thus on 4–5 July, at the request of Chennault, ICD aircraft flew in a quantity of 75-mm. howitzers, ammunition, and other equipment and evacuated some 150 persons and 61 tons of freight from the Kweilin area. Between 1 July and 30 September, ATC delivered a total of more than 300 tons of ammunition and equipment at Kweilin for the Chinese forces defending the city. Early in November, when the fall of Liuchow was imminent, division aircraft, in a total of forty-four trips, evacuated 298 passengers and a weight of passengers and cargo amounting in all to 138 tons. To counter the Japanese advance in December, over 18,000 troops of the Fifty-seventh Chinese Army were moved from Hsian on the Yellow River to Chanyi. At the same time the worsening tactical situation led to the return by air from Burma to China of the 14th and 22d Chinese Divisions and other units of the Sixth Chinese Army. The Tenth Air Force was in control of this operation, and the India-China Division did little more than supply planes and personnel. Still the C-46's of the ATC transported over 14,000 troops out of a total of 25,354 men carried.[67] If these and other special missions had the effect of reducing the weight of cargo which might have been delivered to the Fourteenth Air Force and other consignees in China, they bore with equal relevance upon the basic mission of the entire India-China transport operation.

The deployment of the B-29 units of the XX Bomber Command to China,† beginning with the first flights from the United States on 26 March 1944 gave the India-China Wing a new customer and increased the pressure on the wing's Hump potential. As early as February the wing was given an allocation of 1,650 tons firm, and 2,275 tons possible, to be delivered that month for XX Bomber Command (MATTERHORN project), though a failure on the part of the shipping

---

* All ATC Wings were raised to Division status, 1 July 1944.

† See Vol. V, 52, 78–79.

organizations to have the cargo available in Assam kept actual deliveries down to 381 tons. In March, however, ATC aircraft hauled some 3,602 tons, roughly three-eighths of the Hump tonnage for the month, to stock the new command's bases in the vicinity of Chengtu with aviation gas and other supplies.* At that time ATC had twenty C-87's devoted directly to the MATTERHORN haul which had been provided by XX Bomber Command. The cargo capacity allocated by the theater for the delivery of supplies to XX Bomber Command, and the quantities delivered thereon, varied greatly from month to month, but by the end of the year nearly 30,000 tons, according to ATC figures, had been hauled to XX Bomber Command units, and another 4,573 tons to the 312th Fighter Wing, a Fourteenth Air Force organization assigned to defend the four large B-29 bases in China. A very large portion of the total, over 13,000 tons, was delivered under great pressure in October and November in connection with missions against Formosa.[68]

Long before that, mounting demands had compelled AAF and ATC headquarters to face the problem of further augmenting the Hump lift. As early as March 1944 three key officers of ATC headquarters, the Chief of Staff, Brig. Gen. Bob E. Nowland, and his Assistant Chiefs of Staff for Operations and for Priorities and Traffic, Cols. Harold R. Harris and Ray W. Ireland, on returning from inspection of the India-China Wing, reported that the ATC would have to increase its Hump commitments or some other agency would move in. "The pressure for additional supplies in China," they wrote, "is actually only just beginning and we must constructively plan to expand faster than we have been called upon to undertake to date or else fall behind the war procession in the near future."[69]

Both the theater and the India-Burma Sector, AAF, were increasingly eager to see the Hump lift expanded. In June General Stratemeyer appointed a board of officers, headed by Brig. Gen. William D. Old, to study what action might be taken by the several agencies in the CBI. The board made various specific suggestions to the India-China Wing and to various theater agencies and arrived at the rather obvious conclusions that substantial gains could be made by more efficient use of existing resources and by adding to those resources. The first conclusion was substantiated by the India-China Wing in June

* For variant figures on this operation and an explanation of the lack of agreement among the several authorities, see Vol. V, 81–90.

when it delivered a record 15,845 tons of cargo to China. The truth of the second was demonstrated by the achievements of the next six months.[70]

While General Old's board was at work, Brig. Gen. William H. Tunner, Commanding General of ATC's Ferrying Division, and Col. James H. Douglas, Jr., ATC Deputy Chief of Staff, were also studying the problem on the ground. They reported that the China-bound capacity of the route could be built up to 20,500 tons in October, 27,500 in November, and 31,000 in December if certain specified conditions were met. First, the theater was to make available three suitable airfields in eastern Bengal, one each by 15 August, 15 September, and 15 October. The AAF should provide at least fifteen hundred experienced mechanics for shipment overseas before 1 September. Transport aircraft already allocated to ATC must be delivered on schedule. By 1 October the CBI should provide service and repair units capable of furnishing both supply and third- and fourth-echelon maintenance for the enlarged fleet. Finally, landing facilities and gasoline were to be made available in the Myitkyina area.[71]

The augmentation plan, accepted by General George and submitted to General Arnold on 3 July 1944, was quickly approved by the War Department. Although all its conditions were not met on time, the actual record of deliveries over the Hump far exceeded the planned accomplishment, month by month, as indicated in the following table:[72]

1944	Proposed Deliveries in Tons	Actual Deliveries in Tons
August	13,000	23,675
September	14,000	22,314
October	20,500	24,715
November	27,500	34,914
December	31,000	31,935

The average number of aircraft actually in commission on the Hump operation in June was 108.4; in December, 249.6. Aircraft trips to China increased from 3,702 in June to 7,612 in December. This increase in traffic called for more airfields. In China a major improvement was the relief of congestion at Kunming, where much gasoline and time was wasted in bad weather by planes stacked up over the airport, awaiting their turn to let down through the overcast. The opening of Luliang to extensive ATC traffic in August gave Hump aircraft a second all-weather alternate (Chanyi was the first) to Kunming and helped to break this particular bottleneck, even in face of heavier traffic. Increased "long-haul" deliveries to XX Bomber Command airdromes in the Chengtu area increased the total weight of deliveries without putting pressure on the short-range bases near Kunming. Although the largest amount of cargo continued to be dispatched from the six established fields in Assam, the last two months of the year saw the serious beginning of operations across the Hump, with C-54's and C-109's (Liberator-type tankers) from Kurmitola-Tezgaon, newly acquired ATC base in East Bengal. Meanwhile, between July and December, the number of men available in the India-China Division to handle the increased workload more than doubled.[73]

With its greater resources, ATC was able to aid XX Bomber Command while increasing its deliveries to Chennault's heavily reinforced command from 7,439 tons in January, and only 4,988 in March, to 12,448 tons in June, 16,985 in November, and 14,688 in December.[74]

In April 1944, with the establishment of the Allied Air Forces, India-Burma Sector of the CBI, General Stratemeyer's and General Hardin's headquarters, together with those of the CBI Air Service Command, the Eastern Air Command, and the sector's communications, weather, and statistical organizations, were moved from New Delhi to the Calcutta area. There the combined headquarters were located in the buildings of a large jute mill (Hastings Mill) some sixteen miles north of the city. While the discomforts of the new location were numerous, it was only half as far as New Delhi from the Assam bases; with the development of a direct lift from East Bengal to China, the advantages of the new location would become still more obvious.[75] Early in September General Hardin, with well over two years of arduous foreign service to his credit, was recalled to the United States. His successor in the India-China Division was Brig. Gen. William H. Tunner, of ATC's Ferrying Division, who brought with him several key officers from his old staff. What the men surrounding him came to call the "age of big business" in the India-China Division (ICD) was already under way. These men, who brought into practice some of the techniques of large business enterprise, built upon the foundation laid by General Alexander and more particularly General Hardin. The latter had forced Hump deliveries up from 4,624 tons in September 1943 to 23,675 in August 1944.

As a parting tribute the men of the division on 22 August celebrated "Tom Hardin Day," when they delivered 1,300 tons of cargo "over the Rockpile."[76]

Big Business in the Air, 1945

Only the war's end halted the process of augmenting the airlift of the India-China Division. As tonnage increased, there was less and less talk about any figure to be regarded as the maximum possible achievement. General Tunner and his staff acted upon the thesis that virtually any amount could be delivered if only the requisite facilities and men were provided. Under constant pressure for more Hump lift, they continued to press for additional airfields, especially in China and West Bengal, and for improved navigational facilities. At the same time, in a continuing drive for "production," Tunner insisted upon increased efficiency and upon a fuller exploitation of the existing facilities.

Emphasis was directed at aircraft utilization and then by a logical step at aircraft maintenance, long a sore spot in India-China operations. In July 1944 a technical inspector had recommended the establishment of production line maintenance (PLM) at the Assam stations. Such a procedure, already in use in stateside Training Command bases, called for towing the aircraft through a succession of stations, at each of which a fresh group of maintenance men performed specific maintenance operations in which they were presumably specially skilled. General Tunner adopted the idea, and a program of hangar and apron construction to make it feasible was launched. In December Lt. Col. Robert B. White, Division Aircraft Maintenance Officer, wrote the several base commanders, pointing out the advantages of such a system; he anticipated some resistance on the part of engineering officers and attempted to combat their skepticism by stressing the efficiency of the new system.[77]

In an effort to get PLM started, Division headquarters exerted on the bases a degree of pressure which to some extent defeated its purpose. Some of the lines were organized too hastily, as at Jorhat, where the new system was inaugurated on 16 February 1945. Inadequate hangar and parking facilities hampered the program at some stations, lack of necessary equipment at others. Some base commanders and maintenance officers were halfhearted in their attitude toward the new methods, partly in fear of at least a temporary loss of efficiency and thus of Hump tonnage. Many pilots were distrustful of the quality of PLM maintenance and strongly preferred the old way of doing things, in which each airplane was the direct responsibility of a given crew. Slumps after good starts occurred at some bases. Nevertheless, General Tunner reported PLM an over-all success, largely responsible for the rise in the average percentage of assigned aircraft in operation from 78 per cent in January to 85 per cent in July. He reported a 25 per cent reduction in the time required for 100-hour inspections, while the quality of the inspections had improved. He gave PLM the major credit for the steady increase in daily utilization of C-54 aircraft at Tezgaon from an average of 7.51 hours in April to 11.65 hours in July.[78]

The transition to PLM had been made possible by a standard practice of assigning only one type of transport to a given base. By March 1945 each of four Assam bases (Chabua, Sookerating, Mohanbari, and Misamari) had at least 48 C-46's; three (Tezpur, Jorhat, and Shamshernagar) had at least 30 C-87's and/or C-109's; while Tezgaon had an average for the month of 39.3 assigned C-54's. The total number of aircraft available for the Hump operation increased substantially at the beginning of 1945, but thereafter it remained practically constant. The average number in commission for the Hump service in December 1944 was 249.6; in January 1945, 287.4; in February, 336.8; in April, 325.9; in July, 332. Personnel assigned to the Hump bases, likewise, increased only moderately after the first of 1945. From a total of 17,032 military personnel in December, the Hump bases in India jumped to 19,025 in January and reached a peak of 22,359 in April. Thereafter there was a slight decline. In China, where the need for economy of American manpower was extreme, and where ATC did not gain full control of any bases until 1 July 1945, the numbers of military personnel assigned rose from 2,530 in December to 5,959 in August. In addition to military personnel, the India-China Division employed some 47,009 civilians, mostly in manual labor duties such as loading and unloading aircraft.[79]

The most striking increase in eastbound tonnage carried over the Hump came in January, when 44,098 net tons were delivered as against 31,935 tons in December. The increased tonnage of January owed much to the Allied victory in Burma. The use of the Assam bases and of the high Hump routes had been at best a desperate matter of expedience, dictated by the presence of the Japanese forces in

Burma. Now it was most natural to fly increasing amounts of cargo directly from Bengal to China. Even the planes based in Assam could fly farther south and at lower altitudes than in the previous years. And the availability of a relatively low-level route made it feasible, at last, to bring into service the C-54 aircraft whose limited ceiling had made them useless for the excessive altitudes of the northern routes, but which could carry a cargo in excess of seven tons, approximately twice that of a C-109 tanker and 70 per cent greater than that of a C-46. On New Year's Day the direct run by C-54's from the Calcutta area (Barrackpore) to Kunming was inaugurated. As the season advanced, the fields in eastern Bengal (Tezgaon and Kurmitola) sharply increased their contribution to the division's India-China haul.[80]

Trained men, skilfully designed machines, and a succession of military successes had made possible a vast increase in deliveries to China. But the Hump, even along the lower-altitude routes now in regular use, was still a fearsome barrier capable of taking a heavy toll of life and aircraft. This it proved at the turn of the year. In January, 23 major aircraft accidents occurred in the Hump operation; in February, 38; in March, 46. These accidents took a toll of 134 crew members, dead or missing. At division headquarters and in Washington the number of accidents caused increasing concern. At the beginning of the year, General Tunner had warned his base commanders: "In striving for high aircraft utilization, we will *not* sacrifice flying safety. One hour of daily utilization lost can be made up later . . . the loss of one load of passengers and crew can never be recovered." When minor corrective measures failed to halt the accidents, ATC headquarters in early March reacted strongly. Hitherto accidents had normally been considered in relation to thousands of flying hours, or thousands of tons transported, and the ratio had been reduced sharply since January 1944 when there were 1.968 accidents per 1,000 flying hours in the Hump operation. Now, while praising this improvement, General Smith wrote to Tunner that there must "be a substantial reduction in number of accidents per week and per month, irrespective of graphic comparisons with tonnage transported and hours flown."[81]

Under such pressure as this, General Tunner's headquarters in turn increased the pressure upon base commanders. Those officers felt themselves caught between two fires—the continuing demand for tonnage and the new insistence on an absolute decrease in the number of accidents. Col. Francis M. Coates, ICD Chief of Staff, recommended to Tunner at the end of April that flying safety be relegated to a position secondary to Hump tonnage.[82] Ten days earlier General Stratemeyer, seriously disturbed when the India-China Division on the 15th reduced its forecast for April tonnage from 48,000 to 42,000 tons, took the matter up directly with General George in Washington. Stratemeyer presented figures tending to show that the accident rate per flying hours and per sorties was now low in relation to that incurred in combat operations. He flatly urged George to consider the Hump operation a combat job and to modify his accident policy accordingly.[83]

General George insisted that ATC had always regarded the India-China run as a combat operation. While refusing to abandon his drive for a higher standard of safety, he did give Stratemeyer an opportunity to specify any particular rule or regulation which interfered with tonnage objectives. Stratemeyer proposed permitting an increase in the gross take-off and landing weight of C-54 aircraft. More serious than weight limitations, he thought, was ATC's insistence on measuring Hump accidents in terms of actual numbers rather than in relation to hours flown or ton-mile of delivery. General George agreed to follow a relative standard—accidents per thousand airplane hours—rather than the absolute standard.[84]

In spite of the understandable frustration of the base unit commanders in the field, they and their subordinates somehow succeeded in achieving what division headquarters demanded. They increased deliveries over the Hump, and they reduced not only the accident rate but also the total number of accidents a month. The following table tells the story:[85]

1945	Hump Lift (under ATC Control) India to China	No. of Major Accidents (ATC Hump Oprs.)	Accident Rate per Thousand Aircraft Hrs.	No. of Crew Fatalities
January	44,098 net tons	23	0.301	36
February	40,677	28	0.497	50
March	46,545	41	0.580	45
April	44,254	34	0.511	28
May	46,393	13	0.372	24
June	55,386	20	0.323	17
July	71,042	23	0.358	37
August	53,315	8	0.239	11

143

General Tunner believed that an important cause of accidents would be removed with the promised substitution of C-54's for C-109 and C-87 aircraft. The accident rate on the Consolidated types was almost 500 per cent higher than on the C-54's. With this point of view, Stratemeyer and ATC headquarters agreed. A real difficulty, however, lay in finding the requisite C-54's.[86]

One program toward this end, the so-called "272 plan," provided for building the C-54 fleet up to a total of 272 aircraft by October 1945. By April 1946 the India-China Division was to have 540 C-54's and 410 C-46's calculated to produce a Hump lift of 86,300 tons. Because of the existing shortage of the R-2000 engines which powered the C-54 aircraft, ATC headquarters had earlier proposed to return to Florida, for routine engine change and related maintenance, all India-China C-54's as they needed such service. Aircraft in this "maintenance pipeline" were to carry cargo and passengers in each direction in regular traffic schedules of the ATC divisions through which they passed. Of the 272 Skymasters scheduled for the division it was now proposed that a dozen be reserved for training and special missions, while 60, with accrued engine time of between 600 and 800 hours, were always to be in the pipeline, either returning to the United States, undergoing maintenance in Florida, or returning to India. The engine changes, a responsibility of the Caribbean Division, were to be performed at Morrison Field, though temporarily the load was to be shouldered by the ATC base unit at Miami.[87]

The plan called for an expensive building program at Morrison Field. When approval by AAF Headquarters came in April 1945, the contractors were handicapped by a labor shortage, and the work was accordingly delayed. The same shortage of skilled civilian labor plagued the PIPELINE project itself. The military personnel assigned, largely returnees from overseas, were top-heavy in grades and discharge points and extremely light in qualifications for first-class maintenance work on C-54 aircraft. The planes themselves were in poorer condition than had been anticipated. Roughly treated in the Hump service, they required an excessive amount of sheet-metal work and fuel-cell repair. Accordingly, the number of man-hours required to handle a pipeline airplane averaged 5,511.6 in July, as against an advance estimate of 3,500; this meant an average of thirty-four days on the ground at Morrison Field instead of an estimated seven days. The India-China Division complained bitterly of the delays.[88]

By May it was plain that the C-54 fleet would not be able to carry to China the required volume of cargo, particularly since ATC headquarters was hard pressed to procure on schedule the C-54's for the "272 program." When in April ATC delivered only 44,254 tons over the Hump as against an allocation of 48,770 tons, General Stratemeyer in May planned a new augmentation of the Hump service. After the recapture of Rangoon, the India-China Division was reinforced by several tactical organizations whose primary mission had been completed. These were the 7th Bombardment Group, the 308th Bombardment Group, the 443d Troop Carrier Group, and the 3d and 4th Combat Cargo Groups, plus two combat cargo squadrons of the 1st Combat Cargo Group, with the support of the twelve airdrome squadrons. Operational control passed to the India-China Division. Thus the ICD was to fix quotas of tonnage to be delivered by each organization, to prescribe routes and destinations, to establish procedures for dispatching, briefing, air-traffic control, radio, loading, and reporting, and to determine turn-around standards in China. Administrative control was to remain with the parent air force.[89]

In order to provide a base for the 7th Bombardment Group's transport operations, ATC aircraft and personnel transferred from Tezpur to other India-China bases. The 308th Bombardment Group for a while continued to base at Chengtu, flying to Dergaon, India, for cargo. In July 1945 the 308th moved to Rupsi in Assam. The 443d Troop Carrier Group took station at Dinjan, and most of the units of the 3d and 4th Combat Cargo Groups, flying C-46 aircraft, were stationed at Myitkyina North and West. The 3d Combat Cargo Squadron was based at Myitkyina East, the 2d at Bhamo. One of the squadrons of the 3d Combat Cargo Group was stationed at Luliang. Between them the attached tactical organizations had a total of 207 aircraft available on the last day of June, and 261 a month later.[90]

Fitting the tactical organizations into the India-China Division organization was not easy. Their rated personnel, accustomed to looking down on the ATC as a non-combat outfit, at first tended to count their assignment to a non-tactical mission a degrading anticlimax. They were bitterly indignant when they learned that they were to be given a week of special training flights in preparation for flying the Hump. Personal friction between the tactical units and ICD personnel continued, and mutual fault-finding was widespread. However, friction did not prevent the tactical organizations from making a large contribution to the India-China lift. Starting toward the end of June, they carried 6,488 tons that month, over and above the new record total of 48,899 tons hauled in ATC aircraft. Thus they enabled the India-China Division to achieve its first 50,000-ton month. In July the peak was reached when ATC transports lifted 51,418 tons into China and the attached tactical groups nearly 20,000 tons. Even in August, when the pressure had been removed, the attached units lifted more than 11,000 tons eastbound, against 41,727 tons carried in ATC aircraft.[91]

Though the weight of the Hump lift was vastly greater in 1945 than in 1944, its character and recipients changed but little. One major customer for Hump tonnage had withdrawn. This was the XX Bomber Command, which in January absorbed over 12 per cent of the Hump lift. Thereafter, as its missions from China declined and ceased, its receipts by April became practically nil.

Gasoline and oil accounted in 1945 for nearly 60 per cent of all net tonnage carried eastbound over the Hump. Ordnance supplies (including motor vehicles, dismantled for the Hump crossing, and appropriate spare parts, as well as bombs and ammunition) amounted to approximately 15 per cent of the total lift. The balance, roughly a fourth of the total, included passengers, a relatively small quantity of Air Corps technical supplies, PX supplies, and a larger proportion of Quartermaster supplies. As ATC headquarters suggested, when a woman wrote General George protesting the transportation of beer over the Hump, the decisions as to what should be hauled were made by the commanders in the field on the basis of their judgment as to what commodities would make a contribution to military success against the enemy.[92]

The westbound lift across the Hump was always smaller than the eastbound haul and became smaller relatively month by month. By 1945 most aircraft westbound over the Hump flew empty or with small amounts of ballast. Nevertheless, the traffic out of China had made a minor contribution to the prosecution of the war. Aircraft bound from China to Assam, East Bengal, or Calcutta carried a variety of people, including injured and ailing troops on their way to hospitals in the United States. Thousands of Chinese troops were transported from China to India for training or for combat. The planes carried, too, such strategic materials as tungsten ore, tin, hog bristles, mercury, silk, and even green tea (valued as an agent of good will in northern Africa). Though of considerable importance, no one of these commodities possessed sufficiently high priority to win air transportation beyond India.[93]

After the division in October 1944 of the CBI into the India-Burma and China theaters, the commanding general of the China theater (Maj. Gen. Albert C. Wedemeyer) controlled cargo assignment through an agency called Hump Allocation and Control, or more commonly, Humpalco. Each month the India-China Division submitted to Humpalco a presumably firm commitment as to Hump capability for the following month, together with estimates for subsequent months. Near the middle of the month, Humpalco assembled all using organizations in China, at which meeting the total amounts to be allotted each for the coming month were determined. Each organization's allotment was then also broken down into specific amounts of such general categories as aviation gasoline, motor gasoline, and bombs. Within their specific allotments, the users then placed their requisitions with the shipping organizations in India. The general and specific requisitions were transmitted to Humpreg (otherwise Hump Regulating Office), an India-Burma agency which controlled the dispatch of cargo and personnel to China. A given tonnage was assigned to each base for each shipping agency, and the shippers were responsible for placing material at the proper bases.[94]

The end of hostilities cut short India-China Division's plans for further expansion. Kharagpur, a former B-29 base, and three new bases, prepared *ad hoc*, all in West Bengal, were to be transferred to the ATC and were to house 240 C-54's. Even more ambitious was the ORIENT project, also stillborn. Predicated on a long-term occupation of China by American air forces, it called for a series of airlines radiating out from Shanghai to Vladivostok, Harbin, Mukden, Peiping, Lanchow, Hanoi, and Colombo. Russian opposition to any unnecessary contact by foreign powers with areas within the Soviet sphere and the rapid demobilization of U.S. forces killed this scheme.[95]

The proposal was rooted, however, in the expansion which had taken place in the ATC's operations within China proper. Until well into 1944 the Air Transport Command had counted its mission accomplished when the weight of cargo to which it was committed had been unloaded at the existing China bases. That indeed was as much as General Chennault, the principal customer of the Hump airline, wanted the ATC to do, though in many cases the commodities landed at Kunming or another base still had to travel several hundred miles to the user. The internal transportation system Chennault employed in getting aviation gasoline and other supplies to the using squadrons was a crazy combination of Chinese and American trucks, such railroads as the meter gauge line between Kunming and Chanyi, riverboats, sampans, junks, and steamboats. By April 1944 Chennault also had in service eleven C-47's of the 322d Troop Carrier Squadron. B-24's of the 308th Bombardment Group likewise flew intra-China, as well as over-the-Hump transport missions. For long, Chennault vigorously opposed an intra-China air transport service by the ATC, which he thought would put an inordinate burden upon Hump deliveries to the Fourteenth Air Force; further, he insisted that the air force commander ought to control his own supply movements in forward areas. He did not hesitate, however, to ask for the use of ATC planes for emergency deliveries and evacuation in China. Finally, in October 1944, he consented to ATC's basing fifty C-47's in China. He still insisted in December, however, that further expansion by the ATC in China should be postponed until ATC could deliver 15,000 tons a month for air operations only.[96]

The number of aircraft assigned to the India-China Division's intra-China operation remained practically constant (66 to 72) from the beginning of 1945 until after V-J Day, though the proportion of C-46's as compared to C-47's increased materially. These intra-China aircraft were based at Chengkung, Chanyi, Luliang, and Kunming. Intra-China tonnage fluctuated considerably from month to month, with a peak in May of more than 11,000 tons. When idle in China, the intra-China aircraft were used to augment the eastbound Hump lift. After April, however, such runs were very few.[97]

As the scope of ATC operations to and within China expanded, the route across India grew in importance. Although its principal reason for being was to support the Hump operation, it was also an extension of the series of airways extending from the United States through the Azores, and over North Africa, to Karachi. As such, the character of its cargo was very different from that carried over the Hump. The much smaller trans-Indian lift was given over primarily to mail, personnel, and high-priority supplies. The regular traffic was carried by DC-3 and C-46 type planes, with a total average number in commission varying from 76 in February to 60 in May. Their total lift, in terms of manifest tons, ranged from 18,362 in March to 12,083 tons in April.[98]

In 1945, as in the previous year, a substantial share of the India-China Division's capacity was devoted to airlift of troops and their equipment. The troop movements of 1944 had been largely defensive in character. So also was the ROOSTER movement (21 April–11 May 1945), in which the Chinese Sixth Army was transported from Chanyi, Chengkung, Luliang, and Kunming to assist in the defense of the Fourteenth Air Force base at Chihkiang. As a direct result of this airlift, the Japanese were smashed back, with heavy loss of life, and the use of the air base made secure. Generally speaking, however, the movement of troops by the India-China Division in 1945 was by way of support to the Chinese advance which recovered the bases lost in 1944.[99] With the collapse of Japanese resistance, ATC helped move Chinese troops into Shanghai and other forward areas.

Several of these movements were of impressive weight. In the ROOSTER movement the intra-China fleet, reinforced by thirty C-46's from the Assam bases, made 1,648 trips, carrying 25,136 troops, 2,178 horses, and 1,565 tons of equipment and supplies, for a total tonnage of 5,523. At the same time some 369 tons of aviation gasoline were flown into Chihkiang for the Fourteenth Air Force fighters.[100] The DISC project for transporting Chinese troops from Burma to Nanning in southern China was of like magnitude. The first phase was accomplished by the North Burma Air Task Force, but on 23 June ATC was given operational control. By 14 August over 23,000 Chinese troops with their organizational equipment, including nearly 3,000 mules, had been delivered.[101]

One of the 1945 special movements involved the transportation of the Mars Task Force, including 6,235 American ground troops with their equipment, from Burma to China. These soldiers, who had played a grueling part in the recovery of Burma, now became the first American infantry unit assigned to fight in China. They were flown to China points, mostly by ATC C-47's based at Myitkyina, between 14 March and 25 May.[102]

When the war ended, the Allies had to take over control of large areas still, or very recently, occupied by the Japanese. The Tenth Air Force was made responsible for transporting the 6th Chinese Army from Chihkiang, and ATC for moving the 94th Chinese Army from

Liuchow to Shanghai. The India-China Division's C-54's took off from Kurmitola and Tezgaon fully loaded with gasoline; four out of each five of the Skymasters flew to Liuchow, where gas in excess of that needed for a round-trip flight to Shanghai was removed, and the planes were packed with from 80 to 85 Chinese troops, each carrying his field equipment and rifle. As usual when Chinese troops were carried, the aircraft on arrival at their destination reeked with the nauseating odors of vomit and other filth. Between 9 and 29 September 26,237 soldiers made the air journey to Shanghai.[103]

The end of the war inevitably spelled the end of the India-China airline. Its decline was rapid, though not as rapid as most of the men whom the ATC had stationed in Assam, Bengal, and China wished. There were still some tasks for military air transportation to perform in the theater. Until seagoing vessels could unload at Chinese ports, air transports must continue to supply the American forces still retained on duty in China. On the eve of V-J Day General Tunner had directed that the moment of victory should be the signal for removing "the high pressure, daily trip consciousness . . . from each operating base." Since "the primary mission of the base is now safety and service rather than tonnage," Consolidated-type aircraft were to take off only during the day, and gross take-off weights were reduced. The ABLE route, crossing the highest and most dangerous portion of the Hump, was abandoned at once, and other safety measures were put into effect.[104]

Naturally, the eastbound lift of gasoline and other supplies into China declined rapidly. The official figures tell the story: July, 71,042 tons; August, 53,315 tons; September, 39,775 tons; October, 8,646 tons; November, 1,429 tons. At the end of November the Hump was officially closed, though some special mission flights over the route were made thereafter. Meanwhile the India-China Division, stripped in August and September of its attached organizations, had performed the grateful task of flying approximately 47,000 American troops westward across the Hump and thence across India to the embarkation port of Karachi.[105]

From a primitive barnstorming enterprise the air service from India to China had burgeoned into a large-scale operation, far beyond the wildest dreams of the men who assisted at its beginnings. First and last a grand total of some 650,000 tons of gasoline, munitions, other commodities, and men traveled the air route over the Hump into

China, rather more than half of the total in the first nine months of 1945. One must ask in conclusion what this all meant. The tonnage could have been hauled in approximately 70 Liberty ships, if the requisite ports had only been available, or in 6,500 American freight cars, if only a railroad had existed. The Hump airline was born of an emergency, though in the end its size made it difficult for the men who operated it to remember that it was still properly an emergency communication system.

But a fundamental question remains: What good end was served by the emergency delivery of 650,000 tons of this and that into China? Certainly little went directly to the aid of the Chinese people and relatively little to the Chinese armies, though it can be urged that the regime of Chiang Kai-shek would have collapsed without the support of General Chennault's command and that Chennault's men were wholly dependent upon the Hump lift. It can be argued that it helped to prevent the Japanese from overrunning all of China and preserved for the forces of the United Nations a base for launching an air attack upon Japanese shipping, upon vital Japanese industrial installations in eastern China, upon Formosa, and even upon the Japanese homeland. Thus it may have speeded somewhat the conclusion of hostilities against Japan. Most important in the long run, no doubt, the Air Transport Command's crowded airways to China were the proving ground, if not the birthplace, of mass strategic airlift. Here the AAF demonstrated conclusively that a vast quantity of cargo could be delivered by air, even under the most unfavorable circumstances, if only the men who controlled the aircraft, the terminals, and the needed materiel were willing to pay the price in money and in men. In military and civilian circles alike men were forced to modify their thinking regarding the potential of airlift. The India-China experience made it possible to conceive the Berlin airlift of 1948–49 and to operate it successfully. When the Korean War in 1950 required the emergency delivery of large numbers of men and equipment to the Far East, the precedents and the techniques for doing so were at hand.

CHAPTER 6

*　　*　　*　　*　　*　　*　　*　　*　　*　　*　　*

THE NORTHWEST AIR ROUTE
TO ALASKA

THE Air Transport Command's northwest route extended for a distance of 2,210 statute miles from the domestic terminus at Great Falls, Montana, to Anchorage, Alaska. This indeed understates the situation somewhat, since Great Falls itself was remote from the centers of aircraft production in California and along the Atlantic seaboard. Between Great Falls and Anchorage, the route's major bases were located at Edmonton (Alberta), Whitehorse (Yukon Territory), and Fairbanks (Alaska). Although Edmonton lies in the great cultivated plain of western Canada, Whitehorse, Fairbanks, and most of the lesser bases were set in the midst of a vast wilderness whose surface, heavily wooded, provided relatively few easily recognizable landmarks for the pilot flying contact. Especially between Whitehorse and Fairbanks, the terrain, though not comparable with the peaks of the Himalayan Hump, was rugged enough. Even in summer a forced landing in that area was hazardous. But it was the northern winter rather than distance or terrain which furnished the northwest airway with its distinctive hardships and dangers. Radio aids to aerial navigation, as they became available in sufficient quantity, helped, but the Aurora Borealis and related natural phenomena often so distorted the signals as to make them worse than useless. The winter's blanket of snow tended to blot out what visual signpost man or nature had provided for the harassed airman. Winter temperatures, which often fell below minus 50° Fahrenheit, and which passed minus 70° in the record-breaking winter of 1942–43, altered the characteristic properties of such common materials as rubber, antifreeze solutions, even metal, and of course all lubricants. A moment's contact of flesh with metal was painful, if nothing worse; ungloved hands froze in a matter of minutes. In the bitter cold, sustained activity out of doors was impossible; yet much of the work of operating a transport airline or an airway for the delivery of aircraft must be done outdoors.

As seen by the planners in December 1941, the wintry air road northwest was essential for supplying and reinforcing the pitifully small garrison of American forces in Alaska. Such was its principal occasion for being until September 1942, and throughout the war it continued to deliver to the United States' armed forces in Alaska aircraft and aircraft supplies. For three years, however, from September 1942 until September 1945, this airway's primary function was to deliver lend-lease aircraft, nearly 8,000 in all, to the aircrews of the Soviet Union, waiting at Ladd Field, Fairbanks.[1]

Aid to Russia

Originally, it had been supposed that the delivery of aircraft to the Soviet forces would occur not on North American soil but far within the U.S.S.R.[2] Hence the name, ALSIB (Alaska-Siberia), by which the project for delivering aircraft over the northern route to Stalin's airmen was long known by the Ferrying Command and ATC. On at least one occasion General Arnold even offered to provide the transports and to operate across Siberia the transport service, without which aircraft deliveries could not be maintained.[3] One who recalls the difficulties which the Air Transport Command—not always without fault—experienced in dealing with American theater commanders, the Civil Aeronautics Administration (initially responsible for the construction of several bases in Alaska),[4] the Canadian Department of Transport (which at first undertook to build the necessary facilities along the Canadian segment of the ALSIB route),[5] and even its sister branches of the AAF may indulge his imagination in considering what might have been the result had the command actually attempted to run an airline and deliver thousands of planes within Soviet territory.

The planners in the Air Staff and in ATC headquarters were obliged to look beyond 1942 to the day when a vigorous offensive against Japan might be mounted. The value of Siberian bases for such an offensive was obvious. Planners hoped that AAF use of Siberian airfields in ferrying and transport operations might well facilitate their use ultimately in a bomber offensive against the Japanese homeland.[6] Should the Soviet leaders refuse the proferred aid in Siberia, the transfer point could still be fixed, perhaps temporarily, at Nome or Fairbanks. As early as April 1942, Lt. Col. George Brewer, who surveyed the route for the Ferrying Command, recommended strongly the choice of Fairbanks rather than Nome. Nome was 533 air miles nearer Soviet territory but nearer also to Japanese bases. Fairbanks had better existing facilities, could be supplied more readily, and had some relative advantage over Nome in the matter of weather.[7]

Over a year intervened between the first proposal, in August 1941, that lend-lease aircraft destined for the Soviet forces be delivered by way of Alaska and the final decision that this should be done. From April 1942 on, proposal followed proposal and one negotiation succeeded another.[8] The Soviet representatives were as difficult as usual to deal with, refusing today an offer which they had seemed to accept yesterday, only to revive it on the morrow. Yet it must be said that their objections were not wholly without grounds. Many airfields would have to be established and supplied if the planes delivered via Alaska were ultimately to reach the fighting front, no matter who served as their pilots. The ALSIB route offered substantial advantages over its existing alternates—the waterborne route to Archangel, along which German bombers and submarines took heavy toll, and the air-water-air route by way of the Persian Gulf, where greater distance and the abrasive qualities of wind-blown African soil lessened the life of planes and engines. Yet by those alternates, planes were already reaching the Soviet forces in some numbers. Deliveries could continue without any substantial new construction on the part of the U.S.S.R., with a minimum expenditure of time by Soviet ferry pilots, and without providing a basis for pressure to admit American personnel to Soviet territory. Furthermore, the use of the alternate routes did not affect Russo-Japanese relations, whereas there was a chance that the ALSIB project might supply the Japanese with a pretext for a premature act of war against the Soviet Union.[9]

But the United States was persistent,[10] the Soviet need for aircraft was real, the advantages of the northern air route were apparent, and on 3 August 1942 the Soviet government agreed that it could be used. Within three weeks the AAF was to deliver fifty A-20's, twelve B-25's, forty-three P-40's, and fifty P-39's into Soviet hands at Fairbanks. These totals were soon revised downward when Maj. Gen.

Alexander I. Belyaev, chairman of the Soviet government's purchasing commission in the United States, indicated that the Siberian portion of the route was as yet unable to handle so many planes. Meanwhile, after a strenuous round of conferences and co-ordination between representatives of various agencies of the Air Staff, the Air Service Command, the Materiel Command, and the ATC, the advance guard of the aircraft started toward Great Falls. The first of these, five A-20's, reached Fairbanks on 3 September. Then without warning, on 19 September, Belyaev informed General Arnold that his government had determined not to utilize the ALSIB route after all, though it would accept such planes as had already reached Ladd Field. But this decision, too, was reversed, and the flow of aircraft to Fairbanks, halted for a fortnight, was started again. Soviet personnel had assembled at Ladd Field; Russian pilots received instruction on the American aircraft; and on 29 September the first planes accepted by the Soviet Military Mission in Alaska took off for Nome and Siberian points.[11]

The Winter of 1942–43

By that time the northern winter was at hand, with the program of route construction which the Ferrying Command had outlined in April and expanded in June still incomplete. Although U.S. engineer troops had been brought in to supplement the work of Canadian contractors at the Canadian bases, there was still much to do. Since June ATC personnel had been moving into the Canadian bases. Only in late August, however, were the first ATC representatives sent to Ladd Field, first Alaskan base to be so staffed. By the end of October the ATC's Ferrying Division had deployed some 686 men along the airway. Over half were serving at Canadian bases, principally Edmonton; most of the men who had been sent to Alaska were stationed at Ladd Field. These men found their new stations generally unready for heavy traffic and particularly unready for winter. The essential runways had been constructed, and in some cases given a hard surface, but buildings were insufficient to house even permanent party personnel; hangars and warehouses were incomplete or nonexistent. Troops would have to live in tents, "winterized" if they were fortunate, and supplies would have to be stored and aircraft serviced in the open or not at all. An ATC headquarters officer who inspected the route in September reported, moreover, that messes were poor, recreational facilities nil, and morale low. The men faced a pioneering job for which most of them were quite unprepared by previous experience or training. And, though they could not yet know it, they faced the most severe winter which the area had experienced in a generation.[12]

Transport service along the airway was furnished under contract by Northwest Airlines, Inc., and Western Air Lines. Northwest had been operating over the route since March under the nominal supervision, first, of the Ferrying Command and, subsequently, of the ATC. After opening the route in the spring, NWA, aided by planes and men from Western and five other airlines, had done a heroic job of emergency air transport for the Eleventh Air Force and other elements of the Alaska Defense Command at the time of the Japanese attack at Dutch Harbor, 3–5 June. In late September, Northwest had fifteen DC-3 type transports assigned; Western, which flew from the Ogden Air Depot to Anchorage, had four. Canadian authorities, darkly suspicious of the intentions of American commercial airlines operating, under whatever pretext, north of the forty-ninth parallel, had insisted from the start that these operations be shorn of all commercial aspects and were impatient for their complete militarization at the earliest possible moment. Equally impatient for this consummation were some of the military personnel assigned to ATC and the Army Airways Communications System. Through the winter the jealousy was bitter between the carriers' personnel, who had small confidence in the technical skill and efficiency of the military men, and the soldiers, who suspected the airlines' men of serving the company, if necessary, to the disadvantage of their country. To the numerous other factors conducive to low troop morale was added the realization that airlines' employees, in addition to what the typical G.I. counted a most generous pay scale, received bonuses for service outside the United States. It is no wonder that the feeling between the airlines' employees and Uncle Sam's $50-a-month men led often to blows. Responsibility for communications was divided among NWA, AACS, the Signal Corps, CAA, the U.S. Navy, and the RCAF; the communications facilities themselves were far from adequate.[13]

In other respects, too, responsibility was divided. From June until October, Col. Leroy Ponton de Acre, commanding officer of the 7th Ferrying Group at Great Falls, was nominally in charge of the route, under the over-all direction of his immediate superior, Col. William H. Tunner, head of the Ferrying Division, ATC. But channels were particularly involved. The Permanent Joint Board on Defense, Canada–United States, responsible for fundamental policy, had made numerous recommendations regarding the route and its construction. These recommendations, however, were not binding without an affirmative decision by the Canadian government. That given, any change in the details of air-base construction in Canada required the consent of the Department of Transport in distant Ottawa. The commanding officer of Ladd Field was responsible, not to Ponton de Acre or to any other ATC officer, but rather, through the XI Air Force Service Command, to the commanding general of the Eleventh Air Force and in succession to the commanding generals of the Alaska Defense Command and the Western Defense Command. When the Cold Weather Test Detachment returned to the base in October, the pressure on existing facilities was increased. The command relationship was somewhat simplified, however, when Col. Dale V. Gaffney, who headed the Cold Weather Test Detachment, returned to the position of base commander, for in the first of these capacities he was directly responsible to General Arnold.[14]

Meanwhile, ATC headquarters resolved to establish an Alaskan Wing, whose commander should have the authority usual on ATC's overseas airways. The wing was formally activated on 17 October 1942. Its first commanding officer, Col. Thomas L. Mosley, one-time commander of the Ferrying Command's Foreign Wing, set up his headquarters at Edmonton. His executive, Col. George E. Gardner, had recently been vice-president of Northwest Airlines.[15]

Colonel Mosley's assignment could be regarded as a challenge to a vigorous career air officer aged thirty-seven, but his assumption of command could be expected to result in no sudden miracles. In the critical matters of construction, supply, and even the procurement of personnel, he had to depend upon distant authorities.[16] While his letter of instructions gave him operational control over transport aircraft, it did not authorize him to control their schedules or to exercise command control over their crews.[17] To the extent that the carriers were not autonomous, they were responsible, until March 1943, to the Air Transportation Division at distant ATC headquarters rather than to the wing commander. On the other hand, one of the most competent investigators who visited the operation during

157

the winter gave both NWA and Mosley credit for wholehearted and effective co-operation.[18] Mosley's control of the ferrying route was limited by the fact that its starting point, Gore Field at Great Falls, remained under the control of the Ferrying Division and of Colonel Ponton de Acre. Not until February did Mosley and the other ATC wing commanders gain command control of ferrying pilots while they were actually within the wing area.[19]

Nevertheless, during the winter there was some improvement along the northwest route. Thus an expert consultant to the Office of the Quartermaster General, who had found that "confusion reigned supreme," when he passed through Edmonton in May, August, and November, observed in late January 1943 that the situation had been "transformed in a truly miraculous fashion. . . . Colonel Mosley's ability, resourcefulness and untiring enthusiasm," he reported, "have created a machine out of confusion in a scant two months."[20]

As the winter weeks passed, one construction job after another was completed, and more of the needed equipment for cold-weather operations arrived. On the other hand, Fort Nelson and Fort St. John, where the Canadian Department of Transport's well-digging operations had lagged during the summer and autumn, went through most of the winter without any water, whether for drinking, bathing, or fire-fighting, except what the troops could haul from neighboring streams. At Galena, between Fairbanks and Nome, the wells were completed in due time, but the pumps did not arrive. At some of the lesser bases the food supply ran low in quantity and variety. Vienna sausage, redesignated by popular acclaim as "Yukon shrimp," was for a time staple at some northern stations, though some efforts were made to fly in fresh meat and milk. At some of the smaller bases a large proportion of the man-hours of labor available was spent in cutting, usually with hand saws, enough wood to keep the men reasonably warm.[21] Everywhere the excessive cold of the winter months, as one ATC headquarters officer reported at the end of 1942, governed "every action, from the basic individual struggle to keep warm to the operation of airplanes—in itself, it creates the fight for existence; it tempers the most optimistic plans and reduces efficiency to a minimum."[22] Col. Lawrence Fritz, General George's Assistant Chief of Staff, A-3, and somewhat of a cold-weather man himself,* logged about sixty hours of flying time while piloting a DC-3 type transport

* See above, p. 100.

on the route in January; he experienced breaks in refueling hose and trouble with synthetic-rubber hydraulic hose connections because of extreme cold.[23] A less responsible person claimed that a pilot new to the route could follow it accurately enough by the trail of red left by leaking fluid from the succession of aircraft which had preceded him. Greases and oil became nearly solid when planes were left on the ground for any length of time. Coolant in the liquid-cooled P-39's tended to blow out and catch fire both on take-off and in the air.[24]

During the winter of 1942–43, at most of the stations the few men assigned could not even inventory the vast quantities of supplies which had been sent them. These stores, in the absence of warehouses, had been deposited as fancy or circumstance directed. Covered perhaps with tarpaulin, they had presently been buried under the snow. Thus a plane might stand idle at one of the smaller route bases—out of doors, of course, since hangars were long available only at Edmonton and Fairbanks—awaiting parts which might well be present, though not accounted for, under the blanket of snow. Most stations had as yet no personnel capable of doing much more for transient aircraft than to supply them with gasoline and oil or, with good fortune and much labor, to start their motors on a bitter winter's morning. When serious repairs were required, it was necessary to fly in not only the parts but also the mechanics to do the job.[25]

The wonder is that any planes got through. Yet the record shows that, by the end of March, over 400 lend-lease aircraft had reached Fairbanks. Furthermore, 369 had met the exacting requirements of the Soviet Mission there, had been duly accepted by the representatives of our rather difficult ally, and had been flown westward by Soviet pilots. The accepted planes included 106 A-20's, 34 B-25's, 151 P-39's, 48 P-40's, and 30 C-47's.[26] Month by month, the score of lend-lease aircraft which reached Fairbanks ran approximately as follows:[27]

1942		*1943*	
September	50	January	70
October	43	February	102
November	48	March	101
December	7		

During the same period pilots of the Ferrying Division also delivered some 90 planes to the Eleventh Air Force in Alaska and 21 to the Cold Weather Test Detachment.[28]

The American transports on the Alaskan route were hard pressed that winter to take care of the quantities of men and cargo which had been designated for air shipment. Backlogs were a constant problem. While substantial amounts of materiel were moved for the U.S.S.R. and for elements of the Alaska Defense Command, the transports flew in men and supplies essential to the operation of the route as well as some materiel—like the set of band instruments sent to Northway, for instance—which should never have received air priority.[29]

Since August, Northwest Airlines, in addition to its work along the inland route to Alaska, had been serving the Western Defense Command by flights along the coastal route from Seattle to Anchorage. Because the planes assigned to the coastal route often flew inland under certain weather conditions, the wing asked that the operation be placed under its control. This change was made in January 1943, and at the same time, since NWA had its hands full with responsibilities inland, United Air Lines was brought in to take over the coastal route. Like its predecessor, United was permitted to fly inland when weather or other conditions required it.[30]

Still another peripheral transport service of Northwest Airlines finally came under wing direction in the spring of 1943. In the previous summer four light aircraft had been assigned to the Corps of Engineers to support the construction of the Canadian-Alaskan (Alcan) Highway and the Canol Project. These planes were flown by Canadian civilian pilots, but in July 1942 NWA was directed to place the pilots on its payroll and to maintain the planes. With the coming of winter the demands upon this service became increasingly urgent. Pressure from Lt. Gen. Brehon B. Somervell, Commanding General of the Services of Supply, exerted through General Arnold and ATC headquarters, forced NWA to step up the number of flights, using a number of C-47 aircraft. On these flights, essential supplies were carried, usually from Edmonton, to the contractors and troops at work constructing the Canol pipeline, or the winter road which necessarily preceded the pipeline, from Normand Wells and Canol on the Mackenzie River to Whitehorse. At the latter point a refinery, dismantled in Texas, was being put together again. Finally, in March the entire air operation in support of Canol construction was made a responsibility of the Alaskan Wing, and the crews employed thereon were transferred to the wing payroll.[31]

160

The transports flying the wing's main line also aided in the construction and improvement of the Alcan Highway. Here, as well as in the support of the Canol Project, was a mutual relationship of considerable significance. The construction of the highway, which would take much of the burden off the airline, was assisted by the air movement of men and supplies for road-building. Supplies flown in by the NWA contract carriers, as well as some trucked up the highway, helped in the construction of the pipeline, which in turn was intended to supply fuel to wing transports, ferried aircraft, and highway trucks.

During the first months of 1943 it appeared to Colonel Mosley and to his superiors at Washington that the quantity of aviation gasoline required might be a matter of great moment, for this was a period in which most ATC headquarters plans were conceived on a grand scale.* In January the Alaskan Wing, following the Plans Division of ATC headquarters, was thinking in terms of a movement of 5,000 ferried planes a month and of the operation of from 100 to 150 transports. To handle such a volume of traffic, the wing, which that month handled 83 ferried aircraft, submitted a preliminary outline of a plan for constructing the necessary facilities, including a double line of airports. By February, however, the estimate of 60,000 ferried planes a year had been reduced to 7,900. The program of construction which ATC headquarters proposed to handle that more modest load was in May rejected by the Air Staff, on the grounds that the flow of Soviet aircraft over the route would probably not exceed 388 planes a month.[32] Even that goal, however, required a substantial program of additional airway construction.

Changing Conditions

Meanwhile, ATC headquarters, needing a strong man to take charge of operations in North Africa, in March 1943 offered Colonel Mosley that assignment.[33] At the same time, Colonel Gaffney, base commander at Ladd Field and outstanding Air Force authority on cold-weather flying, was asked whether he would be interested in taking command of the wing. Gaffney at once replied in the affirmative but requested that he be accorded better support from higher authority than his predecessor had received.[34] Colonel Mosley left for his new post on 13 April, and Gaffney, following a period of con-

* See above, pp. 39–40.

sultation at ATC headquarters, assumed command of the wing on 9 May. After four months in his new assignment, he was promoted to the rank of brigadier general. As wing, and subsequently division, commander, he gave forceful direction to the ATC's activities in northwestern Canada and Alaska until April 1946, when the division's mission was transferred to the Continental Division of the Command.[35]

During the winter of 1942–43 the Alaskan Wing's personnel more than doubled in number. At the end of March 1943 the wing, by its own accounting, could muster some 240 officers and 1,497 enlisted men, a majority of them at one of the three major bases, Edmonton, Whitehorse, or Fairbanks. At Fort St. John, Fort Nelson, Watson Lake, and Nome the ATC detachments ranged in size from 56 to 71 men. Still smaller ATC contingents were on duty at Galena, Big Delta, Tanacross, Northway, and Grande Prairie.[36] By the end of September the military strength of the wing had doubled once more; 402 officers and 3,296 enlisted men were assigned. At the year's end the wing claimed a total of 5,438 officers and enlisted men, not counting several hundred Air Service Command troops who were on duty within the wing area.[37] The assigned personnel included some 1,200 men who had passed through the Arctic Training School at Fort Buckley, Colorado. Northwest Airlines' employees along the route reached a peak of 948 in February but were down to 437 by the end of 1943.[38]

Much of the time and energy of ATC officers from station level to command headquarters during 1943 was spent in planning for the new construction considered essential to the fulfilment of the Alaskan Wing's mission. Even before any of the plans submitted that year had received the approval of the Operations Division of the General Staff (OPD), it was necessary to undertake preliminary negotiations with the Alaska Defense Command, the Canadian Department of Transport, the Permanent Joint Board on Defense, the Office of the Chief of Army Engineers, and its local representative, the Northwest Division Engineers at Edmonton. In these interchanges ATC officers sought to determine what agencies would be responsible for procuring and shipping the necessary supplies and equipment and for actual construction and what types of labor, American or Canadian, military or civilian, should be employed. The basic construction plans (Plans B and C), presented by ATC headquarters, and modified and sponsored by the Air Staff, were finally approved by OPD on 1 May and 17 June, respectively, but that did not end all difficulites. The resultant War Department directives left the Alaska Defense Command and the Northwest Division Engineers no option but to undertake the work. Still, the ADC's personnel was limited, it had construction projects of its own, and often, because of shipping and priority difficulties, it lacked some of the equipment or supplies or manpower essential for doing a given job at a particular air base. Across the international border, it was still necessary to gain approval of the expansion program from the Permanent Joint Board on Defense and the Canadian cabinet. Even then the Canadian authorities expected to alter layouts which did not fit into their plans for the future development of the airfields.[39]

General Gaffney would no doubt still have won his popular nickname, "The Screaming Eagle of the Yukon," had he had no problems of construction to face. It is easy, however, to understand how even a much milder and more patient commander might have been tempted to indulge himself in an occasional outburst. The situation was assuredly one of prolonged frustration and friction. It was not, of course, a case of conspiracy against a perfect Air Transport Command. The Alaska Defense Command (redesignated the Alaskan Department in November 1943) did not always find ATC's requests or demands entirely reasonable. It is understandable, too, that the Canadian government, which supplied the land, which was to be the ultimate owner of the air bases, and which proposed to pay a major share of the costs of construction, should wish a final voice in their planning, should wish that the sites marked out by the RCAF for future expansion of its facilities should not now be utilized for other purposes, should prefer the employment of Canadian contractors to that of American civilians or the U.S. Army Engineers, and should fear the effect of American employment practices upon the local wage and price structure.[40]

In the end ATC substantially had its way, when construction work on the bases in Canada and also at Northway, Tanacross, and Big Delta was turned over to the Northwest Division Engineers. On the other hand, that agency was required to use Canadian contractors and laborers in the Edmonton area. From Fairbanks west, General Gaffney was obliged to depend upon the Alaska Defense Command. By the end of the year a substantial portion of the new work had been completed. Improved runways, taxi strips, parking aprons, hangars, warehouses, repair shops, laundries, bakeries, mess halls, barracks, and latrines were put into service, one by one, and helped make it possible for the wing to carry a much heavier load in its second winter than it had in the first.[41]

By mid-summer 1944 the northwest route had achieved a large measure of maturity. Construction was all but completed. The division commander no longer lacked personnel and authority needed for the fulfilment of his mission; at the end of July, 949 officers and 8,347 enlisted men were assigned to his organization. During the summer of 1943 he had gained full command of Nome and the lesser Alaskan bases, Galena, Northway, Tanacross, and Big Delta; the service and overhead personnel at those stations had all been transferred to the Air Transport Command. In September 1943 Ladd Field, too, had been assigned to the ATC. Early in 1944 the acquisition of East Base at Great Falls, Montana, had given the Alaskan Wing effective control of the southern terminus of its principal route. A little later Air Service Command personnel performing maintenance and traffic duties came under the direct command of General Gaffney. Rotation was provided within the division, or even elsewhere within the ATC organization, of men long stuck at isolated bases along the route.[42] Now that the remote likelihood of enemy attack, except perhaps at Nome, had long since passed, headquarters officers found time to concern themselves with setting up a program of basic military training for the men of the division. A "plush" mail and passenger service, with airline seats, was inaugurated between Anchorage and Minneapolis. More and more of the transport operation was run on a scheduled basis, with hot in-flight lunches for passengers. A specialized search and rescue organization, established in January, had reached a high level of flexibility and effectiveness. One of the most annoying aspects of summer duty in the north country was attacked by a vigorous program of mosquito control at the bases most seriously affected. Such amenities as built-in chests of drawers and clothes hampers now contributed to the comfort and presumably the morale of troops at some of the more remote bases. Even the preservation of secrecy concerning the operation seemed no longer essential; accordingly, the War Department's Bureau of Public Relations and ATC headquarters, which had long been harassed by reports, rumors, and queries concerning the ALSIB movement, made it and the whole mission of the Alaskan Division public property.[43]

The Ferrying Mission, 1943–45

The most important responsibility of the Alaskan Division continued to be the safe delivery of lend-lease aircraft to the Soviet representatives at Fairbanks. That such deliveries should be accomplished on schedule and in the agreed-upon-volume was a matter of serious importance to President Roosevelt personally; the pressure of his concern, exerted through Harry Hopkins and General Arnold, was felt at least once by the Air Transport Command.[44] As route conditions improved, the task of handling the ALSIB aircraft became increasingly routine; it was fulfilled generally in a manner both satisfactory and unspectacular, though the record of total deliveries at Fairbanks shows considerable fluctuation, month by month:[45]

	1943	1944	1945
January	70	244	310
February	102	178	216
March	101	298	386
April	169	318	309
May	188	246	257
June	329	292	337
July	320	304	157
August	296	403	37*
September	295	350	
October	204	93	
November	317	192	
December	271	246	
Total	2,662	3,164	2,009

* Includes about twenty returned when lend-lease was discontinued.

Of the planes transferred to the U.S.S.R. at Ladd Field, over 5,000—a substantial majority—were fighters, nearly all being Bell aircraft, P-39 Airacobras, or the larger P-63 Kingcobras. The last of the P-39's were delivered in September 1944; the first of the P-63's had been turned over in June 1944. Until June 1943, however, A-20 light bombers had led the list, and the flow of these Douglas planes continued until July 1944. Nearly 100 more were delivered the following summer, in lieu of advanced trainers which could not then be supplied in the desired quantity. First and last, over 1,300 A-20's were transferred to the Soviet Mission at Fairbanks. Less important numerically, but continued throughout the ALSIB movement, was a steady flow of B-25's and C-47's, reaching a total of something over 700 of each.[46] The relatively small number of types ferried over the northwest route lessened the Alaskan Division's problems so far as maintenance was concerned. As mechanics of reasonably satisfactory qualifications were procured, it was possible for them to achieve a high degree of specialization in maintaining the ALSIB aircraft.

The basic factor governing the flow of aircraft was the succession of U.S.–U.S.S.R. protocols, in which the number and types of planes to be delivered to the Soviet Union were agreed upon. But agreements and resulting allocations could not bring about the delivery of aircraft which factory production lines had failed to complete. Once aircraft had left the factory, there were still other factors which could delay their arrival at Fairbanks. If factory production was erratic—end-of-month production surges were a frequent source of annoyance—the Ferrying Division could not always supply enough pilots to move the aircraft promptly. When modifications or winterization, elsewhere than at the factory, were required, extra delays might occur. Bad weather often delayed deliveries and led to their bunching, since single-engine fighters were normally cleared only for contact flying, as were two-engine craft whose pilots lacked instrument ratings. The ferrying pilots themselves sometimes dragged a foot; they tended to resist the Alaskan Division's policy requiring all ferry pilots to be on hand for take-off at 0700 or sunrise, whichever came earlier.[47]

At the end of the run the Soviet representatives had to check every aircraft and often rejected, pending further maintenance, those which fell below their exacting standards. Thus in the autumn of 1944 deliveries were reduced to the lowest figure in nearly two years. Actually, in spite of numerous difficulties, the usual number of planes had reached Fairbanks; the trouble lay in the fact that hundreds of P-63's were grounded there, at various points along the route, or between the factories in western New York and central Montana. And that was due to the Soviet Mission's refusal to accept any more of the planes without certain modifications, which experience had shown important, to strengthen the fuselage. Some 125 civilian mechanics from the Ogden and Sacramento Air Depots, together with inspectors from the Spokane Air Depot, 6 representatives of the Bell Company, and the necessary modification equipment, were flown to Nome and Fairbanks, where modification of most of the planes which had already entered the route was carried out. At Edmonton sixty-two planes were modified by the civilian employees of Aircraft Repair, Ltd., a local firm which, on occasion, had previously served the wing. The work began on 19 and 20 October, and in less than two weeks the modifications were completed. Before that, however, the Soviet Mission refused to accept any more P-63's until a ventral fin had been installed on each. Since the fins could not be made available before 15 December, all movement of ALSIB P-63's from the factory was halted until word was received from Moscow, 9 November, waiving this requirement. Meanwhile, Alaskan Division officers feared that Soviet representatives would decline to accept aircraft on which winterization, requiring 300–350 more man-hours of work per plane, had been delayed by modification. In this case, however, the Soviet Mission agreed to settle for a minimum of winterization.[48]

In flying a typical ALSIB plane from factory to Fairbanks, the facilities of the Alaskan Division were essential. The task, however, was shared by the Ferrying Division, which supplied, and in most cases had trained, the pilots who did the flying.

Procedures for starting the flight of new aircraft from production centers, at first rather complex, were gradually simplified, particularly after May 1944. The key figures in the process were the Ferrying Division's control officers at the several aircraft factories. These officers were notified by Materiel (later Air Technical Service) Command representatives on duty at the same factories of the prospective availability of tested aircraft for flyaway. From the Aircraft Distribution Office in the Dayton area, they learned the destinations of those planes. At the same time they kept in close touch with the Ferrying Group which they represented and which supplied them with pilots possessing proper qualifications for ferrying that type of aircraft. Thus, when a new P-63 was turned over by the Bell factory at Buffalo to the resident Materiel Command representative and by him to the Ferrying Division's control officer, the latter dispatched it in charge of a pilot, normally one belonging to the 3d Ferrying Group, with headquarters at Romulus, Michigan. Stopping at a succession of domestic bases, the pilot would ultimately reach Gore Field at Great Falls, headquarters of the 7th Ferrying Group. There he usually delivered the plane and returned to his home base, with perhaps another ferrying mission en route.[49]

At Great Falls the aircraft received its final processing before leaving the States. If the checks given there by the 34th Subdepot revealed a need for maintenance, it was done on the spot. As a double check the Alaskan Wing, in March 1943, placed a detachment at

Gore Field to conduct inspections and give aircraft a final mechanical clearance, though the 34th Subdepot commander at Great Falls claimed that this was quite superfluous. The entire procedure came under Alaskan Wing control, however, in January 1944, when the subdepot came under the wing's jurisdiction. Clearance having been given, pilots or crews selected by the 7th Ferrying Group took over and flew the plane up the line. The number of stops en route varied greatly, depending, of course, upon the range of the aircraft, mechanical difficulties, and weather conditions. In October 1944, when prolonged bad weather and serious defects in the new P-63 complicated the picture, the median elapsed time between departure of ferried aircraft from Great Falls and their acceptance by the Soviet representatives at Fairbanks was thirteen days. This lag was considerably greater than during the summer months. It was to be much worse before it became better. Before taking off from Great Falls, aircrews were supposed to draw the Arctic clothing which the Alaskan Wing had designated as necessary for one who flew north—and might conceivably be forced down—in the winter. Until September 1944, they were briefed by personnel of their own group organization; thereafter representatives of the Alaskan Division assumed the responsibility. At Fairbanks ferrying pilots delivered their aircraft and returned to Great Falls. The civilian pilots of the contract airlines, who usually flew the ferrying crews back to Great Falls, were often accused of treating these passengers like so much baggage. Certainly, cargo was usually carried along with passengers. The transports were often inadequately heated and lacked oxygen or any real provision for the comfort and convenience of passengers. Meanwhile, at Ladd Field the processing which the ferried aircraft had received at Great Falls was virtually repeated. When Alaskan Wing personnel satisfied themselves that a plane was ready for delivery, there remained the checks performed by the Russians.[50]

At every step in the process described, there was room for friction. Briefing was not always as complete or as helpful as it should have been. Pilots complained of dirty sheets or none, of unwholesome food, of operations officers who insisted that a man push on, even when he thought it dangerous, because of weather or the mechanical condition of his plane, to do so. At some bases and at some periods maintenance personnel were co-operative and efficient; at others, quite the opposite. At the end of the line a man's first desire, naturally, was for food and rest, but diligent priorities and traffic officers sometimes hurried him into the first southbound transport without adequate opportunity for either. In consequence the pilot often got back to Great Falls, considerably the worse for wear, and certainly not anxious to start out on a fresh ferrying assignment.[51]

On the other hand, the pilots were mostly young and often irresponsible. One after another, baffled by the intricacies of supply and too easily stopped by a refusal of suitable equipment, they flew north clad in light, short boots and regulation pinks. At times, certainly, pilots affected carelessness in dress and grooming, and at one time it was rumored in Alaskan Wing circles that at Great Falls a pool paid off to the pilot who grew the longest beard while on duty up the line. Pilots were prone to stay up late, especially at Calgary and Edmonton, and then to report too late for take-off in the morning. Perhaps most serious, from the point of view of those who thought in terms of the safe delivery of a maximum number of planes, many of the pilots were guilty of irregularities in flight procedure and others lacked experience in flying the particular type of plane being delivered.[52]

Such complaints as General Gaffney and his staff made regarding the ferrying pilots, and the responses of the Ferrying Division, were colored by Gaffney's repeated but unsuccessful proposal that the pilots be assigned to the wing, staged at various points along the route, and assigned to fly only relatively short runs of 500 to 750 miles, on which they might become genuinely expert. General Tunner, who commanded the Ferrying Division until the summer of 1944, resisted this recommendation of the Alaskan Wing commander, with arguments both good and bad and, in any event, with complete success. Nor did the friction end finally with the transfer of General Tunner to the India-China Division and the assignment of Brig. Gen. Bob E. Nowland to the command of the Ferrying Division. Meanwhile, deliveries continued. The accident rate, serious enough, fluctuated widely, was usually rather higher in winter than in summer, but in general tended to decline as the war progressed. Model for model, the percentages of accidents compared favorably with those experienced within continental United States.[53]

As the facilities of the northwest route were improved, the Soviet Union chose to have larger proportions of its lend-lease aircraft delivered by that route. Finally, in June 1944, Gen. Leonid G. Rudenko, Chairman of the Soviet Purchasing Commission in Washington, asked that all aircraft called for in the 4th Protocol, arranged that month, be delivered by way of Fairbanks.[54] Even so, there was only one month (August 1944) in which the number of planes delivered to the Soviet Union at Fairbanks exceeded the maximum of 388 forecast by the Air Staff in May 1943.[*]

Transport Operations

The summer and autumn months of 1944 saw not only the peak of ALSIB ferrying but also the highest level of the Alaskan Division's transport operations. Total ton-miles flown by contract carrier and military crews for the division rose gradually from 1,070,956 in January 1943 to 3,087,348 in September 1944, though this record figure was only a little higher than those for July, August, and October of the same year. The best monthly accomplishment in 1945 was nearly as high—2,877,180 ton-miles in June.[55]

Much of these transport operations fell outside the approved Air Transport Command pattern of strategic air support to a military theater. To be sure, the emergency build-up following the Japanese attack on Dutch Harbor in June 1942, when passenger planes from seven airlines were hastily pulled off their regular runs to deliver the means of defense to forward bases near the Aleutians, showed how vitally air transportation might serve a hard-pressed theater commander.[56] Throughout the war elements of the Alaska Defense Command (Alaskan Department) continued to receive mail, passengers, and some cargo, both routine and emergency, by means of ATC transports.[57] A surprisingly small portion of the transport load (18.6 per cent of the Alaskan Wing's ton-mileage in March 1944, 6.7 per cent in June, and only 3.6 per cent in September of the same year) involved the transmission of personnel, equipment, supplies, and mail for the Soviet Union. A much larger portion of the traffic, particularly in the principal channel, Edmonton-Fairbanks, was devoted to maintaining the route itself. Much of it was direct company traffic: the return of ferrying crews, the shipment of supplies to Air Transport Command bases, or the shifting of ATC personnel from one station to another. Furthermore, most of the remaining lift served Army organizations which, during the last two years of the war, had

* See above, p. 165.

no more important mission than to support the ATC's airway to the northwest.[58]

The willingness of the Air Transport Command to initiate regular intratheater services to assist a theater commander is illustrated on a small scale by the Alaskan Wing's operations along the fog-ridden Aleutian chain. This service, which the Eleventh Air Force requested of ATC headquarters during the 1943 Aleutian campaign, was assigned to United Air Lines as contractor. Accordingly, UAL maintained during August and September the service from Anchorage to Adak to move high-priority passengers and mail. Over a year later, when it appeared that a large portion of the Eleventh Air Force's troop-carrier aircraft would be removed, ATC was asked to undertake regular transport operations on the Chain route. Though the troop-carrier organization did not leave, the ATC service, rendered this time by Northwest Airlines, was begun in January 1944, extended in July to Attu, and discontinued only in July 1945. The Canol operation, which grew to a peak in the last four months of 1943, only to disappear soon after the pipeline was completed in February 1944, may also be cited as an intratheater service.[59]

For its operations on the Canol route and for much of its search and rescue work, the Alaskan Wing used light C-64 (Norseman) planes, equipped with pontoons, skis, or wheels as season and circumstance dictated. After May 1945 the division had four C-54's engaged usually in non-stop military service on the coastal run, Seattle to Anchorage. On the main line, Edmonton-Fairbanks, which handled about as much traffic as all the other transport lines of the division put together, the major burden was carried from beginning to end by DC-3's. A few C-46's were assigned in January 1943, and more were expected to the consternation of wing headquarters. Those which came proved of little use, particularly in the Far North. After a time those which were not transferred out of the wing were restricted almost entirely to the relatively easy run between Edmonton and Minneapolis. The purely military operation never overshadowed that of the contract carriers in the Alaskan Wing as it did elsewhere. Even in the fall of 1944, the proportion of the total load which the military carried was less than a third. Thereafter it rose gradually, but only in August 1945, as hostilities came to an end, were the contract airlines withdrawn entirely from the routes of the Alaskan Division.[60]

171

Summary

Serving an inactive theater of operations and an ally whose receipts of lend-lease aircraft remained substantially constant, the Alaskan Division and the northwest route experienced no such astounding growth during the last months of the war as did the Pacific and India-China Divisions and even the European end of the North Atlantic route. Indeed, the story of the airway to the northwest can be briefly summarized: Begun under difficulties of climate and construction comparable with those experienced elsewhere, it struggled through a first hard winter (1942–43) but shortly acquired the necessary facilities and men to support a relatively steady flow of ferried and transport traffic. This it did with increasing efficiency. Throughout its career its commander and his associates worked with an air of expectancy, rooted in the prospect of a large expansion when the time should come for a final push against Japan. When that time came, however, Siberian air bases played no part in the final assault on Japan proper, and not even the B-29 strips built on the Aleutian chain were employed. As a result, the division's routine load continued to be handled in a routine fashion. When the end of hostilities brought an end to the transfer of lend-lease aircraft, the division wound up its affairs and sent its people home.

CHAPTER 7

* * * * * * * * * * *

ACROSS THE PACIFIC

THE victories attained by the Japanese at Pearl Harbor, at Singapore, and in the East Indies made the successful defense of Australia vital, not only for its own sake, but as a base from which to launch an offensive to recover the ground lost and carry the war into the inner defenses of the newly expanded Japanese empire. Australia itself possessed neither the power nor the material resources needed to guarantee its own security, much less to take the offensive against the Japanese. With Britain's forces heavily committed in the Middle East and elsewhere, the responsibility fell chiefly on the United States.

Although support of U.S. and Allied forces in the Southwest Pacific depended mainly upon seaborne transport services, the vital importance of a supplementary air route had been recognized by the War Department early in the fall of 1941. At that time the War Department was greatly concerned with the build-up of U.S. forces for the defense of the Philippines, a defense in which it was expected that the AAF's heavy bombers would play a significant, perhaps decisive, part. The first of the B-17's flown out to Luzon had followed a route from Hawaii by way of Midway and Wake Island to Port Moresby in New Guinea, and thence northwestward to the Philippines. One leg of this route, that from Wake to Port Moresby, was well over 2,100 miles long. More important, the planes had to fly over Japanese-mandated islands in the central Pacific. Consequently, the War Department early in October had agreed to an AAF proposal that an alternate and more secure route through the South Pacific should be developed. When war came, the construction of necessary facilities along this route was not yet complete, but the work was well advanced. Between the 3d and 12th of January 1942, three B-17's passed

173

that way on a flight from Hickam Field through Australia and on into combat over Java. Delay in completing the strip on Christmas Island forced a detour for a landing at the naval air base on Palmyra Island, but Christmas was open to four-engine aircraft by 15 January.*

The new route, at best, was painfully long—more than 7,800 miles from California to Australia. Its longest jump, that from Hamilton Field near San Rafael, California, to Hickam Field, west of Honolulu, was 2,398 statute miles. Hickam was the principal AAF base in the Hawaiian archipelago and, like Pearl Harbor, had suffered severely at the hands of the Japanese on 7 December 1941. It was a well-equipped permanent installation, however, and the damage was quickly repaired. Some 1,346 miles to the south lay Christmas Island, a tiny coral atoll only a few feet above high tide. Next came Canton Island, a still more barren islet, 1,055 miles west and south of Christmas and 1,920 miles out of Hickam Field by direct flight. Its runways, like those on Christmas Island, were rolled coral. Another 1,274-mile flight brought the Australia-bound aircraft to Nandi Airport, a Royal New Zealand Air Force Field on the northwest coast of Viti Levu Island in the Fiji group. The next stop was at Tontouta Airport, near Noumea, capital of the French island of New Caledonia, approximately 850 miles out of Nandi. The last lap of the route, another 915 miles, took the aircraft from Tontouta into the mainland of Australia. Originally, Townsville in Queensland was the intended terminus, but Williamtown, approximately 88 miles northeast of Sydney, and Charleville, some 430 miles inland from Brisbane, actually served as transport and ferrying termini, respectively, until September 1942. Not until 1944 did the Air Transport Command establish a terminal to the north at Townsville, which at first had been too near to enemy air bases and too far from Army and AAF headquarters at Melbourne.[1]

The Air Corps Ferrying Command, and later ATC, was slow to develop services in the Pacific that were comparable to those it provided along the Atlantic routes. As an organization which owed its very origins to the need for assistance to Great Britain and which quickly assumed heavy responsibility for the ferrying of AAF planes within the United States, the command had no part in the early movement of Army aircraft across the Pacific. The first crews taking off from Hamilton Field for the flight to Hawaii were briefed by the Fourth Air Support Command, which continued to render this service

* See Vol. I, 180–82, 192, 228, 374.

until March 1942. The Hawaiian Department had been charged with responsibility for developing the route beyond Hickam Field, and its agencies and the defensive forces stationed along the island chain connecting Hawaii with Australia naturally assumed the obligation to get transient planes through. The route ran through areas in which the Navy not only held the top command but control over essential communications, and it reached its terminus in General MacArthur's Southwest Pacific Area, a command as sensitive to the prerogatives of a combat theater as any to be found the world round. Moreover, in the division of available aircraft for long-range transport services in December 1941, the Navy had received, tacitly at any rate, responsibility for the development of air transport services in the Pacific.

Origins of the Pacific Wing

Although the Ferrying Command at the beginning of the war had its hands more than full in the performance of other duties, it promptly laid claim to the right of clearing all Army planes leaving the West Coast for Pacific destinations. At the end of 1941 plans were being drafted for the establishment of a subordinate headquarters having charge of transpacific ferrying operations. The problem at the moment was to find personnel to man such a headquarters, and the Pacific Sector had its origin in the assignment of 1st Lt. Robert A. Ping to Hamilton Field, where he reported on 3 January 1942. Before the end of the month Ping had personally cleared six LB-30 aircraft to Hickam Field. Gradually, he built up the personnel of the sector and almost singlehandedly procured for it and himself a sector commander of adequate rank in the person of Lt. Col. Karl Truesdell, Jr. At the beginning of March, sector personnel assumed full responsibility for the briefing and clearing of aircraft to be ferried over the Pacific.[2]

During the spring, ferrying operations in that direction increased from 33 departures dispatched by Ferrying Command officers in March to 36 in April, 43 in May, and 64 in June. Although some of these planes were flown by combat crews, others by the Royal Air Force Ferry Command, and still others by civilian employees of Consolidated Aircraft Corporation's Flight and Training Department, most of the 182 aircraft involved were flown by Pacific Sector crews. These ferrying crews, 32 in number, reported to the Pacific Sector during March, April, and May, after an intensive course of training (Project 32)* at Morrison Field, Florida.[3]

During the first four months of 1942 virtually all the ferried planes were destined for the Fifth Air Force in Australia. Indeed, the need for planes in Australia, and for defense of the South Pacific route beyond Hickam, was so urgent that the Seventh Air Force on Hawaii received no reinforcements during this period and was even forced in February to forward 12 of its own 43 heavy bombers to the Southwest Pacific. But all this was changed in May, as hurried preparations were made for the anticipated attack at Midway by the Japanese. Between 18 May and 10 June, no less than 60 B-17's were flown from California to Oahu for reinforcement of the Seventh Air Force. Only 17 of the Seventh's heavy bombers were able to join the attack on the Japanese fleet early in June, and original estimates of their effectiveness have been drastically revised as a result of later study.† But this revision need not detract from the credit due the B-17 crews themselves or from that due the pilots of the Pacific Sector. These men and the crews who flew with them, working with never more than a few hours sleep between flights, delivered a total of 32 B-17's from the mainland to Hawaii during the critical seventeen days, 22 May–7 June. Crews of the 69th and 70th Bombardment Squadrons also flew 26 B-26's in during the same period with the assistance of navigators supplied by the Pacific Sector.[4]

During January and February the Ferrying Command had assisted representatives of the Netherlands East Indies government in arranging for the flight delivery over the South Pacific route of a considerable number of lend-lease B-25's by RAF personnel and crews of Consolidated Aircraft Corporation's Flight and Service Department. The return of some of these and other ferrying crews posed a problem.[5] The scarcity of men qualified to fly aircraft on long-distance overwater flights made it necessary to use the fastest possible means of getting them back to the point where they might start another delivery. It was expected that the Navy, which in the preceding December had taken the responsibility for air transport services in the Pacific and had entered into contract with Pan American Airways as the operating agency for a small fleet of flying boats, would be able to provide this necessary assistance. By February, however, it was be-

* On Project 32, see above, pp. 32–35.
† See Vol. I, 452–62.

coming apparent that the Navy could not return all the Army's ferry-ing crews from Australia to the United States as promptly as military requirements demanded. When the problem became acute, General Arnold on 29 March 1942 directed Colonel George, who was about to take command of the Ferrying Command, to secure two British LB-30's and open a transport service between Honolulu and Austra-lia.[6]

The two transports, which were reconditioned by the Consolidated Aircraft Corporation and flown by crews provided on contract with that corporation, normally made a through run from California to Australia and back. A survey round-trip flight, with John A. Mc-Makin, chief of the company's Flight and Transport Department, as pilot, was made early in April, and on the 23d Consolidated opened a regular service.* The distance from California to Hawaii made any expansion of this service dependent upon procurement of additional four-engine aircraft. Although two-engine planes often made the flight, they were of necessity too heavily laden with fuel to carry either cargo or passengers. But four additional LB-30's were added to the fleet in May, and during that month fifteen westbound flights de-parted Hamilton Field, carrying in the aggregate 120 passengers, near-ly a ton of mail, and almost 13 tons of freight. Thereafter the size of the airlift grew rapidly, and the westward movement of critical freight, mail, and key personnel soon equaled and then surpassed in relative importance the eastbound transportation of ferrying crews which had led to the beginning of the service.[7]

After the Ferrying Command had been redesignated the Air Trans-port Command, the Pacific Sector in July became the South Pacific Wing. The crews formerly assigned to it passed now to the control of the Ferrying Division of ATC, and the new wing, like its counter-parts in the Atlantic, became responsible for the general supervision of all Army transport and ferrying activity within the area of its con-trol.[8] But the South Pacific Wing, despite its name, actually exercised little authority beyond Hamilton Field in California. Wing personnel at Hamilton were now numerous enough to perform their required tasks, but in the Pacific the only personnel properly assigned to the Air Transport Command in July 1942 were Maj. Fred K. Dupuy, control officer at the Australian end of the route, and Capt. H. Ray Millard, Depuy's successor in mid-August. Seven sergeants, hand-

* This service was operated by Consairways, a subsidiary of Consolidated.

picked by Captain Millard before his departure from Hamilton Field, reached Australia by water late in August to begin careers of endless toil. Also two officers arrived by air to assist Millard, but in between California and Australia ATC enjoyed no real control. At Hickam Field the supervision of ATC operations was exercised by Lt. Col. Gordon Blake, whose transfer from the Seventh Air Force to the Air Transport Command had been flatly and successfully refused by the Hawaiian Department. Blake depended upon the 7th Airways Detachment of the Seventh Air Force and the 19th Troop Carrier Squadron, whose primary mission was to supply air transportation within the archipelago. Not until October was the wing successful in securing the placement of Capt. Arthur W. Stephenson, a veteran airline pilot, as ATC control officer at Hickam Field. At Christmas and Canton islands, Nandi Airport, and Plaines des Gaiacs, which in June replaced Tontouta as the New Caledonia stop of aircraft Australia-bound, other numbered airways detachments of the Seventh Air Force continued to handle ferried and transport planes on behalf of ATC. They had from one to four officers apiece and by October approximately the authorized strength of fifty enlisted men each.[9]

Although ATC had its own officers at the Australian terminus of the line, it took these officers nearly four months to get disentangled from the control of an intratheater air transport organization known as the Directorate of Air Transport (DAT). The directorate, headed by Group Capt. Harold Gatty of the RAAF, late Pan American Airways representative in Australia, was handling a varied and heavy mission with a motley lot of land planes and flying boats—Australian, Dutch, American; some of them transport aircraft of various models and ages, and some transformed bombers. When the New Guinea campaign opened in September, the directorate helped move thousands of troops by air while undertaking the direct air supply of all forward combat forces.[10]

When Major Dupuy arrived in May 1942, the headquarters of Lt. Gen. George H. Brett, Commanding General of the Allied Air Forces, encouraged him to set up his office in Sydney, though the transport shuttle inaugurated the previous month by Consolidated made use of the airport at Williamtown, 88 miles to the northeast. Dupuy's activities were placed under the control of the theater air force and more particularly under that of DAT. Priorities, loading policy, and times of departure were fixed by Group Captain Gatty's office in Melbourne. The handful of enlisted men who did the actual physical work of caring for the transpacific transports while they were in Australia belonged to a unit properly subject to DAT, but, when Millard succeeded Dupuy, he gathered evidence of what he counted unreasonable interference by Gatty's headquarters with the overseas transport operation. With this evidence in September he managed to persuade Maj. Gen. George C. Kenney, the new theater air commander, that ATC operations should be free of Gatty's control.[11]

Millard's account of the episode does not suggest that Kenney's concession resulted from his acceptance of ATC's new concept of independence from theater control. As Millard reported it, Kenney called personally to ask him how many belly tanks he could send to Plaines des Gaiacs on an ATC LB-30. Millard seized the opportunity to inform the general that he was not permitted to load theater cargo without the permission of Gatty's organization and then went on to give in detail the record of interference which ATC operations had experienced. Two days later—and quite informally—Kenney told Millard, as the latter subsequently recalled the conversation, "I told the group captain that he was busy enough with his internal show and that he had better run that and let Millard run his."[12] The Air Transport Command thereby won in the Southwest Pacific Area a greater degree of autonomy, but just how much remained to be seen.

Meanwhile, when theater headquarters moved northward from Melbourne to Brisbane, ATC's operations had been transferred to Amberley Field, 24 miles southwest of the latter city. Amberley now became the terminus for ferried aircraft and the turn-around point for transport planes.[13] The small ATC contingent located there, aided by such men as Millard was able to borrow from friendly organizations on the field, handled an increasing volume of traffic as the antipodean spring came on. Earlier, at the time of the Midway battle, the need for the emergency movement of supplies and personnel to Hawaii and of ferrying crews back to California had resulted in the diversion of the five Liberators then in transport service on the Pacific route. When the emergency was over, the Hawaiian Department, without so much as a by-your-leave to Washington headquarters, diverted most of the transport to the task of eliminating the backlog on the run between Hawaii and Australia. Meanwhile mail and personnel for Australia piled up in California. The regular through service had hardly been restored when Lt. Gen. Delos C. Emmons, Commanding General of the Hawaiian Department, cabled General Arnold that the Hawaiian Air Depot could not properly do its job of engine overhaul for organizations in the Pacific area without adequate air transportation for the delivery of engines. In view of the increased demands for regular air transport from theater commanders, it was fortunate that a delivery of additional four-engine transports, virtually the first C-87's, was made in September. In anticipation of this increment, ATC headquarters looked around for crews. United Air Lines, already flying one of the command's domestic routes, accepted the responsibility. United ground and flight personnel were briefed by Consolidated's experienced representatives, and on 23 September the first United plane left Hamilton Field for Australia. In October and November the two contract carriers placed at Amberley Field a joint maintenance crew of a dozen or so men, who thereupon took over the maintenance responsibilities previously carried by the 22d Service Group of the V Air Force Service Command. By the end of 1942 the two contract carriers were operating a total of 15 Liberator-type aircraft on the route, with a schedule of thirteen round-trip flights weekly between California and Australia. The cargo dispatched westbound from Hamilton Field in December reached a total of 107 tons.[14]

The new service, though of vital importance, was still far from satisfactory. Little or no provision was made for the comfort of passengers in flight, and the housing and messing facilities available at various points along the route, notably Plaines des Gaiacs, were primitive enough. More serious was the persistent weakness in communications; as late as November, planes leaving Plaines des Gaiacs commonly arrived at their Australian destination before the radio message announcing their approach. It was still impossible to attain full utilization of the available lift, and operations were often hampered by the assertion of authority over priorities by local theater and island commanders.[15]

In fact, the whole Pacific route operation at the end of 1942 was still, in the eyes of Generals Arnold and George, "very much of a barnstorming setup—without proper organization, standardization, maintenance or discipline."[16] In order to bring it up to the desired standard, a major and obvious step forward was necessary—the assignment of a sufficient number of well-qualified personnel under direct ATC control to each of the stations along the route. Two new ferrying groups and their subordinate squadrons had been duly authorized and activated in California, as early as November 1942, in order to supply personnel for the operation of the ATC bases in Hawaii, Australia, and the intervening points; the Seventh Air Force also had consented to the transfer of its 7th Airways Detachments to the Air Transport Command. In January 1943 the Pacific Wing, commanded by Brig. Gen. William O. Ryan, was established with headquarters at Hickam Field. But ATC faced difficulty in procuring enough qualified personnel to bring up to strength the groups and squadrons it had activated for assignment to South and Southwest Pacific stations. Substantial numbers of men moved out in March, April, and May, and by the end of July 1943 there were nearly three thousand officers and enlisted men assigned to the Pacific Wing. Personnel continued to be shipped out, even in excess of the authorized strength of existing units though not of operational needs, until the War Department, in October 1943, finally approved a manning table which allowed the wing 794 officers, 24 warrant officers, and 6,341 enlisted men.* Meanwhile, with the existing units overstrength, deserved promotions could not be made, and the wing found it difficult, though not impossible, to defend its cries for additional personnel. Nevertheless, at the end of the year the wing's roster showed approximately 5,000 men.[17]

With the establishment of the Pacific Wing, ATC operations in California and over the air route to Hickam became the sole concern of the Hamilton Field headquarters, now renamed the West Coast Wing. It soon became apparent, however, that the whole route from California to Australia was essentially one and needed a unified command. In May, accordingly, General Ryan was directed to take command of the West Coast Wing as well as of the Pacific Wing, and soon the two organizations were completely merged, with General Ryan's headquarters remaining at Hickam Field.[18]

Unified control under General Ryan's direction and a modest increase in assigned aircraft and personnel (particularly experienced operations officers) enabled the Pacific Wing, by the end of 1943, to build a better through route. Ryan, who had understood that he was sent out "for the purpose of creating an airline over the Pacific which would handle cargo, passengers, and mail, as well as the movement of combat units and replacement combat crews and airplanes in the safest

---

* For a discussion of the new exact manning tables, see above, pp. 48–49.

and the most efficient and expeditious manner possible," at the year's end could feel that his mission had been accomplished. In September the transport operations of the contract carriers were at length placed on a regularly scheduled basis, easing the traffic problems at stations along the route and the sporadic demands on major maintenance facilities of Consairways at San Diego and of United Air Lines at San Francisco. One result was the reduction of aircraft time lost for maintenance at the California bases. At the end of the year Consairways reluctantly complied with ATC's demand that it transfer its major maintenance operations to the Fairfield-Suisun Army Air Field, midway between San Francisco and Sacramento.[19]

During the course of the year the number of transport aircraft assigned to United and Consairways for the Pacific operation rose from 15 to 29, and at the end of December the scheduled traffic along the main line (Hamilton Field to Amberley) amounted to twenty round-trip flights a week. The westbound lift from California, 107 tons in December 1942, had risen to 355 tons in December 1943. Meanwhile ferrying operations had continued apace. During the year ATC had conducted some 1,515 planes, mostly heavy and medium bombers, down the line to General Kenney's Fifth Air Force in Australia, to Maj. Gen. Nathan Twining's Thirteenth Air Force in New Caledonia, or to the Seventh Air Force in the Hawaiian Islands.[20]

In addition, ATC had undertaken a variety of special missions. When, in May 1943, the Fifth Air Force attributed a series of B-24 crashes to weakness in the plane's horizontal stabilizer, ATC responded to Kenney's appeal for air shipment of modified stabilizers by sending out eight sets to Port Moresby. Because of the size of the stabilizers, a C-54A, normally operated by American Airlines over the Atlantic route, was sent to the Pacific to carry the first half of the consignment and incidentally was the first C-54 to reach those parts. The second consignment of stabilizers was delivered by the first C-54 assigned United for regular contract operation over the Pacific routes.[21]

During a trip through the Pacific Ocean areas in March and April, General George had committed ATC to special services for both General Kenney in the Southwest Pacific and Lt. Gen. Millard F. Harmon in the South Pacific. For the Southwest Pacific area George agreed to establish an intratheater shuttle running from Port Moresby through Townsville and Amberley Field to Sydney. Served by five

C-47's flown by military crews sent out specifically for the job, the shuttle transported combat personnel of the Fifth Air Force, on leave from New Guinea, to the rest and recreational facilities available at the Australian metropolis. The C-47's, procured from the Troop Carrier Command's allotment, reached Australia in July and were presently put to work. Somewhat oversupplied with crews, who thus did a minimum of flying and a maximum of resting, the shuttle was called the "Sacktime Line." Its morale value was considerable, though at the end of the year DAT and the 54th Troop Carrier Wing were carrying a larger share of the leave personnel.[22] Already, at General Harmon's urgent request, ATC in February 1943 had sent out a C-87, operated by United Air Lines personnel, for a similar leave shuttle from Espiritu Santo in the New Hebrides group through Plaines des Gaiacs to Auckland, New Zealand. The one Liberator was entirely insufficient, and most of the combat crews on leave continued to be carried by SOPAC's intratheater air transport organization, the South Pacific Combat Air Transport Command (SCAT). Three C-87's were in service by January 1944, when military crews replaced those supplied by United Air Lines, and the terminus of the operation was pushed northward to Guadalcanal.[23]

Early in 1942, AAF and Ferrying Command headquarters had been planning an alternate route, or routes, that for safety would run farther south than did the original South Pacific airway. In time, hard fighting on Guadalcanal eliminated the risk that had first inspired the plan, but a secondary consideration survived—the hope that pursuit aircraft might be ferried down to the South Pacific and Southwest Pacific. Various islands and combinations of islands were suggested for these purposes at one time or another, and airfields were constructed below Christmas on Penrhyn Island, at Bora Bora in the Society Islands, and on Aitutaki in the Cook group. Navy air facilities at Tutuila were also made available. However, a proposed assembly depot in the South Pacific was never established, and very few pursuit planes were ferried through the Pacific areas.[24] Between 23 December 1942 and 7 January 1943 an experimental flight of nine P-38's, assembled at Hickam Field, was ferried to New Caledonia by Ferrying Division pilots. Two B-24's, en route to Australia, served as lead and weather aircraft, and Capt. Austin F. Lytle, a veteran pilot, went along to co-ordinate the flight. The planes went by way of Hilo, Christmas Island, Canton, Tutuila, and Nandi Airport. The longest jump from Hilo to Christmas involved a flight of six and a half hours. Difficulties met en route were considered not insurmountable, but no further movements of this sort took place.[25]

In April 1943, while there was still talk of establishing an assembly point at Bora Bora, the Pacific Wing inaugurated its so-called "milk run," serving bases on the alternate ferrying route. Military crews, flying C-87 aircraft, started at Hickam Field, stopped at Christmas, Penrhyn, Bora Bora, Aitutaki, and Tutuila, and reached the end of the run at Nandi. The "milk run" carried mail, periodicals, films, and miscellaneous supplies to the military and naval personnel stationed on the several islands. It was, in fact, a morale-building service, continuing long after Allied advances had canceled the strategic importance of the islands. As Thirteenth Air Force personnel stationed there moved northward, the "milk run" came to serve primarily ATC detachments and service troops stationed on the islands to make possible ATC operations through them. After plans for the Bora Bora assembly plant were dropped, ATC officers at Hickam Field and at Washington sought relief from this obligation, but theater commanders, the Navy, and the Air Staff were slow to agree. Eventually, the Navy, which had permanent establishments at Tutuila and Bora Bora, agreed to supply a shuttle service from Tutuila to Penrhyn, Bora Bora, and Aitutaki, and in August 1944, the ATC abandoned its "milk run."[26]

The Main Line Swings Northward

In the winter of 1942–43 the Air Transport Command had been encouraged by Air Staff spokesmen to expect the assignment of from 1,400 to 2,633 transport aircraft during 1943,* and ATC's planners, with imaginations quite capable of contemplating a transport fleet of that magnitude, had been engaged in correspondingly optimistic planning for expansion of its services. Accordingly, when General George traveled through the Pacific areas in March and April of 1943, he predicted that by the end of the year some 127 four-engine aircraft, most of them flown by military crews, would be at work on the Pacific routes. Without curtailing service on the existing main airline, General George and his subordinates proposed to use the additional planes to establish a transport route farther north and nearer combat operations in both the South Pacific and the Southwest Pacific areas. A new main line would run from Canton Island via Funafuti and Espiritu

* See above, pp. 39–40.

Santo to Townsville in Australia. As soon as feasible, it would be extended to Guadalcanal and Port Moresby. General George's itinerary was followed by officers from wing and command headquarters, whose job it was to prepare in detail for the expanded operation.[27]

The end of the year, however, found the transpacific route served by only 29 ATC transports, still flown by the contract carriers over the old main line. In November, Capt. Richard M. Davis, an alert ATC officer who was the headquarters specialist on Pacific problems, had traveled through the Pacific Wing and conversed with representatives of the theaters concerned. He found the ATC still delivering cargo to the Thirteenth Air Force in New Caledonia, though most of the elements of the Thirteenth had moved or were moving north, and though Guadalcanal was now the main supply point for the South Pacific area. Similarly, he found that Townsville and Port Moresby, the latter more than 1,300 miles north of Brisbane, had supplanted that center as the chief Air Corps supply points for the Southwest Pacific area. No one then expected the Air Transport Command to operate regular schedules into an area of active combat, but Davis considered it hard to defend lagging so far behind the actual advancement of combat areas. Indignant and chagrined at the failure of ATC to adjust its operations to the changed military picture, Davis wrote from Auckland to his immediate superior: "We are largely overshadowed by other air transport agencies which make us look like a peace-time, post-war, commercial air route to Australia, not really involved in the struggle and *really* 'allergic to combat.' "[28] Following his return to Washington, Davis on 18 December submitted a strong report to General George in which he declared:

> For about six months, the South Pacific and Southwest Pacific areas have represented enormous wastes of air transportation. This has been due, in part at least, to our failure to deliver the goods to the *place* where they are needed, since every pound of cargo and a great many passengers, carried by us to these theaters, has had to be trans-shipped, at least once, often more, to reach its destination. . . . In retrospect it is evident that the plan tentatively agreed upon last spring at Hickam of immediately swinging a portion of the Pacific route through Espiritu Santo to Townsville with a view to operations into Guadalcanal and Port Moresby as soon thereafter as practicable should not have been discarded by this headquarters.[29]

The fact that the responsibility had to be shared by the Pacific Wing, ATC headquarters, and the two theaters most directly concerned may help to explain but does not excuse the failure to swing the route northward in 1943. The wing had succeeded, notably in its main task of building up a strong main line to Australia, but the effort had too largely absorbed its energies. It had failed to keep closely enough in touch with the combat theaters and their needs. The theaters in turn, though concerned in November to know why ATC operations had not been shifted northward, had been slow to request direct air shipment to their new and more northerly bases. Air Transport Command headquarters had been obliged in June and July 1943 to cut its plans for the Pacific operation sharply and repeatedly when it became apparent that nothing like the expected number of four-engine transports and crews could be sent into the Pacific areas that season. Then, too, it had become necessary to devote all the available resources of the command to meeting the so-called "July–September objective" set for the India-China Wing of the ATC by the President. Even though ATC headquarters diverted every available new crew and plane, especially C-87's, to the India-China Wing, it was December before the President's goal was reached. With this achievement finally in sight, and with Captain Davis' recommendations of 18 December before him, General George turned back to the Pacific problem. On 21 December he adopted that officer's views and in no uncertain manner directed General Ryan to institute at once a service from Canton through Espiritu Santo to Guadalcanal, Port Moresby, and Townsville.[30]

Even so, it was 10 February 1944 before United Air Lines, using C-54's and C-87's, established a daily service out of Hamilton Field by way of Hickam and Canton to Guadalcanal. Thence half the planes were to fly directly to Townsville, the other half to Townsville via Port Moresby. Until August Consairways continued to serve the Amberley terminal with from seven to eleven trips weekly.[31] This first northward swing of the transpacific transport service came so late that it barely missed being an anticlimax. By May 1944, the larger part of United Air Lines' transpacific lift offloaded at Port Moresby had to be picked up by DAT aircraft for transfer, two hundred miles across the Owen Stanley Mountains, to Nadzab, which was fast replacing Port Moresby as the major base of supply for campaigns in northern New Guinea.[32]

ATC's move into Port Moresby was badly planned and virtually unco-ordinated with other interested organizations. Two lieutenants and a handful of enlisted men were sent up to shift for themselves and somehow to prepare the necessary facilities at the terminus of the new transpacific service to New Guinea. Construction was under way at Ward's Drome, which long had served as terminal of the C-47 leave shuttle, when, a week before the arrival of the first UAL transport, Brig. Gen. Paul H. Prentiss of the 54th Troop Carrier Wing directed the ATC contingent to move to the superior Jackson's Drome, some miles distant. The Fifth Air Force was now on its way out of the area, with the result that new construction was forbidden and normal channels of supply were completely disrupted. The ATC men were able to procure reasonably satisfactory living quarters—by New Guinea standards—only after the movement of another outfit to Nadzab in mid-March. The station was sadly undermanned and overworked in its early months, especially after 3 March, when the transpacific schedules to Port Moresby were doubled to two trips a day. As late as 31 March, there were only three officers and 29 enlisted men at the station.[33] That these men did the job required of them in a reasonably satisfactory manner apparently reflected no special credit belonging to Pacific Wing Headquarters. The ATC Air Inspector's representative, who arrived in March, put the situation thus:

> It seems to be the policy in this Wing to activate a Station by simply writing a general order of activation, and assigning an officer and one or two enlisted men without furnishing them with any written instructions regarding housing and supply or furnishing them with any publications or technical orders. The new commanding officers are not even briefed in their new duties. Consequently when they arrive at their new Stations, they are forced to shift for themselves, and are at the mercy of other components of the AAF, and other commanders who do not regard the ATC in too favorable a manner. This results in the new commanding officer being forced into a system of trade and barter for his requirements. This generally takes the form of trading cigarettes and liquor for the desired services or materials. . . .

It was, accordingly, recommended that wing headquarters in the activation of future stations have an officer, or officers, of sufficient rank and experience visit the proposed base "and make all necessary plans and arrangements with the commanders of the organizations occupying the base at that time."[34]

At the end of May it was estimated that 80 per cent of all cargo brought into the Southwest Pacific by ATC was directed to the theater's air service command and that 90 per cent of this was destined for Nadzab. By that time, General MacArthur's command had virtually completed its conquest of the key points in northern New Guinea and the lesser islands adjacent. After negotiations between

Col. Richard W. Pears, Wing Operations Chief, and General MacArthur's headquarters, it had been agreed on 24 May that Consairways, then operating one and a half round trips daily into Amberley Field, should move its terminus to Nadzab and provide the same number of trips to that destination. Theater representatives agreed that the necessary facilities, supplies, and equipment would be furnished ATC at Nadzab. Following through, a team of high-ranking wing officers flew to Nadzab, where ATC's plans and requirements were discussed exhaustively with the chief of staff of the advanced echelon of the Fifth Air Force, its supply officer, its chief engineer, and the supply officer of the local service command. An operations area and a camp site were selected, necessary technical supply and engineering buildings were requested, and arrangements made for AACS and weather services. In short, wing headquarters, through the aggressive action of its representatives, now demonstrated how well it had learned the lesson taught by the bumbling beginnings at Port Moresby and emphasized by the report of the air inspector thereon. The first ATC cadre, commanded initially by a lieutenant colonel rather than by a lieutenant, arrived at Nadzab on 6 June. It was speedily reinforced; the intratheater service, about to be greatly augmented, was extended from Port Moresby to Nadzab on 23 June; and the Air Service Command assisted with the maintenance load. On 5 August, Consairways began to run two trips daily into Nadzab from Hamilton Field by way of Hickam Field, Canton, and Guadalcanal. Ten days later United Air Lines moved out of Townsville entirely and began a service of two trips daily to Nadzab over the same route. At the same time and on the insistence of the South Pacific and Southwest Pacific theaters, a through service rendered by military crews flying C-54 aircraft over the old route through the Fiji Islands and New Caledonia to Amberley Field on alternate days was set up.[35]

Thereafter, ATC moved its terminal points forward as the combat forces advanced, but the pattern set at Nadzab for the establishment of new stations could not be followed. Theater agencies, struggling to support a fast-moving combat organization, frequently defaulted on their obligations to ATC—not through ill will, or jealousy, or negligence, or even shortsightedness, but simply through inability to do the job without leaving something more important undone. Thus it was that, on more than one Pacific field, ATC facilities, housing, mess halls, water systems, and even roadways were constructed by clerks and aircraft maintenance men with a minimum of training and almost no tools for such work. Nor was the position of the ATC unique. The Fifth Air Force, too, repeatedly complained that the airdrome facilities which it required for planned combat operations were provided too late or not at all. The scarcity of engineering units and equipment was very real, and the demands for their services were tremendous. Late in the war the Pacific Division tried two other methods. One was to man a new station, not by a new base unit assembled from various quarters, but by transferring an existing unit bodily from a station where service was no longer required. Then the division secured a pair of self-sufficient mobile construction units, capable of supplying a new station with the requisite facilities in time, but unfortunately they came too late to benefit ATC greatly.[36]

Intratheater Service in the Southwest Pacific Area

In one active theater of operations after another, circumstances had led to the establishment by the Air Transport Command of scheduled intratheater services, in addition to the long-range, strategic, intertheater services which constituted the ATC's primary transport mission. The command's largest single operation, the delivery of air cargo from India into China, was such an intratheater service until the breakup of the CBI theater in October 1944. Others were developed as the combat zone moved forward in North Africa during 1943–44 and in Europe, especially after the liberation of Paris in August 1944. ATC headquarters felt that no other agency was so well qualified as the ATC itself to provide regularly scheduled transport operations, whether within a single theater or between the Zone of Interior and a particular theater. Eventually, theater commanders came to see in the ATC, if not the best possible agency for supplying intratheater air transportation, at least an organization through which they might acquire additional transport aircraft and crews for some specific function. Into this category fall the requests of Generals Harmon and Kenney for the leave shuttles which the ATC inaugurated in February 1943 to serve the Thirteenth Air Force and in July of the same year to serve the Fifth Air Force.*

By December 1943, General Kenney was casting about for addi-

* See above, pp. 182–83.

tional aircraft of all categories, including transports. Air transportation was especially important in the Southwest Pacific Area. The distances within the Australian continent and from Australian points to New Guinea, the inadequacy of rail and highway facilities throughout the area, the scarcity and vulnerability of available water transport, and the failure as yet to swing ATC's intertheater main line northward, all highlighted the increasing need for air transport. In the direct support of combat operations, troop-carrier groups of the Fifth Air Force performed a host of tactical missions. The Directorate of Air Transport controlled the Australian airlines, several squadrons of the RAAF, and the squadrons of the American 374th Troop Carrier Group. Though primarily responsible for the movement of cargo from the Brisbane area to points north, the military elements under DAT continued to be called upon for direct support of troops in the combat areas. This was in accord with Kenney's policy of flexible use of air transport, but each diversion of this character meant the temporary collapse of the orderly flow of supplies from the rear areas to the depots supplying the combat elements. Forward or back, nevertheless, the several elements of DAT in November 1943 hauled cargo and passengers to the extent of 7,500 tons, more than the ATC tonnage over the Himalayan Hump that same month.[37]

New Year's Day 1944 found General Kenney and members of his staff, including Col. Ray T. Elsmore, then Director of Air Transport, flying to Washington, where he presented his needs for additional aircraft. In Washington, General Kenney talked to General George about the transport needs of the SWPA and proposed that the ATC set up a pair of transport squadrons to operate under his control with Colonel Elsmore in command. General George favored a scheduled operation in accordance with normal ATC practice and under direct ATC command. He proposed that the ATC, operating approximately a hundred two-engine transports (the use of C-46's was originally contemplated) should take over DAT's operations in the rear areas, thus freeing the latter's troop-carrier squadrons for full-time service forward. Apparently, the two generals reached an agreement that this should be done, though General Kenney later admitted that what he really preferred was the direct allocation to the theater of a comparable number of aircraft and crews.[38]

Early in March Col. Robert M. Love, Deputy Chief of Staff of the Air Transport Command, went to Australia to continue conversations with General Kenney regarding necessary arrangements for setting up the proposed intratheater service. Love soon discovered that Kenney was still thinking in terms of the Air Transport Command's providing planes, personnel, and maintenance for a service to be completely controlled by Kenney or by theater headquarters. Informed of this situation, George radioed Kenney, recalling their previous correspondence and conversation and urging that Kenney's program would not produce an efficient air transport operation. With General Arnold's concurrence, he proposed that ATC be given a clearly defined job to do in the SWPA, in which ATC would fly whatever routes and carry whatever cargo General Kenney might direct.[39]

General Kenney insisted that he must have final control over every plane in the Southwest Pacific Area and that the ATC should enter the intratheater picture with the same status as the other elements which DAT controlled. Colonel Love was supported in his arguments by Maj. Gen. Laurence S. Kuter, Assistant Chief of Air Staff, Plans, who was then in the SWPA, and eventually General Kenney came around to the ATC position and agreed positively that DAT should exercise no command functions over the intratheater service which ATC proposed to render on a route from Melbourne to Nadzab. His message, replying to General George, may be paraphrased in part as follows: "To the extent of their current capacity, your operators will be informed what the job is, where it is, and what the priorities are; we will not, however, tell them how to do it."[40]

The agreements reached were put into final form on 13 April, when Love addressed an official letter on behalf of his chief to General MacArthur summarizing his understanding of the matter, while General Kenney's chief of staff indicated Kenney's concurrence in a letter addressed to General George. The approval of Lt. Gen. Richard K. Sutherland, MacArthur's chief of staff, was immediately forthcoming, and on 18 April the agreement was formally confirmed in an adjutant general's letter from SWPA headquarters. Here was something closely akin to an exchange of diplomatic notes between two sovereign states, if not to a formal treaty.

Service was to be furnished initially on the route: Brisbane, Townsville, Port Moresby, and Nadzab. ATC indicated its intention of providing a hundred C-47 aircraft for the shuttle, twenty-five each in May, June, July, and August. It was agreed that third- and fourth-echelon maintenance should be the responsibility of the theater's air service command and that the theater would aid with first- and second-echelon maintenance until ATC could do the job. The V Air Service Command had already ordered the engines, accessories, and spare parts needed to keep the shuttle aircraft in operation. It was agreed that "the appropriate authority designated by the theater will govern what traffic is to be carried, the priorities therefor and the stations between which service is needed, but that operational and administrative control will be exercised by ATC consistent with existing policies and procedures." General Kenney had intended that the Directorate of Air Transport should be the "appropriate authority designated by the theater"; on this, however, he was overruled by General MacArthur's headquarters, which decided that Col. Charles H. Unger, the Chief Regulating Officer of SWPA, should exercise the responsibility.[41]

Another item in the Kenney-Love agreement, as approved by GHQ, SWPA, called for the organization by ATC of a wing or sector in the Southwest Pacific Area. After some hesitation, ATC headquarters, with AAF and War Department concurrence, determined to elevate all its existing wings to the status of divisions and to organize three wings—the Southwest Pacific, the Central Pacific, and the West Coast Wings—within the Pacific Division. General Ryan became division commander, and Brig. Gen. Edward H. Alexander, who had been the first executive officer of the Ferrying Command, air adviser to General Stilwell in the CBI theater, and commanding general successively of ATC's India-China and Caribbean Wings, was selected to command the Southwest Pacific Wing. Meanwhile, Col. Chester Charles, ATC commanding officer at Townsville, and one of the ablest officers in the Pacific Wing, was ordered to take charge of preparations for the intratheater operation.[42]

With the aid of wing headquarters and with the best of co-operation from SWPA personnel, Colonel Charles perfected plans for inaugurating the service. The first of the planes and crews destined for the operation reached Amberley Field on 3 June, and subsequently went on to Nadzab. On 26 June the new intratheater service was inaugurated, and by the end of the month it was supplying four round trips daily, in addition to a daily Sydney-to-Nadzab leave shuttle.[43]

On 5 July General Alexander arrived in Australia to assume command of the proposed Southwest Pacific Wing. By 1 August he had eliminated a maintenance bottleneck by arranging for the air shipment of a hundred and fifty mechanics from Hamilton Field, and other badly needed personnel had been procured. Some 76 C-47's were on hand, and the remaining 29 were already en route. Within another week, the new wing was operating seventeen C-47 schedules daily between Australia and New Guinea; and Finschhafen had already been added to the points served. In addition, General MacArthur had given the wing operational control of two C-54's which the ATC had supplied him earlier in the year for a series of special missions to Mindanao. These planes were providing service on alternate days between Brisbane and Hollandia. Generals MacArthur, Sutherland, and Kenney had all expressed their satisfaction with ATC's entrance into the theater with the corollary hope that it would release existing troop-carrier units for tactical operations. None of General Alexander's requests for assistance had been refused. Meanwhile, requests for additional schedules were piling up, though Alexander took the position that none should be added until he had enough planes and men to keep it going.[44]

The jurisdiction of the Southwest Pacific Wing was expanded in August to take in another intratheater operation, arranged in May between South Pacific Area headquarters and Colonel Pears to relieve SCAT of its rear-area responsibilities. In SOPAC the ATC with fifteen C-47's based at Guadalcanal had inaugurated in July five daily schedules each way between Tontouta, Espiritu Santo, and Guadalcanal. The South Pacific and Central Pacific areas were shortly combined under the designation of the Pacific Ocean Areas, while the Thirteenth Air Force, chief ATC customer in the former South Pacific Area, was joined with the Fifth Air Force to constitute the Far Eastern Air Forces under General Kenney's command. It seemed logical, therefore, to place what had originally been two distinct intratheater services under the control of the Southwest Pacific Wing. The more easterly of the two shuttles early devoted a good deal of its lift to the air evacuation of casualties from Guadalcanal to the general hospital at Espiritu Santo. Subsequently, hospital facilities at Guadalcanal were built up, and between September and January the wing's C-47's evacuated numerous casualties of the Palau campaign from Manus Island via Los Negros to Guadalcanal and Finschhafen.

Many patients continued to be transferred from Guadalcanal to Espiritu Santo and Tontouta.[45]

The function of the SWP Wing was to aid the combat forces in every way that organized military air transport might, excepting only tactical operations. Encouraged by the zeal of General Alexander, the wing's story from the beginning of the intratheater service in June 1944 until Luzon had been made secure a year later was highlighted by constant revision of schedules for the ATC fleet of C-47's as their services were repeatedly advanced into more forward areas. As early as August 1944, 70 per cent of the traffic carried by the entire Pacific Division originated at stations within the Southwest Pacific Wing.[46]

The original main artery—Brisbane-Townsville-Nadzab—was extended northwest to Hollandia in September, while service south of Townsville was cut. A new shuttle was begun in eastern New Guinea, from Nadzab to Milne Bay via Lae, Finschhafen, and Dobodura. In October, with nothing but mopping-up operations left for the ground forces in New Guinea, Hollandia became the jumping-off point for new landings in Leyte. In preparation for the move, wing aircraft shuttled men and material about from point to point at the behest of GHQ, SWPA. At the beginning of September they flew a portion of General MacArthur's headquarters from Brisbane to Hollandia, making it possible for GHQ to carry on with the loss of only half a day's work. A month later General Alexander, eager to maintain the intimate relationship between wing and theater headquarters, moved to Hollandia, where his headquarters opened officially on 19 October.[47]

Almost at that moment American troops were landing on Leyte, and a month later General Alexander moved thither, this time preceding by a few days the portion of GHQ which was flown in by ATC. The movement of GHQ personnel and cargo proceeded smoothly for two of the three days, 26–28 November, which had been set aside for the movement. On the evening of the 27th, four C-54's and four C-47's were loaded, ready to take off early on the 28th, when the Chief Regulating Officer, GHQ, was notified that 16 tons of critical ordnance materiel, must reach Leyte the next day. He decided to dispatch the ordnance materiel instead of the loads already aboard the C-54's, and with the aid of practically every man on the ATC base at Hollandia the transfer was completed in about two hours. The movement of GHQ's air echelon was completed on 30 November. Wing personnel moved up to Leyte largely by waterborne transportation, with some confusion in the order of arrival of the several shipments. The air echelon flew up during the first week of the new year, and on 6 January, wing headquarters was officially reopened amid the mud and rice paddies of Tacloban airfield. In the final move of wing headquarters to Manila, the echelons arrived in proper order, and headquarters opened in its new location on 25 March. Between 12 and 14 April the wing aided in a third forward movement of GHQ, flying some 822 men from Leyte to Manila. Finally, between 28 April and 2 May, wing aircraft in a total of forty trips transferred the headquarters of General Kenney's Far Eastern Air Force to Manila.[48]

When the first ATC detachment arrived at Leyte on 31 October, the Tacloban airstrip, with over two hundred fighter and bomber aircraft jammed into the available standing room and with enemy air attacks routine, was still very much in the combat area. Well into the new year, the continuing campaign restricted sharply the number of ATC landings which could be permitted at Tacloban. Nevertheless, the wing in November 1944 made thirty-six trips into Leyte, fifteen with C-54's, and twenty-one with C-47 aircraft. At the beginning of February 1945, schedules called for ten daily arrivals there of intratheater aircraft. Nadzab and Port Moresby had been virtually abandoned by ATC at the beginning of the preceding December, by which time the transpacific transport service had moved its major terminal to Biak, and the intratheater service now counted as its key stations Biak, Hollandia, and Finschhafen, in that order.[49] The transportation of personnel was an especially important function for the SWP Wing; in each of the four months extending from October 1944 through January 1945, the number of passengers carried exceeded thirty thousand. In every month of the wing's history the weight of passengers and their baggage hauled was considerably in excess of that of miscellaneous cargo. The passengers included troops on their way to combat, VIP's headed either way, and many thousands of casualties on their way back to hospitals in the theater or beyond. The amount of mail carried fluctuated; in May 1945 it amounted to nearly 20 per cent of the total airlift. As the wing moved nearer to the advancing front, the combat forces had little except battle casualties to ship back. In April and May 1945, northbound planes of the wing were loaded to 95 per cent of their capacity; on the backhaul the figure for both months was only 49 per cent. During its first full year of service, the wing's pilots set a phenomenal safety record—290,000,000 passenger miles flown without a single fatality.[50]

Enemy action was still in progress on the Quezon airstrip at Manila, and Japanese forces were still in Manila City, when the first ATC plane reached that area on 16 February 1945. By June, with the liberation of the archipelago substantially accomplished, the need for the wing's intratheater service had declined sharply. ATC personnel were removed from all bases in Australia, except that near Brisbane, which remained the terminus for twice-weekly services from California and from Manila. In July the roll-up of all New Guinea bases got under way, and Southwest Pacific Wing personnel were made available for transfer to the hard-pressed Central Pacific Wing.[51]

Expanded Operations, 1944–45

The rapid northward shift during 1944 of the Southwest Pacific terminus of the transpacific operations—from Brisbane to Townsville and Port Moresby, from both to Nadzab, and then to Biak—was the prelude to further movements by which the entire transpacific service was swung northward and materially shortened. Early in January 1944, ATC C-54's, which since the preceding November had been evacuating casualties of the campaign for Tarawa, moved forward to a base on that island for the evacuation of casualties in the ensuing campaign for control of the Marshall Islands. By the end of May air evacuation planes were landing at Kwajalein, chief of the Marshalls, and the next month found them flying eastward with some eight hundred patients, mostly men wounded in the battle for Saipan. By mid-August they were loading patients on Saipan itself. In November the air evacuation planes began going into Leyte on a special mission basis, sending patients eastward to Saipan or even, via Kwajalein, Johnston Island, and Oahu, to California.[52]

Air evacuation planes caried cargo and passengers on their westward flights, and the air evacuation routes soon became those of general transpacific air transport operations. Thus on 15 December 1944 the first regularly scheduled transport service was instituted between Hamilton Field and Leyte by way of the central Pacific. Guam soon became the major ATC base in the Marianas, and from there the first ATC plane flew to Okinawa on 8 April 1945, just a week after the initial landings there of the Tenth Army. The service thus inaugurated had been carefully planned to combine the delivery of vital supplies with the evacuation of casualties. Meanwhile, the route from California to the Southwest Pacific Area through Tarawa, Los Negros, and Biak had been extended early in March to Leyte.[53]

The story of the later operations of ATC in the Pacific, however, is much more than that merely of new or extended flying routes. Much of the ATC traffic west of Oahu stopped short of the Philippines and the Ryukyus. By January 1945, Guam and Saipan had become major termini for both ferrying and transport operations, as they had become focal points for the direct attack upon the Japanese home islands. Headquarters of the Seventh Air Force was moved to Saipan in December 1944. The next month, Fleet Admiral Chester W. Nimitz, Commander-in-Chief, Pacific Ocean Areas, moved his headquarters from Oahu to Guam. Since October, the ATC had been helping move XXI Bomber Command to its station in the Marianas, where its B-29's began on 25 November 1944 its attack on the Japanese homeland. In January 1945 the Central Pacific Wing transferred its headquarters from Hickam Field to Guam.[54]

The establishment of the XXI Bomber Command in its island bases and the support of its strategic bombing operations constituted a major part of the Central Pacific Wing's mission, as of the ATC in the Pacific. Briefly, it involved monitoring the delivery of B-29 bombers by combat crews to their Marianas bases, the moving by transport aircraft of the air echelon of the several wings of that command, and the constant support of its bombing operations by scheduled air transport service from the homeland. The responsibilities of the ATC in ferrying the big bombers and in transporting men and materiel from the United States or Oahu did not differ in kind from those made familiar through earlier service for the Fifth or the Far Eastern Air Forces. The only significant variation lay in the bigness and top-secret character of the very-long-range bombers, in the magnitude of the movement, and in the well-founded hope that they might serve to shorten the war materially. In any event, the movement illustrated almost classically the role of strategic air transportation in support of strategic bombing.

In preparation for ferrying the B-29's, the Air Transport Command had acquired Mather Field near Sacramento, California, as a point of departure and had spotted B-29 parts at John Rodgers Airport (Naval Air Station, Honolulu), on Kwajalein, and at Saipan, the major ATC stations on the proposed route. A special engineering detachment, whose members had been carefully trained in the maintenance of B-29 aircraft, was sent out to instruct maintenance personnel along the route. Heavy maintenance equipment required in maintaining the huge bombers was procured and moved by water to the several bases. Special precautions were taken to guard the security of the movement. As always it was necessary to process and brief the combat crews who were to fly their own planes across the Pacific. The B-29 groups were in general better prepared for the long overwater flight than most of the tactical outfits which had preceded them; but, for many crews, flying the Pacific was itself a major adventure, and all that could be done by way of careful briefing or to stimulate the confidence of the fliers was very much to the good. Begun early in October, the movement proceeded with little delay, and by the end of the month some 58 of the heavy bombers had reached Saipan. Eighty B-29's went through in November, 104 in December, and 127 in January 1945. The flow continued into 1945, and in June the XXI Bomber Command received a record total of 237 B-29's, including the thousandth Superfortress to make the flight.[55]

The growing ability of the United States during 1944 and 1945 to concentrate troops and aircraft in the Pacific reflected the upsurge of industrial production, as well as the approaching end of the war in Europe. The peak in transpacific ferrying, not only of B-29's but of aircraft generally, was reached in June 1945. In that month 570 planes were flown out from California for delivery, chiefly to the combat air forces. Total deliveries of aircraft rose from 1,592 in 1943 to 2,545 in 1944 and to more than 3,200 in the first eight months of 1945.[56]

More spectacular was the increased size and capacity of ATC's Pacific transport fleet. In January 1944, military crews assigned to the Pacific Wing were operating on the Tarawa-Hickam run five C-54's especially designed for and assigned to the air evacuation of casualties. United Air Lines was flying nine more C-54's under contract on the transpacific route. Between them, United and Consairways had a total of nineteen Liberator-type planes in the through transport service between the United States and Australia.[57] Before the end of 1944, not only was ATC planning on a Pacific fleet of

160 four-engine planes but the attainment of that objective was already in sight. United Air Lines had gradually exchanged its C-87's for C-54's, as they became available, and since August had operated a fleet of twenty C-54's. Consairways at the year's end had a total of fifteen C-87's in service. Both of the contract carriers achieved a remarkably high record in the daily utilization of aircraft assigned to them. The greatest increase in the airlift over the Pacific came, however, from the additional C-54 aircraft operated by military crews. This fleet grew from 7 in February, to 30 in August, to 86 in December 1944, and to 130 in April 1945.[58]

By June 1945, OPD had approved an airlift in the following December of 3,759 tons monthly from Hawaii to the forward areas. To meet this requirement, ATC estimated that it would need a total of 243 four-engine transports and personnel to the number of 42,000 by the end of the year, with physical facilities in proportion. At the end of July, military crews were flying a total of 147 C-54's on the Pacific routes, the contract carriers between them 38 four-engine aircraft. The weight of cargo, passengers, and mail carried had climbed steadily. In December 1943 the actual lift westbound from the Hawaiian Islands—always larger than the haul from California to Hawaii, thanks to the smaller load of fuel required—amounted to 494 tons. The next December it was 1,618 tons, and in July 1945 it reached the imposing figure of 3,483 tons.[59]

Back in 1943, when it had seemed all but impossible to meet the personnel needs of ATC's Pacific operation, and when OPD was cutting down on ATC's manning table requests for the Pacific Wing, General George remarked to a key wing officer that, when German resistance collapsed, "They will pour such heat on in the Pacific that we will have all we can do to handle it."[60] He predicted that ATC would be able to write its own ticket on requirements, with no questions asked. So indeed it proved, and that in advance of the German collapse. Personnel assigned to the Pacific Wing at the beginning of 1944 totaled hardly 5,000. By July the 10,000 mark was passed, and by the end of October this figure had more than doubled, to enable the three wings of the reorganized Pacific Division to carry the added load involved in the B-29 movement, the increased support given the Seventh Air Force, the growth of air evacuation activities, and the expansion of the Southwest Pacific Wing's shuttles in preparation for the Philippine invasion, not to mention the enlarged transpacific transport operation. During the early months of 1945, division personnel continued to increase, though at a lower rate. By the end of April, the roster included over 24,000 men and women; at the end of July, over 27,000. In August, however, with assignment of many more aircraft and the transfer to ATC of command jurisdiction over the Hawaiian Air Depot and Hickam Field, it jumped to 37,600, and in September to over 41,600 officers and enlisted personnel. The tremendous growth of the Pacific Division made a further reorganization inevitable. The authority of the several wing commanders was strengthened while the division commander, who surrendered some functions and staff personnel to the wings, retained effective over-all control of the entire operation.[61]

To speed up redeployment for the final push against Japan, ATC headquarters at the beginning of summer in 1945 made three proposals which were put into effect: (1) a vigorous attempt to increase the use of aircraft already assigned to the Pacific Division; (2) the routing of new C-54's assigned to the India-China Division westward across the Pacific; and (3) a shift from the Atlantic to the Pacific of the maintenance services through which the India-China Division had heretofore returned its C-54's to Morrison Field in Florida for engine changes and 600-hour checks. Early in July, representatives of the command presented to General Arnold and then to General Marshall a plan for the further augmentation of the Pacific airlift that was projected well into 1946. This plan called for the immediate diversion of some 196 planes from the GREEN PROJECT in the North Atlantic* and, after November, of large numbers of new aircraft originally intended for the India-China Division. But such sweeping measures were not considered necessary. In order to meet an estimated need for air transport of 10,000 combat troops monthly above prior commitments, from the United States to forward areas in the Pacific, ATC during the early days of August shifted some 95 C-54's from its North Atlantic and North African services and from the Ferrying Division to its Pacific routes. This last program for expanding the Pacific airlift was known to ATC personnel as the PURPLE PROJECT.[62]

Meanwhile the scope of ATC's Pacific schedules increased to a point which must have seemed fabulous to the men whose memory of military air transport in the Pacific ran back to 1942. Schedules

* See below, pp. 216–25.

published at the beginning of August 1945 called for six daily shuttle flights, four with LB-30's and two with C-54's, between the West Coast and Hickam Field, nine C-54 flights daily between the West Coast and the Marianas, in addition to three between Hickam Field and the Marianas. Five C-54 flights daily were scheduled to run from the West Coast to Okinawa, and five more from the West Coast to Manila. An additional daily shuttle linked the Marianas with Manila. Consairways' LB-30's provided one daily schedule to Biak and another to Guadalcanal. Twice weekly, Consairways continued to run a flight over the old route from California to Australia. In all, there were twenty-seven round-trip flights scheduled daily between California and Oahu; twenty-four and a fraction between Oahu and forward points in the Pacific.[63] Because aircraft operations depend on weather and on the mechanical condition of the available planes, flights were not always operated as scheduled. By the end of hostilities, however, the Pacific Division made it a practice to stage spare C-54's at key stations, in order to keep cancellations from mechanical causes to a minimum. Desperate and moderately successful measures had also been taken to improve the quality of maintenance given the military C-54's; as a result, the aircraft utilization record of the division crept up slowly during the first half of 1945.[64]

Mission 75

At the beginning of August 1945 the operations of the Pacific Division were still geared to the continuing needs of General Spaatz's United States Strategic Air Force and to the buildup of General MacArthur's U.S. Army Forces in the Pacific, which had been charged with invasion of the island of Kyushu on 1 November 1945. The division also supplemented the airlift supplied by NATS to Admiral Nimitz, the Navy's Commander-in-Chief for the Pacific. Plans for the coming invasion of the Japanese home islands assigned to ATC no new or distinctive responsibilities, but the situation became suddenly quite different with the brightening prospect that Japan might surrender in advance of the invasion. In July General MacArthur's staff had begun preparation of a plan, coded BLACK-LIST, for the occupation of Japan in the event of an early surrender. Early in August, General Arnold urged Kenney to include the extensive use of heavy transport aircraft in the occupation program and promised 180 C-54's for that purpose by 15 August. Accordingly,

BLACKLIST was expanded to include BAKER-SIXTY, which proposed the use of transport planes to land the 11th Airborne Division and perhaps the 27th Infantry Division, as well as advanced echelons of GHQ, the Far Eastern Air Forces, and other headquarters, in a critical portion of the Tokyo plain.

The Far Eastern Air Forces, which was placed in operational control of the project, was to supply 100 C-47's and 272 C-46's; the Air Transport Command at least 180 operational C-54's. General Alexander, whose Southwest Pacific Wing was then "rolling up" its bases in New Guinea and Australia, and transferring personnel to the Central Pacific Wing, was summoned to MacArthur's headquarters on 9 August and informed of the role which ATC was intended to play. Two days later, General Ryan placed him in full charge of ATC's part of the operation. ATC headquarters in Washington, first apprised of the project in a series of urgent messages from Alexander on 13 August, promptly gave the needed authority for the diversion of ATC aircraft. To prevent confusion, General Ryan shortly designated all activity relating to the concentration of ATC aircraft in the western Pacific area and their mission there as the Pacific Division's MISSION 75.[65]

Aircraft operated by military crews were speedily withdrawn from the transpacific schedules, which were left to the planes operated by Consairways and United Air Lines. Some 33 C-54's from the North Atlantic Division, 38 from the North African Division, and 16 drawn from the Ferrying Division and new production converged upon Kadena airfield in Okinawa. New Skymasters being ferried westward to the India-China Division were diverted, in defiance of conventional ATC doctrine but with the blessing of ATC headquarters. Soon General Alexander had at his direct disposal a grand total of 202 C-54's. By the end of the month the C-54's operated by military crews under Pacific Division orders totaled 267, not including the 41 four-engine transports flying with United Air Lines and Consairways crews.[66]

On 14 August the first MISSION 75 aircraft flew from Nichols Field at Manila to Okinawa, where Kadena, constructed as an advanced base for B-29's but as yet unused for that purpose, offered a magnificent 7,500-foot coral runway and with ninety hardstands, each capable, with crowding, of accommodating two Skymasters. Except for these fundamentals, however, the airfield "was completely unadorned by any works of man." Communications equipment was quickly set up and a control tower built. Tentage supplied essential housing. Ground transportation and messing facilities capable of serving thousands of hot meals daily were provided by the co-operation of various organizations, notably elements of the 59th Air Service Group. Spare parts were assembled for emergency maintenance. Maximum load limits, 25- and 50-hour checks, and pilot qualifications minima were all waived for the time being. Arrangements were made for the aircraft to receive their 100-hour checks at Harmon Field on Guam. Weather data were supplied by destroyers of the U.S.N.'s Seventh Fleet, stationed at intervals of 100 miles along the route. A weather squadron moved over from Manila to give the best possible synoptic weather information for the briefing of flight crews. The 54th Troop Carrier Wing, delegated by FEAF to supervise the entire operation, prepared an elaborate flight plan, calling for take-offs from Kadena at three-minute intervals. D Day, planned for 26 August, was postponed until 30 August on account of typhoon weather in the Ryukyus and in the areas approaching Honshu itself. By 28 August, however, the weather had cleared; on that day 15 ATC C-54's and 30 Troop Carrier C-47's, laden with aviation gasoline, oil, and a handful of FEAF communications men, made what might be termed an orientation and supply flight to the designated Japanese target, Atsugi Airport, 16 miles southwest of Tokyo.[67]

Promptly on 30 August the operation proper began. Thirteen days later it was brought to a successful conclusion, without a single fatal aircraft accident. In 1,336 C-54 flights, the 11th Airborne Division (reinforced), the 27th Infantry Division, the advanced echelons of General MacArthur's headquarters, of Far Eastern Air Forces, and of the Eighth Army, plus the initial ATC detachment, were flown into Atsugi airdrome. In all, over 23,000 troops, 924 jeeps, 9 disassembled liaison aircraft, 329 other vehicles and pieces of equipment, including tractors, bulldozers, and 6 × 6 trucks, made the flight from Okinawa to Atsugi. In addition, 2,348 barrels of gasoline and oil and rations to the amount of over 900 tons were offloaded at Atsugi. More than seven thousand released prisoners of war and internees of sixteen different nationalities were brought back to Okinawa, on the first or second lap of their repatriation journeys. In addition to these primary aspects of the movement, ATC personnel performed two related special missions at the request of General MacArthur's headquarters. On 19 August Col. Earl T. Ricks, ATC Director of Operations for MIS-

SION 75, flew the Japanese armistice delegates from Ie Shima near Okinawa to Manila; the next day he returned them to Ie Shima. Then, on 23–24 August, another ATC crew flew to Vladivostok in order to carry to Manila Lt. Gen. Kuzma M. Derevyanko, Russian representative to the pre-surrender conference, and his staff.[68]

MISSION 75 was a magnificent demonstration of what could be done with the transport aircraft of 1945 and a magnificent climax to the role which air transport had played in the Pacific war. Yet its significance should not be exaggerated. On the best day of the landings, with the combined efforts of the 54th Troop Carrier Wing and ATC, no more than seventy-five hundred men were offloaded. In the face of active resistance, nothing like this number could have been landed, and those landed unquestionably would have been overwhelmed by the defenders. In short, the project was feasible only in the absence of effective opposition.[69]

CHAPTER 8

*　　*　　*　　*　　*　　*　　*　　*　　*　　*　　*

TRAFFIC HOMEWARD BOUND

THROUGHOUT all its career, down to the eve of victory in 1945, the Air Transport Command was principally preoccupied with the outbound movement of aircraft, men, and materiel from the United States to overseas theaters or to points where aircraft and materiel could be transferred to friendly powers. That there should be some homeward-bound traffic, however, was inevitable. Mail proceeded in both directions; ferrying pilots, in the system early adopted by the Ferrying Command, had to be returned to their home bases; scarce materials of strategic value in the war effort were flown to American ports on ATC transports; thousands of sick and wounded soldiers flew homeward on ATC planes equipped for air evacuation; and aircraft no longer needed in the theaters were ferried back home. After V-E Day under ATC direction vast numbers of planes and men flew home for redeployment to the Pacific or separation from service.

As early as 1942, pilots of the Ferrying Division after delivering new aircraft to destinations overseas were on occasion directed to ferry war-weary aircraft back to the United States. Thus in November 1942, several ferry pilots who had delivered new P-40's to the Eleventh Air Force at Elmendorf Field, Anchorage, Alaska, were ordered to return old P-36's and P-38's to the United States.[1] The loss of one P-36 from a mechanical failure, and the narrow escape of its pilot, gives some indication of why more of such planes were not returned. Overseas air bases were reluctant to expend on discarded aircraft the amount of maintenance required for a safe trip home. Ferrying crews, on the other hand, were even more unwilling to fly back a plane in a questionable state of repair.[2] Only a small fraction of the planes which had gone out to the theaters were ever returned in this

205

fashion. During the twelve-month period extending from 1 April 1944 until 31 March 1945, some 842 military aircraft were ferried back to the United States, as against 22,144 delivered overseas.[3]

Throughout 1942 and the early part of 1943, with enemy submarine action continuing to take a large toll of waterborne shipments, air transportation of a minimum of strategic materials was essential to certain aspects of war production. The Board of Economic Warfare on behalf of the War Production Board, which decided on needs, procured and stocked backlogs of such essential materials at airports on the ATC routes. Such materials included high-quality block mica from Karachi and South America and quartz crystals from South America (both products indispensable in the manufacture of radio parts and equipment). Tantalite, used in producing radio and radar apparatus, and special alloy steels required for cutting tools were flown from Brazil and the Belgian Congo. Beryl, which in the form of an alloy was used in manufacturing a variety of delicate instruments, came also from Brazil, while rotenone-bearing roots and powder for use in insecticides were brought from various parts of South America. For a time in 1942 rubber was carried when other inbound cargoes were not available. During the twenty-week period between 6 December 1942 and 24 April 1943, the Naval Air Transport Service, ATC, and the contract carriers working under their direction together flew from the east coast of South America to the United States a total of 970.9 tons of such strategic materials. In the first quarter of 1943 ATC aircraft also lifted some 985 tons of strategic cargo from China to India, while Chinese National Aviation Corporation planes brought out 1,038 tons. The largest elements in this tonnage were tungsten, tin, silk, hog bristles, and mercury. The need for these commodities from China was not usually great enough, however, to justify their shipment west of India by air.[4]

Air Evacuation

A far more significant phase of the ATC's homeward-bound traffic consisted of the air evacuation of sick, wounded, and injured men from some point outside the United States to another and from various foreign bases homeward. This service the Ferrying Command early provided on an informal and spontaneous basis, utilizing a fleet of transports moving along its several routes. From many places sick or injured could be moved to adequate hospital facilities only by air.

Patients, whether belonging to the Ferrying Command or not, were thus moved by Ferrying Command aircraft as a matter of course.[5]

When the Ferrying Command was reorganized in June 1942 as the Air Transport Command, its formal statement of mission contained no definite reference to air evacuation. On the other hand, its general responsibility for "the transportation by air of personnel . . . for all War Department agencies, except those served by Troop Carrier units as hereinafter set forth,"[6] could certainly be construed to include the air transportation of sick and wounded personnel upon the request of any agency of the War Department. The responsibility was made more specific when on 28 August 1942 Brig. Gen. Thomas J. Hanley, Jr., Assistant Chief of the Air Staff, A-4, directed General George to

make available in transport airplanes the necessary aircraft equipment to facilitate air evacuation of personnel casualties to the United States from such bases as Alaska, Canada, New Foundland, Greenland, Labrador, the Caribbean and other theatres wherever practicable and in accordance with priorities and approved plans of the Air Surgeon.[7]

No special airplanes were to be provided for this evacuation, which was to be conducted in connection with the routine operations of transports.[8]

The Air Transport Command accepted this instruction as an amplification of its mission, and a series of conferences attended by medical, operations, priorities, and traffic personnel was held to explore its implications. Little was known about the problems involved. The conferees discussed such detailed questions as the number of patients which various types of transports could accommodate, methods of fastening litters in place, the optimum levels for evacuation flights, oxygen and cabin heating for high-level flights, the medical personnel and supplies required, the priorities to be granted those personnel as well as their patients, and hospital facilities at ATC's domestic terminals.[9] Meanwhile Troop Carrier units assigned to the active theaters had already flown large numbers of casualties from airstrips close to the front to points of relative safety. Military Air Evacuation squadrons, consisting of medical officers, flight nurses, and medical department enlisted technicians, were trained at Bowman Field near Louisville, Kentucky, and assigned to the theaters.[10]

In March 1943, AAF Headquarters outlined the procedures which ATC should follow. As yet its service was "on a small scale for exceptional and selected cases."[11] Thus, in January 1943, the first month for which any pertinent records are available, ATC flew eighty patients from one foreign base to another and brought thirty-three patients home to the United States.[12] Progress was slow. Transport aircraft were still quite scarce, and bottlenecks developed in selecting and installing for the air evacuation program suitable equipment which would not hamper the use of the planes for other purposes. As late as 28 September 1943, a forthright ATC officer reported to his immediate chief, Col. Ray W. Ireland, Assistant Chief of Staff, Priorities and Traffic, that "the Air Transport Command is not prepared to transport such wounded."[13]

By that time, nevertheless, the number of air evacuations by the ATC was increasing. From the 113 listed in January 1943, the figure rose gradually to 1,332 in October and 2,160 in December. Meanwhile Military Air Evacuation squadrons were assigned to the ATC and dispatched to some of the critical points along the overseas airways.[14] As experience with air evacuation was accumulated, and more of the transports were equipped with litter supports, the demand for the service increased, and it became an increasingly significant part of the ATC's mission. In December the Commanding General, AAF, was made "responsible for the development . . . and operation of air evacuation" not only "between overseas theaters and the United States" but also "within the United States." This last was an additional task, and, like the rest of General Arnold's responsibilities for air evacuation, it naturally devolved largely upon ATC. As the Ferrying Division contained the ATC's most reliable source of military flight crews, it seemed the logical organization to handle the command's new duties. In April 1944, accordingly, the Ferrying Division carried out its first planned domestic flights for moving patients from one hospital to another within the Zone of the Interior.[15]

The growing importance of air evacuation by ATC planes is most readily suggested by the following table:[16]

NUMBER OF PATIENTS EVACUATED BY ATC

	Total*	Domestic	Foreign to Foreign	Foreign to U.S.
1943	8,767	. . . . .	5,507	3,260
1944	117,151	38,320	47,060	31,771
1945	212,819	76,230	50,182	86,407

* An individual patient may well appear three times in this tabulation, first, for instance, as an evacuee wounded, say, in the battle for Saipan, and flown from Kwajalein to Hickam Field on Oahu (3d column, "Foreign to Foreign"); next, ordinarily after an interval of treatment, from Hickam Field to Hamilton Field, California (4th column, "Foreign to U.S."); and, finally, from that base to the domestic general hospital nearest his home or best suited for the treatment which he required.

The number of sick and wounded men which ATC was called upon to transport depended, first, upon the number of combat casualties; second, upon the requests of theater commanders for air evacuation. If those commanders or their staff surgeons doubted the wisdom or value of moving casualties by air, and had any alternative at their disposal, they might make few requests. Thus, as late as the first half of 1944, only a few patients were evacuated by air from Northwest Africa.[17] Even when the commander thought well of air evacuation, he or his priority board had always to balance the need against other requirements for limited air transport space and to remember that the return to station of medical evacuation personnel would require space which might otherwise be devoted to priority cargo moving toward his theater. On the other hand, the patient, whether evacuated by air or sea, lightened supply requirements by the ten tons needed every three months to sustain him and his attendants in an overseas hospital.[18]

In 1942 and 1943 a seemingly disproportionate share of the ATC's air evacuation flights originated in the Alaskan Wing, in much of whose territory there was no ready alternative for moving patients.[19] During the early months of 1944, the India-China Wing led all ATC Wings in the number of air evacuations. Relatively few of the patients involved, however, were flown all the way from China or even Assam to the United States. Most of the India-China Wing's air evacuation flights were intratheater operations which theoretically should have been carried out by theater troop-carrier planes. But since the local troop-carrier command professed inability to do the job and asked help, the wing assumed the responsibility. The early 1944 peak of the wing's air evacuation activities reflected particularly the casualties resulting from the Japanese attack on the Imphal area and from the severe fighting in Burma.[20] From June 1944, however, until the end of hostilities in ETO, the Southwest Pacific Area and the Pacific Ocean Areas supplied ATC with most of its overseas air evacuation traffic.[21]

By the summer of 1944 the techniques of moving sick and wounded men by air had been standardized and ATC had acquired a large fleet of C-54 transports, its only aircraft suitable for long, overwater evacuation flights. In the Pacific areas ten or more of these planes had already been equipped to carry from twenty to twenty-eight litter patients, arranged in tiers, four litters high. On the North Atlantic route, where only one C-54 had previously been so equipped, additional aircraft were now supplied with the Evans-type litter supports, in preparation for the flow of casualties which would follow the Normandy invasion.

Even in advance of the cross-Channel landings, a substantial number of patients was sent home by way of the North and Middle Atlantic routes in an effort to clear United Kingdom hospitals for the inevitable wave of invasion casualties. This served to test the detailed procedures which the North Atlantic Wing had worked out for the heavy task ahead.[22] On 22 June the first invasion casualties to return homeward by way of the North Atlantic airway left Prestwick; two days later they landed at Mitchel Field, New York. On 29 June the first plane exclusively loaded with invasion casualties, ten litter and four ambulatory cases, reached Mitchel Field.[23]

Theater surgeons selected patients for air evacuation, and such theater agencies as troop-carrier aircraft and surface vessels brought them to the point of aerial embarkation. There flight surgeons assigned to the ATC screened them to determine whether they could make the journey without harm. The conclusion was ultimately reached, however, that most patients who could be moved at all (some exceptions were detailed in an official ATC memorandum) might safely be moved by air. The death of patients in the course of ATC evacuation movements was extremely rare. The basis on which theater officers selected patients for air evacuation varied somewhat from time to time and from theater to theater, but generally the following categories were chosen: (1) those who needed treatment which could not be given in the theater; (2) patients who were expected to undergo a long convalescence and could not be returned to duty for a long time, variously estimated at from 30 to 180 days; (3) those who were expected to die but could be sent home without lessening their chances of survival. The need for emptying forward area and intermediate hospitals was mixed with humane consideration for the patients and their families.[24]

Fork lifts, inclined ramps, and teams of litter-bearers working at different levels were used in loading litter patients into the lofty cabins of C-54 aircraft and in unloading them at their destination. Ordinarily, one or two flight nurses, specially trained in air evacuation, and a Medical Corps enlisted technician accompanied an aircraft fully or partly occupied by patients. At intermediate points in a long flight, the medical air evacuation team was often replaced by another; when not relieved, the team, however weary, had to carry on for another leg of the trip. The condition and behavior of the patients varied greatly, of course, but the usual report was that the men were generally reluctant, even if able, to call for care or assistance and that attendants had to watch them closely to detect their needs. The long flights were tiresome, especially to men already weakened by injuries, but the knowledge that the end of the trip would bring them to the homeland had a therapeutic value. This was true even of psychotic patients, who at a rate of five in a planeload were evacuated in considerable numbers from Southwest Pacific Area hospitals. Medical officers concluded, finally, that the speed of air evacuation made it at once the cleanest and the most comfortable method of evacuating patients.[25]

The Air Transport Command's share in air evacuation from the European theater was in one sense a static operation, though routes and techniques changed as the months passed. For the first half-year after the Normandy landings, virtually all patients were placed on board at Prestwick. Only in December 1944 did the command begin to load wounded at Paris.[26] In the Central and Southwest Pacific areas, however, there was constant shifting both of routes and of pickup points. The procession of victories made yesterday's battleground tomorrow's port of aerial embarkation. The early casualties of the Tarawa campaign, moved by Navy surface vessels and troop-carrier planes to Funafuti in the Ellice Islands, were flown by ATC crews from Funafuti to Hickam Field. Tarawa in turn became the loading point for men wounded in the campaign for Kwajalein. That island secured, it was used to start those wounded at Saipan on their flight to Hickam Field. Next, Saipan served as pickup point for men wounded, not only on the other islands of the Marianas, but also on Leyte. Shortly thereafter, in November 1944, ATC craft pushed into the combat zone itself and began loading casualties on Leyte for transportation both to Saipan and to Biak. Casualties from Iwo Jima were picked up, beginning in February 1945, at Guam and Saipan. On 8 April, D plus 7, the Pacific Division began removing casualties from Okinawa, though conditions there were still very primitive and the struggle for the island was far from won. Manila became a starting point for air evacuation flights on 8 June, a week after Nichols Field was opened to regular C-54 traffic.[27]

In 1944 a fifth of all the patients brought back to the United States flew by ATC aircraft.[28] The program made a strong appeal to the imagination of a generous and sympathetic people, eager to do what they could for the boys. Air evacuation duty was not easy; the nurses and technicians who cared for the evacuees during the long hours of overwater flight bore more responsibility than their counterparts at work in non-mobile hospitals. But there was a peculiar satisfaction in the job, derived in part from the gratitude of men who appreciated the swift passage from combat or a field hospital to Oahu, or, even better, to the United States. One soldier who had just reached Hamilton Field from Saipan expressed the reaction of many: "It's just like dying and going to Heaven when you first get here. I tell you it's a wonderful feeling."[29] What it meant to the parents, wives, and sweethearts of the wounded or ailing men requires no rhetorical embellishment and no conventional documentation.

Redeployment of Aircraft

Operating under a basic war plan which provided for disposing of the European adversary before turning to direct a final blow at the enemy on the other side of the globe, the American high command was obliged to plan far in advance for the day when men and weapons might be transferred from one theater of war to the other. Each echelon of command in Washington developed such plans for redeployment. Those framed at ATC headquarters were begun well over a year before V-E Day.[30] In September 1944 the Chief of the Air Staff outlined a general division of responsibility in connection with such redeployment between the several assistant chiefs of the Air Staff, other Air Force agencies, and the Air Transport Command. Emphasis thus far was placed upon the flight of aircraft and their crews from the European or Mediterranean theaters to the Pacific.[31] Such a movement would provide reinforcements needed for victory against Japan, would scale down U.S. air forces in England and on the Continent to essential garrison units, and would give veteran aircrews a welcome trip home during the move from Europe to the Far East.[32]

During the summer of 1944, ATC endeavored to gain control of, and improve the facilities of, necessary staging bases in California in anticipation of the increased flow of ferried aircraft across the Pacific.[33] Other aspects of the problem were considered, too, and by September ATC headquarters was ready to distribute to the commanders of the several divisions concerned a top-secret plan for the movement from the European and Mediterranean theaters to the United States. The divisions, in turn, made detailed plans for their share in this program. The project as a whole was for some reason still classified as top secret on 30 April 1945, but, when ATC headquarters on 5 May 1945 issued its revised instructions to the field, the classification had been reduced to "restricted."[34]

The Air Transport Command's task, designated WHITE PROJECT, involved the return to America of some 2,825 heavy bombers from the European theater, and 1,240 from the Mediterranean theater. These, with varying numbers of passengers, were to be flown to the United States by full combat crews. All three major Atlantic routes were to be utilized. One version of the plan called for fifty or sixty aircraft a day to fly the North Atlantic route from Valley in Wales through Iceland; twelve a day from the European theater and from five to twenty from MTO were to follow the Central Atlantic route through the Azores. Some twenty-five bombers a day were to fly home by the lengthy South Atlantic route.[35]

Meanwhile in April the eastward flow of aircraft for the European war ground to a halt. First to be held up were all four-engine bombers (B-24's and B-17's) not equipped with radar; then, all heavy bombers; and, finally, on 28 April 1945, other types of aircraft. This allowed almost a month's lull in which to prepare for the reverse ferrying movement. WHITE PROJECT got under way on 20 May 1945, when seventy-one bombers took off from Valley and a smaller number from Marrakech, Morocco, for the long-awaited homeward trip.[36]

Originally planned to last only through August, the WHITE PROJECT was extended to 31 October 1945. The westward flow of heavy bombers had hardly started when ATC received instructions to assume comparable responsibility for the homeward flight of an estimated 1,000 twin-engine bombers and transports from ETO and MTO.[37] It was taken for granted that crews which had flown a given type of aircraft in combat or in troop-carrier service should fly it home. At the same time there was no disposition to challenge the established principle that aircraft and crews en route east or west should be subject to the control of ATC, one of whose specialties was the direction of the overwater ferrying of aircraft.[38]

There were difficulties, of course. ATC officers in the field had to co-ordinate WHITE PROJECT flights not only with the regular ATC transport flights in each direction and with some ferrying of new transports eastward to the India-China Division but also with the parallel and enormous GREEN PROJECT for the return of personnel to the United States. When it was decided to make Bradley Field at Windsor Locks, Connecticut, the principal domestic terminus for planes flown home under North Atlantic Division control, division officers feared that the First Air Force base would not be able to handle the daily traffic. Actually, Bradley Field carried its part most successfully. So did Hunter Field (Third Air Force) at Savannah, Georgia, the normal port of debarkation for aircraft redeployed over the southern route.[39]

Processing of the aircraft for redeployment was the responsibility of the theater air forces. All planes were to receive 100-hour inspections, to be tested for fuel and oil consumption, and to be equipped with the safety devices required by ATC. Pilots were to hold a current instrument card or to be certified as qualified for instrument flying. Celestial navigators were to undergo a six-hour refresher course. Individual health certificates and baggage examinations were to be completed before personnel were cleared to ATC. Officers were allowed only forty pounds of personal baggage; enlisted men, thirty. Aircraft in flight from staging areas to ATC acceptance points remained under the operational control of the theater.[40]

At acceptance points the ATC saw that each aircraft and crew met necessary safety requirements for the projected flight, briefed the crews, checked the aircraft for weight and balance requirements, and dispatched the flights. At the ports of debarkation in the United States, crews and passengers underwent initial processing by base personnel, were transported to the ASF staging facilities at Charleston, South Carolina (from Hunter Field), or at Camp Myles Standish, Massachusetts (from northern bases). After further processing, they received orders giving them thirty days at their respective homes for what was ponderously termed "rehabilitation, recovery, and recuperation." At the aerial ports aircraft passed briefly into the custody of the base, then were released to the Ferrying Division, which flew them, as directed by the Aircraft Distribution Office, either to Air Technical Service Command depots (there to be reconditioned for service in the Pacific) or to Reconstruction Finance Corporation storage fields as surplus.[41]

The operation involved little that was new to the ATC of 1945. Still it was not easy to maintain a completely steady flow of redeployed aircraft through the air channels used. The air forces from which the planes came did not prepare them at a regular rate. Weather delays were inevitable. Maintenance en route was time-consuming, especially for those planes which were more war-worn than had been contemplated. Maintenance personnel carried by the planes proved unable to perform as much of the maintenance along the way as had been expected, for gunners and clerks were all too often sent forward in the guise of maintenance men. Especially among the surplus aircraft was the need for maintenance a substantial burden. Minor annoyances included crews without health certificates, baggage well in excess of the authorized limits, forbidden pets, and weapons smuggled aboard. On the North Atlantic route there was a small epidemic of ditchings, inspired by faulty fuel gauges.[42] The total accident rate was extremely low, however. By and large, the movement was successful, though the early Japanese surrender made it a homecoming and little more. No unit flown home for reassignment to the Pacific ever served in that theater.[43]

Most of the planes from Europe or North Africa had completed the passage by the end of August. During the course of the project, 5,965 aircraft made the westward crossing of the Atlantic (some 4,000 from ETO and more than 1,900 from the Mediterranean theater), all but 521 by the close of August. Most of the 4,182 heavy bombers made the homeward flight in June or July. The passage of two-engine aircraft began in June and was substantially completed during July and August. The last large contingent consisted of 433 Flying Fortresses, which came home in September and October via the South Atlantic airway.[44]

In all, some 3,224 aircraft came by way of the North Atlantic, as against 2,282 which followed the South Atlantic route via Dakar, Brazil, and the Caribbean Islands. Some 459 heavy bombers flew the Middle Atlantic route through the Azores. Most heavy bombers traveled the North Atlantic airway, however, as did nearly all the 212 C-46's. All the 348 returned B-25's, most of the A-26's, and a substantial majority of the DC-3 type transports took the South Atlantic route.[45] In spite of delays caused by en route maintenance, most of the planes moved swiftly on the homeward way.[46]

The WHITE PROJECT became more of a personnel movement than had been expected. In addition to 50,764 crew members, an average of more than 8 to a plane, the planes brought home an additional 33,850 passengers, many of them aircrew men. In all, the returnees numbered over 84,000, a substantial figure by any standard.[47]

Redeployment of Men

The WHITE PROJECT required little more than a reversal of
the direction of the flow of aircraft whose control had long been a
major function of ATC. More revolutionary in its demands upon the
ATC organization was the GREEN PROJECT, a parallel program
for flying some 50,000 passengers a month from Europe to the United
States. Even that was a logical extension of one of the ATC's basic
responsibilities, the transportation by air of passengers for War Department agencies. In this case it was the War Department itself
which was to be served. The original purpose was to fly home for
rest leave troops whose services would shortly be required in the
war against Japan. ATC, which in March had flown about 12,500
passengers from the European and Mediterranean theaters to the
United States, was now directed to fly home from those theaters
approximately four times as many each month. To make this possible,
ATC strength was suddenly augmented by the transfer of some
33,000 men, most of whom had formerly been assigned to combat
bomber groups, theater troop-carrier groups, or their supporting organizations. At the same time ATC received some 256 troop-carrier
C-47's, in addition to the previously planned increment of C-54
aircraft.

The new transport assignment fell into the lap of the ATC in mid-
April. Directed to study the feasibility of flying some 50,000 passengers a month from ETO and MTO to the United States, ATC on
12 April transmitted to AAF Headquarters a plan for the substantial
fulfilment of this mission.[48] The plan was approved orally by the Air
Staff and OPD, and a formal directive came down from OPD to
General Arnold, 17 April. The Air Staff passed the directive on,
three days later, with the characteristic proviso that it should involve
"no reduction . . . in the currently scheduled buildup of air lift from
India to China."[49]

The Air Transport Command had never been unduly modest in
its requests for the construction of facilities which might assist in
the fulfilment of its assigned mission, but now the demands were
deliberately kept down, except in the North African Division, where
additional billeting, messing, recreational, maintenance, and other
needed facilities, at an estimated cost of $311,119.77, were ordered
at Cazes Air Base near Casablanca, at Port Lyautey, and at Dakar.

The timely withdrawal of the Fourth Fleet from the Atlantic made available to ATC at Belém and Natal, in Brazil, Navy quarters and supplies which largely obviated the need for new construction there. To house troops debarking at Miami until their movement by rail to an ASF installation, some 285 hutments were moved from Atlantic Beach, near Jacksonville, Florida, and set up at the Miami base.[50] On the other hand, there was nothing modest, and nothing unreasonable either, about the command's personnel requirements. To meet them, OPD directed the transfer to the ATC of five heavy-bomber groups and four troop-carrier groups, each with four flight squadrons, plus the normal supporting organizations—service groups, air engineering squadrons, air maintenance squadons, quartermaster and medical supply platoons, and quartermaster truck companies. The aircraft of the bomb groups were not needed, but those of the troop-carrier outfits were. Based and inspected at Waller Field, Trinidad, the transports were to provide a major portion of the airlift from Natal to the southern port of debarkation at Miami.[51]

Early plans were changed somewhat, both before the movement began officially on 15 June and thereafter. ATC was directed to raise its monthly airlift westbound from Europe gradually to 50,000 passengers in July, using all the Atlantic airways to capacity. The project was expected to continue until March 1946.[52]

The planners decided to send 40 per cent of the airlift via the circuitous South Atlantic route, 50 per cent by the mid-Atlantic routes from Orly or Casablanca through the Azores, and only 10 per cent along the North Atlantic airway. One obvious reason for this division was the fact that the North Atlantic route was already pretty well saturated by the westbound flight of WHITE PROJECT bombers. Another argument derived from balancing the passenger capacity of C-54 aircraft and the gasoline load required for various hops across the Atlantic. A C-54 which could carry only twenty-two or twenty-three passengers westward against the head winds on the Prestwick-Stephenville route could take forty from Casablanca to Dakar, and again from Dakar to Natal. From Natal to Miami a succession of relatively short hops and an abundance of base facilities made it possible to utilize the abundant C-46's and superabundant C-47's, carrying thirty and twenty passengers, respectively, thus saving the C-54's for the war against Japan.[53]

The North African Division, relatively close to the source of manpower, was quickly supplied with its reinforcement of approximately 7,000 men. The South Atlantic and Caribbean Divisions were not quite so fortunate. The air echelons of the troop-carrier groups began arriving at Waller Field 19 May 1945, following by six days a portion of the advance echelon which had arrived on ATC transports. The pilots and co-pilots were checked and in many cases found to fall short of ATC's requirements. The Caribbean and South Atlantic Divisions put them to school and ultimately accepted most of them as meeting basic requirements. The ground echelons moved slowly by water. The *General Gordon*, carrying 3,578 such troops, docked at Port of Spain, Trinidad, on 27 May. The *General Richardson*, with 5,053 men, followed within a week, and the *Admiral Aberle* brought 3,182 more on 17 June. During six weeks of confusion personnel officers and enlisted men of the Caribbean and South Atlantic Divisions hastily screened the newcomers and divided them between the two divisions, with as much impartiality as was possible in the matter of wanted skilled workers and unwanted high-point men, eligible for early discharge. The interdivisional allocation duly made, the men were assigned to their respective bases. As the support personnel moved out to their several stations, nearly 5,000 remained at Waller Field, where "one of the largest line maintenance bases in existence" was suddenly created* to care for the entire fleet of C-47's.[54]

Although the South Atlantic and Caribbean Divisions received the number of additional "bodies" required for the task at hand, they can hardly be said to have acquired an equivalent number of "souls." Morale of the new men, both there and in the North African Division, was exceedingly low. Through a typical "foulup," some of the bomber groups designated for transfer to ATC were senior in months of overseas service to some whose men they were called upon to speed homeward. Furthermore, the ATC had no use for many of the specialties which men of the combat groups had acquired, so that many enlisted men of high grade had either to be retrained in a new specialty, declared surplus, or assigned to relatively non-skilled duties as truck drivers, guards, or minor clerks.[55] Finally, the transfer was all too complete. Many of the bomber and troop-carrier squadrons had been allowed to understand, all erroneously, that they were to preserve their separate status, assist the ATC for a few months as

---

* At the beginning of the project ATC strength at Waller Field included only eleven officers and eighty-three enlisted men.

units, and then fly on homeward. Instead the groups and squadrons were disbanded, and the men transferred as individuals.[56]

Col. Thomas D. Ferguson, Commanding Officer of the South Atlantic Division, in an attempt to boost the morale of these men stated: "You are not working for the ATC—you *are* the ATC and you are working for Uncle Sugar and a one-way trip to the States and your families."[57] But no one was convinced by this slogan. It was small comfort to the homesick airmen, proud of their old outfits and long accustomed to sneer at ATC personnel as "Allergic to Combat," or to dub them the "Army (or "Association") of Terrified Civilians." On the other hand, veteran ATC propeller specialists and electricians were not inclined to genuflect before men of like SSN who had won battle stars for service at a bomber base far removed from the scenes of aerial combat. In spite of friction and frustration, the wearers of battle stars went to work at Natal and Fortaleza, Dakar and Casablanca, Waller Field and Borinquen, as directed. But the problem of morale persisted as long as the GREEN PROJECT lasted. Something approaching a strike among the men assigned to aircraft maintenance took place at Waller Field, 30 July–2 August. When Colonel Ferguson heard officers of his major base, Parnamirim Field, Natal, enlivening an officers' club dance with their rendition of a song whose principal theme was "To Hell with the ATC," he felt obliged to direct the base commander, Col. John M. Price, one-time commanding officer of the 460th Bombardment Group, to prevent a repetition of the episode.[58]

At the beginning of the project, the North Atlantic Division, the Ferrying Division, and the several contract carriers (Pan American, TWA, American Airlines, and American Export Airlines) together were operating some 165 C-54's on the North Atlantic and Middle Atlantic routes. The North African Division, commanded by Brig. Gen. James S. Stowell, had received by 12 August some 87 Skymasters. To fly these planes, some of the division's C-46 pilots were upgraded, but the NAFD also received some fifty-five first pilots from the discontinued Central African Division and a number of full crews from the Caribbean and Ferrying Divisions.[59]

In planning, ATC had made a distinction between normal passenger traffic and GREEN PROJECT passengers. The latter consisted of persons (with their baggage) specifically designated by the theater. They carried no tickets, but instead each man wore a green-colored tag. Similar tags identified his baggage. Even the instruction pamphlet distributed by ATC to all "GREEN" passengers at ports of aerial embarkation was printed on green paper. The "Green Manifest" passengers, specially handled and processed by the theaters before their delivery to ATC, were expected to require a minimum of processing from the ATC. On arrival in the United States they were turned over almost immediately to Army Service Forces. "Normal traffic," cleared through established priority channels and handled on an individual basis, included "individuals traveling to the United States on temporary duty, leave or furlough from the theater to return to the theater; civilians; foreign nationals; medical evacuees, and Air Transport Command personnel." Once the GREEN PROJECT got under way, an attempt was made to carry normal transatlantic traffic in general on contract carrier C-54's of the North Atlantic Division, based in New York and Washington, or on the Ferrying Division's C-54's, based at Wilmington.[60]

A few hundred passengers handled in accordance with project procedures flew homeward in May, and nearly 2,500 men of the GREEN PROJECT reached the United States during the first fifteen days of June, before its official beginning. How the project developed in relation both to normal traffic and the targets set up for it is summarized in the table which follows:[61]

THE GREEN PROJECT

Month 1945	Original Target (Total Passengers, Westbound)	Revised Target	Accomplishment			
			Green Manifest	Air Evacuees	Other "Normal Traffic"	Total
May	16,000	....	695	7,468	12,219	20,382
June	27,500	....	13,649	5,876	10,589	30,114
July	36,000	43,760	37,704	6,127	6,683	50,514
August	50,600	50,600	36,682	5,578	5,714	47,974
1–15 Sept.	25,300	17,500*	12,378	1,382	3,315	17,075
Total		....	101,108	26,431	38,520	166,059

* Target as reduced about 10 August 1945.

Though the CBI theaters, Persian Gulf Command, and Africa–Middle East theaters together supplied over 10,000 GREEN PROJECT passengers, the overwhelming numbers came from the European and Mediterranean theaters. Indeed, from May through September ETO provided a clear majority both of the Green Manifest travelers and of the normal traffic.[62] But Orly Field near Paris, and

Prestwick, the major European ports of aerial embarkation for westward flight by ATC craft, handled only a lesser fraction of the Green Manifest passengers. Casablanca, take-off point for virtually all South Atlantic, and most Middle Atlantic flights, was the hub of the system. Converted B-17's belonging to the Eighth and Fifteenth Air Forces, and operating entirely outside the ATC organization, brought the men from staging areas at Istres Airport, Marseille, and at Pomigliano and Pisa airports in Italy, to the Port Lyautey Naval Air Station or to the Cazes Air Base, Casablanca. At these points the men came under ATC control and boarded a C-54 for the first stage of their transatlantic flight, either to the Azores or to Natal by way of Dakar. In August the use of Port Lyautey was abandoned, and all the traffic was concentrated at Cazes. At the peak of the movement, 8 August, that base dispatched 1,775 GREEN PROJECT men southward or westward in a single day.[63]

GREEN PROJECT C-54's normally made the flight from Casablanca to Dakar in seven and a half hours. With a scheduled stop of an hour at Dakar, the big transports, backed by the trade winds, pushed on to Natal, eight hours and fifty minutes away.[64] Two of the ranking commissioned or non-commissioned officers assigned to ride on each C-54 had usually been trained as plane group leaders, to maintain cabin discipline and cleanliness, and to take charge of the passengers if it should be necessary to ditch the ship.[65] At Parnamirim Field, Natal, the travel-weary passengers came into the jurisdiction of the ATC's South Atlantic Division. There, usually after an interval for rest and refreshment, they might be transferred to one of the C-54's operated by Caribbean Division crews on the Natal-Miami run, or one of the twenty C-46's flown largely by Eastern Air Lines personnel for that division. More commonly, however, their planeload of forty was divided into two equal groups, each headed by a plane group leader, and loaded on a pair of C-47's, flown by military pilots, late of a troop-carrier group and now flying for the ATC. The crews, including a navigator only if the flight was at night, took the transports from Natal to Belém, nearly six hours northwest. After a change of crews, the plane went on to Atkinson Field, British Guiana, five and a half hours farther on. The C-47 fleet was so scheduled that regular 25-hour inspections fell due at Atkinson Field for planes northbound. Long before the four-hour task was accomplished, however, the passengers took off on another plane which had arrived earlier and whose inspection had been completed. At Atkinson, too, a fresh crew, from the Caribbean Division, took over. A last stop at Borinquen Field, Puerto Rico, six hours and forty minutes out of Atkinson, was a virtual repetition of that at Belém. Still another crew took over for the final six-hour run to Miami. On an average, the returning soldiers had been en route seventy-two hours from Casablanca. Those who took the more direct route, via the Azores, commonly reached Miami, La Guardia Field (New York), Washington, Presque Isle, or Wilmington, within thirty-six hours after their departure from Casablanca.[66]

There were numerous chances for delay along the way, quite apart from a long wait at or near the port of embarkation. One unavoidable cause, even in summer on the relatively favorable South and Middle Atlantic routes, was weather. In August tropical hurricanes in the Caribbean twice virtually stopped all homeward-bound traffic on the Natal-Miami route.[67] If for any reason, such as a breakdown in maintenance, enough serviceable transports failed to reach such critical points as Casablanca, Lagens, Natal, or Atkinson Field, a backlog would pile up. To take care of such situations as well as weather delays, ATC used what was known as "Station Block Control." That is, each base, as its backlog approached capacity, was entitled to call a halt to flights from the next point east and to ask help from division headquarters in the form of extra sections on established schedules. This system worked tolerably well, yet the rate of flow was never completely steady. On the other hand, passenger backlogs never became completely unmanageable.[68]

From the start, it was clear that ATC could not furnish this mass movement of troops all the refinements of passenger service which had lately become common on the best of its regular transport runs. Still the intent was to make the homeward journey of the GREEN PROJECT men as pleasant as possible.[69] Serious effort was directed toward this end; the service improved as the servers gained experience and as their superiors increasingly stressed the importance of consideration and hospitality in dealing with the passengers. At Natal hot meals were served around the clock to the returning soldiers, who also had an opportunity to exchange dirty clothing for clean. Elsewhere steps were taken to improve the quality of transient messes. Careful planning, based on experience, cut to a minimum the time lost in assigning arriving planeloads to their billets. A spot check at

Natal on 6 July showed that only thirty-five minutes elapsed between the time a load of passengers from the east deplaned and their arrival at their individual bunks in the transient area. Medical dispensaries were set up on the flight lines, so that passengers' minor ailments could be quickly treated and their fitness for further flight determined, but passengers seemed to shun this service lest perchance it might delay their homeward passage. Post exchanges were stocked with a liberal array of souvenirs and other articles which the transients would be likely to purchase, such as Natal boots or silk stockings and perfume for the folks at home. At Natal a package-wrapping room was set up, and free movies were available. Reading matter was provided on board planes and on the ground. The South Atlantic Division, and later the Caribbean Division, supplied their customers with booklets telling them something of the division's organization and of the land and water over which they were to fly.[70]

After some early passengers had suggested it, planes were supplied with blankets to soften bucket seats or to keep the passengers warm at high altitudes. When the backlog at Natal fell so low for a time that men had no opportunity to stop there for a good rest, the South Atlantic Division tried installing eight or nine litters on northbound C-47's, so that passengers might take turns sleeping in modest comfort. The Caribbean Division objected, however, on the ground that the weight of the litters, even though not enough to top the permissible gross weight limits, lessened the margin of safety.[71]

This last was a prime consideration. Elaborate precautions were taken. A string of seaborne vessels, British, American, and Brazilian, stood watch on the surface of the Atlantic under the airways. B-17's equipped to drop boats and amphibious aircraft took station at critical points along the routes. Before emplaning, passengers saw films instructing them in safety precautions and ditching procedures.[72] Care paid off, for the whole project was completed without the loss of a life. The worst accident of the entire movement occurred on 24 June, when a C-47 on instruments between Belém and Atkinson Field, flew into two thunderstorms, and in the turbulence fifteen passengers were injured, four enough to require treatment at the Atkinson Field station hospital.[73]

At the ports of debarkation Green Manifest passengers bypassed the usual customs and quarantine procedures and were quickly taken to billets to await the arrival of surface transportation which took them out of the control of the ATC and delivered them to the Army Service Forces. Thereafter they were sent either to a separation center or to their homes for thirty days of temporary duty prior to receiving a new assignment.[74]

At the end of their air journey, passengers were given an opportunity to record their impressions or criticisms. It must be remembered that many of ATC's ranking officers were on leave from civilian airlines and that they were interested in converting potential American passengers to air travel. Comments on the GREEN PROJEST were predominantly favorable. There were complaints and suggestions, of course. Some men thought that they should have been issued summer uniforms for travel through the tropics, others naturally complained of delays experienced, particularly at European staging centers, where some men claimed to have been held as long as six weeks. Many would have appreciated maps of the countries over which they had flown and more information about those regions. But the large majority responded gratefully to the efforts which had been made for their comfort, to the apparent advantages of air travel, and to the efficiency and dispatch with which they had been handled at the Air Transport Command bases en route. One infantryman wrote: "I have enjoyed my trip . . . and would like to see everyone in the ETO get the chance to fly home. . . ." Another was impressed by the consideration shown the passengers: "The air crews are very courteous regardless of rank, and being a private myself, I know."[75]

Like much of the other planning in the spring of 1945, the GREEN PROJECT was predicated on the belief that the war against Japan might not be concluded before the following spring. But early in August, as the Japanese surrender became imminent, new commitments to the Pacific forced ATC to transfer to its Pacific routes eighty-two C-54's, most of which were then in use on the GREEN PROJECT.* As a result, by 10 August GREEN PROJECT goals had been cut from 50,000 to 35,000 a month.[76] By 22 August some seventy of the C-54's so hastily withdrawn from the Atlantic routes and ten more from new production had reached the West Coast.[77]

With the end of all hostilities, ATC once more restudied the GREEN PROJECT. On 23 August General George recommended that the westbound passenger lift across the Atlantic be reduced to

* See above, p. 200.

10,000 persons a month. Since surface shipping capable of moving about 350,000 monthly was operating between the United States and Europe, continuation of the airlift at the current rate for another seven months could speed the end of demobilization from Europe by only fifteen days. Cutting back the project to 10,000 persons a month would enable the ATC to release approximately 150 of the GREEN PROJECT C-47's operating on the Natal-Miami line, about half of the 227 C-54's still in service on the project, and some 30,000 officers and enlisted men then assigned to bases in the Caribbean, South Atlantic, and North African Divisions. Likewise, the four bombardment groups still delivering passengers to the ATC at Casablanca might be relieved.[78] Within four days, General Marshall approved this recommendation, and orders presently went out to terminate the GREEN PROJECT on 10 September and to cut the transatlantic lift to 10,000 westbound passengers monthly.[79] The special procedures for handling passengers continued in use until the end of September. By that time the remnants of the project fleet had brought home from North African, South Atlantic, and Caribbean bases a major portion of the men whose labors had made possible the air journey homeward of over 166,000 of their fellow soldiers.[80]

When the GREEN PROJECT goals were reduced in mid-August, fifty C-47's, formerly based at Waller Field and used on the Natal-Miami circuit, together with their crews and some maintenance personnel, were transferred to Morrison Field, West Palm Beach, Florida. After the crews had received instruction for flying within the Zone of Interior, they were put to work, 20 August, flying PURPLE PROJECT* support personnel from Miami to the Charleston Army Air Field, South Carolina. By 4 September 1,671 men had been moved. Before this, part of the fleet had been withdrawn to provide the air transportation from Miami to San Antonio, Texas, of Brig. Gen. Ray L. Owens' AAF Redistribution Center. Between 30 August and 7 September, 2,029 of Owens' men moved out in a total of 112 C-47 flights.[81]

Meanwhile, on 27 August, at the request of the War Department, ATC inaugurated still another project which reflected the end-of-the-war wealth of aircraft available. This was the TRANSCON PROJECT, designed to carry first 25,000, then 40,000, troops monthly between the East and West coasts, in order to relieve some

---

* See above, p. 200.

of the extremely heavy pressure on rail transportation produced by the monthly return of hundreds of thousands of troops from overseas. Soldiers transported under this new project were to carry ASF orders designating them as TRANSCON passengers. Ferrying Division supervised the whole movement, and its Military Air Transport Service C-47's ultimately carried a major share of the passengers. Four contract carriers, American Airlines, Northwest Airlines, United Air Lines, and Transcontinental and Western Air, Inc., also shared in the movement. Each of the contract carriers employed in the project fifteen new C-47B's, specially delivered, and pilots released for this purpose from military service. In December American Airlines received twenty-two C-54's to be used for TRANSCON. When the job was finished, 1 April 1946, 171,579 troops had been afforded coast-to-coast transportation.[82]

With victory in the Pacific achieved, and the heart of the Japanese empire under American occupation, a final homeward movement, the SUNSET PROJECT, developed. Inaugurated 27 September 1945, it called for the return to the United States of B-29's from the Eighth and Twentieth Air Forces, and B-24's from the Far East Air Force, as well as some two-engine bombers and cargo craft not required by the occupational forces. Like the WHITE PROJECT planes, those of the SUNSET PROJECT were accepted by ATC for overseas flight, after inspection at Manila, Okinawa, and various B-29 bases in the Marianas. They were flown by combat crews operating under ATC control and carried passengers assigned as extra crew members, all being eligible for separation from service. The returning aircraft passed through the Marianas, Kwajalein, Johnston Island, and John Rodgers Field (Oahu) to Mather Field, California. The flow continued through the rest of the year and on into 1946. By New Year's Day, 653 B-29's and 601 B-24's had made the homeward journey, though the discharge of hundreds of experienced aircraft mechanics left the Pacific Division hard pressed to perform the necessary maintenance en route. In all, 1,308 very heavy and heavy bombers returned to the United States under the original SUNSET PROJECT designation.[83]

Of all the aerial redeployment programs of 1945, the GREEN PROJECT was the most impressive. It illustrates the capacity of the War Department, and particularly of the mature Air Transport Command, to plan an air transportation operation of tremendous magnitude and to carry it out in a completely effective fashion. At a word from Washington supplies of every kind were procured and transported to the points where they would be needed. Several thousand men were moved by air and water and were put to work again, often at entirely unfamiliar assignments, thousands of miles from their previous duty stations. It is no wonder that the mimeographed Standard Operating Procedures prepared for the project in several of the participating divisions ran to over seventy-five pages. It was a tremendous demonstration of the mass airlift of manpower, certainly the most striking of those marking the end of the war. Within less than five months, over 166,000 passengers—50,514 in a single month—were flown across the Atlantic without a single fatality. Nothing like it had happened before. What its sequel might be—for peace or war—in a day of larger, more efficient air transports, was a challenge which demanded little of the imagination of the men who had had a part in it.

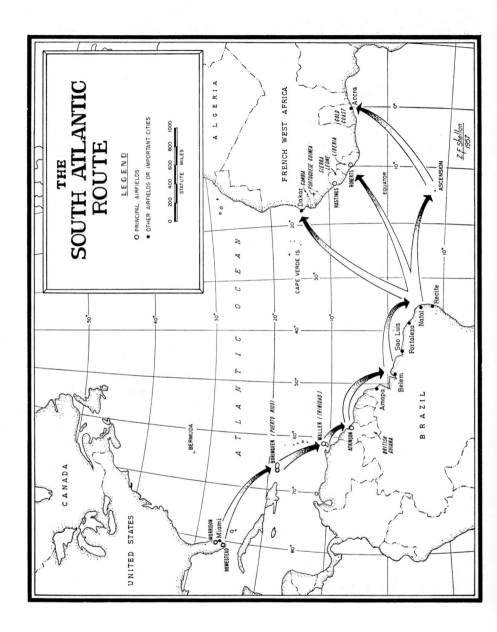

THE
SOUTH ATLANTIC
ROUTE

LEGEND

○ PRINCIPAL AIRFIELDS

• OTHER AIRFIELDS OR IMPORTANT CITIES

0   200   400   600   800   1000
STATUTE MILES

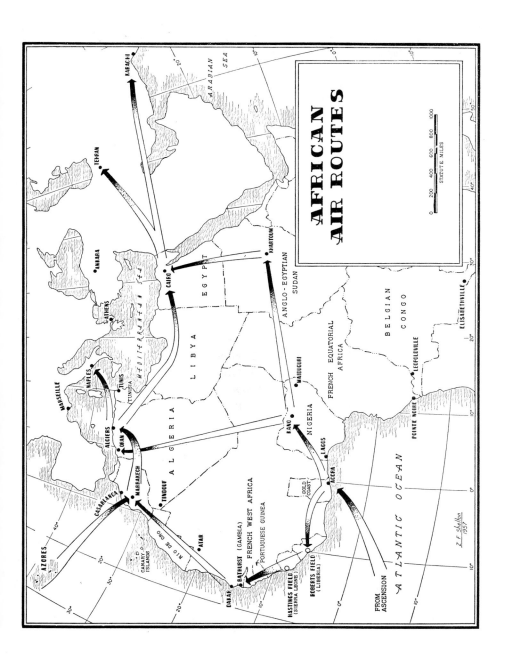

AFRICAN AIR ROUTES

STATUTE MILES
0   200   400   600   800   1000

Z. F. Shelton
1957

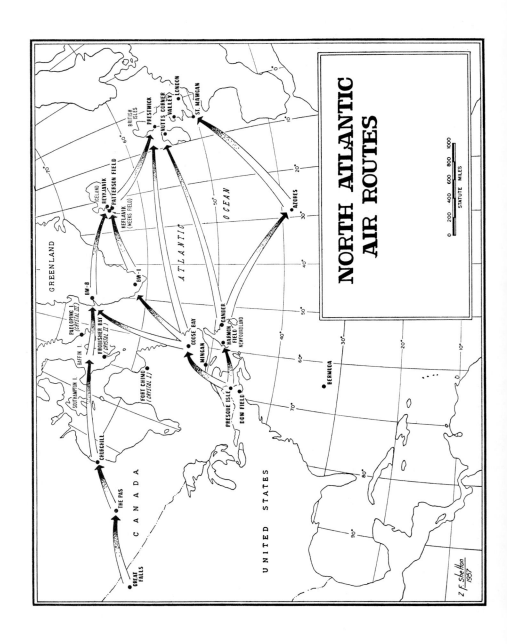

NORTH ATLANTIC
AIR ROUTES

Z F. Shelton
1957

230

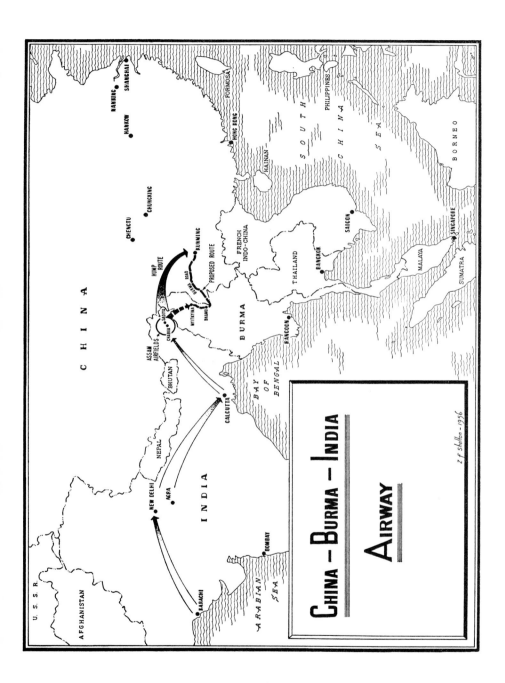

CHINA – BURMA – INDIA

AIRWAY

Z F Shelton - 1956

231

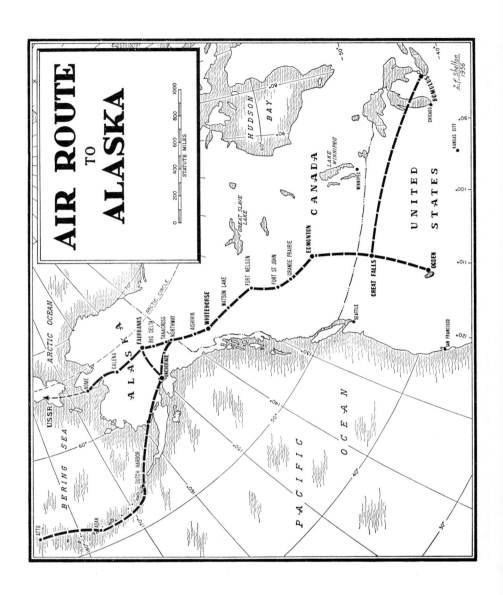

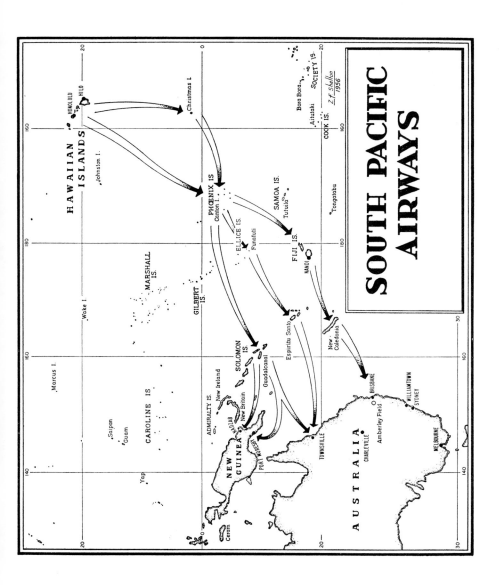

SOUTH PACIFIC AIRWAYS

Z.F. Shelton
1956

233

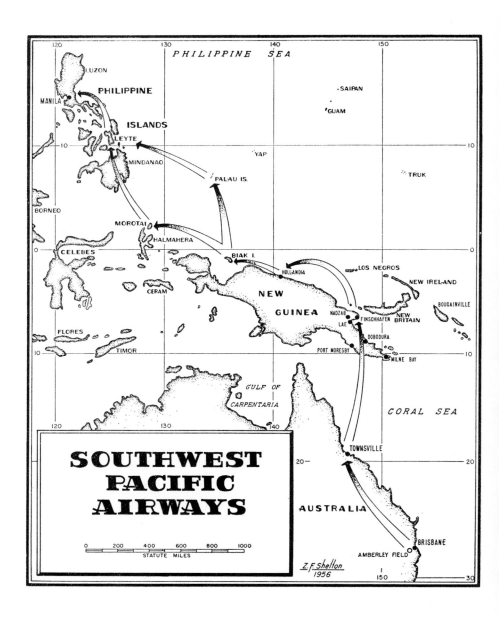

120 130 PHILIPPINE SEA 140 150

LUZON
PHILIPPINE · SAIPAN
MANILA ISLANDS · GUAM
LEYTE 10 YAP TRUK 10
MINDANAO PALAU IS.
BORNEO
MOROTAI
CELEBES HALMAHERA 0 BIAK I. HOLLANDIA LOS NEGROS 0
CERAM NEW IRELAND
NEW GUINEA BOUGAINVILLE
FLORES NADZAB FINSCHHAFEN NEW
LAE BRITAIN
TIMOR DOBODURA
10 PORT MORESBY MILNE BAY 10

GULF OF
CARPENTARIA CORAL SEA

120 130 140

**SOUTHWEST
PACIFIC
AIRWAYS** TOWNSVILLE 20— 20

AUSTRALIA
0 200 400 600 800 1000
STATUTE MILES BRISBANE
AMBERLEY FIELD
Z.F.Shelton
1956 150 30

234

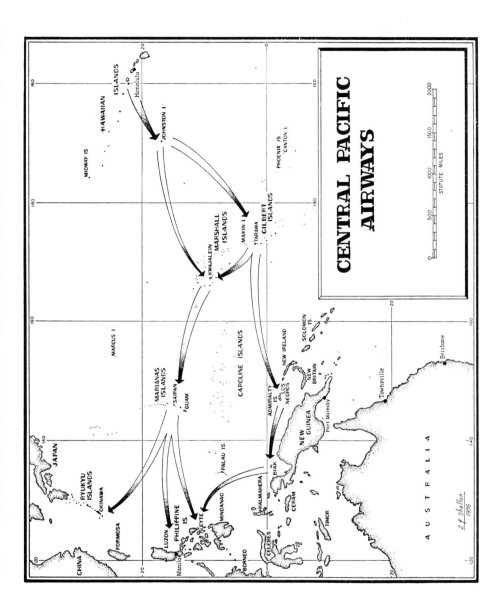

CENTRAL PACIFIC AIRWAYS

STATUTE MILES
0   500   1000   1500   2000

235

SECTION II

*   *   *   *   *   *   *   *   *   *   *

AVIATION ENGINEERS

CHAPTER 9

*   *   *   *   *   *   *   *   *   *   *

THE AVIATION ENGINEERS
IN AFRICA AND EUROPE

A T THE time of the outbreak of the European war General Arnold was negotiating with the Chief of Engineers for a special engineer unit to work with the air forces. The original conception was that small groups of skilled construction and engineering troops, trained intimately with air units, would be easily available to patch up airfields damaged by bombing, camouflage them, and, if necessary, defend them. They might also be prepared to accompany air task forces for light construction of airfields in forward areas. Soon after the German invasion of Poland the Corps of Engineers accepted the general outline, and on 4 June 1940 the newly reactivated 21st Engineers (General Service) Regiment, which had a proud history in the St.-Mihiel and Meuse-Argonne offensives of World War I, was redesignated the 21st Engineers (Aviation) Regiment at Fort Benning, Georgia. It thus became the parent unit of the aviation engineers who at their peak, in February 1945, would number 117,851 officers and men.[1]

The new organization, which was commanded by Lt. Col. Donald A. Davison, was transferred promptly to Langley Field, Virginia. There, the 21st gradually filled its cadres, almost altogether from recruits to the Regular Army, revamped its training according to the new mission, and experimented with such innovations as portable runways. It was not yet expected that the aviation engineers would ever engage in heavy construction, and in peacetime there was no function for them at all. In November 1940 the Corps of Engineers received the responsibility for Air Corps construction,* and Davison, who was

* See Vol. VI, 135.

by then Engineer, GHQ Air Force, began to discuss with the Chief of Engineers a more ambitious scope for the employment of the aviation engineers. A study of the methods of building airfields for the RAF in France during the preceding year, which was carried out in England in the winter of 1940–41 by Capt. Rudolph E. Smyser, Jr., led to the conclusion that the British system relied too much on army engineers. Instead of imitating this method, the Air Corps and the Engineers worked out by mid-1941 a plan under which the air forces should be endowed with men and equipment to build their own bases in forward areas, even if heavy construction was required.

The Aviation Engineer Battalion

The new approach represented a departure not only from previous Air Corps conceptions but from the practices of other major powers. In the brief experience available for study, it seemed that invading forces had only to take over and adapt to their own use the air facilities they found in occupied areas. Nations on a protracted defensive usually enjoyed abundant supply of civilian labor and conventional engineers to construct whatever they required. Without foreseeing the problems that were so soon to face them in building air bases on distant coral islands, in jungles, or in deserts, the handful of Engineer officers on duty with the Air Corps devised in 1941 what proved to be an excellent means to meet the challenge. This was the self-contained aviation engineer battalion, a unit that would form the core of aviation engineering efforts during World War II. Originally established with twenty-seven Engineer officers and 761 enlisted men, the battalion was designed to be capable "of independently constructing an advanced airdrome and all appurtenances."[2] It would have a lavish amount of equipment, numbering 220 items for construction and 146 vehicles—diesel tractors with bulldozers, carry-all scrapers, graders, gasoline shovels, rollers, mixers, air compressors, drills, trucks, trailers, asphalting and concreting equipment, rock crushers, draglines, and pumps—for its mission.[3] Only in the United States could engineers plan on such a scale.

During the months before Pearl Harbor the aviation engineers expanded rapidly. There was plenty of equipment, and the men required little training, for the expanding Army included many men who had construction and engineering experience in civil life. Davison was transferred to England and replaced by Col. Stuart C. Godfrey, who served as ranking air engineer of the AAF from 1941 until December 1943. Already, companies of aviation engineers were shipping to the Philippines, Greenland, Alaska, the Caribbean, and the Hawaiian Islands to participate in airfield construction.* The growing 21st Regiment at Langley Field continued its training and experimentation. During the Carolina maneuvers its troops constructed the first field airdrome in the United States with a runway of pierced-steel plank and camouflaged the airport at Laurens, South Carolina. General Arnold, whose vision and ambition for the Air Corps lay behind the program for the aviation engineers, took occasion in October 1941 to praise the performance of the 21st Regiment and to stress the importance to the air force of the military engineer, who was not a mere assistant, he said, "but one of us."[4] But during the prewar months the aviation engineers worked less with the air officers, with whom there was neither precedent nor immediate occasion for intimacy, than with the Corps of Engineers. Of paramount interest then was the testing of pierced-steel plank, the lighter prefabricated bituminous and square-mesh landing mats, various items of equipment, and portable hangars. In most cases it was to take the aviation engineers a long time to establish themselves with the air force in a close working relationship.[5]

The beginning of the war found the aviation engineers with twelve battalions scattered rather widely. The 804th Engineer Aviation Battalion (EAB) was based on Oahu, where it came under fire in the opening action and immediately went to work repairing Hickam Field. In the following chaotic days all engineers—aviation, army, and civilian—built emergency fighter fields and, for one of the few occasions during the war, completed elaborate camouflage measures. Early in January 1942 the 804th functioned as a unit on Kualoa Field, where the men hurriedly built a turf landing strip and laid steel mat. Then it was expanded and strengthened barely in time for bombers to use it during the Battle of Midway. Detachments of the 804th were on Christmas Island helping construct an airdrome for the South Pacific

* The contribution of aviation engineer units to the development of bases along the North and South Atlantic air routes was necessarily limited. In the latter case, the primary responsibility for an Airport Development Program in foreign territory from the Caribbean to Africa had been assigned to Pan American Airways by an agreement with the U.S. government made as early as November 1940 (see Vol. I, 321). In the North Atlantic, the work was shared by British, Canadian, and U.S. engineers, both military and civilian. Not only did the conception of the aviation engineer battalion emphasize direct assistance to combat forces but the pressing needs immediately before and after Pearl Harbor dictated commitment of most of the newly created units to combat areas.

ferry route and on Canton Island beginning an Army airfield.* For almost two years the 804th and the other battalions which joined it continued to work under civilian or Army control as requirements dictated, mainly anonymously, helping to make the Hawaiian Islands the springboard for the war in the Pacific. As bomber bases, revetments, avgas storage facilities, underground shops, sheltered runways, and tunnels were built, the engineering task was both varied and formidable. The labor performed during this long period was to provide experienced and highly skilled engineers for the air bases that had to be built for the great offensives of 1944 and 1945.[6]

In the Philippines the role of the aviation engineers was initially far less productive. After a journey of almost five months, the 803d EAB, which was sent as a modest reinforcement of the engineering resources that were straining to build heavy-bomber bases, had just begun its labors when the Japanese attacked. Like others in those days, the aviation engineers performed miracles, repairing airfields helterskelter, scraping out emergency runways in a few hours, dodging bombs, and pitching in for all types of work. By the first days of 1942 the battalion was on Bataan. There the men laid out airstrips, erected bridges, built emplacements for guns and searchlights, strung out barbed wire, and fought as combat troops. At last Bataan was overrun, and two companies of the 803d were captured. Company A made it to Corregidor, where for three months its men tried to keep Kindley Field in operation despite the shelling and bombing, the sickness, and failing hopes. A few of them lived to tell the story.[7]

Since June 1941 the 807th EAB had been in Alaska, where airfields were being developed on a low priority. Just before Pearl Harbor the decision was made to construct an air base on Umnak Island, one of the easternmost of the Aleutians, to defend the naval facilities at Dutch Harbor. The probability of a Japanese attack in this area after the war began moved the task into first priority,† and in January 1942 the 807th shipped off to begin the job. It turned out that no suitable docking areas were available on Umnak, a circumstance that was to become very familiar in the Pacific war, and the troops camped in discomfort for weeks on a neighboring island. Finally, another detachment of the 807th landed on Umnak by barge, chose the site, and began to strip it for the laying of the steel mat. When the transport

* See Vol. I, 180–84, 192–93.

† See Vol. I, 304–7.

with the steel planks arrived in March, the 807th unloaded them, ferried across the rough channel in barges, and carried the planks by hand to the beach on Umnak. Despite fearful winds and snows, the organization acquitted itself well. Even though the mat proved very unsatisfactory for some weeks, the job was finally completed, and the base served for fighters and heavy bombers. This operation was the first of the dramatic construction jobs undertaken by a single aviation engineer battalion.[8] Its success justified the battalion as a unit competent for airfield building under the most difficult conditions, and the Umnak achievement became famous among the engineers, both for the difficulties under which it was carried through and the lessons that could be deduced.

These early operations under wartime conditions made it plain that engineering demands were going to be far greater than anyone had expected. The crucial role of aviation, which was recognized by the elevated stature and mission of the Army Air Forces as organized in March 1942, emphasized the importance of rapid air-base construction. No longer could ample civilian labor forces and skills be assumed available; in the Pacific airdromes would have to be built in areas that were uncivilized or uninhabited. All the men and machines and much of the supplies would have to come from the United States. Their movement would be accomplished over extreme distances by shipping facilities that were already critically short and bound to become worse. Nor could the Americans plan on imitating the Axis aggressors, transferring their air units from the homeland to stolen bases in captured areas. Our aircraft, it was expected, would require larger and more elaborate bases than the Axis planes did, and, by the time the enemy was dislodged, his airdromes would probably be in no condition for ready utilization. Above all, speed was imperative, especially in the Pacific, for, before airplanes could operate, bases must be prepared.

The fortunate development of the self-contained engineer aviation battalion proved a sound basis on which to build the construction force necessary for the global task. Even had there been time, there was no need to make any major changes in the battalion organization but for a small increase in the number of men and a gradual substitution of several items of heavy equipment. Between December 1941 and December 1942 the number of such battalions increased from 12 to 51, and three-fifths of them were overseas by the end of the first year of war.[9] The Corps of Engineers supplied the officers as soon as they were trained. Most of the enlisted men, at least during 1942, were volunteers, men who had construction or engineering experience and therefore required little training. Certainly, they got little in the States.[10] From the first the aviation engineers had a special pride, that of performing constructive work in a destructive war, but, more than that, they had the *esprit de corps* of professionals who knew their job. The officers, especially, were jealous of the castle shoulder patches and insignia they wore and protested attempts made later in the war to substitute for them the wings and propellers of the Air Corps.[11] During the early part of the war the most limiting factor was transportation, not men and machines.

The air engineer at Headquarters, AAF, monitored the over-all functioning of the aviation engineers from his office under A-4. Brig. Gen. Stuart C. Godfrey held this position until December 1943, when he went to India to supervise the construction of B-29 bases. It had been planned to replace him with Brig. Gen. Donald A. Davison,[12] who by that time had distinguished himself in the North African campaign, but Davison died suddenly, and Col. George Mayo served as air engineer until the end of the war. The Washington office was modest in size, and its subordinate position on General Arnold's staff illustrated the relatively scant amount of business concerning the aviation engineers that Headquarters, AAF, handled. Nor did the air engineer possess any significant command function. The Corps of Engineers provided the officers as soon as they emerged from Fort Belvoir or other sources. Enlisted men went from Jefferson Barracks directly to one of the continental air forces for unit training, and then usually overseas, where the theater commander had complete control over them. It was the Operations Division, War Department General Staff, not the air engineer, which distributed the battalions on the basis of strategic necessity and availability of shipping. Only through personal inspection tours, correspondence, and such publications as the excellent journal, *Aviation Engineer Notes*,[13] could the air engineer exert any influence on the aviation engineers. Continuous liaison with the Corps of Engineers and the AAF Materiel Command permitted a close supervision of equipment, but the original types proved so adequate that no radical changes were recommended or made.

Notwithstanding its position in Washington, the air engineer's office steadily sought to increase the stature of aviation engineer organizations in the overseas air forces, an undertaking that had General Arnold's indorsement. During the first months it appeared that aviation engineers would be fed into the theaters piecemeal and merged with Army, Navy, and civilian engineering forces to work on construction projects too urgent to be affected by jurisdictional problems. The North African campaign afforded the first opportunity to experiment with the employment of aviation engineers as such. Their performance was so gratifying that an engineer command was finally established for the Northwest African Air Forces, a precedent that was followed in the invasion of Europe in 1944 with equally good results. In the Southwest Pacific and later in the Western Pacific theaters, the aviation engineers worked from first to last under the theater engineer, usually undistinguishably from other engineer units. It was almost the same in India and Burma and in the South Pacific and Pacific Ocean area, despite a different organization on paper and some important exceptions. Apart from informal pressure to place aviation engineers under air force commanders, Headquarters, AAF, secured the publication of an immediate-action War Department letter in August 1943 stating that aviation engineer units were organized and trained for employment with the air forces in combat theaters and that the normal employment of such units was in an assigned status with the air forces. Yet the final paragraph removed any mandatory quality of the letter by the words: "Nothing in the foregoing will be interpreted to restrict the authority of the theater or similar commander in making such readjustments of organization and employment of his forces as may be required to meet conditions peculiar to his theater."[14] Despite complaints from top air commanders that War Department policy was being disregarded,[15] Headquarters, AAF, could not tell a theater commander how to use the forces at his disposal.[16]

It was not intended that the standard type battalion, however employed, would remain the sole contribution of the aviation engineers. During the spring of 1942, when plans for an early invasion of Europe were under consideration, General Godfrey developed a project for an airborne engineer battalion.[17] Descending by parachute with or ahead of other airborne troops, this unit would patch up captured airdromes with hand tools and then be promptly reinforced by glider-borne engineers carrying such light equipment as miniature tractors, scrapers, rollers, mixer, and a supply of pistols, rifles, submachine guns, flares, and radio equipment. The Chief of Engineers agreed to assist in the development of this organization. Training began promptly at Westover Field, Massachusetts, and continued for some months there and with the Troop Carrier Command at Stout Field, Indiana. As finally authorized, the airborne battalion would have approximately twenty-eight officers and five hunderd enlisted men, a medical section, and a chaplain.[18] General Godfrey, who had great expectations for this unit, said the battalion would have a good deal of punch for its size, would not take up much tonnage, and could get places in a hurry.[19] Sixteen airborne battalions had been organized by the end of 1943, but, in spite of three dramatic instances of effective employment in North Africa, Burma, and New Guinea, air force commanders overseas resisted the enthusiasm of the air engineer. The opportunities were too rare, and the equipment was too light. Most of the airborne units spent the war working with the conventional battalions, ultimately exchanging their equipment for heavier pieces. Similarly, the air engineer worked out plans for special aviation engineer units, such as topographic companies to make aeronautical and target charts, camouflage battalions, petroleum distribution companies, and fire-fighting platoons. All these were to work intimately with the combat air forces as aviation engineers.[20] But such plans faltered and were only partially implemented when it became apparent that other agencies could perform these functions or that they scarcely needed to be performed at all. Thus the standard battalion, which justified itself so early in the war, remained the key unit of the aviation engineers.[21]

A Beginning in Britain

For some months prior to Pearl Harbor a group of aviation engineers had been in England studying the probable development of extensive air installations for American bombers and fighters. Already, the main outlines had been settled. The Americans would occupy bases in the general area around Huntingdon and East Anglia, some of them to be vacated by the RAF and others to be constructed. The British were to retain ownership and provide much of the labor and materials under a reverse lend-lease arrangement. Most of the equipment, however, and a large number of engineering and construction troops, would have to come from the United States.* After Pearl Harbor the Americans began the requisite shipments, two aviation

* See Vol. I, 632.

engineer battalions departing in January 1942. In view of the complicated ramifications of the vast construction program envisioned, all responsibility for its fulfilment was concentrated in the Army Services of Supply (SOS). Thus the Eighth Air Force exercised almost no control over the aviation engineer units, although its own engineer officers participated in some of the supervision of the program as well as the planning. Only in matters of airdrome camouflage and fire-fighting did aviation engineers fall under the command of air forces in England.[22]

According to the unit histories of the sixteen aviation engineer battalions which went to England during the first year of the war, the pattern of experience was more or less uniform and far less dramatic than that of those units who went to the Pacific. The Atlantic crossing was generally tense but uneventful. The landing in Scotland or Liverpool, the rail trip to an obscure town in East Anglia, and the first acquaintance with English fog and rain produced similar reactions of curiosity and complaint. Sometimes the battalions would house themselves in tent camps or Nissen huts for many months before they were allowed to build better posts, but at least they enjoyed settled living conditions. A period of experimentation with British trucks and equipment ensued during the interval, never less than several weeks, before their own and very welcome machinery arrived. The aviation engineers worked cordially, on the whole, with British civilians who, on construction projects, sometimes outnumbered them two and a half to one. Mud they contended with and cursed. Airdrome construction was simplified by following the prevailing British designs for three concrete runways, perimeter taxiways, hardstands, and dispersed housing. Usually, the aviation engineers completed their job and moved a few miles to start another one without seeing a single airplane land or take off. During slack periods they attended specialist schools to improve (or in many cases, to acquire) a knowledge of operating equipment and other skills that upgraded the capabilities of the engineers as a whole. The usual hour per day of drill, along with the climate and the seeming endlessness of the construction projects, insured that morale did not soar.[23]

The problems had to do mainly with the fact that equipment was so long delayed, often at docks in the United Kingdom. This condition made some aviation engineer officers bitter over criticisms to the effect that their troops were insufficiently trained, for they would much have preferred to give them unit training in the States with their equipment instead of having them sent prematurely overseas and separated from their equipment for long weeks. The materials furnished by the British were also a source of complaint, as well as the lack of skill and efficiency sometimes attributed to the civilian force. And if it was simple enough to construct the airdromes, the problem of drainage in England was formidable. The runways began to show premature signs of wear during the great aerial offensives of 1944 and required much effort for repair.[24] The frequent changes in plan disturbed the planners on the higher levels, but for aviation engineers there were always more construction jobs than they could handle. If they did not build one thing, they worked on another. On the whole, even if one battalion historian described the English period as the darkest hour for his unit,[25] life was comfortable compared to other theaters. Men became acquainted with their machines and their tasks, and even if some found they were not suited to the rough life of an engineer and if the dreary months in kerosene-lit, cold tents and huts seemed interminable, they were acquiring priceless experience. When the invasion of Normandy came, they were highly skilled and superbly equipped.

North Africa

For the North African landings in November 1942 four of the aviation engineer battalions stationed in England judged to be the best were picked: the 809th, 814th, 815th, and 817th.[26] Their mission was to accompany the assault forces and to provide airfields around Oran, as two British construction companies were to do east of Algiers. In western Morocco the 21st Engineer Aviation Regiment, the original aviation engineer unit, would land directly from the United States, as would the 871st Airborne, which had been hurriedly put together at Westover Field just in time to make the sailing. Brig. Gen. Donald A. Davison was engineer for the Allied forces, and Col. John C. Colonna served as engineer both for the newly created Twelfth Air Force and the XII Air Service Command.[27] Although command difficulties were to arise, the principle of air force supervision of its own construction was established at the outset.

The landings at Casablanca and Port Lyautey saw the 21st Regiment unloading on D Day. Some of its men engaged in sporadic combat. Within three days the regiment moved into two airfields seized from the French, where there was little to do but fill in soft spots and bomb craters. This was fortunate, for the unloading of the regiment's equipment had been marked by much confusion—an experience which carried an obvious lesson as to the need for more systematic loading in the later invasions. At Oran conditions were even more exasperating. The 814th EAB, after being cramped for two weeks aboard ship, walked twelve miles to its project, only to fill in holes, dig up duds, and remain idle because its heavy equipment had been appropriated by someone else. The 815th had lost most of its key equipment at sea, when the ship carrying it had been sunk. The 809th's equipment was on a ship that had developed engine trouble two days out of England and had turned back! The 817th had no such hard luck and got to work on La Senia Airport fairly promptly, but difficulties in unloading and successfully claiming its property made the operation a memorable example of confusion the officers were determined to avoid in the future. The brightest spot in the picture was that sufficient pierced-steel landing mat had been provided to help defeat the African weather.[28]

In Morocco the aviation engineers were able to improve and utilize existing airstrips readily enough and to begin construction on a large all-weather base near Casablanca. But at Oran and Algiers, which were nearer the front and accordingly more crucial, heavy rains had created an almost desperate situation. Near each of those cities was an air base with hard-surfaced runways, but they could scarcely be used because aircraft had to park on the strips in preference to sinking and sticking in the adjacent mud. Aside from offering a concentrated target to the enemy, this situation virtually held up the Allied air war. On 2 December 1942 General Davison flew to the village of Talergma, located on a high, flat plateau between the Saharan and the Maritime Atlas Mountains near the Tunisian boundary, where the French had informed him dry weather usually prevailed. Davison walked about until he had satisfied himself the soil combination was good. Later in the day a party of aviation engineers moved in from the coast and with the assistance of Arabs began at once to clear the first of several airstrips. Other troops of the 809th EAB soon came in by air and truck, and by 13 December a B-26 landed smoothly on the packed runway. The completion of other strips relieved congestion at Oran and Algiers by allowing the removal of the medium bombers and most of the fighters to the Talergma area.[29]

By that time General Doolittle was demanding a dry base closer to the front for his heavy bombers. Again relying on French advice, General Davison on 12 December explored a large sandy expanse near Biskra, which was still deeper in the Sahara, and again found a promising location. Because the conventional battalions of aviation engineers were already being utilized in many localities, Davison summoned the airborne engineers of whom so much was expected in Washington. In one of the most publicized operations of the aviation engineers during the war, two companies of the 871st Airborne Engineer Aviation Battalion loaded their midget equipment into fifty-six C-47's and flew in from Morocco, almost a thousand miles away. They landed at Youks-les-Bains, rode their equipment or walked to the site at Biskra, which they reached on the evening of 13 December, and began work immediately. After twenty-four hours' labor, an earth runway was ready to receive the first B-17's from Oran.[30] The aircraft were now out of the mud. Until March 1943, when spring winds blew sand in such quantities as to make operations impossible, Biskra remained a major base for the heavies.

Not heartening achievement, but disappointment, attended another operation of the airborne engineers. On 7 December the 888th Airborne Engineer Aviation Company was flown from Morocco to Tebessa, just west of the boundary between Algeria and Tunisia. Just as the group got to work it rained, and it was soon lamentably apparent that the miniature equipment was not equal to the job. In spite of machines borrowed from nearby British construction groups, fifteen days were required to scrape out an earthen runway.[31] Soon the airborne company was sent back to the rear area, and the 814th EAB was brought in to complete the task. After a very rough ride in a ramshackle Algerian train and in trucks, members of the 814th EAB plunged into foxholes before plunging into the job.[32] They completed a cluster of dry-weather fields and even an all-weather field at Thelepte, just as the Germans broke through the Kasserine Pass. These fields had to be abandoned temporarily, but oddly enough most of the supplies and equipment were recovered when the Germans were driven out. The failure of the 888th Company overshadowed the success of the 871st Battalion, with the result that air commanders in North Africa adopted what Washington regarded as "a narrow view" of the potentialities of airborne aviation engineers.[33] The story would be the same in other theaters.

After Kasserine, events went better for the engineers, who had been under criticism for falling behind the pace demanded by combat commanders.[34] The rains lessened, and then stopped. More engineers arrived, and the experiences of the past weeks hardened the troops both to the hostile African climate and to repeated German air attacks. The next job was to prepare fighter bases in the Sbeitla area of central Tunisia for support of the ground forces in their effort to expel the Germans from Africa. After receiving the request, the aviation engineers provided five fields within seventy-two hours. The 814th Battalion, which carried out most of the work, demonstrated a marked improvement in mobility—in fact, it achieved almost the ideal by racing from one job to another. Within a few days the Sbeitla fields were too far in the rear, but the 814th was able to create new fighter fields in the Le Sers area within a matter of hours. Its efforts contributed significantly to the final and victorious offensive in Tunisia.[35]

Meanwhile, other units of aviation engineers were constructing airfields from which Allied planes could protect convoys sailing along the coastline from southern Morocco on the Atlantic coast almost to Tripoli. Since supply problems were already aggravating all other difficulties in the North African operations, it was all the more frustrating that shortages of equipment and mud delayed this program of airfield construction. The base at Bône, which for a long time served as the easternmost port available to the Allies, proved the most difficult but perhaps the most rewarding to build. The area was under Axis air attack, and the engineering problem was formidable. Mountains ran into the sea, leaving as the only possible site for an airfield a delta in the Seybouse River mouth. This area was pure mud, a commodity already highly unpopular. The solution was to bring in vast amounts of sand, which lay on the wrong side of the river. For this task the 21st Regiment received all the heavy equipment in the area and set to work. The men built a sand causeway across the river, a roadway on the delta, and began to bring in sand from the dunes. It was not so much the stubborn German air campaign against the troops as the threat of rain that made the outcome of this bold decision so problematical. Any substantial rainfall would wash away the road and cause the river to rise and destroy the causeway. General Davison decided to gamble on the weather, for he had only fourteen days to complete the air base or see the port at Bône closed down. Somehow it did not rain for a few days, and the unconventional passage was finished and the sand spread over the mud delta. On the last day of the time limit, the base was finished and the steel plank laid. Then a cloudburst conveniently packed the sand after the final plank went down. Soon the aviation engineers received the most gratifying of rewards when a B-26 in trouble landed safely on the runway at Bône—a runway the pilot did not know existed until he providentially sighted it.[36]

Out of the North African operations came not only priceless experience but a pattern for command that proved highly successful in both the MTO and the ETO. AAF leaders had won a crucial point when the aviation engineers were assigned to the air force rather than to Service of Supply, as had been the case in England. At one time General Davison indicated his willingness to turn over all construction work to SOS in the hope that more might be accomplished, but General Godfrey, the air engineer in Washington, was insistent that the air forces retain control. Shortly after Maj. Gen. Carl Spaatz assumed command of the Northwest African Air Forces (NAAF) in February 1943, he made Davison chief aviation engineer and Colonel Colonna his assistant. Thereafter, NAAF spelled out all requirements, and XII Air Service Command did the work as directed. Difficulties of command remained on lower levels, but they were usually decided in favor of the operational leaders. Complications arose in the last stages of the Tunisian campaign when the engineer of the U.S. First Army disagreed with the priorities fixed by NAAF for airfield construction in his area. But once more the air forces won their point, and a directive from Allied Forces Headquarters on 23 April 1943 established the overriding authority of the NAAF aviation engineer regarding the construction of airdromes.[37]

By this time the aviation engineer units were spread all the way across the theater, usually working as small detachments rather than as battalions to complete tactical bases in Tunisia and to enlarge airdromes in the Tellergma area for the heavies. Ammunition and fuel dumps, as well as drinking-water supply, became responsibilities of the aviation engineers. The more elaborate bases called for cross-runways and more lavish facilities. But not until the North African campaign was over could such luxuries as shower houses, storage buildings, kitchens, post exchanges, and recreational buildings claim the labor of the aviation engineers.[38]

The achievements of the aviation engineers in North Africa were matters for discreet boasting, notwithstanding some of the early fumbles and setbacks. By the end of the campaign there were ten battalions in the theater. They had built or improved 129 airdromes. British and American engineers had constructed a new airfield on the average of every two days, using less than one-half the number of engineers supposedly required by the War Department troop basis.[39] The wholehearted appreciation expressed by various air leaders was very gratifying to General Godfrey, who saw that the comments circulated. It was General Spaatz, perhaps, whose praise carried the most weight. In a letter to General Arnold he spoke of the aviation engineers as being "as nearly indispensable to the AAF as is possible to ascribe to any single branch thereof." Everywhere he had gone, he continued, "it has been the same story, efficiency, willingness, intelligent application, all resulting in praiseworthy completion of tasks in such short intervals of time as to be considered fantastic when judged by peacetime standards."[40] But even this encomium could not include an appraisal of thousands of mines and booby traps removed, of a few enemy planes shot down, of hours spent in foxholes, of round-the-clock toil in mud or sandstorms, or of casualties suffered.

With the invasion of Sicily impending, the aviation engineers worked on bases in Tunisia for combat planes and troop carriers, a simple enough task now that the rains had ceased and the soil was good. More complicated were the new requirements for fighter fields on tiny islands in the Mediterranean. The British were expanding their bases on Malta, and another airfield could be squeezed on minute Gozo, which lay just to the north. One company of the 2d Battalion, 21st Regiment, began work there on 8 June 1943. They had to destroy stone walls, smooth out ancient terraces, and bring in 70,000 bags of sand from Malta. By working day and night, the aviation engineers and three hundred civilians had two fighter runways of compacted earth ready on 20 June, a week ahead of schedule, a feat that won the praise of Air Marshal Tedder, although, as it turned out, the usefulness of the field was limited by its tendency to become too dusty or muddy.[41]

A detachment of the 888th Airborne Engineers accompanied the men who occupied Pantelleria after the memorable bombing on 11 June 1943. The elaborate underground facilities constructed by the Italians were almost intact, but the runway was strewn with the wreckage of airplanes and had about two hundred bomb blasts. Since the enemy was still attacking the occupying forces, it was imperative to have a fighter runway as soon as possible. Aided by sappers from the Army engineers and by Italian prisoners, the group had this runway ready in six hours. It was a rough one—a small area of the Italian field containing the least damage and bounded by flags, debris, and drums—but it served. On the next day the engineers filled the craters more thoroughly and dozed them. Again marking the repaired area, this time with sheets, they had it operational for P-40's in short order. The 888th spent about three months on the island and in some measure compensated for their earlier failure, or that of their equipment, at Tebessa. The men put the water and power plant into operation and, with the help of a captured shovel, repaired the roads. Then they restored the bakery and central refrigerator, cleared the town, and built showers and kitchens for themselves. For aviation engineers here as in so many other places leisurely reconstruction of war-torn areas followed feverish activities in combat. It was almost the same on Lampedusa, another Italian island which surrendered after bombardment, where fifty men of the 817th Battalion moved in and restored the logistics of civilized life.[42]

Sicily

Aviation engineer officers were afterward inclined to complain that they had been left out of the planning for the Sicilian operation,[43] but the Allies knew very little of soil conditions on the island, and the only recourse was to place the engineers ashore as soon as possible in the belief that they could discover a way to base the aircraft. The general pattern was for the British to construct forward fields behind their own ground forces and for the Americans to support the U.S. Seventh Army in the western sector. For the invasion phase itself, Army engineers were to control the distribution of all supplies and equipment needed for construction. Advanced details of three aviation engineer battalions (the 809th, 814th, and 815th) were to land on D Day and repair captured airfields or carve out new ones as necessary. Until the sailing, all the men could do was work on their equipment, which most of them liked to do, and undergo training in the art of staying alive in combat, which most of them bitterly resented, even though the North African experience had indicated they were far from expert in such matters.[44]

On D Day, 10 July 1943, a small detachment of the 814th Engineers, attached temporarily to the 19th Engineer Combat Regiment, dragged their equipment from the landing craft to the beaches and proceeded inland to a large captured airdrome at Comiso. It took only a little time to repair the craters in its runway, partly because the Germans had left an asphalt plant behind. Next the men of the 814th EAB groped their way to Biscari, putting its field back into operation within four days, the worst aspect of the task being the burial of the enemy dead found there. The twelve aviation engineers of the 809th EAB, who landed with the 1st Division at Gela, were less successful. Some equipment was lost, and a paneled emergency airstrip prepared on D Day was overrun by the Germans on the next day. Moving on 12 July to the former main enemy base at Ponte Olivo, which was said to be cleared, the engineers found it intricately mined and under artillery fire. The painstaking work of removing the mines and filling the small craters took all night; by 13 July, however, the field was operational and out of the enemy's artillery range. A field near the landing beach, later known as Gela East, had been crisscrossed by barbed wire. Three hours after the handful of engineers with the aid of prisoners of war started to clear it, a damaged Fortress was able to land. Soon the airdrome was ready for emergency use on larger scale, although the troops lacked fuel, oil, equipment, and, much of the time, rations and water. The arrival of the 809th EAB and its machinery made it possible to finish the rehabilitation of Ponte Olivo and Gela East and to begin a dry-weather field at Gela West within a few days. During this phase of the invasion, the aviation engineers had been subjected to German shells, strafings, and the devilish thermal bombs scattered at night, all of which caused casualties but scarcely held up the work of reconstruction.[45]

On the westernmost American beach, at Licata, a company of the 815th EAB landed despite dive bombers and strafing German planes and sent a survey party to examine an airfield the Allies hoped to rehabilitate. The engineer in charge decided it would be simpler to construct a new runway, and this the troops did within two days, although most of their heavy equipment was still on the beaches. Allied aircraft descended on the runway in numbers and took off on tactical support missions. Since service troops had not arrived, the aviation engineers had to refuel and rearm the fighters for almost a week. Within a few days the German attacks abruptly ceased, not only at Licata, but in the whole invasion area, and the engineers, now with their three battalions at almost full strength, had bases ready for 34 fighter squdarons on 20 July.[46] For the most part the battalions were well equipped and had managed to retain contact with their equipment. Hectic as the first few days on Sicily were, the aviation engineers had performed very creditably.

Around the first of August 1943 the 814th EAB moved to the western end of Sicily, which had just been seized. Its Company C quickly rehabilitated the former Axis base at Castelvetrano to permit air transports to come in and evacuate the wounded. Two other bases were repaired, those at Sciacca and Borizzo. The 809th EAB completed its work at Ponte Olivo and Gela East airstrips, its labors interrupted only once by the requirement to build dummy airfields to attract German bombers. Some of the 815th's engineers accompanied the Third Division as it crossed Sicily from south to north, a journey which taxed the skill and patience of the men in moving their heavy machinery along the treacherous mountain roads of the island. Once on the northern side, the 815th cleared in a few hours a captured airdrome near Palermo and scratched out bases for fighters and transports east of the city. The withdrawal of the Germans indicated that the battle for Sicily was won. The aviation engineers had done what they were supposed to do. Even the weather had been good, a circumstance so rare when things went badly, so unremarked when they went well. For the next few weeks the aviation engineers worked on barracks, water points, electric power systems, and other necessities that were only frills during combat phases of an operation. Soon the 809th and 814th were preparing thirteen fields, mostly dry-weather, to support projected troop-carrier operations. These fields were scattered over Sicily, and the engineering problems varied with the locality, but none proved formidable. All the bases were ready a day or two before the completion date, 31 August.[47]

The next operation—the invasion of Italy—was already under way. For the crucial landing at Salerno the short range of the Spitfires posed a problem. The British fighters would be indispensable for protection of the invasion beaches, and the only area in Sicily close enough to Salerno was a small strip of coastal plain on the Milazzo peninsula. The moutains crowded the plain so closely that airfields would have to be laid out end to end with two miles in between, and other safety factors would have to be disregarded. That was the way it had to be if the Salerno landings were to be supported by Spitfires, and the 815th EAB duly constructed five runways according to this plan. Much of the work was performed by Italians, whose pay probably failed to compensate for the destruction of their vineyards. Equipment left behind by the Germans was useful. The chief hazard was dust, which became such a deterrent and nuisance the aviation engineers piped water in from the sea for sprinkling and later borrowed some oil from the Royal Navy. The job was finished on time, and the fields served the Spitfires for the Salerno operation. Even the dangers posed by the proximity of the mountains did not result in the loss of a single aircraft. The only sour note in the operation was the hurried dispatch of a detachment of the 815th EAB to Catania, on the eastern side of Sicily, in reply to an urgent call for airfield and road construction. As it turned out, the airdrome was not feasible, and the engineers, pulled away from the Milazzo job, worked on a road until they were withdrawn for more important tasks in Italy. Air engineers grumbled that road construction should have been the job of the Army engineers.[48]

The problem of command came up during the climax of the Sicilian operation. The aviation engineers had amply proved their unique importance to the air forces. But now, the airfields in North Africa and Sicily required maintenance for sustained operations, and the Italian campaign loomed, along with the project to base heavy bombers on the Italian peninsula for the strategic bombardment of Germany. Theater commanders were receptive to pressure from General Godfrey at Headquarters, AAF, and from General Davison at NAAF and other aviation engineers in the theater, to offer more recognition to the organization. Furthermore, plans for the great continental invasion in 1944 from England were reaching a decisive stage that called for an intimate relationship between aviation engineers and the tactical air forces. Although the prevailing scheme of control had functioned well in North Africa and Sicily, too many conflicts arose between the operational air commanders and the air service commanders on the lower administrative levels. Keeping well in mind the needs of the forthcoming operation OVERLORD and, indeed, conferring with Maj. Gen. Lewis H. Brereton, who was designated to command the tactical air forces in that understaking, the NAAF commanders agreed in August 1943 to permit General Davison to assume direct control of the aviation engineers, who were accordingly withdrawn from the Air Service Command. After some shuffling of responsibilities and titles, the next and last step came on 22 October 1943, when General Eisenhower authorized the establishment of a provisional engineer command for the Twelfth Air Force, which soon became the provisional AAF Engineer Command (MTO) and provided the pattern for the renowned IX Engineer Command.[49]

Italy and Southern France

The critical landings at Salerno in September 1943 provided another opportunity for the aviation engineers to perform their unique services in support of an amphibious invasion. It had been planned that an advance party of the 817th EAB would land on D Day with the American forces which were to seize Paestum. Since fighter support of the ground forces was greatly restricted by the distance to the bases back in Sicily, the engineers were to make ready a landing strip in urgent haste. On D Day, 9 September, the party unloaded and headed for the proposed site just before dark. But enemy opposition made the area unsafe, and another site had to be chosen after nightfall by engineers walking about with flashlights and under enemy fire. The site they picked was certain to be dusty, and it was evident that large trees would have to be cleared away, a ditch filled, crops of cotton, wheat, and tomatoes destroyed. As the advance group made its survey, two companies of engineers de-waterproofed their equipment, an irksome task, and moved up. At dawn they started to work, and before evening they had produced a runway 4,000 feet long—graded, rolled, and adorned with enough taxiways and dispersal areas to accommodate several squadrons. They controlled the dust by borrowing water trailers from another unit and sprinkling extensively. Allied fighters were using the field the day after it was ready. Here, as in Sicily, the aviation engineers had to service the airplanes for some days, even bringing gasoline and ammunition from the beach.[50]

The need for more runways was still urgent, for the Germans were resisting tenaciously. On 13 September the 817th EAB began construction on an airstrip beside the Sele River, where a marsh had been drained by the Italians to provide a wheat field. The aviation engineers had scarcely begun work when a German counterattack came so close to the site that equipment had to be pulled away for a day. Again, water trailers were borrowed to keep the dust down, and, after the field became usable on 18 September, the engineers brought up supplies and serviced the planes. By that time work had begun on another site, which the surveyors had selected despite obvious disadvantages. The field, Capaccio, lay too close to the hills and was so dry that great cracks crisscrossed the area, but it had to be put in shape for emergency purposes. This was "cow-pasture" construction, as the engineers called it. But marked out, rolled, graded, and sprinkled, Capaccio was ready for fighters within a day. There was no time to consider wind currents and safe approaches. Fighter planes desperately needed fields on the beachhead to support the beleaguered ground forces, and aviation engineers scratched the airstrips out as fast as they could.[51]

Since it might rain at any time during that season, the high command was nervous about getting an all-weather field ready in the Salerno area. The British construction group tried at Montecorvino an unorthodox measure on an old Italian sod field, which they scraped over once and then covered with mat. The experiment served well enough for emergency needs. The 817th Engineers, working now at battalion strength, undertook a more ambitious project at Gaudo. Since Italian labor was abundantly available and a quarry only three miles away, they scraped down to a subgrade of gravel and stone dust and then laid a rock course and finally steel mat. Early in November Gaudo was ready as an all-weather field.[52]

The next mission was the construction of all-weather bases in the Naples area. The able and experienced British 15th Airdrome Construction Group went to work on two permanent facilities there. Company C of the 815th EAB joined the British organization in October 1943, fresh from a two-week experiment at Cercola, near the base of Mt. Vesuvius. Clearing away ancient buildings and filling wells had been routine enough, but using fresh volcanic ash from brooding Vesuvius as a substitute material for paving runways was indeed novel. Farther away, the British and other companies of the 815th worked on all-weather bases at Marcianise and Santa Maria. Marcianise proved to be a slow job because rain fell on fifty of the seventy-three days required for building it. At Santa Maria, higher headquarters changed plans at least five times, with the result that the aviation engineers were put to work and called off repeatedly. In the end, it remained a dry-weather field.[53]

For the Anzio landings the 815th Engineers again built a base,

Castelvolturno, for the short-ranged Spitfires. This airdrome was located on a coastal strip near the mouth of the Volturno River, about 80 miles south of the invasion area. If mud in southern Italy had immobilized much of the heavy equipment, at least here the beach sand permitted its operation. Malaria seemed the worst threat as the 815th Engineers began work on 1 December 1943. It turned out, however, that the malignant Italian weather of that memorable winter caught up with them. Rains caused ground water to rise to a point that flooded much of the runway, but the steel mat was laid in time for the field to be used as planned for the Anzio operation. The aviation engineers by planting rye grass even hoped to conquer a future dust problem. Another site in the vicinity, Lago, was also a responsibility of the heavily taxed 815th EAB. Compared with Castelvolturno, it proved fairly simple to build.[54]

A complex of bases for heavy bombers and long-range fighters in the Heel of Italy and in the Foggia area was expected to have a decisive bearing on the success of the strategic air offensive, and the provision of these airdromes became first priority in the engineer command. Nearly all the steel mat in the theater was concentrated on this program, although the British finally won a few concessions for the Desert Air Force, which was to need bases up the eastern coast of Italy. As soon as the Desert Air Force moved out of the Heel, the 21st Engineer Aviation Regiment and the 809th and 385th Battalions came in to enlarge and strengthen the existing fields of Lecce, San Pancrazio, Mandura, Brindisi, Gioia, and Grottaglie, all of them for Fifteenth Air Force heavy bombers but Grottaglie, which was to be a fighter base. The deadline for this reconstruction was 31 October 1943, but the slow arrival of the aviation engineers pushed it back to 10 November, and it was actually in December before the heavies could be based in the Heel.[55]

The aviation engineers ran into trouble from the first, originally because of the difficulties in moving equipment on schedule, then because of unexpectedly evil weather, but ultimately because the job had been underestimated, not by the engineers themselves so much as by higher commanders who were eager to get the strategic air force over Germany by the southern route. At Lecce the silty soil was saturated by rain and the natural drainage so poor that the runway was not operational until February 1944. Manduria received bombers in December, but only because pierced-steel plank had been laid on its existing surface, and such effort was required to maintain it that there was nothing left for further construction. The steel plank runway at Gioia disintegrated quickly under use. The aviation engineers scooped muck out and piled it as high as fifteen feet on each side of the runway. They used rock to raise the runway above the water. It was almost the same story at Brindisi and San Pancrazio. The winter of 1943–44 in the Heel was a nightmare of buckling runways, frenzied repairs, mud, water—and neglect of other construction. In one sense, at least, it was fortunate that the slower tempo of heavy-bomber operations at that time kept the air-base situation from being more critical than it was.

The Foggia job had also appeared deceptively simple. There, a fairly level plain with a flat spread of sand and clay and abundant rock quarries seemed to offer an opportunity for rapid airfield development. The new construction involved eight airdromes. The first, Foggia Main, went off well enough. Units of the 21st Regiment and the 814th and 845th Battalions had one runway, with steel plank on a compacted fill of caliche, ready by 1 December and another by the last of January. Drainage proved good in spite of the volume of rainfall. To the east of Foggia Main, at Foggia #2, the aviation engineers laid steel plank directly on an old sod field, a measure that sometimes worked, but in this case it proved necessary to raise the mat thirteen times during the next few months and to smooth out the runway. The airdromes known as Giulia, San Giovanni, and Toretto had high water tables and poor natural drainage. The engineers finally had to cut a deep runway and leave it open until the weather straightened out before laying gravel, compacting, and placing the steel mat. At the other fields, Foggia #1, Foggia #2, and Foggia #7, the situation was similar—a long effort to secure minimum drainage, the rather timorous laying of steel mat, and the repeated repairs and refills. Every frustration dogged the aviation engineers in their efforts toward continuous maintenance. Yet the Foggia runways were at least usable by January 1944, even if other construction lagged three months behind schedule. Naturally, living conditions for the overworked engineer troops were dismal, for they could build little for their own comfort until the all-weather bases were completed.[56]

In western Italy a lull developed for the first months of 1944. Thirty men of the 815th EAB went with British construction units to the Anzio beachhead, but the rest of the battalion departed for the rear, hoping for a rest after such a long stint of airfield development. Instead, they built camp facilities for MAAF personnel and, later, quarters for general officers in the royal gardens at Caserta. When Vesuvius erupted and fallen ash had immobilized eighty-two B-25's, the aviation engineers cleared a road so that the stricken Mitchells could be taxied away. Many other jobs came their way—hauling gravel, improving all sorts of facilities, expanding and developing existing airdromes.[57] Perhaps they were luckier than they realized. In other theaters aviation engineers were often employed on construction jobs that had no relation to air force needs and frequently worked longer hours under worse conditions.

The Allied offensive of May–August 1944 into northern Italy brought back the 815th, 817th, and 835th Battalions to more urgent activities. The 815th built a dry-weather field in the former Anzio beachhead, this time finding enough oil to hold the dust down, and rehabilitated a captured air base after removing several hundred Teller mines the Germans had left behind for their benefit. Following the ground forces they moved into Rome and readied three airfields, where most of the labor was a matter of removing booby traps and mines. They had only six hours to get Roma Littoria in readiness to receive transports coming in to evacuate the wounded, but that was time enough. Then the 815th continued northward, repairing cratered runways and doing whatever had to be done to make captured airdromes suitable for Allied planes. Since German air opposition was so light, Allied fighters could be used more and more for bombing and strafing. This called for lengthening airdromes from time to time, but this was not formidable work for experienced aviation engineers. Their chief concern these days was German artillery, which often remained in the vicinity of the airfields that needed repair. As noted, the 835th Battalion was concerned in these operations, having finished its hard, wet winter in the Heel, as was the 817th, which interrupted its work in Corsica for the renewed Italian offensive.[58]

The problem of constructing air bases on Corsica proved extremely vexatious, if ultimately rewarding. The tactical air forces required bases there for operations against Italy and, eventually, southern France. Only four captured airfields were available for development, and all of them were inadequate for American aircraft. And other airdromes would need to be built, despite the mountainous character of the island. Fortunately, many Frenchmen and Italian prisoners

could be utilized as a labor force, and two companies of French aviation engineers were on hand. Dry-weather fields for transports and
fighters were constructed and even some for medium bombers. These
last, of course, received hard-surfacing and steel mat, as materials and
effort became available.[59] Less labor was required for the Axis airfields on Sardinia, where most of them needed little but mine removal.
But the construction of a medium-bomber base at Decimomannu included the novelty of widening the runway to more than a thousand
feet to permit six B-26's to take off simultaneously.[60]

The first aviation engineer unit to reach Corsica had an unusual
history. This 812th Engineer Aviation Battalion, a Negro organization, had shipped out from Charleston, South Carolina, in May 1942
to build bases in south-central Africa on the substitute ferry route.*
They put in at Freetown, Sierra Leone, had leave in the Union of
South Africa, and finally arrived at Mombasa, Kenya, where they
took a train into the interior. Apparently the men were much amused
by the sight of giraffes loping and monkeys cavorting beside the
rickety railroad. Once they had erected a tent camp in the tall grass
of Kenya, where they had planned to work with the Royal Engineers
on an airfield, they actually completed all they were destined to do
in that area. Suddenly they were on their way back to the coast and
found themselves on ships bound for Egypt. After some days of
sight-seeing there, they piled into trucks and bumped for 900 miles
or so across the desert to Benghazi, where for a time they were the
only American engineers. There they stabilized a base for Ninth Air
Force B-24's that bombed Ploesti and built a pipeline from the sea
to keep the airfield sprinkled. After hauling sand and picking up rocks
for an interval, the unit sailed for Sicily toward the last of 1943, and
then to Corsica in January 1944. For six months they worked around
the clock on airfield development, after which followed ten months
of comparative leisure on the picturesque island.[61] If the itinerary of
the 812th Engineers was unusually colorful, the spurts of hard labor,
the long waits, the sudden changes, and the enjoyment of opportunities available were typical of the wartime life of aviation engineers.

Very elaborate planning for aviation engineer operations preceded
the invasion of southern France. Since a slow and difficult campaign
was expected, with the autumn rains beginning at an awkward stage,
the AAF Engineer Command (MTO) developed unusually detailed

* See above, pp. 54–55.

intelligence dossiers on existing airdromes and on soil and terrain conditions. Six aviation engineer battalions were to land as soon as possible and begin all-weather base construction. The 809th EAB carried out its assignment with dispatch, landing in the beachhead area, clearing the mines and grapevines from a virgin site previously selected, and having it in order to receive Spitfires by D plus 4. The other battalions had a similar experience, encountering little opposition, unloading equipment promptly, and going to work on sites where mines and obstructions offered the only challenge. Not so the 887th Engineer Airborne Company, which had a very bad time of it. All the gliders which bore this unit made crash landings, some of them very rough, and almost a third of the entire company sustained injuries. But this unfortunate operation was the exception; elsewhere the aviation engineers found DRAGOON almost so easy as to constitute a mere exercise. Before long the ground forces were advancing so rapidly the aviation engineers had difficulty keeping up with the line of advance. There was scarcely any need to scratch out airstrips. Soon, two of the six battalions were sent back to Italy, and, by early 1945, all of them had been returned.[62]

It was not altogether a holiday in southern France, however. The Germans had been unusually thorough and ingenious, even for Germans, in mining two of the airfields near the landing. The aviation engineers were by now well experienced in these matters, but they took unusual care to watch out for new tricks on every captured installation. It was dust rather than mud which interfered most with the work of enlarging the runways. This time the aviation engineers were better prepared with water trailers and oil than they had been in Africa, Sicily, and Italy. Filling in craters made by Allied bombs was time-consuming, although French civilians were hired to do much of the labor. In employing the French, difficulties appeared. Some of the first French contractors engaged for this purpose turned out to be in bad standing with the French underground, and political problems had to be met or ignored in order to get the work done. Finally, all hiring was routed through the French labor organization. As always, supplies were short. Sometimes it was a matter of gasoline and diesel oil, sometimes of rations and clothes, but in no case was the lack more than a matter of irritation, not of breakdown. In all, the aviation engineers constructed four new airfields and converted twenty-one existing bases to Allied use. It was an impressive record even for a pushover campaign. The whole affair had gone off better than expected.[63]

In Italy the cluster of air bases in the Foggia, Naples, and Rome areas had long since been improved to support a heavier pace of air operations. With the invasion of France going well, the aviation engineers in Italy received as reinforcements the units that had gone with DRAGOON. There was still enough work to keep them busy, for the approach of autumn weather called for the laying of pierced-steel plank on the former dry-weather fields. As the Allied front moved north, Pisa, Florence, and Pontedera were captured, and their airfields were cleared of debris, patched up, and enlarged. By the end of the war, only fifteen airfields in western Italy were required for tactical operations, only a third of the number the aviation engineers had built or repaired.[64] The twenty-five bases for the Fifteenth Air Force heavy bombers, however, and all the collateral construction required as the strategic air offensive continued, absorbed the constant effort of the aviation engineers until the end of the war.

The Invasion of Western Europe

During the early planning phase of operation OVERLORD the air and engineer officers in England determined to continue and to improve the system, which had worked so well in North Africa and Italy. A fast-moving tactical air force, they reasoned, would need to be self-supporting in the matter of airfield development and to enjoy extreme flexibility in directing engineering troops to repair or construct airdromes on short notice. The intensification of invasion planning in October 1943 bore a direct relationship to the establishment of the engineer command that month in North Africa. Indeed, General Brereton, who was about to move to England with the Ninth Air Force, had participated in the discussions leading to the creation of the engineer command. Once in England, Brereton's staff conferred extensively with Colonel Smyser, who had for more than two years served as engineer with the Eighth Air Force, and other officers who had been working on OVERLORD plans. The plan they devised called for the establishment of an engineer command in the United Kingdom to handle the transfer of aviation engineers from the Eighth to the Ninth Air Force, the training for the invasion, and then the development of airfields on the Continent as the Ninth required them.[65]

The War Department, however, proved reluctant to authorize such a command, perhaps because a precedent might be set for Ordnance, Signal, Chemical Warfare, and other services to elevate their stature. A decision was postponed for some months, during which the Ninth Air Force proceeded to absorb most of the aviation engineer units in England. At length the War Department refused to establish the engineer command. No prohibition, however, stood against the authority of the theater commander to create a provisional command, as had been done in the MTO, and on 30 March 1944 the Ninth Air Force received permission to activate the headquarters of the IX Engineer Command. On 1 July 1944 the command itself, as a provisional organization, came into official existence, though by that time it was very much in business in France. The 17,000 officers and men in sixteen aviation engineer battalions were grouped under four regimental headquarters plus three airborne battalions and a camouflage battalion. Brig. Gen. James B. Newman, Jr., became the first commanding general of the IX Engineer Command.[66]

For OVERLORD the IX Engineer Command had the pick of the aviation engineers stationed in England. Nearly all its troops had been in the theater for many months and were highly experienced in the construction of airdromes. But the task ahead called for different skills, such as removal of mines and booby traps, the rapid scraping-out of landing fields on virgin sites for fighters and transports, the laying of portable landing mats, and repair of captured airdromes. Since the officers were specialists and the men were already seasoned and able, not more than two months of new training was deemed necessary. At Great Barrington and other centers the aviation engineers came and went in unsteady flows during the first part of 1944 to practice the techniques they would soon use in operating as mobile units under enemy fire. The men needed above all further training in dodging bombs, bullets, and shells and in firing. Otherwise, it was simple enough to teach them the mysteries of dewaterproofing equipment and to assure that operators of heavy equipment would be available to the extent of three trained men for each major piece. Some of the troops got a little practice in preparing advanced landing grounds and laying portable mats, but not as much as had been specified. This deficiency did not show up later in France, however. In fact, the rather haphazard quality of pre-invasion training had no untoward results. The aviation engineers were already good! At higher levels, of course, planning for D Day had to do with acquiring intelligence on terrain and soil conditions in the invasion area, the apportionment of tonnage to get the equipment across, and decisions regarding the types of landing mat to be used on various proposed runways. Subsequent evaluations revealed no important defects in the preparations of the aviation engineers for OVERLORD.[67]

The first aviation engineers ashore on D Day were detachments of the 819th EAB. They landed on UTAH beach a little after H plus 4, a bit seasick after two days on their LST's. The men waded about two hundred yards to the beach, only to see their machinery bog down in mud on their dispersal area. Seven hours later they had extricated the equipment and moved to the proposed site of an emergency landing strip. This first mission they completed in three hours, whereupon they dug foxholes to protect themselves from steady sniper fire. It was harder at OMAHA beach. Point-blank fire kept the detachment of the 834th Engineer Aviation Battalion from landing at all on D Day. After another night aboard ship, the men finally unloaded at another point in the face of moderate fire. But moving the equipment to the beach proved very difficult because of the numerous obstacles placed by the Germans, and even after reaching land the unit had to wait disconsolately and exposed all day until the ground forces captured their proposed site. The men of the 820th EAB were also unable to land on D Day at the selected point, their Rhino ferry having once been turned back by a Navy patrol and later in the day struck by an enemy shell. On the next day, after having been towed to the beach, they spent many uneasy hours in the invasion area awaiting the capture of the proposed airfield site. When the delay continued, the 820th went ahead and developed a landing strip at St. Laurent-sur-Mer on D plus 3, and transports immediately began to fly in supplies and evacuate the wounded. This unplanned field on OMAHA beach turned out to be the first operational American airdrome in France, and an average of one hundred C-47's landed there daily for the first six weeks. Soon the scheduled advanced landing ground at St. Pierre du Mont was finished and occupied by a squadron of P-47's, the first Allied aircraft to be based in France since 1940.[68]

During the first week after D Day aviation engineers continued to arrive as planned, increment after increment in successive shipments. Once ashore, the officers would identify their equipment and claim it in person, sometimes with considerable insistence. Then the detachments would seek the earlier arrivals of their units and join them, often after a good deal of confusion. Usually they quickly completed the emergency landing strips, the rearming and refueling strips, and the advanced landing grounds called for in the well-memorized plans. The jobs were finished expeditiously unless German fire kept the troops under cover for too long intervals. There were casualties among the aviation engineers, but far fewer than expected. There were vexations and difficulties. Yet things really went very well. Of all the sites selected before the landing, only one proved unsuitable.[69] Men and machines were all the invasion commanders had expected them to be. As General Newman wrote, the first units ashore were admittedly not the worst of the aviation engineers, although even the worst were "damned good."[70] The men themselves were keyed up by the challenge and well rewarded when they watched transports and fighters land on their runways almost the moment they were finished. It had not been that way in the impersonal construction of the mammoth airdromes in England. The spirits of the men were also quickened when they captured a few Germans and shot several snipers. Their work was judged "superb"[71] and "miraculous."[72]

The expansion of the invasion beachhead to the rim of Normandy and to Cherbourg occasioned a few revisions in the program for airfield construction. Fighter-bombers rather than fighters were needed because of the absence of the enemy's air force and the stubbornness of his ground forces. Thus several of the 3,600-foot runways had to be increased to 5,000 feet, with all the attendant problems of grading, filling, compacting, and laying of square-mesh track or prefabricated hessian surfacing. Then the Ninth Air Force decided to base medium bombers on the Continent, a radical revision of plans which the engineers met by putting the three airborne battalions to work. By early August the aviation engineers were widely scattered over the liberated area, building or improving airfields which the Allies put to immediate use. At that time, seventeen of the fighter-bomber fields were hard-surfaced and two medium-bomber fields had pierced-steel plank runways.[73]

In spite of the remarkable achievements of the aviation engineers, their program was falling behind schedule. The primary reason was the retarded timetable of the ground-force advance, which left too little space open to airfield development. Also the need for transport fields had been underestimated, and extra labor had to be directed to remedy that condition. There were other difficulties. The great storm of D plus 13 had delayed the unloading of mat for several days. And it proved more time-consuming to doze through the orchards and hedgerows of Normandy than the planners had anticipated. Sustained labor during the long daylight hours of the European summer overcame most of these problems, and the long spell of good weather in June and July was a priceless boon. By the last of July many units of the aviation engineers had nothing to do. Some of them even dug tanks so French farmers could water their cattle.[74]

The breakout of the ground forces quickly solved the problem of idleness by providing ample sites for new airfield development. At this point the aviation engineers were grouped into two brigades to construct airfields under the immediate direction of the IX Tactical Air Command in the U.S. Third Army area and the XIX Tactical Air Command in the U.S. First Army zone. The 1st EA Brigade was commanded by Col. Karl B. Schilling, and the 2d was under Col. Rudolph E. Smyser. The general pattern was for a brigade to build or rehabilitate "clutches" of several airfields as close to the front as possible to serve each tactical air command or medium-bombardment wing. Engineer reconnaissance parties would accompany the advancing forces and locate suitable airfield sites. Later in the Battle of France they flew over airdromes or sites, making preliminary selections. Once the location of the prospective clutch had been determined, the battalions moved up as quickly as they could obtain transportation and pass through the inevitable ovations in French villages. The switching of battalions from one brigade to another was easily managed, and the flexible system was almost ideal for the fast-moving war.[75]

Fanning out over Brittany, the aviation engineer units repaired or scraped out a few fields, but the rapid ground advance eastward soon left these fields in the rear area, and the two brigades moved on to the Le Mans area, which ground reconnaissance teams had already combed for choice sites. At this stage it was often easier to build new airdromes, for the bombers of the Allies and the retreating Germans had destroyed most of the existing air bases. By the middle of August most of the aviation engineers had arrived in Le Mans with their equipment. Moving the men and machines was not the problem. As General Newman said, "Even though we are a menace on the road because of the length of our columns and weight of our material, we grab large areas, and drain water transport, I have yet to hear a single complaint."[76] Supply was a problem here, as it was in all other phases of the aviation engineer war. At Le Mans the solution was to borrow a large fleet of trucks from IX Air Force Service Command and open a route to Cherbourg. For several weeks drivers operated day and night, sleeping in their trucks and eating cold rations, until the moutains of supplies needed for air bases had been brought forward. But just when this problem came under control, the luck of the engineers with the weather ran out. Heavy rains delayed construction and forced the men to repair soggy runways and buckling landing mats repeatedly.[77]

Fortunately, no real delay in air operations resulted from the misadventures at Le Mans. Soon clutches in the Paris and Chartres area were available for rehabilitation. Three key officers of IX Engineer Command were killed as they reconnoitered the famous Le Bourget Field north of Paris. At Chartres aviation engineers had the thrill of capturing the German base commander as he sought to escape by bicycle. Now that the Allies were deep in France, the captured airdromes were less damaged. Most of them had been cratered, to be sure, but it was simple to fill up the holes. And while the Germans had mined nearly all the airfields, they had retreated so abruptly they failed to detonate their mines, and the aviation engineers were good at removing them. In the Paris area the damage was worse than in most other places, and energetic measures were needed to place the fields in condition to receive food-bearing transports, many of which landed on grassy strips marked out by the aviation engineers. At the Orly field alone 400 transport planes came in on 29 August. The rehabilitation of the six airdromes in the Paris area for military operations required more substantial efforts. The opening of the railway to Cherbourg greatly facilitated this work, and the first train to enter liberated Paris carried airfield surfacing materials.[78]

The speed with which the Allied armies advanced north and east of Paris in September 1944 stretched the resources of IX Engineer Command and its two brigades. The Le Mans fields were being completed, and those at Paris were still absorbing much effort. Yet landing grounds in the wake of the Allied advance were also needed. Luckily, most of the captured airfields could be made operational within a short time, and, if not, the aviation engineers were able to scrape out sod fields for transports, at this point of the war the most critical type of aircraft. The skill of even small groups of aviation engineers gratified the commanders and aroused the admiration of the Germans. By now it was taken for granted that the engineers would deliver whatever was demanded. The tactical air commands merely specified the kind of base they needed and the general location, leaving all other matters to the constructing unit, which was usually the battalion. The battalions were rotated a good deal from forward to rear areas after hard stints of work, though units in the rear area worked too. Some of them came to be recognized as specialists in concrete or asphalt construction, or in laying pierced-steel plank or square-mesh track, and were employed accordingly. After working on an airdrome for a day or so, a battalion might move two hundred miles to another job. Once the 834th EAB traveled five hundred and fifty miles between assignments. Accustomed to shifting for themselves, aviation engineer officers often had to finagle to obtain supplies. One trick was to remove AAF markings from their jeeps and uniforms so as not to prejudice hardhearted Army supply men who regarded the air forces as too lavishly endowed with the good things of life. This isolation and independence some of the battalion commanders relished. Others felt orphaned and unappreciated. In any event, the aviation engineers did their jobs so well that air force headquarters left them alone.[79]

By autumn, when the armies were at the Siegfried Line, IX Engineer Command had provided a surplus of airfields. During the next months, which everyone earnestly proclaimed were the coldest and wettest known in Europe for generations, some of the airfields in the rear areas had to be improved. On many runways a product invented by the Canadians, the so-called prefabricated hessian mat, which was cloth coated with bitumen, had been laid because it was light and easy to handle. With bad weather looming or at hand, it was necessary to make many repairs or if possible to replace mat with pierced-steel plank. Hangars were constructed to protect the airplanes, and many airdromes were enlarged and improved. New construction was needed in the Toul-Nancy-Verdun area, where the 2d Brigade was concentrated. There the aviation engineers started work while shells were still falling. Then the cold rains began, and there was repeated trouble with pilots who taxied their planes over the graded runways in defiance of orders. The availability of civilian labor, gravel pits, rock quarries, and rubble from damaged villages made somewhat easier what was, in general, an uphill task. As a consolation, the aviation engineers were usually out of pup tents and in real barracks by then, and the proximity of Paris as a recreational area brightened the dark autumn months.[80]

The men of the 1st Brigade spent the autumn mostly in Belgium, repairing airfields and preparing all-weather bases for fighter-bombers. They too were often bogged down in slush and mud. The construction work was difficult, for the high water table was sometimes so close to the surface that earth-moving was likely to have unpredictable results. Civilian labor was available and welcome, although most of the workers were very old or very young, and the troops carried the real burden. Flying bombs and occasional strafings added to the hazards and discomforts of the troops. Then came the Ardennes counteroffensive, which threatened not only the air bases but some of the units themselves, who had to be pulled back hurriedly. Only one American airdrome, Hagenau, was actually overrun by the Germans, and the aviation engineers had the unique experience of burying bombs on the runways and setting them off. The New Year's Day attack by the German Air Force did some damage and, still worse, gave such a scare that the Ninth Air Force demanded a very extensive program of erecting revetments around the hardstands. This undertaking did not proceed very far, however, because of the February thaws and attendant problems of keeping the airfields operational. And then came the advance into Germany.[81]

The engineer command structure had worked so well that General Newman went to Washington in October 1944 to secure authorization of a table of organization and equipment for an over-all engineer command, which he felt would reduce manpower and perfect the centralized control of the aviation engineers. While he had enthusiastic support for this proposal in AAF Headquarters, the War Department again declined to approve it. At length, in February 1945, the theater effected the changes it desired on the usual provisional basis, shifting IX Engineer Command from the Ninth Air Force to USSTAF. Even if it were no longer an exclusively Ninth Air Force organization, the name "IX Engineer Command" was so widely and favorably known that it was retained. In April 1945 the final reorganization resulted in Engineer Command, USSTAF (Provisional), under which IX Engineer Command continued to control its two brigades plus a third organized for maintenance in rear areas. By then there were about 23,000 aviation engineers in the theater. Colonel Mayo, the air engineer at AAF Headquarters, described the organization as being "as nearly ideal as is practicable for a theater of this nature."[82]

After the failure of the Ardennes counteroffensive the aviation engineers began work on their first project in Germany, an advanced landing ground at Düren utilizing both lanes of an *Autobahn*. But this field was within range of enemy artillery and had to be abandoned. Instead, an old German runway at Aachen was renovated by sandwiching rocks, cinders, and two types of mats as a base for the pierced-steel plank, which turned out to involve far more effort than expected. Similarly, at Maastricht, in the Netherlands, the 846th Battalion began a runway on frozen ground which thawed too soon and left a mess which could be remedied only by extensive fillings of gravel. This in turn called for a road heavy enough to support the trucks carrying the gravel from the pits, and the difficulties continued to pile up until the 846th had undergone an experience worthy of the aviation engineers in New Guinea. The bases in France and Belgium were by now enlarged and improved, and most of the battalions were concentrated near the German frontier when the final invasion got under way.[83] If the first experiences at the border had been ominous, no less so were the rumors and publicity forecasting a massive redeployment of the aviation engineers to finish the war in the Pacific. This news fell on the very unreceptive ears of troops who had already been overseas for two and three years.[84]

The over-all plan for airfield construction in Germany called for the provision of strips for fighters and transports, the rehabilitation of captured airdromes, and the building of at least ten heavy-bomber bases and other installations for the occupation air force. West of the Rhine things went as expected. Engineer observers examined German airfields still occupied by the enemy from the nose of reconnaissance planes and decided if they would do. The repairs were sometimes extensive but never beyond the capacities of the aviation engineers, who had now a vast experience. Mines and obstructions left by the Germans were the only serious vexations. The skill of the engineers in preparing fields for the airborne operation VARSITY won a commendation from General Brereton.[85]

When the Allies crossed the Rhine, the problem of air supply for rapidly advancing units became so critical that the aviation engineers had to undertake an extensive program of building strips for transports. This was easy work, however, especially since the weather was good. Sod fields were used when possible. German civilians and prisoners could be drawn on for labor. The aviation engineers, along with other Allied units, almost romped through the rest of the stricken Reich. If the Germans plowed up the airfields, the aviation engineers had tractors and graders to smooth them out promptly. When there were craters, it was only a matter of hours until gravel had been located and dumped in them and surfacing placed on the holes. Sometimes the aviation engineers got ahead of their own supplies, or the Army would not let them take their equipment across bridges, or snipers lingered at the airfields; but none of these interfered with their successes. Most of the airfields were ready for days before the air forces were able to occupy them. Reaching Pilsen in Czechoslovakia and Salzburg in Austria, the aviation engineers halted, their mission completed.[86]

There was every reason for the aviation engineers to share the pride of the Allied forces for the victory in Europe. Nothing had gone seriously wrong, and the absence of criticism made all the more convincing the commendations that came their way. They suffered fewer casualties than had been expected, 119 altogether, including 30 killed and 12 missing in action. As in other theaters, many of the men suffered back injuries from the continual jarring of graders. Their morale had been very high for most of the campaign since D Day. Doing an essential job, largely left alone, and proud, if not careful, of their splendid equipment, the aviation engineers had the unusual wartime satisfaction of performing constructive work that was seldom routine enough to become boring. And while they were not ordinarily in immediate danger, they derived vicarious stimulation from their proximity to combat to whose outcome they contributed so much. Their main achievement, the building or repair of at least 241 airdromes from Normandy to Austria in less than a year, could scarcely be assessed beyond the acknowledgment that it was essential to victory.[87]

Many of the officers among the aviation engineers, and probably many of the enlisted men, felt that they were taken for granted by the air forces. They believed that they had been left out of planning and slighted in matters of supply, which was always bad and sometimes "execrable,"[88] as one of them declared. They objected strongly to proposals that the Corps of Engineers castles be removed from their uniforms and replaced with the wings and propellers of the Air Corps.[89] There was the matter of professional pride which was more precious to them than organizational loyalty. If the European experience had done little to persuade the aviation engineers to submerge their identity in the AAF, the reverse was not true. The air commanders greatly valued the work of their engineers and, both in the theater and in Washington, hoped to incorporate them as an integral part of a future independent air force.

CHAPTER 10

*   *   *   *   *   *   *   *   *   *   *

AVIATION ENGINEERS
IN THE WAR WITH JAPAN

AVIATION engineers committed to the Japanese war had a
more varied experience than did their colleagues in the European war. Climatic conditions ranged from the Arctic storms
of the Aleutian Islands to the tropical heat of the South Pacific. The
engineers had also to make adjustments to varying patterns of command. In the North, Central, and South Pacific Areas, the ultimate
authority belonged to the Navy. In the Southwest Pacific the top
command was an Army one, and it was there that the Army's aviation
engineers played their largest role in the Pacific campaigns.

SWPA

The rout of Allied forces from the Philippines and the East Indies
early in 1942 made Australia the inevitable base for rally and recovery, unless it too should fall. Airfields in the northern area of this continent around Darwin were the most urgent construction requirement
when the 808th Engineer Aviation Battalion, the first in that theater,
moved up by rail from the south in February. The 808th EAB had
practically no stateside training, but, like many of the original engineer units, it was composed of men who already were specialists.
Halted during the bombings of Darwin at the town of Katherine, the
battalion set up camp and began to scrape out airstrips, in which undertaking it was joined by an Army engineer unit in March. For more
than three months the engineers cleared sites, often beginning by at-
taching a cable between two tractors and cutting the growth, and
then graded and graveled them so that fighters and transports could
operate. In all, seven fields were in usable condition for dry weather

276

when the 808th suddenly departed for Port Moresby, New Guinea, in July 1942, to improve one of the airfields near that port which the Allies had to hold at all cost. The remaining construction in the Darwin area was left to Army and Australian engineers. The aviation engineers, it seems, were pleased to leave behind the importunities and bureaucratic procedures of the Australian government and to get closer to the war.[1]

In New Guinea the problems were far worse than any planner had anticipated in the days before the war: the distances, the absence of docks and roads, the jungles and mountains, health and morale, and the ever insufficient forces to accomplish urgent tasks in one of the most primitive parts of the world. Since engineering and construction forces were so limited and equipment so precious, all resources were pooled under Brig. Gen. Hugh J. Casey, who had come down from the Philippines with General MacArthur and was Chief Engineer for GHQ, SWPA. Thus aviation engineers and Army engineers and sometimes Seabees labored on whatever engineering projects had to be completed—the two hundred runways built between Australia and Okinawa, roads, camp sites, docks, hospitals, depots, storage facilities, and many other construction jobs—with little or no effort to segregate aviation engineers for purely air force tasks. In February 1943, a few months after he had assumed command of Allied Air Forces and the Fifth Air Force, Maj. Gen. George C. Kenney formally requested that the aviation engineers be assigned to him. General Casey vigorously opposed any such arrangement, contending that with engineering resources so limited it would be unwise to assign the units exclusively to any one command. If the Fifth Air Force had even operational control of the aviation engineers, he maintained, the familiar problems of insufficient equipment, supplies, spare parts, and lubricants would remain, and two engineering agencies would complicate rather than simplify the problems of planning. Besides, the construction of airfields was integrally tied to the building of roads, docks, warehouses, and oil storage. Casey's point of view prevailed at GHQ, and Kenney received official notification that the Services of Supply would continue to be responsible for all new construction, including airdromes, and that engineer units would be regarded as a pool under the direction of the Chief Engineer, SWPA. It was considered desirable, "in order to permit the Air Force to concentrate primarily on its tactical mission, to relieve that Force as much as possible of major or specialist service work." This decision remained unchanged throughout the war in that theater, although it was often criticized in AAF Headquarters, more so there, it seems, than in General Kenney's command.[2]

Such matters were not of primary concern in 1942, when the desperate situation created by the Japanese movement into southeastern New Guinea and the Solomons called for urgent construction work rather than dissension over command problems. The AAF needed extensive facilities that had to be developed under enemy action in remote locations on a very primitive island. An underequipped Army engineer unit had undertaken the improvement of Jackson Drome, as it was eventually called, near the harbor of Port Moresby, but, amid dodging bombs, unloading ships, and servicing aircraft, this group had not prepared the field for all-weather use. The 808th EAB took over, working night and day and also enduring frequent Japanese bombings. Heavy rains began sooner than expected and saturated the clay shale base of the runways, making it necessary to install a costly system of underground French drains and to repave and reseal the runways with bitumen. If planned bombing missions were not curtailed by this delay, air operations in general suffered. It was eight months before Jackson Drome was finally completed, although operations went on during much of the construction period, and Army engineers extended and improved other airdromes in the vicinity. Two-thirds of the 808th's men were diverted on one occasion to create a new airfield, Durand Drome, to accommodate B-17's whose missions could not await the development of the original runways at Jackson Drome. The aviation engineers had Durand ready in only three weeks, clearing the jungle, hard-surfacing the runway, and sealing it with bitumen. After the Fortresses used it on several occasions, pierced-steel matting was laid, a sequence that did not make for stability of the subgrade.[3]

Already, the engineers realized that many textbook practices would have to be abandoned. In the matter of site selection there was little to go on but common sense and the luck or skill of the surveying parties. The unpredictability of the rainfall in New Guinea complicated every problem, and, since runways had to be placed in readiness without delays, the engineers on occasion took chances with drainage conditions. In a number of cases expensive reconstruction was necessary; General Casey later complained that insufficient attention had sometimes been given to drainage. The standard military airdrome with three intersecting runways, all of them 300 or 400 feet wide, was out of the question during those early months. Only one runway was really necessary, since the winds were usually gentle and came from the same direction for part of the year and from the opposite direction for the other part. No such luxury as an airfield for each type of airplane could be afforded. Instead, the engineers cleared off jungle sites, slowly dozing the big trees, and, respectful of falling coconuts, created a landing area for transports bringing in men and materials. The next stage was to lengthen and improve the runway for fighters, and then to stabilize the base for the pavement and steel matting that would support the bombers. In time all types of aircraft would probably use the airdrome. Long after operations had begun, there might be sufficient labor, usually in the form of newly arrived aviation engineers, to construct something more than the barest essentials around the runways. By that time the experienced aviation engineer units would be developing new bases elsewhere in New Guinea or nearby islands.[4]

It was demonstrated many times that the unification of engineering resources in the theater was not inevitably a detriment to air force effort. Army engineers, for example, were employed in November 1942 to construct airstrips in the Dobodura area to permit air operations against the Japanese threat to nearby Buna. Using hand sickles, machetes, axes, and bayonets, they cleared sites for transports bringing in bulldozers, tractors, and graders. By the end of the year there were facilities for combat aircraft. Early in 1943 Army engineers in the Dobodura area also built Horando Drome, which was used by P-38's during the Battle of the Bismarck Sea. This construction job involved an impressive air shuttle of men and machines from Port Moresby to complete the base, which was promptly used for the reinforcement of ground units and evacuation of the wounded. By July 1943 the 808th EAB, after a long stint at Port Moresby, joined the Army engineers in the Dobodura area. The 808th had even enjoyed a few weeks of rest in Australia, which General Kenney noted the unit had earned and badly needed, and which was to be its last respite from toil until 1945. Under the combined efforts of Army and aviation engineers and with the assistance of native labor, Dobodura became an elaborate base area for air operations, staging, and storage which served until late in 1944.[5]

Meanwhile, one of the three most notable instances of airborne aviation engineer employment during the war took place in July 1943.* The Allies needed a base for fighters near the Lae-Salamau area, which they proposed to seize in September; this base might also serve for refueling bombers that were neutralizing the formidable Japanese air and naval establishment at Wewak. In order to locate a suitable site, Lt. Everette E. Frazier, an aviation engineer on duty with the Fifth Air Force, explored tropical forested areas with an Australian officer and a few natives. On such expeditions into enemy-held territory the natives could be relied on up to a point, although they were likely to tell the visitor only what they thought he wanted to hear. Secrecy was difficult to maintain, for the porters changed with each village, and drummed messages carried news all over the area. Yet, if the white man had weapons, medicine, and a sympathetic attitude, he could count on much co-operation. Frazier found a possible location and made his way back to Fifth Air Force headquarters. Another secret visit, this time by Brig. Gen. Paul B. Wurtsmith of V Bomber Command, resulted in the selection of an abandoned airstrip at Tsili Tsili. The air engineer of the Fifth Air Force, Lt. Col. Ward T. Abbott, took charge of the project. On 10 July 1943, a company of the 871st Airborne Engineer Aviation Battalion, which had been working at Port Moresby for the brief period since its arrival in the theater, flew in C-47's to the site with light bulldozers, graders, carry-alls, and mowers. As the company set to work, natives cleared bogus airstrips in the vicinity to attract Japanese attention, which was soon forthcoming in the way of bombings. But the construction at Tsili Tsili went on undetected, a little delayed when the other companies of the 871st were unable to fly in for ten days because of bad weather. By that time the graded runway could accommodate 150 transports a day. Soon there was another runway and seventy-five handstands, and the new base was serving its purpose.[6]

The achievement at Tsili Tsili aroused great enthusiasm among the leaders of the aviation engineers and came to be widely publicized. Dramatic as it was, however, and important as it proved in operations against Wewak and Lae, overseas commanders were not enthusiastic about the airborne aviation engineers. As General Kenney had written before the operation, the airborne battalion was simply not the equivalent of the regular battalion for airdrome construction.[7] It had only two-thirds the number of men, and its equipment was neither heavy

* The others were in North Africa and in Burma.

nor sturdy enough for major construction. The real need in the theater in engineering matters was for an abundance of engineers, construction troops, and powerful equipment. When airborne battalions arrived, the commanders felt they were being short-changed. Even at Tsili Tsili a regular battalion, its equipment broken down for air shipment and reassembled, might have served better. The scrapers that were used proved so light that kunai grass clogged them, tractors had to be repaired almost constantly, and the miniature graders danced along the surface of the ground.[8] While airborne aviation engineers were employed on at least two other occasions in New Guinea, the 871st at Nadzab and, with the 872d, at Gusap in the Markham Valley, there was little for them to do but perform routine work in the rear. They regarded themselves as orphan units.[9] Late in 1944 most of the airborne battalions turned in their midget equipment for heavier machines or were absorbed in conventional battalions.

Despite the sober reflections about the merits of the airborne aviation engineers, the 871st flew from Tsili Tsili to Nadzab on 7 September 1943, just two days after the massive airborne landing there. Without pause the men set to work on airstrips, putting one of them in readiness so that four days later as many as 420 transports landed. At this point the 842d Engineer Aviation Battalion relieved it in order to lay a gravel base for steel plank to support fighters before the rainy season began. This task completed, the 842d EAB went to work on a project which would become only too familiar—road-building. During its career in the theater only one-tenth of its time was devoted to airdrome construction. In this case it was the notorious stretch of twenty-five miles between the littered harbor at Lae and the base at Nadzab, where, after sixty days of infuriating labor in drenching rains, the 842d "literally floated that road into Nadzab." Hated though it was, this road made it possible to move the heavy equipment up to Nadzab, where a complex of airfields and a mammoth base were developed. The heavily used main airfield gratifyingly represented "an airport construction engineer's dream," built as it was on an old, dry river bed with a soil of well-graded gravel. By the end of the year four fighter squadrons and two medium-bomber squadrons were based there.[10]

While Nadzab was under construction, the 871st and the 872d Airborne Engineer Battalions were flown far to the west and up the Markham Valley to another site chosen by Captain Frazier (he got

the Legion of Merit and malaria as a result) soon after his promotion
following the Tsili Tsili exploit. As in the previous case, an adjacent
site was actually developed, one at a place the Americans called
Gusap, where excellent soil conditions and even a pleasant climate
prevailed. The development of an all-weather base, however, was beyond the capacity of the miniature equipment of the airborne units,
although the men worked doggedly night and day. At length, larger
machinery was disassembled and flown in and the heaviest pieces sent
overland through territory that was uncertainly in friendly hands. By
the end of 1943 the fighter runway was completed and the steel plank
laid. As often happened in the theater, the fighters had moved in,
substantially before the airdrome was ready. As almost never happened in the theater, reports went back from Gusap that living conditions were not too bad.[11]

During the last months of 1943, while construction was going on
apace at Nadzab and Gusap, the unexpectedly rapid conquest of
Finschhafen made possible the establishment of a large air base on the
rugged Huon peninsula. The veteran 808th EAB was assigned this
mission. Its survey party chose a site a half-mile from a harbor, only
to learn that the Navy was unwilling to risk its landing craft there.
Therefore, the aviation engineers hacked a broad path through a
typically dense rain forest and built a road and a bridge to link the
proposed airdrome with the anchored ships, laboriously dragged the
equipment up, and now found that the Navy had changed its mind
about the unsuitability of the original harbor. Despite this wasted
effort, which could scarcely be regarded philosophically, the 808th
created in two months a suitable runway but still had much to do. At
this point the Fifth Air Force hindered the engineers by swamping the
new airdrome with dozens of fighters. Much confusion resulted from
this stunning influx, and much chagrin over the interrupted work
schedule. Yet the fighters proved very useful in waging the war, and
in time Finschhafen received the attention planned for it, eventually
becoming a major staging and storage base.[12]

Aviation engineer battalions were reaching the theater during the
last of 1943 in a modest but helpful flow, although they usually arrived
long before their equipment, were undertrained and had to learn by
doing, and often were cast ashore with little notion of who their
parent command might be. The consequence of this last situation was
that orders were likely to rain in upon the battalion commanders from

all sides, for so much construction work had to be done. At length, the units would be sent somewhere and receive a formidable mission. The 856th Engineer Aviation Battalion, a Negro unit which had trained extensively for desert operations, joined Army and Navy engineers to complete the airdrome on the rain-drenched Kiriwina Island. The 864th and 1913th EAB's landed at Cape Gloucester in January 1944, followed soon by the 841st EAB, to establish facilities for the air forces in an area that threatened to rival any of the horrors offered by New Guinea. The aviation engineers had hoped to utilize captured Japanese strips, but, as usual, these proved so inadequate it was hard to see how even the unpampered enemy could ever have used them. Extensive clearing and grading had to be undertaken by these inexperienced units. Heavy rains fell almost every day, and it was necessary to haul red volcanic ash from a point eight steaming, muddy miles away with trucks that were always breaking down. When the steel mat finally arrived, someone had omitted to include clips, and an exasperating delay ensued. All these misadventures threw the aviation engineers behind schedule so that the runway was not ready until mid-March 1944. The climate had proved as bad as prophesied, and the runway was none too satisfactory, for its muddy subbase kept seeping through after heavy rains.[13]

The development of air facilities at Saidor, up the coast from Finschhafen, during the early months of 1944 was not expected to be a difficult assignment, since an old Australian airdrome was available. The much-employed 808th EAB and the newly arrived 863d EAB moved in, only to learn that orders had arrived to double the expected capacity of the base. GHQ chided the planners for not having co-ordinated the requirements better beforehand. This was little comfort to the aviation engineers, who received as reinforcement only the relatively untried 860th EAB. All had a wretched time of it. Rain fell almost incessantly during the grading and compacting period. Food was so short that in one battalion the average loss of weight was thirty pounds a man. Worse yet, the men even ran out of cigarettes soon after the landing. Also, the inexperienced 863d built its hardstands too small and had to expend much effort trying to remedy the error. Even after the runway was finished, soft spots developed, probably because jeeps and trucks had been driven indiscriminately over it at a critical stage. Finally, by May 1944, Saidor was completed. It was a useful air base if an evil memory to many aviation engineers.[14]

The next lunge forward was the daring assault on Hollandia, where a major base was planned. As many as 25,000 engineer troops were scheduled to develop Hollandia, including nine engineer aviation battalions and three airborne battalions, and for the first time in this theater very detailed preparations were possible. Yet, Hollandia proved very disappointing when an inspection of the proposed base site confirmed the earlier skepticism of General Kenney and General Whitehead that the mammoth facilities projected could be developed. Only enough airfield construction to support the next operation was permitted, and this proved adequate.[15] A better site lay about a hundred miles west of Hollandia on an island which came to be known as Wakde. It was quite small, but the Japanese had cut away much of a coconut plantation for an airstrip. On D Day, 17 May 1944, the 836th Engineer Aviation Battalion landed with the task force. This battalion had languished at Nadzab, like so many aviation engineer units, after it first arrived pulling "about everything in the Engineer book." Probably its most appreciated job there was the Avineer Playhouse, a huge outdoor theater which was surely the largest in the SWPA. Then it had distinguished itself by constructing Mokerang airdrome in the Admiralties in three weeks, for which General Kenney commended the unit. Not only had the Mokerang job itself been difficult, involving removal of coconut trees and the use of unfamiliar coral, but it was performed in a zone otherwise developed by the Seabees and the Army engineers, and the 836th EAB had given no cause for unfavorable comparison.[16]

Now at Wakde, the 836th aviation engineers became probably the first of their type to engage in extensive combat. Under enemy fire they unloaded and tackled the cratered, debris-littered airstrip left by the Japanese. For several days they were under sporadic attack by Japanese infantrymen and even saw some of their precious vehicles fired. Yet, on D plus 4 they had a fighter runway ready. Almost at once patrol planes, fighters, and transports crammed the area. It was from this runway that PB4Y's made the first aerial reconnaissance of the Philippines since early 1942. Despite all the traffic and pressure, construction proceeded on a continuous schedule. The aviation engineers laid coral and sealed the runway with bitumen, built taxiways and other essential facilities, and then enlarged the runway. Wakde satisfactorily supplemented the disappointing bases at Hollandia.[17]

The next operation, Biak, on 27 May 1944 again had aviation engi-

AVIATION ENGINEER (AIRBORNE) WITH LIGHT EQUIPMENT
BROADWAY, BURMA

CLEARING THE STRIP

AVIATION ENGINEERS ON MIDDLEBURG ISLAND

LAYING STEEL MAT

Digging Coral for Base

Finished Strip, Thirteen Days Later

NATIVE HELP FOR THE AVIATION ENGINEERS

GUAM

HEAVY EQUIPMENT

ICELAND

REPLACING STEEL MAT WITH CONCRETE, GREENLAND

BUILDING B-29 BASE AT ISLEY FIELD, SAIPAN

AVIATION ENGINEER STYLE

BUILDING RUNWAYS IN INDIA

NATIVE STYLE

GUARDING AVIATION ENGINEERS FROM JAPANESE SNIPERS, GUAM

neers in the assault force, the 860th, 863d, and 864th Battalions. About a fifth of the men in the 863d EAB had enjoyed a rest in Australia following their hardships at Saidor. The others had utilized the interval to recover their weight and to patch up their battered equipment, for already the aviation engineers knew that it was futile to expect replacements. The passage to Biak, with an entire battalion on four LST's as a rule, was hot and otherwise uncomfortable, but at least the men and machines stayed together. And the men enjoyed a massacre of Japanese airplanes which attacked their convoy. The landing at Biak proved unusually hard. For almost two weeks the engineers unloaded, dodged shells, built roads, and carried supplies. Finally, they got through to the abandoned Japanese airstrip at Mokmer and began to fill the craters. Yet artillery fire was such that they managed to work for only twelve hours during the first three days, spending the remainder of the time under cover or helping the hard-pressed combat troops. Much behind schedule, the aviation engineers at length carried out the airfield construction required on Biak.[18]

In addition to the delays imposed by the fierce Japanese resistance on Biak, frustrations regarding the extreme shortage of supplies and equipment were far worse than usual. Only two large tractors of the eighteen authorized were available for the three battalions. Extensive improvisation and repair taxed the ingenuity of the men, and cannibalization of machine parts jeopardized personal relations, for usually the equipment operators had a paternal pride in their machinery. One of the battalion commanders wrote: "It is difficult to understand why strong measures are not taken to correct this deplorable and demoralizing condition." Perhaps so, but the truth was that this condition was general in the theater—even worse than elsewhere—and remained so until the war was almost over. The aviation engineers also noted without equanimity that Air Corps ground personnel received more issues of food than they did and enjoyed such luxuries as refrigeration. Another complaint arose from the custom of keeping the aviation engineers in ignorance of their mission until they landed on the beachhead, thus denying the officers an adequate opportunity to make plans or, as a battalion commander put it, "of performing such duties expected of an engineer aviation." Dreadful living conditions, casualties, and typhus plagued the men, but they accomplished their job. They suffered as much or worse when the airfield construction program expanded to Owi Island, three miles from Biak. The project was suddenly planned, the weather was terrible, and sickness reached epidemic proportions. Yet within ten days the 860th EAB, 864th EAB, and the Seabees had readied an airfield from which the Philippines were bombed for the first time in more than two years.[19]

Noemfoor Island, where the Japanese had worked about 2,500 Javanese to death on airfield development, was the next steppingstone. Except for three partially cleared airstrips, the coral island was one dense rain forest. After Cyclone Task Force landed with, unexpectedly, no opposition, the 1874th Engineer Aviation Battalion and units of Army and Australian engineers bulldozed their way through the island to enable reconnaissance parties to make their soil tests and surveys. Soon the improvement at Kornasoren, Namber, and Kamiri airstrips began, but the task involved more grading and filling than had been expected, and GHQ boosted the assignment by directing a great expansion at Kornasoren. The engineers fell behind schedule. They also had to provide for a supply of oil and aviation gasoline, and this task called for extensive underwater blasting to erect coral jetties and the laying of sixteen miles of pipe. The surf was so high at Noemfoor that ships could never unload easily there, and eventually the Allies abandoned their plan to develop the island into an extensive base. Like Biak, Noemfoor was not up to air force expectations.[20]

The assault on Cape Sansapor began on 30 July 1944. The reconnaissance party of the task force turned up good sites for airfield development near the village of Mar on the offshore island, Middelburg. Only at the latter were aviation engineers employed, the competent 836th Battalion. Having landed originally at Cape Sansapor, the 836th constructed a sand jetty at Middelburg, where coral reefs prevented landing by the LST's, and defied Japanese raiders by shuttling equipment at night with the floodlights on. The runway site on the little island proved so sandy that coral had to be dug out from the ocean floor at low tides. Once it was compacted, the four companies competed with one another in laying the pierced-steel mat. The aviation engineers, and the Army unit which jointed them, underwent the usual deprivations, air raids, and primitive living conditions, but by now most of them were used to such a life. The job went ahead gratifyingly, the airfield being readied two days ahead of schedule. Then came the phase of constructing bulk-oil storage tanks and facilities for the care of aircraft and, whenever a moment could be stolen, the improvement of living quarters. Like other troops on distant bases, the aviation engineers knew by now they had to look after themselves in matters of housekeeping. More important, the base they provided enabled the Thirteenth Air Force to move far to the west and to begin its campaign against the Philippines and Borneo.[21]

By now everyone knew that each pause should be relished, for another operation would begin only too soon. The men relaxed, often in the useful way of working on their machines. Then would come the alerting orders and the packing, waterproofing, and loading. Always too early, it seemed, they would finish the task and board the LST's, only to wait in cramped quarters until the GI cruise began. Enemy action seldom endangered them seriously and often raised their spirits, or at least broke the monotony. The men liked to keep track of the number of times they had crossed the Equator. Even the officers seldom knew what kind of job awaited them or where it would be. Work there would be, they knew, and Japanese, sickness, and infuriating mechanical and technical problems. Yet they were a seasoned group, and they probably never doubted they would do what was needed and move on to another assignment. They generally felt, as most of the troops in the SWPA seemed to do, that they were unsung and unappreciated.

The Morotai operation was clearly crucial, for its bases would permit the AAF to support the planned landings in the Philippines. Here the air commanders for once had the authority to locate the sites for airfields, an assignment which GHQ engineers apparently thought they bungled, for the locations had to be changed.[22] Three battalions of aviation engineers, the 836th, 841st, and 1876th, were included with the Army, Australian, and later Seabee construction forces. The aviation engineers arrived on 21 September 1944, several days after the initial landing, and found that the surf and sand had already claimed several heavy pieces of equipment. Their camp site consisted mainly of foxholes. The inevitable rain soon began. The task of the 836th EAB was the construction of the Pitoe runway, which "resembled a hog wallow of gigantic proportions," although it was high and dry compared to the sites other units had. It developed at once that far more material than usual would have to be removed. Then Morotai coral proved unexpectedly hard, so that a number of small, shallow pits had to be dug, thus aggravating the hauling problem when there were already too few vehicles. If native labor was not available, at least neither were Japanese snipers in any appreciable number. Although Pitoe was made into a hard-surfaced heavy-bomber base in slightly more than three weeks, a nearby airdrome called Wama was developed only after heroic efforts. Great quantities of debris had to be removed, about 5,000 large coconut trees had to be pushed over by bulldozers, most of them individually, and elaborate drainage facilities installed. Within two weeks the runway was operational, and then pierced-steel mat was laid on the coral base. In all, the construction job had gone very well. Morotai acquired the reputation of being the most efficient engineering job ever conducted in the SWPA to that date.[23]

One of the battalion commanders afterward wrote that the construction on Morotai had been carefully controlled and directed and that a good spirit had prevailed. Yet, he added, almost all the details had been irritating. Nails, for example, were almost unobtainable. Orders had dribbled in on the aviation engineers from a variety of sources. Everybody seemed to want to borrow their equipment, usually to improve living quarters, but the engineers had learned to be hardhearted in such matters. Supply channels were so choked that irregular methods alone got results. This situation involved the politics of the base, knowing the right people, and the successful approach. In addition to the usual sprains and back injuries, the men had suffered particularly from skin disorders on Morotai. And, while it was bad enough for aviation engineers to see companion units of the Army work less and live better, the presence of the Seabees in the vicinity was almost disastrous to morale. Not only did the Navy construction forces enjoy comfortable quarters, refrigeration, and higher ratings, but they received much better publicity back home. When at last the lightening of labor came with the completion of the construction job, another affliction of an imperfect world appeared. This was a determined program of basic training and combat drill which the aviation engineers must have realized, however much they grumbled, was a needed preparation for future hazards in the Philippines.[24]

The Philippines

To provide the logistical services required for the invasion of the Philippines in October 1944, an advanced echelon of Army service forces called ASCOM was created. Of the 37,000 engineer troops in the theater, 14,000 were assigned to ASCOM. Aviation engineers continued to be pooled with other construction forces and were fed into

ASCOM as they arrived from the rear or the States. The air engineers on duty with Far East Air Forces headquarters, or with the Fifth and Thirteenth Air Forces, served essentially as planning and liaison officers, not commanding or even supervising the aviation engineers but participating with GHQ in over-all planning. The decision to seize Leyte instead of Mindanao disregarded the engineering problems involved in such a move, especially with respect to air-base construction. There was very little information about the obscure island, and such as the planners possessed proved to be erroneous as to existing Japanese fields, soil conditions, and rainfall.[25] The ensuing brush with disaster because of a lack of airfields for the AAF and the "terrible disappointment"[26] that Leyte constituted in this respect were consequences of a calculated risk for which the Army assumed full responsibility.[27] The failure of the engineers to provide the bases when needed was not caused by their lack of effort or skill.

The memorable hardships at Tacloban airstrip just after the landing of 20 October 1944 involved only one aviation engineer battalion, the 1881st, which worked with two Army construction companies. The attacks of Japanese *kamikaze* and other aircraft, the appalling overcrowding of the strip, and the emergency use of the runway by naval planes have already been related.* In spite of these difficulties, the engineers laid steel mat and prepared dispersal areas for fighters only one day behind schedule.[28] By then the rains had begun, and it was becoming apparent that Filipino laborers, who had been weakened by hunger and then sated with captured Japanese stores, were not likely to be as helpful as expected. The experienced 808th Battalion landed on the beachhead on A plus 3, charged with the rehabilitation of the former Japanese airfield at Dulag, to the south of Tacloban. Scarcely had the men collected themselves when stranded naval aircraft began to land. Equipment had to be moved off the runway, the planes serviced and pulled out of the mud. Then the rains started, and enemy attacks began. Within a few days the 821st and 842d Engineer Aviation Battalions joined the 808th EAB and during the few rainless hours of the day began to spread gravel and sand over the runway. A flash flood intervened to submerge the only gravel pit and drown out many of the trucks. Finally, steel mat had to be laid on the road so the revived trucks could make it to the runway. By mid-

* See Vol. V, 356–74.

November fighters could land and take off at Dulag, but the unfortunate field never became the principal base it was expected to be.[29]

Meanwhile, reconnaissance into the interior revealed supposedly more promising sites. The 1906th Engineer Aviation Battalion and a battalion of Seabees worked over a dry-weather strip at Bayug, which abruptly became a nightmare of mud when the dry weather ceased. Yet the Fifth Air Force was desperate for bases on Leyte, so, disregarding the rules, the engineers laid steel mat on the graded mud. Before this experiment could be judged, the Japanese dropped paratroopers on Bayug and other fields, a sensational event which had no lasting military effect, but which delayed work and gave the engineers the right to regard themselves as combat troops. Not until late in December was Bayug usable on any scale, and it was never favored as a landing area because of the unstable base below the steel planks. Two other projected airstrips on Leyte which had absorbed some effort of the engineers to little purpose, Buri and San Pablo, were abandoned. Only Tanauan, which lay on the beach and had good drainage, offered much hope. Yet two objections loomed. At the south approach of the proposed runway stood a steep rocky hill. And on the site itself lay the command post of General Kruger, who had obligingly moved out of the engineers' way at Tacloban. Both difficulties figuratively dissolved in the face of necessity, and within eighteen days two battalions of aviation engineers removed the jungle growth, added coral, compacted it with sheepsfoot and smooth rollers, and laid steel mat. Tanauan proved to be a good airfield, and the hill was apparently no hazard at all. In fact, the pilots seemed to enjoy skimming over it and dropping as suddenly as they could onto the runway.[30]

Airfield construction was only a fraction of the engineer effort on Leyte. After Mindoro and Luzon became available, the engineers who remained on Leyte added to Tacloban and Tanauan airdromes, but devoted most of their labors to such necessities as roads, port facilities, oil storage, hospitals, prisoner-of-war stockades, depots, and other construction. Even if the air forces were only too happy to get out of Leyte, the island became a formidable base for other purposes. The aviation engineers who arrived there during the winter of 1944–45 generally expected to enjoy civilization, but the mud and the backwardness of the population disenchanted many of them, and they were glad to move on eventually to Luzon. One battalion even reported that its morale reached bottom in Leyte—that after a long tour of duty on New Guinea! The diversion of the aviation engineers from airfield construction or even air force construction continued to trouble both the air engineer in Washington and air officers in the theater, but GHQ, SWPA, did not relax its grip. At the end of the Philippines campaign, it was estimated that far more than half the effort of the aviation engineers had been devoted to construction unrelated to the air forces. But, of course, many Army engineers labored for the AAF.[31]

Mindoro largely remedied the deficiencies of Leyte as an air base. The southwestern tip of the island contained an area with good soil and not too much moisture. Three aviation engineer battalions comprised a large majority of the engineer troops in the task force that landed on the island on 15 December 1944. Exactly on schedule the airstrip (Hill Field) was readied for fighters, a circumstance that proved highly fortunate. The 8th Fighter Group arrived just in time to break up a punishing Japanese air attack. A few days later work at Elmore Field was interrupted when the Japanese fleet lobbed shells onto the runway and fired the gasoline storage tanks. The engineers pitched in to service the B-25's and fighters which were flying against the naval forces from a base that was not even officially operational. The destruction of fuel by this attack, the untimely loss of a ship bearing mat, plus enemy raids and rain, threw the schedule somewhat behind for Murtha and McGuire dromes on Mindoro. As a consequence of this situation and logistical problems in general, the landings on Luzon were postponed almost three weeks.[32]

Fourteen aviation engineer battalions comprised approximately a third or more of the vast construction forces assembled to develop Luzon into the predominant base of the western Pacific. While other engineers repaired roads and bridges and otherwise facilitated the advance of the ground forces following the landings at Lingayen Gulf on 9 January 1945, aviation engineers, merged almost indistinguishably with other units, began to rehabilitate airfields. The first mission involved a turf strip in the beachhead area. The 810th Engineer Aviation Battalion, just arrived from Biak, landed on 15 January without its equipment because of a high surf. Luckily, the job was simple. Four hundred civilians were hired to fill in the craters and to lay palm fronds to keep propeller backwash from blowing sand through the steel mat. When the mat and machines were finally unloaded, construction went fast, and the field soon was ready for the Fifth Air

Force. The second site on the beachhead proved to have too high a water table, so the engineers chose one in a rice paddy in Mangaldan. In five days it was serviceable as a dry-weather field, although heavy bombers soon ruined it through overuse. Meanwhile, the 841st EAB refurbished the former enemy airstrip at Mabalacat, and, just as Clark Field was being captured, the 863d EAB moved in to fill up the craters in the concrete runway made by American bombs. Filipino labor was invaluable here, but many other inhabitants tore at the hearts of the engineers by standing hungrily, apparently not in vain, beside the chow lines.[33]

During the first half of 1945 thirty-six aviation engineer battalions, the largest number in any one theater, were concentrated in the Philippines. When an engineer construction command (ENCOM) was established in March 1945 under Maj. Gen. Leif J. Sverdrup, the engineer forces on Luzon came within its control.[34] FEAF's construction program centered about five major airdromes and extensive depots. Within a week after its capture Clark Field became a much-used American base again. Nichols, Nielson, Floridablanca, and Porac were the scenes of great construction activity during the hot and dusty months of early 1945. The three-shift day, seven days a week, which had always prevailed when necessary in the theater, became standard for month after month. Japanese saboteurs were a nuisance, though not as much so as pilferers. Filipino labor was willing but often not mechanical-minded or, after years of deprivation in that hot climate, notably energetic. Yet the attractions of Manila and the greatly increased flow of recreational supplies and comforts made life much pleasanter for many aviation engineers.

The scattered battalions in those last months of the war had little in common. Some worked more or less desultorily in Leyte or elsewhere on miscellaneous construction. Others had urgent missions to improve or rebuild airfields to support a war that was still on, not only on Luzon, but on Panay, Mindanao, and other islands. Some battalions, like the 863d, performed such work as repairing railroad bridges to permit the first trains to enter Manila, and constructing piers while the city was still under fire. The 857th EAB drew the assignment of providing comfortable quarters for GHQ in Manila. Prefabricated huts, water and sewer pipes, an electrical lighting system, and sidewalks were installed under the watchful eyes of the brass at GHQ who were eager to get settled. The 872d Airborne and kindred units became or joined standard battalions, sometimes with a little sadness. Also, there were a few problem battalions, understrength, often idle, and demoralized. The 855th EAB, for example, had been involved in a race riot during training days in California. A few months later a fourth of its men were lost when a Japanese torpedo sank the ship carrying the battalion to the Southwest Pacific. It had never recovered, either in numbers or in spirit, and Col. George Mayo, visiting air engineer from Washington, found the unit in bad shape when he saw it at Nichols Field in 1945.[35]

This inspection by Colonel Mayo was indeed exhaustive. After he had visited almost every aviation engineer battalion in the theater, he wrote up his impressions for General Kenney and later submitted a more detailed report to General Arnold.[36] On the whole, Mayo thought morale was reasonably high despite lack of leaves and rest, alleged discrimination against the engineers, and denial of recognition. Most of the units were well trained, but by civilian and theater experience, not by stateside instruction. Supply, he thought, was inadequate and unorganized, a point that aviation engineer battalion commanders could enlarge upon with more vigorous language. Authorized equipment had generally furnished in the beginning, but it was badly worn, and maintenance was sometimes totally inadequate. The personnel situation was quite bad because too many battalions were understrength and opportunities for promotion were altogether too few, especially for the officers and men who had served in the theater the longest. Finally, the employment of the aviation engineers, he held, was faulty, for air commanders could not obtain needed construction without going through interminable channels and having their demands weighed against all others. The shifting of aviation engineers from one command to another, to task force, Army, ENCOM, and so on, had been detrimental to both morale and efficiency. Justified as these and other criticisms were, the work of the engineers, whether they were aviation, Army, Navy, or Australian, spoke for itself. The impressive feats of engineering in the long campaign from Australia to Okinawa permit no overwhelmingly negative appraisal of the system under which they were achieved.

Alaska

The Japanese occupation of Kiska and Attu in June 1942 provoked the Americans into an ambitious program of base-building, for the airdrome they had already made at Umnak was too distant to support sustained attacks on the western Aleutians. Despite many objections, including the estimate that three or four months might be required to build an air base on it, Adak Island was chosen for first development. At midnight on 31 August 1942 two companies of the 807th Engineer Aviation Battalion followed the assault party in a howling gale onto this little-known island. High surf and continuing bad weather interfered with the unloading, so that a more sheltered beach had to be found for the tossing barges and other assorted craft, one of which, the one carrying the runway mat, was lost. The aviation engineers sank two barges to provide a dock and transferred their equipment by crane while officers hurriedly surveyed the island to locate a suitable airfield site. Since a Japanese attack might come at any time, the heavy construction machines had to be dispersed, and roads had to be scraped to permit this. After all, the nearest source of replacement was in Seattle.[37]

What followed was a fine engineering job that became the boast of the aviation engineers. In only ten days the 807th had an adequate base for fighters. It was located on a sand-covered flat on the lower valley of a creek, an area formerly covered by sea water at high tide. The trick was to throw up a dike between tides to keep the ocean out. This done expeditiously, the aviation engineers then diverted the creek by dozing a substitute channel and erecting levees. Next they picked up rocks by hand and hauled them off, and then with timber attached to a tractor dragged the area until it was smooth. Grading, packing, and the laying of steel mat followed easily enough. By 10 September AAF aircraft started to come in, and on 14 September they initiated attacks on the Japanese at Kiska. Not until the end of the month did the enemy discover the new base at Adak, which by that time had taxiways, buildings, hangars, shops, hardstandings, and a permanent drainage system. In fact, Adak proved so satisfactory that a bomber runway was developed, also in less time than expected, and again considerable ingenuity came into play. In this case, the aviation engineers excavated sand from the flat and filled in with tundra brought from the hills. Not only the speed but the excellence of American construction practices contrasted with those of the enemy, who on Kiska and Attu employed convict labor with almost no equipment but midget dump trucks to scrape out bumpy airstrips.[38]

By early 1943 the American forces moved into Amchitka, which was adjacent to Kiska. Here they had a run of bad luck, the winter weather being extremely severe, the enemy raiding from time to time during the construction, and the job itself proving harder than had been estimated. Removing hills and filling gullies required five weeks instead of the two or three planned for, but by the middle of February a steel-matted fighter base was in operation. The 813th Engineer Aviation Battalion and the 896th Engineer Aviation Company carried out this job. The 896th Company was an experimental unit which the Air Engineer, Brig. Gen. Stuart C. Godfrey, hoped would illustrate the usefulness of aviation engineers operating directly under air force control, in this case the Eleventh Air Force, rather than under the theater command. While no fundamental change in the command structure resulted from this experiment, most of the air force headquarters overseas later received companies of aviation engineers for small jobs.[39]

The climactic undertaking of the aviation engineers of the Aleutians came with the assault on Attu. On 30 May 1943, two weeks after the initial landing, about one-third of the 807th Battalion unloaded at Massacre Bay. In the week before the equipment arrived the men made the necessary surveys and soil tests and set up camp. Fighting was still going on, rains fell, and the temperature was still uncomfortably low. But nothing interfered with the construction work, which was essentially a matter of removing tundra, stabilizing sand, and laying steel mat. It was all done eleven days after the work commenced. The runway was not overly suitable, for drainage was difficult and the mat did not rest securely on the sandy base. However, the total Japanese evacuation of the Aleutians shortly afterward reduced the importance of the airdrome and its problems. For another year the aviation engineers remained in the Alaskan area improving bases and engaging in miscellaneous construction tasks. Eventually the well-experienced 807th and 813th Battalions went back to the States for rest and then to very demanding tasks in the western Pacific.[40]

The South Pacific

The desperate fighting in the South Pacific during 1942 gave urgent importance to airdrome construction in the remote and undeveloped islands of that area. The situation would have proved still more critical had the shortage of construction forces not been matched by the unavailability of aircraft.[41] Army engineers and Marines had begun airfield building there in early 1942, and eventually an impressive flow of the civilian Naval Construction Battalions (Seabees) satisfied the most critical requirements of the air forces. Since this was primarily a Navy theater, command functions in construction matters came under the direction of naval officers. By 1943, however, the Thirteenth Air Force assumed control of aviation engineer battalions through its air service command, an arrangement which worked out to general satisfaction.[42] While the operations of the aviation engineers were less crucial and less spectacular than those of the Seabees, their contribution was significant. Tontouta, the most important air base on New Caledonia, and also one of the most highly developed in the entire theater, was largely the work of the 811th Engineer Aviation Battalion. Plaines des Gaiacs, on the northern end of New Caledonia, was the product of the 810th Battalion, like the 811th, a Negro unit which remained on the island for two years and then went on to further toil in the western Pacific.

The early career of the 810th illustrated many of the human and functional problems that arose during the first years of the war in the South Pacific. Crediting a rumor that they were going to a cold climate, the men stored their suntans and sweltered in winter uniforms for five weeks as their transport made its way in the spring of 1942 to Noumea, the port of New Caledonia. For three weeks, until their equipment came, they unloaded ships, often under enemy bombings. When their machinery arrived, they had to move it more than a hundred miles over a mountainous trail to the construction site, a task that necessitated felling trees, reinforcing bridges, fording streams, and, if their training was like that of most aviation engineers, learning how to operate the heavy pieces. On the way the troops frequently cheered themselves up by singing and in fact often seemed to be in a holiday mood. The runway at Plaines des Gaiacs they placed in condition for fighters to use in time for the Battle of the Coral Sea. During this emergency they also unloaded fuel for the aircraft from a nearby grounded tanker. The major construction at Plaines des Gaiacs went on for some months. Mangrove trees were cleared, the runway was lengthened and improved, and machinery broke down and was repaired. The problem of dust they overcame with calcium chloride treatment. Later, when rains impended, they made the runway all-weather by tapping a surface iron-ore pit and rolling the red iron oxide on the base repeatedly. When it became available, steel mat was laid. Hard work, improvisation, and common sense solved all problems in that unfamiliar atmosphere. Finally, the men made themselves a comfortable camp on the native pattern, with roofs of heavy mat grass, and continued to work on various construction jobs, building a dock at the northern harbor of New Caledonia, roads, and storage facilities. Relations with the natives were extremely cordial. Still, a reporter had reason to describe the 810th EAB in 1944 as a forgotten and unvisited unit. And in 1945 the Air Engineer pointed out that the battalion, by that time in the Philippines, had never been in a rest camp. Nostalgic veterans of New Caledonia might have disagreed.[43]

Another battalion had a good time of it on the more developed Fiji Islands. This was the 821st EAB, which went directly there after being quartered a week in the Cow Palace at San Francisco awaiting ship early in 1942. Debarking at Fiji, the men made an eighteen-mile trip to the site, a mass of weeds and brush, which they soon transformed into a fighter field known as Narewa and a pleasant enough camp. Later they worked with Seabees in construction in the Nandi area and other parts of the island. Finally, in early 1944, the 821st EAB went to the Russell Islands to build camps, roads, cemeteries, hospitals, and tank farms. Here they were amused by parrots and annoyed by rats, enervated by malaria, and made miserable by the rainfall.[44]

The 828th Engineer Aviation Battalion joined the Seabees in the later stages of reconstructing the famous Munda airfield on New Georgia. This pattern was typical of aviation engineer employment in the South Pacific. The Seabees performed most of the construction, and the aviation engineers were pulled in as auxiliaries. While full of admiration for the way the Seabees handled the urgent jobs, air officers could scarcely refrain from expressing envy of the ample equipment, sufficient numbers, good living conditions, and considerable publicity the rival forces enjoyed. Yet they noted that the civilian Seabees, who were older than the aviation engineers, could not stand up as well to combat conditions and the strain of unrelenting labor that the latter performed round the clock during the rather frequent emergency periods of the Pacific war.[45]

When the Navy's Central Pacific campaign got under way in 1943, there were air bases to be built on the atolls of the Gilbert and Ellice Islands. Here again, aviation engineers supported the Seabees. The 804th Engineer Aviation Battalion, experienced through its long labors in the Hawaiian Islands, sent a detachment on 1 September 1943 to Baker Island, where the only structure was a lighthouse and the only inhabitants were birds. In ten days the men had a runway cleared, graded, and surfaced with steel mat, and a squadron of P-40's came in to protect the aviation engineers as further construction went on. After finishing parking mats and hardstands for fighters and bombers, as well as Quonset huts and mess halls, the 804th moved on, leaving the remainder of the job to the Seabees. Late in November 1943 the 804th EAB appeared on the coconut-forested Makin Island, where Starmann Field was to be built. The previously chosen site proved too marshy, and the substituted area forced the aviation engineers to familiarize themselves with the approved method of removing coconut trees, a skill the troops in SWPA had already attained. It would not do to strike the trunk normally, for it would break and leave a cumbersome root mass to be dug up. Rather, the blow must be high to tip the trunk, the upturned root slowly dozed up, and the entire tree dragged off by tractors. The threat to operators of falling coconuts quickly lost its humorous aspect. Agility in dodging seemed the only reliable defense, for reinforced headgear or umbrellas scarcely served. As for Starmann Field, work went on with the usual 24-hour daily schedule despite rain and Japanese air attacks and snipers. The aviation engineers had only one respite, five hours on Christmas Day. By that time the steel mat had been laid and fighters were operating. Ready rooms, control towers, communications facilities, water towers, tank farms, and living quarters had to be completed. Perhaps there was a trace of smugness in the report by the aviation engineers that the Seabees, unfortunately, had fallen behind schedule in their kindred projects on nearby islands.[46]

Starmann Field was ready to support heavy bombers of the Seventh Air Force which participated in the assault on Kwajalein. In February 1944 the 854th Engineer Aviation Battalion, which had also gained experience in the Hawaiian Islands, began to unload the day after the invasion. The battle was in progress, and the engineers helped bury the dead. They planned to rehabilitate the Japanese strip by laying Marston mat, which they had brought along, but Navy pilots objected to landing their fighters on such a surface. The aviation engineers had to abandon their plan, not without many caustic observations, and search for suitable grade and subgrade materials. At last they found coarse coral rock and sand which was acceptable and, after working without respite for twelve days, had a runway available to receive a damaged TBF. As the runway was improved and extended and buildings erected, what the aviation engineers took to be a whimsical desire to remove the control tower to another location again brought tensions with the Navy to the stage of energetic discussion. Of course, the Navy had its way. In time, the airdrome on Kwajalein became a major base for combat and transport aircraft, one of the key steppingstones across the Pacific. Guam and Saipan would be the next major undertakings.[47]

China-Burma-India

Aviation engineer operations in China and India during the first two years of the war scarcely fulfilled the purpose for which the battalions had been organized. In China there were not battalions at all, but only a small core of officers under Capt. Henry A. Byroade, who advised General Chennault and oversaw to some degree the Chinese construction of airfields. In India the Tenth Air Force needed and desired air bases but depended on British supervision and Indian labor to provide them.[48] All of the five aviation engineer battalions (the 823d, 848th, 849th, 858th, and 1883d) which reached the theater during 1942 and 1943 were Negro units. As soon as they arrived, they fell under the command of the Corps of Engineers in the Services of Supply to participate in building the Ledo (later Stilwell) Road. The first white battalion, the 853d EAB, came in the first weeks of 1944, late and crippled by a tragedy. Obtaining its training largely in flood control during a rising of the Mississippi in 1943, the 853d had shipped to Algeria, where for a few weeks the men performed small-scale construction. Late in November, while sailing to India, more than half the battalion was lost after an aerial torpedo launched by a German airplane struck its ship near Sicily. When the survivors arrived in India, they were put to work near Calcutta doing mostly quarrying and small jobs for several months.[49]

The other battalions had reached the Ledo Road after a prodigious amount of traveling. They went on ships by way of Africa, usually to Bombay, and then moved for days on slow trains across India to the Bhramaputra River. Steamers took them up the river to a point where railways connected with Burma, and another train ride ensued. At last they would join the construction forces on the Ledo Road. Each battalion would work on a segment of a few miles and leapfrog to another. Their morale seems to have been surprisingly high, considering the distance from home, the rainy season, malaria, and the familiar catalogue of other hardships. Usually they worked on a 24-hour-day schedule seven days a week, but they often lived in bamboo and thatched houses that were not uncomfortable. The enemy seldom molested them. Burmese villages offered certain interests and attractions, and the town of Ledo was reported to be almost as good to visit as a stateside city. The alternation of laboring in the jungle lowlands and the highest mountain chain in the world, in cold and heat, in dust and floods, they seem to have accepted without undue complaint. The work itself was monotonous only in its abundance, for each mile presented a challenge to the ingenuity of the men and the sturdiness of their equipment. Both were equal to it. They hauled rocks, dug ditches, laid culverts, rolled roadbeds, erected bridges, dozed out bamboo jungles, and fought erosion on mountain slopes where the road should be. They occasionally scraped out airstrips, although the air forces had a low opinion of their quality. The aviation engineers had some sense of reward in seeing the Ledo Road take shape.[50]

At last, in January 1945, the road was finished, and some of the battalions—by now there were eight of them—began to move into China, where their services had long been coveted. The 858th EAB was the first to go, taking its heavy equipment more than a thousand miles over the famous road it had helped to build. The 1891st EAB perhaps traveled even more miles in going into China, or so its claim reads. An account by the historian of the 1880th related with pride that every piece of his unit's equipment made it safely, although gravity seemed to have been defied. The men stopped to patch the road they tore up and occasionally had to scramble to save a heavy machine from sliding off into space. Every man had to work his passage by driving the cherrypickers, carry-alls, trucks, tractors, scrapers, and other equipment in relays around the sharp curves. Sometimes appreciative inhabitants applauded when a particularly difficult corner was negotiated. Often it rained. Loads had to be reduced to get a machine across bridges. Once a Bailey bridge, described with assurance as the longest of its type in the world, began to sag with several heavy pieces on it over a fearful torrent. But this and other hazards had no disastrous outcome. When the aviation engineers arrived in China, they received ovations worthy of the liberators of France or the Philippines. Toward the end of the war, when the Chinese armies were melting away, truck-drivers of the 1880th EAB were imperiled by trigger-happy

Chinese soldiers who would shoot if denied rides. Soon all these incidents were only memories. The war was over, and the aviation engineers were going home.[51]

The airborne aviation engineers demonstrated in Burma that they were handy to have around, a point most overseas air commanders had at times doubted. On Christmas Day, 1943, the 900th Airborne Aviation Engineer Company was flown to Shingbwiyang, beyond the head of the Ledo Road, to construct the first airfield behind enemy lines in Burma. On 5 March 1944, this unit participated with the celebrated Chindits and commandos led by General Wingate and Col. Philip G. Cochran in a brilliant exploit, descending by gliders at night deep into enemy territory. Two men were killed, and almost all of them had very rough landings. The troops at once began to work with their miniature equipment to clear a landing strip for transports, which arrived the following night. Soon they had five fair-weather airstrips ready, averaging one a day. Then they became combat troops to defend the airstrips against Japanese infantrymen. General Godfrey praised the engineers for a marvel of daring and efficient planning, and General Arnold congratulated the 900th Company.[52]

The exploit at Myitkyina, directed by Col. Manuel J. Asensio, air engineer of the Tenth Air Force, was another bright spot in a somewhat frustrating campaign. Company A of the 879th airborne engineers took off in transports and gliders on 17 May 1944, with Brig. Gen. William D. Old piloting the lead plane. After a rough ride, all the gliders crashed-landed, but only four men were hurt. The company commander was greeted with the words, "You are in the way!" Perhaps it seemed that way as mortar shells fell and Zeroes strafed and bombed. Yet the engineers rallied and fought back. Hand grenades apparently saved them from enemy infantrymen. Soon they scraped out airstrips which accommodated fleets of transports over the next months. The whole area long remained dependent on air supply. Emergencies arose repeatedly, as on 29–30 July when a monsoon storm almost flooded the Americans out. Somehow the aviation engineers managed to keep the fields in operation. When it became apparent that the Japanese were likely to hold out at Myitkyina for a long period, the Tenth Air Force began to fly in standard aviation engineer battalions with heavy equipment, which of course had to be disassembled and packed and then put together again. In all, four such battalions went to Myitkyina. It was the only area in the whole theater

301

where the aviation engineers worked in strength under air force control.[53]

Late in 1943 General Godfrey was transferred from Washington to the China-Burma-India theater. The development of the MATTERHORN project for basing B-29's in CBI had the highest priority in the theater in addition to the steady impulses of pressure from General Arnold himself. Godfrey envisaged his new job as one of establishing standards and supervising the B-29 bases in the Bengal area, getting the airborne forces into operation under the Tenth Air Force, and overseeing construction in China for the Fourteenth Air Force. For this mission he asked to be designated, and was, Air Engineer, Air Forces, CBI.[54] The Tenth Air Force assumed direction of airfield construction in Burma, and, in China, General Chennault, acting usually through his air engineer, Col. Henry A. Byroade, had immediate control of airdrome building. But, since aviation engineers and their equipment did not reach China in any numbers until early 1945, the work there was performed by hundreds of thousands of Chinese working under local contractors.* In the building of B-29 bases in the Bengal area, British, Indian, and U.S. Army officials had a considerable hand. In all, General Godfrey's position was about as complicated and unsatisfactory as other aspects of command in that theater proved to be.

The construction of permanent airdromes for B-29's in southern Bengal—at Kharagpur, Chakulia, Piardoba, and Dudhkundi—was a frustrating and generally disappointing affair. The unrelenting pressure from Washington was not always necessary or helpful. In the theater, XX Bomber Command vigorously insisted that the work proceed in spite of infuriating and bewildering delays. In February 1944 its commander, Brig. Gen. Kenneth B. Wolfe, complained of the complicated system of getting approval, "this God-awful system of who does what kind of work, when and how," of dissension and arguments. In May he expressed impatience with the stock answers to charges of lack of progress. There was little remedial action the aviation engineers could take. There were only four battalions in the area, including the handicapped 853d EAB and three others that arrived tardily and weeks ahead of their equipment. Importunities to bring the aviation engineers down from the Ledo Road were of little avail. British and Indian authorities procured materials and labor. The Army

* See Vol. V, 65–71.

Service Forces had the ultimate control of logistical matters. In May 1944 General Godfrey, while recognizing the variety of problems, expressed his opinion that things were going as well as possible under the circumstances. After trimming many of the requirements and cutting corners, the construction forces had the bases ready to receive Superforts in April and May 1944 and finished by September.[55]

The aviation engineers, numbering more than half the 6,000 or so U.S. construction troops, labored in heat and dust, mud and rain. The excavation, grading, hauling, laying of concrete, and building of hangars and shops went on as rapidly as the availability of materials permitted. Lavish use was made of Indian laborers, perhaps 27,000 of of them, including women, who carried supplies on head trays. While the Americans believed they overcame various taboos and showed the British a few tricks about securing co-operation from the natives, the workers were often exasperating. They wasted time riding equipment for fun and often pilfered. Rain was likely to scatter them and keep them away for too long a time. Local police and contractors manipulated petty rackets that sometimes discouraged the Indians from working at all. In spite of these vexations, the aviation engineers probably regarded their daily routine as preferable to that of their comrades on the Ledo Road or in the jungles of Burma.[56]

The construction of very-heavy-bomber bases in China went better. Here the job could properly be appraised as stupendous. The immediate control of the program by the Fourteenth Air Force and the availability of hundreds of thousands of workers, most of them apparently cheerful and willing, averted some of the frustrations of the kindred project in India. Between January and May 1944, when the B-29 bases in the Chengtu area were built, a few dozen aviation engineers planned and directed the work, choosing sites near materials they would need and selecting the necessary combination of rocks and sand for the runways. The labor itself was performed by the Chinese, whose social problems in disturbing the good earth and building by hand the vast bases caught the imagination of the American press. Much less inspiring and less publicized were the negotiations with the Chinese government, for the bases proved extremely costly. And for some reason the Chinese proved much less competent at maintaining the runways than in constructing them. After early 1945, when the Ledo Road was opened, aviation engineers could reach China in significant numbers with their heavy equipment, but now the B-29's had moved out of China. In the few months that remained of war, the engineers did not need to inaugurate large engineering projects.[57]

POA

The last phases of the Pacific war brought the aviation engineers a staggering load of work in the Marianas, where airfields were constructed for the B-29's of XXI Bomber Command.* Until close to the end of hostilities fifteen battalions labored to this purpose. The early planning for the great air bases in the Marianas was carried out in the headquarters of the Seventh Air Force at a time when the engineers of that diminutive organization had little data with which to prepare estimates. Even though representatives of XXI Bomber Command participated toward the end of the planning, many requirements were seriously underestimated. Thus the aviation engineers found themselves with tasks and schedules beyond their capabilities and often fell behind. Moreover, data for Guam were inadequate when it came to planning air bases of such magnitude, while for Saipan, which had been under German and Japanese rule, there was scarcely any intelligence at all. Finally, the command situation was a chronic source of dissatisfaction to air engineers. Administratively, they were under Army Air Forces, Pacific Ocean Area (AAFPOA), but for materials and supplies they depended on Army garrison forces. Island commanders had operational control of their work, and, in the last analysis, Admiral Nimitz, Commander-in-Chief, Pacific Ocean Area (CINCPOA), made the important decisions. This situation permitted such "processing" that it might take weeks to obtain approval for a job requiring only a few hours to complete.[58]

Five aviation engineer battalions (the 804th, 805th, 806th, 1878th, and 1894th) performed the major airfield construction on Saipan. The seasoned 804th EAB went ashore on 20 June 1944, five days after the assault. Moving the equipment over a wide pock-marked coral reef to the shore, which was dominated by a 50-foot rock bluff, was a formidable task itself, involving dozing a path over the reef and wading through chest-deep water. Then a cut had to be blasted through the bluff, but, in spite of these obstacles, on the second day after landing a platoon began working on the former Japanese strip at Aslito. The men filled the holes and made good use of a captured Japanese roller, so that within 24 hours a P-47 could land. After four days the

---

* See Vol. V, 512–25, for general discussion of B-29 bases in the Pacific.

aviation engineers had placed a short Marston mat on the runway, had laid a pipe to the ocean to bring in sea water, and had started two coral quarries. Whereupon about 300 Japanese infantrymen overran the field, brandishing axes and automatic weapons. The aviation engineers dropped their tools and grabbed rifles to help drive the enemy away.[59]

The counterattack was only an incident, however unnerving. More serious interference came when the Japanese began to bomb and strafe the construction troops and kept it up for days. Tropical rains worsened spirits and working conditions but, of course, did not prevent labor. After reinforcements arrived, the engineers were grouped in a construction unit that proceeded to make Aslito (later Isley Field) a base fit for the Superforts. It was hard work. Saipan was hot and overcrowded. Mud alternated with palls of dust. There was no time to build a bivouac area, for construction went on day and night, and all equipment was absorbed. For months the troops had no fresh food. Half the trucks broke down at one time, and all of them at one time or another. The road from the coral pits to the runway was ruinous on vehicles, and replacements were unobtainable. Most of the aviation engineers were not accustomed to working with coral, which was harder than anticipated, and found they had a great deal to learn. Nearly every foot had to be blasted. In October a typhoon threatened disaster to the bombers that had recently arrived. Aviation engineers devised rings in their welding shops to anchor the aircraft. In November a Japanese plane crashed into the camp area and burned.[60] Later that month a loaded American bomber blew up on the runway. Of this experience, Brig. Gen. Haywood S. Hansell, Jr., wrote: "Our engineers and our fire people did a job that would warm your heart—the engineers in particular I cannot speak too highly of. They took their large equipment, the big bulldozers and scoops and went to work immediately on the flaming bomber and gas truck in spite of personnel bombs and exploding ammunition. They piled the debris of the bomber into two heaps and pushed dirt on it. Later they drove their 20-ton bulldozers over these flaming heaps. The flames came up through the tractors and all around the drivers but it didn't stop them."[61]

While the concrete runways were being finished at Isley Field, other projects intended for Saipan underwent considerable change. The island was more rugged than had appeared from aerial photographs, and fewer bases could be developed there. Lt. Gen. Millard F. Harmon secured a revision of the construction program by offering to base all four groups of the 73d Wing on two 8,500-foot runways at Isley Field, thus reducing the total building program on Saipan, and to use another strip for spare bombers and other aircraft. Then, six operational runways would be built on the small island of Tinian, between Guam and Saipan. He also reversed earlier plans for dispersed housing areas and agreed to place the camps near the bases. By February 1945, when Isley Field was entirely completed, it was clear that the aviation engineer effort had been twice the estimates. It was not surprising that morale had been low during the worst phases—that the commanders had sometimes had to draw on such reservoirs of faith and hope as they possessed in order to see the job through. It had also been vexing in the extreme to have parts and supplies trickle in, improperly marked and incomplete, and too often seized by another organization. Once the aviation engineers even stripped a former Japanese sugar mill in order to obtain such humble items as boilers, pipes, and valves. Their own living conditions were primitive, and, when the 73d Wing settled down on Saipan, its men found no such niceties as mess halls, showers, and latrines ready for them.[62]

Construction on Tinian did not involve the aviation engineers, since the Seabees had the assignment. That they also got along slowly, notwithstanding their envied equipment, ratings, and luxuries, was possibly some grim consolation to the strained aviation engineers. The development of air bases on Guam had been delayed by Japanese resistance and the Navy's concern for its own construction. The coral was just as hard on Guam as on Saipan, and the supply system as choked. The climate was hotter, and, with the Navy in full control of construction, the aviation engineers occasionally burned with indignation, as when two battalions were pulled off airfield construction early in 1945 to work on a Navy project. Furthermore, the eight battalions which eventually reached Guam had a generally lower level of ability than those on Saipan. Two had been the subject of a scathing inspector-general report at the port of embarkation. Most of them had not received adequate training in the States, and, unlike the first battalions early in the war, their men usually had little if any civilian experience in construction.[63]

The main projects on Guam for the aviation engineers were construction of an air depot and two B-29 bases, North and Northwest

Fields. In the case of North Field the air engineer and his party worked their way over miles of jungle tracks lined with Japanese corpses to find a suitable site. The trail was so bad the machinery could not reach the location until extensive clearing had taken place, largely through the efforts of the 854th Engineer Aviation Battalion. By November 1944 work started, and late in February 1945 the first B-29 mission flew from the base. It was not a poor record. Northwest Field had been chosen after an air inspection by General Hansell and Col. W. E. Robinson, the XXI Bomber Command engineer. Seabees and two aviation engineer battalions, the 1886th and 1889th, started the work, which went on from January to June 1945. One-fourth of the time was absorbed in rooting out the jungle. On Guam, as on Saipan, there was no effort available for the construction of suitable camps. Aviation engineers had grown accustomed to primitive living conditions, but the men of the 314th Bomb Wing were perhaps justifiably chagrined on arriving to find their permanent housing area not even cleared. On the whole, the morale of the engineers in Guam was rather low, even if a vital engineering construction program had been completed.[64]

Okinawa, secured after hard battles between 1 April and 31 July 1945, was expected to become a vast air, sea, and ground force base for the final assault on the Japanese homeland. Soon after the landings the chief engineer of GHQ, Army Forces in the Pacific (AFPAC),* made a reconnaissance and proposed that very-heavy-bomber bases be added to the ambitious airfield construction program already scheduled. In all, twenty-six aviation engineer battalions reached Okinawa before the surrender to work under the direction of AFPAC, along with Army construction forces and Seabees. One of them, the 811th EAB, once in New Caledonia, went on to work in the hot volcanic soil of Iwo Jima. The aviation engineers on Okinawa seemed to come from everywhere, from the Philippines, Guadalcanal, Alaska, Guam, and the States. One battalion, the 801st EAB, had spent most of the war on the Azores. It had the unusual opportunity of comparing the hurricane endured there with the great typhoon of October 1945 on Okinawa. Once on Okinawa, many of the experienced aviation engineers prudently assured themselves of comfortable camps before beginning the grading, opening the quarries, and setting up the asphalt plants in preparation for airfield construction. Serious work

* See Vol. V, 682–83.

began in July, and by the time the war ended Okinawa was well on the way to becoming a formidable base.

Had World War II continued a few months longer, ninety-three battalions of aviation engineers would have been at work in the western Pacific—according to plans, many of them veteran units of the European theater.[65] The mammoth construction program for Okinawa went on in peacetime and under different auspices. Most of the aviation engineers went home, probably to participate in the greatest building boom in American history.

SECTION III

* * * * * * * * * * *

WEATHER AND COMMUNICATIONS

CHAPTER 11

*   *   *   *   *   *   *   *   *   *   *

THE AAF WEATHER SERVICE

J UST as a ground commander must know the terrain over which
his troops and supplies move, so did the successful air commander of World War II depend upon uninterrupted and fresh
intelligence regarding the atmospheric "terrain" in which his forces
operated. The vertical dimension of his three-dimensional battlefield
was no less significant than its length and breadth. Atmospheric conditions thousands of feet above the ground determined the pathways
open to his aircraft, and weather hundreds of miles away could be of
greater military significance than a storm over his own headquarters.
For this indispensable information the air commander relied on the
delicate instruments and skilled personnel of his weather services. By
the end of the war those services had come almost to be taken for
granted, so much so that little thought was any longer given to the
near-miracle they represented.[1]

When the war began, modern meteorology, with its special dependence for the purposes of weather forecasting upon analytical study
of the movement of air masses, was still a youthful branch of scientific
investigation. Its principles and techniques had been developed first
by the Scandinavians as a result of having been shut off from customary weather intelligence by the combatant powers in the first World
War. The new approach began to influence meteorological studies in
American universities and technical institutes only in the later years
of the 1920's, just in time to serve the needs of a rapidly growing
commercial air transport system. Systematic and scientific weather reporting was still limited very largely to the European and North
American segments of the globe, and wartime interruptions of normal opportunities for communication promised increased difficulty in
efforts to extend adequate weather services into more than one stra-

tegically critical area. The general tendency for weather to move from west to east, together with the prospect that the Americans would enjoy the full assistance of Britain's well-developed weather services, promised an advantage over the enemy in Europe. On the other side of the globe, the Japanese had the advantage. The swift and sweeping southward advance of their forces after Pearl Harbor closed to all Allied reporting a vast area of major significance to weather in the Pacific Ocean. On the mainland of Asia, China and India remained in friendly hands, but the weather data that could be secured from those territories obviously would depend very greatly upon such services as could be developed by the Allied armed forces. Similarly, along the more critical of the new air routes, including those across the Atlantic, the facilities for both collecting and disseminating information on weather had to be developed along with the routes themselves.

Although weather could significantly affect a variety of military operations and was especially important to the success of an amphibious landing, weather had its greatest continuing importance for air operations. The Japanese took advantage of bad weather in the mid-Pacific to screen their approach to Pearl Harbor in December 1941. Some fifteen months later, a miscalculation in the Bismarck Sea cost them dearly, when the storm under whose cover their convoy sought to reinforce Lae in New Guinea dissipated, and the Fifth Air Force won a major victory.* On the other side of the world, the heavy concentration of enemy fighters encountered by the Eighth Air Force attacking Schweinfurt on 14 October 1943 was a direct result of accurate forecasting by the German weather services. Because this target lay in the only part of Germany in which daylight bombing seemed to be possible under prevailing weather conditions, the Germans massed their fighters in such a way as to inflict on the Eighth Air Force the highest percentage of loss it had suffered to date.† To take but one other example from tactical operations, the weather forecast determined the timing of the "Big Week" of AAF bombing over Europe in February 1944.‡ Meanwhile, the ferrying of aircraft and the increasingly important development of air transport services depended fundamentally upon the growing military weather services, which became in time quite literally world-encircling.

* See Vol. IV, 141–46.
† See Vol. II, 699–704.   ‡ See Vol. III, 31 ff.

The AAF Weather Service

On the eve of war the U.S. Weather Bureau maintained a modern and efficient system of weather reporting for the continental United States. Although many facets of American life had come to rely on the regular and increasingly dependable reports of this service, the most important of recent developments in the Bureau's activities had been undertaken in the interest of commercial aviation. Across the country, in thirteen districts, forecast centers were maintained at key airports to provide for pilots route forecasts that added greatly to the safety of aircraft flights, both civil and military. The Army, in whose interest the federal government had first undertaken the development of a weather service, depended also upon a supplementary organization of its own embracing some thirty weather stations in the United States and another half-dozen located in overseas possessions.[2] The responsibility for equipping and manning these stations belonged originally to the Signal Corps, but most of them were operated for the special benefit of the Air Corps. Accordingly, the War Department in 1937 had reassigned the responsibility for operation and control of these stations to the Chief of the Air Corps.[3] The Signal Corps continued to be responsible for the development, procurement, storage, and issue of meteorological equipment until late in 1945. Coast and field artillery, ordnance, and chemical warfare units might provide for themselves weather facilities peculiar to their needs, but the Air Corps, as chief user, now took over the primary obligation for meeting the Army's need for special weather services.[4]

As war became imminent, the original plans for expansion of the AAF's weather services were extremely modest. Personnel needs fell into two general categories: (1) men sufficiently trained to serve as forecasters and (2) those who had the skill to serve as observers for the collection of data pertinent to exact forecasting. Standards for recruitment were high. Not only did the performance of these tasks demand a high order of intelligence and some background in mathematics and physics but also policy gave preference in the training of forecasters to officers who were experienced pilots. Especially qualified pilots who applied for the training were sent at the rate of eight each year to study at the Massachusetts Institute of Technology and the California Institute of Technology. In September 1937 a special school was opened at Patterson Field for the training of enlisted men as forecasters in a six-month course. Approximately fifty men were graduated each year. Observers at first received their training on the job at AAF weather stations. In September 1939 a special school for observers was established at Scott Field, with an entering class of seven men who were committed to a three-month course of study.[5] Early in the next year the two schools were moved to Chanute Field and incorporated into the Air Corps Technical School.

By the summer of 1940, when France fell and the fate of England hung on the Battle of Britain, it became apparent that all previous planning for the weather services fell far short of the need. In July a special committee representing the Weather Bureau, the Army, and the Navy reported an inventory of qualified forecasters in the nation distributed as follows: the Weather Bureau, 150; civil airlines, 94; Army, 62; Navy, 46; educational and other institutions, 25. Immediate requirements for increases in these numbers showed for the Army 175, for the Navy 80, and for the Weather Bureau from 25 to 30. It was recommended that the government seek the co-operation of universities offering suitable programs in meteorology as the best way to meet these deficiencies.[6]

Negotiations for this purpose already had been opened with the Massachusetts Institute of Technology, the California Institute of Technology, the University of California at Los Angeles, New York University, and the University of Chicago, all of which had well-established programs of study in meteorology. An original plan for the Air Corps to enroll 40 students in these institutions was modified by the end of August, at General Arnold's insistence, to provide for a total of 150. Recruitment of qualified applicants was to be pressed among "washouts" from pilot training and among students in educational institutions on a promise of training in cadet status. Additional help in the event of war was expected from a program, inaugurated simultaneously under the leadership of the Weather Bureau and the sponsorship of the Civilian Pilots Training Program, for the training of an additional 100 meteorologists. By October 1940, the Air Corps had almost 150 recruits launched on a nine-month course of study at one or another of the participating universities.[7] The members of the first class had been assigned to duty several months before Pearl Harbor, and the second class of 180 had been in school long enough to be graduated in February 1942, six weeks ahead of schedule.

This addition gave the AAF some 330 trained weather officers, but it was now estimated that total needs would be 1,000. By downward adjustment of educational standards for recruitment and with the aid to recruitment that came from the outbreak of war, the AAF entered 440 cadet students in March and another 400 in September. By that time the estimated requirement for weather officers had jumped to 4,000, and at the end of the year, as plans for a 273-group air force became firm, the goal had been placed at 10,000 weather officers by 1 January 1945.[8] The hope of meeting any such goal as this depended upon finding some solution to the problem of recruitment. Because of the special educational qualifications that were required for advanced meteorological training, this problem had been considered acute almost from the beginning of the program. Recruitment by other services and the drafting of young men at the age of eighteen promised that the supply of candidates having the academic prerequisites for study of meteorology would soon be exhausted. Accordingly, the AAF entered into agreements with some twenty additional universities and colleges for the inauguration in 1943 of an elaborate program of premeteorological training. Enlistment of applicants in an enlisted-reserve status was intended to assure protection of the students from the draft until they were qualified for admission to cadet status.[9] The plan, after some opposition in the Air Staff, was approved in November 1942.

Unhappily, the whole program rested upon a gross overestimate of actual needs. How gross was soon made apparent to Maj. Gen. Barney M. Giles, Assistant Chief of Air Staff, Operations, Commitments and Requirements (OC&R), who in May 1943 insisted that by the end of that year the AAF would have enough weather officers to meet all its needs through 1944. The estimated number, counting in the graduates of December 1943, was 4,500—less than half the total called for in existing programs.[10] This estimate of needs did not take into account the possibility of expanded requirements in 1945, but experience proved it to be a far more accurate figure than any which had been used for planning since the earlier days of the war emergency. After a good deal of discussion, it was decided that the class entering upon advanced training in October 1943 would be the last. Even so, the AAF trained many more weather officers than it needed. Of the approximately 6,200 who were trained, over 1,800 were assigned to other duties.[11] The inexperience of staff officers in a new area of military activity, miscalculation as to the most effective organization of weather services in combat zones,* the keen competition for especially qualified personnel during the hasty upbuilding of the armed forces, and the extraordinary size and complexity of the AAF's total expansion—these and other factors contributed to this costly blunder. In looking back, it may be well to recall the psychology of the first months of war. A weather officer responding to General Giles's criticism of the program in 1943 could insist, quite seriously and with some impunity, that wars were lost through shortages, not overages.

Whatever else may be said about the AAF's meteorological training program, it promptly met the needs of a rapidly expanded weather service. After the transfer of responsibility from the Signal Corps, a Meteorological Section had been established in the Office of the Chief of Air Corps. The United States was divided into three (later four) weather regions, in each of which was stationed a meteorological squadron broken down into such detachments as were required to man its several stations. For administrative purposes the squadrons functioned under a group headquarters located at Bolling Field, Washington, D.C. As the service developed, weather stations of different types were taken over from the Signal Corps or were organized to meet new requirements in an expanding Air Corps. Some of these, as at major air bases, provided forecasting services through 24 hours each day. Others maintained regular observing services and provided forecasts as required. Still others functioned only for the purpose of accumulating data on the weather pertinent to the forecasting operations of other stations. The allotment of personnel to each station varied greatly and according to need. At major installations a station weather officer was in charge. At others a noncommissioned officer as station chief bore the responsibility.[12] By the time of Pearl Harbor the service could boast a personnel roster of 4,300 officers and men.[13]

The pattern of organization developed for the Zone of the Interior had been extended overseas by a TAG letter of 18 November 1941.[14] Weather detachments in the Philippines, the Caribbean, Hawaii, and the North Atlantic were redesignated, respectively, as the 5th, 6th, 7th, and 8th Weather Squadrons and were given control of all

---

* It had been assumed, for example, that weather officers would have to be assigned at squadron levels, but experience later argued against this practice.

INFLATING WEATHER BALLOON, KEFLAVIK, ICELAND

LAUNCHING WEATHER BALLOON

MARIANAS ISLANDS

READING METEOROLOGICAL INSTRUMENTS

THEODOLITE OPERATOR, GREENLAND BASE

weather activity in their respective regions. The squadron commander in each region thus became, as was the practice in the continental U.S., the regional control officer. To provide better services along the increasingly busy South Atlantic air route, a ninth region and squadron were activated in July 1942. A 10th Weather Region, embracing India, Burma, and China, had been established in the previous month, and the 11th had been created in May 1942 for Alaska, where the AAF shared responsibility with the Weather Bureau, the Civil Aeronautics Administration, and the Navy for observation and forecasting in an especially difficult area. The 12th Weather Squadron assumed the responsibility for serving the Twelfth Air Force in Northwest Africa late in 1942. And so it went. By the end of 1942 a total of nineteen regions had been established.[15] This number was subsequently increased and regional boundaries were redrawn as experience seemed to require. By the spring of 1945 the AAF was operating all told some 900 weather stations, of which more than 600 lay outside the continental United States.[16]

Problems of liaison and control were many and varied. A Defense Meteorological Committee, representing the Weather Bureau, the Army, and the Navy, functioned from as early as the summer of 1940 to co-ordinate civil and military programs. Later, in 1942, this committee found formal place in the developing organization of the Joint Chiefs of Staff as the Joint Meteorological Committee. Under the Combined Chiefs a Combined Meteorological Committee effected necessary liaison with our British ally on such matters as the exchange of weather information, security regulations, codes, and avoidance of unnecessary duplication of services. After the liberation of France, the rehabilitation of French weather services and co-ordination of their activities with the then well-established Allied services paid good dividends. Less successful were efforts to win the co-operation of our Russian ally, although the Russian attitude relented somewhat after 1943. In North America and in the South and Southwest Pacific co-operation with the Canadians, Australians, and New Zealanders was close and effective. Typical of such co-operation was the establishment of jointly administered regional weather controls, stations organized and equipped for meteorological study and forecast for a large geographical area.[17]

More difficult were questions involving command relations within the Army and even within the air arm itself. From the beginning, experienced weather officers in the Air Corps recognized the central importance of developing a well-integrated and unified service. But the very dichotomy which marked the organization of the Air Corps after the establishment of the GHQ Air Force in 1935 brought up troublesome questions. The obligation to organize, train, and equip weather units belonged to the Office, Chief of Air Corps (OCAC), but the GHQ Air Force, as the combat organization of the Air Corps, controlled bases and tactical units to which weather personnel were assigned. What control over the operations of widely dispersed weather units could OCAC exercise in the interest of common procedures and an indispensable exchange of services? And what influence could GHQ Air Force properly have over the development of doctrines and policies which molded the weather units assigned to its command? These were questions already familiar in more than one department of the Air Corps' activity.* Some aid to their solution came with the decision in 1939 to make the Commanding General, GHQ Air Force, subject to the "supervision" of the Chief of the Air Corps and from the establishment of the AAF in June 1941, when the Combat Command, successor to the GHQ Force, was made subordinate to the Chief of the AAF.† Help was also found in the concept of technical supervision, through which a headquarters not having command over a particular unit might prescribe common procedures for all such units in "technical" matters.‡ More or less successful efforts were also made to protect especially trained personnel from assignments, including temporary ones, that were wasteful of their special skills. But the problem lingered on until the abolition of the Combat Command in the reorganization of March 1942.[18]

Thereafter, the more important of such issues involved units assigned to overseas theaters. Traditionally, the prerogative of the theater commander in a combat zone was inviolable, and yet the effective operation of a world-wide weather service necessarily required a measure of centralized supervision and control. Weather units committed to overseas service were assigned originally to the several theaters or area commands, with no reservation other than

* See, for example, Vol. I, 32; VI, 364.

† See Vol. VI, 11–35, for a study of organizational developments from 1939 to 1942.

‡ In an amendment to AAF Regulation 105-2 of 3 February 1944, technical supervision was for the first time officially defined for the weather service as that "normally exercised through technical orders and specifications necessary for the control and supervision of operating procedures peculiar to the AAF Weather Service."

that of technical supervision by the appropriate AAF agency. There were a variety of ways in which the AAF could exert a helpful influence. It could secure by negotiation protective clauses in War Department Regulations that were in some particulars binding on all theater commanders. The growing autonomy of the AAF as a service having separate representation on agencies of the Joint and Combined Chiefs of Staff provided other and helpful channels of influence. Nevertheless, the problem found no clean-cut resolution until virtually the end of the war.

Part of the difficulty lay in the inability of the AAF to settle certain of its own internal problems of organization.[19] In the reorganization of March 1942 the responsibilities of the earlier Weather Section devolved upon the Director of Technical Services, in whose office at AAF Headquarters was established a Directorate of Weather. The new Director of Weather, Col. Don Z. Zimmerman, within a few months had taken significant steps toward integrating all weather personnel and units within the United States into an organization directly responsible to the directorate. Base units and tactical units theretofore belonging to the Combat Command were transferred to the control of one or another of the four weather regions. Some thought had been given before March 1942 to the creation of a separate weather command, but one of the principles on which the reorganization of that month rested was a belief that AAF Headquarters could function for both the shaping of policy and the direction of operations. This belief, however, was soon abandoned. The policy governing another reorganization, effective in March 1943, was to get operations out of Washington. Consequently, the directorates were abolished, and responsibility for direct supervision of the AAF Weather Service (so designated in 1942) was transferred to the newly created Flight Control Command with headquarters in Winston-Salem, North Carolina. For the exercise of this responsibility, the command activated the Weather Wing on 14 April 1943 and soon thereafter located the wing's headquarters in Asheville, North Carolina.[20]

In July 1943 the Weather Wing became an independent unit by its reassignment to the direct control of AAF Headquarters, where a newly created Weather Division in OC&R assumed supervisory responsibility for the AAF Weather Service.[21] The Weather Wing at Asheville controlled all weather units assigned to the AAF but had no authority over units assigned to combat theaters except for the technical control it exercised over certain procedures. Through the next two years there was much discussion of the organizational and jurisdictional problems presented by these arrangements, and, finally, in July 1945, a thoroughgoing reorganization was begun. The Weather Wing became Headquarters, AAF Weather Service (AAFWS); the Weather Division was abolished and its personnel assigned to Headquarters, AAFWS, at Asheville; a new Chief of the AAF Weather Service, with office in Washington, was made directly responsible to General Arnold and would serve as Arnold's top adviser on all questions relating to weather service. The concept was one already adopted in the fields of air transport and air communications: to concentrate full responsibility in a single command and to give to it operational control of all pertinent services. As the war came to an end a few weeks later, action had been begun for the reassignment of weather units throughout the world to the operational control of the new command.[22]

Operations—Europe, Africa, the Far East

The most impressive achievement of the AAF Weather Service was the extension of its vital activity overseas. That story falls naturally into two parts: (1) the extension of weather services eastward across the Atlantic to battle stations in Europe and Africa and thence across the Middle East to India, Burma, and China and (2) the extension of these same services westward from the United States across the Pacific.

Early flights along the South Atlantic air route depended very largely for weather intelligence upon the meteorologists of Panair do Brasil, subsidiary of Pan American Airways. During 1941 the AAF activated nine weather stations in Puerto Rico, Panama, the Canal Zone, British Guiana, the Virgin Islands, and the British West Indies. But when war came, just after the establishment of the 6th Weather Region,* the AAF still operated a very incomplete service, and shortages of equipment and personnel continued for several months thereafter to plague responsible officers. Local training of enlisted forecasters at Albrook Field in the Canal Zone provided some help in meeting the shortage of personnel. Gradually, needed equipment came through, and the creation of a 9th Weather Region in

* See above, p. 316.

July 1942 helped to solve administrative problems attendant upon an expanding service to ATC and tactical units flying out by way of Brazil to Africa, the Middle East, and the Far East.[23]

The first American weather personnel to serve along the North Atlantic airways arrived at Gander Field, Newfoundland, on 9 March 1941, to support the 21st Reconnaissance Squadron, then on anti-submarine patrol. Three weather officers and ten enlisted men worked alongside Canadian personnel and used Canadian facilities until American equipment became available. Within two months they were turning out synoptic maps of the North Atlantic. With American occupation of the Atlantic steppingstones and the development of an air ferry and transport route to Great Britain, Gander Field ultimately became the nucleus of a weather net that reached from North America to the British Isles.[24]

The many Atlantic storms originating in the Far North underscored the need for timely and reliable weather data from northern Canada and Greenland. To help fill this gap, six enlisted men accompanied the United States Marine Corps task force that landed at Narsarssuak (BLUIE WEST 1) on 6 July 1941 to assume protective custody of Greenland. Their mission was to establish a weather station and support flight operations at the air base to be built there. Three months later a weather detachment arrived at BLUIE WEST 8, on Greenland's west coast just above the Arctic Circle. This station provided a strategically located post for the observation of air masses moving out of the polar region. Before the end of the year, the third Greenland weather installation was established at BLUIE EAST 2, near Angmagssalik, on the east side of the big island. Danish stations in Greenland, with new American radio and meteorological equipment, became integral parts of the AAF weather net.[25]

In the meantime, on 1 September 1941, an air weather detachment of seven men which landed with the first American task force in Iceland had started operations at Reykjavik. For several weeks weather data available there were meager, even when they included reports secured by walking to the British station a mile away or by rowing out to an American destroyer in the harbor. Fortunately, the demand for weather services in Iceland did not become pressing until the great increase in air traffic over the North Atlantic route in the summer of 1942.[26]

The three Crystal stations, in northern Quebec and on Baffin and

Padloping islands, were favorably located to observe the movement of polar air masses.* If and when the projected Crimson Route from western Canada across Hudson Bay to Greenland were opened, these Crystal stations would be needed to support flight operations.[27] This completed the growing roster of weather installations in or near the North Atlantic at the end of 1941. Weather and communications from Iceland to the British Isles remained a British responsibility.

Approximately fifty American weather officers and men were on duty in the north. In effect, each station provided a more or less independent forecasting service tailored to meet the needs of an individual base. At best, such a disunited weather service could be of but limited value to users of a transoceanic ferrying and transport route. Forecasters still drew weather maps on the basis of data they knew to be almost fragmentary. But, gradually, the more serious gaps in the weather-reporting net were filled by the opening of new stations and the improvement of communications facilities. The Azores were included in 1943 with the opening of the station at Lagens.[28]

Men assigned to the lonely and rugged North Atlantic weather stations had to be hand-picked for emotional stability and physical stamina. Those who pioneered BLUIE WEST 8 had no contact with the outside world, except by radio, from the departure of the last surface vessel in December 1941 until the arrival of the first aircraft on the newly built airfield four months later. Men at other northern stations endured comparable intervals between mail calls. Stations at Mecatina and Indian House Lake, in Quebec, were completely inaccessible by land and water and had to be established and supplied wholly by air. Subzero weather and high winds played havoc with housing and with equipment designed for use in more temperate climates. But there were compensations. Wild game occasionally offered welcome variation of diet. The men were kept busy and so physically fit. At BLUIE WEST 8 the commanding officer taught his men to ski. Almost everywhere, morale was reported good.[29]

To assist fighter aircraft headed for the British Isles as part of the BOLERO movement in the summer of 1942, weather reconnaissance flights were first tried. Experience emphasized the desirability of a regular weather reconnaissance program to support all air traffic, and by 1943 three B-25 type aircraft shuttled between Presque Isle, Goose Bay, and Gander on weather flights, while three B-17's based in New-

* See above, pp. 93–94.

foundland provided coverage from 500 to 800 miles eastward over the Atlantic.* Beginning in January 1944, three specially equipped C-54's flew between North American bases and the British Isles, to fill the mid-ocean gap where storms could maintain themselves without revealing their behavior. Each C-54 carried two weather officers specially trained to observe weather from the air. The aircraft generally flew directly across the Atlantic but might return to the United States by way of Iceland or Greenland or along North African–Azores routes if necessary because of bad weather. Qualified observers also made in-flight observations from regularly scheduled C-54's crossing the Atlantic. Navy and Coast Guard vessels stationed along the airways provided additional coverage at surface level.[30]

Aerial reconnaissance as a regular feature of operations along the southeastern route did not start until the spring of 1943. Forecasters carried on Air Transport Command flights in both directions between Atkinson Field, in British Guiana, and Belém transmitted on-the-spot weather reports to ground stations and to aircraft in flight. Improved weather briefing was an incidental benefit, as weather personnel learned to talk the language of the aircrews and acquired a firsthand understanding of their needs. In spite of such advantages, route weather missions flown one or two hours ahead of scheduled flights proved disappointing; they were too early to benefit other aircraft by air-to-air radio and too late to provide detailed information to forecasters.[31] By contrast, area reconnaissance, when begun in 1944, proved so successful that weather became thereafter a negligible cause of aircraft losses. Weather stations at Waller (Trinidad), Belém, and Morrison fields each had two aircraft used for area reconnaissance, and a seventh was kept in reserve at Miami, Florida.[32]

As air traffic across the Atlantic increased, differences between American and British methods of processing weather information led to confusion and then to demands for separate services. Consequently, and on recommendation of a joint RAF-AAF board, North Atlantic terminals offered both American and British weather services. After July 1943 American aircraft flying the North Atlantic were under the watchful eyes of AAF weather and operations personnel. Forecasting was done chiefly at mainline stations through which traffic passed en route to and from Prestwick, Scotland. Transatlantic brief-

* See below, pp. 332–33.

ing of flight crews was done first at Gander Field and later at the American base at Harmon Field, also in Newfoundland.[33]

AAF units in the British Isles were almost completely dependent on British weather services during their first months of operation in the United Kingdom. Extensive use of British weather maps and instruments procured through reverse lend-lease saved both time and shipping space, but at the cost of some confusion in supply procedures. Synoptic reports from AAF stations were transmitted over British nets, since it was mid-1944 before American teletype equipment was generally available. The 18th Weather Squadron was sent to England in August 1942 as token of a plan to make the Eighth Air Force ultimately independent of its British ally.[34]

Weather operations in Africa began in support of the transport and ferrying route across Central Africa that had been pioneered by the British and that was further developed by Pan American Airways for the movement of aircraft and supplies from the United States to the Middle East.* By June 1942 some nine weather officers and sixty enlisted weathermen were on duty at various points extending from Accra on the Gold Coast to Egypt. A newly activated 19th Weather Squadron established its headquarters at Accra during the summer, with responsibilities reaching all the way into the Middle East, where the Ninth Air Force was beginning to operate, and southward to cover an emergency air route being developed below the Equator against the possibility of an Axis victory in the north.[35] By the end of the year the responsibilities of the 19th Squadron reached from Accra to the border of India.

The 10th Weather Squadron, with headquarters at Delhi in India, faced one of the more difficult assignments in the AAF—to assist in the support of China by way of the famed "Hump" air route. Shorthanded, as were most AAF organizations in CBI during the earlier part of the war, the 10th Weather Squadron found the reports supplied by the meteorological department of the Indian government ill suited to its needs. Worse still was the situation across the Hump at Kunming, where a single officer and six enlisted men depended primarily upon data collected through a Chinese air warning system that was far more expert at spotting Japanese planes than in observing developments pertinent to weather forecasting.[36]

Between Kunming and Dinjan in India, AAF planes shuttled along

* See above, p. 46.

a route already famous for its stormy weather. The route passed through the turbulent meeting place of three major Eurasian air masses. Low-pressure masses from the west moved along the main ranges of the Himalayas to the Hump, where highs from the Sea of Bengal clashed with Siberian lows. As late as January 1945, when earlier shortages of men, material, and experience had been very largely overcome, a single storm over the Hump cost ATC nine aircraft and 31 persons killed or missing.[37] This, to be sure, was one for the record, but throughout the war unfavorable weather remained the greatest single cause of fluctuations in the flow of air traffic between India and China.

Not a little bickering marked the relations between the 10th Weather Region and the India-China Wing of ATC, which was hard pressed to meet fantastic goals for tonnages delivered across the Hump. Dissatisfaction with the situation in India and China probably contributed to ATC's bid in the latter half of 1943 for control of weather services along air routes on which ATC was the principal user.* Bickering continued,[38] but the record of the Weather Service in CBI was not wholly one of frustration. When the B-29's of XX Bomber Command began operations from Indian bases against Japan and Southeast Asia in 1944, the new responsibilities were met successfully. Chinese reverses at the hands of Japanese ground forces soon drastically reduced the coverage provided by China's air warning net, but a newly established weather central at Chengtu offset this disadvantage. The progress of U.S. naval forces in the Pacific made possible the provision of up-to-date reports from submarines and other vessels on duty along the Chinese and Japanese coasts. In return, Chengtu was able to provide weather reports of use to fleet units operating in the Pacific.[39]

Asiatic weather still held many mysteries, and the Superforts depended finally on weather planes, fully armed B-29's which flew ahead on the route of attack to send back a last-minute report.† But the Russians were now more co-operative in supplying information regarding weather in Siberia, and, with the aid of observations by American personnel on the Asiatic mainland, the Allies were begin-

---

* Actually, however, the experiment with a transfer of weather units to ATC came in the Caribbean and the South Atlantic. Strongly protested by weather officers looking toward an integrated and unified weather system, the experiment was abandoned at the end of the year.

† See below, pp. 333–34.

ning to turn the tables on the Japanese. It was often possible to predict today tomorrow's weather in Japan or in the Philippines.[40] For assistance in strikes against Southeast Asia some help came from OSS agents operating behind enemy lines.[41]

Meanwhile, back along the air route from the United States the responsibilities of the Weather Service had been greatly extended as a result of Allied campaigns in North Africa and the Mediterranean. The transfer of the weather service from the Signal Corps to the Air Corps in 1937 had made the latter organization the Army's primary agent in all matters relating to weather intelligence. In other words, the Air Corps was obligated to provide such services as other arms might require of it. Actually, little thought was given to the problem until late summer 1942, when the impending invasion of North Africa naturally tended to raise the question. Alert to the possibility that the ground and service forces might develop independent services of their own in the absence of forehanded action by the AAF, General Arnold urged that the Director of Weather give immediate attention to the problem.[42] There soon came from the War Department General Staff a proposal for a unified national weather service to be established at the Joint Chiefs' level—one that would combine the services of the Army, Navy, and Weather Bureau in one organization fully equipped to meet all needs, including studies pertinent to general military planning. The discussion continued into the winter but ended with a decision which left existing arrangements basically unchanged.* Thereafter, as before, the AAF Weather Service developed an organization existing primarily for the support of air operations, but now it had a new sense of its obligations to sister services.[43] In the United States the AAF Weather Service intensified its efforts to advertise among ground and service organizations the assistance it was equipped to give. It also gave new thought to the services it might render.

The general pattern that would be followed in combat theaters was foretold by developments in North Africa. The 12th Weather Squadron, some of its components shipped out from the United States and others purloined from personnel in the United Kingdom, was assigned to the Twelfth Air Force. Thus the squadron commander, who also

---

* The subject was more than once revived thereafter, as in a proposal of 1943 to use surplus meteorological officers in the AAF for the staffing of a separate organization for the ground and service forces. See above, p. 315.

served as regional control officer, became weather officer for the ranking air commander in the theater, through whom the theater commander could easily secure such assistance as he might require for his operations. The demands at first were not too heavy. They increased as plans were drafted for amphibious assaults on Sicily and Italy in 1943, but the work of the Weather Service continued to be overwhelmingly concerned with air operations. As personnel became available, weather officers were assigned at each echelon down to the combat group level. After the Axis forces had been cleared out of North Africa, responsibility for weather service to an increasing air transport activity through the region fell also on the 12th Squadron. Eventually, in August 1944, the 12th moved its headquarters forward to Caserta in Italy, and a newly created 13th Squadron took over at Algiers with responsibility for Northwest Africa. In time, it too moved forward, leaving to the 19th Squadron, with headquarters now at Cairo, full responsibility for Africa and the Middle East.[44]

Experience soon had demonstrated that the concept of fixed weather stations, borrowed from the practice within the United States, was ill suited to the fluid conditions of a combat theater such as was Northwest Africa. After weather stations operating close to the fighting front had come close to being overrun by momentarily successful enemy forces during the first winter, the need for mobility was impressed upon authorities both in the theater and at home. Later extremely mobile unit equipment was provided for squadrons supporting tactical operations.[45] The establishment of the Fifteenth Air Force late in 1943, for collaboration with the Eighth Air Force in fulfilling the objectives of the Combined Bomber Offensive, brought new responsibilities and a need for closer liaison with weather services in the British Isles. The normal assistance of the weather squadron was supplemented after November 1943 by the establishment of a special weather reconnaissance detachment of six P-38 pilots and twenty-two enlisted men who operated under the immediate direction of the weather officer of the Fifteenth Air Force. Its duty was to send weather planes ahead of the bombers for a final check on weather over the target which might result either in cancellation of a planned mission or diversion to alternate targets.[46] However great the progress of weather forecasting, the science was not yet perfected.

The experience gained in North Africa and the Mediterranean was turned to good advantage in preparations for the climactic invasion of western Europe. Meantime, the 18th Weather Squadron in Britain had developed an organization adapted to the peculiar requirements of the strategic bombing operations of the Eighth Air Force. Squadron headquarters were located at air force headquarters. Subordinate headquarters were established for each of the three combat divisions, for each combat wing, and for each combat group. Forecasts sent down from the weather central at headquarters were interpreted with reference to local problems of take-off and assembly, but otherwise they remained unchanged.[47] The 18th Squadron also served the needs of ATC at British terminals. In a variety of ways the British continued to assist.

A second weather squadron, the 21st, was sent to England during the summer of 1943 for assignment to VIII Air Support Command, forerunner of the Ninth Air Force soon to be established for direct support of the coming invasion of Europe. It was a fully mobile outfit, equipped and trained for movement with the army across the Channel and into Germany. Its commander became the weather officer for the Ninth Air Force on its activation in October.[48] After the establishment in January 1944 of USSTAF, a joint headquarters through which General Spaatz exercised operational control of the strategic bombing of the Eighth and Fifteenth Air Forces and administrative control over the Eighth and Ninth Air Forces, the office of Director of Weather Services was created in February at that headquarters. In the following March General Eisenhower assigned to USSTAF the responsibility for providing and co-ordinating weather services for all U.S. forces in the European Theater of Operations. In the preparation of forecasts that would control the timing of the assault in Normandy, the new office shared responsibility with the weather centrals of the British Admiralty and of the RAF.[49]

After the invasion had been mounted, several adjustments of organization gave needed flexibility to a service in which one part, still basically the old 18th Squadron, remained in Britain to serve from its fixed stations the heavy bombers of the Eighth Air Force while the other moved onto the Continent in close support of the tactical forces of the Ninth Air Force. There were now no serious shortages. The experience of three years of war had taught its lessons. Performance was good.

Operations—Pacific

When the Japanese attacked Pearl Harbor, the recently activated 7th Weather Squadron in Hawaii had four weather stations in operation—located at Hickam and Wheeler Fields on Oahu, at Homestead Field on Molokai, and at the newly developed air base on Christmas Island.[50] In the effort to extend the South Pacific air route southwestward to Australia and then to the Philippines, which currently was the highest priority project affecting Pacific air operations, help could be expected from the national weather services of New Zealand and Australia. What could be expected, it soon became all too apparent, of the 5th Weather Squadron in the Philippines was highly problematical.

By summer 1942 detachments of the 7th Squadron had been located at key points along the route leading down from Hawaii to the Southwest Pacific. A joint weather central had been established at Noumea in New Caledonia through co-operation of New Zealand, the U.S. Navy, and the AAF.[51] In Australia, to which General MacArthur had transferred his headquarters after the fall of the Philippines, arrangements were being made for an Allied Air Force Meteorological Service. For the moment the heaviest responsibilities fell upon the Australian Meteorological Service and the RAAF Meteorological Service. A handful of AAF weather personnel had found their way to the new theater, and a 15th Weather Squadron had been activated for assignment to the Southwest Pacific in the preceding April, but this unit did not reach its station until mid-August. Assigned to the Fifth Air Force with headquarters at Brisbane, its commander became regional control officer and staff weather officer for Maj. Gen. George C. Kenney, MacArthur's newly arrived air commander. Its activities were closely co-ordinated with those of the RAAF weather service to avoid unnecessary duplication, but in practice and by agreement the 15th Squadron concentrated its efforts on meeting the peculiar needs of the Fifth Air Force, U.S. component of the Allied Air Forces.[52]

For the South Pacific, where the First Division of the U.S. Marine Corps had begun the arduous campaign for the Solomons in August, a 17th Weather Squadron was activated in September 1942. Personnel of the 7th Squadron already on duty along the South Pacific air route were transferred to the new squadron, but not until December was the 17th fully in place with headquarters at Noumea. The squadron was assigned to Maj. Gen. Millard Harmon, an airman commanding U.S. Army Forces in the South Pacific.[53] As in Australia, there was close collaboration among the Allies and between the American services in the accumulation of weather data—through reports from ships at sea, aircraft in flight, coast watchers behind enemy lines, and trained observers posted at strategic spots. To this joint effort the 17th Squadron contributed its share, but its primary obligation was to function as a source of weather intelligence for the flyers of the newly created Thirteenth Air Force and for ATC and tactical planes on their way through the area.

It was difficult to get enough equipment, and manpower shortages continued for a time to be embarrassing. Nearly all newly arrived weather personnel required from a few days to six weeks of additional training in subject matter that ranged from the basic principles of weather to studies in tropical weather analysis, route forecasts, and the briefing of aircrews.[54]

Across the Pacific in Alaska the attack on Pearl Harbor brought new concern for approaches to the North American continent that lay uncomfortably close to Japan itself. The Air Corps had maintained a weather detachment at Ladd Field, Fairbanks, since 1940 and had added installations at Anchorage, Yakutat, and on Annette Island. Within three months after the beginning of war, new stations were established at Nome, Northway, Naknek, Fort Randall, and on Umnak Island, farthest west of all stations before the Japanese attack on Dutch Harbor in June 1942. With Japanese forces occupying Attu and Kiska out along the Aleutian chain, U.S. forces occupied Adak late in the summer and opened there a weather station in October. Early in 1943 the line had been pushed out to Amchitka, whence it was extended by the end of the summer to Attu and Kiska, from which the Japanese withdrew in advance of landings by U.S. assault forces in August 1943.[55]

Weather in the Alaskan area had a threefold importance for the war effort. First, it affected, and often disastrously, air and other operations in that area. Despite the heroic efforts of weather personnel and close co-operation among representatives of the AAF, the Navy, the CAA, and the U.S. Weather Bureau, no great success was achieved in overcoming the natural disadvantages of the area for combat air operations. Indeed, as has been recorded elsewhere in this history, it was the weather which perhaps in the last analysis ultimately "relegated the Alaska-Aleutians area to the place of a relatively inactive theater."* But it was not alone for the sake of local operations that the weather services of the 11th Region were performed. The fuller information made available for this area was pertinent to a better understanding of weather conditions over much of the North American continent and of the Pacific. And no less important was the assistance rendered in keeping open a vital air supply line to our Russian allies.† In this last task, the 11th Squadron shared responsibility with the 16th Weather Squadron established in August 1942 for a region that embraced the Pacific Northwest, both of the U.S. and of Canada.[56] The men who thus helped to keep this line open endured hardships very similar to those experienced by weather personnel serving in the North Atlantic.‡

Until the launching in 1943 of the Navy-directed offensive in the central Pacific and of MacArthur's victorious drive along the New Guinea coast, arrangements for AAF weather services in the Pacific followed more or less conventional patterns. Weather stations tended to be of the "fixed" variety, and, despite close co-operation with other services in the operation of joint weather centrals, AAF units attended to the needs primarily of their own forces. When the battleline began to move northward, new requirements for mobility appeared. Fifth Air Force sought and secured enlargement of manning and equipment tables to provide for additional detachments needed in the forward movement of MacArthur's island-hopping campaign. The 7th Region sent forward into the Gilberts and the Carolines mobile ("packaged") weather units equipped to follow the assault forces ashore and to provide almost immediate service at any captured airfield. Enlarged geographical areas of responsibility, together with the need for adjustment to changing command arrangements, gave utility to the organization of provisional group headquarters for administrative control of weather units. Thus, in the summer of 1944, Army Air Force, Pacific Ocean Areas (AAFPOA), the superior headquarters established for all Army units operating in the central Pacific, created a provisional group with jurisdiction over the 7th and 17th

---

* See Vol. IV, 363. † See above, pp. 165–70.

‡ The men put on station at St. Mathews Island in the Bering Sea in September 1943 for observation of ice conditions and air masses from Siberia saw no one from the outside until May 1944.

Weather Squadrons. The Thirteenth Air Force having now moved forward from the Solomons into the Southwest Pacific and having been teamed with the Fifth Air Force under the Far East Air Forces (FEAF), Kenney also resorted to a provisional group for administrative control of the 15th Squadron and a newly assigned 20th Weather Squadron.[57]

In the Pacific, as in Europe, combat commanders found it necessary to supplement normal weather services with special reconnaissance flights to determine more exactly weather conditions over specific target areas. This need had not been wholly unanticipated, especially for an area in which the enemy's initial victories had closed off to normal reporting a vast and important segment of the globe. As early as November 1941 it had been proposed at AAF Headquarters that several weather reconnaissance squadrons be organized with special equipment and manning tables to include trained weather observers. Finally, in August 1942 a test squadron was established at Patterson Field, Ohio, but the experiment failed to develop into a coherent program.[58] Instead, requests from theater commanders for assignment of weather squadrons were met with the suggestion that they establish for themselves such services as were needed on the assurance that AAF Headquarters would assist in getting the planes desired. The Fifteenth Air Force used P-38's. The Eighth at one time equipped a unit with Mosquitoes for service primarily as "pathfinders" through the uncertain weather of western Europe. Elsewhere any plane that was available and had the necessary range might be pressed into service, and often weather reconnaissance might become an additional duty for regular reconnaissance services. Thus weather reconnaissance usually served the immediate and specific ends of determining the weather over target, or the route that was open to target, rather than the more general purpose, as originally planned, of increasing the information available for study and forecast of weather in a large geographical area.

Only in two instances did services comparable to those originally considered develop. In 1943 the test squadron at Patterson Field was equipped with B-25's and was later redesignated the 1st Weather Reconnaissance Squadron Air Route (Medium), for service with ATC along the North and South Atlantic air routes. In time, experience demonstrated, as previously noted,* that area reconnaissance paid

* See above, p. 323.

the higher dividends. The 3d Weather Reconnaissance Squadron (Heavy) began operations for ATC early in 1945, with one flight taking over the heavy bombers already assigned to weather missions in the North Atlantic and another flying off the northwest coast of the United States.[59]

In the end, the AAF added two more weather reconnaissance squadrons, both of them assigned to theaters in which the B-29 was deployed. The 2d WRS, activated early in 1944, was sent to CBI, where its planes served XX Bomber Command and the Fourteenth Air Force in China and Eastern Air Command in Burma. The fourth weather recco squadron, the 655th Bombardment Squadron (H), went to the aid of XXI Bomber Command, whose B-29's on Saipan and Guam in late 1944 took over from XX Bomber Command the task of bombarding the Japanese homeland. Activated in August 1944 and fully in place by the following spring with an advanced echelon on Iwo Jima, the unit was redesignated the 55th Reconnaissance Squadron (VLR), Weather, in June 1945.[60]

The 7th and 17th Weather Squadrons had been consolidated in the preceding November, a move which left the augmented 7th Squadron with full responsibility throughout POA. This squadron, in turn, had been deactivated in February 1945, its personnel and equipment being assigned to the newly formed AAF Weather Services, POA. Its responsibilities covered a wide range of activities: a continuing service for transient planes along old and newly developed air routes, assistance for tactical planes operating against bypassed enemy garrisons in the Solomons and the Gilberts or flying against such newer targets as Truk and Iwo Jima, and participation in the operation of the joint weather central on Guam.[61] But the heaviest obligation was to the B-29's, whose strikes against Japanese targets carried them into one of the more turbulent weather regions of the world. Some assistance in predicting the weather over the northwest Pacific came now from China* and from Russia, although Russian reports were usually so delayed as to be of limited value.[62] Help came also from the increasing number of U.S. Navy vessels operating close in to the Chinese and Japanese shores. Like air forces in other theaters, however, XXI Bomber Command had to rely finally on air reconnaissance. P-51's, P-61's, B-24's—all these were used, but only the B-29 and its adaptation for reconnaissance purposes, the F-13, had the full reach required.

* See above, p. 325.

As the planes became available, they were used both for regular scheduled weather recco flights and as weather planes flying in advance of the striking forces.

At war's end the organization of weather services in the Pacific was undergoing still another shift. This time plans called for a single service for the entire Pacific area and its assignment to the Pacific command that would direct the climactic invasion of Japan. Fortunately, that invasion became unnecessary, and the assignment was made instead to the newly independent AAF Weather Services.

Technical and Other Problems

The AAF Weather Service contributed significantly to an extraordinary growth of meteorological science during the war years. It is often difficult, however, to separate the AAF's contribution to this growth from that made by other agencies, especially those belonging to the U.S. Weather Bureau and to the U.S. Navy. Collaboration among these three services was particularly close in the area of experimental research. Close relations were also maintained by each of them, often on a joint basis, with university research centers, from whose staffs many of the key men in the government services had been temporarily borrowed. An exchange of experience came naturally among the relatively small number of leaders who were expert in the field, and the pressure of wartime demands added its own encouragement to this practice.

In general, the AAF Weather Service may be described as primarily a "user"—that is to say, its energies were very largely absorbed in the organization, training, and equipping of weather units to meet the peculiar needs of its own combat and transport forces. For necessary development and improvement of meteorological equipment, it looked throughout the war years to the Signal Corps, with which a close liaison was maintained in the office of the Chief Signal Officer at Fort Monmouth, New Jersey. To this office the AAF specified its requirements. Research thus initiated was centered, with rare exceptions, in the Meteorological Branch, Eatontown Signal Laboratory, of the Signal Corps. Service and field tests were supervised by the AAF Board at the Eglin Field Proving Ground and at the AAF Tactical Center at Orlando, Florida, where all testing was eventually centered with the heaviest responsibility assigned to the 26th Weather Squadron. Acceptance of an item by the AAF still left to the Signal Corps full responsibility for its procurement or production in the quantity desired. Throughout the war approximately 90 per cent of the meteorological projects undertaken by the Signal Corps were initiated at the request of the AAF.[63] Under this arrangement, the AAF's contribution to technological achievement depended very largely on the sharpness with which it defined its problems and the effectiveness with which it passed on to the laboratory the field experience of the user.

This is a role that in the modern age of technology is by no means to be despised, and in return for what it borrowed in the way of aid from other services the AAF had much to offer. Here and there it initiated research programs of its own, some of them involving no doubt a certain duplication of the efforts made by other services, but some of them also contributing to the solution of problems common to all the services. More important, the AAF's far-flung weather stations extended systematic reporting into many regions hitherto uncovered or but imperfectly covered, with results of great benefit to all who were concerned with the problems of forecasting. Its weather reconnaissance missions supplemented available data with reports from regions in which no fixed station could be established. As the operator of the world's most extensive and elaborate system of airways, and with a dozen combat air forces in daily need of accurate weather data, the AAF's records provided a valuable check on the several techniques tested for forecasting. Especially helpful were the data made available on long-range forecasts. AAF pilots, as did Navy pilots, pioneered in the use of special radar equipment for the penetration and observation of storms which had always been a principal hazard to flying. AAF planes patrolling the Caribbean gave timely hurricane warnings for civilian as well as military agencies and tracked the hurricanes so closely that ATC soon turned the disturbances to advantage by plotting courses for its transports that offered the help of tail winds resulting from the storms.[64]

The risk from storms presented an especially important problem in many areas through which the AAF was forced to fly long missions both of transport and of combat. In addition to the help that came from an increasing reliance upon regular area reconnaissance flights, assistance was had from self-contained automatic stations put down in remote regions. Radar, sensitive to electrical discharges and other convective disturbances within a storm, made it possible late in the war to locate and plot the course of storms many miles away from the points of observation. A three-station network, with stations in New Jersey, Bermuda, and Florida, was in operation by June 1944. In May 1945 a "sferics" network was also established for round-the-clock operations in the central Pacific.[65] Still another adaptation of radar that proved especially helpful to air operations was the rawinsonde which made possible the measurement of wind velocity and direction at high altitudes without the necessity for optical tracking heretofore required.[66]

An administrative and operational problem that frequently intruded its questions into the development of the AAF Weather Service was one of communications. The value of weather reports depended so heavily upon their freshness, and upon the completeness of their coverage, that any weather service necessarily depended for its effectiveness upon an elaborate communications network. The channels of communication for the collection and dissemination of weather intelligence were varied and included those under civilian as well as military control, but the Weather Service's dependence on the Army Airways Communication System was especially heavy. AAF policy forbade the development of a competing system and assigned to AACS full responsibility for the transmission of weather communications. The division of responsibilities, however, could not be quite so neat as this policy dictated. Special requirements, as in the extension of facilities into regions where there was no other demand for service or in experiments with facsimile transmission of weather reports, encouraged development of independent communications facilities. Here and there, among other places in India, strong sentiment in favor of having the Weather Service operate its own communications system developed. But this sentiment was overruled at headquarters, in Asheville as well as in Washington. A Communications Facilities Section of the Weather Service was kept busy in the continuing effort to see that communications needs were met and to maintain the necessary liaison with other agencies.[67]

The problem of communications became the more difficult because of the need for adequate security in the transmission of weather reports. The public release of weather information by commercial radio stations and in the press was promptly discontinued after the Pearl Harbor attack, but it took time to work out the details of an effective security policy. AAF Regulation 105-1, issued 6 March 1942, directed that all data pertaining to weather less than seven days old be classified as confidential and that dissemination of information on the weather be limited to members of the armed forces or their representatives. No weather reports or forecasts were to be broadcast or transmitted after 19 March, except in emergencies endangering life or property. Control towers, AACS radio stations, and aircraft in flight were to transmit weather data only in code.[68]

After fears of enemy attack on U.S. cities had subsided,* policy was further clarified in AAF Regulation 105-1, issued 18 September 1943. Domestic weather information was classified as restricted or above, according to its character, and that originating outside the United States was classified in accordance with current directives of the War and Navy Departments. Displays of information in weather stations were to be adequate for operational needs but accessible only to authorized personnel. Control towers and AACS radio stations were to transmit only in prescribed forms, using appropriate scrambles. Aircraft in flight were to disclose weather information by radio only on specific orders of competent authority and when using a cipher approved by the War Department. These restrictions could be relaxed in cases of emergency, but only to the extent necessary to protect life and the aircraft involved. The Weather Bureau and the CAA would provide weather information to military pilots on non-military airdromes upon presentation of proper identification.[69] In the following November the Office of Censorship authorized the release within the United States of local weather information on the condition that there be no mention of ceiling, visibility, wind direction, or barometric pressure.

The inherently difficult problem of weather security was further complicated by its international character, particularly along North Atlantic routes and in adjacent parts of the United States and Canada. Because the United Kingdom was within range of German bombers, the British were determined that the enemy should not get from them the slightest hint as to weather moving eastward across the Atlantic. They insisted that the need for weather data should take precedence over security only in real emergencies. AAF spokesmen took a directly opposite stand. They contended that it was better to take such risks than to deprive friendly forces of needed intelligence on weather conditions. Both the Army and the Weather Bureau maintained that the need for weather security decreased as Allied forces gained air and

* See Vol. VI, 112–16.

ground superiority. But only after 6 May 1945 were weather reports from all of northwestern Euope, except the coastal areas, broadcast in the clear.[70]

Elsewhere, too, authorities showed little hurry to lift wartime weather security restrictions. Weather security in the Caribbean area, in Mexico, and in South America was relaxed in the fall of 1943, but the Canadian government, in conformity with British policy, continued to enforce rigid restrictions east of the 80th meridian. In Alaska, U.S. authorities did not relax regulations until November 1944, and then only partially. The Aleutians remained subject to tight controls, as did, of course, the whole Pacific area until the final surrender of the Japanese in August 1945.[71]

* * * * * * * * * * *

CHAPTER 12

THE ARMY AIRWAYS
COMMUNICATIONS SYSTEM

THE tempo, range, and scale of air operations in World War II greatly multiplied the need for fast and reliable communications. Unified command, centralized flight control, flexibility in the employment of tactical aircraft—all this and much more in the areas of combat operations depended upon an effective system of communications. So, too, did the movement of ferried and transport aircraft along the military airways discussed in preceding chapters, as did the provision of data on which dependable predictions of weather could be made. Radio and wire facilities had literally to circle the globe and at the same time to provide point-to-point, air-to-ground, or ground-to-air communication as the need might dictate. The exchange in some instances required transmission of the human voice; in others, a homing signal for the aid of distraught navigators or the simplified and complex languages of code. Installations might be as complicated as those serving a great city or so simple as to find shelter in a tent, a native hut, or some improvised structure. Whatever the circumstances of the individual unit, it had its place in a larger system that was as vital to air warfare as ammunition or fuel.

The Air Corps had been slow to develop its own system of communications. Having had its beginning as an organization subordinate to the Signal Corps, the Army's air arm continued to depend upon the Signal Corps for communications services even after its own elevation to corps status in 1926. Army aviators had been quick to test the possibilities of air-to-ground and ground-to-air communication opened up by the invention of radio, but not until the 1930's were the technical problems so far overcome as to make radio standard equipment on all Army planes. Indeed, the difficulty experienced in developing an effective shield against interference from the engine, the size and weight of early radio equipment, and the additional risk of fire arising from the wiring of the first sets had engendered some hostility on the part of pilots to the use of radio. It had not been uncommon for them to escape an assumed risk simply by "losing" the equipment, but this attitude was short-lived. As the Aeronautics Branch of the Department of Commerce, established under the provisions of the Air Commerce Act of 1926, developed a modern system of airways throughout the United States, the navigational and other aids provided along charted routes became a standard dependence of military as of other aviation.[1]

Army Airways

Although the civil airways were of great aid to the Air Corps, they had been developed primarily for the assistance of commercial aviation. They served chiefly to link the main cities, whereas many of the Army's airfields were scattered, for strategic and other reasons, at points somewhat remote from the heavier concentrations of population. A flight of ten B-10 bombers, under the command of Lt. Col. Henry H. Arnold, from Bolling Field to Alaska and return in 1934 served to focus attention on the Army's need for airways routed according to the special requirements of national defense.[2] The flight also demonstrated the dependability of recently developed radio equipment, with results affecting the attitude at all levels within the Air Corps toward the whole problem of communications. As the facility and safety of Air Corps operations came increasingly to depend upon the most modern methods of communication, Air Corps leaders experienced a growing dissatisfaction with existing arrangements.

Those arrangements placed the primary responsibility for air communications on local air-base commanders, who usually were required to route all communications between bases through normal Army channels. With the increasing speed of aircraft, it was not uncommon for a plane or flight moving from one base to another to reach its destination in advance of the message advising that it was on the way. In 1934, after his flight to Alaska, Arnold advocated the establishment of a separate Army communications system for the exclusive use of military aircraft. Such a system should provide alerted point-to-point communications for the transmission of flight plans and operating orders, and one or more of its stations should be able at any time to establish radio contact with aircraft in flight. The network would disseminate weather information to interested parties and exercise traffic control over all arrivals and departures at military airfields. A subcommittee of the Air Corps Technical Committee having reviewed the proposal in 1937, on 15 November 1938 the Army Airways Communications System (AACS) was established.[3]

AACS was charged with "the operation of all fixed Air Corps radio facilities installed for the purpose of facilitating air traffic between Army Flying Fields in the Continental United States."[4] In order to assure centralized control, the system was placed under the immediate direction of the Chief of the Air Corps. The United States was divided into three communications regions, with headquarters located as follows: the 1st at March Field, California; the 2d at Langley Field, Virginia; and the 3d at Barksdale Field, Louisiana. To each of these regions one of three newly created communications squadrons was assigned. The procurement and installation of communications equipment remained a responsibility of the Chief Signal Officer. Base commanders continued to be responsible for housekeeping, discipline, and administrative control over AACS personnel, but the traditional authority of the base commander was now definitely limited in the interest of a centralized direction of operations throughout the system. Air-ground and ground-air contacts, point-to-point messages relating to the movement of aircraft, control of military air traffic, and the provision of navigational aids—all these came within the province of the new system.

At headquarters in Washington there had been a staff office for advice on communications questions since 1920. In 1938 the responsibility belonged to the Communications Section of the Training and Operations Division, and on that section fell the burden of inaugurating the new system. A control officer was assigned to each of the three regional commands. As commanding officer of the region's communications squadron, to which communications personnel within the region were assigned, he exercised operational control over the several detachments stationed at Air Corps bases falling within his jurisdiction.[5] The transition was marked by some misunderstanding and not a little difficulty. But by 1940, when the expansion of the Air Corps was moving into high gear, the Army's air arm had made a beginning toward the development of a unified system of communications. In a rearrangement and reassignment of responsibilities in November of that year, a fourth region and squadron, embracing the southeastern states, was added to the system.[6]

The organization of each region, and of its assigned squadron, remained flexible. With his squadron divided into detachments shaped by the peculiar needs of each station within the region, the regional control officer (RCO) lived at first a very peripatetic life as he sought to give practical meaning to the concept of centralized control over the operations of units which still belonged while off duty to local commanders. If the RCO in the earlier days felt that he could perform his mission only at the risk of a court-martial, it is not surprising. He was usually a junior officer, and even his superiors in Washington lacked the rank that was needed to make the support of headquarters awesome.

The AACS had to keep abreast of technological progress stimulated by the demands of wartime conditions and by inter-Allied co-operation in such an area as that of radar. An organization which first had only to use the telephone, the telegraph, and the radio soon faced a need to master equipment of the most diversified sort in the field of electronics. At the end of the war AACS depended upon the services of four times as many different specialists as at the beginning.[7] It operated control towers, radio ranges, homing beacons, "loran" installations, instrument-approach and ground-control-approach facilities, elaborate message centers, and no less elaborate encoding and decoding equipment for transmission of thousands of messages each day. It monitored the traffic along a world-wide system of military airways. It also helped to collect and then disseminated information regarding the weather in all parts of the world.

Problems of recruitment and training in the early days of AACS were complicated by the need to provide detachments for overseas service. As the AAF extended its commitments outside the United States, domestic stations experienced repeated raids on their more experienced and skilled personnel for the purpose of manning new installations overseas. Indeed, a major function of the original domestic regions soon became that of activating, manning, and training special detachments for service outside the United States.

In the effort to strengthen national defenses in the Caribbean and to facilitate the movement of aircraft along the South Atlantic air route, a total of nine communications stations had been brought into operation by the time of Pearl Harbor.[8] Most of them were manned by AACS detachments. In the North Atlantic, the AACS installation that went on the air at Gander Field, Newfoundland, in March 1941 was charged primarily with the dissemination of weather information, as was that at BLUIE WEST 1, the Greenland station which began operations on 21 August. A second Greenland station, originally intended for weather collection and dissemination only, was established at BLUIE WEST 8, on the island's west coast and almost on the Arctic Circle. During the following November, personnel of the 33d Fighter Squadron installed communications equipment at the Reykjavik Airport, which shortly thereafter had the first AACS station in Iceland. Farther west, the three Crystal stations had been established in Baffinland and northern Quebec,* along the projected Crimson Route from the Middle West to Europe by way of Hudson Bay and Greenland. Weather and communications detachments at these outposts were strategically located to report storms that might threaten more southerly sea and air routes. By December 1941 the new communications system in the North Atlantic reached northeastward from the United States as far as Iceland and included ten stations manned by 70 AACS personnel.[9]

In the meantime, on the other side of the North American continent, small beginnings were being made in the central Pacific and Alaska. There was almost nothing on which to build. Although Pan American Airways operated a passenger service between the United States and the Philippines and had projected a branch line from Hawaii to New Zealand and Australia, its communications facilities were geared to its own limited requirements. The establishment of an Air Corps Detachment, Communications, at Hickam Field, Hawaii, early in 1941, was followed by the extension of military airways communications to other installations in the Hawaiian Islands and by survey flights to the Philippines. In addition, a so-called "Airways radio net" that handled point-to-point communications between airfields in Hawaii was used by the 18th Composite Wing for training in gunnery, navigation, and field work. In the meantime, Army, Navy, and CAA responsibilities for the development of aviation in Alaska were allocated at a conference in the office of General Arnold on 27 July 1940. In accordance with this allocation, the AACS installed com-

* See Vol. I, 345-47.

munications facilities at Ladd Field (Fairbanks) and Elmendorf Field (Anchorage). A minor installation on Annette Island, near Ketchikan, in 1941 began copying weather from CAA and Navy broadcasts. Although the AACS station at Yakutat, a coastal point between Anchorage and Ketchikan, did little more than transmit weather data and flight notices, even those operations were hampered by technical difficulties and a shortage of power-plant equipment.[10]

As the war clouds lowered, the AAF gained many advantages from the highly developed state of commercial communications in the United States. It was possible to recruit from civilian life a sufficient number of experts in telephone and telegraph operation, radio broadcasting, and airline communication to offset in some degree the fact that the peacetime Air Corps had very few officers trained in these fields.[11] Further help came from the readiness of Britain to lend assistance, not only by making available to AAF planes the services of its own installations, but by permitting the Americans to share both the equipment and the experience of British agencies. Early flights into Britain depended wholly upon British communications facilities beyond Iceland, as later would the first AAF combat units to be stationed in the British Isles.

Nevertheless, the AAF had to undertake an expanding training program for communications officers and a large number of technical specialists.* The responsibility for implementing this program fell chiefly upon the AAF Training Command. Altogether, more than 200,000 trainees completed the radio courses given by the Training Command between July 1939 and V-J Day. Considerably smaller, but no less important, was a radar training program which began in the autumn of 1941 and produced by V-J Day more than 85,000 graduates, most of them trained for ground technical duties. The majority of officers receiving radar training were flyers, but many others also qualified for electronics work. Separate crytographic schools, with terms of four weeks, were conducted for officers and enlisted men.[12]

Because of the limited number of experienced civilian radio mechanics, the Air Service Command established a civilian training program that ultimately provided instruction for 10,000 of its employees. The first programs were instituted at Sacramento, beginning in July 1941, and at San Antonio, Middletown, and Fairfield early in 1942.

* See Vol. VI, 637–41.

Eventually, civilian instruction was given on three levels: pre-service training, upgrade training, and supervisor training. In addition, special training for military personnel in the use of recently developed equipment was provided.[13] Even so, experience forced AACS units to depend heavily upon in-service training. Only by training on the job did it prove possible to keep up with the demands of an ever expanding communications system into which new and improved equipment was repeatedly introduced.

Until 1944 the Signal Corps continued to be responsible for the procurement and supply of all air communications equipment. In October of that year and in response to a long-standing demand by AAF leaders, the responsibility for the development, purchase, and storage of all communications and radar equipment peculiar to air operations was transferred from the Signal Corps to the AAF. The change, which involved a procurement program with an average value of one billion dollars per war year, was completed early in 1945.[14]

The traditional concept that the theater commander should have full control over all installations and personnel within the geographical limits of his command governed the early assignments of AACS detachments to stations outside the United States. AACS necessarily retained some control over technical questions and procedures, but it lacked both the organization and the authority necessary to assure the development of a truly unified system of AAF communications. The first step toward achievement of a more effective organization came with the extension overseas of the squadron and region to embrace the detachments stationed in a given geographical area, as with the 6th and 7th Regions established early in 1942 for the Caribbean and the South Pacific, respectively. By the end of 1942 ten overseas regions had been established, each with its own squadron and RCO; in the following May there were seventeen.[15] February 1943 had brought another step toward unified control in the activation of five area headquarters for the North Atlantic, the Caribbean, Africa, the Northwest, and the Pacific.[16] These area headquarters, each having supervision over more than one region, enabled the AACS to achieve a better co-ordination of communications activity in the several regions.

This improvement in organization, however, was not sufficient in itself to overcome the basic difficulty arising from uncertainty as to where the ultimate authority lay. The experience of AACS paralleled very closely that of ATC. In the effort to maintain and improve services along a growing system of world airways, each underwent experiences that argued strongly for centralized control and led to demands for limitations on the prerogative of theater commanders. ATC, a chief customer of AACS, was especially sensitive to this need and, while fighting its own battle for a single system of strategic air routes, lent its support to the demands of AACS. A TAG letter of 9 March 1943 undertook to clarify the problem by reminding all commands that AACS functioned as "the War Department's agency, operated by the Commanding General, Army Air Forces, to facilitate the operations of service aircraft over the military airways."[17] Theater commands were restricted to "local administrative and disciplinary control," and the right of AACS to dispose its personnel and equipment as it saw fit was positively affirmed.

The victory, however, was not yet complete, as was indicated by the shifting fortunes of AACS in the reorganization of the AAF at this time. Since March 1942 AACS headquarters had been in the Directorate of Communications, a suboffice of the Director of Technical Services at AAF Headquarters. With the decision to abandon the system of headquarters directorates and to move all operations into the field, AACS passed to the Communications Wing of the newly created Flight Control Command, a command having jurisdiction only in the Zone of Interior.* During the summer of 1943 assignment of AACS overseas regions to ATC or theater commands seemed to indicate a drastic reversal of the previous trend toward centralization. But this new trend was soon countered by the separation of AACS from the Flight Control Command and reassignment of the Communications Wing to the control of AAF Headquarters. With its own headquarters now located in Asheville, North Carolina, the wing operated as an independent unit under the general supervision of the AC/AS, Operations, Commitments, and Requirements. On 15 May 1944 AACS became an independent activity enjoying the full status of a "command" and having now for the first time a bulk allotment of personnel for assignment to its subordinate units. Simultaneously, the command was reorganized into eight wings with headquarters at Chicago, Casablanca, Anchorage, Calcutta, London, Manchester (New Hampshire), Honolulu, and Miami.[18] The new wings absorbed the former areas and regions and received communications groups which were in turn broken down into squadrons and detach-

* For discussion of AAF organization, see Vol. VI, chap. 2.

ments suited to the needs of the particular geographical areas over which the wings held jurisdiction.

It could hardly be said that this action settled all questions. As with the Air Transport Command, AACS was primarily concerned with the lines of air communication joining the United States to its many and far-flung battle lines. Its airways ran through a variety of commands and theaters in order to reach others, and the terminal points of its services often reached into the more forward areas of combat. A clean-cut settlement of all jurisdictional issues was not to be expected, but to a remarkable extent AACS did represent at the close of war a world-wide airway service. It operated then more than 700 stations located in more than 100 countries and serving more than 100,000 miles of airways. To man these installations and to assure their necessary co-ordination, AACS had a roster of 4,500 officers and enlisted personnel to a number exceeding 45,000.[19]

Across the Atlantic and the Pacific

When war came in December 1941, AACS services across the North Atlantic reached no farther east than Iceland. The link with Britain was not established until July 1942, when, in connection with the air movement of the Eighth Air Force to its British bases, a code room and message center were established at Prestwick, Scotland. The first airdromes taken over by AAF units had RAF communications facilities, which continued to be staffed largely by RAF technical personnel. Wire services for AAF operations were provided by the British General Post Office, in accordance with an agreement between General Arnold and Air Chief Marshal Sir Charles Portal.[20] Not until December 1942 did AAF and British authorities reach agreement on fundamental questions affecting the control of flights between Iceland and the British Isles that opened the way for a full-scale extension of the AACS into Britain.*

Unfamiliar operational problems continued to plague North Atlantic communications, as costly experience proved the ineffectiveness of radio techniques that were satisfactory farther south. Delicate equipment had to be heated before it would function in subzero temperatures. Radio reception was frequently disrupted by aurora borealis, which caused fade-outs for as long as sixteen days at some stations. There was no way of overcoming this quirk of nature until radio

* See above, pp. 95–97.

operators turned to unauthorized low frequencies and found that they worked. Where so much of the earth's surface was covered with solid ice, deep sand, or marshes, the normally simple matter of providing electrical grounds for radio equipment assumed major proportions. Rocky soil and strong winds made it difficult to keep shallow-rooted antenna upright at stations in Greenland and Iceland. Under such primitive conditions, common throughout the North, the breakage rate for all types of equipment was abnormally high.[21]

Service at isolated northern outposts was hard on personnel no less than on equipment. In winter, the men lived in a monotonous world of ice and desolation, where gales drifted snow in average temperatures of 50 degrees below zero. From early autumn, when the northern ice forced the last ship to retreat to civilization, until the thaws of late spring permitted the first vessel to return, the men saw no living thing except their dogs and perhaps a few Eskimos. The prefabricated wooden buildings, used in almost all stations until replaced by Nissen huts, were too light to give adequate protection from the wind and cold. A generally low level of radio discipline was aggravated, no doubt, by the discomfort, loneliness, and sheer boredom of operators and aircrews. In any case, the limited circuits were often overloaded with aimless chatter between operators or with needless, and poorly worded or overclassified, messages. During a single night in July 1942, eleven "urgent" messages were filed at BW-1 for transmission to Goose Bay, although "nothing short of the melting of the Greenland Ice Cap," as one observer put it, could have justified that number.[22]

Some confusion also grew out of Anglo-American disagreement as to communications security in the North Atlantic. The British insisted on the use of a complex code, in keeping with the principle that it was better to lose an occasional aircraft than to endanger the weather security of the entire United Kingdom. By contrast, the American position was that security measures should never be so complicated that they hampered operations and that the complexity of codes should be determined by the ability of personnel to use them. Much coded weather was regarded as useless, or even misleading, to those for whose benefit it was processed. Conditions improved somewhat with better training and supervision of operators and the installation of additional equipment.[23]

While these northern airways from the American arsenal to the

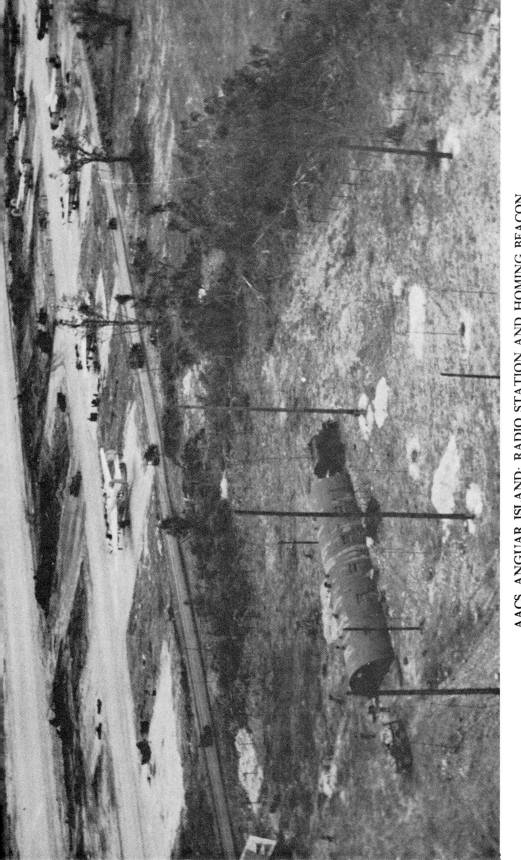

AACS, ANGUAR ISLAND: RADIO STATION AND HOMING BEACON

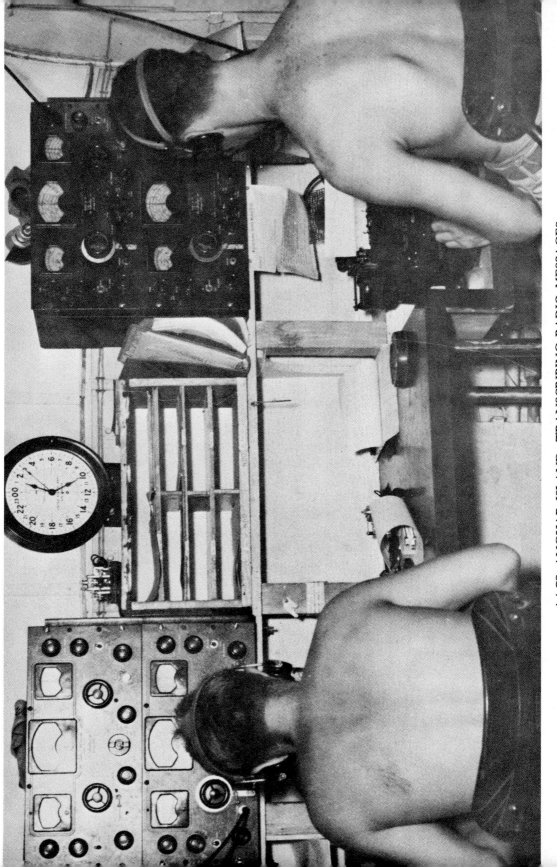

AACS, ANGUAR ISLAND: TRANSCRIBING RADIO MESSAGES

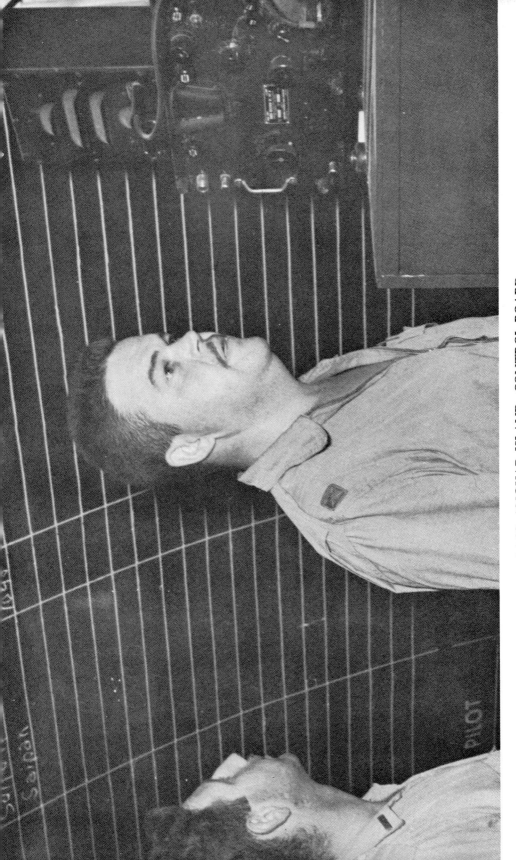

AACS, ANGUAR ISLAND: CONTROL BOARD

AACS CONTROL TOWER, MYITKYINA, BURMA

British Isles were being developed, another was being pushed across the South Atlantic from Natal, near the tip of the Brazilian bulge, where the first AACS installation was established in May 1942. The first United States air communications detachment to serve in Africa arrived at Accra, on the Gold Coast, in June, to take over from Pan American Airways the operation of radio facilities along the African segment of an air route to the Middle East and India. Nearly all the stations were poorly equipped, and the coming of military personnel did not result in any notable immediate improvement. Part of the meager communications resources in Africa had to be diverted to support a more southern route being developed through Pointe Noire, Leopoldville, Elisabethville, and Nairobi, against the chance that Axis victories might make the more direct airway untenable. With new demands on men and equipment resulting from the Allied invasion of North Africa in November 1942, several months were required to bring services across Africa to the Middle East up to desired standards.[24]

Fortunately, British facilities in the Middle East could be counted upon to supplement those that could be made available by the United States. An American detachment of four enlisted men had been established at Abadan in Iran as early as May 1942 for assistance of the Douglas Aircraft Corporation in the assembly and delivery of lend-lease planes to Russia. But not until the early months of 1943 did it prove possible for the AAF to develop in the Middle East communications that were adequate for its expanding needs.[25] In India, too, only the very substantial aid of our British allies had made it possible for the Tenth Air Force to establish a rudimentary communications net linking Karachi and other points on the route across India to China. An AACS squadron had been activated at Bolling Field in the spring of 1942 for assignment to the Tenth Air Force, but that squadron and its equipment did not reach India until the following fall. Under the leadership of Maj. Walter B. Berg, who had been Arnold's crew chief on the 1934 flight to Alaska, the 10th Squadron worked to perfect a communications net having its chief focal points at Karachi, Chabua, and Kunming—along the air route joining the Middle East and China. With an increase in personnel that permitted the 10th Squadron to release all but a few of the men on loan from the British by the spring of 1943, with assignment at that time of the squadron to AACS, with the activation of a 25th Squadron in the summer to have charge of a new region extending from Chabua into China and southward in Burma, and with the establishment of an Asiatic Airways Communications Area in the fall of 1943, a co-ordinated line of communications now reached all the way from Miami across the Atlantic, Africa, the Middle East, and India into China.[26]

Radio communication between the Asiatic mainland and the Southwest Pacific gave some reality to the concept of a world-encircling system of communications. But the story of the development of the airways across the Pacific is actually separate and somewhat different from that already recounted. The first major extension of airways communications facilities in the Pacific after December 1941 was directed toward completion of an air supply line to the South Pacific and Australia. Four principal island stations—on Christmas, Canton, Nandi, and New Caledonia—were established by the summer of 1942. At the end of that year, AAF communications services had been extended into Australia. The first two of the long chain of AACS stations that eventually reached northward from Australia toward Japan were established at Port Moresby and Milne Bay, New Guinea, early in 1943.[27]

In the meantime, needs much farther north were demanding the attention of high-level military planners. The vulnerability of American naval outposts in the Pacific gave added urgency to the early strengthening of air defenses in the Aleutians and along the Gulf of Alaska. Six months after the outbreak of hostilities, which is to say at the time of Japan's invasion of the Aleutians, AACS still had only nine stations in Alaska, manned by fewer than eighty officers and men. Part of their radio equipment had been procured from "ham" operators and from stations of the CAA, the Bureau of Indian Affairs, or civilian airlines. Under such circumstances, standardization of operating and maintenance procedures was hardly feasible. Here, as in the North Atlantic, radio fade-outs were common, and extremely low temperatures played havoc with sensitive instruments. Notoriously unreliable weather conditions and almost complete lack of satisfactory charts made it necessary to provide on-the-spot guidance of aircraft in flight over western Alaska and the Aleutians. Nowhere in Alaska was there an adequate aircraft warning system, and the two radar sets in the territory offered far from satisfactory protection. For that reason, both AACS and the Navy established radar beacons to support the air offensive against Kiska and Attu and later the bombing of the Kurile Islands. Beginning in November 1943, the AACS station at Amchitka transmitted weather data intercepted from Chungking, China, thus greatly lengthening the period for which it was feasible to make weather forecasts in the North Pacific.[28]

In a region where each user of communications had such meager facilities, co-operation became a necessity. In August 1942, therefore, a joint communications board was established to pool CAA, PAA-Navy, and AACS facilities and to co-ordinate plans for future expansion. Although AAF Headquarters two months later directed AACS to supervise and control CAA facilities in Alaska, duplication of activities continued to be serious, especially along the coastal route east of Anchorage. This airway was used by the United States Navy and Coast Guard and by the Royal Canadian Air Force as well as by several AAF agencies. In order to prevent utter confusion, these users formulated a standard procedure for clearance and control of air traffic and incorporated it in the original joint Army-Navy-Canadian agreement. However, the large number of military agencies operating in Alaska and western Canada delayed a clear-cut definition of responsibilities until after the formation of a Joint Army-Navy-Alaskan Aircraft Control Committee late in 1943.[29]

The first wartime communications along the air route to Alaska by way of Edmonton and Whitehorse were provided under Army contract by Northwest Airlines, the company that had pioneered the route as a civilian airway. But, when tactical units and Canadian forces also used the route, misunderstandings resulted from the different procedures followed by the Canadian authorities, the contract carrier, and AACS personnel. To end the confusion, the Canadian government insisted that the entire transport and ferrying operation through Canada be militarized. As a result, Northwest Airlines gave up its communications facilities, but only after strong pressure was exerted by the Alaskan Division of the Air Transport Command. With the building of the Alaskan Highway, stations along the northwest route were linked to the United States by land teletype. The line reached Whitehorse in June 1943, and Fairbanks four months later, but the circuit was often out of commission because of wire breakage, lack of spare parts, or a shortage of trained personnel.[30] Nevertheless, it relieved the crowded radio channels and improved the systematic collection of weather information in a hitherto neglected part of North America.

Airways to Tokyo

Nowhere were arrangements for communications services more complex than in the Pacific. An early need for hard-pressed Army and Navy units to pool their resources in the face of threatened disaster set a pattern, or lack of pattern, that was perpetuated by the complexity of command arrangements in the Pacific area.

AAF and Navy doctrines differed radically as to the desirable extent of centralization of communications facilities in areas occupied by both services. Because the South Pacific was a Navy theater, all communications personnel and equipment on each island were pooled to form a single signal center that served air, ground, and naval units. The Navy held that the communications responsibilities of the Thirteenth Air Force were limited to its own internal wire facilities and to the operation of radio equipment in its own aircraft. Although aircraft warning and fighter control units were administered by Thirteenth Air Force Headquarters, they were in many cases under the operational control of island commands or other non–Air Force units. Radio facilities for inter-island administrative traffic of the Thirteenth Air Force were furnished by the island commands or, in their absence, by Navy signal centers. The system of communications used in the Southwest Pacific Area, an Army command, was naturally more satisfactory to the AAF. There each headquarters had its own signal center, connected laterally to adjacent headquarters and vertically to higher and lower echelons in the chain of command.[31]

Assignment of communications duties in the Southwest Pacific varied with time and circumstances. Initial responsibility for air communications was at first vested in the tactical units, with the AACS becoming responsible for control towers and most other navigational aids only after installation of more or less permanent facilities. In 1943 this policy was changed to assign such responsibility to AACS immediately upon the capture or completion of an airstrip. For that reason, AACS mobile control-tower teams were formed to serve with tactical forces. In some cases they were not far behind the assault troops who hit the beach or spearheaded an advance. Before the launching of an offensive, the staff communications officers of the co-operating air, ground, and naval forces met in conference to co-ordinate requirements and allocate functions. Initial control of air-ground operations was vested in the Navy if the landing area was beyond the most efficient range of land-based installations. Requests for tactical air support of ground forces during the landing phases of an assault were directed by the naval commander, who either assigned the mission to carrier-based planes or relayed the request to appropriate AAF headquarters. As soon as the assault area was consolidated and airstrips prepared, an air task force assumed responsibility for tactical air operations.[32]

During the early stages of the war, minimum communications requirements were met only because air operations were on a small scale and because communications personnel often worked twelve to sixteen hours a day. But, unfortunately, operators could work at their best only six hours a day for five days a week when the flow of messages was heavy. Many of them became psychiatric cases when pushed beyond their endurance.[33] Some detachments were stationed in isolated places where they had to be self-sufficient. Under such circumstances, control-tower operators, radio operators, radio mechanics, and cryptographic technicians doubled as cooks or carpenters or for the performance of whatever other work had to be done. Some commanders established provisional communications units and placed their members on detached service wherever they were most urgently needed. This makeshift helped get the job done, but it was injurious to morale. Enlisted men sometimes went several months without being paid, and many of them complained that they had missed overdue promotions bcause of absence from their regular units.[34]

Personnel shortages were matched by equipment shortages, and maintenance problems were aggravated by inadequate protection of equipment from the weather. Communications units generally had to make the best of inferior sites and housing, because they had to get on the air as soon as possible and were not prepared to do engineering work. It was not uncommon for radio operators to stand ankle deep in mud while sending important operational messages or for rain water to seep through cracks in the roof and drip on communications equipment and message paper. Such primitive conditions were improved with the arrival of additional personnel and the erection of better buildings at the more important stations, but in out-of-the-way places the period of rugged pioneering continued almost to the end of the war. Non-tropicalized communications equipment broke down at an alarming rate, as fungus coated delicate instruments and salt water rusted metal surfaces. This forced operating personnel to perform higher-echelon maintenance than would have been necessary if normal replacements and repair facilities had been available. Procurement procedures prescribed by higher headquarters were often too slow to meet immediate needs. More than one unit learned that critical equipment might, on occasion, be secured more readily "through the judicious use of a bottle of liquor" than through official requisitions. An official evaluation board reported that "of greatest value in the procurement of spare parts was a good supply sergeant who was friendly with neighboring, invariably well supplied, Navy units." Such informal "borrowing" from other services, and a project system that used available equipment to its maximum effectiveness, made it possible to provide at least minimum communications facilities despite shortages of equipment.[35]

After 1942 the AACS was forced repeatedly to adjust its organization in the Pacific to the demands of several advancing battlefronts. The original detachments stationed in Hawaii and down along the South Pacific chain of air bases had been given regional control by activation on 19 February 1942 of the 7th Army Airways Communications Region, with jurisdiction extending through but not beyond New Caledonia. The region's main task, at first, was to assist in the movement of aircraft down the chain to Australia and in the establishment of air defenses along the newly developing air route. The beginning of the Solomons offensive later in the year brought additional responsibilities. On Christmas Eve 1942 AACS put its first station in the Solomons into operation at Henderson Field. On 21 January 1943, in the same month that saw the activation of the Thirteenth Air Force, the responsibility for the area embracing the Fiji Islands, the New Hebrides, New Caledonia, and the Solomons was assigned to a newly activated 20th AACR. This left the 7th to concentrate on obligations pointing its attention toward the Gilberts, the Marshalls, and, in time, the Marianas. Already, on 11 January 1943, the Pacific Airways Communications Area (PACA) had been activated at Hickam Field for control of the two regions.[36]

The introduction of AACS facilities into Australia, where AAF units falling back from the Philippines and the Netherlands East Indies at first depended heavily upon the communications services that could be provided by the Australians, came more slowly. In late summer 1942 the 5th Army Communications Squadron, originally intended for service in the Philippines, was assigned to Gen. George C. Kenney's Fifth Air Force in Australia. The squadron's job, as subsequently defined, was to provide communications facilities at Brisbane that would establish a proper terminal for the airway reaching across the Pacific from California and to provide standard services for Army planes in Australia, with special attention to the need for linking rear bases with forward airdromes. At Amberley Field, some 30 miles from Brisbane, the first AACS station in Australia went into operation on 5 December 1942, thereby completing a network of airway communications extending from San Francisco through Hawaii and the South Pacific to Brisbane. By the end of February 1943 two stations had been established in the immediate neighborhood of Port Moresby in New Guinea and another southeastward some 250 miles on New Guinea's Papuan coast. The conquest of Buna had also been followed up by efforts resulting in the early opening of additional stations for point-to-point communication, traffic control, and weather reporting at Dobodura and on the islands of Woodlark and Kiriwina. Meanwhile, a beginning had been made in the development of a network of stations in northern and northeastern Australia.[37]

The pattern of activity thus set in the early operations of the South and Southwest Pacific Areas was to be repeated again and again as the Fifth, Thirteenth, and Seventh Air Forces collaborated with ground and naval units to push the Japanese back along the coast of New Guinea, up the island chain of the Solomons, and out of the Gilberts and the Marshalls. Across beach after beach, or in one of the earliest planes to land on hastily prepared or repaired strips, advanced AACS detachments followed on the heels of assaulting forces to establish emergency facilities that would be improved, as the provision of men and equipment permitted, for incorporation into an expanding and increasingly diversified communications network. As the lines of advance in the Solomons and New Guinea converged to set the stage for a climactic assault on the Philippines, and as plans were being perfected in the central Pacific for seizure of the Marianas, AACS adjusted its organization to meet new demands. In keeping with a recent decision in Washington for redesignation of AACS units, the Pacific Airways Communications Area became on 15 May 1944 the 7th AACS Wing with jurisdiction over the 5th, 7th, and 20th Squadrons—now redesignated, respectively, as the 68th, 70th, and 71st AACS Groups.[38] The subdivision of the groups into squadrons, and of squadrons into detachments, gave to the AACS in the Pacific, as elsewhere, a superior structure for the accomplishment of its mission. No less important was the establishment of a common headquarters for the combat zones of the Pacific war.

Biak, Saipan, Guam, Leyte, Luzon, Iwo Jima, Okinawa—all found their way into the history of the 7th Wing, as finally did Tokyo. When news of the Japanese proposal for surrender came, the 7th Wing and more especially the 68th Group received orders to fly into Atsugi Airfield, below Tokyo, the communications equipment and personnel necessary for guidance and reception of the great transports scheduled to "fly in" the first contingent of the occupation troops. AACS's mission was to provide navigational aids, point-to-point communication with Okinawa, air-to-ground communication for planes in flight, weather data, and traffic control. A special unit of hand-picked men was quickly organized, put through a trial exercise at Clark Field near Manila, and flown to Okinawa to await the signal from higher headquarters. On the morning of 28 August 1945 some two dozen C-47's (one of them a fully equipped mobile radio station) flew from Okinawa to Atsugi carrying technical equipment and technicians, many of them belonging to the AACS, for the establishment of an emergency air base in Japan's homeland.[39] And so were men long accustomed to follow combat troops ashore put in a position to welcome combat units as they reached the war's last beachhead.

Before turning from the Pacific to other areas, two communications units intended to reduce duplication of Army and Navy facilities should be noted. One was the Oceanic Air Traffic Center (OATC) established in November 1943 as a clearing-house for flight authorization, information, and control with offices at San Francisco and Hickam Field, Hawaii. Originally concerned only with the movement of aircraft between the mainland and Hawaii, OATC extended its services westward early in 1945. The other was the Joint Airways Communications System, Pacific (JACSPAC). It depended for the most part upon AACS facilities, but it used certain of the Navy's facilities. Both ATC and the Naval Air Transport Service looked to JACSPAC for operational communications, and so were unnecessary duplications avoided.[40]

China-Burma-India

In CBI the 10th AACS Squadron, operating as a unit of the Tenth Air Force, struggled through the winter of 1942–43 to establish communications facilities linking India and China and at the same time to render such assistance as it could to tactical operations in Burma. The squadron was reassigned to AACS in April 1943, and in July its responsibilities were divided with a newly assigned 25th Squadron. The 10th retained responsibility for India and Burma, except for Assam, and the 25th, with headquarters at Chabua, took up the task of providing communications along the famed "Hump" route into China. In the fall, as previously noted, the Asiatic Airways Communications Area (AACA) was introduced as a superior headquarters for the two squadrons.[41] These developments followed a pattern of organization that was becoming familiar throughout AACS at the time. More important is the fact that they also reflected a growing concern at the highest level of command for the assistance of China. The Fourteenth Air Force recently had been activated, and ATC had been given targets for cargo deliveries over the Hump that were staggering by comparison with anything theretofore achieved.*

For the Hump and its defending forces, the 10th Squadron had managed to put into operation nine stations—three on the China side of the Himalayas and six on the India side—of which Chabua in Assam and Kunming in China were the chief, as was the 10th's station at Karachi the chief link joining Chabua with Khartoum and other points along the airways of Africa. To man its stations, the 25th took over from the 10th a complement of 16 officers and 168 enlisted men who often worked on twelve-hour shifts while they waited for reinforcements that would bring strength up to 77 officers and 540 men. The 10th Squadron began its separate operations with another nine stations, of which the one at Delhi, where military headquarters in CBI tended to concentrate, and the one at Karachi, gateway to India, were the chief. With a complement to begin with of 31 officers and 141 enlisted men, the 10th AACS Squadron had many members who also knew, day after day, what a twelve-hour tour of duty meant.[42] When AACA gave way in May 1944 to the 4th AACS Wing, the new wing took charge of more than a hundred and twenty stations.[43] The wing included the 1st Tactical Group, a unit organized specifically for assistance of the B-29's of XX Bomber Command.[44]

More than one of the AACS stations in CBI were now major installations embodying some of the more advanced technical equipment and skill of the society that had placed them "on the other side

* See above, pp. 124–28.

of the world." Some were limited by geographical considerations, by the lack of an adequate source of power, or by the speed of military developments to makeshift facilities that depended ultimately for their effectiveness upon the men who manned them. These were men to whom the G.I. term of "sweating it out" became something quite literal in the climate of India or Assam, men who often knew in China or in Burma the meaning of repeated enemy attacks, and men who experienced the isolation of duty in remote mountain stations or in the jungles of Burma.

Beginning in December 1943 the AACS had undertaken to provide tactical communications in Southeast Asia at the request of the Fourteenth Air Force and other combat units. Its first two stations for that purpose were established in eastern China, to support air operations against Japanese shipping in the China Sea and against enemy troops and supply concentrations in the Changsha area. Other facilities were installed in the Imphal-Kohima region, where enemy ground forces had broken into India and almost reached the railroad from Assam to Bengal. Farther south, stations were established at Bangalore and Ceylon for the support of amphibious operations of the Southeast Asia Command. During the spring of 1944, eight others were set up to assist air and ground forces operating in China, India, and Burma.[45]

In spite of these new and enlarged installations, air communications in eastern and southeastern Asia continued to present a serious problem. The lack of adequately powered radio aids to navigation seriously limited bad-weather operations. Shortages of personnel and equipment to handle point-to-point communications caused overloaded channels and delayed reception of weather and other tactical information at command headquarters. Outdated or inaccurate weather data were especially injurious to air-transport operations and directly affected the air supply of forward bases.[46]

In MTO and ETO

Two AACS squadrons, the 13th and the 14th, were activated on 18 April 1942 for service in Africa. First to leave the United States was the 13th, whose advanced detachment reached Accra in the following June. By November, when the invasion of Northwest Africa occurred, the 26 officers and 261 enlisted men of the 13th Squadron had taken over from Pan American Airways all communications services across Africa to Khartoum. Meanwhile, the 14th

Squadron had directed its attention to the alternate route running eastward along a line south of the Equator—a route then under development but soon to be abandoned.[47]

The invasion of Northwest Africa on 8 November imposed new and especially heavy responsibilities on the men and equipment of both squadrons. An 18th Squadron had been activated in the United States during October for assignment to the Twelfth Air Force in North Africa, but not until the end of the year did it reach its station. In the intervening weeks the men of the 13th and 14th Squadrons had pushed a line of communications facilities northward from Accra and Kano to Bathurst, Dakar, Oran, Casablanca, Marrakech, and Algiers, thus helping to establish a vital link between terminals of the South Atlantic air route and the new battlefront.* Many of the officers and men detached for temporary and emergency duties in the north were destined finally for reassignment to the 18th Squadron. From the 14th Squadron also came much of the strength of a newly activated 19th Squadron, which assumed at the end of the year responsibility for the region extending eastward toward Karachi in India.[48] In March 1943, the Twelfth Air Force having yielded its claim to its own squadron, the 13th, 14th, 18th, and 19th Squadrons came under the control of the newly activated African Airways Communications Area.[49]

The area's components had rendered significant aid to the extension of air transport into a new combat zone while continuing to maintain and strengthen through transport services to the Near and Far East. It had been possible also to provide some assistance for tactical operations, especially in the collection and dissemination of weather intelligence, but not enough to overcome the general dissatisfaction with communications that continued to be expressed throughout the North African campaign.[50] Critical shortages of personnel and equipment were overcome in time, as were other deficiencies attributable to inexperience and to the haste with which the whole North African venture was undertaken. AACS was fortunate in the growing tendency to view its responsibility as something restricted to the maintenance of communications between the front and its rear areas.

After the conquest of Tunisia in May, the invasion of Sicily came next, on 9 July 1943. The 18th Squadron sent its first detachment into Sicily on 4 August, and by 6 September it had two stations in opera-

* See above, pp. 64–65, 72–73.

tion, at Palermo and Catania.[51] From Sicily the next jump was into Italy, where, by the end of 1943, AACS stations had been established at Naples and Bari. Two others were added, one on the island of Sardinia and another on Corsica.[52] By 15 May 1944, when the African Airways Communications Area gave way to the 2d AACS Wing in keeping with a plan for the reorganization and redesignation of units throughout the AACS, the new wing embraced some fifty major installations in Africa, the Middle East, and Italy. Already, area head-quarters had been moved up the coast to Casablanca in order better to meet the growing responsibility for transport traffic now heavily concentrated along North African airways linking the Atlantic routes with the Middle East, Russia, and India.* The more southerly route from Accra to Khartoum had now a declining importance, and by the end of the war its personnel were being transferred to other areas in preparation for the abandonment of what originally had been the special province of the pioneer 13th Squadron.[53]

As the focus of combat operations moved up the Italian boot, the 18th Squadron in March 1944 had been divided for administrative convenience into European and African sectors, each of which re-ceived a separate AACS group in the reorganization that followed in May. The 58th Group in Italy served chiefly to link the combat zone with rear areas in Northwest Africa, and so with transport and ferry routes reaching back across the Atlantic to the United States. Although it provided valued assistance to units participating in the invasion of southern France in the late summer of 1944, the 58th had no direct part to play in that invasion. But, when ATC later found it necessary to extend its services into southern France, the 58th AACS Squadron led the way. At the end of hostilities the 58th Group was transferred to the 5th AACS Wing in Europe.[54]

Although the 5th Wing dated back only to May 1944, some of its components had a history reaching back into 1942, when the first AAF combat units reached the British Isles. These units had found ready at hand an elaborate and extremely modern system of wire, radio, and radar communications for the control of air traffic over the United Kingdom. By agreement with British authorities, the Eighth Air Force adapted its procedures to the existing network and adopted for the most part British communications equipment. Only as AAF forces grew into the mighty armadas of 1944 and 1945,

---

* See above, pp. 86–91.

which is to say only very slowly, did they seek to establish supplementary services of their own.

The first AACS detachment in Britain—two officers and nine enlisted men—reached Prestwick on 1 July 1942 for the purpose of providing such assistance as it could render to the current movement of the Eighth Air Force across the North Atlantic. In the attempt to work out a satisfactory agreement for the provision of American communications services along the last leg of the North Atlantic hop, an agreement was reached with the British in December 1942 that resulted in the establishment by the summer of 1943 of seven AACS stations in Great Britain and three in Northern Ireland.[55] And so the AACS found its primary function in Britain, as in so many other parts of the world, to be that of providing effective terminal communications for transoceanic airways. The first AACS personnel had come to Britain on detached service from units stationed out along the North Atlantic route from Newfoundland to Iceland, but, as their numbers grew, they were reassigned in April 1943 to a newly activated 24th AACS Squadron and Region. At the end of 1943 this squadron had 16 stations, 65 officers, and 481 enlisted men.[56]

Although the 24th had begun to assume responsibility for the operation of ranges and beacons of some importance to combat units, its chief task was still that of monitoring and guiding the AAF traffic which flowed from or into the transatlantic airways, including the one which joined Britain with Northwest Africa. It was a traffic that steadily mounted in volume as the build-up for the coming invasion of Normandy continued through the winter and spring, and on the eve of that invasion AACS became involved in an ill-conceived and none too successful attempt to establish a complete system of traffic control within the British Isles.[57] In Britain to the end of the war, success in the field of communications depended upon acceptance of the idea that U.S. facilities complemented, instead of replacing, the admirable facilities already established by British agencies.

Meantime, the AACS found a proper outlet for its developing ambitions in plans for the invasion of Normandy. The 24th Squadron readily accepted proposals in the fall of 1943 that it organize, equip, and train mobile communications units that would follow the invading forces into Europe and thus prepare the way for assumption by the AACS of responsibility for more or less fixed installations that would help to extend standard airway services into Europe in support of advancing combat forces.[58] The first AACS detachment reached Normandy on 17 June 1944 (D plus 11), the second four days later, both of them going on the air near the St.-Laurent strip.[59] Other detachments followed, especially after the breakout at St.-Lo in July, and by September AACS had reached Paris. Meantime, Detachments G and H, first on the Continent, had moved forward seven times each.[60] At the beginning of spring 1945, AACS counted among its more than twenty-five stations in Belgium and France those at Liége, Reims, Étain, Ablon, Péronne, Lunéville, Lyon, Le Havre, Chartres, Dijon, St.-Germain, and Orly.[61] Early in April the first detachment crossed the German frontier, and others soon followed. In little more than a month the war was over.

In western Europe, as in the Mediterranean and other parts of the world, the job of AACS had been not so much to extend the line of battle as to bring the line of communications leading back to the homeland up to the battle line. It was a job of critical importance to services of supply that depended especially upon air transport, and so does the achievement of the most advanced AACS detachments bear testimony to the need for those units and men who, all along the line, labored to keep the traffic flowing.

SECTION IV

* * * * * * * * * * *

MEDICINE, MORALE, AND AIR-SEA RESCUE

*   *   *   *   *   *   *   *   *   *   *

CHAPTER 13

THE MEDICAL SERVICE
OF THE AAF

THE story of the medical support of the Army Air Forces in World War II has been told elsewhere fully and competently.[1] The present account, by contrast, makes no pretense at detailed coverage but attempts only to emphasize the unique problems that were encountered and the solutions that enabled the air arm to accomplish its war mission. The dominant feature of the program was the clear recognition of the central role of the individual flyer. The majority of line officers, responsible for the expansion of the Air Corps after 1939 and for its transformation into the Army Air Forces, were experienced flyers. During their years of training they had been intimately associated with the small group of medical officers who as pioneer flight surgeons were then creating the discipline of aviation medicine. In addition to a love of flying, these two groups had many common bonds, personal and professional, which were sources of mutual respect and strength. Regardless of how large the AAF became, its commanders rarely forgot that victory depended upon the individual fighter pilot and the small, interdependent aircrew of the bomber or other multiplace aircraft. As important as the machines were, they were obviously useless without the men to fly them courageously and effectively. The principal function of the medical service, therefore, was the care of the flyer.

No attempt will be made here to review what may be called the normal clinical activities of the physician in uniform. The personnel of the AAF benefited from all the advances in medical science that were contemporaneous with World War II: the sulfa drugs, penicillin, and more effective definitive surgery, to name only a few. In this general area the medical service of the AAF adopted two important practices and demonstrated their value well in advance of the medical departments of the Army and Navy. These were the early ambulation of the postsurgical patient and the aggressive physical rehabilitation of the sick and wounded.[2]

These two clinical practices, plus a desire to retain administrative control over personnel who required special procedures in AAF hospitals, precipitated an administrative conflict between the Surgeon General of the Army (SG) and the chief medical officer of the AAF. Other conflicts with the SG concerned the need for a specialized medical service for flying personnel and the command relationship between the line and the medical service. These controversies which were carried on in the upper echelons of the military establishment will be described, briefly, below. It is enough to say at this point that the writer is convinced that the conditions of flying create a number of medical problems sufficiently important and sufficiently unique to justify the specialty career of flight surgeon and the discipline known as aviation medicine.

The Flight Surgeon

The term "flight surgeon" was coined in 1918 to designate those officers of the Medical Corps, United States Army, who had been trained in the Air Service Medical School and assigned to duty with Air Service units.* During the 1930's the rapid mechanical developments of aircraft, the increased knowledge of the physiological consequences of flight and air combat, and the prospects of mobilization resulted in frequent alterations in the type and extent of instruction and experience required for the rating of flight surgeon.[3] After July 1940 the requirements and training were substantially the following: a desire, willingness, and aptitude to practice aviation medicine; an interest in aviation generally and a desire to participate regularly and frequently in aerial flight; graduation from a Class A medical school, followed by at least a one-year rotating internship; and completion of the approximately 300-hour course at the School of Aviation Medicine (SAM).

After graduation from SAM the medical officer qualified for the rating of Aviation Medical Examiner. After a year's duty with the AAF, and after having flown at least 50 hours in military aircraft, he was then eligible—if otherwise qualified—for the designation of flight

* See below, p. 376.

surgeon. The duties of the flight surgeon may be epitomized as follows:[4]

1. To dispense routine medical services, including the management of trau-
matic injuries.
2. To select candidates for flying training, with special emphasis on the oph-
thalmological, cardiovascular, and neuropsychiatric phases of the examination.
3. To provide "care of the flyer," i.e., to study the effect of flight on the
pilot (and aircrewman), act as his confidant and adviser, and also to act as an
intermediary in medical matters between the flyer, his commanding officer, and
higher medical authority.
4. To investigate the effect of flight and seek remedies for those environmental conditions which may have an adverse, or a limiting, influence.

So cursory a description of the prescribed role of the flight surgeon
in military aviation ignores perforce the many ambivalences in the
three-way relationship of the doctor, the flyer, and the commander.
Since most of the difficulties of the medical service were related directly to interpersonal problems, the actualities deserve some consideration.

As scientific investigators, flight surgeons studied exhaustively, and
attempted to quantitate, the physical, physiological, and psychological
stresses of flying. Such research enabled engineers to design equipment (e.g., oxygen-supply systems, instrument-training systems, and
soundproofing) permitting men to fly the machines that were built.
Equally important were the studies of survival in such circumstances
as bail-outs at high altitude and high speed, ditching, air-sea rescue
operations, and the like. Most experiments testing safety devices and
survival procedures were carried out by flight surgeons themselves,
nearly always at great personal hazard. Their willingness to risk their
lives for the benefit of others and their ingenuity in reducing some of
the perils of flight earned for the corps of flight surgeons the universal
respect in which they are held by airmen. In contrast to this was the
threatening aspect of the flight surgeon in the selection process and in
the continuing evaluation which is comprehended by the term "the
care of the flyer." Here conflict was inevitable. On the one hand, the
flyer grounded by the doctor's decision had his career thwarted, his
status altered, and his pay reduced. On the other hand, the doctor's
decision that he was fit to fly could send the combat aviator suffering
from physical illness, anxiety, or fear of flying back to perils that were
only too real or could force him to become insubordinate if he refused
to fly.

At the squadron level the flight surgeon served the commander as personal adviser on the human factors in this small segment of a great weapons system. In this capacity it was his duty to keep as many men fit for flying as possible and to help the airmen under his care to function to the limit of their capacity. At the same time he was expected to be the confidant, adviser, and private physician to the individual flyer whom he was assigned to serve. A balanced discharge of these often mutually antagonistic responsibilities is called the art of aviation medicine. At the squadron (or unit) level, where personal contacts were closest, the art was practiced, in general, fairly well. But each higher echelon also had a flight surgeon, to whom the squadron doctor reported, who served as adviser on human factors to his commander. The senior physician dealt with the disposition of individual cases, with the combat capabilities of the subordinate commands, and with policy matters such as tours of duty, rotation, rest, and the like. On the one hand, the flight surgeon of the higher echelon attempted to interpret and justify to his commander the actions and recommendations of the unit physicians. On the other hand, the commander was under constant pressure from higher commands to keep as many men flying as possible. In turn, the medical officer was required to exert constant pressure on his medical subordinates for a course of action favorable to the war effort, even though it often appeared to him to be prejudicial to the flyers. It is not surprising that there was friction between the practitioners of the art of war and of the art of aviation medicine. Attempts to reduce this friction were legion, as evidenced by a steady stream of innovations, directives, and experimental procedures, but no perfect solution was possible.

Aviation Medicine

Aviation medicine began with the realization that individuals varied in their reactions to the circumstances of flight. Before World War I attention was directed principally to the physical fitness of the flyer, and the earliest work was concerned with the establishment of minimum physical standards. From the outset it was evident that the body's capacity to adjust to the special conditions of flight was a limiting factor in the utilization of aircraft. The unusual stresses encountered in flying, which are the subject matter of aviation medicine, may be described as follows.

1. *Physical.* As we move from the earth's surface into space, the

atmosphere becomes less dense, and the temperature lower. At an altitude of about 10,000 feet symptoms develop, because of decreased oxygen in the blood; at 18,000–25,000 feet most individuals lose consciousness and are close to death. Using ordinary (i.e., non-pressurized) oxygen-supply systems, an altitude of 40,000–45,000 feet is barely tolerable. Using pressure oxygen systems, the limiting altitude is in the neighborhood of 90,000–100,000 feet.

2. *Gravitational.* As aircraft were driven faster by improved engines, the typical maneuvers of flight (and particularly combat flight), such as acceleration, turns, dives, and the pull-outs from dives, generated centrifugal forces on the blood and tissues of the pilot, the magnitude of which is measured in G's, or multiples of the force of gravity. The clinical significance of such gravitational stresses is related to the length of time over which they are sustained. Protective devices, known as anti-G suits, were devised which counteracted to a limited extent these powerful forces.

3. *Physiological.* When the human body is exposed to physical and gravitational stresses, adaptive and compensatory physiological mechanisms come into action, and survival depends upon the adequacy of the response. A knowledge of the nature of these compensatory reactions is necessary in order to develop protective devices and to establish the limits within which the aviator can function. The stresses that the combat flyer encounters daily exist nowhere else, and the study of them requires such devices as low-pressure chambers and the giant human centrifuge as well as the usual equipment of the laboratory.

4. *Psychological.* Military and civil aviation ceased to be a daytime, fair-weather occupation during the 1920's. The development of instrument flying grew out of psychological studies of the means by which man is able to orient, or fails to orient, himself in flight when all spatial reference points are absent.[5] Likewise, the significance of other psychological attributes, such as depth perception, reaction time, and ability to tolerate rotary and confused motion, has a bearing on the capacity to fly safely.

5. *Emotional.* Even after years of study, the emotional aspects of flying are poorly understood. No one who has studied successful flyers will deny that their psychic constitutions are unique and that there is a fairly consistent configuration of their personality structure. The act of flying yields a distinct gratification, particularly to the pilot, and it appears that this libidinal devotion serves the airman as a power-

369

ful shield against the threat of failure and death. The existence of strong emotional currents in flyers, and the inadequate perception of their meaning by non-flyers, led inevitably to conflict at all levels where command or authority was shared by the two groups.[6] Such conflict was intensified by the mystical unity of the flyers against all others. This attitude was epitomized by Malraux when he said, "Aviation united them as childbirth makes all women one."

These five areas, then, provide the subject matter for the specialty of aviation medicine. To a remarkable extent the medical scientist has been able to keep step with the aeronautical engineer, and the planes that have been produced can be flown safely. Long before Pearl Harbor, the leaders of the Air Corps recognized the need for collaboration between aviation medicine and aircraft design. This recognition came from realization of the discrepancy between aircraft performance and human tolerance and from realization that the human element was the weakest link in the air weapons system that the Air Corps was attempting to create in the 1930's. At that time the medical research activities of the Air Corps were concentrated in the School of Aviation Medicine, being concerned primarily with selection procedures and physiological and psychological studies of individual flyers. The concept of a need for "human engineering" developed from the experiences of Lt. Col. Malcolm C. Grow, MC, who divided his time between air duties as flight surgeon at Patterson Field, Ohio, and as informal consultant to the Equipment Branch, Engineering Division, at Wright Field, Ohio. In 1934 he established the Laboratory of the Aero Medical Research Unit at Wright Field, with Capt. Harry G. Armstrong, MC, USA, as co-founder.* The broad mission of the unit was to investigate all medical problems with reference to Air Corps material, problems of flight in which tactical efficiency is correlated with the machine, medical problems arising from and related to engineering advances, and the effects of flight on man.

The laboratory expanded rapidly and to a remarkable degree accomplished its mission. Concurrently, the research program of SAM was accelerated, although the emphasis there continued to be directed to the investigation of psychophysiological problems.[7] The American genius for improvisation, expansion, and improvement functioned in

---

* These two pioneers of aeromedical research carried heavy responsibilities throughout World War II. In 1946 Maj. Gen. M. C. Grow was appointed Air Surgeon and at the end of his term was succeeded by Maj. Gen. H. G. Armstrong.

its characteristic manner, and, when the United States entered the war, aviation medicine was full fledged, and the human factor was no longer the weakest link in military aviation.[8]

Administrative Problems

As a matter of expediency the Army Air Forces, in June 1941, wanted to accept as little immediate responsibility as possible for such services and housekeeping chores as were then adequately discharged by the Army's Services of Supply. Among them was the medical service, which was provided in part by Army medical officers assigned to the Chief of the Medical Division, Office, Chief of Air Corps, and in part by hospitals and dispensaries ultimately responsible to the Surgeon General of the Army. There were enough problems involved in the expansion program to argue for deferment of some long-range objectives, but there can be no doubt that air force planners looked forward to the development of a fully integrated air weapons system. Implicit in the concept of a weapons system, whatever its mission was to become, was the need for organic control—if not of every element, at least of the key components. Since the establishment of the Aero Medical Research Unit (1934) the Air Corps had been committed, in doctrine as well as in practice, to the parity of the human factor and the "hardware." It was inevitable that in time an unrelenting campaign would be waged for the establishment of an independent medical service responsible only to the Chief of the Army Air Forces.*

The unique emotional configuration of the flyer, the complexities of modern aircraft, and the exiguous nature of aerial warfare made it evident to the air staff that the expanding force must retain to the greatest extent possible the characteristics of an elite corps.† No one seriously challenged the air staff's decision not to lower intellectual and physical standards for aviation cadets. Hence there was no serious objection to the AAF's requirement that only those enlistees and in-

---

* The campaign for an organic medical service for the AAF really began when Col. David N. W. Grant, MC, was appointed Acting Chief of the Medical Division, OCAC, on 12 October 1939. This able physician and administrator continued to serve as the chief medical officer of the air arm throughout the expansion period and the war. Frequent reorganization of the medical service was necessary to cope with the rapid development of the AAF, and on 30 October 1941 Colonel Grant was designated "The Air Surgeon." Subsequently he was promoted to brigadier general and in 1943 to major general. He retired in 1946 after twenty-nine years of service, fifteen of which were with the air force.

† It was not quite so straightforward as the following summary makes it seem. See Vol. VI, 537 ff.

ductees whose AGCT score placed them in Classes I and II should be considered for pilot and aircrew training. It was only necessary to examine a contemporary bombardment plane like the B-17 to realize that the ground crewmen who serviced it needed to be far more dexterous and far better equipped intellectually than the men who serviced the ubiquitous jeep, for example. Serious resistance, however, was encountered to a corollary proposition that this fledgling force required its own medical service. As a matter of fact, the medical service of the AAF finally achieved about the same degree of virtual autonomy as did the air arm itself in June 1941, but the freedom gained involved a time-consuming and often acrimonious controversy between the medical officers assigned to the Office of the Air Surgeon and those in the Office of the Surgeon General of the Army.

The imaginative ones among the pioneers of military aviation and their medical colleagues, who were beginning to call themselves "flight surgeons," insisted from the days of World War I that an effective air force should have an organic medical service responsible only to the chief of the force. In the years between 1917, when Lt. Col. Theodore C. Lyster, MC, first made the proposal, and 1947, when the United States Air Force was established, efforts to develop such a service varied greatly with respect to individual enthusiasm and official resistance or support. Inevitably, the long campaign was confused by recurring "battles of memos," *ad hoc* committees, and compromises. Incompletely concealed by the verbiage that enshrouded the long struggle, there can be discerned two themes and a number of variations on them which are worthy of consideration.

The two themes were the revolutionary nature of air power and the equal importance of men and machines in an air weapons system. The variations can be abstracted most conveniently in the form of the following propositions.

The airplane is a revolutionary weapon that demands a tightly knit but flexible organization as modern as the instrument itself. The flyer must have a flight surgeon who understands his problems, who is responsive to his needs, who is able to participate in every phase of the development of the new air weapon, and who is under the authority of the same commander. The ideal flight surgeon must share the convictions of the flyer concerning the revolutionary nature of air power and should regard the challenge to participate in aviation medicine as equivalent to the challenge in other areas of medical research. The leaders of military aviation had acquired an experimental attitude that stood in contrast to the intrenched conservatism of the General Staff. Flyers, including flight surgeons, should be free to develop American air power according to their own dreams, restricted only by the financial resources of the country and their own capabilities. The geographical limitations that provided a logical basis for the operational plans of the Army Medical Department were meaningless to an air force whose planes compressed time and distance. And, finally, since the human resources of the Air Force were considered equivalent in importance to the planes, and since the air arm provided all levels of maintenance for the latter, why should not the commander provide and control all levels of maintenance and repair (i.e., hospitalization) for the men without whom the planes were useless?

As a sort of counterpoint to these themes and variations one senses the unique personality of the airman—the visionary—who has rejected the good earth for the boundless air. One feels, rather than perceives directly, the spirit of defiance toward conventional attitudes and traditional authority. In spite of this, the flyers and their volunteer flight surgeons were realists enough to know that simply wanting a separate medical service would not achieve it. Such a service, like autonomy in any branch of the air arm, must be gained in a piecemeal manner, with the exertion of steady, opportunistic pressure, and in the end it was the demands of war rather than sheer logic that brought success.

In this context the first objective of the medical service of the AAF was to achieve an administrative situation where the chief of the medical service was responsible directly to, and only to, the chief of the air service (whatever his current designation might be).[9] This was a unique concept for a military organization when it was first proposed in 1917, and in terms of management relationships it is still a unique concept. The theory behind the objective is very simple: in an air force—or in any other large enterprise, for that matter—the welfare of the human factor is as important as any other consideration which is the normal concern of top management (e.g., raw materials and plans). Accordingly, the chief medical officer of the organization should be directly responsible to the chief executive; he should be a member of the top echelon of control, and he should not be required to present advice and recommendations and receive directives on policy and/or operations through the medium of a non-medical administrator (e.g., a G-1 or G-4, or the Commanding General, Army

Service Forces, or the personnel manager). If the health and the welfare of manpower are important, the chief executive should have direct access to his chosen medical adviser, and vice versa.

To a physician, this proposition seems self-evident; but it is quite apparent that it is not, and has not been, equally evident to most military and civilian administrators. This staff relationship has been the normal procedure in the Air Corps, the Army Air Forces, and the present U.S. Air Force. Prior to the establishment of the USAF the relationship was not always unequivocal,[10] but it was operationally effective, and it had the force of assuring that the medical needs of airmen were the direct concern of the highest echelon of command. In terms of human relationships, the devotion of AAF management to the philosophy of the parity of the human factor and the hardware, and the success with which it was implemented, represents a real contribution to the managerial aspect of our society.

The next objective—a medical service independent of the Surgeon General of the Army—was a logical consequence of the first, but its achievement was complicated by the traditional policies of the Medical Department. In the normal course of War Department operations it was customary for a Medical Corps officer to be assigned as surgeon to the staff of the commander of a major component such as a corps area, an army, or an overseas theater. This officer was directly responsible to his commanding officer, but he was also responsible to the Surgeon General for the execution of his military medical functions in compliance with the approved practices of the latter's office. Professional standards, tables of organization and equipment, hospitalization procedures, disposition procedures, and research and development (to name only a few) were centralized functions controlled by policies established in the office of the SG. There was, therefore, no strain at all in assigning an officer as Chief, Medical Division, Office of the Chief of the Air Corps, and in stating that he was responsible to the Chief; but the medical mission that he executed, and the manner in which he executed it, and the tools and personnel that he could requisition or develop remained to a very large extent within the control of the Surgeon General. Offsetting this limitation to some extent was the willingness of the Air Corps to use its own funds in support of medical projects peculiar to its own needs, as in the establishment of the School of Aviation Medicine in 1919 and the Aero Medical Research Unit in 1934. The failure of the SG to accept full responsibility and the degree of independence for the Air Corps that came through financial control of such organizations represented significant steps toward a separate medical service for the air arm.

A military medical organization has three important components: a physical examination service; a field medical service, which includes the handling of battle casualties and provisions for ambulatory care (e.g., sick call); and a hospitalization service. In the agitation for a separate air medical service early in World War II one encounters little to indicate that the planners wanted separate air force hospitals under the same terms of control as for the physical examination and the field medical services. There were probably sound enough reasons for the failure to campaign for such hospitals early in the game. The Surgeon General may have been willing to delegate control of physical examinations (an unpleasant task at best) to the flight surgeons; but he resisted stoutly all attempts to relocate the field medical service until the pressures of expansion and the experiences of combat overrode the chronic objections. The fact that the Air Surgeon developed an effective hospital system around the stateside air-base station hospitals and the aviation medical dispensaries (i.e., the equivalent of a field medical service) did not weaken in the least the resolve of the SG to defend his general hospital system* to the limit of the patience of all concerned, including the Chief of Staff. The vast system of named general hospitals was one of the few military medical activities over which the Surgeon General had complete control. In actuality, the completeness of his control fluctuated as a result of organizational changes in the War Department, and there was a period subsequent to the March 1942 reorganization when the SG found himself receiving policy and other directives from a higher echelon, the Hospitalization and Evacuation Branch of the Special Staff of the Commanding General, Army Service Forces.[11] In any case, it was evident that there would be no voluntary relinquishing of general hospitals on the

---

* In the nomenclature of the Medical Department, general hospitals were large establishments organized to render definitive medical service to any type of case, however complex, and to determine eligibility for separation from the service on medical grounds. The general hospitals in the Zone of Interior were designated as named general hospitals (e.g., Walter Reed) and, as exempted stations of the War Department, were under the control of the SG rather than the command of the military district in which they were located. Overseas general hospitals in World War II were numbered, were zone-of-communications installations, and were under the control of the Commanding General, Army Service Forces.

part of the SG just because the Air Surgeon wanted to round out his medical service.

It is instructive to examine briefly the stepwise manner in which the air medical service emancipated itself from parental control, considering only what appear to be the critical phases of the separation process, with approximate dates and cursory comments.[12]

1. *Pilot selection and classification.* The first physical examination requirement for flyers was prepared by the Surgeon General's office in 1912 at the request of the Aviation School, Signal Corps. In spite of its many revisions the physical examination test alone was an inadequate basis for selection when measured by the high fatality rate in trainees during World War I. On 19 January 1918, the Aviation Section, Signal Corps, established the Air Service Medical Research Laboratory at Mineola, New York, with Col. W. H. Wilmer, MC, as director, to study the factors responsible for pilot failure and thus to improve the selection process. From that time on the aviators and the flight surgeons retained the initiative in research and development of methods to reduce the loss in manpower and planes resulting from inadequate pilot selection and human failure. The impetus and the funds for these continuing studies came from the budget of the air arm.

2. *School of Aviation Medicine.* The first school of aviation medicine was the School for Flight Surgeons established in 1918 in conjunction with the Air Service Medical Research Laboratory at Mineola, later moved to Mitchel Field, New York. The school taught the practical application of the research being done at the laboratory, particularly the performance of the new tests: the Altitude Classification Examination, the Personality Study, and the Physical Tests of Efficiency. In February 1921 the school was recognized by the War Department as a special service school. It thus became exempt from the jurisdiction of the corps area commander and was directly under the Chief of Air Service. In November 1922 its name was changed to the School of Aviation Medicine. Subsequently it was moved (1926) to Brooks Field, Texas, and then (1931) to Randolph Field, Texas, its present location.

3. *Research laboratories.* The first aviation medicine laboratory and the first school for flight surgeons became a single unit, concerned almost exclusively with the evaluation of the reactions of the individual aviator to the conditions of flight. As the aircraft development

376

program progressed, the need of a laboratory for "human engineering" became apparent, and in 1934 the Air Corps authorized the Aero Medical Research Unit at Wright Field.* Its mission was to collaborate with aeronautical engineers on every aspect of military aircraft development that involved the human factor.

4. *Administration of aviation medicine.* The medical unit responsible for pilot selection, the care of the flyer, and other matters related to aviation medicine has had many names and many organizational assignments.[10] The first such unit was the Medical Department, Air Division, Signal Corps, activated 17 September 1917. This activity was returned to the Surgeon General's control on 9 May 1918, presumably in connection with the creation of the Air Service on the 20th. The activity, including the same medical officer personnel, was then designated the Air Service Division, OSG. It remained in this administrative location until 14 March 1919, when the Surgeon General abolished the division and delegated its functions to the Chief Surgeon, Air Service. Operational control was never regained by the SG, and it appears that control of policy moved steadily away from the Army's Medical Department from that time on.

5. *Procurement of aviation medical personnel.* In the years between the two world wars, candidates for flight surgeon training and for careers in aviation medicine were members of the Medical Corps assigned to the School of Aviation Medicine at their own request. This system, which was adequate for peacetime, broke down completely in 1941. By the spring of 1942, the Surgeon General reported to the War Department that he had been unable to fill the 1,500 places for Medical Corps officers allotted to the AAF.[13] A number of factors were responsible for this poor showing, chief of which were the temper of times, the unnecessarily complicated procurement procedure, and ineffective recruiting publicity. The Air Surgeon worked out an informal agreement with the SG, which was tantamount to permission to do his own recruiting, to process for the SG the paperwork of applicants who expressed a desire for service with the AAF. On this basis an aggressive and imaginative recruitment campaign was initiated, which included press releases in professional journals and regular news media, personal solicitation, and informational packets. In spite of the persistence of red tape in Washington, the Air Surgeon was able to fill his first procurement objective of 2,000 Medical Corps

* See above, p. 370.

officers between 21 March 1942 and 1 July 1942. Similar techniques were applied to meet objectives for other specialized medical personnel. In terms of long-range objectives the Air Surgeon's recruiting program brought into his medical service a high proportion of Board-qualified specialists,* as well as a substantial number of Fellows of the American College of Surgeons and the American College of Physicians. These well-trained physicians were to play a key role in the hospitalization system of the AAF.

6. *Exemption of air-base installations.* The revision of Army Regulation 95–5, 20 June 1941, established the Army Air Forces, and defined the status, function, and organization of the air arm. Among the provisions of AR 95-5 was the delegation to the Commanding General, Air Force Combat Command, of "command and control of all AFCC Stations [air bases] and all personnel, units, and installations thereon, including station complement personnel and activities." Similar provisions applied to the Chief of the Air Corps with respect to Air Corps stations. As a result of this action, personnel at all air bases passed into the control of the AAF. In this way, an extensive system of station hospitals and aviation medical dispensaries was added to the responsibilities of the Air Surgeon.

7. *The convalescent centers.* The medical service of the AAF, willing to benefit from the experience of its RAF counterpart with "flying fatigue," "operational fatigue," "staleness," or whatever name was currently in vogue, began to plan for the reception of such cases well in advance of their appearance. In the European Theater of Operations rehabilitation centers were requested by the Surgeon, Eighth Air Force, in July 1942, were authorized by the Commanding General, ETOUSA, in August 1942, and were established forthwith.[14] In the United States the Air Surgeon at the same time initiated requests for authority to operate comparable facilities for AAF personnel returned from overseas. The validity of the request and the proposal for AAF control were challenged by the SG, but ultimately the Chief of Staff, with the Secretary of War's personal approval, authorized convalescent centers of the type desired. Approximately nine

---

* A number of quasi-official bodies have been organized (e.g., the American Board of Internal Medicine) to examine and certify physicians who wish to be designated as specialists because of advanced training and special interest. These boards specify minimum educational requirements and conduct written and oral examinations on which to base certification. Within the medical profession, the term "specialist" is largely restricted to individuals certified by one of nineteen specialty boards.

months after the Commanding General, AAF, asked permission to do so, the first eight centers were activated, and one—the station hospital at Coral Gables, Florida—was granted authority to function as a general hospital but only for the purpose of reclassifying officers for limited service and for appearance before retirement boards.[15]

8. *Hospitalization.* Throughout the war the problem of hospitalization of AAF personnel was never resolved to the satisfaction of anyone. In November 1943 the Air Surgeon controlled approximately 75,000 beds in about 350 station hospitals and dispensaries in the Zone of Interior.[16] In the theaters the air forces controlled only the beds in their aviation medical dispensaries and in some rehabilitation centers. The philosophy of war, tradition, and prestige were inextricably involved in the controversy over hospitalization. Neither of the contending parties won, and in retrospect it is fair to say that the extreme attitudes of the partisans on either side reflected no credit on the medical profession.

By the end of the war the medical service of the AAF could review its accomplishments with justifiable pride. From the 800 Medical Corps officers on hand at the time of Pearl Harbor, it had expanded until, in November 1943, approximately 16,000 doctors were on duty in air stations throughout the world, providing superior medical care for the aircrewmen of 234 combat groups, 135 of which were overseas,* as well as for the noncombat personnel who made up 60–80 per cent of the global air force. Medical problems that were as revolutionary as the planes that generated them had to be faced and solved. In the absence of traditional solutions the air arm's medical service had to improvise, experiment, and innovate on a grand scale. The youthful leadership of the service, and its close partnership with pioneering line and engineering officers, was equal to the challenge, and, although the administration was often severely strained, the mission was accomplished.

Operations

The operations of the air medical service in the field of aviation medicine is discussed here in a functional manner. Subdivision of the material on a geographical basis is neither feasible nor valid, for the speed of military aircraft in World War II reduced the significance

* See Vol. VI, 424.

of such terms as "zone of interior," "zone of communications," and the "front."

In spite of the large numbers involved, the individual flyer continued to occupy the central position in aviation medicine and to provide the stimulus for aeromedical research. Every flight surgeon was a potential investigator, and the best of them contributed magnificently to our knowledge of men under stress. Moreover, it can be said truthfully that every aviator was a research problem, so little was known that needed to be understood. Thus for the leaders of aviation medicine each day's problems, crises, and crashes led directly to experimental attempts to understand, solve, or avert them. Fortunately, the whole AAF operated pretty much on an experimental basis, so it was easy to obtain co-operation and support for any study that was stimulated by an obvious problem. Flight surgeons moved about rapidly among the special laboratories, the training stations, the schools, the proving grounds, and the theaters of operations. New ideas and new solutions were at a premium, and many projects were put into operation prematurely, to be withdrawn later when the validation study turned out to be negative. The entire air arm was composed of men in a hurry who knew where they wanted to go but had to learn how to get there.

Because it was easier to make changes in the procedures for men than to remodel the machines, one has the impression that the human factor was subjected to more experimentation than the hardware. Since it is not possible to review all the schemes that were tried and rejected, attention necessarily will be directed to the main currents and to the successful programs.

The strength of the AAF's medical service rested on its strong orientation toward the welfare of the individual flyer. The fact that all the senior air commanders were successful aviators made them uniformly sympathetic to what may be considered the official attitude. However, as military commanders they had to subordinate concern for individuals to the tactical and strategic missions of their commands and to think of the maximum number of men and machines that were available each day. Bookkeeping on the human factor was necessary so that the rate of attrition of manpower did not exceed the rate of loss of planes. Sick and injured men were as easily understood as defective and damaged aircraft. Men who were unwilling to fly, or unable to fly, or who, when flying, were dangerous to others posed an entirely different problem. An additional complication was the particularly poignant nature of the classical dilemma of the commander in the case of air combat units. It may be hard to think of a regiment of infantry or a battleship's complement in terms of individuals, but it was not hard for the air group commander to think of the pilot officers in his fighter squadrons in this way. In spite of this inevitable personal identification, successful air commanders appear to have been as uncompromising in their demands on combat personnel as were the officers of the other arms. It is entirely possible that senior air officers, both line and medical, were able to repress their feelings of guilt by dependence upon "objective" assessments of the combat capability of their men. To this end a large number of "psychological tests" were devised, tested, and usually invalidated. "The remarkable pretense at prediction of success and failure in combat, common to [air] medical and line officers alike, suggests a widespread defense against the emotional impact of combat—the denial that fear of mutilation and death are in themselves strong enough to change a man, and the assertion that more important factors are whether he has wet his bed past the age of six or whether he can take orders or whether he is a competent flyer."[17] The relevance of these remarks will become evident as the discussion progresses.

The reader is asked to bear in mind the fact that the medical service of the AAF was responsible not only for aviation medicine but also for the health of all air force personnel, except those admitted to hospitals outside the control of the Air Surgeon.

Selection and Classification of Aircrewmen

When the expansion of the Air Corps was authorized in 1938, the Medical Division had a well-established doctrine of pilot selection based on principles prescribed by the Air Service Medical Research Laboratory in 1918–19 and elaborated over the succeeding years at the School of Aviation Medicine. In brief, the ideal pilot was preferably a graduate of the Military or Naval Academy who wanted to become a flyer, was a well-nigh perfect physical specimen of superior intelligence, and had scored in the upper deciles of tests of physical efficiency, altitude classification, co-ordination, and the like. The battery of tests to which the candidate was subjected varied from year to year depending on current medical thinking and on the attitudes of senior flight surgeons. The majority of the procedures had never been submitted to a searching scrutiny by biostatistical techniques, since this science as it applied to test evaluation was just coming out of its infancy. Most of the tests were based on the concept that the stresses of flight were physical and that failure to adapt to such stresses was due to a substandard physiological constitution—a concept that was seldom criticized seriously at that time. The pilot-training program of the Air Corps before 1938 never graduated more than 250 flyers per year, so that there was plenty of time and personnel for an exhaustive study of the type of tests then in use. In 1939 the physical disqualification rate was 73 per cent of the applicants, and eliminations during training averaged around 40–50 per cent. In round numbers the Medical Division had to deal with no more than 1,800 candidates for pilot training each year.

The Air Corps expansion program* confronted the Medical Division with a new set of problems inherent in the mass production of aircrewmen. In June 1938 the strength of the Corps stood at 20,196, of which approximately 10 per cent were commissioned officers. Six years later the AAF would number 2,372,292, with 388,295 commissioned officers on duty. During the entire period of expansion and war, 194,000 young men successfully completed pilot training, and more than twice that number received their wings as aircrewmen (e.g., bombardiers, navigators, and gunners). There seems never to have been any question about the propriety of delegating the task of selection and classification to the medical service, and the successive procurement objectives did not alter the service's confidence in its ability to do the job. The projected work load of the flight surgeons and aviation medical examiners is shown in the following table:[†]

Program	Date Formulated	Annual Graduation Rate of Pilots	Number of Cadets Entering Program*	Number of Applicants Needed[†]
24-group...Fall 1938		1,200	2,200	12,000
41-group...Spring 1939		7,000	14,000	70,000
54-group...Spring 1940		12,000	24,000	120,000
84-group...Spring 1941		30,000	60,000	300,000

* Based on 50 per cent elimination rate.
† Based on 80 per cent physical disqualification rate.

This programing contained some slack, which was just as well, since no one could be sure that manpower and materiel procurement

* For a detailed account of the program, see Vol. VI, chap. 13.
† See also Vol. VI, 434.

would meet the ambitious schedule. The prediction of applicants needed was based on the round-number estimate that only one-fifth of the applicants could pass the aviation-cadet qualifying examinations. Actually, the rate of rejection in 1939 was 73.2 per cent, and realistic downgrading of the physical and mental qualifications reduced the reject rate to 50.3 per cent by the time the United States entered the war. Likewise, eliminations from pilot training for the whole six-year period turned out to be 39 per cent instead of the 50 per cent scheduled. The majority of the eliminees could be reclassified as aircrewmen, so that they were not entirely lost to the AAF. In any case, the magnitude of the task ahead suggested that the Medical Division had to streamline and facilitate its selection program. Two important actions were taken for this purpose.* First, a program was developed to predict the aptitudes of aviation cadets and to put the classification of aircrewmen on a positive basis. Second, in the selection process, the emphasis was changed from the pilot to the aircrewman (i.e., pilot, bombardier, navigator, and flight engineer, whether commissioned or not).

The impetus for these changes came from two directions. On the one hand, flight surgeons at SAM in the spring of 1941 obtained a grant of $600,000 for the development of aptitude tests that would indicate an applicant's general potentialities, practical judgment, and capacity to absorb instruction. To implement this program, a psychology section was organized under Col. John C. Flanagan in the Medical Division, OCAC, and subsequently psychology units were established at SAM and at Maxwell Field and other preflight training centers. On the other hand, the Air Corps Technical Training Command (TTC) was seeking special tests to screen high-school graduates for training as bombardiers and navigators, a group that TTC's experts were convinced would afford better material than eliminees from pilot training. At the same time, because of concern for meeting training quotas, Brig. Gen. Carl Spaatz, Chief of Air Staff, became convinced that the AAF would have to adopt a revised testing program. Considering the existing system of educational requirements archaic because it placed "too much emphasis on formal education which may mean nothing and . . . no emphasis on native intelligence which may mean everything," General Spaatz directed A-1 to make a thorough renovation of regulations governing the requirements for

* Vol. VI, 489-91.

selecting flying cadets. This task was undertaken by the three OCAC divisions concerned—Personnel, Training and Operations, and Medical—at a series of conferences extending from 28 November to 3 December 1941. As a result it was recommended that thereafter all applicants for flying training, on passing an aviation-cadet qualifying examination (to be prepared by the Medical Division), should be qualified simply as aviation cadets (aircrew). Specific assignments for those thus qualified would then be determined by special classification tests administered at one of the three training centers. These tests were to be designed to measure the aptitude of each trainee for pilot, bombardier, and navigator training. To accomplish this latter objective, the research project of the Training Command was transferred to the Medical Division and combined with the pilot-selection project.

Although these actions were precipitated by the realities of preparation for total war, they were not unforeseen and represented, in fact, a steady drift of the thinking of aviation medicine with respect to the unsuccessful flyer. In World War I, failures were attributed to physical deficiencies: "chronic digestive disturbances, chronic constipation, or indigestion, or intestinal disorders tending to produce dizziness, headache or to impair vision."[18] The influence of physiologists after 1919 shifted the onus of failure to physiological mechanisms incapable of coping with reduced oxygen tension, cold, and gravitational forces. In the years before 1939, this concept was expanded, and to it was added the psychologists' theory that failure also stemmed from inadequate psychomotor co-ordination and from inability to learn. At the time of the expansion program the technique employed to elicit disqualifying features other than physical and psychological ones was a biographical personality inventory called the Adaptability Rating for Military Aeronautics. The psychiatric phase of this rating was fairly primitive. In fact, prior to Pearl Harbor, psychiatry was not primarily concerned in the selection process, and instruction for flight surgeons was confined largely to the recognition of the major psychoses.

The change in selection regulations was recommended just before the attack on Pearl Harbor, when the elaborate program of the psychologists was still in the stage of choosing and evaluating tests and of procuring test equipment. The declaration of war left the Air Surgeon no choice but to start processing applicants on the new basis and at once. From the outset there was insufficient time for the elaborate battery of psychomotor and performance tests that had been projected, and simple, electrically scored paper-and-pencil tests had to be substituted wherever possible. The complex tests were carried out on samples of flying candidates to provide material for later validation. So far as the Air Surgeon's office was concerned, the psychological tests turned out to be unsatisfactory predictors of failure, and in the fall of 1942 it was deemed necessary to reinstate a perfunctory neuropsychiatric examination which had been deleted in favor of certain attitude and aptitude tests.[19] The details of the operation of the aircrew classification program are described elsewhere and need not be reviewed here.*

With the onset of hostilities the Medical Division was faced with the problem of processing a flood of aircrew candidates with a trickle of medical officers, who themselves required indoctrination and training. In February 1941 the War Department had authorized establishment of three Air Corps replacement training centers for classification and preflight instruction of candidates for pilot, bombardier, and navigator training. There was some realignment of the planning, and, finally, the classification centers of the Flying Training Command were established at Nashville, Tennessee, San Antonio, Texas, and Santa Ana, California.

The newly commissioned medical officers were assigned to these classification centers for a six-week practical training course. Initially, half their time was devoted to in-service training as members of the medical processing unit, which executed the medical portion of the cadet examination in production-line fashion. The balance of their time was scheduled for a variety of didactic exercises to familiarize them with medical administration and to introduce them to the problems and the philosophy of aviation medicine. There is probably no job in medicine more boring than to perform routine physical examinations day after day on healthy, willing recruits. In spite of this well-known fact, the rapid rotation of assignments in the processing unit, the excellent organization, and the enthusiastic co-operation of young physicians in a novel situation all resulted in a thoroughly

---

* See Vol. VI, 549-56, where General Arnold is quoted as saying: "The Aviation Psychology program paid off in time, lives, and money saved, and through its selection of the raw material has aided in the establishment of an effective air force. This has been done at a total cost of less than $5 per candidate tested." Whatever the cost may have been, the air surgeons were less impressed with results than was General Arnold.

effective performance. From contemporary records there is no evidence that the medical processing units ever became bottlenecks in the classification program, nor is there any reason to believe that the high standards of the physical examination were seriously compromised. It was a remarkable achievement to adapt successfully production methods to a selection-classification process to which senior air officers, line and medical, attached so much significance.*

From the earliest days of military aviation, doctors and psychologists have served as selectors, and it is pertinent to compare the success of their efforts in two world wars, twenty-five years apart. In World War I the selection process was successful in 55 per cent of the candidates admitted to flying training; of 20,773 men who were passed by the selection boards, 11,438 completed the course.[20] In World War II the selection classification was successful in 61 per cent; of 318,000 men who entered flight training, 193,400 graduated as pilots.† Since the prediction of success is only 10 per cent more reliable, it would appear that criticism of World War I standards as "based almost entirely on empirical grounds" could also apply to the standards used in World War II.[21] Regardless of this, it appears that responsible line officers of the AAF were well satisfied with the performance of the medical service in aircrew selection. It is entirely possible that this satisfaction was due to the not so obvious fact that this was an area of decision for which command was not responsible.

Throughout the entire period of the wartime flight-training program there was increasing interest in the evaluation of the various

---

* In reflecting on this process, this writer has wondered why the responsibility for aircrew selection and classification should ever have been delegated to or assumed by the medical service. If success in military aviation (or any sort of flying for that matter) depended solely on physical fitness (theory of World War I), or on a combination of physical-psychological fitness and teachability (theory of the years between the wars), and not on something else, the job obviously belonged to the medical service. Moreover, medical educators, and graduate science educators (e.g., psychologists, physiologists, and the like), had always done a fine job of selecting candidates for advanced training in their own professions. In any good medical school eliminees should not exceed 10 per cent, and the same ought to be true for a major university's graduate school. But this degree of success in selecting for one's own profession has no bearing on the ability to select for some other profession, such as flying. This raises, of course, the question of something else being involved in the makeup of the successful aviator in addition to the factors postulated by the medical service. It seems evident that the doctors and psychologists were failing to recognize some predictor of success or failure in flying that they were able to recognize intuitively in the candidates for their own profession. This is, of course, speculation, but the plain fact is that the selection process was not much more efficient in 1942 than it was in 1918.

† See Vol. VI, 577–78.

tests used. The large volume of recruits permitted rapid accumulation of sufficiently large samples of data for analysis. The AAF was statistically minded and, in addition to having business machines and computers, was able to call on biostatisticians and operations analysts for consultation. There was probably never a time when accepted medical procedures were subjected to so competent a scrutiny. Many were rejected entirely, and few of the elaborate routines escaped unscathed. A particularly striking example was the Schneider Index, a method of evaluating cardiovascular fitness developed by one of the fathers of aviation medicine. When the business machines got through with the index, it was evident that the only significant element was the differential between blood pressure measured in the reclining and the standing positions. This could be measured very simply and required less time and no need for consulting tables and summing-up scores. In the evaluation of susceptibility to motion sickness, the Barany-chair test was another casualty; it was replaced by a simple swing test. Most of the complex psychological tests of co-ordination and psychomotor function and the majority of the simple pencil-and-paper tests to evaluate personality and aptitude also failed to demonstrate validity when tested by modern methods. All these considerations end up in the same place: regardless of how carefully or how casually a group of men was selected for military flying, about 40–50 per cent washed out.

The Care of the Flyer: Training

The principal function of the medical service of the AAF is described by the term "the care of the flyer." The concept of the flight surgeon and his role in the care of the flyer was originated during the first World War by Col. Theodore C. Lyster, MC, USA, and Maj. Isaac H. Jones, MC, USA, who proposed the organization of a Care of the Flyer Unit in June 1918. Although flight surgeons attached to such units were under the jurisdiction of the post surgeon, the latter was advised that "in all matters relating to the care of the flyer, the Flight Surgeon should be given a free hand and his advice will control." The flight surgeon, on his part, was designated as the adviser to the commanding officer and the flight commander "in all question of fitness of aviators or aviation students to fly."[22] The term —the care of the flyer—was a durable one which is still in use, although the concept of what it comprises has been expanded greatly.

In World War II the flight surgeon was necessarily concerned not only with the individual pilot but also with the aircrew of multi-engined planes as individuals and as a combat team. The shift in emphasis from the single-seated fighter that dominated the air in the first war is demonstrated in the following table:*

Aircraft Acceptances by Type
1 July 1940—August 1945

Type	Total	Per Cent of Total	Men per Plane (Approx.)
Fighter	99,950	34.3	1–2
Bomber	97,810	32.4	3–13
Trainer	57,623	19.3	1–2
Transport	23,929	8.3	2–6
Communication	13,643	4.6	2–4
Reconnaissance	3,918	1.3	1–4
Special purpose	2,420	0.8	...
Total	299,293	100.0	

To man these aircraft in training and operations required about one-fourth of the strength of the AAF. The number of men who completed aircrew training between July 1939 and August 1945 is indicated below:†

Type	Total	Elimination Rate (Approx.) Per Cent
Pilots	193,400	40
Bombardiers	48,000	12
Navigators	50,000	20
Flexible Gunners	297,000	10
Flight Engineers	7,800	9
Radar Observers, bombers	7,600	..
Radar, night fighters	1,000	..
Radar, countermeasures	500	..

The grand total of better than 600,000, plus about another 125,000 eliminees, suggests the magnitude of the flight surgeons' task in the provision of "care of the flyer."

In functional terms this care consisted of the following: (1) to evaluate the influence of concurrent illness and injury on the ability to fly and to provide treatment for such disability; (2) to treat injuries and disorders attributable to flying; (3) to teach and to interpret the physiology of flight (in practice this meant altitude indoctrination and the use of oxygen equipment); (4) to teach the use of and to

* See Vol. VI, 352.

† Adapted from Vol. VI, chap. 17.

evaluate protective devices; (5) to diagnose as accurately as possible symptoms and disability due to emotional reactions; and (6) to help the airman recognize and deal with the tensions and anxieties generated by flight and combat, as well as the tensions and anxieties that may affect any man in the same age group or in the military service.*

The first two items were well within the competence of the average physician who volunteered for medical service with the AAF, and there is every reason to believe that these duties were discharged enthusiastically and satisfactorily.

The next two items involved a specialized knowledge of physiology and modern air force equipment, which the ordinary doctor simply did not possess. The training provided by SAM was supposed to correct this deficiency, but over-all planning failed to the extent that two-thirds of the medical officers in the ETO at the beginning of operations there were not qualified to perform the essential duties of a flight surgeon.[23] This regrettable situation resulted from a number of factors. Because of pressure to meet Eighth Air Force (and other air force) schedules, doctors were assigned overseas before they had received any special training in aviation medicine. Similarly, unit commanders tended to offer the less desirable medical officers when asked to contribute personnel for task forces. Most serious of all, the training then provided at SAM was obviously inadequate because of the large commitment of time to the "64"† (physical) examination and to aspects of military medicine of little use to the flight surgeon in a combat area. Training schedules for medical officers eventually were revamped to provide more tactical and physiological training before assignment overseas; and, in England, on-the-job training was supplied by the Eighth Air Force Provisional Medical Field Service School, Col. Harry G. Armstrong, commanding, which opened its doors on 10 August 1942.

The last two items on the list of "care of the flyer" functions constituted one of the most perplexing problems of military medicine not only in the AAF but also in the Army and the Navy. It was a bigger problem for the air medical service because its existence was recognized, even though there was never a clear scheme for dealing with it other than by the application of the art of aviation medicine. Any attempt to evaluate the extent to which the average flight surgeon

* Cf. statement of duties of a flight surgeon, above, p. 367.

† WD AGO Form 64, Physical Examination for Flying.

was successful in the discharge of these functions necessitates judgments contingent primarily on cultural factors: medical, social, and military. Since the flight surgeon was deeply involved in administrative procedures relating to the emotional reactions of aircrewmen, a brief digression is required to present the background of the problem.

When one explores the field currently defined as psychosomatic medicine, semantics becomes critical, and careful selection of terms is necessary, if the issues are to be understood at all. Instead of using the terms "psychological symptoms" or "psychiatric symptoms," the writer prefers to speak of the role of emotional reactions in the production of symptoms and disability—or, more precisely, of inability to function at the expected level of performance. Contemporary physicians (1940–45) were aware of the fact that acute, overt emotional states (e.g., anger, fear) are accompanied by striking physiological activity (e.g., rapid heart beat, blood-pressure changes, disturbed gastrointestinal function), and the nature of these reactions was generally appreciated. There was considerably less agreement on the extent to which chronic, less obvious, emotional states (e.g., apprehension, anxiety, frustration, tension, desire, fatigue) were accompanied by physiological disturbances, and, if so, what these changes were and how they could be recognized. In an era of medicine when scientific research provided such certainties as the sulfa drugs and the electrocardiogram, it is not surprising that the average physician preferred to devote attention to these and tended to avoid the intellectual effort involved in analysis of so subtle and manifold a situation as the interaction of conflicting emotions and personality in complex present-day man. In addition to this, the relationship between these everyday emotional reactions and grosser disturbances of behavior—the psychoneuroses and psychoses—was not at all clear either to physicians or to psychiatrists. Competing schools of thought peddled conflicting doctrines, all of which lacked the substantial quality of the Law of the Heart or the explanation of the cause of diabetes, for example. It is fair to state that the seventy-odd medical schools of the country were relatively ineffective in teaching this aspect of the practice of medicine. As recently as 1956,[24] a study of general practitioners disclosed that no more than 15–20 per cent were able to deal intelligently and realistically with symptoms of emotional reactions. The average doctor not only is inept in this respect but also is aware of his ineptness, and the usual reaction on his part is indifference and/or hostility to the patient who "has nothing wrong with him" as measured by a conventional physical examination and the usual laboratory tests.

The prevailing attitude of laymen—or of society—to such patients is not much different from that of the average physician. Family and acquaintances are usually aware of the stresses to which the invalid has been exposed, but, since they, and others, have endured comparable vicissitudes, the tendency is to attribute symptom formation and disability to an unrecognized disease, to a character defect, or to unwillingess to bear a fair share of the load, or to downright perversity. If a correct psychosomatic diagnosis is offered, the average layman tends to view it as a sentence, or an alibi, and not as a basis for corrective action. The normal sympathy for the sufferer from a "real disease" (e.g., tuberculosis or a stomach ulcer) is denied the one whose troubles are "all in his head" or "imaginary."

The reaction of the military to this realm of human behavior has always been more extreme than that of society or the medical profession. The deserter, the coward, the victim of the self-inflicted wound, and the "gold-brick," having appeared in every war of which there is any record, were well known to commanders of all nations. The standing procedure for handling these types has varied according to the cultural level of the society and the personalities involved, but it has always been administrative: summary physical or capital punishment, imprisonment at hard labor, or discharge in disgrace. In the "old Army" and the "old Navy" there were no psychiatrists messing around with the men, acting as confidants and intermediaries, and inventing excuses for downright cowardice and insubordination. Senior air commanders, of course, had grown up with flight surgeons and remembered the value of their friendly counsel, and they recalled the artful manner by which a sympathetic doctor could tide a fellow over a bad time. But the commander had made the grade because he had what it took, and these other fellows should be able to do the same if they had the guts and kept a stiff upper lip. Even so, the attitude of air commanders was a little more humane and a little less regimental than that of other military men. This may explain in part why the air force fought so hard for its own medical service and why the Air Surgeon was able to retain direct access to the Commanding General, AAF. The handling of the situation was complicated in the overseas air forces because hospitalization and (to a large extent originally, at least) disposition was a function of the Army Medical Department, which was under the strict control of the line with respect to standing operating procedures for such laggards. The military attitude is essentially a no-nonsense one, which may be suitable for an infantryman, or an AB seaman, or a stevedore in a port battalion, although some doctors challenged this view before the war was over. In the case of the highly trained, almost irreplaceable aircrewman a somewhat more flexible, less arbitrary form of treatment was obviously in order.

These attitudes, which can be interpreted as evidence of a culture lag, had a profound influence on the complex function of the doctor assigned to a military unit. War is a remarkable laboratory, and perceptive physicians learned fast, not only from their own personal reactions to deprivation, hardship, and combat, but also from their patients. Repeated efforts were made by command to establish simple categories and specifications for what were essentially dynamic personality reactions of the greatest complexity.

The foregoing are the elements, greatly simplified, of the dilemma that confronted the flight surgeon who conscientiously tried to discharge the duties implicit in the last two items on the list of "care of the flyer" functions. There was further complication of the deceptively simple statement of the surgeon's duties: to act as confidant and adviser to the airman and also *to act as an intermediary in medical matters between the flyer, his commanding officer, and higher medical authority.** Small wonder that those who knew the business best believed that it required at least three years of close contact with airmen and their problems to become adept in the art of aviation medicine! It is not surprising that the newly recruited and superficially trained flight surgeons had difficulties. The remarkable fact is how well they did in this relatively uncharted area of medicine, guided only by their professional idealism and the experience of the few seasoned flight surgeons who were available in any command. The learning process was difficult and the level of service uneven, but somehow the doctors kept the men flying.

The basic function of the flight surgeon at the combat squadron or group level was to determine whether a man was fit to fly. It was the prerogative of command to determine what sort of aircraft he should fly and what mission he should be assigned. This separation of roles seemed reasonable enough in peacetime and apparently never led to any serious difficulty then or during wartime training. But in combat

* See above, pp. 366–68.

392

zones conflict developed when a man was judged able to fly but not to fly a combat mission. The background of this problem and its ramifications will become evident.

During individual flying training crowded schedules left little time for establishment of a close confidant-adviser relationship between the flyer and the doctor. Moreover, it was evident to everyone that assignment to combat crews would involve a different physician, so that a cadet seldom bothered to make the emotional investment of becoming intimate with a flight surgeon. Serious emotional reactions that could not be handled by the cadet himself were likely to result in his being promptly washed out by a hard-boiled instructor or through a serious or fatal accident. Cadet elimination boards adopted a strict, no-nonsense attitude and were accustomed to depend on the subjective judgments of the flight instructors, whose advice was seldom questioned so long as the elimination rate remained in the 40–60 per cent range. Although flight surgeons sat with these boards, they did not act as intermediaries between the cadet and command; indeed, their primary duty was to help in the cadet's next assignment. Flight training is necessarily ruthless, and the men who survived it had been through a selection process far more rigorous and realistic than anything the psychologists could devise.

Having completed individual training and received his wings, the typical airman was assigned to an operational or replacement training unit at one of the combat crew training stations (CCTS). Here, all the elements of a combat unit, including medical personnel, were assembled for training as a team prior to assignment to operational duties. "When the individual pilot, gunner, or other flying specialist arrived at an OTU or RTU station, his main concern was the character of his crew [or, in the case of the fighter pilot, his squadron]. The crew was the family circle of an air force; each member knew that long hours of work, play, anxiety, and danger would be shared. Naturally, each man hoped to be assigned to a crew [or a squadron] in whose members he had confidence and with whom he would be congenial."* Here also began the unique patient-physician relationship which the flight surgeon (the family doctor) had to develop to serve effectively his men and his commander. The time together prior to combat varied from a few months to a year, and in that time every aspect of the team relationship had to be consolidated. The elimina-

* Vol. VI, 606.

tion rate had decreased with each step in the training program, and at CCTS the unit flight surgeon was intimately involved in cases submitted to the flying evaluation board. By this time the AAF had invested eight to ten months of expensive training in each flyer, and serious consideration was necessarily given to all recommendations or requests for elimination on whatever grounds. In most cases, flying personnel now had their first experience with high-performance military aircraft, and this required training in the use of oxygen equipment and protective devices.

Responsibility with respect to oxygen equipment was twofold. First, each unit commander was responsible for oxygen discipline in his command, and he was required to designate an oxygen equipment officer, usually the assistant operations officer,[25] who had received training through a unit oxygen officers' course given either at SAM or overseas, as at the Eighth Air Force Provisional Medical Field Service School. Second, the medical service was responsible through SAM for altitude (and oxygen) indoctrination of aircrewmen and, through the Aero Medical Research Laboratory, for the development of oxygen equipment and the conduct of investigations to ascertain the physiological requirements of oxygen equipment. A formal procedure to accomplish this, the High-Altitude Indoctrination and Classification Program, was established by an AAF directive, 19 March 1942.[26] This provided for preliminary instruction on altitude flying and oxygen discipline at preflight and flexible-gunnery schools and advanced indoctrination and classification for high-altitude tolerance at CCTS. To implement the program, low-pressure chambers were installed at the three cadet training centers, the seven flexible-gunnery schools, and at various stations of the four continental air forces. Personnel to man these units were trained in SAM's aviation physiology course, attendance at which was required of all flight surgeons. At a typical CCTS each aircrewman received instruction covering the effects of altitude on bodily functions (anoxia, aero-embolism, gastrointestinal cramping, aero-otitis, and effects of cold) and the proper use of his mask and the plane's oxygen system. In addition, each man (in groups of about twenty, under the supervision of a flight surgeon and an aviation physiologist) experienced a 3–4½-hour chamber "flight" to 35,000–40,000 feet. During this flight the symptoms of anoxia were demonstrated, the fitting and use of the face mask was checked, and confidence in the oxygen system was established. Early experience in the ETO with flyers who had not received such indoctrination was so unsatisfactory that the program was accorded high priority and implemented with great diligence. In the AAF Training Command more than 42,000 separate chamber flights were made to train over 620,000 different individuals.[27]

The usefulness of the unit's surgeon at this and later stages in his military career owed much to the special training he had received through a program conducted by the School of Aviation Medicine under the able leadership of its wartime commandant, Col. Eugene G. Reinartz, MC. Between Pearl Harbor and V-J Day, a total of 4,365 physicians completed the aviation medical examiners' course or the flight surgeons' course. (During the same period the failures totaled only 146.)[28] At least an equal number of medical officers and other personnel attended short courses of specialized instruction at SAM. In addition, a variety of special-purpose training was offered for medical officers at the School of Applied Tactics, the Emergency Rescue School, and the School of Air Evacuation, to name only three. The SAM commandant and his staff were kept informed of conditions in the theaters and of apparent deficiencies in the training of medical officers. In general, they were unselfishly responsive to criticisms and suggestions, and the curriculum was revised almost constantly as the war progressed.

Care of the Flyer: Combat

Training accomplished, the combat unit and its flight surgeon moved overseas to the ETO, or to the Mediterranean or the Pacific, or to the China-Burma-India theater, where in each there were unique medical problems as well as those common to the whole AAF. But it is from the experience of the Eighth Air Force, based in England, where combat conditions were the most arduous, that the problems of aviation medicine can be separated with fair confidence from the unfavorable environmental and sanitation conditions that existed in other air theaters. The emphasis on the experience of the Eighth is not intended to minimize the accomplishments of medical personnel elsewhere. It is chosen as an illustrative case simply because the Eighth had the longest experience, the highest casualty rates, and the most reliable statistics.

The war mission of the Eighth Air Force was offensive: to drop hundreds of thousands of tons of high explosives on Hitler's Europe by high-altitude, daylight bombing. The Eighth was the proving agency for the AAF's doctrine of air power implemented by an air weapons system. In Europe the AAF had two excellent heavy bombers—the B-17 and the B-24—in friendly competition with the heavies of the RAF. Opposing these two air forces were the still mighty Luftwaffe and the powerful antiaircraft defenses of the Reich with its excellent guns and rapidly developing air-warning system, which always seemed good enough to the Allied flyers but actually was inferior to the Allied radar. It was most important for American airmen that the Eighth Air Force succeed and to do as well or preferably better than the battle-tested RAF. Command was acutely conscious of all these considerations, and so—to a large extent—were the men. It is within this frame of reference, and with the knowledge that the Eighth was expanding rapidly at the end of its 3,500-mile supply line, that one should examine the care of the flyer program and other aspects of the AAF's medical service. Motivation was very strong, and whether it involved the will to win or the will to outperform the RAF is immaterial; the result was excellent morale in the whole force. It was predictable that the commanding general would expect maximum effort from the two components of his weapons system: the human resources and the materiel. It was also predictable that anyone who interfered with his attempt to squeeze the last bit of service out of his men and planes was in for a fight. It was up to the medical service to assure the maximum availability of manpower.

Headquarters, Eighth Air Force was established 19 May 1942, and Maj. Gen. Carl Spaatz assumed command 18 June. Between that date and the initial all-out strike of the 1st Bombardment Wing on 9 October 1942,* General Spaatz approved most of the recommendations of the Eighth Air Force surgeon that involved care of the flyer, but his failure to support two others were to have a serious effect on the originally high morale of the airmen. One, relating to an unsatisfactory situation in hospitalization and disposition, will be described later.† The other was a request for a decision on the length of the tour of duty. It was obvious to experienced flight surgeons that combat crews and individual fighter pilots could not long tolerate the combined stresses of combat and the anticipated attrition rate if the only limit to their tour of operational duty was personal survival. Based on a "conservative" estimate of 5 per cent loss per mission,

---

* See Vol. II, 220.   † See below, pp. 407–12.

combat crews with little regard for mathematical accuracy realized that they could be wiped out, theoretically, by 20 missions.* As early as the fall of 1942, the Eighth Air Force surgeon, Colonel Grow, urged that combat crews be relieved from operational duty after 15 missions. Flight surgeons watched morale sink during the winter of 1942–43, as the squadrons were depleted more rapidly than the replacements dribbled in. In March 1943 the Eighth Air Force Central Medical Establishment† prepared a study of the consequences of this lack of policy, "Morale in Air Crew Members, Eighth Bomber Command,"[29] and recommended a definite and fixed combat tour. Finally, some seven months after the start of the bomber offensive, Maj. Gen. Ira C. Eaker, then commanding the Eighth Air Force, announced that the tour of duty for bomber crews would be a minimum of 25 missions, and for fighter pilots, 150 missions or 200 operational hours of flying. This decision, combined with a well-balanced leave policy and the use of rest homes and rehabilitation centers, had a favorable effect on morale. Comparable decisions regarding the combat tour were not made in the other air forces until they were forced on command by the pressure of circumstances.

As the offensive of the Eighth Air Force got under way in 1942, flight surgeons encountered five problems in aviation medicine which remained major concerns until the end of hostilities. They were: anoxia, frostbite, aero-otitis, battle wounds, and stress. Attempts to minimize and control these problems became the concern of the school system and the research units of the medical service, and the time and effort devoted to them are incalculable. It is fair to say that each problem had been anticipated to some extent, but actual combat was necessary to underline its urgency and define its scope.‡

---

* Actually, a loss rate of 5 per cent per mission works out to 35 per cent surviving 20 missions. This amendment of the odds could not have afforded much satisfaction even to the most unsophisticated.

† First established 24 July 1942 at PINETREE, England, as Eighth Air Force Provisional Medical Field Service School. It was renamed Eighth Air Force Central Medical Establishment on 9 November 1943 and became the First Central Medical Establishment (CME) in August 1944 (Link and Coleman, *Medical Support of AAF in WW II*, p. 551). Other numbered air forces organized similar establishments.

‡ The medical statistics of the AAF were presented as follows: (1) occupational disorders peculiar to flying, i.e., anoxia, frostbite, aero-otitis; (2) non-occupational disorders, i.e., respiratory disease, venereal disease, neuropsychiatric disorders, injuries; and (3) battle casualties, i.e., wounded or injured in action, killed in action, missing in action. These were reported on the Care of the Flyer Reports, AF Form 203, which included mean strength and individual data on each casualty.

1. *Anoxia.* Combat missions of the Eighth were normally executed at altitudes of 22,000–25,000 feet, so that an adequate continuous supply of oxygen was mandatory. As soon as operations began, the number of reports of fatal and non-fatal anoxia incidents far exceeded the most pessimistic predictions.[30] In non-fatal cases reduced combat efficiency was evident, and on many occasions a mission aborted because of failure of the oxygen system or the appearance of anoxia in a crewman. Fatal cases occasionally occurred without any clear evidence of defect in the equipment. A study by the Eighth Air Force Central Medical Establishment showed that anoxia cases were caused by battle damage to the oxygen system, failure of the quick-disconnect, freezing of the mask, personal errors in the use of the system and ignorance of proper oxygen discipline, and failure of the regulators.

The two obvious remedies were better training and better equipment. In England the Eighth Air Force Provisional Medical Field Service School stepped up its program of training flight surgeons and unit oxygen officers and attempted to provide low-pressure chamber indoctrination for all aircrewmen who had missed it during flight training. A comparable increase in emphasis on high-altitude training at all levels was ordered at SAM and in the Training Command. The equipment problem had been practically overcome at the Aero Medical Research Laboratory in 1941, when captured samples of German demand systems were used as models for a completely new demand system to replace unsatisfactory continuous-flow units. Production and installation of the new system got sidetracked somewhere, and it was not until the spring of 1943 that the new equipment arrived in England in sufficient quantities for installation in all operational aircraft. There were still a few bugs in the masks and valves and the "walk-around" bottles, but the people at Central Medical Establishment soon overcame them. By November 1943 the problem was coming under control, and one year later the Air Surgeon could report that the anoxia incident rate among heavy-bomber crews had dropped from 115.5 per 100,000 man-missions (November 1943) to 23.4 in November 1944. This 80 per cent decrease in incidents was accompanied by a 68 per cent reduction in fatalities, whose rate decreased from 21.6 to 7.1 per 100,000 man-missions over the same period of time.

2. *Frostbite.* At the maximum altitudes flown in the ETO, the air

temperature ranged from —50° to —60° F. Inside bomber and fighter aircraft, temperatures of 0° to —10° F. were the rule except at open gunports in the waist and the tail, where the temperature approximated that outside. In belated anticipation of these conditions the Aero Medical Research Laboratory established a clothing-test unit in the Biophysics Branch early in 1942 to develop individually heated garments for aircrewmen. In spite of the late date of starting, it appears that prototype electrically heated garments were produced in time for issue to waist and tail gunners in the VIII Bomber Command in the fall of 1942. These suits, boots, and gloves were poorly designed and susceptible to electrical failure. Better models came into production after October 1943, and eventually enough were on hand to help control the frostbite problem.

In addition to the equipment deficiency, the aircrews lacked proper indoctrination in the prevention and emergency treatment of frostbite and in the proper use of such protective equipment that was on hand. An energetic training program and advanced instruction of unit equipment officers by the Central Medical Establishment were helpful. Finally, the American genius for improvisation in the field resulted in inclosures for the waist and tail guns, with obvious benefit to the gunners. The magnitude of the frostbite problem was evident from the fact that more than one-half of the casualties (excluding accidents on returning from missions and missing in action) between August 1942 and January 1944 were due to frostbite. Twelve per cent of these were attributed to lack of equipment and 24 per cent to defective equipment. The heavy toll of 19.7 cold injuries per 1,000 man-missions in February 1943 was finally reduced to 0.03 in August 1944. Over the entire period of air operations in the ETO, frostbite was responsible for 3,452 removals from flying status, 35 of which were permanent.[31]

3. *Aero-otitis.* This is an acute or chronic disorder of the middle ear caused initially by inflammation and obstruction of the Eustachian tube, particularly at its entrance into the nasopharynx. In healthy individuals this passage is open, permitting equalization of the air pressure on both sides of the eardrum and free movement of secretions into the nasopharynx. When the upper respiratory passages are inflamed for any reason, air-pressure adjustment fails to occur during ascent, causing pain and hearing loss. At altitude, adjustment eventually occurs, but during descent the external pressure increase is not

balanced, and pain and deafness return. The victim can inflate his middle ears by a forced expiration with the nose and mouth held shut, but this maneuver carries infected secretions into the middle ear. Because of the abnormal conditions resulting from the blocked Eustachian tube, an inflammatory or suppurative otitis media develops. The acute process runs a course of a few days to a few weeks, but in susceptible individuals recurrences are common or a state of chronic infection may develop. When the infection is due to pyogenic bacteria (e.g., streptococci), sulfa drugs and penicillin control the attack promptly. Since most cases are related to a viral infection, drug therapy is useless. Before the development of cabin pressurization, aero-otitis was common, and the disability and discomfort associated with it was a significant factor in the adoption of pressurized cabins in commercial aircraft. In the continental air forces, aero-otitis was the commonest disorder attributed to flying. Factors that favor its development, in addition to respiratory-tract infection, are long exposure to high altitude and gradual ascent and descent. The incidence was twice as great in heavy-bomber crews as in mediums and four times as great in heavies as in fighters because of the difference in rate of climb.

Among the occupational disorders of the Eighth's aircrewmen aero-otitis was the most important, accounting for two-thirds of the temporary removals from flying status. During the whole period of operations there were 8,345 removals for this reason, and, of these, 52 were permanent. The average number of days lost per attack of otitis was eight. Of the non-fatal afflictions of flyers, only battle injuries were more numerous. A great deal of effort was devoted to this problem by a variety of medical specialists, with surprisingly little in the way of significant results. The most popular form of treatment was the destruction of lymphoid tissue at the entrance of the Eustachian tube by means of radium applicators. No well-controlled study of this prophylactic procedure to justify its use has come to the writer's attention. The situation in England was particularly favorable to the development of aero-otitis, because of the high "normal" rate of respiratory infection, the crowded living quarters, and the rapid turnover of personnel. The flight surgeons did all the conventional things—and some unconventional ones—to cope with this problem but were no more successful than anyone else.[32]

4. *Battle casualties.* Casualties* from enemy action were of course

---

* In military medicine "casualties" is the general term for those killed in action (KIA) and those dying of wounds, which together equals total killed; those wounded in action

anticipated by the medical service, but no one knew when the air war got under way what the final reports would look like. RAF experience, so valuable in many areas, was of little aid here, since British bombers operated at night, the AAF by day. Two aspects of battle casualties deserve comment: first, the influence of the casualty rate on morale[33] and, second, the usefulness of protective armor. In this new type of warfare, the majority of casualties were the crews of the planes that never returned. The empty bunks and the new replacements told the story more bitterly than the steady disappearance of familiar aircraft from the hardstands.

The problem is illustrated graphically in the following chart, where the numbers of survivors and the numbers of those killed and missing in action out of a group of 2,051 heavy-bomber crewmen are plotted against the number of operational missions.[34] The risk rate per mission is also shown.*

ATTRITION OF HEAVY-BOMBER AIRCREWMEN

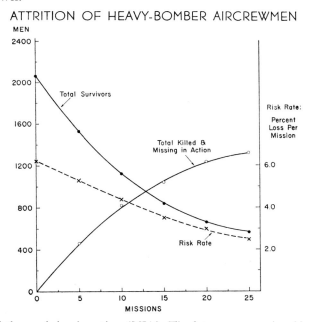

(WIA); and those missing in action (MIA). The latter category is subject to adjustment later, when all the returns are in.

* This graph is constructed from data collected in a study of the attrition rate for heavy-bomber crews in the ETO. The 2,051 flying personnel used in the study were members of the 91st, 94th, 305th, 306th, 381st, and 384th Bombardment Groups. The total survivors are the aircrewmen available for subsequent missions. In addition to the 1,295 airmen killed and missing in action, 197 were lost from the original number for a variety of reasons, including battle wounds. The broken curve indicates the percentage of the survivors killed and missing in action per mission. These data apply to 1943-44.

The average aircrewman may have been handy with dice or cards, but he never understood statistics. The way he interpreted it, the rising curve for the percentage of the group killed and missing in action spelled a steady decrease in his personal chance of survival. He never understood the significance of the broken line showing the risk rate per mission, which became increasingly more favorable as the 25-mission tour progressed. The net result was that the old soldier's protection against anxiety, the delusion that "nothing can happen to me," was replaced by the morale-destroying fixation that "something disastrous must happen to me." There was nothing definite that the flight surgeon could do about this, except talk to the ones that had it worst, prescribe phenobarbital and benzedrine, arrange for a rest leave, and hope for the best.

When the aircrewman who flew against the Nazis said that things were really tough in the ETO and the MTO but everyone else had it pretty good, he was absolutely right, as can be seen in the final tabulation of AAF casualties:

AAF Casualties in All Theaters
December 1941–August 1945*

Theater	Total Casualties	Per Cent of Grand Total	Killed	Wounded	Missing	Strength†
ETO	63,410	52.0	19,876	8,413	35,121	
						610,000
MTO	31,155	25.6	10,223	4,947	15,985	
FEAF	17,237	14.2	6,594	3,005	7,638	......
20th AF	3,415	2.8	576	433	2,406	......
CBI	3,332	2.7	1,263	494	1,575	
						440,000
POA	2,476	2.0	926	882	668	
Alaska	682	0.6	451	53	168	......
Other	160	0.1	152	1	7	......
Grand total	121,867	100.0	40,061	18,238	63,568	

* *AAF Statistical Digest*, Dec. 1945, pp. 49–59.
† Total strength deployed against Germany and Japan, respectively (Vol. VI, 32).

The decision to supply aircrewmen with body armor may seem anachronistic, but it was based on careful studies of wound ballistics initiated by the Surgeon, Eighth Air Force.[35] Colonel Grow was aware of British studies of the wounds received by men engaged in desert warfare: 40–70 per cent of the wounds were caused by low-velocity missiles (i.e., shell fragments, ricochets, and grenade fragments), capable of being intercepted by armored vests and properly designed helmets. Because of the similarity of these missiles to flak, a study of air force battle casualties was ordered in October 1942. The incidence of wounds due to low-velocity missiles in a good sampling was 70 per cent. The Central Medical Establishment then designed and ordered armored vests, half-vests, and sporrans for field trial. Delivery began in March 1943, and, by January 1944, 13,500 flak suits were on hand. Crews resisted the use of the armor at first, but an energetic demonstration campaign and the obvious protection afforded converted the majority of airmen. In addition to the flak suits, seats were armored, and flak screens and flak pads resistant to low-velocity missiles were installed in most planes. The results are seen in the following table:

Effect of Body Armor on Casualty Rates

	Unarmored	Armored
Total number of individuals struck by missiles*	508	495
Per cent killed	35	21
Per cent injured	65	16
Per cent uninjured, or injured so little as to remain on duty	0	62
Per cent of aircraft receiving battle damage per mission†	26.5	21.5

* In ETO.

† This figure is included to indicate the comparable intensity of enemy resistance during the early part of the campaign, when aircrewmen were unarmored, and the latter part, when armor was generally used.

5. *Stress.* When stress and its sequelae come up for consideration, the comfortable realm of definite clinical entities and reliable statistics is left behind. There is only a wasteland in which to wander, filled with shadows of theories, dusty slogans, and dire predictions. Everyone knew that military service, particularly combat, was bound to be rugged. The stresses to which men would be subjected were many, and they could occur singly or in any conceivable combination. In a preceding section* attention was directed to the contemporary attitude of physicians and others to emotional reactions to stresses as the basis for symptom formation and disability. Experienced physicians have no idea how to predict how much stress a given person can tolerate, nor are they at all certain that exposure to stress to the limit of tolerance is instrinsically harmful. If the medical service had any common tacit policy in this respect, it was to help the men carry on to the limit of their capacity, and then perhaps fly a few more missions.

As an official policy spelled out in directives, such a plan would

* See above, pp. 390–92.

have been futile at best and destructive of morale at worst. As implemented by sympathetic, perceptive flight surgeons, responsive to the high goals of command and eager to help their charges conduct themselves as men, the unwritten plan worked magnificently. Psychologists and psychiatrists presented arguments, proposals, nomenclatures, and warnings which only served to confuse the issue. Twelve years after the end of the war one fails to see the grave psychic consequences of pushing men to—and beyond—what many then considered the breaking point. By the pragmatic test of war, the airman tolerated magnificently all the stresses that he encountered. No one knows the extent or the variety of the symptom-producing emotional reactions that occurred along the way, but remarkably few men permitted these reactions to produce disability. Statistics are meaningless on the various emotional states: anxiety reaction, fatigue, fear of flying, aeroneurosis, or what-not. The figures that count are the temporary removals from flying status—of which there were only 3,067 for the entire war period in the ETO. In addition, there were only 1,042 permanent removals from flying status for anxiety reactions; and if one adds other probably related entities, such as insubordination, the total is only 1,576, or less than 1.5 per cent of the combat force.[36] This force had been badly mauled by the Luftwaffe and the inclement weather of northern Europe—to the extent that its casualties numbered 63,000, while some 60,000 aircrewmen successfully completed the prescribed tour of duty.[37] The flyers in the other theaters did just about as well.

It is quite evident that the morale of the men who finished their combat tours had been exceptionally well sustained and that the effort devoted to the care of the flyer had paid off handsomely.

A Day in the Life of a Flight Surgeon

The complex duties of the flight surgeon assigned to a heavy-bomber squadron are illustrated by the following "log" of a typical bad day. This is what it was like in England, or Guadalcanal, or Nadzab, or Tunisia. The composite presented derives from many sources:

0400   Up early for briefing at Group—coffee and crackers there. This will be another maximum effort strike for which we have 53 planes available, but only 50 crews. Weather foul—a twelve hour trip. After briefing, checked oxygen equipment myself for the 2 new crews. . . .

0500   In the ambulance on the line for takeoff. There are only 2 of us on duty —another is off at school somewhere and the group surgeon is at a meeting.

0510   Called to sick bay. Lt. . . . carried in by his crewmen, too weak to climb into the aircraft—Diarrhea all night—Bad chow?—Too much whiskey?—Or nerves? He's stayed in his hut smoking and drinking since the last strike when his buddy got a direct hit and exploded. Crew looked relieved when I grounded him, and the sergeant made out the hospital ticket.

0540   One of ours—Capt. . . . lost power on takeoff—crashed into the Channel— burned—Poor devils! Air-sea got there quick but no survivors.

0550   One of the new crews lost an engine half-way down the field—skidded off the runway and nosed over gently. No one hurt but the waist gunner who broke an arm when he jumped out—sergeant puts a temporary splint on him; and I take the pilot who's shaking bad to my quarters for a few stiff drinks—When he relaxes, I give him a seconal and my driver takes him to his hut. Lucky!

0630   Everyone airborne—to breakfast.

0700   Sick call: 2 or 3 men with bronchitis (or malaria, or diarrhea) to over-crowd the already full dispensary. Couple of fellows getting edgy—head-aches—dizzy spells: gave them appointments to come back later for a little quiet talk. Usual dressings—all o.k. Sergeant and I work on the reports— Reports!

0930   The other flight surgeon and I flip to see who will stick around for the cripples and the aborts—I won—so my driver and I start off for rounds in the hospitals. Raining.

1000   . . . Station Hospital. All our men in surgery doing fine, except Lt. . . . who has minor flak wounds of the abdomen—says he can't eat. Talked with him for half hour or so—he's edgy—his crew has ditched twice and some-body has been hurt on every one of their 10 missions—I think he's had it and suggested to the ward officer that he'd do better in the general hospital —he won't be fit to fly for months.

1100   The colonel called me to his office and raised hell about one of our men who went AWOL during the night—the kid is a tail gunner that I sent in with acute amebic dysentery—we're not permitted to treat it in dispensary now! I'd seen the kid on the flight line this morning and wondered how he got out so soon. Some guys. . . .

1200   Lunch at the hospital. Picked up some stuff from the pharmacy and from medical supply—very generous fellows. . . .

1300   . . . General Hospital. Several of our mob got in here when they got lost in the fog and crashed nearby. Doctor on the officer's ward wanted to talk to me about the pilot, Capt. . . . , who it seems is very morose, won't talk about the war, his family, or anything else for that matter. His broken ribs and chest injuries are doing all right, but the doc has requested a psychi-atric consultation. I told him to forget it—B's always quiet, and of course he feels bad about smashing up his plane—she'd always been lucky until that trip—he only thinks about planes and women and won't talk much about either of them—He's an iron man and his crew idolizes him—he needs a psychiatrist like I do—The young doctor is not convinced and we have quite a debate—says he knows when a man is cracking up. I say wait a bit, let me talk to B. I'll manage to get B out before they do anything drastic. . . .

1400 Sat in on a Disposition Board involving some of our men—what a riot!
One of our mechanics with headaches that they said was due to hostility
to his lieutenant—they think he better be sent back. I know better: his
headaches are hangovers from the rotten moonshine he and his pals are
making somewhere on the base—we'll probably lose him even though he's
a good mechanic, overhung or not. . . .

1430 On the way back to the field passed our ambulance—stopped—four of
our men with fairly serious injuries from flak and a crash when their cripple
came in—not too bad, but too much for our sick bay to handle . . .

1500 Talked with men with nerves—one had a "Dear John" letter which I had
to read—the other just needed some one to talk to—They'll be all right with
some phenobarb and a little more rest—twelve hours a day, seven days a
week in the shops can get a little rugged for some of the boys—The last
man, a navigator is worried about his ability to do his job—he's loused up
a couple of trips and they only got back because of plain dumb luck—
I can't make out whether he's stupid, or beginning to crack up—we'll talk
some more tomorrow. . . .

1610 Back in the ambulance on the line, "sweating out" the returns as the fog
begins to roll in. . . . Our radio brings us all the chatter between the tower
and the planes. . . . Priority in landing goes to the planes with wounded
men aboard—there are only 2 this time—one gets down safely—moderate
flak and machine gun wounds which can be patched up when we get all
the planes in—The other couldn't get its wheels down so we all raced over
to the crash strip, and ran along with her as she came in—a messy landing—
cartwheeled—then caught on fire. The crash crew got there first and had
foam on her and we got all the men but the copilot who was pinned in the
debris. We were working on him when the gun belts started to go, and
then the fire started again in the cabin so we couldn't get back—the radio-
man said he died on the way in, and that's the way it looked to me, the few
seconds I had to see him. Two other planes missing—one was seen going
down over the target—no one knew what happened to the other. According to my form card this is a little worse than average for a tough mission
—but not bad considering. . . .

1700 Helped serve at the aircrew bar after interrogation—all who feel the need
of medicinal whiskey get it courtesy of the Air Surgeon—bless him! No
one very edgy, except Lt. . . . , who has just lost the second roommate in a
fortnight as our Allies say—Later at the club, I played gin rummy with him
and we philosophized about luck and life and things. . . .

1730 Dinner—the mess is getting worse—food too greasy—mess attendants not
too clean—the kitchen will get a thorough inspection and the mess sergeant
will get chewed tomorrow. . . .

1830 Made rounds in the dispensary with my partner—everyone doing well,
thanks to sulfa, paregoric and phenobarb—Only a few men for evening sick
call—a special one that I run for the men who are too busy on the line for
the regular one—Sergeant and I worked up the reports on the day's casualties—Crash crew brought in the body from the burned plane—described
the wounds—he may not have been dead when they crashed—made out the
report, tagged the body and sent it off to the Graves people. . . .

1930 Back to the . . . General Hospital for a medical meeting—the Wing Surgeon thinks we should all be there—and attendance is taken—one goes—Not

a bad clinic on hepatitis and frostbite—some good ideas—there was a social hour afterwards and I ran into a classmate that just came over. . . .

2300   Back home—and to bed—too tired to write home.

0200   Sergeant wakened me—one of the armorers has DT's and is sitting in his hut shooting the snakes with his .45. I took the gun away from him, and we got him to the sick bay where some IV amytal finally put him out—and so to bed again.

Hospitalization

The hospital care of AAF personnel was the basis for a dispute that began with the expansion program and continued to V-J Day. The details of the controversy are given exhaustively elsewhere.[38] The problem of command control and the prerogatives of the Surgeon General of the Army and of the Air Surgeon, respectively, loom large in the voluminous official correspondence on the subject. As is often the case, the fundamental issues were relatively simple, and they can be understood best by briefly describing the system as it operated during the war years and by considering the personnel procedures involved in the hospitalization of a typical infantryman and a typical aircrewman.

In the Zone of the Interior (ZI) a recruit, or an officer, assigned to infantry received his training in one of the four continental army areas. When sick or injured, he was sent to a post station hospital under the control of the Army Service Forces or, in the case of a special school, under the control of the Surgeon, Army Ground Forces. If the condition requiring hospitalization was minor (directives specified cases properly treated in station hospitals), the infantryman remained on the rolls of his company and on discharge returned to it. For a major condition, or if apparently unfit for further military service, the soldier was transferred to a named general hospital and dropped from the rolls of his company, which could now requisition a replacement with the appropriate military occupational specialty (MOS). In the general hospital the soldier was picked up on the morning report of the detachment of patients. After receiving maximum benefit from this hospitalization, if fit for duty, he was shipped to a replacement depot for assignment on the basis of his MOS, but there was almost no likelihood that he would return to his original unit. If he was not fit for duty, the hospital disposition board recommended the appropriate type of separation from the service.

In a theater of operations the wounded, sick, or injured infantryman moved backward along a medical evacuation chain. So long as the reason for hospitalization did not require him to move farther to the rear than the field medical service of the division or corps (medical battalion installations and evacuation hospital), he remained under the control of the army commander but was not necessarily returned to his own company. He was sent, usually through a replacement unit, to some understrength company. If the disability was more severe, he entered the numbered station and general hospital system of the zone of communications which was under the control of the theater Services of Supply. From there on procedures paralleled those in the ZI.

In theory, then, the soldier was an interchangeable part of the war machine, whose assignment depended upon his MOS. The system was designed to keep ground-force units up to combat strength, utilizing the table of organization and the MOS as the basis for assignment from a replacement unit.

Procedures within the AAF were conditioned by a different attitude toward the airman. During individual flying training, and in the preliminary training of ground-duty personnel, the practice with respect to hospitalization was similar to that of the Army except that the station hospitals of air bases and other air installations were under the command of the AAF and, therefore, under control of the Air Surgeon. Transfer of a patient to a named general hospital was seldom ordered, except when disposition as unfit for further duty was contemplated, for the station hospitals as a rule were exceptionally competent professionally. Even at this early level of training the AAF tended to consider its human resources not so much as interchangeable parts but rather as members of individual teams, whose *esprit de corps* was a vital element. When aircrewmen were assigned to a combat crew training station, this official attitude became an increasingly important consideration with respect to hospitalization. As members of an aircrew or a fighter squadron, the flyers and ground-duty personnel rapidly developed into a team that required mutual interdependence, mutual responsibility, and mutual loyalty. Under these circumstances it was of the utmost importance that the man who had to be hospitalized for a tolerably brief period should return to his own unit and that he should get back as promptly as possible. The AAF accelerated station hospital care to the maximum extent possible, and this helped the individual to retain his allegiance to his unit and his group. An airman who got into a named general hospital was lost not only to his squadron, but the operations of ASF replacement centers were such that he could also be lost to the AAF, although this latter possibility was corrected eventually by War Department directive.

Overseas the problem was serious, for the AAF did not have a field medical service comparable to the medical battalion and the evacuation hospital, except for the 25-bed aviation medical dispensaries. In most theaters, men on sick report could be retained in dispensaries for a limited time only: 96 hours to a week was the rule. The numbered station hospitals on or adjacent to the large air bases and the numbered general hospitals were controlled, as were the bases, by the Services of Supply, responsible to the theater commander. As zone-of-communications installations supporting a combat force, these hospitals were supposed to return to their units battle casualties and the sick and injured who were hospitalized 30 days or less. If released from a hospital after more than 30 days, airmen were sent to an air force replacement depot. In theory there was no assurance that an airman would ever return to his own unit, although in practice most of them did as a result of informal agreements in the various theaters. Where the station hospital staff thought it desirable or when theater medical directives so specified, long-term patients and those requiring disposition were transferred to numbered general hospitals, whose disposition boards tended not to consult the flight surgeons of the airman's unit. To correct this, theater directives usually prohibited disposition of flying personnel, since assignment to flying duty was a prerogative of air command, even though determination of fitness to fly was a medical responsibility.

The difference in the attitude of the Army and the AAF toward their respective human resources is abundantly clear in the medical operations of the ZI and of the theaters. In the complex team activities of an air combat unit, the individual had to be paramount, since personality and group experience were important. Small wonder that flight surgeons complained bitterly about protracted hospitalizations and time-consuming administrative procedures over which they had no control.

In the United States the air-base station hospitals were developed professionally to an extent that provoked frequent complaints from the Surgeon General. The violent nature of aircraft accidents demanded prompt and skilful surgical care which the medical service of the AAF was able to supply as a result of the ambitious physician recruitment program undertaken in 1942, largely by default. Of the 9,000 doctors who volunteered for service with the AAF, 4,000 ranked as specialists, and, by the winter of 1943, the staffing capability of air-base station hospitals was such that approximately 60 per cent of the 239 then in operation were approved for residency training by the American Medical Association and accredited by the American College of Surgeons.[39] Many of these functioned as general hospitals, medically, although they could not perform the administrative functions of disposition.

As a result of a number of factors, including complaints to President Roosevelt about hospital treatment of airmen overseas, the rapidly increasing load of casualties, and exacerbation of the conflict between the Surgeon General of the Army and the Air Surgeon, the regional hospital system was established in April 1944 by WD Circular 140. The provisions of this circular were as follows:

1. The flow of general-hospital-type patients to ZI installations was split so that battle casualties were sent to the named general hospitals and trainee patients to the nearest regional hospital, regardless of command relationships.

2. The Air Surgeon and the Surgeon General each designated 30 of the ZI station hospitals to be under *his* control as regional hospitals, chosen to serve non-overlapping areas.

3. The regional hospitals were staffed to provide definitive care (except for patients requiring specialized treatment at certain named general hospitals, e.g., paraplegics at Lawson General Hospital) and to operate disposition, physical reclassification, and retirement boards.

4. No airman could be separated from the AAF by an Army Service Forces board without the concurrence of the Commanding General, AAF, or his representative.

5. Patients from overseas or from the ZI requiring convalescent care were sent to separate Army or AAF convalescent hospitals, depending on the service to which they belonged.

6. Commanding General, AAF, was charged with the responsibility for air transportation of patients and their medical service in transit.

This adjustment improved and clarified the situation in the United States, but it had no influence overseas. The theater hospitalization problem was never resolved in spite of many memoranda, letters, expressions of opinion, conferences, and plans. Two factors seem to have been responsible for the air staff's lack of willingness to press the issue. In the first place, the current structure of theater command was working well, as measured by the success of combat operations. A drastic revision of the plan for medical support had to be thoroughly justified, and the staff doubted that the situation was quite as intolerable as the medical service kept insisting. Estimates by command flight surgeons of excessive man-days lost due to failure of the AAF to control overseas hospitalization ran as high as 30 per cent;[40] opinions as to the effect of Army doctors on airmen's morale made discouraging reading—almost too discouraging. In the second place, such factual evidence as could be collected did not support these claims. The air staff was statistically minded, and management of the human resources could be handled the same way as aircraft maintenance. Studies were made in the Eighth Air Force which indicated that about 1,000 man-days per month were lost because of the existing system of hospitalization.[41] This worked out to a loss of only a few per cent in the availability of flying personnel and was obviously not sufficiently serious to justify an overhaul of the command structure in the theaters.[42]

Actually it does not appear that the medical care of airmen was inadequate in any important respect: either because they had to be sent to SOS hospitals or because they were retained and cared for illegally in aviation dispensaries. The young doctors who staffed either type of installation had the same basic medical background and approximately the same tools to work with. It is true that the 25-bed aviation medical dispensaries were often overcrowded, and it is also true that the equipment authorized for them was far less adequate than existed in a 250- or 500-bed numbered hospital. But the flight surgeons were energetic and rapidly developed skills in organizing that were not taught in medical school. Commanders of medical supply depots tended to disregard regulations, and highly efficient supply pipelines were developed for items "peculiar to the AAF" that often included medical equipment. In fact, the informal development of medical facilities for the Eighth Air Force was so effective that the theater surgeon, Brig. Gen. Paul Hawley, wrote to TSG, in July 1943, as follows: "I am so fed up with the ability of the Air Forces to obtain in profusion critical items of medical equipment through their own channels, which I am unable to obtain for other components of the Army, that I am resisting strenuously any move to give the Air Force a separate medical service or separate medical supply."[43] The flight surgeons in the other theaters did just about as well.

The Surgeon General and the War Department were not able to prevent the medical corps of the AAF from providing the sort of medical service they wanted their men to have, but it was possible for the SG and those in sympathy with his views to exact a sorry retribution. The victims of official policy were not the sick and wounded but the doctors and the enlisted medical personnel allotted to the AAF. Failure to revise manning tables and failure to recognize the *de facto* conditions retarded promotions and kept the unofficial field medical service of the AAF seriously understaffed and underrated. In spite of this unpleasant situation, and although overworked and inadequately housed, the unit surgeons took excellent care of the men who needed hospitalization of the sort they were able to provide.

Disposition and Tour of Duty

The major responsibility of the medical service was to enable command to get the maximum effort out of flying personnel. A realistic concept of an air weapons system in action required that every resource be utilized to the limit of its capability. In the case of the plane the limit was obvious: when it could no longer fly, a replacement was provided, and the remains were cannibalized or simply shoved aside to be junked later. In the case of the human resources, this realistic practice was not feasible for utilitarian and humanitarian reasons, some of which have a bearing on the disposition procedures of the AAF. In the discussion that follows, attention will be confined to the disposition of the airman considered incapable of further combat flying, regardless of whether the judgment was made by himself, his flight surgeon, his unit commander, or any combination of the three. Certain general comments are necessary to establish a proper perspective for consideration of the ways in which the AAF dealt with the problem.

At the outset of every bitterly contested campaign in World War II there were combat units that dubbed themselves—often with considerable justice—expendables. As a campaign progressed, sound military doctrine provided a system of reserves so that it was possible to rotate the forces in actual contact with the enemy. The theater commander was clearly responsible for the decision to develop and implement such plans depending upon his mission, the extent of enemy resistance, the forces at his disposal, and his estimate of the situation. The disastrous effect on morale of a policy that provided relief only for casualties was recognized, but no one had a clear, quantitative basis for relating attrition to morale, least of all American air commanders who were aggressively using their new weapons for which there was no sufficient background of combat experience. Army and Navy com-

FLIGHT NURSES ARRIVING IN CHINA

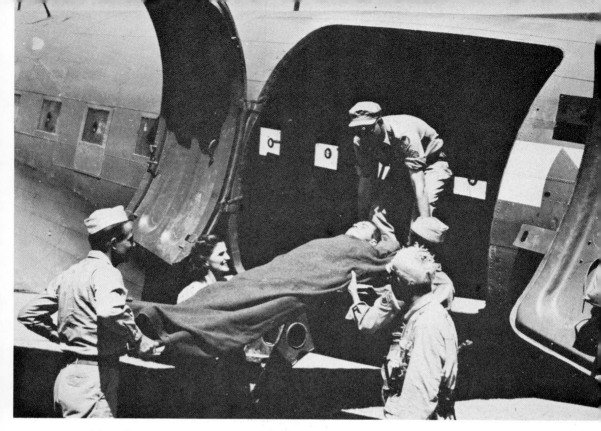

Hand Loading on C-46

AIR EVACUATION FROM CHINA

Hoist Loading on C-54

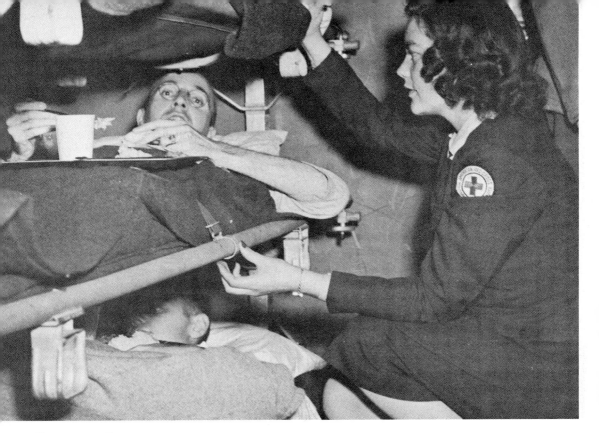

STOPOVER AT ICELAND

AIR EVACUATION

LASHING DOWN ON C-87, CHINA

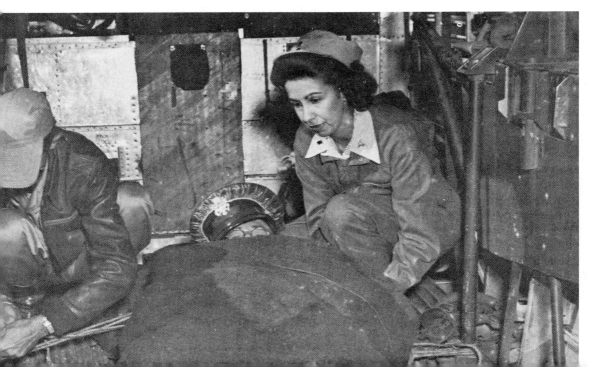

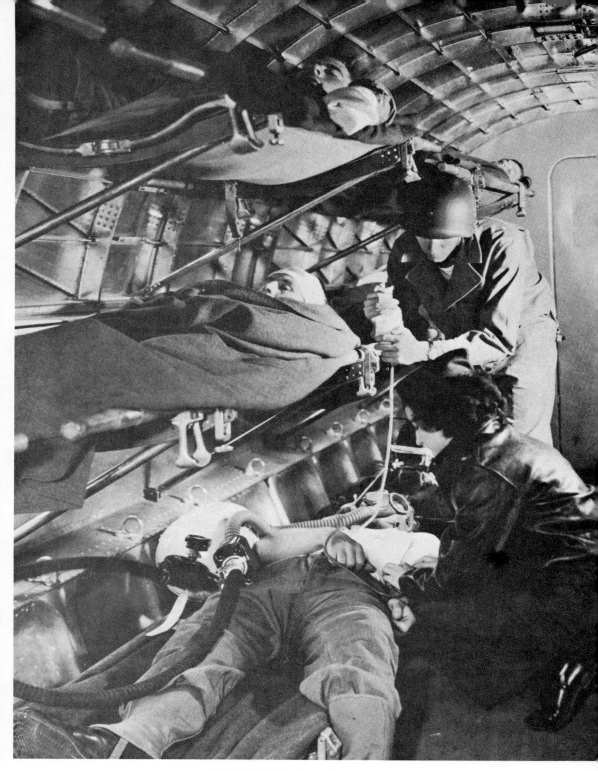

ADMINISTERING BLOOD PLASMA

manders had some (usually) vicarious experience from other wars, but this was relatively useless to the air arm, since the official attitude toward the individual soldier or sailor was simply not comparable to the flyer-centered orientation of the AAF. Each overseas air force, then, had to develop its own policies of relief, rotation, and disposition; and, even when official AAF directives on disposition appeared in 1944, each theater air commander continued to follow, primarily, the patterns that had been evolved to meet the problems peculiar to his own force. It seems obvious that any fair policy with respect to disposition had to be contingent upon and reasonably consistent with the policies establishing tours of combat duty and rotation between combat and rest areas. Unfortunately, in all the overseas air forces, the problem of disposition arose with the onset of hostilities and increased rapidly, whereas directives regarding tours of duty and rotation either were never issued, were late in appearing, or were variable because of delegation of authoity to subordinate commanders.

The fundamental problem of disposition of aircrewmen is stated succinctly in the official medical history:

There were two methods of removing aircrew personnel from flying status. One was administrative and the other was medical. Unfortunately, medical disposition was easier to accomplish and was likely to have less repercussion than administrative disposal. For this reason, line officers took advantage of medical disposition to remove many aircrew personnel which rightly should have been done by administrative measures. This practice placed tremendous responsibility upon the [unit] flight surgeon, and led eventually to the establishment of flying evaluation boards.

There was often a conflict between the medical condition and needs of the individual on the one hand and the tactical situation on the other which demanded full aircrews. This conflict was not easily resolved by the flight surgeon. Each case presented a unique problem. Along with the flyers whose ailments were magnified by their own fatigue were those with prohibitive conditions who wanted to resume flying status in order to serve with their crews. There were occasions, it was believed, where the flight surgeon's opinion was influenced by the necessity of continuing on good terms with his unit commander. Problems posed in the disposition of flying personnel were important because of the potential effects upon the fighting ability of an air force, and hence had to be dealt with in the light of operational experience.

Policies for the disposition of aircrew personnel who developed anxiety reactions* had to be established as the need arose. Throughout the war there was never complete agreement between the line officers, the medical officers and the psychiatrists about the disposition of such personnel, which testifies to the complicated nature of the problem posed by personnel suffering from emotional dis-

---

* The terminology used in this chapter would be: ". . . who developed emotional reactions due to stress."

turbances. In many of the anxiety reaction cases there was no clear-cut distinction which would indicate either medical or administrative aspects. Moreover, after a medical diagnosis was made, the administrative disposition of the individual would determine, in many instances, whether the individual could be salvaged for further duties.[44]

The paramount consideration was the great complexity of military aircraft and the nature of air combat, both of which required that the human component of the weapons system be composed—to the greatest extent possible—of "professional" fighting men. There was really no place in the combat force for the militia-type soldier, the ninety-day wonder, or the citizen-in-arms. The specialized training, the high degree of integration necessary for successful air operations, and the great burden placed on the individual aircrewman in combat all demanded a policy of conservation of manpower. The force, to be effective, had to be an elite force and one that was committed for the duration of hostilities. In this sense the aircrewman could not be considered expendable or replaceable to the same extent as the aircraft, even though the field commander had to be prepared to expend both of them to accomplish his mission. From this standpoint, the utilitarian aspect of unfitness for combat flying, from whatever cause, can be summarized as follows:

1. The man who considers himself unfit for combat flying or who is considered unfit by the flight surgeon or the unit commander is obviously inefficient, and he is thus potentially dangerous to the safety of others, as well as to himself.

2. Men inefficient in one area (e.g., combat) may have considerable efficiency in another assignment.

3. An inefficient man who is capable of endangering another's life arouses in the latter a fierce resentment.

4. A man declared medically unfit for flying has the basis for a future claim against the government for compensation.

5. The medical determination "unfit for flying" precluded disciplinary administrative action, although reassignment was possible.

6. It was manifestly unfair to courageous, highly motivated men when a weakling or a coward was relieved from combat flying solely on medical grounds.[45]

Finally, it is necessary to recall the traditional air force policy mentioned earlier: the flight surgeon determines only fitness for flying, but command determines the type of duty to which a flyer shall be assigned.

Consideration of the human factors in the disposition problem involves both the art of aviation medicine and the art of war. The problem here, in terms of the individual flyer, is the amount of combat he can tolerate and the extent to which his efficiency can be impaired before he is useless or dangerous to his combat unit. Even if the AAF administration had tried to establish a uniform policy for the tolerance of the human factor, it would have been a failure for two reasons: biological variability and the dissimilar nature of the stresses to which flyers were exposed in the various overseas theaters. The greatest difficulties that were encountered by command in the determination of policy regarding fitness to fly have been summarized by Douglas D. Bond in *The Love and Fear of Flying.* They were, first, the openly expressed fear of combat flying, or fear of flying a particular aircraft, or fear of night flying; second, that the severest symptoms of fear of flying were seldom detectable on the ground or seldom persisted for very long after grounding; third, the enormous value placed on physical symptoms by doctors and line officers; and, finally, the ambivalent attitudes on the part of those doing evaluation.

The problem that confronted the medical service and command can be appreciated most readily in terms of *stress* and *strain.* These words are used here approximately in their engineering sense, where stress refers to any sort of adverse influence exerted on a structure (or a person), and where strain implies the deformation or disturbance of the individual resulting from the forces applied. When the strain becomes sufficiently great, failure occurs. In the case of the airman, failure is his inability to fly or his refusal to fly.

Strain may be manifest in a variety of ways: by fatigue, staleness, headache, insomnia, gastrointestinal disturbances, anxiety states, phobic reactions, or regressive reactions (i.e., psychoses), to name only a few. In some cases strain is apparent on the physical examination (e.g., increased pulse rate, tremor, and abnormal breathing). In other cases, strain appears as "psychosomatic" symptoms, with no abnormal physical signs (e.g., vomiting, headache, and dizzy spells). In still others, strain manifests itself as disturbances in behavior (e.g., insubordination, excessive drinking, and inability to concentrate). Presumably, the nature of the strain will depend more upon the constitution and the personality of the individual than upon the sort and the intensity of the stresses that are responsible. Skilful physicians recognize strain intuitively and quantitate it in the same fashion.

Stress is a composite term for all the pressures exerted on the combat flyer in addition to the ordinary vicissitudes of life. It refers to the physical fatigue of long missions at high altitude in the cramped confines of military aircraft; harrowing experiences, such as heavy flak or gunfire damage, ditching, crashes in hostile territory or in remote regions; minor wounds; infections and parasitic disease; unappetizing meals; enervating climate; fear; and a host of other elements, none of which can be quantitated either singly or in combination. Quite obviously, the problem is that of dealing intelligently and realistically with symptoms due to emotional reactions, symptoms due to environmental factors and disease, and the reaction of the total personality to the stresses incurred. As indicated above, not all physicians are able to deal with such problems as effectively as they should. But it seems obvious that intelligent, perceptive doctors should be better qualified to evaluate intuitively such a manifold problem than any layman or board of line officers regardless of their military rank or experience with troops.

The administration of the AAF believed otherwise, and the prerogative of command to determine the disposition of the individual flyer was never relinquished, unless a disqualifying medical diagnosis was made and sustained by a review board, such as those authorized in the several central medical establishments. It is fair to say that throughout the war the attitude of administration toward the ineffective flyer was much more consistent than the attitude of the doctors. Professional differences of opinion are no novelty, and they are particularly common when the problem is the interpretation of emotional reactions as a cause of symptoms and disability. Calling a psychiatrist into consultation often adds to the confusion, and such was the case during the war. The consultants of the Neuropsychiatric Division introduced new terms and new concepts that were no more useful as guidelines in the administration of the disposition process than the ones the flight surgeons had been using all along. In fact, the attitude of the average psychiatrist toward a man with "flying fatigue" was a great deal more permissive than that of the average flight surgeon, who usually knew the man pretty well and had "sweated out" some bad times with him before.

At the start of hostilities there were few precedents and no clear policy for handling men who were to fail because of strain. The man who refused to fly because of openly expressed fear was given a Standard Form 64 examination to determine whether or not he was "medically fit to fly." In the absence of disqualifying physical findings, he was seen by a psychiatrist, and, if his finding was "abnormal fear of flying, no psychoneurosis or psychosis found," the aircrewman was ordered to appear before a flying evaluation board convened by command. This board could recommend reassignment to other flying duties, or to non-flying duty, or it could recommend a court-martial at which the flyer could lose his wings, be demoted and reassigned to ground duty in the theater, or be subjected to even more severe disciplinary action. If the finding was "psychoneurosis," the case was handled through medical channels. If fear was not openly expressed but the flight surgeon believed that the "anxiety" was incapacitating, he could disqualify the flyer on the medical examination (e.g., manifested by rapid heart rate). Under these circumstances, no disciplinary action was taken, but the man was reassigned, and the diagnosis was accepted by the commander as an excuse for the man's failure, as well as an explanation of it. Such grounded men stayed on duty with their group and, because of shortages of qualified ground-duty personnel, often were advanced in rank more rapidly than their squadron mates who remained on flying status. The effect on morale was obvious, and in 1944 command ruled[46] that the doctors could not disqualify a flyer on medical grounds if any administrative action was contemplated, such as reassignment to other flying or to non-flying duty.

At this point the flight surgeons lost the privilege of grounding a man for anything except symptomatic medical conditions or well-established neuropsychiatric disorders: psychoneuroses and psychoses. The large number of flyers who showed evidence of strain between these extremes had to be referred to a central medical establishment for evaluation on a complex basis prescribed by the AAF. When the administration took a hand in diagnosis, the sensitive care of the flyer relationship was compromised, and this led inevitably to degradation in diagnosis and disordered medical statistics. All the problem cases had to be fitted into one or two categories, whose components were vulnerable to criticism because of the lack of quantitative criteria for stress and predisposition.

The first category was secondary flying fatigue (also called "operational exhaustion," "combat stress reaction," and other terms). Anxiety had developed, physical signs were evident, creditable amount of emotional trauma (i.e., stress) had been sustained, and there was no neurotic predisposition. In such a case no disciplinary action was proposed, and the airman was reassigned to noncombat duty. The second category was lack of moral fiber (also called "fear reaction" and "temperamentally unsuited for flying"). In this condition anxiety had

417

developed, but there had been too little trauma (i.e., stress), and there was no neurotic predisposition. In such a case a man was considered medically qualified for flying, and disciplinary action was required (i.e., demotion, loss of wings, or other action). The boards that made these determinations included senior flight surgeons, but the authority of the board remained vested in the line-officer members.

The flight surgeon retained the right to recognize simple or primary flying fatigue and could authorize rest leave, subject to constantly changing theater directives. It should be evident that, when the theater had no official policy regarding the length of the tour of duty or the rotation of combat crews, the judicious use of rest leaves was a powerful instrument for the maintenance of morale and combat effectiveness. Just the fact that rest areas existed to which a man could retreat for a week or two helped him to cope with the hopeless feeling that he was expendable. Where the attrition rate was heaviest, it helped him to suppress the feeling that his number had to come up sooner or later; and, most of all, it provided an opportunity to convalesce from minor occupational incidents, such as aero-otitis, aero-sinusitis, malaria, or superficial flak wounds, away from the petty annoyances of a service hospital. Happily, the red tape involved in ordering rest leave was kept at a minimum, and, in most commands, the judgment of the unit surgeon was final.

The policy of rest leave originated in World War I and was abundantly justified then and in the second war. For many flyers one of the few pleasant memories was a rest leave in some lovely resort town or in a charming, private country home. Whether in England, or the Mediterranean, or Australia, or the Vale of Kashmir, the AAF found places where the tired flyer could discard his uniform, sleep as long as he wanted, and spend idle, pleasant days while the mysterious "healing force of nature" accomplished what no schedule of rehabilitation could ever do. Weight was gained, tension relaxed, self-confidence restored; and, even if the venereal disease rate for a month at a place like Ifrane (in Morocco) got as high as 1,400 per 1,000 per annum,[47] it was worthwhile. This was an exceptional situation, however, and VD was never a serious medical problem because of the remarkable effectiveness of sulfadiazine and penicillin. The real benefits of rest leave were derived from the friendly folk who took care of the men and from the restoration of the flyer's belief in the continued existence of a peaceful, orderly world where death and destruction were not the principal goals.

There was never an AAF-wide policy on the granting of such leaves. In England, where the facilities were the most abundant, some heavy-bomber crews began to take rest leave after the third or fourth mission, with most of them going off between the tenth and eighteenth, when they had been on station for two to five months.[48] After a serious crash or an exceptionally harrowing mission, it was customary for the flight surgeon to give the survivors a leave. In the MTO comparable practices prevailed, although an abundance of close-by rest areas was not available until the ground campaign moved into northern Italy. In the Fifth and Thirteenth Air Forces it was the policy to give rest leaves approximately every three months, and the entire flying personnel of a unit might go en masse to Australia or New Zealand. This practice, in combination with the rotation of duty policy of these air forces, yielded excellent results in the maintenance of the health and morale of men operating in an enervating and malarious tropical theater.[49]

Where the rest centers were remote from the combat bases, which was the usual condition everywhere but England, it was necessary to establish air force medical facilities, with skilled flight surgeons in attendance, to supervise the centers. When the SOS hospital system of a theater lacked a convalescent care or rehabilitation program—as was the rule during much of the war in the Pacific—the rest areas functioned as convalescent centers, and flying personnel were ordered to rest leave, when indicated, immediately after discharge from a station or general hospital. As the war progressed, each rest area developed in its own fashion, uniquely adapted to local circumstances. Since no provision had been made for rest-rehabilitation-convalescent facilities in tables of organization and manning tables, staffing of the centers was accomplished on a temporary basis usually under the supervision of the "care of the flyer" section of the central medical establishments. The latter units provided a remarkable degree of flexibility in coping with problems that developed in a theater which had not been—and usually could not have been—anticipated. It is not easy to evaluate with any degree of confidence the contribution of the rest-leave facilities to the success of the war mission of the AAF. As an extension of the "care of the flyer" program it is fair to say that it was one of the most important and successful activities of the medical service.

419

A brief discussion of policies and practices relating to the length of the tour of combat duty and rotation* in the several air theaters is necessary. The basic problem here is the same as the one mentioned above: the utilization of the human resources to the limit of their capability. The limiting factors were interrelated—fatigue and morale —and had no particular relation to casualty rates. As an elite, professional fighting force, the AAF expected to use its highly trained aircrewmen for the duration of hostilities, however long that might be. When the first listless, dejected airmen of the Eighth, the Fifth, and the Thirteenth returned to the United States as a result of medical disposition, command was presented with grave prognoses and dire predictions by some of the physicians and psychiatrists who attended them. Few of these doctors had field experience with professional fighting men, but they knew a beaten man when they saw one. If this was a sample of what aerial combat could do, there was bound to be trouble ahead. Strenuous attempts were made to rehabilitate these men, but the early results were not encouraging.† Actually, the men who appeared in stateside rehabilitation centers in 1943 were a very small fraction of flying personnel overseas, and these had been thoroughly screened in the disposition process. They were anything but representative of the men who were able to carry on. The majority of the aircrewmen who completed prescribed tours of duty or who returned to the United States on orders to training units were in much better condition even though the occurrence of fatigue states—not diagnosed as such on medical records—was high. Of these, the consulting psychiatrist of the Office of the Air Surgeon said in July 1944:[50]

At Redistribution Stations routine examination of returnees sent back on rotation policy after completion of prescribed tours of operational missions indicates that such a policy is absolutely essential for maintenance of flying personnel in the theaters. This examination shows that sometimes as high as 30 per cent of returnees are suffering from operational fatigue, moderate or severe.

---

* Rotation, as used here, refers to the alternation of assignment to combat and noncombat duty in the course of a tour of duty in a theater of operations. This is not to be confused with rotation between a theater and continental United States.

† In the case of flying personnel returned from the Southwest Pacific Area for medical reasons, only 5 per cent were rehabilitated sufficiently to return to flying status. In contrast to this, 60 per cent of men from all other theaters passing through rehabilitation centers were able to return to flying duty. The personnel policies of the SWPA were exceptionally severe for all hands, and approximately the same salvage reports occurred in the case of Army combat personnel. Ask any man who was out there!

The remaining 70 per cent are usually badly played out even if they are not demonstrating actual symptoms.*

Throughout the war, in every air force, there was constant pressure by command surgeons for a fixed tour of duty and some sort of rotational plan. The resistance of theater air commanders to the establishment of a fixed tour of duty is understandable only from the point of view that the AAF was on its mettle and was willing to go all out to demonstrate the correctness of its theory of air power.

Prescribed tours of duty were the rule in the Navy and the Fleet Marine Force, not only for regular personnel but also for airmen. Years of experience with overseas service, isolated stations, and sea duty (a major warship is not so different from an air combat group, when you think about it) formed the basis for a policy to which there were very few exceptions: eighteen months' service outside the continental United States for the Navy, fourteen months for the Marine Corps. Moreover, in naval combat operations the imperative need to service the ships—even during an aggressive, sustained campaign—led to the establishment of a sort of two-platoon system. A destroyer squadron (or cruiser division) would slug it out in the Slot or the North Atlantic for two or three months and then be relieved by a fresh squadron, while it went to a naval base for repairs and refitting. It is true that some of the advanced bases were pretty dull ports (e.g., Espiritu Santo), but at least there was a break in the sea routine. More often than not, some major repair job required a run to Pearl Harbor, or Sydney, or Norfolk, where a decent liberty was possible for all hands.

The Army never worked out a satisfactory policy for its overseas tour of duty; in fact, most of the troops assigned to a theater were there for the duration, and return to the United States (TUS, the orders said) other than as a casualty, or for other medical reasons, was the exception. In combat, rotation of troop units in contact with the enemy was a standing operating procedure, and this practice was obviously related to the necessity of having a substantial fraction (say one-third) of any force in reserve. The length of time in the line (i.e., in actual contact with enemy troops) varied from army to army, depending on local circumstances and the attitude of the commanding

---

* Apparently the consultant believed that a report of 100 per cent incidence of fatigue would force the air staff to "do something." Air staff, presumably with the concurrence of the Air Surgeon, thought otherwise.

general. In some theaters (SWPA was the most extreme case) there were campaigns where the reserves were committed early, and the foot soldier had to take it on the same terms as the airman. For the personnel of the Army Service Forces overseas, there was no policy on tour of duty, no rotation, and almost no rest leave until 1944–45, when the unpopular adjusted service rating (ASR) scheme was instituted.

To describe in simple fashion the situation in the AAF, the following tabulation is offered. Where tours of duty and rotation policies were sufficiently well defined, they are stated, along with summary remarks about the unusual stresses encountered in the particular theater.

EUROPEAN THEATER OF OPERATIONS: EIGHTH AND NINTH AIR FORCES

Tour of Duty: 25–30 missions for heavies and 200+ hours for fighters.
Rotation: None prescribed.
Special Stresses: Very high attrition rate; many casualties due to intense anti-aircraft defense and the Luftwaffe; high incidence of respiratory disease and its complications.

MEDITERRANEAN THEATER OF OPERATIONS: TWELFTH AND FIFTEENTH AIR FORCES

Tour of Duty: Based on an elaborate sortie credit system, related to the probability of completing a tour—averaged 50–60 missions for heavies and 300+ hours for fighters.
Rotation: None prescribed.
Special Stresses: Moderate opposition by Luftwaffe; poor subtropical and desert environmental sanitation, resulting in hepatitis, malaria, and dysentery.

PACIFIC THEATERS: FIFTH AND THIRTEENTH AIR FORCES

Tour of Duty: Not definite; around 500 hours for heavies and 500–600 hours for fighters.
Rotation: Well-enforced policy of 6 weeks of combat, 2 weeks of rest, and 4 weeks of rear-area operational training.
Special Stresses: Missions over water or inaccessible terrain; initially moderately severe but decreasing opposition by Japanese air; poor tropical environmental sanitation, resulting in malaria, scrub typhus, dysentery, and heat.

CHINA-BURMA-INDIA THEATER: TENTH AND FOURTEENTH AIR FORCES

Tour of Duty: None prescribed.
Rotation: None prescribed.
Special Stresses: Missions over inaccessible terrain—Himalayas, jungles, China; poor subtropical environmental sanitation, resulting in dysentery and malaria.

MARIANAS: TWENTIETH AIR FORCE

Tour of Duty: 8–11 months, 400–1,000 hours.
Rotation: None prescribed.
Special Stresses: Very long missions over water to Japan and fear of capture; repeated maximum effort strikes ordered by CG to force surrender without necessity of invasion of the home islands; higher operational than combat loss.

In summary, a fair evaluation of the conflict over the disposition process requires serious criticism of the medical service, particularly the lower echelons—the unit and group flight surgeons. The attitude toward ineffectives on the part of Headquarters, AAF, and air force commanders was much more consistent than that of the doctors. As members of senior staffs, the Air Surgeon and the force surgeons shared the views of the line, and they generally worked in harmony with command to establish medical policies compatible with the AAF's concept of air power. The difficulty was almost entirely with the unit flight surgeons and the psychiatrists. As air force officers and physicians, their position was potentially ambiguous, but their sympathies were clearly with the flyers. As average products of American medical education, their ability to evaluate stress and strain was uneven, often inconsistent, and highly personal; and, as physicians, they were resentful when their judgments and diagnoses were challenged. Had the doctors been united, or even consistent, as to diagnosis and as to their responsibility to the AAF, there might have been relatively little trouble with administration. As it was—and whether he liked it or not—the physician was the subordinate of command and was expected to play on the team at all times. Highly qualified and experienced senior flight surgeons worked with command to develop policies for the medical and administrative treatment and for the further use of men incompetent as a result of illness or failure, and to do this command had to be concerned with diagnosis. The fact that the problems of individual flyers were complex and often unique was insufficient justification for resistance to, and resentment of, an over-all policy.

Comparable comments may be made about the issues involving the tour of duty and rotation. The lower echelons of the medical service were seldom in sympathy with official policy as they perceived it. It is certain, however, from the position of the Air Surgeon in relation to the Commanding General, AAF, and the Air Staff that serious, continuing consideration was given to the medical requirements of flying personnel. Regardless of how the tough policies were formulated and implemented, they can only be measured by the pragmatic test of war. The simple fact is that the policies were sound, and the fraction of aircrewmen who were permanently removed from flying status because they could no longer take it did not exceed a few per cent for the whole period of hostilities. Finally, this writer is not aware of any significant number of ex-airmen who are now disabled because they were driven so hard.

Human Engineering

The concept of human engineering had exerted an increasingly important influence on aircraft design since the establishment of the Aero Medical Research Laboratory at Wright Field in 1934.* During the war years the AAF was able to recruit a great number of physicians and biologists qualified to participate in research involving every aspect of flight. The combined research program of the medical and engineering division had many ramifications, too numerous to describe in detail. The scope of the research is clearly shown in the figure below, a diagram prepared to illustrate the human factors in aircraft design.[51]

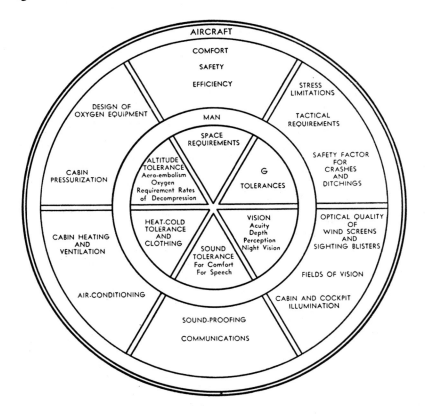

* See above, p. 370.

Fundamentally, flight surgeons were involved in two types of research; an example of each will be discussed briefly. The first type included problems suggested by investigations of serious accidents and incidents during routine, experimental, or combat flying (e.g., freezing of oxygen masks, failure of protective equipment, and death or injury while bailing out). The second consisted of problems presented by the design of aircraft with higher performance characteristics than standard models (e.g., anti-G suits to compensate for gravitational forces developed during high-speed combat maneuvers, survival at altitudes in excess of 40,000 feet, and supersonic flight).

In the first category, an example is the development of the ejection seat to facilitate escape from damaged aircraft. The Flying Safety Branch, AC/AS-3, established in 1942, received reports of all flying accidents. Detailed analyses of crashes led to recommendations for revised training, procedures, and materiel. In 1942, pathologists at SAM began studies of the types of injuries sustained in fatal and non-fatal crashes with the objective of recommending changes in the design of aircraft and of safety devices to improve the chances of survival. A medical division was organized in the Office of Flying Safety (1943) to work with the pathologists and to study the nature of pilot error or pilot failure when it occurred. A problem of particular interest was the reason for failure to use parachutes in cases involving spin or dive crashes. Associated with this problem were the many fatal accidents where the flyer was killed or rendered incapable of using his parachute as a result of colliding with the aircraft while bailing out. The obvious solution was a combination of a seat that could be ejected automatically to throw the flyer clear and a parachute that could be opened automatically if for any reason the man could not operate it. The latter device had been developed at the Aero Medical Research Laboratory as a result of studies of free falls from extreme altitude. A free fall, say, from 35,000 feet to about 15,000 feet, was desirable to get the flyer rapidly down to altitudes where emergency oxygen was not required and where the air temperature was more tolerable. All the problems associated with free falls had been solved: the emergency oxygen unit, parachutes and harnesses to withstand any opening shock that a man could tolerate, and the pressure-sensitive device to open the parachute if the flyer was unable to do so. It was apparent that an ejection device to throw a man clear of a wildly spinning plane had to impart a high initial velocity to the seat and had to be failure-proof.

The human tolerances for acceleration had been worked out in the big human centrifuges as a part of the anti-G suit program, and certainty of function could be assured by using an explosive charge to fire the seat and its occupant out of the plane. The various components of the system were fabricated and assembled, and, as was customary, the critical tests of vertical acceleration and the operation of the entire unit in flight were made by flight surgeon volunteers. The value of the ejection seat was obvious, and ultimately it became standard equipment in certain types of military aircraft.

In the second category, the example to be presented involves the problem of flight at altitudes in excess of 40,000 feet. Aeronautical engineers had solved the problem of engine design to permit flight at 50,000 feet or higher long before aviation medical researchers worked out the human equation to everyone's satisfaction. In the case of the aircraft, the superchargers required to supply enough thin air for the motors could also compress air for the cabin, and cabin pressurization was well established before the war to provide greater comfort and safety for civilian transport planes. It was no problem at all to build a plane to withstand a pressure differential of more than 7 pounds per square inch (psi), and, when fully pressurized, the "altitude" inside the cabin would be about 14,000 feet when the plane itself was at 50,000 feet. For military aircraft, cabin pressurization presented two problems: first, the weight of the compressors and the extra weight of the air frame reduced the aircraft's effective bombload; second (more serious), enemy action was sure to damage the fuselage, resulting in a sudden loss of cabin pressure which exposed the crew to the triple hazards of anoxia, aero-embolism, and explosive decompression.

The first of these hazards had been studied exhaustively at the Aero Medical Laboratory, and it was known that the standard demand mask, delivering 100 per cent oxygen, could not keep the blood fully oxygenated above 35,000 feet and that the absolute limit for the demand system was a bit over 40,000 feet. For flights at higher altitudes pressure-breathing systems were developed, and these extended the limit for adequate oxygenation from 35,000 to around 50,000 feet. Pressure-breathing systems were well enough developed by the winter of 1943/44 that they could be used in photo-reconnaissance planes. (The first such missions were flown over Berlin, February 1944, by the 14th Photo Reconnaissance Squadron, using Spitfires.) The new system created a number of problems and required special indoctrination of the crews, since rapid changes of altitude or rapid changes in the mask pressure could lead to aero-embolism, which was a real hazard in any case above about 45,000 feet.

The second hazard, aero-embolism, is similar to the bends, the caisson-worker's disease, which affects people exposed to a rapid drop in atmospheric pressure. The flight surgeons and the naval medical research people worked together on a problem as serious for divers and submariners as for flyers. What happens in aero-embolism is exactly what happens when a bottle of champagne is opened: there is a rapid drop in the pressure within the bottle, and the gas in the wine expands rapidly, forming bubbles and shooting out the cork. When the pressure surrounding a man drops suddenly, the gas dissolved in the fluids of the body—in this case, nitrogen—expands to form bubbles which obstruct the tiny capillaries that supply oxygen to the tissues. The result is aero-embolism, the predominant symptoms of which are pain in nerves and bone and which, if long continued, may be fatal. It is obvious that the crewman of a pressurized plane were liable to aero-embolism in the event of battle damage to the cabin. The effect on the flyers would be equivalent to a very rapid ascent to the altitude at which the plane was hit. In the case of the flyers, aero-embolism could be minimized by proper use of the pressure-breathing system.

There remained the third hazard—explosive decompression. The human body contains a considerable volume of gas in the lungs and the gastrointestinal system, in addition to the dissolved nitrogen in the blood. The pressure difference between sea level and 40,000 feet will expand this volume of gas 7.6 times. If the expansion (or the ascent) occurs slowly, the increase in volume can be exhaled or expelled without difficulty. However, if the pressure change is instantaneous, there is a real possibility that lung tissue would be damaged or a hollow organ like the stomach ruptured. Studies made before the war suggested that decompression at a rate greater than 5,000 feet per second was hazardous, and rates in excess of this were considered explosive. The urgent need for high-altitude aircraft (to get above the Luftwaffe) was so pressing that further studies were made to set realistic limits of tolerance for rapid decompression. Flight surgeons, using each other as subjects, re-examined the problem in low-pressure chambers reproducing conditions predicted for combat. The two related factors to be determined were the limit of tolerance for rate of pressure change and for extent of pressure change. Keeping the extent, or the differential, constant at 1.8 times, Col. Harry G. Armstrong found that 16,000 feet per second could be tolerated safely. At a rate of 20,000 feet per second, other investigators went from 10,000 to 40,000 feet with only minimal symptoms due to expansion of gas in the bowel. It was now apparent that the most critical factor was the size of the hole in the cabin to be expected from enemy action, since this would control the rate of change of pressure. The engineers provided pressurized planes for the flight surgeons, and battle damage was studied through use of actual weapons. The biggest holes resulted from disintegration of the plastic scanning blisters (observation posts), some of which were 30 inches in diameter. The flight surgeons then went back to their low-pressure chambers to reproduce combat situations, using themselves as subjects. They found that they could tolerate 87 psi per second with few or no symptoms. This condition resulted when a hole 66 inches in diameter was produced in a bomber cabin whose volume was 1,000 cubic feet, pressurized to an altitude of 10,200 feet, and "flying" at an altitude of 35,000 feet. This research program was an integral part of the development of the Superfort, the B-29, and similar studies established safe limits for fighter planes. The way was now clear for production of military aircraft which could be operated safely at the altitudes to which their engines could drive them.

These two accounts of research have been given in some detail in non-technical terms to permit the general reader to appreciate the vital importance of human engineering and of the role that was played by flight surgeons. Dozens of other examples could be offered, for aviation medicine and human engineering were new additions to the biological sciences. There were no authorities to be consulted, no books to go by; these men were writing the books as they went about their duties.

In addition to the research conducted by the Aero Medical Laboratory, SAM, the Flying Safety Branch, and dozens of university medical laboratories under Office of Scientific Research and Development (OSRD) contracts, very significant investigations were made in the field. In England at the 1st Central Medical Establishment, the problems that developed in the ETO, and to some extent those of the MTO also, were studied at firsthand, usually with the active participation of the flight surgeons concerned. It was hoped that the other central medical establishments, particularly the 2d on Guadalcanal, would work the same way. For a variety of reasons neither the 2d nor the 3d ever got an experimental program going, although their staffs collected and analyzed important "care of the flyer" data for studies which formed the basis for research programs in the United States. Research and statistical analysis were key factors in the success of the AAF. From the commanding general down, their significance was appreciated, and there was never any question about funds or priorities for projects which might facilitate any aspect of the war effort.

Post Mortem

The medical service of the AAF played a crucial role in the achievement of victory in the air. It operated the selection-classification program that provided over 600,000 aircrewmen, 194,000 of whom were pilots. In spite of using the latest diagnostic methods, psychological testing, and psychiatric evaluation, this group of successful flyers represented only 61 per cent of the cadets accepted for flying training. In World War I the primitive techniques of the fathers of aviation medicine selected about 20,000 pilot candidates, 55 per cent of whom earned their wings.

The "care of the flyer" program paid handsome dividends. In spite of battle attrition so severe that 77 per cent of the men who flew against the Nazis were casualties, and in spite of disease conditions so bad that malaria rates on Guadalcanal exceeded 1,000 attacks per 1,000 men per year, the doctors kept the aircrews flying. Permanent removals from flying status never exceeded 2 or 3 per cent in any air force for the whole period of the war.

Unauthorized hospitalization in the field, which had to be improvised with equipment begged and borrowed because of the stubborn resistance of the War Department to change, was so successful that all the old arguments collapsed. And when the USAF was established in 1947, the Air Surgeon had a free hand to develop a complete medical service responsive to the needs of the Air Force.

It almost seems that the wartime medical service thrived on controversy, there was so much of it: between the Air Surgeon and the Surgeon General; between flight surgeons and line officers; between flight surgeons and the Air Surgeon; and between the psychiatrists and everyone else. Much of the controversy reflected no credit on

429

the medical profession, but at least the issues were discussed openly, and everyone knew what the doctors thought, even if they disagreed.

The really important principles for which the air medical service fought seem to be correct, and, to the extent that medical support contributed to victory, the Air Surgeon's stand is vindicated. These principles were: (1) in an air weapons system, the human factor is equal in importance to the plane; (2) the chief medical officer of the system must be directly responsible to the chief executive, and this relationship should extend to every echelon of command; and (3) a major combat force must control its own medical service.

CHAPTER 14

*　*　*　*　*　*　*　*　*　*　*

MORALE

FOR more than forty centuries military specialists have explored the subject of morale in an attempt to isolate and master those elusive forces that fire or wet down the spirits of men at arms. The incomplete success of these efforts is indicated by the fact that there is still no commonly accepted definition of morale, nor is there a definitive list of factors which affect morale; and any discussion of the relative importance of various factors is almost bound to lead to disagreement. There are few soldiers, active or discharged, who never have volunteered quick dicta on morale in particular and the Army life in general. But although such opinions, grounded as they may be in steamy memories of Papua or gritty afterthoughts about Cyrenaica, often glow with the heat of felt experience, they do not fill the need for some working definition which will at least serve present purposes. In this chapter,[1] "morale," that "most abused, most misunderstood"[2] term, will be taken to denote an attitude of mind which, when favorable, leads to the willing performance of duty under all conditions, good or bad, and which, when unfavorable, leads to the unwilling or poor performance, even perhaps to non-performance, of duty under the same good or bad conditions.

Neither this nor any other definition can eliminate, however, the difficulties posed by considerations of time and place for anyone who undertakes to assess the morale of the Army Air Forces in World War II. Any statement about morale in the Caribbean during the intense activity of the 1942 submarine crisis, for example, would not apply to the final period of the war when the area had sunk back into relative obscurity and the Sixth Air Force seemed as remote from violent conflict as the Spanish galleon on its shoulder patch. The problem of place is illustrated by the radical contrast between the

431

Eighth Air Force in Britain and the Thirteenth Air Force in the South Pacific. The two air forces lived different lives in different geographical areas with different levels of civilization; they fought different wars under different climatic and combat conditions; and they enjoyed, or suffered with, different priorities and differing degrees of independence, prestige, strength, and fame. These and other distinctions arising in some measure from the accident of place exerted a variable influence on the morale of each organization.

Another obstacle to a precise estimate of morale is the problem of measurement. Traditionally, it has been assumed that the incidence of venereal disease provides a reliable index of troop morale. But actually VD statistics, however full, cannot be evaluated apart from such questions as the availability of women,[3] variations in the incidence of venereal disease among procurable females, the frequency of intercourse, the effectiveness and convenience of prophylactic aids, and the level of soldierly enthusiasm for the healing powers of penicillin. In short, the incidence of VD was conditioned by many factors.

Perhaps the most formidable obstacle to gauging morale correctly in the Army Air Forces is the evaluation of subjective evidence. There are only a few leading documents on morale, and these have limited usefulness. With distinguished exceptions, unit historians—whose work is perhaps the chief quantitative source of information on the subject—did their job perfunctorily as an unwelcome added chore for which they had had no preparation. Some overlooked morale completely, some gave it only a dull glance, and others handled it with a delicacy appropriate to NCO's and junior officers who wrote with one eye on the commanding officer through whose hands the record of the organization's achievements must pass before it ascends to a higher headquarters.[4] There is reason to ponder, for instance, the balance and accuracy as well as the rhetoric of reports which declare that "morale has pierced its highest ebb"; reason to wonder if the acid content of other histories can perhaps be traced to an affliction of the author's spleen; and, in any case, good cause for handling most of the evidence on morale with unusual care.[5]

The inevitable question remains. Is it possible to move past the obscurities of the record to a generalization about morale? The answer is a cautious, rather reluctant "Yes." The available testimony, which of course can never add up to an arithmetically clean sum, appears to justify the following statement: Morale in the Army Air

432

Forces during the second World War hovered, on a rough average, between fair and good. It varied in some degree from man to man, unit to unit, air force to air force; it could soar above "good" to rarefied heights or tumble below "fair" into a black slough; and in all places at all times it reacted with the sensitivity of a compass needle to every change, every shift in conditions. But, extremes and fluctuations aside, morale more often than not seems to have clung to a middle or perhaps slightly higher level. When positive and negative influences tended toward equilibrium, certain basic constants made for a favorable balance. Most airmen never really doubted that they were on the winning side in a great war,[6] and no amount of standard grousing could obliterate the obvious fact that concern for their well-being had generated a remarkable welfare effort—civil and military, public and private—whose effects could be felt from the hill stations of India to the most implausible PW locations inside Germany.[7] And, if all else failed them, airmen could always take comfort in the thought that they might have been in the infantry.[8]

But any generalization about AAF morale, in applying to all men and all units, applies to no man and no unit. The following discussion attempts to add substance to the spare frame of generalization and also to furnish the corrective qualifications that any full-blown statement about the ways of human beings must have. If the discussion at times takes on a dark hue, that coloration undoubtedly reflects in part the concern of most of the documentary material with the problem side of morale and the tendency of men in uniform to speak more of woe than of weal.

In Training

From the earliest days of the war period the AAF grappled energetically, if not always successfully, with the inevitable morale problems produced by the service's explosive expansion. Regulations, field manuals, directives, memoranda, and other forms of injunction, advice, and exhortation provided subordinate commanders, chaplains, and junior officers with prescriptions for safeguarding the morale of the hundreds of thousands of recruits then flooding into AAF basic-training and classification centers.[9] Among other things, the military leader was to know his men, take an interest in their concerns, earn their respect and their loyalty, eschew cursing them, promote their comfort and welfare, be patient, considerate, calm, firm, and vigor-

433

ous, keep the men informed, show enthusiasm, never assign pointless tasks, explain the reasons behind orders, preserve good health, make sure that uniforms fitted, help solve family financial problems, check on laundry facilities, and bid a furloughed soldier a cheery farewell.[10] In such fashion the AAF provided ready-made paper solutions to all matters even tenuously related to morale. Reality, however, shied away from ideality, and nowhere was this more true than in AAF basic-training centers.

The obstacles to high recruit morale at AAF basic-training centers were varied. Many of the men arrived from reception centers in a condition of bruised bafflement after sustaining the first shock of military life. If they expected to find a refuge at such typical stations as Basic Training Center No. 7 at Atlantic City or Basic Training Center No. 9 at Miami Beach, where in 1942 and 1943 surging growth and kaleidoscopic change were normal, they were disappointed. Unit commanders or their representatives greeted trainees with inspirational orientation talks whose quality varied according to the interest and talent of the speaker.[11] Whatever good such sermons may have achieved in replacing bewilderment with an understanding of the aims and methods of basic training, and in creating unit spirit and confidence in the training commander, was often dissipated by experiences that followed. In practice, two-way communication between the separate worlds of recruits and training-group officers was rare. Budding loyalties withered when officers whirled, revolving-door fashion, into and out of training unit commands every two to three weeks or—in one extreme case—six times in a month and when the need to furnish cadres for new organizations set off a series of raids on the permanent party ranks of existing basic-training groups. Jefferson Barracks alone, for example, turned out forty Technical School Squadrons cadres in 1942.[12] Furthermore, instructor officers were in short supply, many had marginal qualifications, regarded their assignment as a punishment for past sins and a bar to future grace, and, whatever their personal feelings may have been, were too sorely beset by multiple duties to pay direct attention to trainees. Permanent party enlisted personnel—especially drill instructors, who as a group were closest to the recruits and played key roles in the basic-training program—also failed to measure up to standards in quantity and quality. Many of them had been picked helter-skelter, were understandably bemused by the starts, stops, and switches of training programs, suffered themselves from contagiously low morale, or were simply incompetent. As time passed and pressures eased, it became possible to improve the permanent party situation, but this upturn came too late to help thousands of trainees who in 1942 and 1943 absorbed from their supervisors little sense of mission or common purpose. There were, of course, exceptions—unit commanders and instructors who tackled their jobs with intelligence and enthusiasm and who were rewarded by fine results.[13]

Job classification and assignment had perhaps a greater influence on trainee morale than any other step in the process of basic training. If necessary, most recruits would probably have been willing to shrug off basic-training-center shortcomings as a price to be paid for the long-run benefits promised by proper classification and assignment. The woes of the drill field were fleeting; but the decisions of classification and assignment sections might, as far as wartime military careers were concerned, endure forever. Contemporary soundings of soldier opinion show that the AAF outstripped the Army Ground Forces and Army Service Forces in giving men the jobs they wanted and for which they felt best qualified. There was, nevertheless, widespread discontent on this score.[14]

In the case of aviation-cadet applicants who had volunteered for induction with the expectation of receiving immediate college training but were instead subjected to psychological and medical tests that barred them from the aircrew program, the trouble was rooted in the excessive zeal of AAF recruiters and, fundamentally, in the sharp competition between the services for manpower.[15] Another serious problem developed when quick shifts in AAF needs jarred and sometimes stalled the carefully crafted machinery of classification and assignment. Theoretically, civilian background, AGCT scores, results of aptitude tests, and personal choice determined the classification of a recruit. But time and again the pressure to fill school quotas by any available means wiped out the good work of classification sections; thus, to the cheerless tune of "exigencies of war," qualified weather-observer candidates set out for radio school, and qualified draftsman candidates in turn went off to auto-mechanics school. Although such instances of misclassification and malassignment were in a minority, they cropped up too often for comfort and dealt a hard blow to the morale of the victims. Admittedly, the erratic appetite of war forced the AAF to reshuffle requirements frequently. Yet

435

there was a strong feeling that better planning could have prevented much grief. Once the damage was done, repairs were difficult. As late as March 1945 the Eighth Air Force, for example, was still struggling to right the wrongs of malassignment.[16]

The clear, direct influence of leadership, training procedures, classification, and assignment on the morale of basic trainees is unquestionable. But the effect of other factors defies easy measurement. Floorless, stoveless tents pitched on marshy ground at Keesler Field, throttling dust at Sheppard Field, rain and muck at Greensboro AAB, and extremes of heat and cold at Jefferson Barracks certainly offered little cause for jubilation. But, though such conditions could aggravate an already bad morale situation, it seems doubtful that they alone would ordinarily create one. Nothing in the record, furthermore, proves that recruits in an uncongenial setting had a markedly lower morale than those who were in the Babylonian environs of Miami Beach.[17] Army Emergency Relief, the American Red Cross, the United Service Organizations, base legal officers and chaplains—all in their several ways gave aid and comfort to trainees and thereby made a definite, if limited, contribution to morale. Similarly, post facilities for relaxation—theaters, service clubs, post exchanges, day rooms, gymnasiums, and libraries—played a useful role by offering diversion and amusement during leisure hours. Their importance, however, could be and was exaggerated. Secretary of War Stimson, never one to deny the worth of off-duty pleasures, bridled at the idea that "the morale of any army could be measured by the number of its recreation halls and canteens."[18] This view, which Stimson spurned as a delusion, was held far more widely than he liked. There was a tendency to try to dispose of morale by tucking it into a separate compartment of army life, where it could safely be left to the ministrations of "morale agencies." According to Stimson, morale depended finally on the training that a soldier received and on his confidence in his military leaders; but in the eyes of the AAF Training Command, among others, it seemed to hinge rather on the energy of the Special Services officer. Thus at Miami Beach, as one chaplain complained, morale was looked upon as the peculiar province of Special Services, whose efforts boiled down to little more than a series of extravaganzas at the Pine Tree Bandshell.[19]

Recreational facilities were especially incapable of undoing the damage done to morale by dislocations such as often occurred at the end of basic training. By that time most recruits, for better or worse, had exhausted the possibilities of basic-training centers. If, for example, they had fared well in classification, they could expect to gain little by marking time on drill fields or in front of mess-hall sinks; and if they had fared badly, a prolonged stay at the scene of disaster promised equally little. For these reasons and perhaps because of native restlessness, there was a general urge to move on to the next step in AAF training as fast as possible. When trainees had high hopes of shipment to schools without protracted delay, their morale reflected that optimism. But, when unco-ordinated training periods and shifting quotas slowed down or damned up the flow to schools, morale sank. The longer men stagnated in pools, the more dispirited they became. Pass and other restrictions which had hobbled them as raw recruits continued to harass them in their new role as casuals; and, though advanced training programs were concocted to keep them profitably occupied, they still spent much of their time—when they were not on KP, guard, and fatigue details—literally as well as figuratively going over ground that was familiar. One battle-eager youngster who went on a drunk after six months of frustration at Atlantic City swore that he knew every brick in the road to the drill field and insisted that he had pushed a broom far enough to cross the adjoining ocean.[20]

Pools of idle manpower were not peculiar to basic-training centers. At one time or another they collected at almost every level of the Zone of Interior training program and, on occasion, both before and after a particular phase of schooling.[21] And, wherever or whenever pools appeared, the predictable consequences were administrative aches and morale pains. The aviation-cadet program, to cite a notable case, was cursed with a pool problem, or a complex of pool problems, of oceanic dimensions from the outbreak of war until V-J Day. An ill-fated combination of all-out recruitment, inadequate facilities for handling the men recruited, and precipitate ups and downs in aircrew requirements led to the accumulation of masses of cadet applicants and cadets waiting, variously, to go on active duty, to enter the college-training program, to get out of college training and into preflight schools, and to escape from post-preflight holding points into the flying schools, where, as many cadets later learned, more pools had formed. Each of these pools became, as might have been expected, a slough of despond. Morale may hit its lowest mark, strangely enough, in the ranks of men who had not even donned uniforms—Air Corps Enlisted Reservists whom the AAF could more readily recruit than absorb.[22] The AAF, pricked by barbs of criticism, argued in self-defense that the fast-changing nature of the war made pools inevitable. Undoubtedly, the argument had force. But there were indications that the pool problem might have been eased and morale stiffened through closer co-operation between Headquarters AAF and the Training Command as well as through a quicker realization by planners that what they regarded as a passing migrane was actually a permanent question which called for a better answer than makeshifts or convulsions of policy.[23]

That morale in the flying and technical training schools of the AAF often fell short of the desired standard should have surprised no one. A military academic machine which previously had existed only in miniature, and which now in three and one-half years produced 670,014 aircraft-maintenance specialists, 128,877 armament specialists, 299,104 radio specialists, 297,318 aerial gunners, 74,400 single-engine pilots, and equally impressive numbers of other specialists,[24] was almost inevitably destined to be troubled by problems arising from hasty construction and human frailty.

In October 1943 an emissary from Headquarters AAF made a five-day inspection of the cadet armament course at Yale and wrote a glowing report on the excellence of the school, the "really first rate"[25] quality of the teaching, and the enthusiasm of the students. But elsewhere, at schools unblessed by ivied comforts, conditions were less idyllic. Tent cities of the kind that once graced Kelly Field, temporary structures which proved pathetically inadequate in winter at Sioux Falls, South Dakota, and in summer at southern bases where 120° F. temperatures were frequent, and general overcrowding at many fields did not nourish high morale.[26] Nevertheless, though the radio students who trudged through the dead cold of a Wisconsin winter night to 0200 classes at Truax Field might not have appreciated the fact, the basic morale problems of AAF schools—like those of recruit-training centers—probably did not spring from physical sources.

Nowhere was this more apparent than among those whose task it was to teach the students—the instructor personnel. Their pains were largely of the spirit and the pocketbook. Complaints of injured morale arose during the protracted delay and confusion that accompanied the commissioning of civilian instructors at preflight schools in 1942, and similar protests resulted, once again from the efforts of overzealous AAF recruiters, who, hard pressed to outbid the Navy and secondary rivals in another phase of the scramble for manpower, had oversold civilians on the rank, promotions, and assignments they might expect upon entry into service. The question of promotions appears to have been the chief focus of discontent among the instructors. Far from real war and its stimuli, sometimes malassigned and keenly aware of their unfitness for their task, and demoralized on occasion by lackluster leadership (always a major morale factor, but one rarely discussed except in generalities) or by the sheer boredom generated by a standardized teaching system which allowed little room for individual initiative,[27] many instructors often tended to lay especially heavy stress on personal rather than organizational goals. Motives aside, there was objectively good cause at times for agitation over the promotion situation. The argument that there never would or could be enough promotions to make every man's cup run over did not comfort those officer instructors whose chances for advancement started to fade early in 1943. One legitimate reason for shutting the doors was that too many men had become eligible for promotion at the same time. But this fact was outweighed in the minds of many instructors by the knowledge that officers in administrative and other favored categories were getting most of the available promotions. Morale and efficiency fell off when hard-working instructors had to plod along as second lieutenants for a year and a half to two years while their more happily situated peers moved ahead of them in rank.[28]

Enlisted instructors, for their part, felt no urge to shed tears over the fate of junior officers who, after all, enjoyed the perquisites and immunities that went with a commission. Their own predicament was worse, and their morale that much more affected. Civilian instructors, for example, not only earned higher pay than enlisted men for equal work, but were free from many of the restrictions that hemmed in military personnel. At the Laredo Central School for Flexible Gunnery officer students were taught by privates who received a full measure of KP and like assignments but no promotions. To the low-rated men on the faculties of other flexible-gunnery schools, the dearth of promotions was injury enough; every graduation day, however, seeming insult was added when a new batch of freshly striped sergeant or staff sergeant gunners rolled off the academic assembly line.[29] Those gunners who went on to armament school at Buckley and Lowry Fields had a catalytic effect on the faculties there, too. Many of them outranked their instructors and believed, furthermore, that after gunnery training they had nothing more to learn about armament. The result was a compound of disciplinary trouble and lowered instructor morale. Some relief came with the adoption of a policy providing that in the future all armorer-gunners would receive armament training before going on to gunnery school and non-commissioned officer status. A more positive balm was the opportunity for instructors to qualify for the cadet armament course, which led to an armament officer's commission. The Training Command also made a number of attempts to raise morale and the quality of teaching by side-stepping Table of Organization restrictions and other obstacles to higher rank for instructors, but these efforts met with incomplete success. Administrative heads continued to be worried by the problem as late as November 1944.[30]

A majority of the students who swarmed into the AAF's school system approached military education with attitudes ranging from willingness to outright enthusiasm.[31] The average airman was inclined at the least to welcome schooling as a forward step along the road to a military career which, if it did not lead to glory, might nevertheless have its satisfactions and postwar uses. Technical training and flying training also offered the immediate attractions of novelty, inherent interest, and, for some, excitement. There were, of course, shortcomings in working conditions, living conditions, and other areas of school life, but such departures from perfection were half-expected and wryly accepted by men who had already sloughed off their illusions during the shakeout process of basic training or cadet classification. More positively, administrative efforts to ease or end irritants had a therapeutic effect on morale. Student protests, for example, over the damage that had resulted from the piling of purely military training on top of a full program of technical training led by early 1943 to a sharp cutback in military activity at schools. To cite another case, the gradual elimination of night shifts—long an object of mass reprobation—gave students more sleep and time to recharge their energies and served as a tonic to their spirits.[32] And the use of such incentives as promotions, competition, and enhanced opportunity based on merit similarly helped to revive flagging morale. So it was that most men went through the school phase of military life, sometimes cast down by adversity or the repellent drabness of their work,[33] perhaps more often buoyed by a different set of influences. This majority group, like any group, undoubtedly had its morale problems, but they were not usually of the virulent kind.[34] The real trouble lay elsewhere.

The glider-pilot program produced the most spectacular case of mass low morale in the record of the Training Command. Haste, ignorance of the nature and conduct of both glider training and operations, uncertainty of purpose, and lack of clear responsibility were at the root of the troubles that developed when, in 1942, the AAF rushed headlong into this new activity. Because the shortage of manpower had made it difficult to round up enough glider-pilot candidates during a period in which the program's goals shot up more than seven fold, extravagant advertising—with its stress on money, rank, and thrills—and lowered physical standards became the order of the day. The resulting enlistments overwhelmed the glider schools. Large pools of waiting men gathered. Then, as the entire program was drastically cut back in the spring of 1943, when about three-fourths of the hapless trainees were reassigned, morale dropped even lower to become "an extremely serious and almost insurmountable . . . problem."[35] Of the survivors, many were dropped on physical grounds just before graduation. It was not until that late hour that they underwent physical examinations.[36]

The misfortunes that plagued the glider program were confined, fortunately, to a small segment of the AAF school network. No such isolation occurred, or was possible, in the case of men who had been eliminated from the various aviation-cadet programs. A high percentage of these washouts not only suffered from their own personal disappointment but constituted a menace of epidemic proportions to the morale of those with whom they came in contact. At Scott Field disgruntled eliminees who had been shunted into radio school showed no desire to mend their fortunes and behaved dourly enough to provoke a senior officer into denouncing them as sources of contagious rot.[37] Similarly, the great majority of flying-school eliminees in the cadet armament course at Lowry Field early in 1942 appear to have earned for themselves nothing more distinguished than the epithet "defeatist."[38] Administrators were also hard pressed to cope with the cadets who came to navigation or bombardment schools after being washed out of pilot training. Here the curriculum deserved a good measure of the blame for the eliminees' bleak mood, for until 1943

these reluctant navigators or bombardiers were forced to grind
through the same preflight course they had already completed during
their pilot-training days. Morale rose when an overhaul of the flying-
school system finally put an end to this pointless repetition. There
were those who felt, however, that the whole eliminee problem might
never have arisen if attempts had been made to quarantine washouts
and minister to their morale before they went on to new assignments.
Whether or not the Training Command had the time and personnel
for a campaign of mass rehabilitation is questionable. But the success
of at least one experiment in careful reorientation in 1944 suggests
that such an investment of effort might have yielded liberal dividends.[39]

The great majority of combat veterans who flowed into the training mill fresh from overseas duty were afflicted, like cadet washouts,
with infectiously poor morale. Again, as had been the case with the
washouts, responsibility for this condition was mixed. For their part,
the authorities charged with the classification and training of returnees generally tackled the job with the best intentions. Unfortunately,
a gap of remarkable breadth separated theory from common practice.
Thus, when demand waxed for the use of combat veterans as instructors, returnees suddenly found themselves tagged as pedagogues—
whether or not they yearned for the role or had the talent to play it.
Those who voluntarily went to an instructors school got along well,
but those who looked upon their new career as a grievous form of
involuntary servitude soon showed characteristic signs of maladjust-
ment and poor morale. They clashed with permanent party men,
failed courses with disturbing frequency, and aroused serious concern
over their attitude.[40]

Virtually every technical or flying school carried on its rolls a
number of men whose morale had allegedly been damaged by faulty
classification or malassignment. True enough, the machinery of classification and assignment did function more than once with the fine
discrimination of a bulldozer, but its behavior hardly accounts for
all the claimed injuries. In many instances students seemed to be
suffering more from the frustration of personal plans and preferences
than from actual mishandling. This was perhaps especially true after
the crisis mood of the first eleven months of the war had faded[41] without being replaced, in the case of rootless trainees, by some counter-
force like organizational pride or the pull of leadership that might have

helped men through the process of subordinating individual desires to the demands of military necessity. Reports from technical schools spoke of the problem of dealing with recalcitrant students who either objected to the kind of training they received or wanted no training at all. Their low spirits probably sank further under the added weight of a feeling of futility when it became known that, in spite of orders from Headquarters AAF, newly acquired specialist skills were frequently going to waste in operational units.[42] Flying schools had troubles of their own. Some small-sized pilots, for example, raised an outcry over their assignment to fighters, while others of all dimensions were just as outraged by assignment to bombers. Harassed training authorities tried to hew to a policy of voluntary assignment, but there were times when an urgent need for manpower—especially in the heavy-bomber program—forced them to override personal choices. The resultant drop in morale had to be accepted as one of the costs of an emergency situation.[43]

As the many tributary streams of air and ground specialists flowed from their sources in the Training Command and merged to form units, new morale factors came into play, and familiar ones took on new force. Once in a regularly constituted organization, men who had hitherto drifted through individual training as individuals found themselves in a changed world. For the first time—in most cases—they actually belonged to a unit with a permanence, a meaning, and a clearly defined purpose that Training Command school squadrons (whose numerical designations quickly faded into a half-forgotten blur) had seemed to lack. There might be tumult and confusion during the early weeks of an infant organization's life, but in good time a feeling of identification with the unit began to well up in men—and with that emotion came a lift in spirits. The speed with which *esprit de corps* developed varied with the rate of personnel turnover, the availability of equipment and facilities for a prompt start on training, and—above all else—the quality of leadership shown by senior officers.[44]

Though it would be hard to claim that physical conditions had no effect on morale at isolated bases like Blythe, in the California desert, where summer heat was terrific,[45] other factors generally exerted a graver influence. The most dramatic of these was a fear of flying in certain aircraft. There was nothing new about the phenomenon. It had cropped up in World War I when the DH-4 won temporary notoriety as the "Flying Coffin." Two decades later the Spitfire—finest

443

of Britain's fighters—also encountered much whispering suspicion after the occurrence of several crashes marked by wing collapse. In their turn, at least a half-dozen American aircraft of World War II became objects of worry and controversy. The P-38 came in for its share of criticism early in 1942 when a series of accidents involving this novel fighter set off a wave of applications for transfer to bomber units. The excitement died down and the wave of applications ebbed as pilots gradually mastered the airplane's quirks. At about the same time the B-26 became the center of a greater furor whose echoes reverberated in General Arnold's office. Almost from the day of its first delivery to AAF organizations, this medium bomber proved difficult to maintain and—much worse—dangerous for raw pilots to fly. As disaster followed disaster, a mood of panic spread from one B-26 base to the next and helped to add to the accident rate. The situation became so serious that, when an opportunity for transfer arose, every eligible pilot in the 320th Bombardment Group (M), with the exception of the commanding officer and his executive, either formally or informally stated a desire to escape from B-26 training to a safer kind of flying. It took changes in design, combined with lectures and aerial demonstrations, to convince crewmen that the B-26 would behave as well as any other airplane if handled properly.[46] The Second Air Force, which concentrated on four-engined bomber-crew training, had its share of grief—first with the B-24 and later with the B-29. Trouble with these aircraft—as with others that came before them or after them—stemmed from inadequate maintenance work, combat-crew deficiencies, faulty supervision of the training program, and the maddening bugs that mar the early record of almost every untried airplane. During 1942 and 1943 the B-24 had the sorry distinction of being the Second Air Force's "problem plane." In 1943 alone, 850 Second Air Force combat crewmen went to their deaths in 298 B-24 accidents. The air of mystery that enshrouded many of these disasters had a doubly chilling effect on the morale of untouched crews. Four baffling crashes in rapid-fire order at Alamagordo, New Mexico, for example, led Gen. N. B. Forrest to report: "The people down there are scared to death of their airplanes and it is very bad."[47] Morale congealed almost as dangerously in the 34th Bombardment Group (H), which lost 7 B-24's and 43 crewmen during a six-week stay at Salinas, California.[48] The B-24—like the P-38 and the B-26—ultimately went

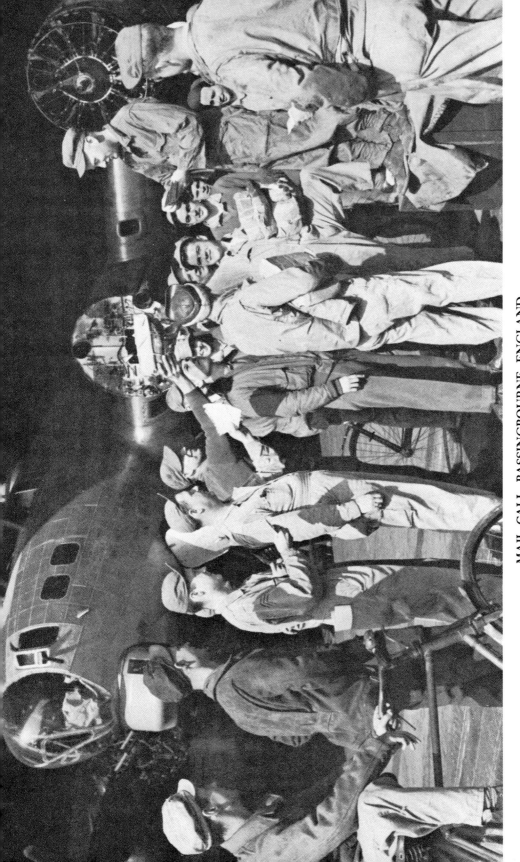

MAIL CALL, BASSINGBOURNE, ENGLAND

G.I. Style, Fighter Base, England

DANCING

Kanaka Style, B-29 Base, Saipan

On Tour of Pacific Bases

AAF ENTERTAINERS

At Thirteenth Air Force Base

VOTING SERVICE, SEVENTH AIR FORCE

CELEBRITIES: AT NAM LIP, BURMA

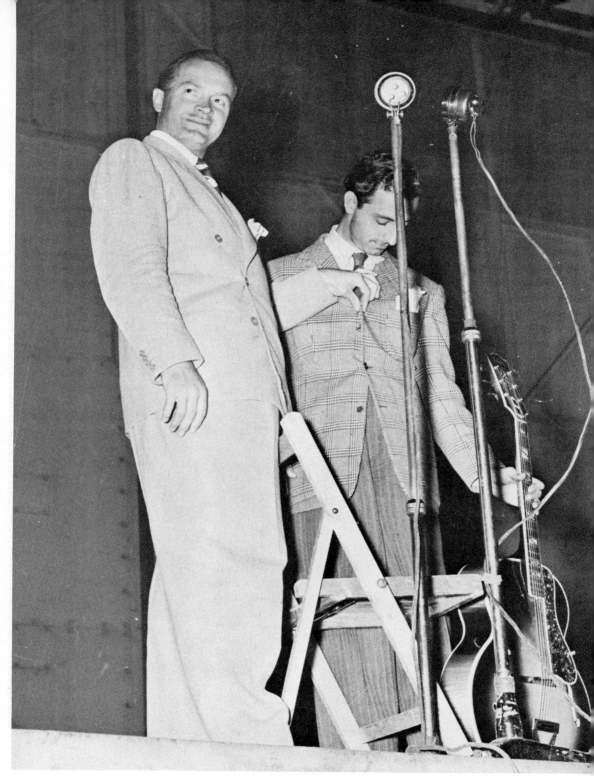

CELEBRITIES: AT AIR DEPOT IN ENGLAND

CELEBRITIES: AT BOMBER BASE IN ENGLAND

CELEBRITIES: AT AIR BASE IN LANCASHIRE, ENGLAND

ATHLETICS, EIGHTH AIR FORCE BASE, ENGLAND

EASTER SUNRISE SERVICE, THIRTEENTH AIR FORCE

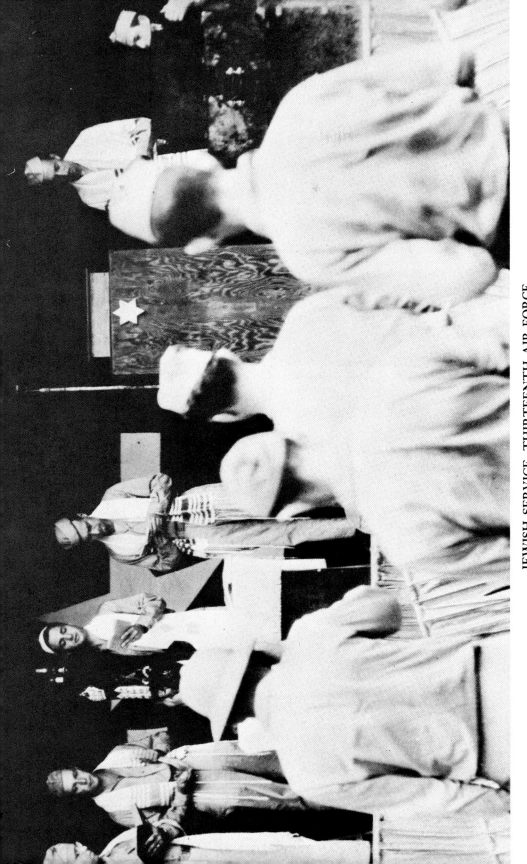

JEWISH SERVICE, THIRTEENTH AIR FORCE

At ATC Base

ENLISTED MEN'S CLUBS IN INDIA

At Air Depot, Panagarh

on to a notable record in combat, but not until many apprentice airmen had contributed heavily in lives and spirit to its trying-out.

Overcrowding at airfields, lack of convenient recreational facilities, and drastic shortages of housing for dependents[49] were familiar but minor morale factors at this stage of the training program. Though these discomforts may have caused individual cases of discontent, most men in operational training units had by this time learned to shrug them off or accept them as the facts of Army life in wartime. But the issue of promotions was something rather new to the alumni of flying schools and technical schools who manned the organizations that were taking shape in the continental air forces. A majority of these men had spent most of their military lives in one form or another of individual training. As casuals they had moved about in a rigidly controlled economy where promotions either came automatically to all trainees in good standing at some point in the schooling process or were not open to any of them. Now, in the more flexible world of the numbered air forces, officers and enlisted men alike scanned bulletin boards and followed the latest Table of Organization developments with an interest that fed on high hopes of personal advancement. The general tendency to promote men to within one step of the maximum rank or grade allowed for their positions served as a spur to morale.[50]

The question of leaves and furloughs also began to loom larger on the horizon as airmen realized that their time in the Zone of Interior was running out. For most of them there had been little or no chance to break away from military routine—except on passes—until they reached the end of Training Command schooling. Between that point and their date of departure from the United States, they could normally expect—as a matter of policy—a leave or furlough of up to fifteen days, plus travel time. This last chance for a visit home might come before, during, or after OTU or RTU phase training—depending on schedules or unlooked-for lulls in activity brought on by a dearth of airplanes. In the case of unassigned men who had not received unit training, it might not come short of arrival at Overseas Replacement Depots. Early or late, these leaves and furloughs were a boon to morale.[51] But, whenever they were unduly delayed, cut down, or written off, a decline in morale followed. Such was the experience of units of the XII Air Force Service Command which had abandoned pre-embarkation furloughs in the rush to meet TORCH commitments in 1942; and such was also the experience of the Training Command and the Second Air Force after they had adopted similar emergency measures in the spring and summer of 1944 in order to fill their obligations to the OVERLORD forces in Europe and the B-29 project in the Pacific.[52] At the Greensboro, North Carolina, ORD during this period, the moratorium on furloughs in combination with spit-and-polish discipline helped to send the court-martial rate soaring; while out in Kansas a senior general officer unwittingly made a difficult situation worse by declaring during an inspection of the 40th Bombardment Group (VH) that the group's combat crews ought to have seven days of leave—a respite which they could not get and did not get because of the urgent need to modify their B-29's and fly them away by a set date. The crisis soon passed, after provoking a near-mutiny at one base, and by November the Second Air Force could report that over 99 per cent of the men processed for transfer overseas by its 21st Wing had had leaves or furloughs at some time during the previous six months.[53]

Overseas

The approach of overseas movement usually acted as a signal for the appearance of an ailment that came to be known as "gangplankitis." Its symptoms ran the gamut from nervous tremors to AWOL and desertion. It could crop up anywhere—at training fields, staging areas, overseas replacement depots, and ports of embarkation—and whether it would occur in mild or intense form was something no one could predict with certainty. Generally speaking, severe seizures were most likely to develop when organizational ties were weak or—as in the case of individual replacements who belonged to no unit—non-existent; when leaves or furloughs and even passes were banned; and when men had long weeks of idleness in which to consult their fears of the unknown reaches beyond the piers of San Francisco or the runways of Morrison Field, Florida. But "gangplankitis" normally presented no grave problems. If the prospect of leave-taking aroused some qualms, it also generated a surge of excitement and high spirits powerful enough to overcome the drag of other factors.[54]

During the journey overseas the likelihood of morale difficulties tended to vary with the length of the trip: the longer the passage, the greater the problem. Those who traveled by air might praise or damn the assets and liabilities of such stopover points as Presque Isle, Borinquen Field, Goose Bay, Hickam Field, Natal, BLUIE WEST No. 1, and Kwajalein. But these reactions were more or less fleeting. Movement by air usually offered the virtues of speed—except along the North Atlantic route in winter, which at least provided the compensation of Iceland's Danish pastry—and variety. It mattered little if the food at a base in Trinidad were wretched; within twenty-four hours the complainants might be enjoying a meal in a hotel at Belém, Brazil. Similarly, if the sight of Ascension caused dismay, it did so only for a day.[55] Men in ships were less fortunate. Few wartime voyages resembled the 27th Bombardment Group's journey to the Philippines in November 1941 aboard the *President Coolidge:* the liner was comfortable and uncrowded, the diet—"steaks, squabs, cheeses of all kinds"[56]—astonishing. After Pearl Harbor, those who traveled fastest along the shortest routes generally fared best. During a quick run from New York to the Firth of Clyde on the *Queen Mary*, cramped quarters, dismal food, and other shortcomings ranked only as passing irritations. But on many longer voyages—especially through equatorial seas—the heat, the overcrowding, the lack of ventilation, the surfeit of strange stews and other dubious dishes, the stench from overflowing commodes, the shortage of recreational facilities, and the nerve-grinding tedium of spending up to thirty-eight consecutive days aboard ship could blend into a corrosive mixture. Many of the discomforts and deficiencies were unavoidable, but, as anger boiled up over such affronts as gross inequities in food and food service, this fact was often forgotten.[57]

The chances of war brought American airmen into overseas settings that varied radically in nature and effect. Units could consider themselves thrice blessed if their movement orders took them to stations in a temperature zone where climate was tolerable, disease was no grave menace (save to the careless and incontinent), and living quarters were reminiscent of what they had known in stations in the United States. The worst that could be said of Eighth Air Force housing in Britain during 1942 and 1943 was that it did not equal the standards of permanent Zone of Interior installations. In southeastern Australia, facilities at Tocumwal and Melbourne struck Maj. Gen. George C. Kenney as perhaps even too comfortable to be militarily useful. And in China, during the summer of 1942, Kunming offered to the startled men of the 23d Fighter Group a magnificent locale and accommodations that were as gratifying as they were unexpected.[58]

But East Anglia, New South Wales, and the valleys of Yunnan

were not the world. Elsewhere, from Shemya to Biak, from Youks-les-Bains to Espiritu Santo, airmen too often encountered conditions that subjected them to mass trials by fever and chill, dehydration and deluge, dust and slough, monsoon, khamsin, and williwaw. There was nothing temperate about the heat of Darwin and the north Australian bush country, the suffocating, clinging damp of the Papuan jungles, the bleakness and cold of the Alaskan mainland, the interminable grayness of the Aleutian chain, Bengal's mixture of sun and stench, and the Libyan Desert's winter blend of sandstorms and inundations. There was nothing reminiscent about the scrap-and-tincan dugouts that dotted the landscape at forward fields in Algeria, the washed-out tents at Magrun—"a hell hole if there ever was one"[59]—in Cyrenaica, unwinterized Eleventh Air Force quarters at Elmendorf, the charnel-house atmosphere of Tarawa, Kwajalein, and other devastated atolls in the central Pacific, and the insect-ridden, snake-ridden, lizard-ridden, unfloored and unscreened pyramidal tents at bases in New Guinea. Nor was there any dearth of menace, or at least misery, in the onslaught of afflictions like malaria, dengue fever, scrub typhus, diarrhea and dysentery ("Karachi Crouch," "Delhi Belly"),[60] schistosomiasis, boils, abscesses, tropical ulcers, fungus infections ("Guinea Crud," "Jungle Rot"),[61] furunculosis, filiriasis, and "fevers of unknown origin."[62]

During the early stages of combat operations, however, morale held up far better than might have been expected, in spite of physical conditions that ranged from poor to appalling. Disease, of course, could and did have a depressing effect. Malaria, for example, helped to drain reserves of strength and will in stricken organizations like the 11th Bombardment Group in the New Hebrides and Lower Solomons and the Fifth Fighter Command in Papua. Chronic dysentery had a similar if less extreme effect on personnel of the India-China Wing of the Air Transport Command. Perhaps equally depressing were the glaring contrasts that existed between the living standards of senior officers and their men in India in mid-1942 or between sailors and their poor relations of the Army on islands of the south and central Pacific at any date.[63] But these cases fall far short of telling the whole story of morale in physical adversity. Given the spur of crisis, the compulsion of responsibility, the elemental pull of leadership, the feeling of pride in their unit, the excitement of participation in great undertakings, and the belief that all concerned were sharing and suffering alike, air crewmen and ground crewmen in all theaters not only endured privation but did what they had to do with a drive and a spirit that many of them could never again summon up in later, physically easier, periods after the wear and tear of overseas life had taken its toll. Morale in some Twelfth Air Force units was never higher than during the winter months at Thelepte and other forward bases in North Africa when conditions were at their worst. On the other side of the world, verve, enthusiasm, and sense of purpose carried many Eleventh Air Force men through the hectic days and hard times of 1942; but these had largely dissipated by 1944, to be replaced by the "demoralizing and depressing"[64] influence of Aleutian fog and inaction.[65]

The challenge of physical hardship might serve as a short-term stimulus to fresh and eager troops, but there was no power of uplift in ill-cooked mutton and tinned stew. "Poor food" ranked as one of the most frequently, most persistently voiced grievances of airmen in theaters of operations. The fact that available edibles usually met nutritional requirements signified nothing to overseas veterans whose stomachs turned automatically at the sight of the spongy contents of a Vienna sausage can. Complaints about diet could cover everything from unfamiliar British Empire staples to camel meat and dehydrated American vegetables. They could reflect the eternal presence of canned U.S. Army Quartermaster C, K, and B rations in the Pacific or the absence of same in China. They could refer to foodstuffs themselves or to the peculiar things that cooks sometimes did with those foodstuffs. They might mean only what they seemed to mean; they might also be indicative of a growing mood of restlessness, weariness, or resentment. In any case, sustained and vehement protests over dietary inadequacies spelled trouble: the longer the duration of the chorus, the greater the probability that morale was ebbing.[66]

Food was not a major problem in western Europe and the Mediterranean. Though difficulties arose, they were usually neither permanent nor serious. The quality of cooking often left much to be desired, but airmen generally accepted this shortcoming, however sourly, as another one of the facts of Army life—a condition that mess training and other measures might relieve but never eliminate. British rations, which rarely failed to evoke a bristling reaction, made only a brief, early appearance at AAF messes in Great Britain and disappeared as soon as supplies began to flow in regularly from the Zone of Interior. Thenceforth, aside from mutterings about monotony and the talents of GI chefs, there were few complaints in the ETO over a diet that usually contained a variety of fresh foods. When Ninth Air Force units began their series of skips and jumps across France in 1944, K rations dominated menus at times. But not many men fretted about this temporarily limited fare during a period of action and movement.[67] In Northwest Africa and the Middle East, where transportation never kept pace with demand, and supply lines had to reach far beyond port and refrigeration facilities, diet became a touchy issue in the months after the curtain-raising excitement of TORCH and El Alamein had faded. Rear-area units, according to the time-honored pattern, suffered least. When fresh meat began to arrive early in 1943, they received it first and most frequently. At less accessible bases up front, where the arrival of a stray planeload of frozen meat was a holiday event, men had to make do with what quickly became a dreary diet of British rations and the usual array of canned American hashes, stews, and luncheon meats. Fortunately, trading talents quickly came into play, and more than one mattress cover ("sleep-sleep")[68] changed hands in return for native chickens, eggs, and tangerines. Haphazard barter had its limitations, however, and the food question showed signs of developing into a disturbing problem just at the time that Allied forces moved into Sicily, Italy, and Sardinia. After the move into Europe, there soon followed a remarkable improvement in troop menus as fresh meats and dairy products poured into the refrigeration storage facilities of ports like Naples, Bari, and Cagliari and then flowed out to consuming units with increasing regularity. As butter, steaks, pork chops, and "the long 'Coney Island' hot-dog"[69] made their welcome appearances, morale rose and diet ceased to be an issue of real consequence in the Mediterranean.[70]

Airmen were less fortunate east of Suez. In Asia and out across the Pacific food rarely failed to be an issue of consequence from the beginning of the war until its final stages. Except at rear-area installations in India, Australia, and Hawaii, or at forward bases in the Aleutians, where by 1944 chicken every Sunday had become a commonplace, dissatisfaction with available fare developed into and remained a chronic complaint of the overwhelming majority of air units. Conditions varied widely from Lingling to Sansapor and Saipan, but at all these bases a persistently unsatisfying diet damaged morale.[71]

In isolated China, which, logistically speaking, lay at the end of the known world, AAF organizations were dependent upon the Chinese

War Area Service Corps for the bulk of their food and for its preparation as well. The system aroused more protest than praise. Airmen at CWASC hostels variously complained about the monotony of diet, objected to the dearth of vegetables, described water-buffalo meat—which at times made up 90 per cent of the meat issue—as sickening, and reported that unsanitary kitchen conditions had caused numerous cases of dystentery. But, in spite of the pressure of repeated assertions that morale had suffered as a result of these conditions, little could be done either to reform the hostel organization or to procure American food. Eggs and rice remained life-sustaining standbys for men who dreamed of C rations. No such yearning existed, however, on the other side of the Hump in Assam, where the lack of refrigeration facilities necessitated a diet of canned QM foods. Here the problem of coping endlessly with hash and the military version of Spam was one that taxed the ingenuity of GI chefs and the morale of the clientele.[72]

In the Pacific the combination of long, often attenuated, supply lines and grossly inadequate refrigeration facilities—both ashore and afloat—created an almost insurmountable barrier to a satisfactory diet for Army forces. Airmen nevertheless tried every conceivable way of getting through, above, or around that barrier. They attempted, with mixed success, to improve the preparation of the Australian and American canned rations and dehydrated vegetables that formed their basic menu. They resorted to cajolery, letters of request through channels, barter with the Navy out of channels, smuggling, thievery, special buying arrangements in Australia and Hawaii, the rigging-up of makeshift coolers, and the use of everything from C-46's to P-38's for "fat-cat" shipments of extra supplies to forward areas. But these expedients provided only sporadic relief at best. The ultimate solution of the problem lay beyond the control of air units, whose efforts to lay hands on palatable foods and the precious "reefers" in which to store them were either informal or illegal, depending on the observer's viewpoint. Official responsibility for refrigeration rested with the theater engineers, who were hampered both by shortages and by the strait jacket of War Department Tables of Equipment. Jurisdiction over the procurement and shipment of rations belonged to the Services of Supply, whose hotly criticized operations reflected only too faithfully the fact that—for Army purposes, at least—there were not ···ough refrigerated cargo vessels or transport aircraft to go around.

The situation remained serious until the winter of 1944–45. By then GI veterans of an endless succession of jungles and coral outcroppings had had more than enough time to wonder, as they poked at their bully beef or contemplated peanut butter, why neighboring naval forces never seemed to have to do without the refrigerators, the fresh foods, and other material blessings that could make wartime existence in the torrid regions of the Pacific more tolerable.[73]

On the Ground

A number of factors shaped the morale of AAF ground personnel as they went about their daily rounds. That the most dramatic factor of all—peril to life, limb, and mind from enemy air attack—exerted perhaps the least influence was a matter of the fortunes of war. American mechanics, clerks, and administrators were no less vulnerable than their foes to the shattering effects of sustained aerial assault. But, generally speaking, only those AAF units in the most advanced areas during the early phases of a campaign ever underwent a pounding. They could be badly hurt. The Japanese fragmentation bombs that rained down upon Port Moresby, the concentrated bombing and strafing inflicted upon Twelfth Air Force men at Thelepte, the beating administered to Fifth Air Force Service Command truck-drivers who worked round the clock on the Oro Bay–Dobodura supply run, and the punishment meted out to signalmen and other personnel at Wakde and Biak all strained morale and undermined endurance. Yet these cases were exceptional. Most air organizations either never came within striking distance of Axis aviation or were shielded effectively by local Allied air superiority and the enemy's gradual descent into a defensive strategy. During the last half of the war enemy raiders intruded so infrequently upon the calm of many bases that one of their rare, ineffectual appearances was more likely to result in an upsurge rather than a sinking of spirits.[74]

A more serious threat than enemy bombs to the stamina and morale of noncombat personnel under certain conditions was overwork. In New Guinea, the New Hebrides, the Solomons, and the Gilberts shortages of personnel (especially in the skilled categories) and equipment put a heavy burden on the manpower available. Maintenance men who toiled long hours seven days a week under cruelly difficult conditions could hold up for a time but not indefinitely. When overwork sank from the exalted status of an all-out emergency effort to the level of routine, unrelieved drudgery, the danger of a drop in strength, productivity, and morale developed.[75] Though the problems posed by exhaustion came to the fore most quickly in dismal settings like Guadalcanal and Tulagi, they were by no means confined to the torrid zone. In China, for example, the commander of the veteran 23d Fighter Group warned Headquarters Fourteenth Air Force in November 1943 that his undermanned, underequipped organization could not stand the strain of overwork much longer "without a serious decline in efficiency and . . . morale."[76]

As long as the tempo of ground activity normally stayed below the danger line, hard work could serve as a powerful stimulus to unit morale and performance. This was especially true in the case of ground personnel who were able to see a close and direct connection between their labors and the prosecution of the war. In days of crisis, when that relationship stood out with naked clarity, noncombat men reacted magnificently to the challenge of the hour. Maintenance crews of fighter and bomber squadrons at Nome, Adak, and Umnak, during 1942, toiled up to sixty-five and seventy hours at a stretch in zero weather, snowstorms, and one-hundred-mile-an-hour gales and emerged from the ordeal in good spirits. They had done something worthwhile, and they knew it. At Causeway, Tunisia, the ground men of the 79th Fighter Group uncomplainingly labored sixteen hours a day during a vital period of operations against the Afrika Corps. Line crews and other ground-section personnel at Eighth Air Force stations in England earned a glowing tribute for the way in which they met the crushing requirement of maximum aircraft availability that went into effect on 2 June 1944 and lasted until two weeks after the Normandy landings.[77] When unit activities went forward at a less hectic pace, the virtues of work were still apparent to observers and toilers alike. A Seventh Air Force bombardment squadron characteristically reported from Guam in 1944 that "everybody is too busy to feel sorry for themselves."[78] Eight months later the squadron's parent organization—a group whose morale aches were legion—echoed the refrain from Okinawa with the comment that the workload left "little time for contemplation" and thereby helped the days to "pass more swiftly."[79] Non-tactical units voiced similar sentiments. The smoothly functioning 3d Air Depot Group at Agra, India, for example, found that "hard work and less idle time" strengthened morale by seeming to shorten the long months and years of an overseas tour of noncombat duty. Here, too, was an affirmation of faith in the principle that "the faster time flies, the sooner our return to the States."[80]

There were limits, however. Ground personnel who could be counted upon to pour all their strength into the execution of any militarily useful task looked with contempt and disgust upon chores that were transparently worthless. Make-work projects led nowhere and achieved nothing more constructive than waste motion. Almost every airman had had at one time or another an unpleasant taste of such enterprises in the Zone of Interior; overseas, they were even less palatable. This was particularly true in veteran organizations like the Twelfth Air Force Service Command, where the concocting of make-work schemes in 1945 kept men "busy" but damaged morale.[81] Enlisted men harbored an even more intense antipathy to work details or projects involving special comforts and privileges for officers. The commanding officer of Headquarters Squadron, USASTAF, for example, protested against the practice of detailing his men to construction work on an officers' club at a time when there was no dayroom for enlisted men and when a wide gap in living standards already existed between officers and enlisted men. An engineering officer at a lower echelon in the central Pacific was equally critical of the practice of repeatedly pushing aside work that would improve living conditions for enlisted personnel in order to proceed with the apparently unnecessary rehabilitation of high-ranking officers' quarters. Enlisted ground personnel, particularly in areas where the sounds of combat were faint, had a bottomless capacity for indignation against what they took to be flagrant discrimination. Cases like these were all that was needed to transform latent resentment against officers into steaming wrath.[82]

Despite all efforts to avoid sags in the rate of operations, almost all units inevitably experienced spells of inactivity. Bad weather, shortages of equipment, snarled shipping schedules, unpredictable twists of events, and a number of other factors might be responsible for enforced idleness. Whatever the cause, the effect was likely to be unhealthy. Airmen, whose devotion to sack time was proverbial, of course welcomed a respite from the grinding demands of a period of stress, but they had no desire to vegetate. Long days and weeks of marking time had little appeal for ground personnel, who saw in the fastest possible progress toward victory the only sure path to their supreme goal—home. The urge to get on with the war may have been strongest where opportunities for diversion were few and the environment was hostile; it was, nevertheless, universal. Whenever an atmosphere of frustrating calm descended on units, morale dropped. This was true at Suichwan, China, where the 11th Bombardment Squadron was washed out of active status by winter rains. It applied with equal force to the 41st Bombardment Group's wait for something to happen at Makin Island. Thirteenth Air Force units also suffered from declining morale when there was little for them to do during the operational slowdown of the summer of 1944. Inactivity at two such widely separated points as Barking Sands, Kauai, and a troop-carrier station in Britain produced a common effect of homesickness and wilted spirits.[83] In the Twelfth Air Force Service Command the story was essentially the same, and the conclusion obvious: "A unit must not be allowed to go through a long period of idleness."[84] This dictum might have included individuals as well as organizations: "insufficient occupation" was an epidemic affliction of flight surgeons in the Mediterranean.[85]

In backwater sectors and inactive theaters the inability of many men to see how their drab duties had anything to do with the events described in *Stars and Stripes* and *The Daily Pacifican* frequently produced a disheartening sense of futility. This condition could also be detected at times in the ground echelons of tactical units like the 325th Fighter Group in Italy, but, generally speaking, there was a good deal of truth in the slogan, "the nearer the front, the higher the morale."[86] Behind this cliché lay something more than a conviction that time raced at Tacloban and Leyte and dragged in the Caribbean. Pride, self-respect, and sensitivity to the opinions of others ("And what did you do in the war?") were also involved. On Morotai, morale flourished in bombardment units whose men "knew they were contributing a goodly share toward the winning of the war."[87] In India, the feeling that they had "participated,"[88] however vicariously, in successful combat missions helped to keep up the spirits of mechanics in a bombardment maintenance squadron. On Tinian and Okinawa "justifiable pride" in "concrete accomplishment,"[89] and the fact that all personnel—ground as well as combat—could measure the grief visited upon the enemy through their joint efforts, contributed heavily to an outlook of optimism.[90] But in rear areas,* frustration often outweighed such compensations as a relatively high standard of living and immunity from sudden death. A special services officer pictured morale as "a tremendous problem"[91] in the Aleutians after the withdrawal of the Japanese had reduced numbers of Eleventh Air Force men to a routine of sitting on their hands in a cold mist. Obsession with "a feeling of unimportance"[92] was perhaps just as strong at air depots in England, where one observer advocated a policy of sending depot personnel on temporary duty to combat units in order that they might see tangible evidence of the worth of their work. In the Mediterranean, men in AAFSC/MTO units that were still stationed at African bases many months after the tide of war had swept into Europe also found it difficult to believe that their efforts had any military significance. This mood may well have been most acute in the rear echelons of the Thirteenth Air Force Service Command, whose personnel could draw small comfort from the conviction that they were stagnating in the middle of nowhere ("What was the name of that island again?") as members of a forgotten air force in a secondary theater of operations.[93] There were ways, however, of combating the negative mood that was so common among service personnel. In the Fifth Air Force Service Command, for example, intelligence officers carried on a steady and at least partly successful educational campaign that was designed to show how the prosaic labors of non-combat units had made the triumphs of the Fifth Air Force possible. The spur of competition also helped to keep men out of the doldrums, as did the careful exploitation of the individual airman's pride in his resourcefulness and skill.[94]

One fairly certain antidote for rear-area depression and restlessness was forward movement. Pulling up stakes might mean confusion and disruption, exhausting effort and physical misery, but these liabilities were overshadowed in the minds of most men by the excitement of a change of scene and the knowledge that every forward stride along the highways to Berlin and Tokyo brought home, paradoxically enough, that much closer. Another encouraging aspect of a move was that it promised to carry men nearer to the combat zone. The experience of the 43d Service Group of the Ninth Air Force in the Middle East was typical. When the 98th and 376th Bombardment Groups

---

* The term was more figurative than real in air forces like the Eighth, where air depots were within cycling distance of the nearest bomber airdromes.

ceased operations at Bengasi and flew on to a more active sector, morale slumped in the 43d, which had been left behind to contend with dust storms instead of the enemy. For a few weeks, "everybody was in the dumps."[95] But, as soon as the group received orders to trek west, morale soared. "We were moving, our prayers had been answered."[96] Halfway around the world, where a change of station could usually be defined as a shift from a developed jungle site to an undeveloped jungle site, service units of the Fifth and Thirteenth Air Forces also reacted buoyantly to the arrival of movement orders.[97]

In the Air

Some of the workday factors that affected the morale of AAF non-combat personnel had a similar, perhaps even more acute, influence on combat crewmen. Enemy air raids on forward AAF bases taxed the nerves, energies, and spirits of air and ground men alike: "Washing Machine Charlie" in the Solomons and his Luftwaffe cousins in Tunisia were no respecters of persons. Nevertheless, as hard as it may have been for a bleary-eyed mechanic to drag himself through his daily routine after the tension and loss of sleep caused by shelling and bombing, it was probably still harder for a pilot who had undergone the same tearing stress to face up without respite to the rigors of air combat. True enough, combat fliers had the opportunity—denied their earth-bound comrades—to hit back at the enemy, but there were times when, in their raw-nerved state, they were hardly disposed to snatch at the opportunity. Similarly, though overwork might grind non-combat men down to a condition of deep-seated fatigue, reduced efficiency, and lowered morale, it could actually shatter combat personnel. A steady diet of sixteen-hour days at workstands was harsh fare, but nowhere as harsh as an almost equally steady diet of long overwater missions, flown against odds, without benefit of fighter escort or adequate air-sea rescue facilities. It was no accident that, at a time of critical manpower shortages, the punch-drunk survivors of the early air battles in the Philippines and Java had to be sent home, while weary ground crewmen were still considered capable of holding on. Idleness, too, could weigh more heavily upon combat men than ground men. Service personnel may have become restive and disheartened as they fidgeted about, waiting for constructive employment; but they experienced nothing like the mounting pressure to which bomber crews were subjected during the day-by-day ordeal of

457

starts, stops, and postponements that preceded the first Eighth Air Force mass assault on Berlin and the first XXI Bomber Command strike against Tokyo.[98]

Of those morale factors peculiar to combat operations, attrition was among the most prominent. The average flier, of course, came to battle with every expectation that there would be casualties, though he might be jolted when he first encountered them. Battle losses did not of themselves automatically make for low morale. More often than not, they impinged only upon the consciousness of those close to the men who had gone down; others experienced only fleeting twinges of regret and unease. In terms of unit morale, the important thing about attrition was not that it occurred but how it occurred. In a battle-hardened squadron, for example, the loss of an obscure replacement pilot might have no effect whatever on morale. But if the man who was shot down turned out to be the squadron commander— as was the case in the 314th Fighter Squadron of the Ninth Air Force —or another key figure, the loss could come as "a terrific blow" to the entire unit.[99] The mental consequences of casualties hinged also upon the rate of operations. In bombardment groups of the Eighth Air Force, where the count of missions ran into the hundreds, losses were almost an organic part of the daily routine and could normally be absorbed without any impairment of morale. A different situation existed, however, in the western Aleutians, where the level of operations in 1944 was so low that losses tended to stand out more dramatically than elsewhere: an antishipping sweep that cost one B-25 crew threw "a cloud of gloom"[100] over the 77th Bombardment Squadron.

In spite of dissenting opinions,[101] there seems to be little doubt that heavy casualties exerted an intense downward pressure on morale. The gray atmosphere they created in the 17th Bombardment Group in North Africa and their "depressing effect"[102] on bomber crews in the South Pacific during the spring months of 1944 were typical. When heavy losses occurred in concentrated form, the pressure on morale increased acutely. The shock of calamitous attrition in the Ploesti low-level mission of 1 August 1943, for example, hit the 98th Bombardment Group with "tremendous" force.[103] Disaster at the hands of German fighters during the Vicenza raid of 28 December 1943 reduced the 512th Bombardment Squadron of the Fifteenth Air Force to a condition of stunned bewilderment over the "immensity"[104] of its loss and was a major factor behind the withdrawal of the unit from combat two days later. When the 512th went back on operational status, its worried new crews showed too much of a tendency, for a time, to discover mechanical troubles early in a mission and head for home. In the Pacific, according to General Kenney, the casualties sustained by the XIII Bomber Command in the Balikpapan strikes of 30 September and 3 October 1944 brought the morale of the surviving crews "close to the breaking point."[105] Catastrophes that resulted from noncombat causes were scarcely less demoralizing. The Fifth Air Force was badly shaken by the tragic loss on "Black Sunday"[106]—16 April 1944—of thirty-one fighters which had returned safely from an attack on the Tadji area only to be sealed off from their home bases by a fatal barrier of cloud and fog. The ATC's India-China Division also had reason to remember "the black days of January 6–8, 1945,"[107] when a storm over the Hump destroyed nine transport airplanes.

Prompt replacement of killed, missing, wounded, and worn-out airmen was essential to the preservation or restoration of good combat morale. In the case of units whose attrition rates were moderate, a steady supply of new pilots or crews acted more as a preventive of trouble than anything else. But, for squadrons and groups that had been numbed by disaster, an immediate influx of reinforcements had the life-giving quality of a blood transfusion. It counteracted tendencies toward disintegration, helped to bring the organization out of a condition of shock, and started the healing process. Though new faces often were a painful reminder of old ones, their appearance came as a reassuring sign of renewal and continuity and put an end to the sinking sensation induced by the sight of empty crew quarters and blocks of vacant seats at mess-hall tables. But, whether losses were severe or relatively light, morale suffered in some degree when the replacement flow failed to keep pace with needs. This happened in England and North Africa during the somber days of the winter of 1942–43 when fighter pilots or bomber crewmen needed little imagination to realize that their shrinking numbers meant lowered striking power and effectiveness, increased strain and risk, and, if enough help did not come soon, the mathematical probability of extinction for all. Fortunately enough, by late winter and spring the situation improved, and with the improvement came a rise in spirits.[108]

When convinced that the mission was worth the cost, air crewmen could stand up to the hazards and losses of combat operations with remarkable steadfastness. A belief of that kind charged the Liberator

459

crews who participated in the Ploesti mission of 1 August 1943 with
an electrical enthusiasm before the raid and later speeded their recovery from its staggering exactions. The same assurance helped to sustain Eighth Air Force morale during the daylight air battles over Germany in the summer of 1943 and Twentieth Air Force morale during
the night strikes against Honshu in the spring of 1945.[109] In the Alaskan Department, however, the frequently voiced feeling that "the
risks and casualties encountered had been very high for the results
gained against the enemy"[110] acted as a drag on morale; cloud banks
in the Aleutians and canneries in the Kurils were not inspiring targets.
The B-25 and B-24 airmen of the Seventh Air Force extracted just as
little satisfaction from their discouraging task of flying an endless
series of neutralizing sorties against Marcus, Truk, Nauru, Ponape,
and other bypassed excrescences on the vast surface of the central
Pacific.[111] Although the soured mood of many fliers in the two small-
est Pacific air forces was to a great extent the unavoidable result of the
role they had to play, in North Africa a like temper appears to have
been caused by weak co-ordination between command intelligence
agencies and front-line units. Pilots who lacked an understanding of
what they had done and why they had done it "often felt that the missions were a waste of time, material and life."[112]

Success or failure in combat had perhaps as compelling an influence
on the ebb and flow of morale as any other single factor. Combat personnel who had gone through much and traveled far on the long uphill pull to the climax of aerial battle were bound to reflect in attitude
and behavior their unit's ability or inability to accomplish its assigned
mission. This held true no matter what the casualty rate might be, no
matter how important or unimportant the objective. Though the
heavy losses sustained in the great strategic attacks of 1943 against
Ploesti and targets deep within the Reich initially hit bomber-crew
morale with concussive force, crewmen could draw renewed strength
not only from the conviction that the objective justified the cost but
also from the proud belief—sometimes unfounded—that they had succeeded in doing what they had set out to do.[113] One of the dispiriting
things about air warfare in the central and north Pacific sectors, on
the other hand, was the fact that fliers often had no way of knowing
whether they had accomplished anything or not; and, not knowing,
they were often inclined to assume the latter. "Lack of confidence in
results" went hand in hand with "rock-bottom morale"[114] in an

Eleventh Air Force B-24 squadron in 1942. Ascertainably good results had a tonic effect, whether the objective was a ball-bearing plant at Erkner, a formation of Me-109's in the Middle East, or a Japanese concentration at Wewak, whereas poor performance had the opposite effect, whether the hapless units involved were missing petty targets in Micronesia, middling targets in the coastal areas of northwestern Europe, or major targets in the Mediterranean.[115] Appropriately enough, the 41st Bombardment Group's chart illustrating the number of enemy aircraft shot down and ships sunk was known as the "Morale Board."[116] In India the repeated failure of Tenth Air Force bombers to destroy completely a single bridge in Burma during 1943 —before the accidental discovery, on 1 January 1944, of the right bombing tactic—plunged combat men into a mood of worried gloom that contrasted sharply with the brimming confidence and high spirits of the crews of the 7th Bombardment Group, in April 1945, on the occasion of their one hundredth successful bridge-busting attack.[117] In the Mediterranean the same kind of contrast in moods could be seen in the 17th Bombardment Group, which, much to the "disgust" of its fliers, was pulled out of action in October 1943 because of bombing inefficiency, went through retraining, and in a matter of a few months was able to boast about its record of "almost unbeliev-able" bombing accuracy.[118]

Fighter pilots who were troubled by misgivings about the worth of escort work had only to head for the nearest bomber field to learn that their big brothers looked upon them as knights-errant whose very presence sent spirits up and losses down. The veteran of the Eighth Air Force's 305th Bombardment Group who described Spit-fires and P-47's as looking "pretty sweet"[119] when they shepherded limping B-17's safely home understated the feelings of bomber men. To combat crews few sights were lovelier than friendly fighters circling around bomber formations during the quiet stretches of a mission or more breathtaking than their sudden appearance at an instant of ultimate extremity. Bomber crewmen who had ever stared straight at an onrushing FW-190 for long seconds before catching a glimpse of a P-51 on its tail would not soon forget the emotions of that moment.

There may have been some uncertainty concerning the extent to which full fighter protection could cut bomber attrition (predictions ran as high as 75 per cent), but all parties agreed that the cut would

461

be substantial and the benefit to morale immense. Unfortunately, unanimous agreement on the merits of escort fighters and the crying need for them did not solve the painful problems of range extension, production, and allocation; and, until those problems were solved, virtually all bomber forces had to make do with only part-time fighter cover or no cover at all. P-38's and P-51's did not reach the Tenth Air Force, for example, before the latter part of 1943. In the central Pacific, Seventh Air Force bombers rarely received any assistance before the last weeks of the war. The Fifth Air Force, after a hard beginning, fared better than the Seventh, but its supply of P-38's was limited by priorities favoring the ETO and MTO. And it was not until the fall of 1944 that Liberator crewmen of the Thirteenth Air Force were finally relieved of "that particular kind of lonesomeness they feel when the only fighters they see are enemy fighters."[120] In Europe and the Mediterranean, escort presented no great difficulties during the early phase of operations, when American bombers generally concentrated on peripheral targets where the opposition was spotty. The cover furnished by fighters of limited range in this period of shallow penetrations saved a number of B-17 crews and, according to General Spaatz, gave a healthy lift to morale. But in 1943, when deep thrusts into savagely defended territory carried heavy bombers far beyond the reach of the friendly fighters then available, a crisis of serious dimensions developed. The emergency did not pass until enough P-51's and P-38's were on hand to shield USSTAF bomber forces. The Eighth Air Force was out of danger by early 1944, the Fifteenth a few months later. But, even after the crisis had ended, events continued to illustrate the profound influence of escort: in July 1944 a few lapses in fighter support were enough to cause a serious fall in Eighth Air Force bomber-crew morale.[121]

Aerial combat in World War II subjected human beings to emotional and physical stresses which mankind had never known before. The demands on fliers may or may not have been more severe than those imposed upon men engaged in surface warfare. But they were new as well as harsh, and that quality of newness, strangeness, and unfamiliarity brought an added dimension to the ordeal of battle. Wherever airmen flew—whether it was through the flak-smudged atmosphere four miles above Vienna, the forbidding emptiness of the Pacific and the Bay of Bengal, or the "nightmare of searchlights, tracers, rockets, and . . . smoke"[122] over Tokyo—they entered that new dimension of strain. All efforts to mitigate the tensions, fears, and dangers that were part of air operations, and to give airmen every possible assistance should they come to grief, contributed in some degree to the making or maintenance of good morale. The protection that newly developed body armor, for example, gave to bomber crews of the Eighth Air Force in 1943 yielded benefits that were mental as well as material and led to the wholesale adoption of the lifesaving equipment.* There was no hiding place in a B-17, and any gadget or garb that lessened a crewman's feeling of naked vulnerability to all missiles was likely to have a comforting effect. Similarly, something as minor as the improvisation of an extra safety belt that would keep gunners from being sucked out of a pressurized B-29 if a blister gave way, also heartened crewmen.[123] On a larger scale and in an entirely different sphere, such brilliantly successful undertakings as Operation REUNION—the mass aerial evacuation of more than 1,100 American PW's from Rumania to Italy in 1944—improved the morale of thousands of MAAF fliers by offering them abundant proof that, if they were shot down and survived, they would not be forgotten. Air-sea rescue operations were perhaps an even greater boon to morale. Navy lifeguard submarines in the Yellow Sea apparently never saved any XX Bomber Command personnel, but the B-29 crews "just felt better knowing they were there."[124]

Elsewhere many hundreds of fighter pilots and bomber crewmen received more direct aid from activities of an astonishing array of Australian coast watchers, lifeguard submarines, picket destroyers, crash boats, PT boats, DUKW's, RAF Hudsons, L-5's, PBY and PBM Dumbos, B-29 Superdumbos, B-17 Flying Dutchmen, and P-51 Josephines. The air-sea rescue campaign—faltering and limited at first but later highly organized and increasingly effective—produced a series of spectacular rescues before it had run its course. And tales of men picked up in Kavieng Harbor or pulled out of the North Sea never failed to bring an upsurge of spirits.[125] By 1945 the waters over which American airmen flew seemed appreciably narrower than they had been in 1943, when Maj. Gen. Willis Hale wrote from Funafuti: "So into the ocean they go and we have failed to recover a single man."[126]

---

* See above, pp. 402–3.

Recognition for Work Done

The recognition given combat men for their feats was remarkably diverse. It might take the form of gross tons of newspaper and magazine publicity for the ETO air forces, three precious bottles of Scotch awarded by General Kenney on one occasion, trophies, oral and written commendations, battle-participation stars, unit citations, or the "little bits of pretty ribbon"[127] that symbolized the Air Medal, Distinguished Flying Cross, Silver Star, and other personal decorations. Whatever the form, recognition was sweet, and morale thrived on it. Even inaccurate publicity was acceptable, as long as it sounded a laudatory note. But, when accolades were few or delayed, morale did less well.

The men of the smaller air forces did not relish the comparative obscurity in which they carried out their hard but subordinate tasks. Sarcastic references to the aura of glamour and reknown that surrounded "the self-styled 'big league' Air Forces"[128] betrayed the Seventh Air Force's sensitivity over its neglected state. B-24 men of the Thirteenth Air Force—weary of toiling in the shadow of the Fifth Air Force—were equally touchy and complained bitterly that their missions had been slighted or ignored. Combat awards and decorations served as a valuable complement to, or—if need be—substitute for, the kind of morale-building headlines that the XIII Bomber Command craved. But the good that awards and decorations could do depended to some extent upon the speed with which they were recommended, processed, and formally presented. The universal stress on the need for quick action bespoke a conviction that delay robbed decorations of part of their worth. Minor morale crises developed in units of the Twelfth and Seventh Air Forces when approval of recommendations for the Air Medal took as long as six months. It was only natural for men who knew that they were poor insurance risks to want to receive their honors while they were still alive. The beneficial effects of awards and decorations could also be lessened when combat men thought—rightly or wrongly—that they were being discriminated against. In NWAAF, for example, fighter pilots claimed that their bomber brethren had harvested a disproportionately large share of the available honors; junior officers and NCO's often took a bilious view of the battle decorations pressed upon senior officers; and, when standards governing decorations were tightened, fliers who had already met the requirements of the old standards protested angrily that they were being cheated. Sharp variations in standards from air force to air force and theater to theater provoked just as much irritation. These differences, of course, represented a necessary adaptation to varying combat conditions. There was a feeling, nevertheless, that the excessive largesse of some air forces had cheapened the DFC and Air Medal. Fifteenth Air Force men pointedly suggested that it might be a good idea to stamp their conservatively awarded DFC's with the number 15 in order to distinguish them from Eighth Air Force DFC's. But the Fifteenth, too, was not above suspicion of inflationary activity. Between August 1942 and 29 December 1944, one of its heavy bombardment groups distributed a total of 15,544 Air Medals and Oak Leaf Clusters.[129]

The recognition that ground personnel received for their services fell far short of that accorded to fliers. This was natural, normal, and traditional. It was just as natural, normal, and traditional for large numbers of noncombat men—especially in service units—to resent their status of inferiority and to feel that they deserved far more than they got in the way of praise and glory. Even those combat organizations which complained most bitterly of anonymity probably won more public attention than the average service unit. The thrill enjoyed by the men of AAFSC/MTO's 17th Repair Squadron when they saw pictures of the airplane assembly work done by them in Iran was an experience denied to most ground personnel. Not only was there scant applause "to split the ears of the Groundlings" but the awards and decorations open to them were limited either in number or prestige.

The DSM, of course, belonged to a starry world that the average ground man never laid eyes upon. Less exalted in nature, the Legion of Merit also lay beyond normal sight and reach, except when it was improperly pressed into service in an effort to honor achievements that would otherwise have gone unrecognized.[130] Below the Legion of Merit was a void. Until late in the war, non-flying enlisted men could ordinarily hope for no greater glory than the Good Conduct Medal, which was handed out with such indiscriminate prodigality as to become more an object of GI humor than respect. The institution of the Bronze Star Medal in 1944 gave promise of filling the gap between the Legion of Merit and the Good Conduct Medal. The new decoration was at first hailed as "a means of rewarding the ground crews for the wonderful work they have been doing,"[131] but it apparently did not come into wide enough use to achieve maximum effect.[132] In service units, battle-participation credits probably became a hotter issue than decorations. Service personnel in all operational theaters protested bitterly and at length over War Department and theater policies (based, with some changes, upon a surface-bound conception of the nature and extent of combat zones and campaigns) that deprived them of some, if not all, of the battle stars which had been awarded to ground men of bomber and fighter groups for doing the same kind of work that they were doing at the same time and—often—in the same place. What began as an expression of wounded pride became something much more intense in 1945 when service personnel learned, to their dismay, that each battle star was worth five discharge points. AAF commanders, aware of the harm done to morale by such inequities, attempted to secure a redress of service-unit grievances but made little headway. The battle-star issue remained a sore point up to the end of the war.[133]

Promotions, like battle stars, had a twofold value. At one stroke, they appeased the airman's appetite for recognition and added to his income. Whether AAF personnel cherished the added rank and prestige more than the added pay is hard to say. Most of them were content to leave analysis of their motivations to others and to concentrate instead on the pursuit of whatever prizes were available. Fliers and ground men, surgeons and chaplains, and colonels and privates, with visions of stars and stripes in their heads, all awaited the latest word concerning prospects for advancement with an interest that never flagged. Naturally, when the news was promising or promotion orders actually came through, morale climbed—with the rate of ascent varying according to the number of men involved, the categories affected, and—as always—the counter or complementary influence of other factors like combat losses. Promotions had an especially rousing effect if they arrived with a rush after a spell of drought; such, for example, was the case with the 500th Bombardment Group on Saipan. But, whenever they were inordinately delayed or blocked for some reason, a morale problem developed.[134] Forward echelon men who might otherwise have shrugged off their failure to win prompt promotion became wrathful as soon as they heard tales of how men in rear areas and the Zone of Interior had managed to clamber up the ladder of rank with the greatest of ease and speed.

Unfortunately, these tales often had more of a ring of truth to them than the usual run of GI stories and rumors. In May 1942 an anonymous lieutenant in the Southwest Pacific summed up the matter of promotion inequities succinctly when he told his commanding officer, "Colonel, we are being dumped on."[135] The colonel agreed, but that did not help matters. The same note of protest was sounded by many other men in SWPA and other theaters.[136]

At about the same time, the Eleventh Air Force faced a somewhat different difficulty. Its headache was one of channels and their length. All Eleventh Air Force recommendations for officer promotions had to go first to the Alaska Defense Command, from there to the Western Defense Command, and from the Western Defense Command on to Washington, where Headquarters AAF passed them to The Adjutant General for final action. The result, of course, was wasted time and motion until the War Department provided a remedy in September 1942 by granting to the Eleventh authority over its own promotions. The India-China Wing of ATC suffered from the same kind of difficulty during the period when it had to route promotion recommendations through Headquarters ATC in Washington. But even after Maj. Gen. Harold L. George, Commanding General of ATC, had voluntarily abandoned his authority to the theater in an effort to hasten action, conditions did not improve. The India-China Wing had simply exchanged the disadvantages of red tape for the limitations of the T/O.[137]

That complaints inevitably arose in all theaters over the baneful effect of T/O restrictions was not surprising. Tables of Organization were by their very nature finite; the ambitions which they checked were not. Feelings on the subject faithfully reflected locale. In July 1943 Maj. Gen. George E. Stratemeyer, while still Chief of the Air Staff in Washington, took a calm view of what he described as budgetary and War Department policy restraints on promotions. Writing to Maj. Gen. Ira C. Eaker in England, he noted that the promotion question was under study and that action would duly follow.[138] Two months later, after General Stratemeyer had assumed command of the India-Burma Sector, China-Burma-India, his tone and outlook changed radically. In a letter to his successor on 4 September, he capped a plea for extra grades and ratings with the exhortation, "For God's sake, give us some help." "All I am trying to do," he added, "is build up morale and the least that can be done back there is to support me when I . . . only want to spend a few more of Uncle Sam's dollars."[139]

The predicament in which General Stratemeyer found himself was already quite familiar to AAF commanders overseas. There were either not enough promotions to go around under existing T/O's, especially in units that operated at above-normal strengths; or, in the case of provisional organizations, there was no T/O at all. Efforts to secure wholesale reforms usually foundered on the rocks of War Department resistance. Air force commanders had better luck at winning piecemeal concessions, which, if they did not cure morale ills, at least eased them. The Tenth Air Force, for example, gained permission early in 1943 to promote fifty second lieutenants in spite of T/O barriers; the Twelfth Air Force twice succeeded in getting extra allotments of grades; and in the Southwest Pacific the Fifth Air Force received some special dispensations. During 1943 and 1944 the War Department made further concessions on a general basis by liberalizing promotion requirements for second lieutenants and privates.

The largest promotion problem of all, however, not only defied solution but—during the last year of the war—steadily worsened. The War Department's policy of furnishing replacements in grade wiped out almost all hope of advancement for thousands of overseas veterans and thereby dealt a damaging blow to morale. Officers and enlisted men who had worked hard and waited long for the opportunity to fill T/O vacancies that called for higher grades and ratings watched bitterly as replacement personnel fresh from the Zone of Interior moved straight into those coveted openings. The chorus of protests against "high-ranking replacements"—the term soon became anathema—was loud and sustained. The War Department nevertheless held to its policy rather than accept the alternatives of arbitrary demotion of the only personnel available for overseas shipment or the abandonment of T/O standards. Not until the summer of 1945, when the mass exodus from overseas theaters had gotten under way, did relief come.[140]

Off Duty

During leisure hours, when there was time to look away from a world circumscribed by pistons, flak, and third carbons, the thoughts of thousands of airmen turned first and foremost toward home. Therein lay the importance of mail to morale. Letters (with the usual snapshots inclosed), personal parcels, and periodicals not only linked men overseas with the people and places they had left behind but served also as tangible symbols of the homeland for which airmen longed with an aching desire that at times bordered on the obsessive. Mail from home was not, however, an unmixed blessing. Letters bearing news of feminine faithlessness and other calamities like family illness and death hit the men who received them hard. But the anger, concern, and grief that came of such bad tidings were essentially private and touched only isolated individuals.[141] The general run of mail, on the other hand, had an altogether healthy influence on morale. Letters and parcels contributed notably to the high spirits that prevailed when activities were going smoothly and provided a measure of cheer in situations that were otherwise quite cheerless. Airmen asked one thing above all of the Army Postal Service—a steady flow of mail. Given that, they were volubly grateful. It was not unusual for a unit to single out reliable mail service as "the biggest morale booster,"[142] especially if that service happened to coincide with the Christmas season. But, as soon as mail deliveries slowed down or stopped, reports of a sag in morale followed with automatic regularity. The sag was likely to become more pronounced if, after a five-month delay, holiday packages finally arrived with their contents scrambled into a wierd hash.[143]

Complaints of poor mail service cropped up most frequently in 1942 and the first half of 1943. In this early period, cargo space on air transports was at a premium and had to be fought for—not always with success. Shipments of second-class matter bound for such end-of-the-line points as India and China had to run a gantlet of thieves en route—again not always with success. In a number of instances the postal system was simply inadequate to meet the mounting demands that were made upon it. Probably the most serious complaint came in November 1942 from a representative of Headquarters AAF who, after returning from a tour of the Eleventh Air Force, charged the Army with neglect of overseas mail delivery. In time, however, service improved immensely, though up to the end of the war there were still sporadic lags and delays—particularly when units were in the throes of movement, when ships with mail aboard were diverted from their original destinations because of operational necessity, and when communications with outlying areas broke down. But these lapses could not obscure the fact that over the long pull the Army Postal

469

Service performed a task of unprecedented difficulty and complexity with a skill, ingenuity, and reliability that benefited morale greatly.[144]

However pleasurable mail may have been, it alone could scarcely exorcise the twin specters of boredom and brooding which threatened the morale of airmen during off-duty hours. Few men had either the desire or the mental energy to devote all their spare time to the ritual of reading and re-reading letters and writing replies. Other diversions were needed. The least complicated of these, in material terms, were GI bull sessions and games of chance. The former, which required only people and a willingness to range back and forth over the eternal subjects of women, war, home, food, and the merits and demerits of various makes of American automobiles, won a high place—though often by default—on the list of leisure-time activities. The latter, hardly more complicated, called only for the same people plus a deck of cards or a pair of dice. Thousands of airmen everywhere found some escape in long sessions of bridge, poker, pinochle, and crap games.[145]

But virtually all other recreational pursuits, even one so essentially simple and private as reading, reflected in varying degree the influence of the factors of time, place, and logistics. In the European and Mediterranean theaters, which benefited from relatively short lines of communications and abundant local resources, recreation presented no serious problems except during the North African phase of operations, when forward units lacked either the facilities or the equipment for most leisure-time activities, and later during periods of movement on the continent of Europe, when some organizations temporarily spurted beyond the effective reach of the American Red Cross, Army Special Services, and other agencies.[146] Generally, however, airmen in the two theaters had ample opportunity for off-duty diversion. Many availed themselves of the hospitality of their Allies and cobelligerents; and all, according to their tastes, found some form of pleasure in the cities and towns of Britain, France, Belgium, Luxembourg, Italy, and North Africa, where cultural and historical monuments could be seen at almost every step, where entertainment was to be had in innumerable opera houses, bistros, and music halls, where beer, wine, brandy, and gin answered the need for relaxation and stupefaction, and where the company of women of differing social stations could be enjoyed for differing social purposes.[147]

The program of officially sponsored recreational activities got off to a fast if uneven start in both theaters and before long expanded to awesome dimensions. Special Services offered movie showings (easily the most consistently popular form of diversion in all theaters and the one credited with doing the most good for morale), supplied athletic gear and equipment, ran hobby shops, distributed scarce radios, phonographs, and P.A. systems, sponsored USO show tours of AAF bases, organized dozens of all-soldier shows like "Skirts," which played 212 times in Britain before 260,000 spectators (including Queen Mother Mary), became involved in radio broadcasting in Italy, produced a rodeo at Foggia, superintended a "Tea Bowl" football game in England and a "Spaghetti Bowl" game in Italy, had a hand in track and field meets, organized fifty dance orchestras in the Fifteenth Air Force and over five hundred basketball teams in the Eighth Air Force, initiated a series of symphonic concerts and operatic performances in Naples, and fostered an interest in art among airmen in Britain.[148]

Information and Education Sections* were scarcely less active at their somewhat more staid tasks of setting up and conducting off-duty schools, supplying and running unit libraries, establishing newspapers, distributing news maps, copies of *Stars and Stripes, Yank*, and other publications, arranging for courses at Oxford, Cambridge, and other institutions, and both encouraging and facilitating enrolments in United States Armed Forces Institute and university extension courses.[149] Working alongside Special Services and I and E, the American Red Cross also made a major contribution to the program of leisure-time relaxation. Its activities included the management of hundreds of off-base service clubs, ranging from modest centers in provincial towns to huge and elaborate establishments in cities like London and Naples, Aero Clubs (complete with American hostesses) at airfields, wandering clubmobiles, rest homes, beach clubhouses, and outdoor pavilions. Its offerings were equally diverse, running the gamut from the inevitable doughnuts and coffee to books, radios, phonographs, musical instruments, Ping-Pong tables, sports events, educational tours, sightseeing tours, dances, forums, and sleeping facilities. There seems to have been general agreement that, despite occasional lapses and shortcomings, Special Services, I and E, and the Red Cross, aided and abetted by indefatigable chaplains and the USO, not only provided airmen with a goodly measure of amuse-

* I and E had operated as a part of Special Services until the latter part of 1944.

ment, diversion, and edification but also helped substantially to keep AWOL, courts-martial, and VD rates down.[150]

In Asia and the Pacific most airmen quickly learned not to expect too much in the way of recreational opportunities or facilities. Only units in rear areas or at fields in China could enjoy the benefits of being based at or near centers of civilization. The rest, for at least the greater part of the war, had to adjust themselves to an existence almost devoid of women, normally potable beverages, and other amenities that were commonplace elsewhere. Informal and organized off-duty activities alike suffered from crippling handicaps imposed by shortages of equipment and transportation, low priorities, and the length of lines of communication. Reports from the CBI and the several Pacific theaters during the first two years of the war were filled with complaints about enervating monotony and the dearth of movie equipment, "live" entertainment, athletic gear, books, periodicals, newspapers, club buildings, and the like. There was no choice, however, but to make shift with what was available or could be bought, borrowed, bartered, or stolen.[151] Men therefore sat in the rain watching movies and waited patiently when projectors broke. They hailed Joe E. Brown with delight during his pioneering tour of the Southwest Pacific and welcomed the USO troupes that preceded and followed him—especially those with girls in the cast. They depended on the helpful Japanese for radio entertainment until Army broadcasting stations were established in 1944. And they played softball, volleyball, and basketball when and where they could.[152]

Special Services, I and E, the Red Cross, and other agencies all had to grapple with the problem of carrying out their regular tasks under irregular conditions. They did surprisingly well and earned widespread praise for their contributions to the maintenance of good morale.[153] Special Services distributed its meager allotment of supplies and hunted for more, promoted the usual sports events and shows, tried to keep the flow of films moving, and established and ran not only dayrooms and clubs but also a gold-mining camp and a ski lodge.[154] I and E Sections gave out news, published newspapers, set up war rooms, organized quizzes, and played a leading role in the founding of off-duty schools like Fox Hole Military Academy, Angaur Prep, Suribachi College, and Fifth Air Force University.[155] The Red Cross, though it came under criticism at times in the Southwest Pacific and CBI, generally functioned as well as circumstances permitted. It staffed rest camps in Australia, operated from tents in the central Pacific, had charge of full-scale establishments in the Philippines, mass-produced doughnuts in the Admiralties, specialized in hot coffee on Tarawa, and won legendary fame for the hamburgers served at its canteen in Gaya, India.[156]

The need to supplement the ordinary off-duty recreational activities with periodic intratheater leaves for both combat and non-flying personnel was recognized in all operational air forces. Commanders and flight surgeons alike accepted the proposition that short spells of relief from the drab and wearing routine of overseas military life were essential to the maintenance of efficiency, health, and good morale. In Europe and the Mediterranean, where rest facilities and transportation were generally available, the leave program got under way early and went forward without serious interruption. Airmen en masse swarmed through Britain on holiday trips, thronged into Paris to sample its delights, and enjoyed the attractions of such superb rest centers as Cannes and Capri.[157] In the CBI conditions were less satisfactory. Nevertheless, personnel in India managed to relax at hill station rest camps like Darjeeling and Shillong during the hot season and in Calcutta, Lucknow, and other cities when cool weather came on. Airmen in China made use of the limited facilities at Camp Schiel, Tsuyung, and Kunming.[158]

In the Pacific, vast distances, frequent shortages of accommodations in rear areas, and a chronic lack of transportation conspired to make the leave program as much a source of raging frustration as a builder of morale. No amount of pleading, warning, and cajoling could conjure up enough aircraft to carry all the men who needed rest to havens in Australia, New Zealand, and the Hawaiian Islands. Combat personnel understandably had first call on aircraft space when and if it was available. Ground men could only wait in disgust until their names climbed to the top of long leave lists. The Fifth Air Force tried to hew to a policy of giving non-combat men a week in Australia for every six months endured in New Guinea. Few, however, received their leaves on time. Most waited at least ten months, some as long as eighteen.[159] V Air Force Service Command Negro troops, whose poor morale reflected such familiar phenomena as low status and discriminatory treatment, had even greater cause for disgust. According to an intelligence report, "the lack of a rest area and rest leaves for colored personnel" had a serious and inflammatory effect on Negro units.[160] The leave situation in the Pacific deteriorated, if anything, as the war entered its last year. FEAF's movement to the northwest made it increasingly difficult to fly men to Australia and resulted in the gradual elimination of leaves to that area.[161] In the central Pacific, air units were similarly moving beyond the reach of their rest areas. The situation led Maj. Gen. Curtis LeMay to propose, as a temporary substitute for trips to Hawaii, that two luxury liners be brought to the Marianas and used as floating rest camps for his B-29 crewmen. Lack of shipping, however, blocked the realization of this idea.[162]

For the overwhelming majority of airmen, overseas leaves were only temporary medicine—essential but no cure whatsoever for a fierce, growing desire to get back home. The longing for rotation implied no lack of patriotism. It was instead simply the elemental reaction of ordinary human beings to the exactions of war and prolonged separation from the people, places, and things they valued most.[163] Under these circumstances the twists and turns, ups and downs, of rotation policy were bound to have a major effect on morale.[164] Rotation policy was conditioned above all by three factors: the availability of replacements, the intensity of operations, and estimates of the ability of men to stand up to various kinds of strain. These factors explain why combat men were ultimately rotated in large numbers and ground men were not and why within the combat-crew relief program there were marked fluctuations in the rotation rate.

The early realization that after a certain number of missions or combat hours—varying according to the nature, intensity, and locale of operations—a hypothetical average flier would decline in efficiency and, if not relieved in time, "burn out" led to the development of a decentralized system of aircrew rotation.[165] Battle-weary veterans were to be transferred to the Zone of Interior, where, it was felt, they could best recover from their experiences before going on to another combat tour or other activities. The aircrew rotation system never functioned, however, in a vacuum. Senior air force commanders were expected to carry out their missions—General Arnold was emphatic on that point[166]—in spite of the fact that the flow of replacements up to the last year of the war rarely if ever seemed adequate to cover attrition, allow for relief, and still leave enough men to meet mounting operational commitments. An impossible situation soon

474

arose. Combat men eventually went home, but some air forces had to hold back rotation, and others—like the Eighth—were forced to scrap the rotation programs they had established. Headquarters AAF was deluged by a torrent of anguished pleas for more replacements, reports of impending or actual combat-crew exhaustion, and warnings that the involuntary policy of slow rotation or no rotation that had been forced on the overseas air forces was doing grave damage to flier morale. Headquarters AAF, for its part, replied with assurances that replacements were being trained and rushed to the theaters as fast as was humanly possible and expressed the hope that by some future date—1944 was usually given—a peak supply of replacements combined with a drop in attrition would make possible the establishment or restoration of a consistent and steady process of rotation. The long-awaited day of personnel plenty did finally come in the summer of 1944, and thereafter combat-crew rotation was at most a minor issue.[167]

Ground personnel began the war with few illusions about rotation. The lack of manpower reserves made normal replacement of non-combat men a virtual impossibility.[168] Nothing could change that harsh fact. Nevertheless, as time passed, commanders and flight surgeons in the Pacific and CBI pointed out with increasing urgency the debilitating effect of climate and working and living conditions on the energy and morale of the men in their charge. They also insisted again and again that it was absolutely essential to give those men some goal to aim for, some hope of escape "short of the indefinite end of the war or collapse."[169] An already bad morale situation became perhaps worse whenever hopes for an effectual program of relief were periodically raised, then dashed. A scheme calling for the rotation of 5 per cent of AAF ground personnel per month was abandoned in March 1943 before it ever got under way and constituted "the most crushing blow to morale experience during the period."[170] A War Department plan for rotation at the token rate of one-half of 1 per cent per month actually went into effect in 1943 but in the long run probably caused more misunderstanding and bitterness than good. No sooner was the program launched than eligibility standards were raised. Later changes created further restrictions. But even then, with all but the most grizzled veterans eliminated from eligibility, the program still ran far behind schedule. Coming on the heels of the aborted rotation plans was a project for granting thirty days (later forty-five) of temporary duty in the Zone of Interior to qualified personnel who agreed to return to the theater for another year. The TDY program appears to have functioned with some success, but it came too late and affected too few men to repair the damage done to morale by confusion, delay, and half-extended, half-retracted promises.[171]

Though leadership received far less attention than rotation as a morale factor, it nevertheless exerted a strong influence—perhaps stronger than that of any other single factor. There was widespread agreement that unit morale acted as "a complete barometer and gauge of the fighting spirit, capacity for leadership, and general all-round ability of the . . . commander."[172] What constituted effective leadership varied according to the circumstances and the personality of the officer in command. But certain fundamental traits appear to have been essential. These included vigor, aggressiveness, fairness, firmness without arbitrary harshness, a lively interest in the welfare of all personnel, and, perhaps most important of all, the ability to inspire confidence by demonstrating both a grasp of the work at hand and a capacity for doing it.[173] That many officers, especially those with the least experience, lacked one or more of these qualities is beyond question and not too surprising. Each shortcoming was usually reflected in lessened efficiency and lowered morale, whether the unit involved was large or small. Despite a number of somewhat strident complaints about poor leadership, the AAF—a very human organization working in an imperfect world—appears to have done a creditable job in the selection of its leaders. The record of senior officers, like that of their juniors, was mixed. Conspicuous failures occurred, but they stood out as exceptions. Senior commanders by and large knew their work and did it, understood their responsibilities and fulfilled them, placed a high valuation on the well-being of their men and fought for it. They led; they took care of their own. In so doing, they contributed richly to the maintenance of good morale from the beginning of the war to the end.[174]

Fifth Air Force B-24 Spotting Survivors

AIR-SEA RESCUE

Thirteenth Air Force Catalina Taxiing In for a Pick-up

APPROACH OF RAFTS TO NAVY PBY

RESCUE OF GENERAL TWINING AND CREW IN CORAL SEA

RESCUER SWIMMING OUT WITH LINE

Coming Ashore

Safe after Six Days on a Raft

CATALINA PICK-UPS

*   *   *   *   *   *   *   *   *   *   *

CHAPTER 15

AIR-SEA RESCUE

THE rescue of airmen forced down at sea became for the AAF a problem of increasing importance in the course of World War II. This was especially true in the Pacific, where the first desperate fighting took place and where the AAF eventually committed no less than five air forces to operations which regularly demanded over-water flight, often for great distances. In the European and North African theaters air combat more commonly occurred over land, but there, too, provision had to be made for rescue of the many American airmen who were forced down into the waters around the British Isles or into the Mediterranean Sea. The expanding activity of the Air Transport Command reinforced the need to find, sustain, and rescue airmen who were down at sea for whatever cause—enemy action, want of fuel, mechanical failure, or human error.

Sentiment played an important part in the effort to provide rescue services, but there was much more involved than mere sentiment. Air-sea rescue paid off in distinct military advantages. Not only did it help sustain the morale of combat crews. It also saved for later combat service pilots and crewmen who had been trained at great expense of time and money and who often had the priceless advantage of combat experience.

In 1941 the AAF was poorly prepared in terms either of experience or of equipment to meet its need for rescue operations at sea. Fortunately, help was forthcoming from the U.S. Navy and from our Allies. Navy planes, surface vessels, and submarines drew no service lines when receiving a report that some flier was down at sea, and within the limits of its resources the Navy readily assumed responsibility in areas of its primary jurisdiction for the rescue of Army as well as Navy fliers. Similarly, in the European theater Britain's well-organized and experienced air-sea rescue service accepted the responsibility for saving U.S. aircrews who came down in the North Sea and the English Channel. By formal agreement between the RAF and the Eighth Air Force in September 1942 it was stipulated that the Americans would not duplicate the rescue services the British could provide. Instead, American crews would be protected by the existing British service, to which the AAF would contribute planes and other assistance as the scale of its operations expanded.[1] British agencies carried the same responsibilities in the waters off India and Burma. In the North African campaign the main burden fell on the U.S. and Royal navies and on the Royal Air Force. In all parts of the world the AAF's planes frequently participated in rescue searches, whether the flier were its own or some other, but not until 1943 did the Army Air Forces seek a significant degree of self-sufficiency by training and equipping special air-sea rescue squadrons of its own.

The Question of Responsibility

Traditionally, the American military services had divided the responsibility for aircraft accidents as follows: in land areas they were handled by the nearest Air Corps base; at sea, by the Navy. Each service undertook to train and indoctrinate its own crews and to provide them with emergency equipment—parachutes, flares, life-preservers and life-rafts, special rations, and medical supplies. Within the AAF, provision for air-sea rescue had been considered a command rather than a headquarters responsibility. Each command was expected to provide for its own needs, including negotiation for such assistance as might be required of a sister service. The obligation resting upon AAF Headquarters was to provide needed material assistance and to see that crews received a necessary indoctrination as part of their regular training.

These limited responsibilities passed, during a reorganization of AAF Headquarters in the spring of 1942 that was distinguished by the establishment of a system of directorates for the control of operations,* to the Director of Traffic Control and Regulations. In a minor reshuffling of offices two months later, the job was given to the Director of Flying Safety. In March 1943, when AAF Headquarters experi-

---

* See Vol. VI, 33–36. The system of directorates was an effort to separate the operating from the policy-making agencies in AAF Hq. When the experiment failed, the tendency was to move operations out of AAF Hq. and into the hands of subordinate field agencies.

enced its third major reorganization in as many years, air-sea rescue was assigned to a newly activated Flight Control Command at Winston-Salem, North Carolina. This decision, however, was soon reversed.[2] On 25 August 1943 the responsibility was reassigned to a newly created Emergency Rescue Branch in the Pentagon office of the AC/AS, Operations, Commitments, and Requirements (OC&R).[3]

The decision to bring the job back to Washington has a simple explanation. Until the summer of 1943 the scale of AAF combat operations had been sufficiently limited to make possible a continuing dependence upon the assistance of friendly services or upon a policy of providing additional planes and equipment for those air forces which found it necessary to organize supplementary rescue services of their own. But it had now to be assumed that AAF commitments to combat operations by the spring of 1944 would reach a total that would impose upon the several air forces a new obligation to look out for their own airmen. Especially significant was the prospect that AAF forces in the Pacific, including those equipped with the cherished very-long-range B-29, would soon have a strength far exceeding the totals originally planned for 1944. No less important were proposals by the Navy which elevated the issue of air-sea rescue to the highest level of policy.

The problem of achieving some better co-ordination of effort between the Navy and the AAF, and a closer liaison with interested Allied services, had been under discussion by agencies of the Joint Chiefs of Staff since the spring of 1943.[4] Closer integration of existing services promised savings in personnel and materiel. It was also felt that greater efforts were needed for the establishment of common rescue procedures among the several participating forces. But it proved easier to agree on the need for improvement than upon the best means for its achievement. The Navy argued that the rescue function should be turned over to the U.S. Coast Guard, a step that would represent a logical expansion of the latter's traditional mission and at the same time would release Army and Navy personnel for other duties. The AAF preferred to depend upon co-ordination of effort through a new liaison committee representing the several services and the Maritime Commission. On 18 August 1943 the Joint Chiefs of Staff instructed the Joint Administrative Committee (JAC) to study the problem.[5]

In the same month the AAF drafted plans to make itself as self-sufficient as was possible by organizing seven air-sea rescue squadrons, each to be equipped with PBY's for rescue operations, with L-5's for liaison, and with AT-7's or AT-11's for utility purposes.[6] The schedule called for completion of the program by the spring of 1944 in accordance with a plan to assign most of the new units to the Pacific air forces. The question of assignment was critical. Throughout most of the Pacific the Navy held the top commands, and Navy doctrine favored a principle of area coverage, with rescue units assigned for operational control to a variety of area or island commands. In opposition to this policy, the AAF insisted that its rescue units should serve as integral parts of a theater air force, in the belief that this practice would guarantee the greatest possible flexibility in their employment.[7] It was an old question of debate between the Navy and the AAF, and one that was never fully resolved.

The AAF won a victory in the deliberations of the JAC, which concluded that the Coast Guard, despite its enviable tradition as a rescue agency, would face insurmountable obstacles should it have to expand its responsibilities to include all air-sea rescue. Instead, the committee recommended that the Navy and the AAF continue the development of separate services but that a new agency be established in Washington for their co-ordination. On 15 February 1944, the Joint Chiefs of Staff asked the Secretary of the Navy to establish such an agency. The new board was headed by the Commandant of the Coast Guard and included representatives of the Navy, the AAF, and the ASF. It undertook to advance pertinent research, to disseminate information that would encourage a closer co-ordination of operations and procedures, and to maintain liaison with responsible agencies in Allied countries.[8]

AAF leaders still feared that the Navy wished to turn over full responsibility to the Coast Guard, and they objected to proposals that the new office station liaison officers in the several theaters with powers of direct communication on the ground that this would add executive functions to a body that had been intended to be no more than an advisory agency.[9] The continuing differences helped to strengthen the conviction among AAF leaders that an air force, in this as in other particulars, should be as self-sufficient as is possible, a development not without influence on the policies of the postwar Air Force. But during the war a very considerable disparity continued to exist between policy and achievement. Although the program of August 1943 for the creation of seven emergency rescue (ER) squadrons had been scheduled for completion by the spring of 1944, there were only two such units in operation in the following summer. Another had become operational by the end of the year, in the Southwest Pacific, but the others did not achieve that status until 1945 and some of them only at the very close of the war.* Thus the AAF's move for self-sufficiency in this particular respect began late and fell far short of the success attained in other fields. Perhaps it was this record that persuaded General George of ATC to advocate, as late as March 1945, the turning-over of full responsibility for rescue services along the transocean airlines to the Navy.[10]

An Evaluation

Despite the tardiness and incompleteness of the AAF's efforts to provide its own emergency rescue squadrons, the record suggests that a growing awareness at AAF Headquarters of the importance of air-sea rescue paid good dividends. It is impossible to gauge with mathematical accuracy the degree of success achieved in air-sea rescue during the war. Many airmen reported in distress were later lost to accident or enemy action without a chance to ditch or bail out. Others, who went down near hostile shores after broadcasting distress signals, were picked up by the enemy. Yet, however lacking in finality, available statistics for almost every theater showed a marked improvement in performance. In 1943 only 28 per cent of Eighth Air Force crews reported as in distress were saved. By April 1944 the figure had risen to 43 per cent for bomber crews and to 38 per cent for fighter pilots. In September approximately 90 per cent of AAF crews forced down at sea in the ETO were recovered. By the end of March 1945 a total of 1,972 American airmen had been saved by British or U.S. rescue units in the North Sea, the English Channel, or other waters around Great Britain. Even then, on the eve of Germany's surrender, there could be no relaxing, for the Eighth Air Force still had ditchings involving some fifty lives per month.[11]

An equally impressive record was being achieved in the Pacific, in spite of the greater distances and areas involved. Between July 1943 and April 1945 air-sea rescue units working with the Fifth Air Force saved 1,841 persons, 360 of them in the month of January 1945, when the Fifth had its own emergency rescue squadron. During the three months before 1 March 1945 an average of two B-29's were ditched

---

* See below, pp. 499–500.

in each strike against the Japanese home islands. During the preceding
November and December 34.4 per cent of downed crewmen had been
picked out of the water, but in January only 12.6 per cent were rescued. A complicated command system added to the natural difficulties,
but closer liaison with the Navy was worked out, and greater stress
was placed upon indoctrination of crews.[12] The record began to improve immediately, if not steadily; in March rescues rose to 74 per
cent, in May to 80 per cent, and in the whole nine months of missions
from the Marianas just half—654 out of 1,310—of the Superfort crewmen reported down were rescued. No one grudged the effort involved, but it was on a scale as lavish as most matters connected with
the VHB program. When the last B-29 strike was staged on 14
August 1945, about 2,400 men, or one-fourth of those participating
in the mission, were on air-sea rescue duty.[13]

The chances of survival and rescue for airmen forced down at sea
depended on a number of factors. The skill and coolness of individuals
after a bail-out or forced landing at sea were of first importance.
Weather conditions counted heavily. So did luck. So did the prompt-
ness with which rescuers came. The ditching characteristics of aircraft might spell the difference between survival and death; rescue
equipment carried on the aircraft or used by the ASR units might be
the deciding factor.

Some planes ditched better than others, chiefly because of basic design, though this was largely adventitious. Flying Fortresses ditched
well because of a rugged structure and a hydrodynamic shape that
prevented porpoising or diving under the surface as the plane hit the
water. Since the low midwing absorbed part of the initial shock and
added buoyancy, an undamaged B-17 might float half an hour or
more. Even with one wing damaged, it usually floated topside up long
enough for the crew to escape. The high wing design of the Liberators was conversely a disadvantage. In a forced landing at sea the
fuselage had to absorb the whole impact, and often the bomb-bay
doors would fly open and the plane would break in two, either just
forward or aft of the wing roots. Thus the survival record in ditchings
was much higher for B-17's than for B-24's. In ten ditchings under
favorable conditions by Liberators belonging to the Thirteenth Air
Force, there was an average of one death each.[14] It was 29 April 1944
before the ETO reported its first wholly successful B-24 ditching,
when a Liberator went down forty miles northeast of Cromer, Eng-

land, and floated long enough for the whole crew to escape.[15] The very heavy B-29 was unpredictable; it might crack up in ditching, or it might remain afloat long enough to allow an orderly escape of the crew. Its basic design and high flotation, if the pressurized cabin remained undamaged, balanced against its huge weight and high landing speed. In the very first B-29 mission, against Bangkok on 5 June 1944, one Superfort, ditched in the Bay of Bengal, floated ashore next day.[16]

Fighter craft were notoriously hard to ditch safely. Only once was the P-51 known to have ditched successfully, and this minor miracle could not be repeated deliberately, since the pilot lost consciousness and therewith all memory of his technique. Normally, the radiator scoop of the Mustang plowed the plane under at impact. The average time between impact and submersion for a fighter was less than twenty seconds, and in that short span the pilot had to recover from the shock of impact, release the canopy, climb from the cockpit, and inflate his life-jacket or life-raft. Hence it became the practice under most conditions for fighter pilots to bail out rather than risk ditching.[17]

With bombers and most other multi-engined planes, ditching was the preferred procedure. It gave the survivors a chance to get into life-rafts without being immersed in cold water. This was more important in the North Atlantic than in those Pacific Ocean areas where the water was warmer. It was rare that an airman survived more than two or three hours in the cold waters of the North Sea or English Channel, and, consequently, it was dangerous to parachute into the sea without a life-raft or a good chance of an early pickup. Conversely, if rescue ships were near at hand, bailing out might be less hazardous than trying to ditch a badly damaged plane or one with poor flotation qualities. Perhaps, most important of all, ditching, where even moderately successful, kept the crew together as a team, a physical and morale advantage.[18]

In both ditching and parachuting, many airmen were killed because prescribed safety equipment was not carried, or was not properly installed, or was not used according to instructions. Throughout the war there was a constant search for better survival equipment, but in this matter, as in so many others, it was easier to invent a new gadget or improve an old one than to train aircrew members to get the best out of whatever was currently available.

The importance of training is illustrated by the comparative record of Navy and AAF crews ditching multi-engined planes in the Pacific.

In this difficult feat the Navy was much more successful, putting down B-24's or B-34's without casualties under conditions similar to those costing AAF B-24's or B-25's losses up to 30 or 40 per cent. Navy pilots had a better understanding of the sea and could judge from its surface the direction of the wind. The proper approach was upwind across the waves if the wind were strong, but otherwise along the top of the swell. AAF pilots too often glided into the water instead of stalling in, tail down, which reduced the danger of bouncing on the rough surface. Too frequently outside openings, except those used for escape hatches, were not closed, and the doors between compartments, which if secured would check the flow of water from bow to stern, were left open. Poor air discipline made ditching very hazardous, especially when pilots put down without sufficient warning or when crew members failed to take their designated ditching station and posture. Crewmen were frequently injured during a ditching when unsecured equipment, which, if not essential to survival should have been jettisoned, was tumbled about inside the plane. Obviously, an airman if injured had less chance to make a successful escape from a sinking aircraft.[19]

Air-Sea Rescue Equipment

According to the view adopted by the Air Staff, the AAF, through whatever agency it might appoint, was responsible for the development and procurement of ASR equipment. This included the survival items carried on board each aircraft destined for flight over water, items carried on board rescue planes, and the rescue planes themselves. Little had been done in this respect before the eve of World War II. The Navy's jealous concern for its prerogatives discouraged Air Corps flights over the ocean. There was little money for research and development of any sort, and the procurement of rescue items had a very low order of priority. Nor was there much uniformity; identical aircraft often carried different types of equipment, sometimes ill suited to the requirements of a particular plane or locality; and it was consequently impossible to standardize procedure. The chief needs were means of keeping survivors afloat, provision of survival kits, ways of locating the airmen downed at sea, and means of bringing them home.[20] In spite of a late start, marked improvements were made in each of these categories.

It was important to keep a ditched plane afloat as long as possible, certainly until the crew could enter their life-rafts. Attempts to build watertight compartments into the tail, wings, and fuselage of military aircraft had proved impractical by the mid-thirties. The Air Corps had tried also equipping some planes with rubberized-fabric gas bags, to be inflated with carbon dioxide in the case of ditching. Thereafter, the search for built-in buoyancy remained dormant until 1943, when Second Air Force members suggested a similar gas-bag system for B-17's. The complete equipment weighed only 300 pounds and required no structural change in the bomber. Its advocates argued that the British use of flotation equipment had produced a much better record in rescues than that of the AAF.[21] The suggestion brought no results; by that time the AAF was more interested in developing a satisfactory life-raft than in experimenting with equipment to keep the whole plane afloat.

The ideal life-raft should be light in weight, small in bulk when deflated, and have stowage room for food, water, and other survival items. It—even the largest raft—should be easy to launch from ditched aircraft, be rugged enough to stand buffeting by rough seas, and be capable of being steered. To find a satisfactory balance of all these requirements took years. The first life-rafts procured for the Air Corps were a type used by sportsmen, bought on the open market in 1927. That year the Air Corps accepted a specially designed four-man raft, which was discarded in 1931 as too bulky for use. During the next five years the Materiel Division Equipment Laboratory at Wright Field developed a number of models of one- and two-man rafts, none wholly satisfactory. By 1938 most Air Corps planes were being equipped with such rafts.[22]

When the war came, the AAF followed the lead of Pan American Airways in changing to rubberized-fabric life-rafts without bladders. A five-man raft, Type A-3, was standardized in 1943. It had a design similar to that of a Navy raft and used the same fabric, a compound of natural rubber and cotton, considered more resilient than synthetic rubber and nylon. A change in the position of the bulkhead in the outer casing gave greater stability in case of a partial deflation. A newer model, Type A-3A, appeared in 1944. With one 10-inch seat, two water-ballast pockets, and a lifeline that doubled as a boarding ladder, the A-3A weighed only 36 pounds net; it measured 98 by 60 inches in size. By the end of 1944 about 150,000 Type A-3 and A-3A rafts had been delivered. Meanwhile, the AAF Materiel Center developed a seven-man raft, Type E, for dropping from rescue aircraft. It proved so satisfactory that it was soon made standard equipment for all planes making over-water flights with more than four men aboard.[23]

For some time before Pearl Harbor two-man rafts had been used in pursuit planes, but in August 1942 the AAF adopted a Navy one-man raft, Model AN-R-2A. Issued to each crew member in aircraft of three places or less, it was attached to the parachute harness either as a seat pack or back pad. It was not satisfactory; it had to be blown up by mouth, and it was hard to board under usual ditching conditions. Also its weather cover and patching kit were considered inadequate by some users. Modifications were hard to secure, since the design was Navy.[24]

Before the end of 1943, however, Wright Field had copies of and was testing an RAF individual dinghy, equipped with sail, water pocket, spray shield, collapsible hand pump, hand-held signals, and sea anchor. In the ETO American fliers had preferred this dinghy to any U.S. model, but in May 1944 the AAF adopted Type C-2, with a rated capacity of 350 pounds and with a wider range of accessories, including a sea anchor, keel, larger water pocket, and better sails.[25]

The limited capacity of life-rafts made imperative a careful scrutiny of basic accessories. Designers weighed the relative emergency merits of navigational aids, signaling devices, food, water, and shelter. Most selections were the result of a series of compromises. Selections for the one-man raft were particularly difficult to make, since both the raft and its accessories were carried on the flier's person. In 1942 the one-man AN-R-2A raft's equipment was simple: repair kit, bailing bucket, two paddles, concertina pump, two bullet-hole plugs, sea anchor, can of drinking water, seat pad, and two hand paddles. No food was included. In 1944 distress-signal flares, a sponge, signaling mirror, and desalting kit were added. Standard multi-place raft accessories included also fishing tackle, first-aid kits, and a packet of religious booklets. Devices used to attract the attention of rescue searchers comprised signal mirrors, sea-marker dyes, colored smoke, and, where possible, a Gibson Girl radio.[26]

No item was more vital to the airman in a raft than a supply of drinking water; this was especially true in the hot reaches of the Pacific. After tests in December 1942, Arnold ordered the immediate procurement of the Delano Sunstill, "not something Materiel Command thinks is better."[27] This still, weighing only two and one-half pounds and simple to operate, could produce under proper conditions about one pint of water per day. Unfortunately, deliveries were delayed for a whole year. Meanwhile, Materiel Command tried to incorporate into one unit the best features of all known solar stills but failed because of the reluctance of civilian manufacturers to share trade secrets. In December 1944 the U.S. government secured the patent rights to the Gallowhun Sunstill, and, in January, Wright Field invited bids on 350,000 units built to Gallowhun specifications. However, subsequent tests showed that the Higgins Sunstill could produce twice as much drinking water as the Gallowhun type, and efforts were made to standardize the Higgins still. Because of this series of delays, which Arnold's curt remark seems to have foreseen, sun stills did not come into general use until near the end of the war. Progress had been made earlier in the development of a desalting kit, and by September 1944 they were being issued. These kits took most of the salts from sea water by chemical precipitation and filtering, but the materials in the kit were subject to deterioration.[28]

Life-preservers must provide dependable buoyancy without too much bulk, and early preference had leaned toward the highly reliable kapok jacket which could not be deflated by a bullet hole or snag. After the middle thirties, however, the need to reduce bulk and the improvement of inflation devices turned the AAF to the use of pneumatic preservers. During the early part of the war the AAF was a common user of the Navy's Type B-4, but it proved unsatisfactory because it would not keep an airman in full flying clothes afloat. A new rubberized-fabric vest, Type B-5, was developed by the AAF in 1944, designed to keep the face of an unconscious person out of the water and to exert less pressure on the wearer's body.[29]

In November 1943 the Materiel Command's Equipment Laboratory began work on an airborne lifeboat, which could be dropped to survivors who could not be picked up by surface craft, submarines, or seaplanes. Specifications were released to the Higgins Company in the spring of 1944 for a 27-foot boat, with two engines which would give a speed of 8 knots. Delivery was slow, lagging behind orders until January 1945. The boat proved satisfactory in operation. When carried by a B-17, it could be faired into its belly so as to produce little additional drag, resulting in a loss of only 6 miles per hour. Dropped by parachute, the boat was usually released at a speed of 120 m.p.h. from an altitude of 1,500 feet. Attempts to use the B-25 as a lifeboat carrier proved unsuccessful. In March 1945 the AAF began the modification of B-29's to enable them to carry large lifeboats for use in connection with VHB operations against Japan. The British, too, produced, shortly before V-E Day, a large airborne boat, 30 feet long and 3,000 pounds in weight and carrying twenty men. It had a cruising radius of 300 miles and could be refueled from the air and sailed by an inexperienced crew.[30]

In the European theater the AAF, because of this tardy development of its own lifeboats, was long dependent upon the British Air/Sea Rescue Service. The first rescue using an AAF airborne lifeboat was in early April 1945 off the coast of Denmark. Six men were adrift in a raft; the waves were high, whipped by a 50-knot wind. RAF Warwicks dropped three lifeboats, but all had broken in the rough water or drifted away. A B-17 of the 5th Emergency Rescue Squadron dropped its boat. Ninety seconds after it had hit the water, the six men were aboard. Twelve minutes later they had the engine running and were heading for England. They survived a bad storm but then, having run out of gas, drifted at the mercy of the seas. On the third day a torpedo boat homed in on the lifeboat's Gibson Girl and brought the men home.[31]

A second successful drop was made on 1 May by the 1st Emergency Rescue Squadron to a fighter pilot in the midst of a minefield outside Trieste harbor. The pilot rated the operation "perfect," and he spoke with some authority, having already been rescued twice in boats dropped by the British.[32]

This pilot's confidence in air-sea rescue procedures and equipment, and his own skilful co-operation, represented a change since the early days of the war. Perhaps half of VIII Bomber Command's crews had been accustomed to flying without parachutes, partly because the weight and bulk hampered their free movement about the ship at high altitudes. B-17 pilots and co-pilots felt it useless to comply with parachute regulations when their equipment offered them so little chance for survival. After testing the Pioneer Model P3-B-24 chute in combat, the 92d Bombardment Group found it suitable for most persons and conditions. By January 1943 the Eighth Air Force had received 400 of this type, and 10,000 were on order. One-man rafts could be worn with the new model parachute, though at some cost in comfort.[33]

Detachable breast-pack parachutes gave greater freedom of movement, but crewmen preferred the greater security of the back pack. Men were sometimes thrown from a plane without having a chance to grab a chest chute or missed catching it in a bad spin. Sometimes the attachment snaps did not work. Late in 1943 the AAF adopted a four-point quick-release box, similar to the RAF type for use on seat and quick-attachable parachute harnesses, and modified the back-type B-8 harness for use with this box. All production of the new harnesses and parachutes was earmarked for combat theaters, and existing stocks of the old types were issued to units in the United States.[34]

Experiments with parachute emergency kits and rations had begun well before the war. The first kit, developed in 1934, proved unsatisfactory, and, between 1939 and 1941, separate kits were developed for the tropics and the Arctic. With the United States involved in literally world-wide war, the Equipment Laboratory began to look for a single universal **parachute emergency kit**. In June 1943, 25,000 new B-4 kits were ordered, but production difficulties and the decision to use up existing stocks of jungle and arctic kits delayed overseas delivery of the B-4's until well into 1944. Continued dissatisfaction with pad-type kits led to production of the C-1 Emergency Sustenance Vest in 1944. Easy to put on in a hurry, the vest did not restrict movement or interfere with the parachute harness and was relatively comfortable. Of some 200,000 ordered, nearly 16,000 were delivered during 1944. When standard survival kits were not available, substitutes were designed and procured locally and at times these were preferred to the regular issue.[35] In the first rescue of a B-29 crew from the Indian Ocean, survivors credited the recovery of the wounded to the drugs contained in a homemade vest worn by a flight engineer.*

Larger kits containing rations and supplies were designed for carrying in tactical planes or for dropping to crews in distress. Most kits contained items that were specialized according to climate and terrain. This specialization produced a confusing variety of kits, and, unfortunately, the early endeavors at standardization were hampered by delays and by misunderstandings between personnel overseas, in Washington, and at Wright Field. Eventually, in the spring of 1945, it was agreed to use one basic 25-pound kit for all areas, but the decision came too late to help. Larger aerial delivery kits, weighing from 110 to 210 pounds, were designed for dropping by parachute to men who were stranded. They contained rations, clothing, first-aid material,

* See Vol. V, 97.

gun, flares, tents, and water; the selection of items differed according to the area for which it was designed. As in most cases of resupply by air, much of the emergency sustenance material was lost or ruined in the drop.[36]

Responsibility for developing a ration suitable for stowage in life-rafts was shared by Wright Field and the Army Quartermaster Subsistence Research Laboratory in Chicago. The first bail-out ration, developed in 1934, was primarily for fliers forced down on land. It was compounded of bitter chocolate, powdered skimmed milk, oat flour, and cocoa fat and was packaged in four-ounce cakes, each with a food value of about 600 calories. Palatable and a source of quick energy, this cake remained the standard emergency ration until the appearance of the Army's K ration in 1941. The K ration, however, was too bulky, too poorly packaged for use at sea, and too thirst-provoking. In 1942 the Materiel Command developed a package containing an Army D ration bar, dextrose tablets, bouillon powder, and chewing gum. In developing life-raft ration A in 1943, the Quartermaster, profiting by Navy and British experience, doubled the calorie count of the K ration and reduced its tendency to provoke thirst. Ration A was unsatisfactory, however, because of its bulk, its deficiency of vitamins, and its poor packaging. In June of that year VIII Bomber Command was authorized to procure from the British 9,000 Mark II emergency rations for issue at the rate of ten per heavy bomber.[37] A year later the Ninth Air Force was still repacking U.S. life-raft rations in Mark II tins.

In January 1945 procurement specifications called for an AAF ration including the new type A candy unit (or equivalent), sugar-coated gum, and vitamin tablets. Rations were designed for five or six man-days. Chewing gum was prized as a deterrent to thirst and as a handy mastic to plug a hole or seal a can. Benzedrine tablets were sometimes supplied to be used as last-resort stimulants. The rations issued Eighth and Ninth Air Force crews were calculated to last only seven days, considered the maximum period of endurance for airmen ditching in the waters around Britain. Rations carried in airborne life-boats were more generous both in quantity and in food value. One developed in 1944 contained about 1,500 calories per man per day.[38]

The most difficult task in air-sea rescue was probably that of sighting the survivors. Various devices were used by those down at sea to attract the attention of searchers—flags, mirrors, sea markers, and flares. Each had some utility, and each could be carried in a small raft, but all were effective only at short range. The obvious need was a radio transmitter. This requirement was recognized early in the war and was emphasized by such dramatic episodes as the long voyage of Capt. Eddie Rickenbacker's party in 1942 and the six-day exposure of Brig. Gen. Nathan F. Twining and fourteen airmen between Guadalcanal and Espiritu Santo in 1943.[39]

The first portable radio transmitter for this purpose was the SCR-578, widely known as the Gibson Girl. By July 1942 this transmitter was being carried in bombers and transport planes leaving for combat theaters, but it was not universally used until a year later. Later improvements, tested in the spring of 1944, provided accurate fixes from bearings 1,000–1,500 miles away, roughly ten times the effective range of the standard model.[40] In practice, however, the value of the SCR-578 to men adrift in a life-raft depended less on the rated power of the transmitter than on the ability of the survivors to get the antenna up. When the kite or balloon, used to raise the antenna into the air, lacked sufficient lift, two to three hundred feet of antenna wire sagged into the water, and radiation was severely affected. The British had tried launching the antenna with a Very pistol, but this attempt was unsatisfactory and was abandoned in 1943 in favor of the American method. Even with the antenna up and the transmitter in working order, the set was useless if the detachable handle of the built-in hand generator was lost.[41]

To afford long-range navigational aids and fixes, the SCR-578 was modified in the spring of 1945 to broadcast distress signals automatically on two frequencies: 500 kilocycles for homing of search aircraft and 8280 kilocycles, the world-wide emergency frequency for aircraft. During the last few months of the war the SCR-578 was being replaced by the AN/ERT-3 automatic two-frequency transmitter, which was distributed in the Pacific theaters as rapidly as it became available.[42] American manufacture of a self-contained British radio transmitter, which could be homed on by aircraft equipped either with ASC Mark II or with US SCR-521 radios, was considered, but the plan did not go through.[43]

This continued search for a better homing device was not a confession of the utter failure of the Gibson Girl. It had admirable features, which offset its weaknesses, and many airmen owe their lives to it. Communication failures were often the result of poor air-sea rescue indoctrination or of emotional strain. The crew sometimes neglected to broadcast its position before being forced down—often inadvertently or, in the case of B-29's off Honshu, for fear of disclosing their position to the enemy. Sometimes, too, a crew sent out a distress signal and then, after landing safely, failed to notify the rescue headquarters. In November 1944, for example, a B-25 was lost in bad weather over the Indian Ocean while hunting for a B-29 that had already landed at China Bay in Ceylon. In another incident two B-29 crews that had ditched were located by returning Superforts, yet 38 hours elapsed before the searching unit was notified. In a strike against Tokyo on 24/25 February 1945, sixteen B-29's were in distress at sea, but only one used the distress frequency prescribed by current directives.[44] In other instances B-29 crews discouraged rescue submarines, highly vulnerable to enemy action during a pickup, by broadcasting their positions in the clear. Practices such as these added unnecessarily to the already difficult labors of the rescue units, and the mutual confidence, necessary for good teamwork, of the rescuers and the distressed airmen was damaged.

Navy and AAF experiments with radar for air-sea rescue had little success. Neither service was able to develop light-weight radar sets sensitive enough to find a small rubber raft in rough water and simple enough in maintenance. A device known as a corner reflector, requiring no field maintenance, was developed in 1944 and standardized for joint Army-Navy use. When installed in a dinghy, the radar echo could be detected by radar-equipped aircraft flying at an altitude of 800 feet 16 miles away. If the reflector had been dependable, it would have been a great improvement over visual search, but it was too fragile for use in rough seas. Moreover, it could be used only in connection with radar-equipped search planes, never available in sufficient numbers.[45]

The choice of aircraft for air-sea rescue operations was largely determined by what was available, with such modifications as were useful and possible. Almost all aircraft types were used, including single-engined liaison planes and fighters. For example, long-range P-51D's and P-47N's stationed on Iwo Jima proved valuable for spot searches for B-29's lost along the path to Honshu. But the workhorses of the rescue program were multi-engined planes—Navy Catalinas, British Warwicks, AAF Liberators, Flying Fortresses, and Superfortresses. Each type had advantages, but none combined in desired degree the

492

cardinal virtues: great cruising range and carrying capacity, slow speed for searching operations, ability to land in and take off from rough water, and defensive strength against intruders. Land-based planes always, and seaplanes frequently, teamed up with the surface vessels or submarines that made the actual pickups of survivors. Sometimes, especially during the early part of the war, tactical aircraft were used for search and rescue missions, but that practice was generally considered a stop gap that interfered with combat strikes without providing the best of air-sea rescue service. Increasingly, the more suitable type aircraft were used by units organized and trained for the rescue mission, and the planes themselves underwent modifications of varying degrees of importance. During the war no serious effort was made to design from scratch a plane for air-sea rescue service.

The rescue record of the Catalinas was a spotty one, ranging from some of the most spectacular successes of the war to discouraging failures. Its range and load capacity were satisfactory, its cruising speed ideally slow, but the Catalina had trouble in landing in rough seas and in taxiing with a heavy load aboard. During one period in 1944, CBI's Eastern Air Command reported that half the Catalinas sent on rescue missions cracked up on landing, leaving two planes in trouble instead of one.[46] The Catalina, awkward in flight and lightly armed, was quite vulnerable to enemy attack.

Eastern Air Command used also RAF Warwicks, which could carry the droppable lifeboats possessed by the command. But the Warwicks did not have enough cruising range for the sprawling theater in which EAC operated. In range and in rugged dependability, the Liberator was more satisfactory, but it was too fast for meticulous searching, and its turning radius was so great that spotters on board could easily lose a sighted dinghy as the bomber came about. Nor could the B-24 carry a lifeboat. On balance, however, it was the best plane available, and by January 1945 most emergency rescue crews in the command had converted to Liberators, and in that month they did more flying in support of long-range combat operations than had been done in the previous seven months with twice as many Warwicks.[47] For the long-range work the British Air Ministry proposed to use Lancasters—which it was planning to redeploy in large numbers to the Pacific after victory in Europe—and in the spring of 1945 worked on an airborne lifeboat to fit that famous bomber.

493

AAF officers were dubious when the British tried to equate the Lancaster with the B-29 as a very-long-range aircraft, and on both performance and potentiality they were correct. The unique qualities of the Superfortress were as obvious when it was used for air-sea rescue as for bombing missions. It had the great range and staying power for a search mission of fourteen or fifteen hours, and it was so heavily armed that it could work where other search planes dared not go; in fact, on a number of occasions B-29 rescue planes were able to defend both the airmen in a life-raft and would-be rescuers in a submarine or surface craft from Japanese attacks. It was axiomatic that only a B-29 rescue plane could cover the whole radius of action of B-29 bombers, and the rescue mission became increasingly significant as the weight of attack from the Marianas against the Japanese home islands increased. The first Superforts so used were regular bombers or, more rarely, the F-13 reconnaissance model, fitted out locally with rescue equipment. In 1945 a special rescue model was developed, called the "Superdumbo"—the Catalina had been unofficially named the "Dumbo." The Superdumbo carried extra radio equipment and operators, rafts, provisions, survival kits, radios, and other supplies to be dropped to airmen in the water.[48] Eventually, the rescue B-29 was equipped with a large, powered lifeboat.

Perhaps the most significant addition to the rescuer's equipment late in the war was the helicopter. Its advantages were numerous. It could search minutely the local area in which the fliers were reported as down and could snatch men off a raft under almost any sea conditions. Although of limited range, the helicopter could take off from a small deck, a jungle clearing, or a beach and hence had a high degree of mobility. In May 1944 the Eighth Air Force asked for six helicopters, each capable of carrying a payload of 1,800 pounds, considering them especially valuable for service in foggy weather. During the next twelve months fifteen R-6 helicopters were sent to China and the Southwest Pacific. By June 1945 helicopters were a standard part of the equipment of emergency rescue squadrons, and AAF Headquarters was planning to use 140 of them by the end of the year. The full exploitation of the helicopter as a rescue instrument came after V-J Day, though fortunately before the Korean War.[49]

Actually, most pickups during World War II were made by surface vessels. Submarines were used and did valiant service in waters under enemy control, as did seaplanes, which worked also in other areas. But both the submarine and PBY had tactical and performance weaknesses, and the leading role in the climax of the complex rescue mission—the removal of men from the sea—was usually played by some surface vessel.

The surface-rescue vessels ranged in size from crash boats and motor launches to destroyers, and each type had its virtues and limitations. Because the prime responsibility for air-sea rescue fell to the British in the ETO and CBI and to the U.S. Navy in the Pacific areas, most of the surface craft were outside the purview of the AAF. Nevertheless, the AAF did procure and operate boats of its own.

In 1943 responsibility for operating Army surface vessels in air-sea rescue service was transferred from the Quartermaster Corps to the Army Air Forces. This change in policy, though not at the instance of AAF Headquarters, was in keeping with its doctrine that airmen should have full control of facilities used in emergency rescue. The equipment ranged from 16-foot swamp gliders and 22-foot shallow-draft boats to seagoing vessels up to 104 feet in length. Delivering the largest boats to overseas units proved a difficult problem. To save the wear and tear of a long, rough voyage under their own power, they were shipped as deck loads on larger vessels. Such passage was not always easy to arrange, for there was a constant shortage of deck space, and some overseas ports lacked necessary facilities for the un-loading. The AAF accordingly tried to exchange its 104-foot rescue boats for 63-foot high-speed Navy craft, some of which Arnold had already obtained from Admiral King. Eventually, from the several types the AAF developed a standard 85-foot emergency rescue craft.[50] But no craft was ever designed that combined in satisfactory degree the high speed, long cruising range, and seaworthiness that the AAF sought, and the performance of standard boats was never wholly adequate, even when they worked out of secret harbors or from mother ships far in advance of the bases used by the aircraft whose missions they supported.[51]

Training rescue boats crews was at first left to the appropriate theater commands. But late in 1943 all Quartermaster Corps rescue-boat activities were reassigned to the AAF, and Training Command assumed responsibility for individual training for Emergency Rescue Boat operations. Unit training of boat crews, ranging from four to thirteen men, fell first to the Fourth Air Force, later to the Third.[52]

Rescue Operations

When in September 1942 the Air Ministry agreed to provide air-sea rescue services for the Eighth Air Force, the Eighth was relieved of any immediate necessity of building a service of its own. The British in March 1940 had established a unified system of communications, assuring speedy transmission of emergency calls from airmen forced down in the English Channel or in the North Sea to the closest rescue agencies. In the following August, just as the Battle of Britain approached its peak, a more formal organization of air-sea rescue services was achieved by agreement between the RAF and the Royal Navy. The airplane, used chiefly for search and spotting, was teamed with the surface craft, which usually effected the actual rescue of airmen forced down in waters adjoining the British Isles. An improved communication network made it possible for joint command posts to mobilize the full resources of the services as the emergency might require.[53] Deep-sea searches were made by the Coastal Command, which in January 1943 deployed about forty Hudsons and Ansons in this mission. Searches less than forty miles offshore were handled by RAF Fighter Command groups using Spitfires, Ansons, and Walruses.[54]

In Europe AAF units devised their own ditching procedures and emergency training methods, adapting current RAF practices. Whatever virtue the Eighth Air Force directives may have had, they were ineffective in operation. Ditching drills were often perfunctory, and aircrew indoctrination remained imperfect. Some pilots put an unnecessary strain upon a hard-working service by their reluctance to admit they were in trouble until it was too late to render help easily. There was a widespread feeling that airmen should always bail out of a doomed plane rather than try ditching even when parachuting would mean almost certain death from cold or drowning. Some aircrews were ill informed about their duties in a ditching or crash landing; others lacked skill in the use of life-raft equipment; others were remiss in the use and care of flying clothes. There was little co-ordination between the agencies responsible for the procurement of emergency equipment and the operational units that used it. In time-honored military fashion, some crews hoarded scarce equipment while others suffered serious shortages. Medical officers noted these weaknesses in the air-rescue program with concern, for at times the consequent medical problems almost dwarfed those that were standard among combat fliers.[55]

The fault lay partly with procedure, partly with the equipment. Late in 1942 the life-raft situation was described as "critical, deplorable and confused." In theory an entire bomber crew could get into the large life-raft and help each other while awaiting rescue, but in practice too many airmen who bailed out were drowned because they were unable to reach the raft. Those who parachuted seldom landed close together, especially in bad weather. There was a pressing need for a dependable multi-place raft for the bomber crew that ditched and for a one-man raft or dinghy—in addition to the life-preserver—that could be worn in flight and inflated quickly after hitting the water in a bail-out. British dinghies, though liked by U.S. fliers, were not readily adaptable to their crew positions and were in short supply. For want of standard equipment, Eighth Air Force crews had to get along with makeshifts.[56] Time provided the answer to many of these problems, but, meanwhile, losses of American crews were high when compared with those of British airmen, who depended upon the same rescue agencies.

As the Eighth Air Force surmounted its own peculiar problems of equipment and training, it began to take a share in the actual work of rescue. By the summer of 1943 the 65th Fighter Wing was charged with the operation of a rescue-control station for the specific purpose of fixing the location of American aircraft in distress. In September VIII Bomber Command assigned one bomber per group for search along the routes of its bomber missions upon request for this assistance by Air Sea Rescue. Early in 1944 the 65th's rescue-control detachment, located at Saffron Walden, used fighter aircraft to patrol routes followed by returning bombers. Later, in the spring, the AAF agreed to provide 25 P-47's for these patrols, and the RAF placed 8 Walrus bombers and amphibians on call from Saffron Walden for the rescue of American crews. The Americans at no time undertook the development of a separate rescue service, but they did add over 200 emergency rescue personnel to the theater's troop basis late in 1944 and supplemented available equipment with 6 OA-10A aircraft, the Army's version of the Catalina. The rescue control detachment of the 65th Fighter Wing became the 5th Emergency Rescue Squadron early in 1945.[57]

Similarly, in North Africa and throughout the Mediterranean the AAF depended heavily upon the RAF's superior experience and organization. Not until the summer of 1943 did the AAF have a rescue organization of its own—a detachment equipped with three or four worn-out Catalinas, which had been flown by ATC from Florida. Planes and crews belonged to the Twelfth Air Force, but they operated closely with British units under NAAF's Coastal Command. At the end of the year the crews of this detachment, no doubt because of their experience, were ordered home to serve as instructors at the newly established Emergency Rescue School at Keesler Field in Mississippi, where the AAF now undertook to organize and train its own rescue units. Appropriately, the 1st Emergency Rescue Squadron was assigned to the Mediterranean, where it began operations in April 1944. Early in 1945 two of its three flights were reassigned to India as the nucleus of a newly established 7th Emergency Rescue Squadron.[58]

Thus from the beginning to the end of the European phase of the war, the AAF depended heavily upon its British allies for the rescue of American airmen. It was from the British that the AAF borrowed many of the ideas that shaped the organization of its own emergency rescue service. Since in Europe and Africa the problem was to rescue airmen forced down in the relatively narrow limits of the English Channel, the North Sea, and the Mediterranean, it was natural that rescue services emphasized the partnership of airplane and surface craft. Equally natural, perhaps, was the AAF's tendency to assume that in the development of its own services this partnership should be perpetuated, even to the extent of committing the Air Force to the procurement and operation of a large number of surface craft. But experience—especially in the Pacific, with its much greater distances—was to call this assumption into question before the war had ended.[59]

In the war against Japan the U.S. Navy, like the Royal Navy in the North Atlantic and the Mediterranean, carried the main burden of air-sea rescue. Only in the Southwest Pacific did the Army have the top command and thus, in a sense, the primary responsibility. There, until the summer of 1942, air-sea rescue was handled on an emergency basis with whatever equipment was available. Fortunately, the Royal Australian Air Force possessed a few PBY's, and in August the Fifth Air Force received four of its own. These planes were of great aid in the current attempt to develop a systematic pattern of search in the interest both of reconnaissance and of rescue. As a makeshift air-sea rescue service developed, the responsibility fell largely to the V Fighter Command, which also took the lead in the preparation of manuals for the guidance of pilots forced down in the New Guinea jungles. The Fifth Air Force received its first emergency rescue squadron (2d ERS) only in July 1944. Meanwhile, units of the Seventh Fleet and Navy PBY's had supplemented the resources of the Fifth.[60]

It was in the South Pacific that the Navy's PBY won its fame as the Dumbo. The Dumbo was used to attempt the most hazardous of rescues, and in an astonishing number of instances plane and crew came through the venture successfully.* The courage and dedication of the Dumbo crews helped in a real measure to overcome the shortage of rescue aircraft and survival equipment. The shortage of the latter was so serious that General Twining, commanding the Thirteenth Air Force, was down at sea for six days in January 1943 without the means for radio contact with those who sought his rescue.† After the Thirteenth had completed the successful campaigns of the Solomon Islands and had joined forces with the Fifth under the newly created Far East Air Forces (FEAF), the 2d ERS was assigned to the Thirteenth in October 1944, when the Fifth received the newly arrived 3d ERS.[61] Despite the unaccustomed degree of self-sufficiency made possible by the presence of two AAF rescue units, FEAF continued to receive the assistance of Navy Dumbo squadrons.

On 24 November 1944 the XXI Bomber Command began long-range operations against Japan from Saipan, and the 4th ERS was sent to the central Pacific for support. But it was April 1945 before the 4th ERS was in operation with three of its PBY's at Peleliu. Meanwhile, the rescue service for the B-29's, which had to fly from the Marianas across 1,400 miles of open sea to reach their targets on Honshu, was the subject of negotiation between the AAF and the Navy.

By 1944 the AAF would have liked to have been more independent of the Navy in rescue aid in the Pacific Ocean area than it was prepared to be. It would have preferred to have its own rescue agencies operating under its own command, but this was out of the question. By decision of the Joint Chiefs of Staff, Admiral Nimitz, CINCPOA, was responsible for air-sea rescue. Responsibility in turn was assigned to Vice-Admiral John H. Hoover, who as commander of the Forward Area established the Air-Sea Rescue Task Group under Capt. H. R. Horney, with units at Saipan, Guam, Peleliu, Ulithi, and, after

* For accounts of two of the more daring rescues, see Vol. IV, 265–66, 355.
† See Vol. IV, 79.

February 1945, on Iwo Jima. Surface craft and submarines were made available on request from Captain Horney in accordance with the schedule of B-29 strikes as reported by Headquarters, XXI Bomber Command.* The submarines served as lifeguard stations at regular intervals along the route. Normally, they reached their rendezvous points approximately two hours before the aircraft were due and stayed in position until all planes were accounted for or until further participation in the search seemed unjustified. It was a costly business, for the submarine might be drawn from its regular patrol with a consequent weakening of the blockade that constituted its chief mission. Necessarily, employment of the submarines was restricted to exceptional missions.

The 4th ERS performed valiantly during the few months of combat that remained after its deployment. Its planes and the B-29's of the XXI Bomber Command contributed significantly to the devolpment of a technique of "escort and orbit" that had grown out of a long experience in the Pacific. By providing an escort of rescue planes and by stationing others at stated intervals on the homeward route, the escort and orbit system added greatly to the total effectiveness of rescue efforts. Before the war ended, the AAF had provided eight B-17's equipped for dropping motorboats and a number of B-29 Superdumbos. But it was the Navy—its Dumbos, its surface craft, and its submarines—that did the major part of the work; and it was the U.S. Marine Corps, at a cost of 20,000 casualties, that gave a crippled B-29 a chance to land at Iwo Jima on its way home.

As the end of the war approached, plans for the invasion of Japan called for new efforts to increase rescue forces and to co-ordinate even more effectively rescue activities. The 5th ERS was scheduled for redeployment from ETO to the Pacific. The 6th ERS was assigned to the Fifth Air Force, which put part of the squadron on Okinawa in July. In August two flights of the 7th ERS were transferred to Okinawa from India, where they had assisted the RAF emergency service for the past few months. On 5 August representatives of AAF Headquarters and of the Fifth, Seventh, Thirteenth, and Twentieth Air Forces conferred at Manila. Agreement was reached for publication, after co-ordination with Admiral Nimitz, of instructions that would standardize all procedures in rescue operations during the coming invasion.[62] But on the next day the first A-bomb was dropped on Hiroshima.

* The subject of rescue is fully discussed in Vol. V, 598–607.

SECTION V

* * * * * * * * * * *

WOMEN IN THE AAF

*   *   *   *   *   *   *   *   *   *   *

CHAPTER 16

WOMEN IN THE AAF

WHEN the United States entered World War II, the role of American women in a total war effort had not been clearly defined. That role was to remain a subject of controversy throughout the war. But while congressmen, military planners, the public at large, and women themselves argued over their proper place, the need for women's clerical skills became the opening wedge which resulted in their widespread use in traditional as well as unprecedented jobs, both civilian and military. As the youngest arm, with fewer traditions and inhibitions than the other branches of the Army, the AAF was an enthusiastic employer of women almost from the beginning of the war. Indeed, it used nearly one-half of the peak strength of 100,000 who served in the Women's Army Corps. The effort to bring women into the Army, however, was a long and complicated one and nowhere met with more initial resistance than in the War Department General Staff.

The nation's manpower shortage, which did not begin to become acute until 1942,[1] forced military planners to look with increasing favor on the large reservoir of womanpower. There were already thirteen million women employed in the United States, but there were approximately nineteen million others, between the ages of twenty and sixty, who were not gainfully employed.[2] War Department planners reluctantly regarded the younger women of this group as suitable for several types of jobs within the Army, while advocates of a draft for women urged their use on a wider scale as a means of releasing married men and fathers from selective service.

Proponents of the use of womanpower in the military establishment could find precedents in Allied and American experience during World War I and in Allied experience during the early years of

World War II. In the first conflict small groups of American women were sent overseas as civilian contract employees to serve in such positions as telephone operators, clerical workers, and chauffeurs with the AEF. When requests for a women's corps were turned down in 1918 by the War Department, the AEF borrowed from the British Women's Auxiliary Army Corps. Even for posts within the United States the Army had difficulty in obtaining sufficient numbers of female civil service employees. The Navy was likewise hampered by a shortage of clerical workers; but a neat, if legally dubious, solution was found by interpreting the enlistment law, which covered "any citizen of the United States," to mean that women were not excluded. As a result, during World War I, nearly thirteen thousand women were enlisted in the Navy and Marine Corps, most of them serving as Yeomen (F), with the same status as enlisted men. There is evidence that the Army might have been forced to take similar action if the war had not ended in 1918.[3]

Between wars the Army made several studies of the use of women in the military establishment. Perhaps the most exhaustive and prophetic study was prepared in 1928 by Maj. Everett S. Hughes, who recognized the necessity of using women in any future war. He recommended that women serving overseas and in danger zones be militarized, used "as required in corps areas, branches and theaters of operations, organized according to tables of organization, and accorded the same rights, privileges, and benefits as militarized men."[4] Shunted about from one office to another, with copious indorsements over a period of two years, the Hughes plan was eventually interred in the War Department files, where it remained undiscovered until near the end of 1942.[5]

With the approach of World War II, Army planners late in 1939 again tackled the problem of a women's corps, this time visualizing the possible use of women as "hostesses, librarians, canteen clerks, cooks and waitresses, chauffeurs, messengers, and strolling minstrels." Although the resulting plan, which opposed giving women full military status, was laid aside without further action,[6] pressure mounted from several sources to keep the issue alive. American military observers in England reported on the indispensable women's auxiliaries which they saw in action, and their reports were accompanied by warnings that any American forces sent overseas could not expect to borrow from these auxiliaries because of the British manpower shortage.[7] It was common knowledge, moreover, that in China and Russia women were taking an active part in national defense, doing manual labor, front-line duty, and other tasks traditionally reserved for men. In the United States various women's organizations began to demand opportunities for service in the defense effort, either as civilian volunteers or as military personnel.

The Women's Army Auxiliary Corps

When Representative Edith Nourse Rogers of Massachusetts informed Gen. George C. Marshall in the spring of 1941 that she expected to introduce a bill establishing a women's corps in the Army, the War Department could no longer avoid the issue. Planners in G-1 Division of the General Staff hurriedly outlined the framework for a women's organization which would "meet with War Department approval, so that when it is forced upon us, as it undoubtedly will be, we shall be able to run it our way."[8] Mrs. Rogers incorporated the plan in a bill which she introduced in the House of Representatives on 28 May 1941, calling for establishment of a Women's Army Auxiliary Corps.[9] The bill was referred to the Bureau of the Budget, which, doubtless to the relief of G-1 Division, kept it under consideration for four months, finally recommending in October that the proposed legislation be dropped.[10]

The events of 7 December 1941 quickly changed the attitude of the Bureau of the Budget, which gave its approval to the Rogers bill four days later. War Department officials now pushed to secure passage of the legislation, which Mrs. Rogers felt "would give thousands of our women an opportunity to do their part in winning our war." It would make available, she said, "the work of many women who cannot afford to give their services without compensation."[11] Both the Secretary of War and the Chief of Staff urged congressional approval; even though the manpower shortage was not then acute, Secretary Stimson and General Marshall pointed to the Army's need for women in types of jobs which they traditionally performed better than men. Women in uniform were wanted particularly for the Aircraft Warning Service.*[12]

A year after its introduction the Rogers bill became Public Law 554 on 15 May 1942, when the President signed the bill creating a Women's Army Auxiliary Corps for service with the Army of the

* See below, p. 510.

United States. The measure permitted the enlistment of 150,000 women between the ages of twenty-one and forty-five, but the executive order which established the corps set an initial strength limit of 25,000.

Obtaining the necessary legislation was only the first of many hurdles to be cleared in creation of an effective women's corps. Legal authorization did not guarantee public acceptance of the idea of women serving with the Army. Congressional critics had been unable to defeat the measure, but their opinions and predictions of dire consequences reflected the feelings of a large segment of the public. To some congressmen the measure was "the most ridiculous bill" and "the silliest piece of legislation" within their memory. Another legislator found it "foreign" to the proper American attitude toward women, while still another saw it as a reflection on the nation's men that women should do Army service. The women of the country, said one representative, "those who sew on the buttons, do the cooking, mend the clothing, and do the washing at home," really wanted to stay in the home.[13] Congressional critics were joined by spokesmen for certain religious groups, who were alarmed by this "invasion of the sanctity of the home."[14]

The Army itself was unwilling at first to accept this newest addition to its forces. As one colonel put it, in retrospect, "We had a war to fight, and war was man's business." Women, he felt, "would only clutter it up."[15] The wartime performance of the Wacs* altered the attitude of many commanders, including General Eisenhower, who originally was opposed to women in the Army. His observation of the various British women's services helped to convert him. Later, in North Africa, he found that "many officers were still doubtful of women's usefulness in uniform." But such officers were ignoring the changing requirements of war. "The simple headquarters of a Grant or a Lee," said General Eisenhower after the war, "were gone forever. An army of filing clerks, stenographers, office managers, telephone operators, and chauffeurs had become essential, and it was

---

* The use of abbreviations in this chapter, though perhaps confusing to the reader unacquainted with the chronology of the Corps, is in accordance with War Department practice and authorization. The abbreviations "WAAC" for the Corps and "Waacs" for its members are used with reference to the auxiliary period of the Corps, up to the summer of 1943, before conversion to full Army status was effected. References to the Corps and to its members after that time are made by the use of "WAC" and "Wacs," respectively.

scarcely less than criminal to recruit these from needed manpower when great numbers of highly qualified women were available. From the day they first reached us their reputation as an efficient, effective corps continued to grow."[16]

Despite the fact that they won commanders' plaudits, the Wacs were never able to win unanimous acceptance by the military. To many soldiers the WAC was only a subject for crude jokes and injudicious remarks. Army surveys of soldier opinion, conducted at the request of Col. Oveta Culp Hobby, revealed a decidedly unfavorable attitude toward the women's corps. Only one-fourth of those polled reported that they would like to see a sister or girl friend join the corps. Other surveys showed that one of the reasons women did not join the corps was that almost all of them had heard that the Army was opposed to women in uniform.[17]

Despite an extensive effort by the Army and high-pressure advertising firms to sell the WAC, many eligible women remained unresponsive to appeals for enlistment. Some women disliked the prospect of military routine and the curtailment of personal liberty; some were afraid that they could not stand the reported rigors of training and regimentation. No doubt, the low pay, as compared with wages offered by the war industries, accounted for much of the recruiting difficulty. Many women were unaware of the variety of jobs open to Wacs; the prospect of kitchen police, laundry duty, and other unattractive types of work had no appeal. Unfounded rumors of immorality, given wide circulation by a New York newspaper columnist, did untold damage to all the women's services, undoubtedly causing many potential recruits to shy away from the WAC. Some women complained of the unflattering, "tent-like" uniform; some found the women's organizations in the other armed services more attractive than the WAC. Other women were plainly apathetic to the war effort, apparently feeling that, if the nation really needed them, they would be drafted. This, of course, was a logical view, for the nation had never met its military needs without a draft.

Even a temporary lowering of acceptance standards did not enable the corps to meet its goals. The initial rush of volunteers, composed of the genuinely patriotic, the bored, the curious, the economically depressed, was followed by a slump which the WAC was never able to overcome except during sustained drives. Great Britain had had a similar experience, being unable to fill the ranks of WAAFs,

Wrens, and ATS without national conscription. But the United States was not ready to draft its women, and it was unable to arouse in a majority of women a sense of personal responsibility for helping directly with the war effort. Perhaps a weakness during the early months of the recruitment program lay in some of the advertising copy; over the objections of the WAC director, who preferred a straightforward patriotic appeal, advertising experts aimed most of the appeals at self-interest. WAC benefits and the variety of WAC jobs rather than the nation's needs were stressed, and the attempted "glamourization" not only failed to attract the desired number of recruits but also failed to acquaint prospect recruits with the seriousness of the situation. Other women's services had a similar experience; as summed up by the wartime commander of the SPARS, "We never completely succeeded in putting across the idea that women were really needed and wanted in the armed forces."[18]

The Army, like the other services, found that women could be used in a vastly greater number of jobs than originally contemplated.[19] And the result was a greater demand for women in the services. As early as November 1942 the WAAC strength limit was raised by executive order from 25,000 to the 150,000 authorized by Congress.[20] G-3 had already recommended that the corps be expanded by 1946 to 1,500,000 members. Fantastic as the figure appeared to some War Department officials, it was given solid support by an exhaustive study of Army jobs which were suitable for women. The project, carried out by The Adjutant General's office, was termed "the most comprehensive study ever made of the outer limits to which replacement of men in the United States Army could theoretically be pushed."[21] The classification experts concluded that only 222 of the 628 military occupations listed by the Army were unsuitable for women, and in an acute manpower shortage women could be used in many of the 222 jobs. This finding meant that in the fall of 1942 the Army could use 750,000 women, and it was estimated that by the end of 1943 at least 1,323,400 could be placed in "soldiers'" jobs.[22] Such were the possibilities; the actualities were strikingly different, since the WAC failed by more than 50,000 to reach its original authorized strength of 150,000.

With the Army, Navy, Coast Guard, Marine Corps, and defense plants all trying to recruit women, competition was naturally keen, and controveries arose among the various agencies in their campaigns

AIR WACS WITH EIGHTH AIR FORCE IN ENGLAND
SWITCHBOARD OPERATOR

Teletype Operators

AIR WACS WITH EIGHTH AIR FORCE IN ENGLAND

In Mobile Control Unit Truck

STENOGRAPHER

AIR WACS WITH EIGHTH AIR FORCE IN ENGLAND: BAKERESS T/5

to stimulate enlistments. In the summer of 1943 the Secretary of War and the Secretary of the Navy signed a joint agreement for the recruiting of women, designed to protect the labor supply of industries critical in the prosecution of the war. Further agreements led to the attempted co-ordination of all national newspaper, radio, and motion-picture recruiting activities with the War Manpower Commission and the Office of War Mobilization.[23] As a result WAC recruiters were under tremendous pressure to meet their quotas from an ever narrowing field of prospects and often signed up women who were poor prospects for successful adjustment to life in the Army—women who were trying to escape an undesirable home situation, or joining on a spur-of-the-moment fancy, or attempting to be sent at Uncle Sam's expense to a location near the current boy friend's post.[24]

Voluntary recruitment thus provided one of the persistent headaches for the Women's Army Corps. Other problems stemmed naturally from a program that was frankly experimental in nature, that had to be pieced together from day to day, that found its goals constantly being enlarged before existing quotas could be met—and all carried out in the face of a certain amount of public ridicule, unfavorable publicity, and internal administrative difficulties. Those Wacs who served in the AAF shared in both the triumphs and the comedy of errors which marked the history of the corps. More important, the AAF Wacs, under the capable direction of Lt. Col. Betty Bandel, pointed the way for solution of many of the corps' problems. And their pioneering efforts not only contributed to the winning of the war but also had important implications for the future role of women in the Air Forces.

Air Wacs

It was typical of the AAF, with its long-cherished ideas of independence, to desire a separate women's corps completely independent of the women serving with other branches of the Army.[25] The AAF, furthermore, early recognized the need for full Army status, rather than auxiliary status, for the WAAC. These two ideas were temporarily squelched in November 1942 when General Marshall wrote a note to the Chief of Air Staff: "I believe Colonel [Aubry] Moore this morning took up with Mrs. Hobby the question of her attitude toward a separate women's organization for the Air Corps. I don't like the tone of this at all. I want to be told why they cannot train these women, why the present legal, auxiliary status prevents such training. I don't wish anyone in the Air Corps office to take up without my personal knowledge any question of organizing a separate unit, or any discussion of it except with me first."[26]

Although the AAF could not acquire Waacs on its own terms, it was glad to take them on any basis. During the early months of the existence of the WAAC, the Aircraft Warning Service received top priority in the assignment of women in the AAF. The AWS stations, vital to the nation's defense at a time when enemy air attacks were expected on both coasts, were then being operated by some 6,000 unpaid women volunteers and a few soldiers. But the Air Forces felt that effective operation of the stations required full-time personnel subject to military discipline; this need was met by the assignment of Waacs, who began to arrive at the posts in September 1942 immediately after completing their basic training at Fort Des Moines. These first WAAC companies were so efficient that the AAF, with less than three months' experience in the use of Waacs, discussed with Director Hobby the possibility of obtaining 540,000 more. As the probability of an air attack on the United States appeared to diminish, however, the War Department decided early in 1943 to replace the Waacs with civilians at all Aircraft Warning Stations except those where it was impossible to obtain volunteers.[27] This policy resulted in the reassignment of approximately 3,000 women in March and April 1943, although the AWS managed to keep about half of this number by allotting military vacancies for small clerical detachments at several fighter-command headquarters and other operations and filter centers.[28]

In March 1943 the AAF began to receive its first Waacs for use in posts other than AWS stations. Small companies reported for duty at Chanute and Scott Fields and at the Map Chart Division, Jefferson Barracks, Missouri. In the following month twenty-three WAAC units arrived at air bases in the United States, and by the end of September 171 air bases had Wacs as part of their personnel.[29] To assist in administration of the WAAC program in the AAF, Colonel Hobby in March 1943 sent a carefully selected WAAC officer to the headquarters of each of the major air forces and commands.[30] These liaison officers became the first WAC "staff directors" and soon proved so valuable that the War Department made the position mandatory in each major command and each of the principal subordinate commands using WAC personnel.*[31]

The WAC staff directors were alternately amazed and amused at some of the requests they received. They were the only officers in their commands who had any idea of the organization and administration of the WAC, and there was considerable misunderstanding among the AAF men as to the proper duties for Wacs. One of the most persistent misconceptions was that Wacs should operate Army messes; Air Force officers with visions of food "just like mother baked" frequently recommended that Wacs take over mess duties. War Department policy, however, limited Wac food-service assignments to the maintenance of WAC messes, thus making the women's units self-sustaining.[32] Requests for "laundry companies" and for individual Wacs to perform in "soldier shows" likewise had to be turned down, for the War Department was wary of any duties which might have an adverse effect upon recruiting or upon public opinion. AAF Headquarters, moreover, discouraged the use of Wacs as military police and gate guards.[33]

Also of great concern to staff directors was the matter of housing at air bases and installations scattered over the United States. Not only was construction often behind schedule, but the completed barracks were so flimsy and drab that WAC efficiency and morale were seriously affected. The War Department was, of course, hampered by the critical shortage of building materials and the necessity for speed in securing housing accommodations; no distinction was made between housing for transient troops and that for more or less permanent troops. The lack of privacy was a traditional concomitant of Army life, but many older women "grew nervous and irritable under the strain of living in open, noisy barracks with fifty or a hundred lively girls." And the Wacs who developed back strains in carrying hods of coal no doubt wondered why the AAF could not provide central heating for their barracks.[34]

Morale was further affected in some cases by the training policies of commanding officers who required Wacs to train the same number of hours a day that men did. A sixteen-hour work day was frequently the result, for the women on clerical assignments could not always leave their offices during the day to take training on duty time, as was

---

* At the top of the organization was the Air WAC Officer, adviser to General Arnold.

prescribed. In other cases, Wacs who were assigned to secretarial and clerical jobs in the domestic commands, like enlisted men on such assignments, sometimes wondered why they were in the service when they found themselves doing the same kind of work as the civilian sitting beside them. Their morale was not improved by the knowledge that in some of the busier offices civilian business-machine operators, telephone and TWX operators, and typists were preferred to members of the WAC because they were not called off the job for KP, parades, and other military duties. WAC squadron commanders and civilian personnel officers attempted to explain to both groups that they were needed and that they filled different missions: Wacs could be used as mobile troops and on odd schedules of hours and broken shifts as civilians could not, whereas civilians could be used in numbers which the Wacs could not expect to duplicate.[35] Still, the misunderstanding existing in many offices using both WAC and civilian women clerical workers was not appreciably clarified by such explanations.

What, then, kept up the morale of Wacs serving in the AAF on the home front? They could and did "gripe" like the most discontented GI's. But many of them had an acute sense of responsibility and tremendous personal pride in their squadrons and the higher commands to which they were attached. Because the WAC was experimental and because it was in the public eye, many of its members were anxious to make the organization succeed. Because they were volunteers and because they were women, some of them were determined to prove that they could do their jobs as well as men. But of overriding importance was the knowledge that the AAF wanted them. Although General Arnold was no feminist, he was one of the most powerful champions of the WAC. At the height of the slander campaign against the women's corps, he wrote to the commanding generals of all domestic air forces and commands that any lack of respect for the WAC would not be tolerated on a single air base. He explained that, as more men were shipped overseas, it was necessary "to recognize and use the skill and training of women to the maximum extent possible." This matter, wrote General Arnold in conclusion, "is, in my opinion, one of the key problems to be worked out if the Army Air Forces is to utilize the personnel placed at its disposal in the way which will get our job done, and get it done quickly."[36] This official attitude, which was given wide publicity, helped to reassure relatives of the women and the Wacs themselves that the AAF welcomed them and appreciated their services. Some Wacs undoubtedly remained unconvinced.

WAC officers assigned to AAF Headquarters in Washington were well aware of the cordiality of the Air Forces, for they were allowed to set up a staff organization which was almost ideal under the circumstances. Colonel Bandel, the Air WAC Officer, found that her recommendations were usually given favorable consideration. One of her innovations, which proved to be highly popular and effective, was her practice of sending an informal monthly mimeographed letter to all staff directors, explaining the reasons underlying the actions taken at AAF Headquarters.[37] Even non-AAF WAC staff directors overseas asked to be put on the mailing list, while non-AAF company commanders corresponded regularly with AAF WAC squadron commanders to obtain information on War Department regulations and circulars, which they seldom saw.

Because each major operating division of AAF Headquarters early accepted a WAC officer, Colonel Bandel's Air WAC Division was able to eliminate operating duties and to confine its work to co-ordination of the WAC program, study of field conditions, and formulation of policy recommendations. This system, which other comparable WAC staff sections were able to adopt only later if at all, enabled the AAF to pioneer in the study of WAC utilization and the formulation of policies to remedy weaknesses in the program.[38] One of the contributions of the Air WAC Officer to the more effective use of the corps was her recommendation, approved by the War Department in September 1943, abolishing separate WAC grades. All War Department grade allotments to the major commands were thereafter made without reference to the sex of personnel; except for the limitation upon the number of Wacs that could be furnished any command, either a man or a woman could be placed in any authorized and suitable job. The women were no longer considered an additional allotment, since each station had only one military quota; and the resulting simplification of bookkeeping was a considerable improvement over the cumbersome system of WAC requisitions.[39]

The AAF, like other commands, had been highly pleased and notably relieved when in the summer of 1943 the Women's Army Auxiliary Corps became the Women's Army Corps.[40] This step, placing the corps *in* the Army instead of *with* the Army, corrected a fundamental error which had been growing increasingly obvious.[41] Under the auxiliary system the Army had little more control over

Waacs than over civilian workers. Like civilians, the women could leave the service any time they wished. Naturally, their use on highly secret and mobile work or overseas assignment was severely hampered. On the other hand, the women were not entitled to military benefits even though they performed military duties. With the conversion to Army status, approximately 80 per cent of the women serving with the AAF re-enlisted.[42] Of those who did not, some failed to pass the physical examination, others had acquired new home responsibilities since their original enlistment, and others (neurotics and trouble-makers) were refused re-enlistment by their commanding officers.[43]

TABLE 1

Wacs Assigned to the AAF from July 1943 to July 1945
by Six-Month Intervals

	July 1943	Dec. 1943	July 1944	Dec. 1944	July 1945
In continental U.S.:					
Officers	545	1,758	1,787	1,579	1,522
Enlisted women	16,094	16,082	26,468	29,931	27,449
Total	16,639	17,840	28,255	31,510	28,971
Overseas:					
Officers	.....	.....	184	267	316
Enlisted women	.....	.....	4,034	6,505	6,666
Total	.....	.....	4,218	6,772	6,982
Total:					
Officers	.....	.....	1,971	1,846	1,838
Enlisted women	.....	.....	30,502	36,436	34,115
Total	.....	.....	32,473	38,282	35,953

NOTE.—Peak strength for total AAF Wacs was in January 1945, with 39,323 officers and enlisted women; peak strength within the continental United States was in the same month, with 32,008 officers and enlisted women; peak strength overseas was in April 1945, with 7,601 officers and enlisted women.

The AAF, which had more than 16,000 Waacs in July 1943, still had fewer than 15,000 Wacs in September, although many new units had been assigned to it (see Table 1).[44] The gap between WAC assignments to the AAF and Air Forces' demands for Wacs had now reached wide proportions. In contrast to the 15,000 on duty, the AAF needed more than 130,000 and had an approved quota of 65,000. A new approach to the problem was clearly in order.

What was hoped to be a solution to the problem was an AAF plan which received War Department approval late in August 1943, calling for AAF recruitment of its own Wacs. Regarded by Colonel Bandel as "the most important and most far-reaching of the steps" which the

AAF took in developing the WAC program, the plan enabled the Air Forces to appeal to women directly, promising them job assignments of their choice and assuring them that every effort would be made to assign them to a station of their choice. Similar authority was extended to the Army Ground Forces and Army Service Forces, thus for the first time giving potential Wacs their choice of branch and job category. Although WAC recruitment was still a basic responsibility of the ASF, the other branches merely being allowed to participate in the campaign, the AAF nevertheless entered into the program "with its usual enthusiasm." Because it had personnel at installations in practically every state in the Union, the Training Command was directed to conduct the campaign for the AAF.[45]

With the objective of enlisting at least 46,000, the Training Command opened the campaign in October 1943, blanketing the country with recruiting teams and publicizing the program through every available medium. Coining the phrase "Air Wacs," the AAF incurred the disapproval of the War Department, which feared that the AAF Wacs would be regarded by the public as a "separate corps." The phrase had gained such widespread use, however, that a War Department directive to the AAF could not halt the trend toward regarding Wacs in the AAF as "Air Wacs." Recruits were not promised permanent assignment to a specific AAF command, nor were they promised or denied foreign service. For the most part, the AAF was able to make good on its job-category commitments, although there were some glaring exceptions which commanders attempted to correct as the cases were brought to their attention.[46]

In addition to the Training Command personnel conducting the campaign, several other air commands carried on short recruiting drives of their own, designed to point up the advantages of service with their installations. The Air Transport Command, for example, held out the prospect of eventual assignment to one of its far-flung bases around the world, and within less than a year the ATC increased its WAC strength from 500 to 5,500.

By January 1944 the AAF was recruiting between 2,000 and 2,500 Wacs a month, with this figure remaining constant until the end of the campaign. Although the Training Command stopped its intensive drive in June 1944, Air Wac recruiting, with station and job promises, actually continued until the end of October 1944, when the War Department ended all station and job recruitment of Wacs. After that time, recruits could be promised only general assignment to the Army or to the AAF. From 15 October 1943 to 31 December 1944, when to all intents and purposes AAF Wac recruiting was completed, 27,047 women had enlisted in the Army for service with the AAF, more than all other branches combined but only slightly more than half the number which was the initial objective. It was an expensive campaign, since more than 1,500 officers and enlisted people devoted their full time to it, while hundreds of others were on part-time recruiting duty —and these were in addition to the several thousand ASF personnel of the recruiting service who were accepting WAC enlistments for assignment to the AAF. Though expensive, the campaign was also educational, for it enabled the men of the AAF to learn more about the WAC program, thus contributing to more effective utilization of Wacs. It likewise familiarized the public with the need for women in uniform and probably contributed to public acceptance of women soldiers.[47]

The influx of 27,000 recruits did not pose a major training problem for the AAF. There was no need for elaborate technical training because the majority of women, in contrast to the seventeen- and eighteen-year-old boys being inducted, had a usable skill before they enlisted, often in the highly prized clerical field. The AAF proposed and pioneered in a time-saving policy of avoiding unnecessary training for women already qualified. Basic training was still supplied by the WAC, under the Army Service Forces, and the ASF desired to retain basic graduates for another six to twelve weeks of specialist training as clerks, drivers, cooks, and medical technicians. With the inception of "Air-WAC" recruiting, the AAF refused to allow most of its recruits to be so retained and arranged for immediate shipment to air bases for employment in civilian skills or on-the-job training. In particular, administrative and clerks courses in ASF schools were felt to be of little value in teaching AAF procedures. However, the AAF policy did not prevent specialist training for women who would benefit by it or were highly qualified for it; in fact, the AAF early opened to women virtually its entire roster of job specialties and schools. On 20 November 1943 Wacs were declared eligible to attend any noncombat training course attended by AAF men, provided that the training would in a station commander's opinion increase an individual's job efficiency or would enable her to be utilized in some higher skill for which she had unusual aptitude or civilian background.[48]

The AAF's preference for avoiding nonessential training extended to continuation training of units on field stations. Until the last year of the war, WAC field units operated under the ASF requirement of four hours' weekly repetition of basic courses. These usually had to be given at night and constituted a problem of fatigue and boredom for units spending several years at one station. The AAF therefore sought and obtained War Department approval of a plan making it solely responsible for continuation training of its Wacs, as it was for its men. A simplified procedure thereafter allowed commands to limit training to the non-repetitive weekly orientation hour given all personnel, and prescribed sports and recreation rather than the daily physical training period.

The job training of women was so completely integrated with the entire AAF training program that virtually no separate statistics are available as a basis for comparing the record of the women with male trainees. Obviously, this policy meant that the Wacs had to be as well qualified as men to enroll in and graduate from a training course. It is known only that approximately 2,000 women completed courses in AAF technical schools, including those for Link-trainer instructors, airplane mechanics, sheet-metal workers, weather forecasters, weather observers, electrical specialists of several kinds, teletype operators, control-tower specialists, cryptographers, radio mechanics, parachute riggers, bombsight-maintenance specialists, clerks, photo-laboratory technicians, and photo-interpreters.[49]

The AAF showed no reluctance in opening up its noncombat jobs to women, even jobs which required "unwomanly" mechanical skills. Toward the end of the war there was an increase in the number of women on technical assignments, when it became difficult to obtain enlisted men in the top intelligence brackets required by some of the work. At the peak of WAC enrollment, in January 1945, more than 200 different job categories were filled by enlisted women, while WAC officers held more than 60 different types of jobs in addition to that of company officer. A flexible system of assignment enabled the AAF to use Wacs with special skills found in only a very few women, like those who were skilled as chemists, cartographers, geodetic computers, topographers, sanitary inspectors, and even dog-trainers.[50] But as might be expected, a high percentage—about 50 per cent—of the Air Wacs held administrative or office jobs. These clerks, typists, and stenographers were doing only what they had been doing in civilian life, with the exception that they had to know AAF procedures, organization, and nomenclature.

At the Air Technical Service Command, WAC clerks kept stock records of the thousands of pieces of technical equipment. The Training Command, employing more Wacs than any other AAF unit, found them especially adept at keeping the records of training courses, trainees, and flight hours (see Table 2). In the four domestic air forces, Wacs kept personnel and flight records and staffed the assembly lines through which crews and equipment passed for overseas assignment. Wacs in the Air Transport Command were used in dispatching offices, at information desks, and in process duty at aerial

TABLE 2

Distribution of WAC Personnel among Air Commands
in the United States, January 1945

Training Command	8,904
First Air Force	1,920
Second Air Force	3,528
Third Air Force	3,097
Fourth Air Force	2,140
I Troop Carrier Command	1,046
Materiel Command (ATSC)	3,887
Air Transport Command	3,095
AAF Center (School of Applied Tactics)	857
Personnel Distribution Command	1,572
Other	1,962
Total	32,008

ports of embarkation. One Wac on the latter type of duty, when asked whether she liked her job, replied, "Like it? I've checked in Lord Louis Mountbatten, Winston Churchill, and Sir John Dill in one week. Who wouldn't like it?"[51] The majority of WAC clerical workers, however, never saw Winston Churchill or any other celebrity. They faced one monotonous day after another, each full of routine but necessary paper work, struggling with a typewriter full of pink copies, yellow copies, green copies, and white copies.

Publicity given to the more unusual types of jobs and an over-dramatization of the aviation aspect created the public impression that far more women were employed in flying duty than was actually the case. Relatively few Wacs ever saw the inside of an airplane in the line of duty. Some 20 Wacs were listed as "Air Crew Members" and there was at least one WAC Crew Chief. Women sometimes also made noncombat flights as radio operators. As an experiment, one entire flight line was staffed with WAC mechanics, and there were eventually some 617 women in Airplane Maintenance, 656 Aviation Specialists, and lesser numbers in related jobs. However, since men in these skills usually could be found, and since the need for women's clerical skills continued unabated, no significant attempt was made to train women not already qualified in aviation work.[52]

Negro Wacs in the AAF were employed on the same types of jobs as were other Wacs, although comparatively few Negro women were skilled in clerical and related fields. In accordance with Army policy, the WAC was directed to limit its Negro recruits to 10.6 per cent of its total strength, and the Negroes served in segregated units.[53] At the height of the AAF WAC program, ten Negro units were being utilized, representing about 1,100 women. This number was second only to that used by the Army Services Forces.[54]

The Wac Overseas

The last major development of the AAF's program for the employment of Wacs began in the spring of 1944, when the AAF adopted a comprehensive plan for assignment of WAC clerical workers to the headquarters of combat air forces around the world. WAC units had been serving with some overseas air forces since the summer of 1943, but prior to March 1944 the system for allocating WAC personnel to overseas theaters did not guarantee that an AAF-trained Wac would be assigned to an air organization.

Under War Department rules, each shipment of Wacs for overseas duty was formed by contributions from the Air, Ground, and Service Forces, according to the proportion of Wacs then serving in each of these. The defect in this plan, according to the Air Forces' point of view, was that a Wac skilled in AAF procedures might be assigned to an ASF unit overseas, while a Wac trained in ASF practices might be assigned to an AAF unit. After repeated Air Force prodding, the War Department allowed gradual changes in the system, so that by 10 June 1944 Air, Ground, and Service Forces were each authorized to send its own Wacs outside the Zone of the Interior for assignment to a particular command, provided the theater commander concurred.[55] Because the AAF was willing at the outset to fill overseas requests at its own expense, the air forces around the world received, for the most part, carefully selected, AAF-trained Wacs in numbers greater than the War Department had originally planned to furnish them.

Subordinate commands in the AAF were eventually allowed to send Wacs to overseas stations without reference either to the War Department or to AAF Headquarters. The Air Transport Command had been granted this authority in November 1943. The Army Airways Communications System and AAF Weather Wing soon gained similar authority. Not only in decentralization, but also in guidance of its commands, the AAF was leading the way in this phase of the WAC program; in the opinion of the WAC historian, "no other Army command so thoroughly explained to the field the problems and the best means of selecting women for overseas duty."[56] The AAF required that Wacs selected for such duty be fully qualified, be recommended by the appropriate WAC squadron commander, and, insofar as possible, be desirous of overseas duty.[57]

TABLE 3

WAC Personnel with Air Forces Overseas
January 1945

European theater	2,835
Mediterranean theater	457
Pacific Ocean Area	2
Far East Air Forces	694
China-Burma-India theater	287
Air Transport Command	2,755
Other (AACS, etc.)	285
Total	7,315

Well before this system went into effect, Wacs had been shipped to the Eighth Air Force in England, the first WAC Separate Battalion arriving in July 1943. The satisfactory performance of this unit led to so many requests that by September the Air Force Wacs made up one-half of the total WAC strength in the European Theater of Operations. Requests from other theaters soon poured into AAF Headquarters. From air forces in the China-Burma-India theater, for example, came a request for several hundred Wacs, while the Far East Air Forces asked for more than two thousand. By no means all the requests could be filled, but monthly shipments were begun in April 1944 and continued until January 1945. By that time Wacs were serving with air forces in every major theater of operations (see Table 3).[58]

With a peak strength of approximately 7,000, the AAF WAC overseas program involved a relatively small group of women. But this number was sufficient to demonstrate—even to the most skeptical, apprehensive, and half-amused airmen—that the Air Wacs could contribute to the effective operation of higher headquarters in many different parts of the world. Before WAC units arrived in the theaters, officers charged with their reception often showed concern over the extra trouble which would be required to house and care for female personnel. Visions of disciplinary, health, and morale problems caused some commanders to hesitate in requesting WAC units. The experience of the Wacs overseas soon showed that most of the fears were groundless.

Housing accommodations proved to be bothersome only in the more isolated areas, such as New Guinea, where they were a problem for all troops. In more than one theater headquarters troops enjoyed accommodations frequently superior to those occupied by troops at home, whether men or women. In July 1945, one year after their arrival in India, Air Wacs were reported to have a beauty parlor on the base and Indian laborers to keep their barracks in order. After the headquarters moved up into China in the summer of 1945, about seventy Wacs were transferred to the new station, where they were housed in a modern three-story apartment building, with enough privacy to satisfy the shyest, most introspective Wac; instead of seventy women in one large room, only two or three were assigned to a room, while the mess hall had small tables, each seating four women, and native labor was available to do the general housekeeping and run the mess.[59] In the British Isles, in spite of cold drafty buildings and quaint plumbing facilities, many Wacs had comfortable accommodations in hotels, converted mansions, and schools; in Europe after V-E Day they frequently enjoyed semiprivate rooms, small mess-hall tables with linen and silver, and relief from all fatigue details. In North Africa and New Guinea, women accepted tents and the absence of plumbing facilities in the same spirit as did other troops.[60]

With regard to health, the Wacs in all theaters, like the Army Nurses, proved to be no special problems despite frequent moves necessitated by combat, despite a variety of weather conditions including rain, snow, fog, cold, heat, mud, and humidity, and deprivation of citrus fruit, milk, and other items of normal diet. In the North African and Mediterranean theaters "the annual noneffective rate for

Wacs was less than the comparable nonbattle noneffective rate for men—about 2.7 per 100 strength for Wacs, and 3.6 for all personnel exclusive of battle injuries."[61] During most of the war the attrition rate for Wacs serving in Europe, India, and China was about the same as that for noncombat men. Only in the Southwest Pacific Area was the medical evacuation rate higher for Wacs than for noncombat men; several surveys concluded that non-medical reasons, such as deficiencies in uniforms and supplies, had a major bearing on the high rate of loss, particularly with regard to malaria, dermatitis, and respiratory disorders. Other contributing factors were command policies such as the undue restriction of Wacs in compounds and a failure to provide healthful recreation.[62]

In the matter of discipline and courtesy, the overseas Wacs maintained a high standard. With an uncanny ability to scrounge or to create cleaning and pressing facilities, they frequently gained the reputation of being "the most smartly and neatly dressed troops" at their stations. Violations of regulations and offenses of all types were significant by their negligible numbers. In the North African, Mediterranean, and European theaters the number of courts-martial for Wacs was "extremely small." According to statistics compiled by the Air Provost Marshal, men in the European theater committed offenses from ten to a hundred and fifty times as often as women. "Serious misconduct was lacking, and the advance plans for a group of female military police were never carried out." Disciplinary records in the Southwest Pacific Area showed that most WAC offenses were minor infractions which could be attributed "chiefly to tension, exhaustion, or loss of respect for authority."[63] In all theaters the Wacs' standards of conduct and devotion to duty led to a competitive situation, resulting in improved discipline and courtesy among the male personnel. The general rise in morale, which stemmed from the combined use of men and women, led many commanding officers to requisition additional Wacs. In the words of one officer in the European Division of the ATC, "The Wacs were like a tonic. They gave the men competition on the job and a new interest in social life on the base. The Wac Detachment was the finest morale booster that the base ever had."[64] To both the GI who was homesick for the sight of an American girl and to the general who had not seen an efficient secretary in three years, most Wacs were a welcome addition to the overseas air forces. One group, understandably, sometimes accorded the Wacs a chilly reception—those male soldiers who were assigned to communications, clerical, and administrative jobs which the Wacs were supposed to take over.

A combination of factors led to a generally high level of morale among the overseas Wacs themselves. For one thing, they constituted something of a specialist corps; most of them had been carefully chosen for overseas duty. Naturally, there were defects in the overseas shipment program; but on a statistical average, according to the WAC historian, Wacs in the overseas theaters were "the best educated, the most intelligent, and the most highly skilled of the Corps."[65] Moreover, they were volunteers. Perhaps most important of all, their nearness to combat enabled them to see a direct connection between their jobs and the prosecution of the war. The Wac who typed a weather report could see the men guided by that report returning from their bombing mission. And in her spare time she assisted overworked nurses, helped wounded soldiers write letters home, and volunteered for other hospital duties which brought the war still closer to her.[66]

Wherever overseas WAC morale was low, the chief reasons—as in the United States—were usually poor classification and job assignment. For example, an inspection of the WAC unit in the Far East Air Service Command in February 1945 found no complaints about mud, mosquitoes, heat, tents, or anything except jobs. As soon as classification and job assignment were improved, the complaints diminished. In the European theater there was a tendency on the part of commands to request highly qualified personnel to perform routine tasks. The resulting low morale among Wacs was pronounced; since they had volunteered for certain types of jobs, they felt that their qualifications should be used. When placed in positions which did not keep them fully occupied, they were often highly critical of "Army needs." This complaint, however, was heard only in the early months of Wac assignments to the ETO; as operations were stepped up and male personnel were shifted to combat jobs, the Wacs, being more stationary, came to be depended upon more and more because of their experience on the job and seniority in sections.

Other assignment problems arose from the time lag between placing of requisitions by overseas air forces and arrival of Wacs from the United States. The Eighth Air Force, for example, in October 1943 requested a large number of technical and mechanical specialists who were greatly needed at the time. To fill some of the specialties in the requisition, such as teletypewriter operator and cryptographic technician, certain Wacs were specially trained in the Zone of the Interior. But when the first shipment arrived eight months later, many of the positions had already been filled or the need for them had been altered by the changing operational conditions. The European Division of the ATC was able to absorb some of the specialists, such as airplane-engine mechanics, radio mechanics, airplane electrical mechanics, and parachute riggers and repairmen. Most of these Wacs, however, could not be placed on jobs for which they had been trained. "Many of them griped," reported the ATC historian; "many of them wished they had stayed in the States; most of them were glad to go to work and do their best."[67]

Not all cases of poor classification and job assignment could be attributed to changing operational conditions. Sometimes personnel were misclassified in the Zone of the Interior in order to fill overseas requisitions, and air forces which requested stenographers occasionally received teletype operators or clerk-typists. In other cases, poor job placement could be attributed to commanders' lack of knowledge regarding the expansion of the WAC program and the variety of jobs for which Wacs were qualified. In the European theater more difficulty was experienced in finding suitable assignments for officers than for enlisted women; the personnel officer of the WAC section frequently had to use a good deal of persuasion "to convince certain male officers that a WAC officer's education, experience, civilian and military training could be used to replace a male officer or in lieu of a male officer." This reluctance, as well as the problem of misclassification, was to a large extent overcome with the passage of time.[68]

WAC officers overseas, besides serving as detachment commanders and company officers, also served on such assignments as photo-interpreting, intelligence, operations, fiscal, code and cipher, and inspector general. Enlisted women were assigned to any one of fifty-six different duties. But by far the majority of both officers and enlisted women served as secretaries, clerks, and administrative personnel.[69] Because of the lack of civilian employees overseas, the Wacs' clerical skills were all the more needed. An estimated 90 per cent of Wacs in the overseas air forces were used in such positions, as compared with approximately 50 per cent of the Wacs in the domestic air commands. Overseas employment of the Air Wacs thus lacked the variety experienced by

Wacs in the Zone of the Interior. When Colonel Bandel was touring the ETO in the winter of 1943–44, she found that Wacs working in clerical positions at air bases were fascinated to hear about the jobs, like control-tower operator and Link-trainer instructor, that Wacs in the United States were beginning to do.[70]

Wacs in the ATC European Division reported that "doing a secretarial job overseas is essentially the same as doing it any other place. You take down notes; then you transcribe them and type the letters. As a sideline you learn a thousand-and-one details about the particular type of work being done in your section—Operations, Traffic, Supply and Service, Personnel, etc." For a feeling of satisfaction on the job, however, these same Wacs admitted that overseas service was far better than that in the States, despite certain inconveniences and dangers.[71] Wacs in the Far East Air Forces, sometimes with only a tent for an office, managed to type clean, accurate copy while picking strange insects out of the typewriter and sweltering in the steaming jungles of New Guinea.

Buzz-bomb attacks in the ETO and bombing and sniper attacks in the Pacific constituted ever present dangers. Nowhere were Wacs unnecessarily exposed to danger, but the possibility of enemy capture prevented some commanders in forward positions from using WAC personnel. Under the international Rules of Land Warfare, Wacs were not considered protected personnel, and the enlisted women would not be entitled to officer privileges in the event of capture. Commanding officers who did use Wacs close behind the retreating enemy did not minimize the necessity for safety and security measures.[72] Such commanders clearly explained the situation to the Wacs and warned them of the dangers and discomforts they might expect as they moved forward. General Kenney, for example, who had about two hundred Wacs in his Far East Air Forces headquarters upon its formation in June 1944, talked frankly to the Wacs prior to their moving up to New Guinea. He warned them that his headquarters "would be subject to bombing, it would be the roughest of living conditions, they would probably stand in line in mud up to their ankles in the mess line, the atabrine line, and to get to the shower." The Wacs, thus forewarned, were then flown to Hollandia; they continued to advance with the headquarters, reaching Leyte in the Philippines on 29 November 1944.[73] By the end of April 1945, when General Kenney's entire headquarters had been flown to Fort McKinley, Manila, his WAC contingent numbered 450, as compared with 250 officers and 500 enlisted men.[74] The Far East Air Service Command, as of June 1945, was using 574 Wacs, who, together with the FEAF Wacs, made up approximately 17 per cent of the total WAC strength in the Southwest Pacific Area.[75]

Though a subject of some debate in the War Department, commanders in the Southwest Pacific felt that the advantage of having WAC clerical skills in these successive forward areas outweighed the disadvantage of having to guard their camps and insure their constant protection. In the opinion of many observers, however, theater policies restricting the women to locked compounds in most stations in New Guinea were not only unnecessary but were also unwise. At least in the opinion of the Wacs, the restrictions on their freedom of movement proved to be more of a hardship than "wearing trousers and heavy boots as protection against mud or mosquitoes." Circumstances were somewhat altered as soon as cities like Manila were occupied and headquarters could be set up in permanent buildings.[76]

By January 1945, WAC demobilization planning was begun and nearly all AAF WAC recruiting stopped. By V-E Day the total strength was starting to drop, and Air Wacs were beginning to return from overseas. By V-J Day the Air WAC overseas strength was 1,500 less and the domestic strength 5,000 less than it had been in the peak month of January. During the spring and early summer of 1945, however, Wacs figured in preparations for the Army of Occupation in Europe and for the new U.S. Army Strategic Air Forces then being organized to bring the full weight of the air arm against Japan. An ETO request for Wacs in the Army of Occupation received War Department approval on 12 March, with the Air Forces being directed to supply 1,500 of the required number. Almost 400 women, comprising the first increment of the 1,500, were shipped out in April, and almost 600 more were sent to Europe by midsummer, when the program was halted because of diminishing personnel needs overseas. The new USASTAF, in the meantime, had asked for Wac personnel immediately after its formation, and on 1 August 1945 the AAF was authorized by the War Department to assign Wacs to USASTAF and to send them wherever they were needed, with theater concurrence. Only a few women had been shipped out under this authorization when the war ended, and the whole program for overseas shipment of Wacs came to an abrupt halt.[77]

As the war neared its close, significant evidence of WAC loyalty to the Army was provided by a study made in the ETO.[78] When queried approximately six months prior to V-E Day, members of the Corps revealed the following inclinations:

Would join the WAC again if they knew what they now know about the Army:

Officers   90%   Enlisted women   65%

Would have remained in civilian life:

Officers   3%   Enlisted women   17%

Would join another women's service:

Officers   2%   Enlisted women   3%

No opinion:

Officers   5%   Enlisted women   15%

Might be interested in another term of service if the WAC continued after the present emergency:

Officers   67%   Enlisted women   37%

Would be interested in a reserve status:

Officers   69%   Enlisted women   30%

Prefer a foreign to a continental U.S. assignment:

Officers   85%   Enlisted women   63%

The interest shown in a reserve status and another term of service had a direct bearing on planning for the postwar use of women in the service.

On 29 March 1944 the first of a series of papers had been prepared at AAF Headquarters on the possible use of Wacs in the postwar air force.[79] If there was any doubt in the public mind by the end of the war as to the official Air Force attitude toward the Wacs, it should have been removed by General Arnold's final report to the Secretary of War. At the end of his report he made a series of recommendations on the military air policies he believed that the nation should adopt. With regard to women in uniform, the wartime experience, he pointed out, proved that "these women in the jobs they were qualified to perform were more efficient than men." Since another war might require complete mobilization of all Americans, General Arnold concluded that "a nucleus organization of female soldiers should be maintained in peacetime in order to provide for rapid and efficient expansion in time of national emergency."[80]

Women Airforce Service Pilots

Another innovation in the AAF during World War II, likewise experimental but far more controversial and involving considerably fewer women than the WAC, was the use of women pilots for ferrying and other domestic flying duties. In this case, the AAF was more reluctant to undertake the experiment; but, again, the manpower shortage and the experience of England pointed to the use of women. In mid-1941 there were 2,733 women licensed as pilots in the United States, with 154 holding commercial licenses. Many of these women wished to serve as auxiliaries or reservists in the nation's air defense. Prior to the war, however, and for a short time after Pearl Harbor, the Air Corps took a sternly masculine attitude toward the subject. As early as 1930 the War Department had queried the Air Corps on the possible use of women pilots in the Army, and the Office of the Chief of the Air Corps replied that it was "utterly unfeasible" to take them into the military service, remarking that women were "too high strung for wartime flying."[81]

Ten years later General Arnold, Chief of the Air Corps, turned down a proposal by Plans Division to use approximately one hundred women as co-pilots in transport squadrons and in ferrying single-engine aircraft. In August 1941 he again disapproved of a project to use women in aircraft-ferrying duties, stating that "the use of women pilots serves no military purpose in a country which has adequate manpower at this time." From sources outside the Air Corps came various proposals, one of which eventually was put into effect. In September 1939 the prominent American aviatrix, Jacqueline Cochran, had written to Mrs. Franklin D. Roosevelt regarding the need for planning to use women fliers in a national emergency. "In the field of aviation," she wrote, "the real 'bottle neck' in the long run is likely to be trained pilots." Male pilots could be released for combat duty by assigning women to "all sorts of helpful back of the lines work" such as flying commercial, transport, courier, and ambulance planes. Such a plan, Miss Cochran warned, "requires organization and not at the time of emergency but in advance." Three years after writing this letter, Miss Cochran found herself at the head of just such a program, not in advance of an emergency but in the middle of it.[82]

Miss Cochran's plan looked forward to employment of women pilots on a scale that made an ambitious training program a central feature of the project. A different and more modest proposal was advanced by Mrs. Nancy Harkness Love, another prominent aviatrix, who was employed in non-flying duties by the Air Corps Ferrying Command. Mrs. Love's plan, which gained the support of the Ferrying Command and later the ATC, called for a small group of highly qualified women fliers, who would require little additional training, to help fill the command's growing need for ferry pilots. As it happened, in the confused rush to meet pilot shortages, both plans were put into effect almost simultaneously, General Arnold having conferred with Miss Cochran in the late spring of 1942. In September 1942 the Women's Auxiliary Ferrying Squadron (WAFS) was activated at New Castle, Delaware, under the command of Mrs. Love, while the Women's Flying Training Detachment, under the direction of Miss Cochran, was established in the Flying Training Command.[83]

Two factors, present at the outset, were destined to cause difficulty in the Air Forces' use of women pilots. One was the fact that the women were civilians employed in military and semimilitary tasks. The other was the existence, side by side, of two different concepts regarding the women's pilot program. On the one hand was the idea of a restricted, elite group of well-trained fliers who could make their contribution to the ferrying program almost immediately. Opposed to this idea was the concept of a fairly large number of women pilots who would require an extensive training program and who would then be assigned to a variety of flying duties in order to release men for combat. General Arnold, when confronted with the problem, called a meeting of ATC officials and Miss Cochran and told them that he "would not have two women's pilot organizations in the AAF —that they had to get together." It was a bigger proposition than flying for ATC.[84] The Cochran concept eventually won priority, but command problems continued to hamper the program, for the Ferrying Division of ATC, the chief using agency, needed to have complete control of the pilots assigned to it, whereas Miss Cochran felt that she needed to have complete control of all women pilots in order to carry out the experiment effectively. On 5 August 1943 the WAFS and women pilot trainees were merged into one organization, Women Airforce Service Pilots (WASP), with Miss Cochran becoming Director of Women Pilots.[85] Mrs. Love was made WASP executive with the Ferrying Division of the ATC.

Before the merger was completed, four squadrons of WAFS demonstrated that they were capable of handling much heavier and more difficult types of planes than had been originally expected. At the same time, directives from AAF Headquarters to the Flying Training Command indicated a progressive broadening of the training program for women pilots. In November 1942 General Arnold directed the command to augment such training "to the maximum possible extent." The Air Forces' objective, he wrote, was "to provide at the earliest possible date a sufficient number of women pilots to replace men in every noncombatant flying duty in which it is feasible." Training was now to be provided for women with no previous flying experience as well as for those who were already licensed pilots. Within a few days General Arnold, writing to the Chief of the Air Staff, gave added emphasis to the necessity for using women "in every possible position throughout the Air Forces."[86]

The AAF was unable, however, to use more than a fraction of the number of women who wanted to serve in the WASP; for the WASP, unlike the WAC, never suffered from a dearth of applicants. In all, some 25,000 women applied for admission to the WASP training program; of the 1,830 who were admitted, 1,074 completed the course and were assigned to operational duty. The flood of applications can be explained, at least in part, by the overglamorization resulting from newspaper and magazine stories on the program. Air Force officials attempted, without much success, to tone down the public enthusiasm, at least until the experiment had proved successful. Even routine flights—ordinary, uneventful affairs—often received headline treatment, whereas such flights involving male pilots never aroused public interest. Not only thousands of American women but several hundred Canadian women and some from England and Brazil sought admission. One Canadian woman wrote:

Because we are fighting on the same side in this war rather than against each other, and because one more flier (be he Canuck or Yank) -means one less German, I would like to ask you on bended knee if there will be any chance of accepting me at Sweetwater if I were to go ahead and complete my necessary hours.

P.S.—I am physically fit; have a college degree; can sing the Star Spangled Banner; have never been a nazi spy; and would gladly take out U.S. papers if only it were possible.

All such applications, which could not meet the citizenship requirement, were automatically rejected.[87]

The Director of Women Pilots, in her final report, said: "The selection was entirely a matter of choosing clean-cut, stable-appearing young girls, of proper age, educational background, and height, who could show the required number of flying hours properly noted and certified in a log book." Except for the original group of WAFS, recruitment was handled directly by Miss Cochran's office. Included in the first set of requirements for WASP trainees were American citizenship, high-school education or its equivalent, twenty-one to thirty-five years of age, 200 hours flying time, minimum height of 60 inches, medical examination by an Army flight surgeon, and a personal interview with an authorized recruiting officer. When it appeared from early experience that younger women were more successful in training than older ones, the minimum age for admission was reduced to eighteen and a half; most of the WASPs were under twenty-seven. Experience also proved that it was desirable to admit only those women who were at least 64 inches tall.[88]

Training of the women pilots began in November 1942 in a contract school at Howard Hughes Airport in Houston, Texas. When facilities here proved to be inadequate, the training was gradually shifted to Avenger Field, Sweetwater, Texas. The first program of instruction, consisting of 135 hours of flying training and 180 hours of ground school, provided for a four-month course designed to qualify the pilots "to ferry training type Army Aircraft." Successive modifications in the curriculum were dictated by a declining experience level of the applicants, dissatisfaction with the training program, criticism of the proficiency of the graduates, and plans to use the women on duties other than ferrying. Except for the fact that the women were not training for combat, their course of instruction was essentially the same as that for aviation cadets. The WASPs thus received no gunnery training and very little formation flying and acrobatics, but they went through the usual stalls, loops, spins, lazy-eights, snap rolls, pylon-eights, and chandelles, and they had to be able to recover from any position.[89] The percentage of trainees who "washed out" compared favorably with the elimination rates for male cadets in the Central Flying Training Command. The average elimination rates for WASPs in 1943 was 26 per cent and in 1944 was 47 per cent; cadet elimination rates for the same years varied from slightly less than 25 per cent to over 55 per cent.[90]

Although ferrying was the first and principal duty of WASPs, their usefulness was increased when decisions were made in the fall of 1943 to assign women pilots to the Training Command for operational duties and to initiate special training projects. The latter program included the following:

	Number Entering	Number Graduated
Transition, C-60	16	6
Transition, B-17	17	13
Transition, B-25	20	19
Transition, B-26	57	39
Co-pilot, B-26	24	Discontinued
Advanced instrument	246	232
School of Applied Tactics	460	460

Upon completion of primary training each woman pilot was given the opportunity to indicate her preference as to the type of plane she wished to fly, the location desired as a base, and the members of her class with whom she preferred to be based. In most cases the women indicated that the type of plane was the factor of greatest importance to them. Rating sheets were prepared from daily records on all trainees by flight line, ground school, Link department, physical training department, student officers, and staff advisers. On the basis of these rating sheets and the number of disciplinary demerits, the over-all rating of each graduate was determined. Those trainees with the best over-all ratings were then given their preferences on assignments which came in from the Central Flying Training Command, provided they could fly the type of plane required by the assignment.

Most of the ferrying assignments involved light aircraft, but when the WASP program came to an end on 20 December 1944, women pilots had ferried 77 types of aircraft, including the P-38 and F-5, P-39, P-40, P-63, C-54, C-46, and B-24. The women encountered the same flying conditions and problems as were faced by male pilots, sometimes guarding their own planes at understaffed airfields, sometimes having to improvise refueling facilities, and frequently flying open-cockpit planes in subzero weather. After April 1944 the accident rate rose when pursuit-plane ferrying became the main WASP activity; the higher rate cannot be attributed to any lack of ability, for male pilots had a similar record. For example, in the continental air forces in 1944 the accident rate for single-engine pursuit planes was 1.34 per 1,000 trips flown; for heavy bombers the rate was 0.29.

In spite of their concentration on a more hazardous type of ferrying than that done by male pilots in the division, the WASPs did not complain. The evidence is emphatic, according to the ATC historian, "that women pilots took their turns at making deliveries in entire equality with the men, that they lost no more, if not fewer, days per month from flying status for physiological reasons than did the men." General Arnold stated that it was common for commanding officers to prefer WASPs over male ferry pilots because the woman pilot ordinarily reached her destination a day or two ahead of the time required by a male pilot. The reason: "she didn't carry an address book with her." By specializing in the delivery of aircraft types which did not fit into the pilot transition program, the WASPs during the latter months of their program greatly facilitated the advancement of male pilots from Class I to Class V and thence to overseas duty. And when the WASP went out of existence in December 1944, the women ferry pilots within 27 months had completed 12,650 movements over a distance of approximately 9,224,000 miles—"a record of useful achievement and of solid contribution to the prosecution of the war."[91]

Although the ferrying was done almost entirely by daylight, substantially all the other operational duties were performed by day and night. WASPs were used in tracking and searchlight missions, simulated bombing, smoke-laying and other chemical missions, radio control work, instrument instruction, and administrative and utility flying. In addition, a few exceptionally qualified women were allowed to test rocket-propelled planes, to pilot jet-propelled planes, and to work with radar-controlled targets. On some of these assignments the WASPs encountered difficulties, in a few cases sufficient to discontinue their use in such work. As an experiment some of the women were assigned in the summer of 1943 to target-towing jobs in support of antiaircraft and aerial gunnery training. The test was not carried out under ideal circumstances and was therefore not conclusive; some of the pilots lacked proper training for the work, and certain male personnel connected with the mission tended to protect the women from risk and responsibility. In general, however, the women pilots were considered capable of tow-target work; according to the chief of the Tow Target Section of the Fourth Air Force, they were better adapted to the activity than most pilots returned from combat. In glider-towing duties the WASPs were not successful primarily because operation of the C-60 proved to be physically too strenuous. In 1944 the Eastern and Western Flying Training Commands were asked to undertake an experiment in the use of women pilots as instructors in basic-flying schools for aviation cadets. The almost unanimous opinion of commanding officers, supervisors, and the WASPs themselves was that women should not serve as basic-flying instructors because of the possible morale effect on aviation cadets. WASPs did serve successfully, however, as instrument instructors in the Eastern Flying Training Command.[92]

Much of the difficulty encountered by the WASPs on their various assignments stemmed from the hostility of the male pilots with whom they worked. It was undoubtedly galling to some airmen to see a woman flying a plane which they were not yet qualified to handle. Many officers were skeptical of the women's abilities as well as their sincerity of purpose. But the WASPs had a way of converting NB's (non-believers). As their total of hours and miles flown mounted, doubts about their capabilities and apprehensions based on supposed physical or temperamental weaknesses were either removed or substantially lessened. The Air Surgeon concluded: "It is no longer a matter of speculation that graduate WASPs were adapted physically, mentally, and psychologically to the type of flying assigned. My Surgeons have stated that they stood up well to their job; that the male personnel lost more time due to being grounded."

The resentment and hostility of many officers eventually turned into admiration. "When these girls first came here," said one officer in the 3d Tow-Target Squadron at Camp Davis, "I said I'd be damned if I'd let one of 'em taxi me down the runway. I wanted to hang on to this skin of mine a little longer. Then one day I *had* to give one of the WASPs a check-out flight from here to Charlotte. And now I take it back, every word I said. She was even better than some of my own boys." Of the original fifty WASPs at Camp Davis, fifteen were sent to Camp Stewart, Georgia, to fly special assignments involving much exacting instrument work. One of the Air Force officers working with the women confessed: "Two of the girls are as good as I am at this particular job, and hell, I think *I'm* the best in the Army."[93]

The WASPs were not playgirls. Although under Civil Service, WASP trainees were subject to the same discipline as cadets. The white-glove test was applied in their barracks inspection, and they were allowed only seventy gigs. They faced the same hazards as male pilots, yet had none of the benefits of military status. A total of 37 WASPs lost their lives in aircraft accidents, while 7 suffered major injuries and 29 suffered minor injuries. Reporting to General Arnold on 1 August 1944, Miss Cochran noted that WASPs were "doing the work of an officer freed to serve elsewhere," yet they did not even have "the right to a military funeral." Their civilian status led, on the other hand, to certain administrative problems; there was nothing, for example, to prevent a woman from resigning after having received training at government expense.

As the WASP neared its end, Miss Cochran pointed out that "without militarization there were some inherent organizational weaknesses which might have been very serious to the program except for the loyalty and good sense of the individual WASPs." At the beginning of the program, however, she had considered it unwise to militarize until at least 125 women were trained and assigned to various flying duties. By the time the AAF asked Congress for militarization of the WASP, conditions had so changed that not only was the request denied but the whole program was brought to an abrupt end.[94]

On 30 September 1943 the first of the WASP militarization bills was introduced in the House of Representatives. Both Miss Cochran and General Arnold desired a separate corps headed by a woman colonel similar to the WAC, WAVES, SPAR, and Marine heads. But the War Department consistently opposed such a move, since there was no separate corps for male pilots as distinguished from non-rated AAF officers; instead, it preferred that they be commissioned in the WAC and thus added to some 2,000 "Air WAC" officers already assigned, for whom flying duty was then legally permissible.[95] While the matter was under congressional consideration, the CAA War Training Service program was ended (15 January 1944); moreover, an announcement was made that the AAF college training programs would be terminated on 30 June and that soon thereafter a number of civilian-contract flying schools would be released. The prospective grounding of so many civilian students and instructor pilots led to a flood of indignant letters to congressmen in protest against the militarization and training of women pilots when men pilots were being put into the "walking Army." Male civilian tempers were further inflamed by news that the AAF had begun giving officer training to WASPs at the School of Applied Tactics. Though widely misunderstood, the step had been taken not only in anticipation of the WASPs' militarization but also in the belief that the WASPs would benefit in the performance of their duties from a study of military procedures.

The House Committee on the Civil Service (Ramspeck Committee) then undertook an inquiry into the criticisms made of the WASP program. Its report on 5 June 1944 claimed that the WASP was unnecessary and unjustifiably expensive and recommended that the recruiting and training of inexperienced women pilots be halted.

In addition, rapid changes in the military situation adversely affected the WASP program. The favorable progress of the war, along with a lower attrition rate than had been expected, indicated that there would soon be a surplus of male pilots. Under the circumstances the proposal for militarization, as well as the WASP program itself, was doomed. On 20 December 1944, with graduation of the final class of trainees at Sweetwater, the WASP was deactivated.[96]

At the conclusion of the WASP program there were 916 women pilots on duty with the AAF, assigned as follows:

	Number
Headquarters AAF	1
Training Command	620
Air Transport Command	141
First Air Force	16
Second Air Force	80
Fourth Air Force	37
Weather Wing	11
Proving Ground Command	6
Air Technical Service Command	3
Troop Carrier Command	1

The WASPs had flown approximately 60 million miles on operational duties, with an average for each pilot of 33 hours a month. Through no fault of theirs, by the time the women pilots were ready to make their chief contribution to the war effort, their services were no longer vitally needed. As an experiment to determine the capabilities of women pilots, the program was impeded by the limited opportunities for adequate testing, since wartime pressures gave top priority to operational missions of the various commands. The results of the experiment, therefore, cannot be considered conclusive. But at least the program demonstrated that women are capable of carrying out a variety of flying and aviation administrative duties.[97] It was also demonstrated that some American women were willing to risk their lives in wartime flying assignments even though they and their families were being discriminated against in the matter of compensation and benefits.

Army Nurse Corps

Other women in uniform entitled to wear the regulation AAF shoulder patch in World War II were members of the Army Nurse Corps assigned to the AAF. By 1944 more than 6,500 nurses were so assigned, 6,000 of them on duty at AAF station hospitals. The remaining 500 were flight nurses serving in the air evacuation of the wounded. In contrast with the WAC and WASP, the Army Nurse Corps was well established as an essential organization in time of peace as well as of war. Since nursing was one of the traditional fields of employment for women, the Army nurses did not suffer the ridicule and abuse of women who were pioneering in new occupations, many of which had been exclusively male prior to the war.[98]

On the other hand, flight nurses with the AAF did pioneer in new uses for their skills and at the same time contributed to the relatively low mortality rate of wounded American soldiers in World War II. Air evacuation was a logical development of the air age, obviating the transportation of trainloads of supplies and hundreds of doctors and nurses to the front. Hospitals could thus be established hundreds of miles behind the lines, their remoteness to the front lines aiding the recovery of the wounded. In areas where air-evacuation units operated, the flight nurses boosted the morale of soldiers by their very presence, while the prospect of prompt relief from suffering and of quick treatment in case of emergency further aided front-line morale. Air-evacuation duty, always tense with drama and excitement, seemed to be the perfect answer for those women who "didn't join the Army Nurse Corps to take care of people with measles."[99]

All nurses assigned to the AAF were sent to a training center for four weeks before being sent to AAF station hospitals in the United States. After six months' duty, they became eligible to make application for flight-nurse training. Applicants had to be recommended by the senior flight surgeon of their command as being particularly adapted for the service, and they were required to pass the same physical examinations as all other flying personnel.

Nurses meeting these requirements were sent to the School of Air Evacuation, Bowman Field, Kentucky. So strenuous was the eight-week course of training here that, remarked one observer, each nurse "should have received a medal" simply for completing the course. There were the usual movies, lectures by personnel who had returned from active duty, and routine subjects such as military courtesy, record-keeping, and care of equipment and clothing. The more rigorous phase of the training took place on outdoor maneuvers. After learning how to load and unload a plane, the nurses had parachute drill, gas-mask drill, and practice in crash procedure. They underwent simulated bombing and strafing attacks, as well as wormed their way along the ground under a barrage of live machine-gun bullets. The nurses learned survival procedures under all climatic conditions, and they practiced swimming and rescue work fully clad.

The first class of flight nurses graduated at Bowman Field on 18 February 1943. By the end of that year flight-nurse units were operating in every theater where units of the AAF were assigned. In the Sicilian and Italian campaigns flight nurses arrived as soon as transport planes could be sent to the front. In the Tarawa-Makin campaign, flight nurses helped evacuate the wounded within three days after the first troops landed. Their work at the several fronts carried them right into the danger zone—probably farther than American women had ever gone before—within machine-gun range of the enemy.[100] The risk seemed fully justified, however, in view of the greatly reduced death rate among the wounded. Flight-nurse duty was hazardous, exacting, and strenuous, but it was also rewarding. It was entirely voluntary, and those women who served in air-evacuation units had the satisfaction of knowing that they were helping to save lives and at the same time participating in an exciting new development in wartime medical practices.

A smaller group of women with a special skill served as dietitians at the various air bases. The Medical Department of the Army for many years had employed civilian women as dietitians, giving them a postgraduate course at Walter Reed General Hospital after 1922. The course was open to women between the ages of twenty and forty if they held a Bachelor's degree with a major in food and nutrition or in institutional management. Later the requirements were altered in order to admit more women. After June 1944 the dietitians were commissioned as second lieutenants upon completion of their twelve-month course. Those who were assigned to army air bases were well aware of the relationship between proper diet and air performance. In planning meals, the Air Force dietitian knew that a balanced vitamin intake would aid the aerial gunner and bombardier in hitting their targets, while yellow vegetables would help the pilots' eyes adjust to night flying. Besides planning meals and supervising those who prepared and served the meals, the dietitian also kept records of food costs and was responsible for ordering equipment and supplies. And at bases which were operated on three shifts, she could be assigned to duty any hours of the day or night.[101]

As Civilians

For those women who either could not or did not wish to serve in uniform, there was ample opportunity to aid in the war effort as civilian employees of the AAF. In addition to the greatly needed clerical and administrative skills, civilian women also contributed technical and industrial skills. As early as January 1942 plans were made at AAF Headquarters to employ women in jobs of the latter type, but several months elapsed before opposition, particularly among shopmen, was sufficiently overcome so that the women could be hired in any sizable quantity. By September 1942, when the AAF had 58,125 female employees, it was apparent that the women were "either a necessary evil or a godsend." By June 1943 the number had risen to 151,016, and from that time until the end of the war women comprised about 45 per cent of the total civilian strength.[102]

Depots of the Air Service Command, in particular, depended on newly recruited women for a variety of jobs, many of them dirty, many of them monotonous, but all of them important. Wearing mechanics' overalls and safety turbans, the women checked equipment and cleaned planes; they repaired propeller blades, cleaned spark plugs, and patched up old parts. They camouflaged planes for ocean, arctic, desert, or jungle flying, took care of fur-lined flying suits (which required summer storage), repainted radium dials, riveted, and welded. And while the women were doing these jobs, the AAF was finding it necessary to institute changes in some of its personnel practices. To facilitate the employment of mothers with young children, personnel officers at AAF field installations helped establish child-care services. And the presence of women employees influenced the establishment of nursing service and improved lighting, ventilation, and hygienic facilities.[103]

Women who could not serve full time, either in uniform or as civilians, assisted the nation's air arm in a number of part-time volunteer capacities. Many of them worked in the Aircraft Warning Service, as ground observers or in the information and filter centers.

The Civil Air Patrol, which after 29 April 1943 was under the supervision of the AAF, accepted women volunteers on an equal basis with men. Those with a pilot's license performed all missions except coastal patrol; those not licensed to fly, but still interested in aviation, served as control-tower operator, mechanic, ground-school instructor, radio operator, photographer, first-aid assistant, or airport supervisor. Although women comprised only 10 per cent of the CAP strength, the publicity given to their activities led to the erroneous impression that many more women were participating in the program. Leading magazines carried full-page color ads for such products as cigarettes and refrigerators, featuring women CAP pilots. Some of the men at certain bases resented the fact that they served "anonymously" while the women got all the publicity. It was the policy of the CAP "to play down the female angle" within the 10 per cent proportion of its membership; but, as in the case of the WASPs, advertisers and newspapers continued to spotlight the women's activities.[104]

Other volunteer work, of a somewhat different type, was carried on by women members of AAF families throughout the country. Organized into local AAF women's clubs, they engaged in a wide variety of welfare projects for AAF personnel at almost every air base and in many communities. They assisted in such projects as bond sales, kindergartens, clothing and toy exchanges, lectures, study clubs, U.S.O. activities, mending service, athletic clubs, garden clubs, flower committees, lending libraries, club canteens, and information desks. By 1944, membership in the local organizations totaled 25,000 women; and after 8 February 1944 their work was co-ordinated by the newly formed National Association of Air Forces Women.[105]

One final group, not employed by the AAF, but nevertheless contributing directly to its functioning, was the host of women in the aircraft industry who helped turn out bombers, pursuit planes, transports, and training planes for the AAF. By the late fall of 1943, there were 478,000 women in the aircraft industry, making up 36.5 per cent of the production force, as compared with a fraction of 1 per cent in 1940. At one parachute company, women made up 85 per cent of the total employees in 1944. No doubt many of these women felt a closer relationship with the nation's air effort than did many women in uniform whose assignments seemed only remotely connected with the war.[106]

AIR WAC: WELDER FOR ATC IN INDIA

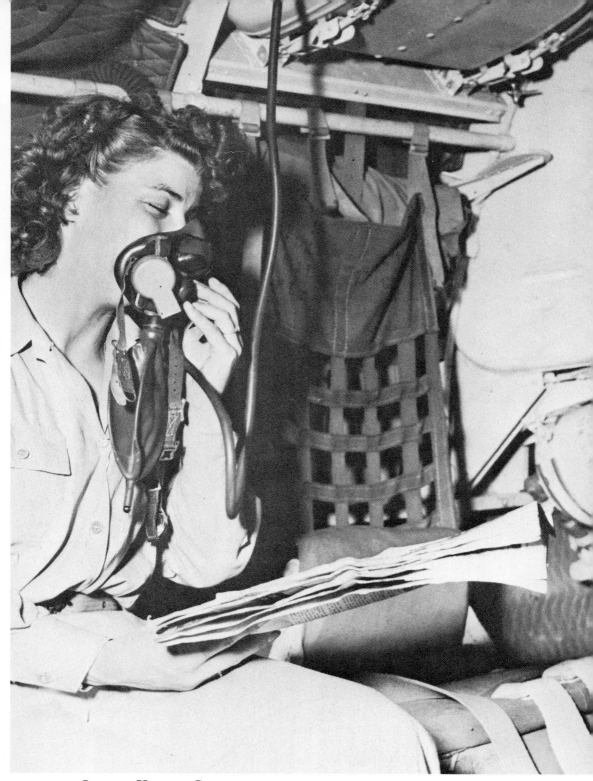

Over the Hump to China,

AIR WACS IN CBI

ARRIVING AT CHUNGKING

AIR WACS IN CBI: RECEPTION AT CHUNGKING

Whether in uniform or as civilians, whether employed by the AAF or volunteering their efforts, women served in a variety of capacities, all of which were necessary to the proper functioning of the Army Air Forces. The total number of uniformed women was small, both in proportion to the number needed and in proportion to the men in the AAF. But it was sufficiently large to demonstrate the effectiveness, the wide range, and the virtually indispensable character of women's skills during wartime. And it was sufficiently small to indicate that, in any future war demanding an all-out effort, the United States probably would be forced to draft its women. Not even the glamour of aviation could overcome the indifference or reluctance to enlist of the majority of eligible women. But those who did participate in the air effort helped to open up the field of military aviation to women, a step which was part of a larger pattern in the emancipation of their sex and in the assumption of the full responsibilities of citizenship regardless of sex.

SECTION VI

* * * * * * * * * * *

REDEPLOYMENT AND DEMOBILIZATION

*   *   *   *   *   *   *   *   *   *   *

CHAPTER 17

REDEPLOYMENT
AND DEMOBILIZATION

REDEPLOYMENT and demobilization are essentially different activities. Both terms imply movement of men and materiel; both include much more than that. Redeployment is the "transfer of a unit, an individual or supplies deployed in an overseas theater to another theater, or to another location within the theater, or to the zone of interior for the purpose of further employment";[1] it entails procurement, supply, and maintenance. To the AAF in World War II redeployment meant, specifically, the transfer of units and equipment from the European and Mediterranean theaters to the Pacific and China-Burma-India theaters. Demobilization is "disbanding military forces; changing over from a war footing to a peacetime footing."[2] It embraces, in addition to the separation of personnel, the termination of contracts, the sale of surplus property, and the disposal of facilities not required in times of peace. Different as are the two concepts, they were always coupled together in the planning that was carried on during the war years. Indeed, the story of the planning is almost all there is to tell about redeployment; for the plans were aborted by the sudden collapse of Japan. Almost as soon as it had begun, redeployment was turned into demobilization.

Demobilizations of the Past

The United States had never been confronted with the problem of such a large-scale redeployment as that contemplated by the military during the years from 1942 to 1945; but demobilization was an old story. Six times before World War II the people of this country had had to muster their forces for war. Six times they had seen those forces—save for an almost infinitesimal body of professional soldiers —hastily returned to civilian life at the end of hostilities. Historical tradition, and more particularly the experience of World War I, argued that all planning for yet another demobilization must take into consideration the strongest popular pressures for a speedy release of the civilian-soldier.

The first major demobilization carried out in the United States was that which followed the Civil War. As in our previous wars, throughout the period of hostilities men were being discharged, as short-term enlistments expired. But no consideration seems to have been given to the problem of postwar demobilization until after Lee surrendered. Then the government was confronted with the task of discharging 1,034,000 Union soldiers.[3] The hastily devised demobilization plan called for each division to be moved intact to one of nine rendezvous areas where, upon the completion of muster and pay rolls, divisions and corps were inactivated. Lesser units were thus considered to have been mustered out of the federal service and were transferred to their home state, or camp of original organization, for the final act of individual separation from the service. With many soldiers simply taking Dutch leave from their units once the fighting stopped, over 600,000 officers and men had been discharged by early August 1865; by the end of the year the total was near 900,000. The one million mark was passed before 30 June 1866, and by 1 November of that year 1,023,021 had been mustered out. A few volunteers were kept in service, for various reasons, more than a year longer; the last volunteer organization was not disbanded until 30 December 1867.[4]

Of World War I a prominent historian has written: "There were times in the history of mobilization in which the government of the United States looked like a madhouse; during demobilization there was lacking even the madhouse in which the crazy might be incarcerated. They were at large."[5] Not until October 1918 did the War Department give any serious thought to the problem of demobilization.[6] After briefly considering demobilization according to length of individual service or the needs of the civilian economy, and after rejecting the suggestion that local draft boards might serve as the agency for separation from service, the Army adopted the simplest method—demobilization by unit. From Armistice Day to the end of 1918 and throughout 1919 the Army had one impelling motive: to relieve itself from the public, journalistic, and congressional pressure by responding to the demand, "Bring the boys home!" And bring them home it did.

Demobilization began on 11 November 1918. Within an hour after the news of the signing of the Armistice reached Washington, separations from the service were taking place.[7] In more than one instance a troop train, loaded with newly sworn-in draftees headed for training camp, was stopped and sent back to its starting point; there the men were immediately discharged from the service. Units in the United States, from development battalions to combat divisions in training, were disbanded or inactivated and their personnel discharged as fast as the necessary processing could be accomplished. As combat divisions and other organizations overseas were declared by General Pershing to be no longer required in the theater, they were shipped back to the United States to be disbanded or inactivated if not required as components of the Regular Army. Thousands of men overseas who had become detached from their organizations, generally because of having been hospitalized, were sent to casual camps such as the one at St. Aignan (known to its inmates as "St. Agony") and held there until service records were received from Tours, the records depository. When a group of some two hundred soldiers had been matched with their service records, the men were organized into a casual company, put in charge of a couple of officers similarly detached from their organizations, and loaded onto the first available States-bound ship. From the port of debarkation the casuals were sent to a camp on the eastern seaboard; there they were held for a few days while groups, one for each of the thirty-odd demobilization centers, were organized. Every soldier was assigned to the group headed for the separation center nearest his home.

Some deviations from the principle of unit demobilization occurred, as in the early discharge of approximately 81,000 soldiers classified as anthracite coal miners, railroad employees, and railway mail clerks.[8] An order issued by the Chief of Staff in February 1919, making eligible for discharge all troops who had been in this country on 11 November 1918, excepted certain categories—Regular Army troops, medical personnel, and soldiers engaged in administrative work connected with demobilization. But the last group complained so bitterly about being kept in service that in March 1919 they were replaced by civilians.[9]

Although the lack of administrative personnel trained in discharge procedures imposed delays on the processes of demobilization, by the end of November 1918 more than 43,000 troops had been discharged. In December a peak of 643,043 separations was reached. During the first half of 1919 men were discharged at rates ranging from 274,479 per month in March to 404,588 in June; by 1 July a total of 2,735,986 had been separated. At the end of November 1919 the total number of separations accomplished was 3,416,066. The strength of the Army was then less than 275,000; by 30 June 1920 it was 209,901.[10]

Rapid as this progress would seem to have been, it was not rapid enough for the troops being discharged or for their families and friends; that being so, it follows that it was not rapid enough for the members of the United States Congress. A flood of correspondence from the Senate and House Office Buildings poured into the War Department; the volume of it, and the fact that every message had to be answered promptly (for such is the feeling of an Executive department toward any member of Congress), greatly impeded the demobilization program. Throughout the demobilization period the Secretary of War, the Chief of Staff, and others who should have been permitted to devote themselves to other purposes were compelled to spend much of their time in what was largely a vain attempt to defend the Army and its policies. While the Army was demobilizing 3,500,000 soldiers, the Navy, which had grown from 65,777 officers and men on 1 April 1917 to 497,030 on 11 November 1918, was returning more than 400,000 men to civilian life.[11]

World War II Plans

United States planning for World War II redeployment and demobilization began early enough to have assured a highly successful operation, had earliness of planning been the only requisite for success. In a message to Congress of 14 January 1942 President Roosevelt charged the National Resources Planning Board (NRPB) with "the preparation of long-range plans . . . for post-war full employment, security, and building America."[12] In response to this mandate, a conference was held in the summer of 1942; present were the members of the NRPB and representatives of the War, Navy, and Labor Departments, the War Manpower Commission, the Veterans Administration, and other federal agencies. Late in 1942 the NRPB published *Post-war Agenda*, outlining plans for demobilization and for many other post-bellum activities. Planning by the NRPB continued into 1943 and culminated in a report, *Demobilization and Readjustment;* this was submitted to the President on 30 June 1943 and was made public on 31 July. The plans outlined in this report had a very considerable impact, since many of the ideas suggested were subsequently put into effect by one or another agency. But the NRPB itself made no further contribution to demobilization planning because the Congress refused to appropriate funds to permit it to operate after fiscal year 1943.[13]

All planning for demobilization during World War II was complicated by the fact that there were really two wars to be taken into account. It was assumed by the planners that the war in Europe would end before the war against Japan, probably a year before. It was also assumed that part of the forces deployed against Germany would have to be redeployed to the Pacific or to the Asiatic mainland, in order to assure the promptest possible end to the Japanese war. The marked differences in the characteristics of the two wars argued that the requirements of redeployment would fall unequally on the several arms and services. It was assumed that redeployment would involve chiefly naval and air forces, while a large percentage of the ground forces would become eligible for demobilization upon the accomplishment of victory in Europe. And this assumption undoubtedly helps to explain the early attention that was given by military leaders to the problem of demobilization.

Serious planning at AAF Headquarters began in the spring of 1943 with the appointment of Col. F. Trubee Davison as the chief of a special staff section—the Special Projects Office (SPO). Its particular mission was described as "legislative planning," and it soon received a directive calling for study of the problems of demobilization and of the postwar air force.[14] Simultaneously, the Chief of Staff called upon the head of the Army Service Forces (ASF), Lt. Gen. Brehon B. Somervell, to "initiate preliminary studies exploring the fields of basic policy and broad planning for demobilization of our military organization after the cessation of hostilities."[15] The result of General Marshall's directive was the establishment in the ASF of the Project Planning Division, headed by Brig. Gen. W. F. Tompkins.[16] There seems to have been some thought that demobilization would become the special responsibility of ASF, but in July the Secretary of War fixed that responsibility in the War Department itself by establishing a Special Planning Division (SPD) as part of the War Department

Special Staff.[17] The Project Planning Division was abolished, and General Tompkins and his staff were transferred to the new division. Colonel Davison, who continued at the head of the SPO, became the AAF representative on SPD. The Army Ground Forces (AGF) had no formal representation but kept in close touch with SPD through the Control Division of the AGF G-1 Section.[18]

Great stress was laid on the necessity for keeping secret the purpose of the new division "in order to avoid a public relaxation in the war effort should it become known that we were deeply involved in preparations for demobilization."[19] This fear of a public reaction was probably well founded. One AAF officer, when he read in a secret document that a group had been organized to engage in demobilization planning, took a red pencil and underlined the word "demobilization," adding a question mark in the margin opposite. Then, below the question mark, he wrote "Already!"[20]

First thoughts naturally tended to favor demobilization by unit. From the military point of view this procedure had every advantage, as a memo of June 1943 from Col. J. H. McCormick of A-1 pointed out to General Arnold.[21] Unit demobilization is simple to administer, it ignores equity and other social considerations on the ground that they lie without the purview of the Army, and it keeps units not yet demobilized at war strength and fully operational. The advantages in other methods had to be admitted: they made it possible to reward individuals who had served longest and sacrificed most by releasing them first and might provide controls that could be helpfully adjusted to the capacity of the civilian economy to reabsorb discharged personnel. But Colonel McCormick, along with other officers concerned, felt that the Army should consult first its own interests and leave to appropriate civilian agencies the primary responsibility for the solution of the nation's social problems. Accordingly, A-1 recommended that standard procedures be based on a plan of unit demobilization.

This inclination to favor unit demobilization probably reflects the feeling at AAF Headquarters that no substantial reduction of the Army's air arm could be expected before the defeat of Japan. In September 1943 Maj. Gen. Thomas T. Handy, Chief of the Operations Division, apparently assumed that as many as 43 air groups would be eligible for demobilization after the defeat of Germany. But this opinion seems to have been corrected within the month, for

General Handy is on record as of 21 September 1943 with the opinion that none of the 112 air groups expected to be released from "the European-African Theater" by the defeat of Germany would be immediately eligible for demobilization.[22]

The Special Planning Division, viewing demobilization as it affected the entire Army and not just the air arm, had been quick to recognize that unit demobilization, however much it might be preferred by the military authorities, would not be acceptable to the American GI's or to their friends and relatives. Its director had expressed to General Marshall the belief that no one of the methods that had been discussed—demobilization by skills, by length of service, by age, and by dependency—would be acceptable by itself, that the determination as to priority of separation would have to be made on the basis of a combination of factors.[23]

Already the AAF had been forced to direct special attention to the particular problems of the war-weary airman who might require return to the United States for rest and recuperation or even separation from the service. On 15 August 1943 the AAF had activated its Redistribution Center at Atlantic City[24] with a mission "to receive all Army Air Forces Personnel returning to the continental United States from overseas, except those returned for hospitalization or on specific assignment, and to receive such Army Air Forces personnel as may be transferred to the Redistribution Centers by continental commands and air forces, and after examination and re-evaluation assign them to appropriate stations, detail them to rest camps or effect their separation from the service."[25] Simultaneously with the establishment of the Redistribution Center, there were activated Redistribution Stations No. 1 and No. 2 at Atlantic City and Miami Beach, Florida, respectively, and rest camps at Lake Lure, North Carolina, Castle Hot Springs, Arizona, and Camp Mystic, Texas. The Redistribution Center, which became the Personnel Distribution Command (PDC) on 1 June 1944, later opened redistribution stations at Santa Monica and Santa Ana in California, at Camp Davis and Greensboro in North Carolina, and at San Antonio, Texas. The PDC also acquired during 1944 and 1945 more than a dozen convalescent hospitals (some of which also served as regional hospitals) and several overseas replacement depots.

For planning purposes it was assumed that the earliest probable date for the termination of the war against Germany was 1 September

1944.[26] On the critical question of method, it was decided that the principle of individual separation would be followed under rules basing the right to separation on multiple factors. In determining those factors, the requirements of the military forces came first; after that, physical condition, length of service, combat service, and dependency were listed in that order. Demobilization was expected to fall into two phases: Period I, the interval between the surrender in Europe and the termination of hostilities in the Orient; and Period II, the final transition to a peacetime basis.[27] After a year of study, during which attention was given not only to redeployment but also to projected requirements for occupation forces in Europe, the War Department published Readjustment Regulation 1-1, issued on 30 August 1944.

Although modified by changes from time to time, RR 1-1 remained to the end the basic plan for the demobilization of enlisted personnel. It provided that the War Department, as soon as a readjustment of the troop basis should become possible, would inform the commanding general of each theater what his new mission was to be and what would be the troop basis proposed for accomplishing that mission. Suggestions from the field commanders would be invited, and then the War Department would decide how many elements from each theater or command would be placed in each of four categories: (1) units to be retained for continued service in their then current commands; (2) those to be transferred from one theater to another or to the United States or from the United States to a theater; (3) those to be reorganized and then put in one or the other of the first two categories; and (4) those to be inactivated or disbanded. Each commanding general would then designate specific organizations to make up his quota of units in each category.*

By the terms of RR 1-1, any married female member of the Army, commissioned or enlisted, was to be separated upon application, regardless of any other consideration, if her husband had been separated. Unmarried female and all male enlisted personnel were to be separated according to a point system based on length of service after 16 September 1940, overseas service, combat service, and parenthood. The War Department would decide how much weight to give to each of

---

* By the spring of 1945 the categories had been changed: (1) units scheduled for direct redeployment to another theater; (2) units scheduled for redeployment through the United States; (3) units to be assigned to the occupation air force; and (4) surplus units and personnel scheduled for return to the United States for inactivation or separation.

the factors constituting the Adjusted Service Rating (ASR) Score and then, after V-E Day, when partial demobilization would be in order, would set a "critical score" at such point that, by the separation of all personnel having that score or a higher one, the Army would be reduced to the size regarded as necessary to win the war against Japan.

The AAF had approved the ASR system for the separation of enlisted personnel, but it strongly objected to subsequent efforts to apply the same policy to commissioned officers. In August 1944, officers might be relieved from active duty under regulations which made provision for relief of those who were over forty-five years of age "for whom no suitable assignments" were available, those whose relief was "essential to national health, safety or interest," and those who could prove "undue hardship."[28] Colonel Davison argued in December 1944 that, no matter how much emphasis might be given to the principle that military necessity came first, the use of a critical score for officers would inevitably lead to pressure for the separation of high-score officers and would, at the same time, impede the separation of officers of marginal efficiency who had low scores and wished to remain in uniform. Colonel Davison pointed out that every officer had accepted his commission voluntarily and insisted that the higher pay and other advantages of commissioned rank imposed on each officer an obligation to remain in the service as long as he was needed.[29] On this point the AAF won a partial victory. RR 1-5, dated 30 April 1945,* provided for an ASR score for officers, but there was to be no critical score, and military need was to be the controlling factor.[30] It was possible under RR 1-5 for the AAF to retain its most capable officers on the ground of their military essentiality and to meet successive reductions of the troop basis by releasing from active duty its less efficient commissioned personnel, along with high-score enlisted men.

AAF leaders were gravely concerned over the possible result of the first public announcement of their plans for Period I. They feared that there might be a disastrous lowering of morale in the AAF when it was revealed that, while there would be partial demobilization for the AGF and ASF, there would be nothing but redeployment for AAF units. General Arnold thought that any very serious morale problem could be averted by emphasizing the vital importance of the

---

* RR 1-2, covering the personnel movements that would be required after V-E Day; RR 1-3, prescribing an athletic and recreational program for Period I (the time between V-E Day and V-J Day); and RR 1-4, setting up an Army educational program, were published on 15 September 1944.

role that the AAF was to play in the Japanese war—the necessity for throwing our entire air potential against Japan in order to minimize losses and hasten the end of the war. At the same time he recognized that AAF personnel, especially those who had long been engaged in service that was hazardous or arduous, or both, were in all fairness as much entitled to be returned to civilian life as were their opposite numbers in the AGF and ASF. Hence he proposed to discharge AAF personnel in the same proportion as the other forces by replacing those released with new inductees and with ground and service personnel whose units would be inactivated but who as individuals would not be eligible for discharge.[31] He thought that a clear statement of this policy, and a promise that AAF personnel redeployed directly to the Pacific could expect early separation or at least rotation to the United States, would go far toward alleviating dissatisfaction.[32]

Redeployment

The redeployment of AAF units had its beginning while plans for the larger movement were still in a formative stage. In the fall of 1943 it was expected that operations in the Mediterranean could be cut back by the following spring to such an extent as to make several units available for transfer to the CBI.[33] The claims of ETO, where the build-up for the coming invasion of western Europe was under way, naturally were given first place.* Nevertheless, the 33d and 81st Fighter Groups were sent to China by way of India in February and March; there they flew P-40's and P-47's for the Fourteenth Air Force.[34] Later, in September, the 33d was transferred to Burma, where it joined the Tenth Air Force.[35] Another addition to the Tenth Air Force was the 12th Bombardment Group (Medium), which left Italy in the early spring of 1944. Originally a B-25 outfit, the group used both B-25's and A-26's in Burma.[36] There was also, in India, an instance of what might be called temporary redeployment. The flying echelons of the 64th Troop Carrier Group and the 4th Troop Carrier Squadron of the 62d Troop Carrier Group left Sicily early in April 1944 for detached service in India; they rejoined the ground echelons, which had remained in Sicily, in June.[37]†

* The very considerable redeployment of units from MTO to ETO in 1943–44 is omitted from this discussion, as are the movements of air units from one Pacific theater to another.

† On 10 December 1944 MAAF ordered Flights A and C of the 1st Emergency Rescue Squadron to proceed—flight echelons via Bengasi, Libya, and water echelons via Bari,

Meanwhile, comprehensive plans were drawn for the eventuality of an early defeat of Germany. At the beginning of February 1944, the "Tompkins Demobilization Plan" assumed that there would be, on 1 September 1944, a total of 154 AAF groups in the European and Mediterranean theaters.* It was expected that after the German surrender 112 groups could be released for redeployment, which would leave in Europe and Africa for an ocupation force 42 groups.[38] Units scheduled for service in CBI would be transferred directly to their new stations. Most of those intended for duty in the Pacific would be redeployed through the United States. Some units would be assigned to the strategic reserve in the Zone of Interior, thereby releasing still other units for assignment to combat duty against Japan. In all circumstances the guiding principle was to preserve the combat efficiency of the unit. But AAF Letter 55-3, which on 10 April 1944 outlined "Policies and Procedures for Redeployment of Army Air Forces," and SPO's "Actions to be Taken by AAF Commanding Generals in ETO and MTO Immediately Following the Defeat of Germany," dated 20 April 1944, recognized the special claim of an airman who had a record of long combat service.[39] Whenever the transfer could be made without too seriously damaging the operational efficiency of the unit concerned, such an individual might be transferred to an organization scheduled for assignment to the strategic reserve in the United States. Understandable and compassionate as was this concession, it promised a most significant qualification of the principle that the combat efficiency of the unit should be the first consideration.

In September 1944 (September had been the earliest anticipated date for Germany's surrender) over-all responsibility for redeployment operations at AAF Headquarters was vested in AC/AS, Operations, Commitments, and Requirements (OC&R). At the same time each AAF Headquarters staff office was called upon to appoint a redeployment officer to co-ordinate with OC&R all matters pertaining to redeployment. Likewise, each continental air force and command was ordered to appoint a redeployment officer to see that the directives and other instructions of OC&R were carried out. AC/AS, OC&R

Italy—to Karachi, India. Both echelons left Bari on 5 January 1945. Flight A was returned to the MTO, less personnel and equipment, and was reassigned to the Twelfth Air Force, effective 12 February 1945 (Admin. Hist., 12th AF, Part I, Sec. 2, pp. 29–30).

* There actually were 149 groups in ETO-MTO on 31 August 1944 (*AAF Stat. Digest, WW II*, p. 6).

immediately delegated his redeployment responsibility to the Theaters Branch of the Commitments Division.[40] Instructions covering redeployment procedures had also been issued to overseas commanders, but in September 1944 the Allied armies in western Europe missed the chance for an early victory over Germany.

Perhaps it was the hard fighting of the winter campaign in Europe, and the prospect that still more hard fighting would be required before Germany could be forced to surrender, that brought a change of attitude toward those who fought. In any case, the AAF announced a new policy early in January 1945. The new plan called for replacement, "to the maximum extent possible," of personnel in units returning to the United States for redeployment with personnel from the continental air forces and commands.[41] This policy was to be interpreted as meaning that commanders would replace at least 50 per cent of the personnel, exclusive of combat crews, with more than one year's overseas service but retain in the unit a sufficient cadre of experienced personnel.

The new policy did not last long. In June it was superseded by a policy that came much closer to 100 per cent replacement. Only the commanding officer, the deputy commander, holders of certain critical MOS's, and any volunteer who would sign a waiver of his right to be separated under the terms of RR 1-1 (the ASR critical score had been set on 12 May 1945 at 85 for men and 44 for women) would continue with the unit in its new assignment. An AAF letter of 18 June undertook to distinguish between those who had completed a full tour of overseas duty and those who could be credited with only a partial tour. In the case of flying personnel, complete tours were defined in terms of specific numbers of missions or hours. For heavy-bomber crews the figure was fixed at 18 missions or 110 hours; for medium- and light-bomber crews, as for fighter pilots, it was 35 missions or 150 hours; and for troop-carrier crews 100 combat hours or 500 hours in the theater. All ground personnel who had left the United States on or after 1 December 1944 were considered to have completed only partial tours. "As a guide," AAF Headquarters advised, "normally 20% of the officers (other than air crews) by grade should be retained in redeployed units." Likewise, "normally 20% of ground enlisted personnel should be retained."[42]

Headquarters, AAF, had called upon its subordinate commands to be prepared to put into effect the AAF plans for redeployment and demobilization immediately upon the announcement of Germany's surrender.[43] The Air Technical Service Command (ATSC), to take a typical example, apparently circulated throughout the command its indorsement to the AAF letter, supplying its subordinate components with much of the information that had been received from Washington and designating certain tasks to be performed at the proper time by specific officers.[44]

The ZI command that was mostly concerned with redeployment, however, was the Continental Air Forces (CAF), which had been activated on 15 December 1944[45] with complete supervision of redeployment as its chief mission.* Temporarily located—at first in the Pentagon and then at Bolling Field—Headquarters, CAF, activated at cadre strength only, spent much of the first part of its existence in preparing for the move to what was intended to be its permanent quarters at Camp Springs, Maryland—renamed, on 7 February 1945, Andrews Field.[46] It will doubtless surprise no one to learn that Headquarters, CAF, when it went out of existence on 21 March 1946, was still at Bolling Field.

Briefly, the AAF plan of redeployment† required that each organization about to be redeployed be screened for the purpose of removing all personnel ineligible for redeployment. Among such personnel would be those found to be physically unqualified for further combat duty and those who, by virtue of high ASR scores, would become eligible for separation before the organization could be redeployed or very soon after its arrival in the new theater.[47] Vacancies caused by these transfers from the organization would be filled with low-score individuals from other organizations in the command, air force, or theater. Thus the unit would leave for its new assignment completely manned with personnel eligible for redeployment.

Except for a few organizations to be redeployed direct to the CBI or the Pacific, units would first return to the United States. Upon

* Other missions were: air defense of the continental United States, joint air-ground training, and formation and command of the continental strategic reserve at the completion of redeployment (AAF Ltr. [C] 20-9 for CG's all air forces and commands, by Lt. Gen. Barney M. Giles, Dep. Comdr. AAF and C/AS, 16 Dec. 1944, sub.: Activation of Headquarters Continental Air Forces). All four of the continental-based air forces were subordinate to the new command, as was also the I Troop Carrier Command.

† The basic authorization for all subsequent redeployment planning was a report prepared by the Joint War Plans Committee (JWPC), an agency of the Joint Chiefs of Staff. This report appeared in April 1944 as a top-secret document under the designation JCS 521/5. It was revised in May and was approved in June as JCS 521/6. There were also later revisions.

arrival there, each unit would proceed at once to an Intermediate Processing Station (IPS), perhaps Bradley Field, Connecticut, or Hunter Field, Georgia, for processing of personnel records, medical examinations, and the like. Within 48 hours, the returnees would be on trains, headed for 30 days of RR&R (recuperation, rehabilitation, and recovery), at the end of which the members of the organization would reconvene at a central assembly station (CAS). There replacements would be provided for any personnel who had, for one reason or another, become ineligible for redeployment; and the unit would then be turned over to the Training Command for conversion or refresher training. Upon the completion of that training, the organization would promptly be sent to the Pacific or the CBI.

That was the plan. Theoretically it was perfect; in practice it was anything but perfect, as the experience of the air forces concerned and the units slated for redeployment will indicate.

The trouble began overseas, where theater commands were slow in making known to lower echelons their redeployment plans. General Eisenhower said[48] that planning in the ETO started in February 1945;* but the tentative "European Theater of Operations Basic Plan for Redeployment and Readjustment" was not revealed until 21 April 1945—very shortly before V-E Day. This plan was approved by WDGS on 30 April and published on 15 May.[49] The overseas commanders should not be judged too harshly, for they were naturally more concerned with winning the war against Germany than they were with planning for future operations against Japan. Nevertheless, the air forces were sorely handicapped by the failure of the theaters to establish any firm plan before V-E Day and by the fact that plans once made were so often and, apparently, so arbitrarily changed. In its history, the Eighth Air Force complained bitterly of the difficulty encountered in meeting the commitments made for that air force by USSTAF and Headquarters, AAF.[50]

The situation in MTO was much the same. The Twelfth Air Force complained that redeployment schedules prepared between November 1944 and the following March were of little value because of the rapidity and frequency with which theater plans were changed. Not until two weeks after V-E Day was there a plan sufficiently firm to

---

* Actually a "Redeployment Planning Group" was established as a special staff section of ETOUSA in November 1944 (GO 118, ETOUSA, 27 Nov. 44) and issued "Redeployment Planning Directive No. 1" on 6 January 1945 (John G. Sparrow, *History of Personnel Demobilization in the United States Army* [Washington, 1951], p. 171).

constitute a ground for action. "The actual forecast, on the basis of which most of the redeployment of this Air Force took place, was not received until 25 May 1945."[51]

Lt. Col. Albert W. Jensen, Twelfth Air Force A-1, revealed graphically in a memo to his commanding general,[52] the harassment to which he was subjected by higher echelons of command. In May, following instructions from higher headquarters—which seemed to him to be logical and to conform with current directives—he withdrew low-score personnel from units being redeployed through the United States and replaced them with high-score personnel. Because almost 65 per cent of the members of the Twelfth Air Force had ASR scores above the critical score of 85 points, such an action seemed imperative if there were to be low-score personnel available for manning the units that were to be redeployed directly. But higher echelons objected to Colonel Jensen's interpretation of redeployment directives, and in June an order was issued calling for the removal of all high-score individuals—except volunteers—from units being redeployed either directly or indirectly. At this time the AC/S, A-1, AAF/MTO advised that units being redeployed through the United States might, if necessary, be shipped out of the theater at cadre strength. At about the same time, however, MTOUSA directed that every unit being redeployed from the MTO must be up to full strength. Such units as had already been sent below strength to staging areas were, before being shipped out, to be brought up to authorized strength by the transfer of personnel, either high score or low, in proper or related MOS. This MTOUSA policy made it necessary to declare essential men who had already been transferred out of four groups scheduled for redeployment in July and to reassign them to their original organizations. Most of the men involved had been overseas for two and a half years and had ASR scores of more than 100 points; they were, understandably, not pleased at the prospect of continued overseas duty, and one of them requested an investigation by an inspector general. At a mass meeting held on 11 July 1945, Colonel Jensen explained to the men why it had been necessary to declare them essential and keep them in groups destined for the Pacific; he promised that they would be the first to be rotated after arrival in the Pacific theater. During the closing minutes of the meeting, however, a telephone call from AAF/MTO revealed that enough low-score men had been discovered in the Fifteenth Air Force to permit cancellation of the reassignments. The Twelfth Air Force would have been spared much grief had AAF/MTO made its discovery a bit sooner.

It was not the overseas air forces alone that suffered from what must have seemed the caprices and vagaries of higher headquarters. The 489th Bombardment Group (H) and the 369th Air Service Group were processed at Bradley Field, Windsor Locks, Connecticut, in the latter part of December 1944.* Personnel of the two groups scattered to their homes for 30 days on TDY for "Rehabilitation, Recuperation, and Recovery." They were to report to the Second Air Force on 22 January 1945. Relatively minor personnel adjustments were contemplated: at least 50 per cent of the ground personnel with more than one year of overseas experience would be replaced, the bombardiers would be given transition training from the Sperry to the Norden bombsight, the navigators would get a refresher course in celestial navigation and instruction in the use of Loran equipment, and the other combat crew members would go to Davis-Monthan Field to receive such refresher training as might be required and to await the arrival of their "fly-away" B-24's. On 23 January Second Air Force was informed that plans had been changed: the 489th was to become a B-29 outfit and the 369th was to be trained for very heavy bombardment (VHB) support. It was "typical of the administrative fumbling which characterized the entire redeployment program," reported the historian of the Second Air Force, "that official word of the redesignation of the 489th as a very heavy bombardment group was not received by Headquarters, Second Air Force, until about 20 March 1945—two months after the decision had been taken. During all this time it was necessary to maintain two rosters of personnel—one for a heavy bombardment group of four squadrons, the other for a very heavy bombardment group of three squadrons—and to report strength, overages, and shortages of personnel on the basis of two different Tables of Organization."[53] The readiness dates, which had been 15 February for the 369th and the ground echelon of the 489th and 1 March for the air and flight echelons of the 489th, were changed to 1 June and 1 August.

It appears that the original intention was to have the Second Air

---

* Some small units had been sent to the United States for redeployment even before this time. The 1st Air Combat Control Squadron, Amphibious, had arrived on 10 October, the 683d Signal Aircraft Warning Company on 7 November, and the 1st Composite Squadron on 18 November. All three were processed by the Third Air Force, the first at Hunter Field and the other two at Gulfport Army Air Field.

Force redeploy 23 combat groups.[54] As it actually turned out, the Second Air Force was made responsible for the conversion and redeployment of four VHB wings, each consisting of four VHB groups and their associated service groups. Of these 32 groups, only one—the 369th Air Service Group—was redeployed; one other—the 489th Bombardment Group (VH)—was at a port of embarkation when the end of the war brought about the cancellation of the sailing. Eleven other bombardment groups and ten service groups belonging to the 47th, 20th, and 96th Bombardment Wings were partially manned; but none had completed training, and only one had been assigned any combat crews at war's end. The groups of the remaining wing, the 13th, existed only on paper.[55]

In addition to the 369th, only two groups—the 319th Bombardment Group and the 514th Air Service Group—were actually redeployed through the United States, both by the First Air Force. The Third and Fourth Air Forces and the I Troop Carrier Command did not complete the redeployment of any major units. Both the First and Third Air Forces operated intermediate processing stations (IPS), the former at Bradley Field, Connecticut, and the latter at Hunter Field, Georgia.[56]

All four ZI air forces and the I Troop Carrier Command operated central assembly stations (CAS). At these installations, according to the original plan, units would receive old members as they returned from their RR&R, screen out any who had become ineligible for redeployment, accept replacements to bring the organization up to authorized strength, and then depart for the base at which they were to be trained for their new mission. In practice, the returnee, upon arrival at the CAS, was assigned to a squadron—frequently "X"—which was just a pool for replacements. If his old organization was one that was to be redeployed, he might or might not be reassigned to it. If he was aware that the reorganized group would have little in common with the outfit he had known, except the designation and a few key personnel, he might not much care whether he rejoined it or cast his lot with a different unit.[57]

The experiences of the first groups to be returned to the United States for redeployment to the Pacific vividly illustrate the best and the worst features of the redeployment program. The story of the 489th Bombardment Group and the 369th Air Service Group has just been told. The next two major units to arrive for redeployment were the 319th Bombardment Group (M) and its associated group, the 514th Air Service Group. The members of these units were processed at Bradley Field in January 1945 and had the same kind of pleasant treatment that had been so much enjoyed by personnel of the 489th Bombardment Group and the 369th Air Service Group some five weeks earlier. " 'Bradley was wonderful,' one of them said. 'I couldn't believe it was the Army—it was so efficient.' "[58] The task of converting the two organizations from B-25's* to A-26's was originally assigned to the Third Air Force; but on 1 February 1945 the groups were assigned to the First Air Force, and their conversion training was carried out at the First Air Force's Columbia Army Air Base, South Carolina.[59]

If there had been doubt in the minds of members of the 319th and 514th about their being in the Army while they were at Bradley Field, that doubt was promptly dispelled when they reassembled, after RR&R, at Columbia AAB. No one factor was responsible for the confusion, the chaos, that surrounded the two groups during the period of their assignment to the First Air Force. The groups' officer and enlisted personnel, Columbia AAB personnel, and the higher echelon headquarters involved—First Air Force, Continental Air Forces, and Army Air Forces—all contributed in various ways and in varying degrees to the mess that existed at Columbia in the spring of 1945. The trouble started overseas, where the groups' administrative personnel had evidently "been more interested in watching operations . . . than in keeping up their paper work."[60] Records were so incomplete that it was estimated "that 75 per cent of the records of the 319th and 65 per cent of those of the 514th had to be completely remade at Columbia."[61] It can well be understood that this situation did nothing to endear the newcomers to such Columbia AAB personnel as had to work overtime to get the group records in shape. Nor did the superciliousness with which members of the groups looked upon permanent party personnel as stay-at-homes do anything to improve relations between group and base personnel; it was particularly galling to those permanent party members who had had quite as much combat experience as any member of the 319th.[62]

When processing got under way at Columbia, and it became apparent that the groups that would go to the Pacific would be very differ-

---

* The 319th Bombardment Group had been converted from B-26's to B-25's in the MTO.

ent from those that had returned from the MTO, morale immediately collapsed. Col. Joseph R. Holzapple, who had commanded the 319th since August 1943, had anticipated that 20 per cent of his personnel would have to be replaced. But when all those with more than one year's overseas service, those with dependent children, those over forty years of age, and those made ineligible by reclassification or medical disqualification had been eliminated, the replacement figure for the two groups proved to be 76 per cent. The eliminees were replaced by fillers from the First Air Force. The organizations contributing personnel were under orders to provide capable, qualified replacements. Some commanders, no doubt, unselfishly sacrificed key men whom they could ill afford to lose; a larger number apparently took advantage of the opportunity to rid themselves of misfits and incompetents. Hence many of the replacements sent to the 319th and 514th proved to be in no wise qualified for the jobs they were expected to perform and had themselves to be replaced.[63]

An equally serious difficulty in remanning the two groups was that many of the men sent as replacements had not had the ten-day furlough required by POM directives. At first the officers of the groups, of Columbia AAB, and of Headquarters, First Air Force, thought that this would make no difference, that men could be sent overseas without furloughs on the ground of military necessity. But it was War Department policy that any man who had not had the required furlough was to be left behind; and the Deputy Chief of Air Staff ruled that that policy must be followed in the case of the 319th and 514th.[64]

It had been intended to have processing and such basic training as might be required all finished before the unit training began. The base officials had expected to supervise the individual training rather closely and then to allow the groups a large measure of independence in their operational training.[65] Since many members of the groups had applied for and received extensions of their RR&R, and since many First Air Force units were slow in supplying fillers, the processing dragged on and had not been completed when training began on 6 March.[66] From that time on training and processing were conflicting activities.

Even after operational training got under way there were difficulties such as conflicts in training schedules and shortages of essential training equipment.[67] Moreover, the Columbia AAB authorities thought it necessary that they should take a larger part in the group training program than had originally been intended; and there was, for a while, some confusion as to the division of responsibility between officers of the base and those of the groups. Nevertheless, "training progressed well enough so that required standards were met by the time the postponed readiness dates rolled around—which is another way of saying that the dates had to be set back in order that training could be finished."[68] The two groups left Columbia for Seattle on 26 April and embarked for Okinawa on 7 May, arriving at their destination on 3 July.[69]

Lest it be thought that Columbia Army Air Base was unique in having troubles, let the situation at Sioux Falls Army Air Field be considered. The Strategic Air Command (SAC) historian wrote, almost a year after the event: "If Sioux Falls wasn't the busiest army air field in the United States during redeployment it certainly was one of the most chaotic. 'Organized confusion' was a term regularly and apparently aptly applied to the situation by the base personnel."[70]

By the summer of 1945 the problem confronting the central assembly stations, of which Sioux Falls was the largest, was not to find fillers for units being redeployed; it was to get rid of returnees for whom there were no facilities for training and entertaining, even, in some instances, for housing and feeding. It was found that almost three-fourths of the officers and more than one-fifth of the enlisted men reassembling at Sioux Falls were eligible for separation; but with the ASF separation centers hopelessly bogged down, separation quotas and transportation to the centers were both lacking. Nor were those eligible for redeployment more fortunate; the overloaded Training Command could not or would not take them. Some found places in permanent party organizations; the rest just waited. During the first ten days of July more than 8,000 individuals had assembled at Sioux Falls to be separated or redeployed. Returnees continued to arrive until, by the end of the month, more than 20,000 had been processed; but only 6,382 had been shipped out. In August more than 30,000 additional returnees were received, and during September almost 8,000. In the three months a total of 48,738 were shipped out, leaving, at the end of September, more than 10,000 awaiting, by that time, not redeployment but separation.[71] As this experience suggests, the problems of demobilization threatened to swamp the machinery established for redeployment.

It is not surprising that, when Japan surrendered in mid-August

1945, the units redeployed from Europe to the Asiatic-Pacific theaters were still insignificant in number. Perhaps the setback AAF planners had suffered when Germany failed to collapse on schedule, in the fall of 1944, caused them to be caught off balance when V-E Day did come, despite the fact that it had been so long in sight; perhaps it was merely the magnitude of the operation that made the redeployment machine so slow in getting under way. It had been the original intention to send many units of the Eighth, Twelfth, and Fifteenth Air Forces (the Ninth was to be the occupation air force in Europe) direct to the Asiatic and Pacific bases from which they could most effectively operate against the Japanese. But on 15 May 1945 the War Department issued a "Revised Redeployment Forecast." This provided that only the headquarters and ancillary units of the VIII Air Force Service Command, two air-service groups, and one fighter-wing headquarters would go direct; all other organizations were to be disbanded or inactivated in the theater or sent to the United States for redeployment to the Pacific, assignment to the strategic reserve, or inactivation.[72]

What actually happened was that Eighth Air Force headquarters was transferred, on 16 July 1945, less personnel and equipment, to Okinawa (it was manned in the new theater by personnel from the XX Bomber Command and from the Zone of Interior, along with a few key figures from the old Eighth Air Force); seven bombardment groups, three fighter groups, and a number of service units were transferred to the Ninth Air Force to become part of the occupation air force; seven of the Eighth's bombardment groups, with their associated service groups, were transferred to the Air Transport Command; and 2,192 heavy bombers, with crews, were used in the HOME RUN (otherwise known as the WHITE plan) project—transporting personnel from the ETO and MTO to the United States. Redeployment began in the Twelfth Air Force even before R (for redeployment) Day—12 May 1945. The movement of the 319th Bombardment Group and the 369th and 514th Air Service Groups to the United States and eventually to Okinawa has already been discussed. A good many other units—among them a fighter group, two bombardment groups, and six air-service groups—had been scheduled for direct redeployment to the Pacific during the spring and summer; instead they were sent to the United States, and most of them were inactivated soon after arrival in the Zone of Interior.* Many other units were disbanded, discontinued, or inactivated in the theater. There is evidence that the Fifteenth Air Force intended to redeploy directly to the Pacific the 734th Military Police Battalion and the 31st and 52d Fighter Groups, as well as a number of other organizations. Instead, the fighter groups were sent to the United States, and what happened to the military-police battalion is a bit of a mystery.† Thus it appears that redeployment from the ETO and MTO was limited to one bombardment group, the 319th, and two air-service groups, the 369th and 514th, all deployed through the United States. No record has been found of any major unit's having been redeployed directly to the CBI or the Pacific between V-E and V-J Days.[73]

Demobilization

Demobilization of the AAF had its beginning before Japan's surrender in August 1945. The AAF had reached its peak strength in military personnel in March, 1944. At that time, 306,889 officers and 2,104,405 enlisted men comprised a total of 2,411,294.‡ During the

* Two flights of the 1st Emergency Rescue Squadron were sent to the CBI in January 1945. Two Twelfth Air Force units, the 35th Fighter Group and the 547th Air Service Group, had got as far on their way to the Pacific as the Panama Canal on V-J Day; with the announcement of the Japanese surrender, orders were changed, and the transport headed for New York.

† The historian of the Fifteenth Air Force wrote: "On 9 June the 734th Military Police Battalion . . . departed the Air Force for the Pacific Ocean Area" (Hist. 15th AF, 1 May–31 July 1945, p. 8). The historian of the 5th Wing, to which the 734th was assigned, says that personnel of the military-police battalion were replaced by a squadron guard made up of individuals selected from various units of the wing (Hist. 5th Wg., June 1945, p. 1); and the unit is omitted from the list of components of the wing given on the title page of the June installment of the wing's history. It is listed, however, in the July and August installments as one of the wing's components.

‡ The following table represents total AAF personnel at the end of the months indicated:

Month	Total	Commissioned	Enlisted	Month	Total	Commissioned	Enlisted
1944				1945			
Mar.	2,411,294	306,889	2,104,405	Nov.	1,200,247	200,152	1,000,095
June	2,372,292	333,401	2,038,891	Dec.	888,769	164,004	724,765
Sept.	2,391,281	357,924	2,033,357	1946			
Dec.	2,359,456	375,973	1,983,483	Jan.	733,786	141,643	592,143
1945				Feb.	564,605	115,243	449,362
Jan.	2,345,068	377,426	1,967,642	Mar.	500,472	102,286	398,186
Feb.	2,324,377	385,111	1,939,266	Apr.	485,151	95,906	389,245
Mar.	2,325,842	385,916	1,939,926	May	472,563	88,746	383,817
Apr.	2,328,534	388,278	1,941,256	June	455,515	81,733	373,782
May	2,310,436	388,295	1,922,141	July	450,626	72,983	377,643
June	2,282,259	381,454	1,900,805	Aug.	441,852	68,452	373,400
July	2,262,092	371,269	1,890,823	Sept.	419,670	65,991	353,679
Aug.	2,253,182	368,344	1,884,838	Oct.	406,802	61,252	345,550
Sept.	1,992,960	310,443	1,682,517	Nov.	373,960	50,722	323,328
Oct.	1,553,867	241,226	1,312,641	Dec.	341,413	49,529	291,884

The low mark in the postwar era was reached in May 1947 with a total of 303,614.

second quarter of 1944 there was a decrease of 65,614 in the number of enlisted men; but the decline in total strength was only 39,002, because in the same period commissioned strength increased by more than 26,000. This loss of enlisted personnel seems to have been attributable largely to involuntary transfers from the AAF to the AGF—transfers that were noticeable especially in the ETO. There was an increase of some 22,000 AAF enlisted personnel in July but a net loss for the third quarter of 1944 amounting to 5,534. Continued losses in the last three months of the year brought the number of enlisted personnel below the 2,000,000 mark—to 1,983,483, as of 1 January 1945. Officer strength continued to increase month by month; at the end of 1944 it was 375,973. The phenomenon of decreasing enlisted strength and increasing officer strength continued through the first five months of 1945; an increase in May brought the number of AAF officers to the peak figure of 388,295; a total of 1,922,141 in enlisted personnel made a combined total of 2,310,436.[74] The decline between 30 May and 31 August was only 57,354, but after V-J Day the reduction in force was greatly accelerated. By the end of 1945 the total strength of the AAF, commissioned and enlisted, was only 888,769. This figure was lowered in January by 154,983; in February by 169,181; and in March by 64,133. Total AAF strength in military personnel at the end of March 1946 was only a little more than half a million.[75]

This rapid demobilization had been made possible by the AAF's assumption of a large part of the responsibility for the separation from the service of its own personnel. The operation of separation centers had initially been assigned to the Army Service Forces, which at the beginning of September 1945 had some twenty-two centers with an estimated total monthly capacity of 300,000. At that time the backlog of those eligible for separation already stood at approximately 500,000, and it was expected that the rate at which veterans were returning from overseas theaters would reach a comparable figure by 1 October. Consequently, on 1 September Headquarters, AAF, called upon CAF to submit a plan for separating AAF personnel at AAF installations. The plan was submitted on 3 September and won prompt approval from Headquarters, AAF. War Department approval was quickly secured; and on 6 September Commanding General, CAF, was directed to undertake the separation of AAF personnel in the Zone of Interior as such personnel became eligible for separation under RR 1-1.[76]

Permanent party personnel of the Personnel Distribution Command

and individuals being processed in PDC installations were to be separated by PDC rather than CAF. This exception in favor of PDC was later countermanded; effective 19 October 1945, CAF was given complete responsibility for AAF separations.[77] In addition, the term of CAF's responsibility was extended beyond the original date of 1 December 1945 "for whatever period is necessary to provide for prompt separation of all eligible personnel in the Z/I, in excess of the capacity of WD separation centers."[78] The CAF promptly set up thirty-two separation bases, all of them being in operation by 26 September. The daily rate of separation rose during the first week of operations from 754 to 2,395, and by 30 September had reached 3,948.[79]

Changes as of 1 October in War Department rules governing separation, one of which was the lowering of the critical score from 80 to 70,* made some 84,500 enlisted men and women eligible for separation. Thus, despite the fact that more than 31,500 were separated during the month of September, the backlog of AAF candidates for separation was larger in early October than it had been in mid-September.[80] However, the AAF separation bases operated with efficiency and dispatch; by 1 November 304,564 members of the AAF had been separated, and there was no backlog.[81] The number of AAF separations during November was 208,945,† and separation bases were being inactivated. By the middle of December, CAF had secured AAF approval of a plan to operate, beginning 1 January 1946, separation bases at only nine installations, with a total daily capacity of 2,800. Having accomplished their mission, these bases were closed between 9 and 18 February 1946. On 20 February CAF announced that its separation program was concluded, with 734,715 officers and enlisted personnel having been processed at AAF separation bases.[82]

* The critical score had been reduced from 85 to 80 on 3 September (*Army-Navy Register,* 8 Sept. 1945, p. 7). On 1 November it was lowered again; enlisted men with ASR scores between 50 and 59, inclusive, and two years of active service, and enlisted women with scores between 29 and 33, inclusive, with one year of active service, became eligible for separation (Daily diary, D&PR Br., AC/AS-1, 31 Oct. 1945). At the end of November an enlisted man who was the father of three or more children under eighteen was entitled to be separated (*ibid.,* 29 Nov. 1945). There were successive lowerings of the critical score, the idea being to have the score at such point by March 1946 that at that time all enlisted men with two years of service would have the number of points required for separation; the point system would then be abolished and two years of service would be the criterion for eligibility for separation (*Army-Navy Register,* 13 Oct. 1945, p. 5).

† This figure is very nearly 70 per cent of the total number of separations at AAF personnel that occurred during the month; only 144,675 were separated by ASF centers, hospitals, and other installations.

No less impressive is the rate of demobilization by unit. Between the Japanese surrender in mid-August 1945 and the following Christmas the AAF was reduced from 218 groups to 109. In other words, the force had been cut in half (by this standard of measurement) within the span of four months, and the rate continued precipitously downward through the first half of 1946. By the end of June the nominal strength of the AAF, then 54 groups, had been cut in half again.* Actually, the real loss in terms of effective strength was much greater than even these figures suggest. A plan of demobilization giving priority of separation to the more experienced and the more expert soon took its toll of every unit, and each unit paid twice. First came the loss of key personnel and then their replacement by men drawn from a variety of sources—men who may have had the right MOS but also had little in common with the older members of the unit beyond a desire for early separation from the service. What had been lost was not only key men but that indefinable quality variously described as morale or spirit which, by whatever name, so largely affects the strength of a military organization. As early as October 1945 Maj. Gen. St. Clair Streett of CAF felt compelled to warn General Arnold that "we will have soon reached a point, if it has not been reached, at which the Army Air Forces can no longer be considered anything more than a symbolic instrument of National Defense."[83] In General Streett's view "a potpourri of warm bodies" was no substitute for an air force.

The postwar transition involved things as well as people. On 30 September 1945 the AAF had 1,895 installations, of which 1,333 were located in the Zone of the Interior.† At the end of the year, the latter figure had been reduced to 429, including auxiliary fields.[84] On V-E Day, to take another example, there were in AAF hands in Europe 24,000 spare aircraft engines, 238,000 long tons of technical supplies, nearly 12,000 special-purpose vehicles, and over 466,000 long tons of bombs and ammunition. By 1 January 1946 USAFE had disposed of 19,006 engines, 126,603 tons of technical supplies, 5,151 vehicles, and

---

* The peak strength of the AAF had been reached in March 1945 at 243 groups. The following shows strength in groups at the close of the indicated months from September 1945 through August 1946: September, 201; October, 178; November, 128; December, 109; January, 89; February, 81; March, 71; April, 65; May, 60; June, 54; July, 52; August, 52.

† The peak figure for installations of all kinds, reached by the end of December 1943, was 2,252 (see Vol. VI, 120).

184,950 tons of bombs and ammunition. With its requirements set at 2,099 in the first category, 36,653 in the second, 3,172 in the third, and 67,500 in the fourth, USAFE found itself at the beginning of 1946 facing the prospect of disposing of 3,234 spare engines, 74,771 tons of technical supplies, 3,669 vehicles, and 213,750 tons of bombs and ammunition.[85]

The AAF's role in the disposal of this and other such property was limited by national administrative and legislative action. Planning for economic demobilization had been begun at the White House level as early as 1943. The Surplus Property Act of October 1944 created the Surplus Property Board and made it responsible for the supervision, care, handling, and disposition of surplus property and for its transfer between government agencies. In response to a directive from the Director of the Office of War Mobilization and Reconversion, the Secretary of War and the Secretary of the Navy established the Army-Navy Liquidation Commission; this agency was charged with the disposal of surplus property located outside the United States except that in U.S. territories and possessions. Executive Order 9541, effective 1 May 1945, transferred the Office of Surplus Property, with jurisdiction over surplus property in the United States and its territories and possessions, from the Treasury Department to the Department of Commerce. Congress acted on 18 September 1945 to replace the Surplus Property Board with the Surplus Property Administration. Executive Order 9630, dated 27 September 1945, abolished the Army-Navy Liquidation Commission and transferred to the State Department all authority over the disposal abroad of surplus property. Executive Order 9643, of 19 October 1945, transferred the Office of Surplus Property from the Department of Commerce to the Reconstruction Finance Corporation; the latter immediately created the War Assets Corporation as its agency for handling surplus property. Still another Executive Order—this one 9689, dated 1 February 1946—made the War Assets Corporation responsible for disposal of most surplus property in the United States. And congressional action on 1 August 1946 made the Department of State the sole disposal agency in overseas areas, except Hawaii, Alaska, Puerto Rico, and the Virgin Islands.[86]

The main responsibility falling thus upon AAF organizations was that of declaring to the appropriate agency such of their material stocks as were to be considered surplus to existing and anticipated needs. A few statistics selected from the great plethora of those available will be sufficient to suggest the scale of these transfers. Much AAF equipment was covered by bulk sales agreements with the British, French, and Italian governments negotiated during 1946, the first being one entered into in March with Great Britain at a contract figure of $532,000,000. By the end of 1946 the Office of the Foreign Liquidation Commissioner in Europe had disposed of AAF property listed at the following totals: airplanes, $47,000,000; airplane and other parts, $274,300,000; bombs and ammunition, $117,800,000.[87] Early reports from the depots of the Far East Air Service Command showed that over 30 per cent of AAF property on hand had been declared surplus by November 1945. The sale of aircraft originally costing $120,000 a piece for a little more than $19,000 each is suggestive of the phenomenal losses sustained in postwar disposal of surplus items.[88] In the ZI, the Air Materiel Command by the end of January 1947 could report a total of $4,800,000,000 in surplus property. Of this total, property worth $226,000,000 had been "transferred, donated, or redistributed"; items worth $843,000,000 had been shipped on War Assets Administration (WAA) instructions; AAF disposal in scrap and salvage accounted for $2,227,000,000; and the remainder—worth $1,504,000,000—had been declared to WAA but was still in AAF possession awaiting instructions from WAA.[89]

Included in the property not declared surplus were some 15,000 aircraft—B-17's, B-24's, B-29's, A-26's, P-47's, P-51's, PT-13's, C-46's, C-47's, and P-80's—that were stored for possible later use by the AAF and reserve organizations. Of 24,114 AAF planes in continental United States on 1 May 1946, there were 8,224 in use, 840 had been declared excess, and 15,050 were in storage.* The storage program presented many difficulties. Of the eight depots employed, some had unfavorable climatic conditions, others limited space. A new technique of cocooning—the plane was covered with a layer of webbing and then sprayed with a liquid which hardened into a protective envelope—promised at first to answer all storage problems. But experience soon proved, despite obvious merits in the technique, that there were bugs to be worked out.[90]

Meanwhile, the end of hostilities had brought to a halt the huge and varied procurement program of the AAF except such parts of it as

---

* The total of aircraft on hand, including those belonging to overseas units, as of that date was just over 36,000.

were necessary for the curtailed operations of the future. A freeze was ordered until all inventories had been checked and all actions involving cancellations, reinstatements, and new procurements had been completely co-ordinated. Simultaneously, General Arnold suspended all modification of aircraft until the AAF could be certain that it was not "shoeing any more dead horses."[91] The Materiel Command's procurement personnel dropped from 25,443 in July 1945 to 8,308 by 1 January 1946, and by the end of 1946 the total was down to 2,871.[92] As wartime procurement gave way to postwar programs, the AAF by 30 July 1946 had contracts for $654,000,000, with twenty-seven aircraft companies, of which total $479,000,000 was for production and $175,000,000 for research and development.[93]

Organization adjustments to the fact of demobilization were rendered additionally complex by a national policy that looked forward to the maintenance of military forces outside our own territories for an indefinite period of time and by the prospect that the AAF might fulfil its ambition for equality with the Army and the Navy in the postwar organization of national defense. Although this last question remained unsettled in any final sense until the enactment of the National Defense Act of 1947, all interim plans were made in the expectation that a long-deferred ambition would be soon achieved. Much less subject to the uncertainties of future policy were the immediate demands for occupation forces in Europe and the Far East, not to mention the intervening bases and air routes that were necessary to the maintenance of those forces.

At the close of the war with Germany in May 1945, the AAF was represented in ETO and MTO by four air forces: the Eighth, Ninth, Twelfth, and Fifteenth. As has been previously noted, the first of these had been selected for redeployment against Japan and reequipped with B-29's. The Ninth, largest of all the wartime air forces and as a tactical organization one of the most diversified in its equipment and potentialities, had been selected as the occupation air force.[94] This left the Twelfth and Fifteenth for inactivation or reassignment. It may seem that the history of each of these great air forces and of their superior headquarters—Mediterranean Allied Air Forces (MAAF) in the MTO and United States Strategic Air Forces (USTAF) in the ETO—should be brought to a neat ending at whatever point of time they ceased to exist or were reassigned. But the end of an air force, like its beginning, presents a bewildering complex of paper actions—activations and inactivations, assignments and reassignments, covering a multitude of subordinate organizations—that has appeal only for those who enjoy the antiquarian's interest in the record for its own sake. Subordinate units may survive the parent organization with designations perpetuating the memory of the parent long after its demise, as in the case of the XII Tactical Air Command, which outlived its parent, the Twelfth Air Force. And so let it be noted here, merely, that the great concentrations of air power which helped to win the war in Europe began soon after the victory to disappear as their units were inactivated, redeployed, or reassigned—some of them looking like themselves in a reincarnation, some of them having no resemblance whatsoever to the original. In time, it became necessary to do something about the superior headquarters which no longer presided over a military force sufficient to have any real utility, and these famous commands might have their ends in nothing more than the inactivation or redesignation of a headquarters squadron. For whatever it may be worth to the historian or the antiquarian, let it be recorded that USSTAF had its ending with the redesignation to Headquarters and Headquarters Squadron, United States Air Forces in Europe (USAFE), on 16 August 1945. MAAF* was dissolved on 31 July 1945, and its AAF functions were taken over by Army Air Forces in the Mediterranean Theater of Operations (AAF/MTO); the latter was discontinued on 1 October 1945. It has already been noted† that Headquarters, Eighth Air Force, was transferred, less personnel and equipment, to Okinawa on 16 July 1945. The Twelfth Air Force was inactivated on 31 August 1945 and the Fifteenth on 15 September of the same year.[95]

Much more to the point is the fact that in March 1946 there were 47,544 members of the AAF in the European theater, and 2,555 in the Mediterranean area.[96] USAFE had set up its headquarters in Wiesbaden, Germany, in September 1945;[97] to the command were assigned the XII Tactical Air Command, with two fighter wings, a reconnaissance group, a photo-reconnaissance group, an air service group, a tactical control group, and other auxiliary units; the European Air Transport Service, with a troop-carrier wing; the European Aviation Engineer Command, with an engineer aviation regiment; the AAF/European Theater Reinforcement Depot; the Base Air Depot Area

---

* MAAF was a joint RAF-AAF operational headquarters.

† See above, p. 565.

573

(at Burtonwood, England); the 40th Bombardment Wing; and the European Air Materiel Command (originally IX Air Force Service Command).[98]

Much larger were the forces (71,959) at that time still deployed in the Pacific under the control of, at first, either United States Army Strategic Air Forces in the Pacific (USASTAF)—the Eighth and Twentieth Air Forces—or Far East Air Forces (FEAF)—the Fifth, Seventh, and Thirteenth Air Forces. However, on 6 December 1945 USASTAF was abolished by the inactivation of its headquarters and headquarters squadron, and FEAF was redesignated Pacific Air Command;[99] the new command assumed jurisdiction over all AAF units in the Pacific except those belonging to the Air Transport Command. The five Pacific Air Forces had a total of six very-heavy-bombardment groups, nine fighter groups, two light-bombardment groups, and two troop-carrier groups, along with three tactical reconnaissance, five air-sea rescue, five night-fighter, two liaison, two tow-target, and two very-long-range photographic-reconnaissance squadrons. The Fifth Air Force was deployed in Japan, the Eighth and Thirteenth in the Philippines, the Twentieth in the Marianas, and the Seventh in Hawaii. There was also the Pacific Air Service Command, later Far East Air Service Command.[100]

In China the AAF was represented in March 1946 by 7,668 of its personnel, who functioned under the control of Headquarters, United States Army Air Forces, China; the command had dwindled from two air forces,* one air service command, and one photographic group to an aggregation comprising one fighter squadron, a two-squadron troop-carrier group, two air-service groups, one air-depot group, one airdrome squadron, two military-police companies, one weather squadron, and one Army Airways Communications System group.[101] In Alaska the Eleventh Air Force had been redesignated Alaskan Air Command (AAC) on 21 December 1945; at the end of March 1946 its components, in addition to its headquarters and headquarters squadron and various service troops, were one fighter group of three squad-

---

* When Rangoon came into Allied hands in May of 1945, the air phase of the war in Burma was virtually concluded; hence the Eastern Air Command, which had exercised jurisdiction over the Tenth Air Force and various other AAF units in the India-Burma theater, was disbanded on 1 June 1945, and the Tenth Air Force was transferred to China to become part of USAAF, China (The Deployment of the AAF to China from India and Events after August 1945, p. 1). The Tenth and Fourteenth Air Forces were inactivated at Seattle, Washington, on 6 January 1946 (GO 1, ASF Seattle POE, 2 Jan. 1946).

rons and one heavy bombardment and one troop-carrier squadron.[102] In the Caribbean the Sixth Air Force was redesignated Caribbean Air Command (CAC) on 31 July 1946; at the time of the redesignation the CAC's personnel strength of 7,934—almost 5,000 greater than it had been at the beginning of 1946—was distributed among fourteen squadrons: four heavy-bombardment, six fighter, two reconnaissance, one troop carrier, and two tow target.[103]

At the end of the war the Air Transport Command (ATC) was operating with nine divisions, eight foreign and one domestic. One year later there were only three—the Atlantic, Pacific, and European Divisions. The Ferrying Division, having taken over the Alaskan Division, was renamed the Continental Division. Then the Continental Division was absorbed by the Atlantic Division, as were also the North Atlantic, South Atlantic, and Caribbean Divisions. The India-China Division terminated its Hump operations in November 1945; its other activities were taken over early in 1946 by the Pacific and North African Divisions. The North African Division, in turn, was taken over by the European Division. In the course of this contraction and consolidation ATC personnel strength was reduced from its August 1945 peak of 209,201 military and 104,667 civilian personnel to 42,090 military and 17,590 civilian personnel in December 1946.[104] The mission of ATC was substantially enlarged in March 1946 when the Army Airways Communications System, the AAF Weather Service, the Aeronautical Chart Service, the Flying Safety Service, and the Air Rescue Service were all assigned to it. But a trend toward an over-all reduction of activity was emphasized in regulations of June 1946 defining ATC's transport operations as "supplementary" to those of U.S. civil air carriers. Upon ATC fell the responsibility for maintaining necessary liaison with the civil airlines, except for such technical matters as might belong to the Materiel Command.

Reorganization of the AAF

In March 1946 ATC had become one of the eight major commands into which the AAF was at that time divided. At the end of the war the AAF's basic organization depended upon the following subordinate commands: Air Technical Service, Air Transport, Training, Proving Ground, and Personnel Distribution, plus the Continental Air Forces, which had as components the I Troop Carrier Command and the four U.S.–based air forces—First, Second, Third, and Fourth. After considering a variety of alternatives, the AAF put into effect on 21 March 1946 a plan providing for the Strategic Air Command, Tactical Air Command, Air Defense Command, Air Materiel Command, Air Training Command, Air Transport Command, Air Proving Ground, and Air University Command. At the same time the CAF was inactivated. Headquarters, CAF, in effect, became Headquarters, SAC. The Second Air Force, at the time when SAC was activated, was relieved from assignment to CAF and assigned to SAC; but a few days later it was inactivated and assigned, in an inactive status, to Air Defense Command. Other CAF components, except the First, Third, and Fourth Air Forces and the IX Troop Carrier Command, were assigned to SAC. Personnel of the Second Air Force were used to man the Fifteenth Air Force, which at this time was reactivated and assigned to SAC.[105] The Air Defense Command (ADC), with headquarters at Mitchel Field, New York, assumed full responsibility for the air defense of the continental United States* and for co-ordinating air defense activity supplied by other services.[106]

The Tactical Air Command (TAC), established first at Tampa, Florida, and moved in the latter part of May 1946 to Langley Field, Virginia, originally had as its components three air forces—the Third, the Ninth, and the Twelfth; with the inactivation of the Third on 1 November 1946, the number was reduced to two.[107] The stated mission of TAC was "to participate in joint operations with ground and/or sea forces; to co-operate with the Air Defense Command in the air defense mission; to operate independently in offensive operations; to train units and personnel for the maintenance of the tactical forces in all parts of the world; to co-operate with Army Ground Forces in training of airborne troops; to perform such special missions as the Commanding General, Army Air Forces may direct."[108] In

---

* To carry out its mission, ADC planned to use six air forces, one for each Army Area. The First Air Force would be responsible for the New York–New England territory. The Eleventh Air Force, reactivated at Olmsted Field, Pennsylvania, on 13 June 1946, would have the region of which the corners are Indiana, Pennsylvania, Virginia, and Kentucky. The Fourteenth Air Force, reactivated at Orlando Army Air Base, Florida, on 24 May 1946 would be assigned the southeastern states—Tennessee, Mississippi, Alabama, North and South Carolina, Georgia, and Florida. The Tenth, reactivated at Brooks Field, on 24 May 1946, would have jurisdiction over New Mexico, Texas, Oklahoma, Arkansas, and Louisiana. The Second Air Force, activated at Fort Crook, Nebraska, on 6 June 1946, would serve Wyoming, Colorado, North and South Dakota, Nebraska, Kansas, Minnesota, Iowa, Missouri, Wisconsin, Illinois, and Michigan. The Fourth Air Force, at Hamilton Field, California, would defend the eight westernmost states.

sum, SAC, TAC, and ADC shared the responsibility for the AAF's combat missions.

The functions and organizational structure of the Air Technical Service Command (ATSC)—which had been created in 1944 by the merger of the Materiel Command and the Air Service Command— were in a state of continual change during 1945. These structural and functional changes varied in nature and degree. Some were total innovations, some were slight revisions of existing structures or practices. All were the result of an attempt to improve ATSC's wartime organization and to make its working structure more suitable for peacetime operations. When ATSC became the Air Materiel Command (AMC) on 9 March 1946, the new command's chief postwar task had already been made clear: to transform a huge, sprawling, production-at-any-price organization into a compact, efficient, cost-conscious and economy-minded concern. The AMC continued to provide logistical and technical support to the AAF in the fields of research and development, procurement, supply, and maintenance, but the emphasis shifted from quantity production for immediate needs to long-range programs which would improve the quality of AAF performance.[109]

Uncertainty as to the ultimate size, form, and functions of various elements of the postwar defense organization exerted a harmful influence on all AMC operations. The Bureau of the Budget, for example, twice proposed to Congress a year's moratorium on all research and development. With the sword of Damocles thus hanging over it, the AMC Engineering Division could not be sure that it had any mission at all. Also acute budgetary troubles began to plague the AMC with attendant reductions in force and cancellation of programs. A formidable workload of essentially unproductive activities had fallen to the command as a result of the war's termination. Vast amounts of aircraft and aeronautical equipment spread out all over the globe had to be disposed of or stored for possible future use. What in normal time would be a relatively minor function then required thousands of employees and produced endless complications. Not only did materiel have to be disposed of but the vastly expanded facilities of the command—and of the whole complex of ZI installations as well —had to be reduced to a size commensurate with new requirements. Stations had to be inactivated, warehouses consolidated, and leased property vacated. The completion of this activity was greatly hampered by the lack of firm planning commitments by higher authority.

The elimination of excess properties was retarded by necessary retention of numerous installations for possible future use (such as for the Air Reserve program), by political pressures in some localities, and by delays in the acceptance of stocks by the War Assets Administration. Another postwar workload was the adjustment, settlement, and disposal of wartime procurement contracts cancelled after V-J Day. This involved task was the preoccupation of the procurement activity of AMC throughout 1946.

At the same time it was necessary for AMC to assume certain new responsibilities, such as the evaluation, for purposes of technical intelligence, of a vast number of captured enemy records. Little wonder that Headquarters, AMC, remained large in proportion to the size of the command throughout 1946. Though the strength of the command was reduced during the year from 166,000 to 99,000, the personnel strength of the headquarters remained constant at about 15,000.[110]

Less difficult was the postwar adjustment of another wartime giant, the AAF Training Command, which had begun to dwindle long before the war ended. Indeed, the decline in technical training began in the middle of 1943 and that in flying training during 1944.[111] After the merger of the Flying Training Command and the Technical Training Command in July 1943, the resultant AAF Training Command (AAFTC) had become an organization of three flying training commands—comprising twenty-two flying training wings—and three technical training commands. At the beginning of 1946 standard pilot training was being conducted at eight Training Command stations, but early in the year it was discontinued at three of these.[112] In August 1945 commissioned strength of AAFTC had been 89,852, and the enlisted strength was 336,648; by the end of the year the command had only 30,118 officers and 129,422 enlisted men. Personnel strength continued to decline throughout the next twelve months, and by the end of 1946 the commissioned strength was 7,866 and the enlisted strength 77,470.[113]

On V-J Day the AAF Proving Ground Command (AAFPGC) at Eglin Field, Florida, was part of the AAF Center. Other components of the center were the AAF School, the AAF Board, and the Arctic, Desert, and Tropic Branch; these three components and Headquarters, AAF Center, were at Orlando, Florida. The AAFPGC consisted of single base units at Aberdeen, Maryland; Edgewood, Maryland; Madison, Indiana; Hope, Arkansas; Tooele, Utah; Huntsville, Alabama; Watertown, South Dakota; Muroc, California; and Pinecastle, Florida, with three base units at Eglin Field, Florida. There was also the Cold Weather Testing Detachment in the Arctic. On 8 March 1946 the AAF Proving Ground Command at Eglin Field became the AAF Proving Ground (AFPG); at the same time the designation AAF Center was dropped, and the headquarters at Orlando became Headquarters, AAF Proving Ground.[114] At the time of the redesignation the military personnel of the command comprised 1,554 officers and 5,741 enlisted personnel. By the end of 1946 officer strength had declined to 544, but enlisted strength had increased to 6,872. On 24 June 1946 the headquarters at Orlando was moved to Eglin Field; thus the installation at Eglin became the AFPGC, and the term AFPG was dropped. Then, on 10 July 1946, the AAF Proving Ground Command was redesignated Air Proving Ground Command (APGC).

On 19 November 1945 the Army Air Forces School had been transferred from Orlando, Florida, to Maxwell Field, Alabama,[115] prewar home of the Air Corps Tactical School.* Early in 1946 plans were being shaped for concentration under one command at Maxwell of all the AAF's specialized schools. By 6 April 1946 these plans had become firm enough to permit the issuance of an AAF regulation defining the functions of a new Air University intended to incorporate, according to a pattern conventional enough in civilian education but new to the military services, all the AAF's advanced educational programs. The adoption of the term "university" found additional justification in the institution's assumption of responsibility for the encouragement of research activity appropriate to the University's educational mission.

Wartime Planning for the Postwar Air Force

In conclusion, a few words should be added on wartime plans for the postwar air force, a responsibility which had been assigned to the Special Projects Office in 1943.† From the beginning of SPO's activity, AAF leaders had talked in terms of an air force of 105 groups.[116] Plans for the deployment of this force, as expressed in September 1943, called for 21 groups to be assigned to the Atlantic, including Europe and Africa (10 very heavy bombardment, 10 fighter and

* See Vol. I, 46–52.

† See above, p. 549.

fighter-bomber, 1 troop carrier); 58 groups to the Pacific and Asia (25 very heavy bombardment, 1 heavy bombardment, 25 fighter and fighter-bomber, 1 reconnaissance, and 6 troop carrier); and 26 groups to the Zone of Interior, Alaska, and the Canal Zone (5 very heavy bombardment, 1 heavy bombardment, 4 medium and light bombardment, 10 fighter and fighter-bomber, 2 reconnaissance, and 4 troop carrier).[117] It was estimated that combat personnel for 105 groups would total more than a half-million men; with the necessary training and transport troops and antiaircraft artillery, the total personnel would be more than a million. At the estimated annual cost of more than $4,000 per man, a "self-contained, complete U.S. Post War Air Force"[118] would require more than four-fifths of the amount that could realistically be expected to be made available, according to one War Department estimate,[119] for all the armed forces of the country.

The men who drafted these proposals were intelligent men—men who were familiar enough with the realities of national and service politics. Perhaps they understood too well the need to establish a bargaining position before entering into the negotiations through which the tax dollar available to the armed services was customarily divided. Perhaps they saw a need, at a time when the independence of the AAF had not yet been conceded, to take the most aggressive position. Perhaps they spoke chiefly for the record. This was a time of war, when the heaviest penalty on a military leader was imposed for asking less than he might need and when the nation asked only what it could do to save itself. Perhaps these airmen, together with leaders of the other armed services, should be credited with some anticipation of a situation in the postwar world that would quickly make prewar standards for military budgets wholly unrealistic. The historian has trouble in going behind the record to interpret such problems of motivation. He can only state that by mid-February 1944 the AAF was ready with its IPWAF (Initial Post War Air Force) Plan which called for an air force of 105 groups (31 very heavy bombardment, 11 heavy bombardment, 4 medium and light bombardment, 45 fighter and fighter-bomber, 3 reconnaissance, and 11 troop carrier), plus 30 separate squadrons (night fighter, photo reconnaissance, tactical reconnaissance, and mapping). The personnel for such a combat force would total 525,000[120] and would have to be complemented by an equal or larger number of troops for administration, training, and other ZI activities.

By 7 July 1944 all War Department planning had come to be based on an assumption that the grand coalition of Great Britain, the Soviet Union, China, and the United States might be perpetuated into the postwar era to stabilize the world situation. Consequently, PWAF Plan No. 2 on that date projected a 105-group air force for the period "after the defeat of Japan and prior to the establishment of an effective organization to maintain peace."[121] Upon the establishment of such an organization, the Air Force would be reduced to a strength of 75 groups.

On 13 November General Marshall, apparently disturbed by the fact that the then current planning—even with PWAF Plan No. 2 substituted for IPWAF—would require an annual outlay for the armed forces of almost $7,000,000,000, directed a resurvey of postwar military strength. This study was to be based on the assumption that the total annual expenditure for the military would be $5,000,000,000, of which the War Department share would be $2,800,000,000. Allowing $1,500,000,000 for Universal Military Training and $200,000,000 for the Reserve, National Guard, and ROTC, the amount left for the Regular Army, including the AAF, would be $1,100,000,000.[122]

The Committee to Re-survey Postwar Strength, on which the AAF representatives were Maj. Gen. Laurence S. Kuter, Col. George P. Baker, and Col. R. C. Moffat, held an organization meeting on 16 November. At the second meeting, held on 27 November, it was agreed that $1,100,000,000 would be sufficient for an Army of 275,000, of whom 25,000 would be officers. It was further decided that 55,000 of the total should go to the ASF, 100,000 to the AGF, and 120,000 to the AAF.[123] The AAF could hardly quarrel with an allocation that gave it more than 43 per cent of the total;* but a 120,000-man air force was a far cry, indeed, from one of 105 or even 75 groups. It was thought in the AAF that a proper distribution of the 120,000 would assign 30,000 to overhead and commands and 40,000 to the training establishment, leaving only 50,000 for the tactical components. That number of combat personnel would suffice for fewer than 20 groups.[124] At their third meeting, held on or before 1 December, the members of the committee considered the possibility

---

* Colonel Davison did point out that such an arbitrary division of strength among the three components—without consideration of the mission of each—did not seem wise (Memo for Advisory Council by Col. F. T. Davison, 13 Dec. 1944; see also Memo for Dir. SPD by Col. Davison, 22 Dec. 1944).

of a postwar Army with 400,000 enlisted men. Such an Army would have made possible an air force of from 20 to 24 groups.[125]

The committee's work ended in *War Department Plan for the Post War Military Establishment*, published in November 1945. This document gives no figures to show the number of enlisted men there were to be in the postwar air force; but, since provision is made for an officers' corps of 25,000,[126] it is safe to assume that a total personnel of 275,000 was what the planners had in mind. Thus there would have been a 16-group, 120,000-man air force.

The fortunes of the AAF-USAF did not sink quite that low. The nadir in groups was reached in June 1950, at which time the USAF could muster only 46 groups,[127] many, if not all, of which were below authorized strength;[128] military personnel at this time totaled 411,-277.[129] The low-water mark in personnel was established in May 1947; at that time the total was only 303,614.[130] But in June 1950 came Korea; and, without ever having reached the minimum size once planned for it, the Air Force began to expand.

NOTES

NOTES

✶ ✶ ✶ ✶ ✶ ✶ ✶ ✶ ✶ ✶ ✶

NOTES TO CHAPTER 1

1. Grover Loening, "Ships over the Sea, Possibilities and Limitations of Air Transport in War," *Foreign Affairs*, XX (Apr. 1942), 490–91.

2. ATSC, Development of Transport Airplanes, pp. 47–51, 85–86, 102–5.

3. Leonard Eiserer, "Army Air Corps Outhauls All Domestic Carriers in Volume of Freight Shipments," *American Aviation*, V (1 Aug. 1941), 6; ATSC, Development of Transport Airplanes, pp. 107–9.

4. ATSC, Development of Transport Airplanes, pp. 108–12, 121–22, 134–44, 202; Materiel Division Consolidated Report for the Month of March, 1942, Sec. II, Part I, 51–54; War Production Board Aircraft Branch Report 8-J, 15 Apr. 1942, Tables 16, 24.

5. ATSC, Development of Transport Airplanes, pp. 10–105, 164–88.

6. Munitions Requirements of the AAF for the Defeat of Our Potential Enemies (short title, AWPD/1).

7. *Ibid.*

8. Statistical Hist. of the Air Transport Command, 29 May 1941—31 May 1948, p. 69. The exact figures, for 31 Aug. 1945, are 1,020 four-engine transports and 2,070 two-engine major transports.

9. Memo for C/AAF from Col. E. L. Naiden, 3 Dec. 1941.

10. Pertinent documents and discussion are found in Administrative Hist. of the Ferrying Command, 29 May 1941—30 June 1942, a study by the Historical Branch of ATC.

11. *Ibid.*, pp. 15–20.

12. Quoted in Administrative Hist. of the Air Transport Command, June 1942—Mar. 1943, p. 33.

13. Administrative Hist. ATC, 1941–42, pp. 66–70.

14. *Ibid.*, pp. 71–83.

15. *Ibid.*, pp. 94–95.

16. *Ibid.*, p. 106.

17. *Ibid.*, especially p. 105, for a list of proposed commissions and appointments in the spring of 1942 from among airline executives. Not all who were desired could be secured.

18. *Ibid.*, pp. 109–19.

19. *Ibid.*, p. 117.

20. AAF General Orders #8, 20 June 1942.

21. Administrative Hist. ATC, June 1942—Mar. 1943, pp. 18–21, 28–31.

22. Quoted *ibid.*, pp. 29–30.

23. *Ibid.*, pp. 31–32.

24. *Ibid.*, pp. 8–18.

25. See especially Oliver La Farge, "Strategic Air Supply," *Air Transport*, II (Sept. 1944), 21–25; and the fuller discussion by the same author in *The Eagle in the Egg* (Boston, 1949). Colonel La Farge was historian of ATC during the war years.

26. Ltr., TAG to Commander-in-Chief, SWPA *et al.*, 6 June 1942.

27. Quoted in Administrative Hist. ATC, June 1942—Mar. 1943, p. 136.

28. *Ibid.*, pp. 137–38, quoting TAG Memo #W95-19-42, 21 Sept. 1942.

29. *Ibid.*, pp. 138–39, quoting TAG Memo #W95-6-43, 26 Feb. 1943.

30. Administrative Hist., Ferrying Command, 1941–42, pp. 124–25.

31. Administrative Hist. ATC, 1942–43, pp. 142–50.

32. E.g., Administrative Hist. ATC, Mar. 1943—July 1944, pp. 194–95.

33. *Ibid.*, p. 197.

34. *Ibid.*, pp. 197–205.

35. *Ibid.*, pp. 205–14, for discussion of this and other problems involving relations with the civil airlines.

36. *Ibid.*, p. 216; Administrative Hist. ATC, 1942–43, p. 204; AAF Stat. Digest, pp. 23, 33.

37. AAF Stat. Digest, p. 300.

38. *Ibid.*, pp. 304–5.

39. *Ibid.*, p. 302.

40. For full discussion of these organizational developments of 1943, see Administrative Hist. ATC, 1942–43 and 1943–44, especially summary discussions at the end of each.

41. Executive Order #8974, 13 Dec. 1941.

42. Minutes of Mtg. of Special Aviation Committee, 14 Dec. 1941.

43. Civil Aeronautics Board, Final Report of Changes in War Air Service Pattern, 18 May 1942—15 Oct. 1945, Table 3. This table gives a breakdown by type and ownership of multiengine transport aircraft owned by domestic air carriers at the end of each month from Sept. 1939 to Aug. 1942. Aircraft owned by Pan American Airways were not included in the table, but this information was supplied by CAB to the ATC Historical Office, 10 Jan. 1947. PAA aircraft are included in the totals given here, which are for 30 Nov. 1941.

44. Memo for Sec. of War from Pres. Roosevelt, 6 May 1942. For distribution of aircraft commandeered and those retained by the airlines, see the following: memo for the Sec. of War from Lt. Gen. H. H. Arnold, 9 May 1942; memo for the Military Director of Civil Aviation from Lt. Gen. H. H. Arnold, 9 May 1942; ltr., L. Welch Pogue, Chm, CAB, to Brig. Gen. Donald H. Connolly, 18 May 1942. When the transaction was finally completed, the airlines were left with only 190 DC-3 type aircraft, the remaining 10 being of the lighter Lockheed Lodestar type. Furthermore, 35 of the DC-3's were operated under contract for the aircargo service of the Air Service Command, so that only 165 actually remained for regularly scheduled commercial operations of the carriers, a reduction of over 50 per cent since the opening of the year.

45. Lt. Col. Oliver La Farge, ATC Historical Officer, ATC Transport Aircraft in World War II: A Study of Types, Performance and Fleet Augmentation, pp. 36–37.

46. Development of Transport Airplanes, pp. 164–67.

47. *Ibid.*, pp. 164–69.

48. *Ibid.*, pp. 169–73

49. *Ibid.*, pp. 173–80

50. *Ibid.*, pp. 180–88, 246; USAF Handbook, Erection and Maintenance Instructions, L-82A Aircraft, 6 Jan. 1947 (Rev. 5 Apr. 1949), Sec. V; AMC, Standard Aircraft Characteristics, C-82A, 23 May 1950.

p. 5; Daily Activity Rpt., M & S, 19 Nov. 1944; Narrative Rpt., C-82 Operation by the Air Transport Command, 28 May 1947; ATC Daily Diary, Opns. Div., 14 Jan. 1947.

51. Most of the information given here on the C-46 is taken from two sources: La Farge, ATC Transport Aircraft, pp. 22–35, and ATSC, Development of Transport Airplanes, pp. 143–63. See also La Farge, Notes on Interview with Major Raymond R. Hajek, AC, Maintenance Engineering, AC/S, Operations, ATC, May 14, 1946.

52. ATC Plans Div., Rpt. on Air Cargo Capacity from India into China during 1943, 8 Jan. 1943; ATC, Estimated Requirements To Meet July and September Objectives for India-China Operation, 23 May 1943.

53. Memo. Rpt. of Meeting on Standardization of Transports, 14 Apr. 1943.

54. These figures are taken from a table given in ATSC Development of Transport Airplanes, p. 162. The June and July delivery figures do not agree with La Farge, ATC Transport Aircraft, p. 22.

55. Hist., Caribbean Division, Air Transport Command, Part IV, p. 84; Part VI, pp. 39–40.

56. Stat. History ATC, pp. 69–70.

57. ATC Daily Dairy, Opns. Div., 7 Aug. 1946.

58. ATSC, Development of Transport Airplanes, pp. 219–21.

59. La Farge, ATC Transport Aircraft, pp. 9–10.

60. *Ibid.*, p. 12; ATSC, Development of Transport Airplanes, pp. 211–19

61. La Farge, ATC Transport Aircraft, pp. 18–21; ATSC, Development of Transport Airplanes, pp. 200–211; Wkly. Rpt. of Activities of ATC, 14 Aug., 4 Sept., 23 Oct., 1942.

62. Interview with Capt. Sidney H. Feldman, Maintenance Engineering, ATC Opns., by Elizabeth A. Herndon, 2 May 1946; Stat. Hist. of the Air Transport Command, p. 69.

63. La Farge, ATC Transport Aircraft, pp. 5–7, 14–18; ATSC, Development of Transport Airplanes, pp. 189–93.

64. See sources cited in n. 63.

65. *Ibid.*; Stat. Hist. ATC, p. 69; OWI, American Air Transport, p. 4.

66. Administrative Hist., Ferrying Command, 29 May 1941—30 June 1942, pp. 27–30; Hist., FC Operations, 29 May–7 Dec. 1941, pp. 18, 33–34.

67. Hist., FC Operations, 7 Dec. 1941–30 June 1942, pp. 35–36.

68. *Ibid.*, pp. 30–31. The ferrying responsibilities of the Ferrying Command and other organizations were restated in AAF Reg. 55-6, 16 Apr. 1942.

69. Hist., FC Operations, 7 Dec. 1941–30 June 1942, pp. 36–37, 40; Procurement and Training of Pilots in the Ferrying Division, ATC, May 1941—Sept. 1945, p. 26.

70. Hist., FC Operations, 7 Dec. 1941–30 June 1942, pp. 39–41; Procurement and Training of Pilots, pp. 81–107.

71. Hist., FC Operations, 7 Dec. 1941–30 June 1942, pp. 37–39, 42.

72. Activities of the Ferrying Division, ATC, 1942, p. 11.

73. Procurement and Training of Pilots, pp. 94–107.

74. Women Pilots in the ATC, pp. 3–10. This study, prepared by the ATC Historical Officer, is a revision and condensation of an earlier work by the Historical Officer of the Ferrying Division, ATC, entitled: Hist. of the Women Pilots of the Ferrying Division, Air Transport Command, Sept. 5, 1942—Dec. 20, 1944.

75. Women Pilots in the ATC, pp. 10–42.

76. *Ibid.*, pp. 53–175.

77. CAA, *Statistical Handbook of Civil Aviation, 1949*, pp. 63, 83.

78. Statistics supplied by Stat. Services Div., Military Air Transport Service, Mar. 1949.

79. Hist., FC Operations, 7 Dec. 1941–30 June 1942, pp. 117–20.

80. *Ibid.*

81. Hist., Caribbean Div., ATC, Part II, pp. 169–78.

82. *Ibid.*, pp. 170–72, 180–81, 190–95, 200–203.

83. *Ibid.*, pp. 181–82, 190–95, 202.

84. *Ibid.*, pp. 178–81.

85. *Ibid.*, pp. 194–95.

86. *Ibid.*, pp. 185–90.

87. *Ibid.*, pp. 198–200; Hist., Ferrying Div., ATC, III, 122–31.

88. Hist., Ferrying Div., ATC, III, 122–31.

89. Hist., Caribbean Div., ATC, Part II, 203–16.

90. Procurement and Training of Pilots, pp. 132–41; Hist., Ferrying Div., ATC, III, 75.

91. Procurement and Training of Pilots, pp. 59–75.

92. *Ibid.*, pp. 76–80.

93. Memo for CG AAF from Col. William H. Tunner, 26 Sept. 1942.

94. Procurement and Training of Pilots, pp. 147–83; Women Pilots in the ATC, pp. 43–52.

95. Memo for CG AAF from Brig. Gen. H. L. George, 14 July 1942.

96. Memo for CG ATC from Brig. Gen. T. J. Hanley, Jr., 21 July 1942.

97. Hist., Domestic Transportation Division, ATC, 15 Mar. 1943—1 Apr. 1944, pp. 44–58. (Cited hereafter as Hist., DTR ATC.)

98. R&R, Brig. Gen. T. J. Hanley, Jr., to Gen. George, 18 Dec. 1942, and comment 1, George to Hanley, 22 Jan. 1943; Program for 1943 and 1944 for ATC, 16 Jan. 1943; ATC Transport Aircraft in World War II, p. 39.

99. R&R, Brig. Gen. O. A. Anderson to ATC, 9 Jan. 1943; Program for 1943 and 1944, Breakdown into ATC Wings, 26 Jan. 1943.

100. Stat. Hist. of ATC, 29 May 1941—31 May 1948, pp. 10, 69–70. Major transports include the heavier two-engine planes, C-46's and C-47's, and the four-engine craft, C-54's and C-87's. Not included are the lighter two-engine types such as the Lockheed Lodestar or C-60.

101. Hist., DTR ATC, pp. 66–77.

102. *Ibid.*, pp. 9–13, 16–19, 83–85, 88.

103. *Ibid.*, pp. 95–104, 111–13.

104. *Ibid.*, pp. 85–87.

105. *Ibid.*, pp. 104–11.

106. Hist., DTR ATC, pp. 87–88.

107. *Ibid.*, pp. 114–15.

108. *Ibid.*, pp. 61–63; Procurement and Training of Pilots, pp. 328–52.

109. Hist., DTR ATC, pp. 63–64, 121–25; Procurement and Training of Pilots, pp. 353–64.

110. Hist., DTR ATC, pp. 19–20, 119–25; Procurement and Training of Pilots, pp. 366–67, 503–11.

111. Procurement and Training of Pilots, pp. 368–79, 484–88, 505–11.

112. *Ibid.*, pp. 489–502; Hist., Ferrying Div., ATC, VI, 182–90.

113. Procurement and Training of Pilots, pp. 515–16; Hist., Ferrying Div., ATC, VI, 95–106, 196–99.

114. Procurement and Training of Pilots, pp. 512–15; Hist., Ferrying Div., ATC, VI, 211–17; VIII, 118–19.

115. Hist., Ferrying Div., ATC, VIII, 114–18.

NOTES TO CHAPTER 2

1. Foreign Ferrying Deliveries, Jan.–June 1942, compiled by ATC Historical Br. Of the total of forty-four bombers ferried to the Southwest Pacific area by late February 1942, eight went by the Pacific route and thirty-six by way of the South Atlantic.

2. Hist., Caribbean Div., ATC, Part II, pp. 6–8; Part III, pp. 57–59.

3. Administrative Hist., Ferrying Command, 29 May 1941—30 June 1942, pp. 83–84.

4. *Ibid.*, pp. 76–89.

5. Ltr., TAG to CG AAF Ferrying Command, 12 June 1942; ltr., TAG to CG ATC, 5 July 1942; Administrative Hist., ATC, June 1942—Mar. 1943, pp. 7–8.

6. Administrative Hist., ATC, June 1942—Mar. 1943, pp. 17–18; ltr., TAG to CG ATC, 19 Mar. 1943; ATC GO 4, 29 Mar. 1943.

7. Administrative Hist., ATC, June 1942—Mar. 1943, pp. 161–64, 191–99.

8. Ltr., TAG to CG AAF Ferrying Command, 12 June 1942; ltr., TAG to CG ATC, 5 July 1942.

9. Hq. Africa–Middle East Wing, ATC, GO 20, 14 Dec. 1943.

10. Ltr., Brig. Gen. H. L. George to Col. Paul E. Burrows, 31 July 1942; Hist., Caribbean Div., ATC, Part III, pp. 14–15.

11. Ltr., TAG to CG AAF *et al.*, 8 June 1943; Hist., Caribbean Div., ATC, Part III, pp. 55–61.

12. Hist., Caribbean Div., ATC, Part III, pp. 95–140.

13. *Ibid.*, pp. 77–94, 187–251.

14. *Ibid.*, pp. 59, 95–96; ltr., Lt. Col. Frank H. Nightingale to CO Caribbean Wing, ATC, 20 Oct. 1942; ltr., Lt. Col. William L. Plummer to CO Overseas Div., Office of the Inspector General, 4 Mar. 1943; ltr., Maj. James C. Jensen to Wing S-3 *et al.*, 11 Sept. 1942; memo for CG ATC from Col. Richard H. Ballard, 23 Oct. 1942.

15. Hist., Caribbean Div., ATC, Part III, pp. 53–65, 96–97, 132–33; Part IV, 1–13.

16. Ltr., Brig. Gen. H. L. George to Col. Robert L. Walsh, 19 June 1942; Hist., South Atlantic Div., ATC, Part II, pp. 2–10.

17. Hist., South Atlantic Div., ATC, Part I, pp. 75–87. For the Airport Development Program, see Vol. I, 321.

18. Hist., South Atlantic Div., ATC, Part II, pp. 12, 19–20.

19. *Ibid.*, Part I, pp. 31–44.

20. *Ibid.*, pp. 12–20; Part II, pp. 12, 18–19, 22–25.

21. *Ibid.*, Part I, pp. 1–44; Part III, pp. 136–202.

22. R&R, ACFC to C/AAF through C/AC, 8 Nov. 1941; memo for C/S from Brig. Gen. Carl Spaatz, 15 Dec. 1941; ltr., Sec. of War Henry L. Stimson to Sec. of State, 19 Dec. 1941.

23. Distances taken from USAF Pilot's Handbook, Africa, April 1949.

24. Hist., Wideawake Field, Ascension Island, ATC, p. 6.

25. Paraphrase of Msg. #568, London to Sec. of State, 7 Feb. 1942, Ann. "A" to JCS 161, 7 Dec. 1942; CCS 28/1, 23 Mar. 1942.

26. Draft of ltr., Sec. of War to Sec. of Navy, 15 Jan. 1942; interview with Col. Philip G. Kemp by Maj. Oliver La Farge, 17 July 1945; Hist., Wideawake Field, Ascension Island, ATC, pp. 7–8.

27. Rpt. on operations at Lawyer by Maj. F. J. Clarke, Corps of Engineers, 30 July 1942; Report on construction of Wideawake Field, incl. to ltr., Capt. Glenn L. Summers, 38th Eng. S-2, to Lt. Col. R. N. Genthon, 13 Oct. 1943; Hist., Wideawake Field, Ascension Island, ATC, pp. 8–24.

28. Ltr., James P. Chapin, Associate Curator of Birds, American Museum of Natural History, to Col. James A. Ronin, 24 Sept. 1942; *Impact*, I (Aug. 1943), 9–10; Louis N. Ridenour, "Wide-awakes through the Windscreen," *Atlantic Monthly*, CLXXIX (Feb. 1947), 108–9; History, Wideawake Field, Ascension Island, ATC, pp. 37–38.

29. Ltr., Maj. Gen. H. L. George to Dr. James B. Chapin, 27 Aug. 1942; ltr., Chapin to Ronin, 24 Sept. 1942; *Impact*, I (Aug. 1943), 9–10; Ridenour in *Atlantic Monthly*, CLXXIX (Feb. 1947), 108–9.

30. Hist., South Atlantic Div., ATC, Part II, pp. 2–10.

31. *Ibid.*, pp. 205–12.

32. Ltr., Brig. Gen. H. L. George to Brig. Gen. Shepler W. Fitzgerald, 15 June 1942; ltr., Gen. G. C. Marshall to CG AAF *et al.*, 16 June 1942; Hist., ATC in Central Africa and the Middle East, Part II, Vol. I, pp. 4–10.

33. Memo for Mr. Brownell from Brig. Gen. Robert Olds, 13 Feb. 1942; msg., Hardin to Ferrying Command, 22 Apr. 1942; ltr., Gen. G. C. Marshall to Louis A. Johnson, 8 July 1942; Lt. Col. George

Kraigher, Reasons for Militarization of PAA–Africa, Ltd., 29 July 1942, incl. to memo to Gen. George from Lt. Col. James H. Douglas, 4 Aug. 1942; msg. AM EW 394A, Hq. AMEW to CG ATC, 6 Aug. 1942; memo re PAA–Africa, 6 Aug. 1942, incl. to ltr., Franklin Gledhill to Lt. Col. James H. Douglas, 6 Aug. 1942; Hist., ATC in Central Africa and the Middle East, Part II, Vol. I, pp. 22–40.

34. Draft of msg., Arnold to Adler, 6 Feb. 1942; memo for Gen. Olds from Col. A. W. Vansman, 7 Feb. 1942; memo for C/AAF from Brig. Gen. Robert Olds, 9 Feb. 1942; directive memo for AAG from Lt. Col. Nathan F. Twining, 12 Feb. 1942; memo for Mr. Brownell from Brig. Gen. Robert Olds, 13 Feb. 1942; ltr., TAG to C/AAF *et al.*, 18 Feb. 1942.

35. Memo re PAA–Africa, 6 Aug. 1942, incl. to ltr., Franklin Gledhill to Lt. Col. James H. Douglas, 6 Aug. 1942; ltr., Brig. Gen. Shepler W. Fitzgerald to Maj. Gen. Harold L. George, 23 Sept. 1942; memo to Mr. J. H. Smith, Jr., from Brig. Gen. S. W. Fitzgerald, 23 Sept. 1942; ltr., American Vice-Consul W. Stratton Anderson, Jr., to Accra Sec. of State, 30 Sept. 1942; ltr., Brig. Gen. S. W. Fitzgerald to Mr. J. H. Smith, Jr., 26 Nov. 1942; ltr., Brig. Gen. S. W. Fitzgerald, 28 Nov. 1942, and 1st Ind., Fitzgerald to CG ATC, 16 Dec. 1942; memo to Col. George A. Brownell from Col. James H. Douglas, Jr., 21 July 1942; Hist., ATC in Central Africa and the Middle East, Part II, Vol. I, pp. 20–40.

36. Hist., Ferrying Division, ATC, III, 138–39.

37. Hist., ATC in Central Africa and the Middle East, Part II, Vol. II, pp. 135–36; Administrative Hist., North African Sector, ATC, pp. 2–4.

38. Foreign Ferrying Deliveries, Jan.–June 1942, compiled by ATC Hist. Br.

39. Foreign Ferrying Deliveries, July–Dec. 1942.

40. Foreign Ferrying Deliveries, Jan.–June 1942; Foreign Ferrying Deliveries, July–Dec. 1942.

41. Hist., Alaskan Div., ATC, II, 269–73.

42. Msg., TAG to CG 3d AF, 24 June 1942; ltr., Brig. Gen. Hume Peabody to CG Ferrying Command, 25 June 1942; memo for Lt. Col. Mason from Oliver La Farge, 29 Dec. 1942; Hist., Caribbean Div., ATC,

Part III, pp. 145–49; Vol. II, pp. 20, 25–26.

43. USAF Historical Studies: No. 108, The AAF in the Middle East: A Study of the Origins of the Ninth Air Force, pp. 75–77; Hist., 57th Fighter Gp.

44. USAF Historical Studies: No. 108, pp. 77–78; Hist., Caribbean Div., ATC, Part III, pp. 145–48; memo for Mason from La Farge, 29 Dec. 1942.

45. USAF Historical Studies: No. 108, pp. 79–80; Hist., 12th Bomb. Gp.; Hist., Caribbean Div., ATC, Part III, pp. 148–49.

46. USAF Historical Studies: No. 108, pp. 77–79.

47. Foreign Ferrying Deliveries, July–Dec. 1942.

48. Col. S. T. Moore, Tactical Employment in the U.S. Army of Transport Aircraft and Gliders in World War II, p. 101.

49. Foreign Ferrying Deliveries, July–Dec. 1942.

50. ATC Stat. Control Div., Summary of Operations of ATC, Annual Chartbook, 1943, p. 15.

51. Ltr., Capt. Bruce Aitchison to CG ATC, 14 Aug. 1942; ltr., Capt. Bruce Aitchison to CG USAFIME, 3 Sept. 1942.

52. Ltr., Aitchison to CG ATC, 14 Aug. 1942.

53. Ltr., Brig. Gen. Harold L. George to CG AAF, 17 June 1942.

54. Ltr., George to Arnold, 12 July 1942, cited in memo for Lt. Col. Mason from Oliver La Farge, 29 Dec. 1942.

55. Memo for Mason from La Farge, 29 Dec. 1942, Table I.

56. Memo for Lt. Col. P. N. Montaque from Capt. Bruce Aitchison, 9 Aug. 1942; ltr., Aitchison to CG ATC, 14 Aug. 1942; ltr., Aitchison to CG USAFIME, 3 Sept. 1942.

57. Wkly. Rpts. of Activities of ATC, 14 Aug., 4 Sept., 1942; Lt. Col. Oliver La Farge, ATC Transport Aircraft in World War II: A Study of Types, Performance and Fleet Augmentation, pp. 18–19.

58. Wkly. Rpt. of Activities of ATC, 16 Oct. 1942.

59. Wkly. Rpt. of Activities of ATC, 1 Jan. 1943; memo for Mason from La Farge, 29 Dec. 1942, Table II.

60. Hist., Caribbean Div., ATC, Part II, pp. 227–28.

61. *Ibid.*, pp. 233–34.

62. *Ibid.*, pp. 164–65; Part III, p. 235.

63. *Ibid.*, Part II, pp. 157–62; Part III, pp. 241–51; Administrative Hist., ATC,

Mar. 1943—July 1944, pp. 178–79; ltr., Col. Charles W. Sullivan to Inspector General, 22 Jan. 1943; memo Regarding Inspector General's Survey of Embarkation, dated 22 Jan. 1943, 1 Mar. 1943.

64. WD Circ. 385, 27 Nov. 1942.

65. Hist., Caribbean Div., ATC, Part III, pp. 247–48.

66. Maj. Howard G. Kurtz, Jr., Air Transport Command Transportation Control Plan, 20 Jan. 1943; Kurtz, Transportation Control System, Proposed Directive, Forms and Graphic Presentation, 23 Feb. 1943; ltr., Maj. Gen. H. L. George to Wing and Division Commanders, 14 May 1943; ltr., George to Wing and Division Commanders, 1 June 1943; ltr., Col. L. G. Fritz to Wing Commanders, 21 June 1943; ltr., Col. R. W. Ireland to Wing and Division Commanders, 14 July 1943; ltr., Maj. Malcolm A. MacIntyre to Wing and Division Commanders, 6 Aug. 1943; ltr., Col. L. G. Fritz to Wing and Division Commanders, 7 Aug. 1943; memo to Priorities & Traffic Officers, ATC, from Maj. Malcolm A. MacIntyre, 21 Aug. 1943; Lt. Col. Oliver La Farge, Control of Strategic Air Transport, 20 Oct. 1945; Administrative Hist., ATC, Mar. 1943—July 1944, pp. 178–81; Hist., Caribbean Div., ATC, Part IV, pp. 41–45.

67. WD Circ. 130, 4 Apr. 1944.

68. Administrative Hist., ATC, Mar. 1943–July 1944, p. 182.

NOTES TO CHAPTER 3

1. Hist., North Africa—the First Phase, AFATC, pp. 1–3; ATC Plans Report #12, Special information assembled for General George for trip leaving Washington 12 Oct. 1942; ATC Plans Rpt. #19, Rpt. and information on possible ATC transatlantic and African ferry routes.

2. ATC Plans Rpt. #12.

3. ATC Plans Rpts. #12 and #19.

4. ATC Plans Rpt. #12.

5. Hist., North Africa—the First Phase, p. 3.

6. Ibid., pp. 6–7; memo for CG ATC from Col. Richard H. Ballard, 23 Oct. 1942.

7. Hist., North Africa—the First Phase, pp. 7–8.

8. ATC Wkly. Rpt., 18 Dec. 1942.

9. A very complete record of the KIT project has been preserved. Upon completion of the project, Col. Reichers, Maj.
Edward A. Abbey, the medical officer, and the various members of the ATC flight crews submitted detailed reports which, with supporting documents, were bound together in a single volume. The account of the project given here is based on these reports and on a brief history, entitled "Kit Project," written by the ATC historian during the war.

10. Reichers Rpt.; Hist., Kit Project.

11. Hist., Kit Project and various reports.

12. Reichers Rpt.

13. Ibid.

14. Ibid.

15. Abbey Rpt.

16. Reichers Rpt.

17. Ibid.

18. Ibid.; Tillman Rpt.

19. Reichers Rpt.; Tillman Rpt.; Hist., Kit Project.

20. Tillman Rpt.; Reichers Rpt.

21. Reichers Rpt.

22. Tillman Rpt.

23. Abbey Rpt.

24. Hist., South Atlantic Div., ATC, Part III, pp. 42–73.

25. Hist., North Africa—the First Phase, pp. 8–9.

26. Ibid., pp. 9–13.

27. Ltr., Brig. Gen. C. R. Smith to M. Pierre Boisson, 15 Dec. 1942; ltr., Boisson to Smith, 17 Dec. 1942; ltr., Smith to Boisson, 17 Dec. 1942; ltr., Rear Adm. William Glassford to Boisson, 20 Dec. 1942.

28. Ltr., Capt. Inslee A. Hopper, Intelligence Officer, 14th Ferrying Group, to Intelligence Officer, Africa–Middle East Wing, 7 Feb. 1943; ATC Station Survey, Eknes Field, Dakar, 15 Jan. 1944; ATC Station Survey, Mallard Field, Dakar, Oct. 1944; Operational Hist., North African Sector, Africa–Middle East Wing, ATC, pp. 5–6, 25–26.

29. Msg., Smith to George, 14 Dec. 1942; Operational Hist., North African Sector, pp. 6–7, 26–27.

30. Administrative Hist., North African Sector, pp. 2–5, 20.

31. Ibid., pp. 8–19, 60–66.

32. Hist., Caribbean Div., ATC, Part III, pp. 158–61 and appendix, "Unit Movements, July 1942, through June 1943."

33. See The Army Air Forces in World War II, II, 129.

34. Hist., Caribbean Div., Part III, 161–62.

35. Hist., 321st Bomb. Gp.

36. ATC Wkly. Rpts., 11 and 18 Dec. 1942; see also Vol. II, 128.

37. Hist., 99th Bomb. Gp.; Hist., Caribbean Div., Part III, appendix, "Unit Movements, July 1942, through June 1943."

38. Operational Hist., North African Sector, pp. 5-6, 25-26, 61-62; Msg. #ATC 2349, Walsh to Fritz, 22 Feb. 1943.

39. Msg. #AMEW 395 J, AMEW to ATC, 13 Jan. 1943.

40. Operational Hist., North African Sector, pp. 62-63.

41. Hist., Ferrying Div., ATC, IV, 204-16; Hist., Caribbean Div., Part III, appendix, "Unit Movements, July 1942, through June 1943."

42. Hist., North African Sector, pp. 61-68A and appendix.

43. Hist., European Wing, ATC, early 1943 to D Day 1944, p. 99 and statistical appendix.

44. Operational Hist., North African Sector, p. 28 and appendix.

45. Msg. #AMEW 212, Fitzgerald to George, 15 Feb. 1943.

46. Operational Hist., North African Sector, p. 36.

47. Ltr., Maj. J. C. Stewart to Chief, Air Priorities Division, ATC, 27 Jan. 1943.

48. See AAF in WW II, II, 619.

49. Hist., European Wing, ATC, early 1943 to D Day 1944, p. 99 and statistical appendix.

50. Ltr., Lt. Col. H. B. Longfellow to Col. R. W. Ireland, 30 Dec. 1942; Msg. #6583, Hartle to George, 20 Jan. 1943; msg., Smith to George, 20 Jan. 1943; Msg. #AMSME 4301, Arnold to Stratemeyer and George, 28 Jan. 1943; ltr., Lt. Col. John de P. T. Hills to Col. R. M. Love, 10 May 1943.

51. Memo for Col. R. J. Smith et al. from Col. L. G. Fritz, 12 Dec. 1942; memo to CO Caribbean Wing, ATC, from Col. P. N. Montague, 12 Dec. 1942.

52. Ltr., George to CG South Atlantic Wing, ATC, et al., 11 Jan. 1943; memo to CG ATC from Maj. Hamilton Heard, 16 Jan. 1943; "North Africa—the First Phase," p. 17.

53. Notes of a discussion between representatives of the U.S.A.A.F. A.T.C. and D.G.O. held in D.G.O.'s office, Bush House, S.E. Wing, 28th December 1942, by Wg. Comdr. P. S. Foss; msg., Air Priorities Sec., Hq. ETOUSA to AGWAR, 28 Dec. 1942; msg., Air Priorities Sec., Hq. ETOUSA

to AGWAR, [28 Dec. 1942]; note of a discussion with representatives of the Air Transport Command at No. 44 Group, Gloucester, on 30th December, 1942 [by Wg. Comdr. P. S. Foss]; ltr., Lt. Col. H. B. Longfellow to Col. R. W. Ireland, 30 Dec. 1942; memo to CG ATC from Maj. Hamilton Heard, 16 Jan. 1943. Major Skelly died shortly after the group reached England; Major Heard then took charge of the negotiations for ATC. See memo to CG ATC from Heard, 18 Jan. 1943, commending Major Skelly for his devotion to duty as chief of the mission prior to his death.

54. Memo to CG ATC from Heard, 16 Jan. 1943.

55. Ltr., George to CG South Atlantic Wing, ATC et al., 11 Jan. 1943.

56. Msg., George to Smith, 23 Jan. 1943; ltr., Capt. Robert B. Hotz to Resident Contract Carrier Supervisor, 11 Feb. 1943; ltr., Lt. Col. James G. Flynn, Jr., to Capt. H. W. Helfert, 20 Feb. 1943.

57. Msg. · #ATC 522, Blake to Smith, 27 Jan. 1943.

58. Msg. #ATC 1005, George to CG AMEW, 6 Feb. 1943.

59. Hist., European Wing, ATC, early 1943 to D Day 1944, Stat. App.

60. Ibid., pp. 26-27.

61. Ibid., pp. 104-5.

62. Ibid., pp. 105-6; AAF in WW II, II, 642-43.

63. Msg. ATC #4013 & 666A, Fritz to CO EWATC, 10 Apr. 1943; msg. ATC #4245, Ireland to CO EWATC, 15 Apr. 1943; msg. ATC #4367, Ireland to Montgomery and Longfellow, 19 Apr. 1943; msg. ATC 1472, Burrows to CG NAWATC and CG ATC, 1 May 1943; msg. ATC #5506, 12 May 1943; ltr., Col. Robert M. Love to CO EWATC, 15 May 1943; ltr., Maj. Robert E. Montgomery to CG AMEW, 5 June 1943; ltr., Col. T. L. Mosley to CG ATC, 18 June 1943; consolidated transport schedules, United States to United Kingdom and North Africa, effective 29 August 1943, incl. to ltr., Lt. Col. James G. Flynn, Jr., to CG NAWATC et al., 20 Aug. 1943; Hist., European Wing, ATC, early 1943 to D Day 1944, pp. 50-51, 89, 91-96; ltr., Lt. Col. James G. Flynn, Jr., to CO EWATC, 15 Sept. 1943, and 1st ind., Col. James C. Jensen to Hq. ATC, 21 Sept. 1943; Hist., European Wing, ATC, early 1943 to D Day 1944, pp. 95-97.

64. Hist., European Wing, ATC, early 943 to D Day 1944, pp. 96–97, 191.

65. *Ibid.*, pp. 191–93; Hist., North African Wing, ATC, 15 Dec. 1943—30 Apr. 1944, pp. 43–45.

66. Maj. Warren W. Wheaton, Rpt. on ATC's participation in Mission 11, incl. in ltr., Wheaton to Brig. Gen. Earl S. Hoag, CG EURD ATC, 18 Aug. 1944; Hist., European Wing, ATC, early 1943 to D Day 1944, pp. 193–95; Hist., North African Wing, ATC, June 1944, pp. 35–41 and App. XXXVIII; ltr., Capt. Harry Rammer to CG NAFW, ATC, 3 July 1944.

67. Ltr., Maj. J. C. Stewart to Chief, Air Priorities Div., ATC, 27 Jan. 1943; Operational Hist., North African Sector, ATC, p. 37.

68. Msg., Smith to George, 22 Jan. 1943; msg., George to Fitzgerald, 4 Feb. 1943; Msg. #9796, Boughner to Ireland, 16 Apr. 1943; memo to Col. Douglas from Brig. Gen. C. R. Smith, 12 May 1943; ltr., Arnold to Spaatz, 17 May 1943; weekly reports of activities of ATC, 29 Jan. and 5 Feb. 1943; Operational Hist., North African Sector, ATC, p. 38.

69. Operational Hist., North African Sector, ATC, pp. 38–39.

70. Hist., Mediterranean Air Transport Service, 25 May 1943—31 May 1944; Administrative Hist., North African Sector, ATC, pp. 20–33; Operational Hist., North African Sector, ATC, pp. 17–22.

71. Administrative Hist., North African Sector, ATC, pp. 22–23.

72. Ltr., Smith to Tedder, 1 June 1943; msg. from Algiers #W1656, Smith to George, 30 May 1943; Administrative Hist., North African Sector, ATC, pp. 23–26.

73. Ltr., Col. T. L. Mosley to George, 22 June 1943; ltr., 1st Lt. Carleton H. Jones to CO North African Sector, 24 July 1943; ltr., Col. T. C. Macaulay to Det. Comdr., 48th Transp. Sq., 30 July 1943; ltr., Col. T. C. Macaulay to Brig. Gen. H. A. Craig, 30 July 1943; ltr., Col. T. L. Mosley to ATC Det. Comdrs., 30 Aug. 1943; Operational Hist., North African Sector, ATC, pp. 18–21; Administrative Hist., North African Sector, ATC, pp. 26–33.

74. Hq. MAC GO 4 [25 May 1943]; Hist., MATS, 25 May 1943—31 May 1944, pp. 2–4; Administrative Hist., North African Sector, ATC, pp. 21–22.

75. Rpt., Col. T. C. Macaulay to Brig. Gen. S. W. Fitzgerald, 19 Apr. 1943; draft ltr., Arnold to Spaatz, 17 May 1943; memo for Gen. Hanley from George, 20 May 1943; draft ltr. to Eisenhower, 21 May 1943, prepared at Hq. ATC for Gen. McNarney's signature.

76. Draft ltr., Arnold to Spaatz, 17 May 1943; draft ltr. to Eisenhower, 21 May 1943; memo to Lt. Col. Samuel E. Gates from Maj. Eliot Bailen, 25 Apr. 1944.

77. Memo to Gates from Bailen, 25 Apr. 1944; msg. from Algiers #395, Smith to George, 14 Jan. 1944.

78. Administrative Hist., North African Sector, ATC, p. 23.

79. Ltr., Smith to Tedder, 1 June 1943; msg. from Algiers #1656, Smith to George, 30 May 1943.

80. Operational Hist., North African Sector, ATC, pp. 47–50; ltrs., Col. T. L. Mosley to George, 9 June 1943 (two ltrs., same date, on same subject); msg. from Algiers #368, Hoag to Ireland, 16 July 1943; msg. from Marrakech #332, Mosley to George, 9. Aug. 1943.

81. Administrative Hist., North African Sector, ATC, pp. 63–65.

82. In connection with North Africa, this policy is implied in the following: memo to Col. Douglas from Brig. Gen. C. R. Smith, 12 May 1943; draft ltr., Arnold to Spaatz, 17 May 1943; draft ltr. to Eisenhower, 21 May 1943. For a more general statement of the policy, see, for example: memo for Gen. Nowland from George, 21 Dec. 1943; memo to Col. Mason from Col. James H. Douglas, 4 Mar. 1944.

83. Ltr., Smith to George, 3 Nov. 1943; msg., Smith (Algiers) to George, 3 Nov. 1943; Hist., MATS, 25 May 1943—31 May 1944, pp. 36–37; Hist., North African Wing, ATC, 15 Dec. 1943—30 Apr. 1944, pp. 21–22, and App. XIV–XVIII.

84. Ltr., Smith to George, 3 Nov. 1943.

85. Hist., North African Wing, ATC, 15 Dec. 1943—30 Apr. 1944, pp. 21–22, 33; June 1944, pp. 31–32.

86. Hist., North African Wing, ATC, 15 Dec. 1943—30 Apr. 1944, pp. 38–39.

87. Hist., North African Wing, ATC, June 1944, p. 31.

88. Hist., North African Wing, ATC, June 1944, p. 33; Hist., North African Wing, July 1944, p. 12 and App. XIV; Hist., North African Div., ATC, Sept.–Nov. 1944, pp. 4–5, 12.

89. Hist., North African Wing, ATC, June 1944, p. 33.

90. Hist., North African Div., ATC, Sept.–Nov. 1944, p. 5.

91. *Ibid.*, pp. 5–9.

92. *Ibid.*, pp. 213–19; Hist., North African Div., ATC, Dec. 1944—Feb. 1945, pp. 7–9; Rpts. of activities of ATC for months ending 15 Oct., 15 Nov., 15 Dec., 1944.

93. Hist., North African Wing, ATC, 15 Dec. 1943—30 Apr. 1944, p. 36; July 1944, pp. 101–19 and App. LXXXI; Hist., North African Div., ATC, Sept.–Nov. 1944, pp. 11–12; 1 Mar.–30 Sept. 1945, p. 27; Report of Activities of ATC for month ending 15 Oct. 1944.

94. Hist., North African Div., ATC, Sept.–Nov. 1944, pp. 92–93; Dec. 1944—Feb. 1945, pp. 115–17.

95. Memo for Gen. Hanley from George, 20 May 1943; draft ltr., Arnold to Spaatz, 17 May 1943; draft ltr. to Eisenhower, 21 May 1943.

96. Memo for Arnold from George, 15 Nov. 1942; memo for CG AAF from Brig. Gen. C. R. Smith, 16 Nov. 1942; msg. #1803, Sec. of State to American Legation, Lisbon, 30 Dec. 1942; msg. #6, American Legation, Lisbon to Sec. of State, 2 Jan. 1943; Short History of U.S. Interest in Aviation Facilities in the Azores, 19 Nov. 1943.

97. Short History of U.S. Interest in Aviation Facilities in the Azores, 19 Nov. 1943 and Tab. G, Report on Status of Development of Facilities in the Azores—Air and Naval.

98. Ltr., AVM G. R. Bromet, Capt. C. H. Sanders and Col. David A. Morris to CG ATC, 1 Dec. 1943; CCS 270/13, 6 Dec. 1943; CCS 270/14, 6 Dec. 1943; Amendment to CCS 270/14, 10 Jan. 1944; ltr., Brig. Gen. Bob E. Nowland, C/S ATC, to CO North Atlantic Wing, ATC, 3 Jan. 1944.

99. Memo for CG AAF from Col. Robert M. Love, 16 Dec. 1943; msg., CM-OUT 9009-759, Marshall to Fuqua, 23 Dec. 1943; msg., 3151, Norweb to Sec. of State, 31 Dec. 1943.

100. Rpts. of Activities of ATC for months ending 15 Dec. 1943 and 15 Jan. 1944.

101. Memo for Lt. Col. J. G. Flynn from Col. L. G. Fritz, 20 Feb. 1943.

102. John F. Davidson, Narrative Rpt. on survey flight C-54A airplane #137273 for the Air Transport Command by American Airlines, 29 Apr. 1943.

103. R&R, George to OC&R, 18 May 1943; ltr., Maj. Fred M. Glass to CG North Atlantic Wing, ATC, 31 May 1943; msg. from Cincinnati ATC 516, Campbell to Dupont, 8 June 1943; ltr., Col. L. G. Fritz to CG North Atlantic Wing, ATC, 8 June 1943.

104. Ltr., Capt. Charles O. Galbraith to Col. Robert H. Baker, May 7 1943; report of Capt. Charles O. Galbraith, incl. to ltr., Maj. Charles G. Conly to CO Ferrying Division, ATC, 12 May 1943; "Two Stops to Cairo," account of Capt. Charles O. Galbraith's survey flight, Gander to Marrakech, incl. in ltr., Maj. Gordon A. Rust to CG ATC, 9 Aug. 1943.

105. Ltr., Col. Harold R. Harris to CO North Atlantic Wing, ATC, *et al.*, 10 Dec. 1943, in Hist., North African Wing, ATC, 15 Dec. 1943—30 Apr. 1944, App. XX.

106. Hist., North African Wing, ATC, 15 Dec. 1943—30 Apr. 1944, pp. 41–43 and App. XXI.

107. Ltr., Harris to CO North Atlantic Wing, ATC, *et al.*, 10 Dec. 1943.

108. *Ibid.*

109. Msg. #ATC 0226, Harris to CO North Atlantic Wing, ATC, *et al.*, 4 Feb. 1944.

110. Hist., Caribbean Division, ATC, Part IV, p. 62.

111. *Ibid.*

112. Hist., Caribbean Div., ATC, Aug. 1944, pp. 37–39.

113. Hist., North African Wing, ATC, 15 Dec. 1943—30 Apr. 1944, pp. 29–30; May 1944, pp. 10–11 and App. VIII.

114. North African Div., ATC, Annual Rpt. 1944, in Hist., North African Div., ATC, Dec. 1944—Feb. 1945, App. I.

115. Hist., North African Wing, ATC, 15 Dec. 1943—30 Apr. 1944, pp. 46–57; May 1944, pp. 19–27 and App. XXX–XXXIII; Rpt. of Activities of ATC for month ending 16 June 1944.

116. Hist., North African Wing, ATC, May 1944, p. 21.

117. North African Div., ATC, Annual Rpt. 1944, p. 22.

NOTES TO CHAPTER 4

1. Hist., North Atlantic Div., ATC, I, Pt. 1, pp. 285–86.

2. *Ibid.*, p. 287; Hist., Ferrying Div., ATC, III (20 June 1942—14 Feb. 1943), 151–56.

3. Hist., North Atlantic Div., I, Pt. 1, pp. 207–8, 323–26, 341–44, and *passim*.

4. *Ibid.*, pp. 210–13, 218–20, 232, 262.

5. Hist., North Atlantic Div., The Crimson Route, pp. 1–12.

6. *Ibid.*, pp. 6–46; memo for CG ATC from Lt. Col. George F. Brewer, sub.: Daily Report—North Atlantic Ferry Route Project, 28 Aug. 1942.

7. Hist., North Atlantic Div., I, Pt. 1, pp. 281–83, 285, 351–52, 373, 387–89; Tables appended to ATC Wkly. Rpt., 9 Oct., 23 Oct., 13 Nov., 27 Nov., 24 Dec., 1942; 1 Jan., 8 Jan., 1943.

8. On the recommendation of ATC, the AAF in the spring of 1943 abandoned the airfields at The Pas, Churchill, and Southhampton Island while those at the CRYSTALS and Mingan were reduced to emergency status. Save for five RAF planes which followed the CRIMSON route to the United Kingdom in the summer, virtually no other use was made of the route by either ferried or transport aircraft. Memo for Captain Bolles from Lt. Col. Robert A. Logan, 3 Dec. 1942; ltr., Maj. George H. Shafer to CG NAW, ATC, sub.: Report of Survey Flight over Crimson Route, 13 Dec. 1942; ltr., Brig. Gen. C. R. Smith, C/S, ATC, to Brig. Gen. Robert W. Harper, AC/AS, A-3, 11 Mar. 1943; memo for C/AS from Brig. Gen. T. J. Hanley, Jr., sub.: Crimson Route, 21 Mar. 1943; memo for C/S from Hanley, sub.: Modification of Crimson Project, 10 Apr. 1943; ltr., Brig. Gen. C. R. Smith to CG AAF, sub.: Modification of Crimson Project, 19 Apr. 1943; memo for Senior U.S. Army Member, Permanent Jt. Bd. on Defense, Canada–United States from Brig. Gen. J. E. Hull, Actg. AC/S, sub.: Modification of the Crimson Project, 29 Apr. 1943; 2d ind. (ltr., AC/AS, Plans, to CG ATC sub.: Crimson Route, 12 Nov. 1943), CO NAW, ATC, to CG ATC, 20 Dec. 1943.

9. Directive memo for CG ATC from C/AS, 22 June 1942.

10. Hist., North Atlantic Div., I, Pt. 1, pp. 215, 225, 227–28, 229–32, 242–44, 277, 279.

11. Ltr., Brig. Gen. B. F. Giles to CG ATC, sub.: Operating Control of the North Atlantic Ferrying Route, 13 Sept. 1942.

12. Memo for Gen. Wedemeyer from Maj. Gen. H. L. George, sub.: Control of North Atlantic Air Route, 12 Nov. 1942.

13. "Discussions between R.A.F. Ferry Command, R.A.F. Delegation, and the Air Transport Command with Respect to Operations over the North and South Atlantic Routes."

14. *Ibid.*, Tab. A.

15. *Ibid.*, Tab. B.

16. *Ibid.*, Tabs. C, E, F.

17. Memo for Gen. Arnold from Maj. Gen. H. L. George, sub.: Meeting of RAF and AAF Representatives at Montreal, Canada, November 16 and 17, 1942—North Atlantic Operations, 18 Nov. 1942.

18. Hist., European Wing, ATC, Early 1943 to D Day 1944, pp. 8–10, 22–24, 39–45.

19. Msg., #6042, Spaatz to Arnold, 18 Jan. 1943, in ATC General's Log; see also *Army Air Forces in World War II*, II, 619.

20. Msg., Smith to George, 20 Jan. 1943; msg., AMSME 4301 Arnold to George, 28 Jan. 1943, in ATC General's Log; Weekly Report of the Activities of the Air Transport Command, 8 Jan. 1943.

21. Msg., ATC #522, George to Smith, 27 Jan. 1943; msg., ATC #1005, George to CG AMEW, 6 Feb. 1943, in ATC General's Log.

22. See *AAF in WW II*, II, 615; msg., #7756, Andrews to George, 9 Mar. 1943; msg., #7866, Andrews to George, 13 Mar. 1943; Weekly Report of the Activities of the Air Transport Command, 12 Mar. 1943.

23. Msg., Wiley to EW and other ATC Wings, 23 Mar. 1943; msg., AAF #2087, Warnock for Bonesteel, Iceland Base Command, 27 Mar. 1943; msg., ATC #110 A, George for CG NAW, 8 Mar. 1943, in ATC General's Log; ltr., Fritz to CG NAW, sub.: Planned Transport Operation—North Atlantic Route—March, April, and May 1943, 7 Mar. 1943; Rpt. of Activities of the ATC for the month ending 15 July 1943.

24. Ltr., Love to Brig. Gen. C. R. Smith, Chief of Staff, ATC, 20 Apr. 1943; Hist., North Atlantic Wing, ATC, II, Pt. I, p. 131; Hist. of the European Wing from Early 1943 until D Day 1944, p. 29.

25. Ltr., Love to Smith, 20 Apr. 1943; msg., ATC #3953, George to CO EWATC, 9 Apr. 1943; msg., ATC #1472, Burrows to CG NAWATC and CG ATC, 1 [May] 1943; msg., ATC #5506, George to Craig, 15 May 1943, in ATC General's Log; Report of Activities of the ATC for the month ending 15 July 1943; Narrative Report Survey Flight C-54A Airplane #137273 for the Air Transport Command by American Airlines, in 29 Apr. 1943, MATS Hist. File.

26. See *AAF in WW II*, II, 308–9, 373–74.

27. Summary of Operations of the Air Transport Command, Annual Chartbook, 1943, p. 15; Report of Activities of the ATC for the month ending 15 Jan. 1944; Hist., North Atlantic Wing, ATC, II, Pt. I, pp. 131–32; Hist., European Wing, 1943–44, p. 99. It should be noted that the historians of the European and North Atlantic Wings, each relying upon his own organization's statistical control section, came up with slightly different figures for aircraft deliveries. During the summer of 1943 the North Atlantic route was used for the delivery of those aircraft, capable of negotiating the route, which were destined for the Ninth, Tenth, Twelfth, and Fourteenth Air Forces. Report of Activities of the Air Transport Command for the month ending 15 June 1943.

28. Hist., North Atlantic Wing, II, Pt. I, p. 132.

29. *Ibid.*, p. 120; Hist., 1386th AAF BU, Meeks Field, Iceland, Sept. 1942—Oct. 1944, ch. 4, pp. 7–10; Hist., ATC in Greenland, pp. 41–44.

30. Hist., North Atlantic Wing, II, Pt. I, p. 119.

31. *Ibid.*, pp. 139–44; Hist., Ferrying Division, IV, 218–23.

32. Ltr., Capt. F. H. Cannon to CG ATC, sub.: ATC I&S Division Intelligence Digest, 13 Aug. 1943; ltr., Maj. W. R. Walner to CG NWA, sub.: Experimental Convoy Flight of P-47 Aircraft, 14 Aug. 1943; ltr., Col. G. D. Campbell, Jr., to CG ATC, sub.: Reports on First Overseas Flight of P-47 Aircraft, 25 Aug. 1943; ATC Intelligence Digest, 24 Aug. 1943.

33. Hist., North Atlantic Wing, II, Pt. I, pp. 127–28, 147. Cf. Vol. I, Pt. I, pp. 284–85; Hist., Ferrying Division, IV, 269.

34. Hist., North Atlantic Wing, ATC, II, Pt. II, pp. 241–43, 245–56. Appropriately, Colonel Fritz was appointed commanding officer of the North Atlantic Wing of the ATC in October 1943.

35. Memo for CG AAF from Brig. Gen. C. R. Smith, sub.: Policy—Ferrying Operations over the North Atlantic Route during the Winter Season of 1943–44, 26 Aug. 1943; memo for Asst. Chief of Air Staff, OC&R, from Smith, sub.: Operation of Combat Type Aircraft over the North Atlantic Route during the Winter Season of 1943–44, 4 Sept. 1943; memo for Lt. Col. Flynn from Maj. Hamilton Heard, sub.: Meeting regarding Winter Ferrying over the North Atlantic, 1 Oct. 1943, in MATS Hist. File.

36. Reports of Activities of the Air Transport Command for the months ending 15 Sept. 1943, 15 Dec. 1943, 15 Feb. 1944, 15 Mar. 1944, 15 Apr. 1944; Hist., North Atlantic Wing, ATC, II, Pt. I, p. 132; Hist. of the European Wing from Early 1943 to D Day 1944, p. 187. See ltr., Col. R. H. Kelly, OC&R to CG ATC, sub.: Operation of Combat Type Aircraft over the North Atlantic Route during the Winter Season 1943–44, 27 Jan. 1944.

37. Hist. of the European Wing from Early 1943 to D Day 1944, pp. 186–87.

38. Ltr., Col. Harold R. Harris, Asst. Chief of Staff, Opns., ATC, to CG's SAW, AMEW, EW, CAW, NAW, sub.: Winter Operations over the North Atlantic Route, 11 Nov. 1943; memo for CG AAF from Maj. Gen. H. L. George, sub.: Temporary Suspension for the Winter Season of Passenger Flights from the U.S. to the U.K. over the North Atlantic Route, 22 Nov. 1942, in MATS Hist. File; Report of Activities of the Air Transport Command for the month ending 15 Dec. 1943.

39. Reports of Activities of the Air Transport Command for the months ending 15 Dec. 1943, 15 Jan. 1944, 15 Mar. 1944.

40. *Ibid.*, 15 July 1944, 15 Aug. 1944; Hist. Record Report European Division, July 1944, p. 8.

41. Hist. of the Ferrying Division, ATC, V, 222–53, 588th AAF BU, Hist. of Snowball, May through September 1944.

42. Reports of Activities of the Air Transport Command for the months ending 15 Aug. 1943, 15 Nov. 1943, 15 Jan. 1944, 15 July 1944. See *AAF in WW II*, II, 345, 654–55.

43. ATC Office of Stat. Control, ATC-SR-2, Traffic, 29 Aug. 1945, p. TF-3; ATC Monthly Reports, 16 June 1944—16 June 1945, incl.

44. ATC Monthly Report, 16 May 1945; ATC Office of Stat. Control, ATC-SR-2, Ferrying Operations, 21 June 1945, p. F-3; *ibid.*, 21 Feb. 1945, p. F-6; *ibid.*, 22 May 1945, p. F-6.

45. EURD, Historical Record Report, July 1944, p. 10; Historical Record Report, November and December 1944, pp. 77–78.

46. ATC Monthly Report, 16 Oct. 1944, 16 Dec. 1944; EURD, Historical Record

Report, September and October 1944, pp. 14–16; Historical Record Report, January to V-E Day 1945, pp. 47–48.

47. ATC Monthly Reports, 16 Oct. 1944, 16 Jan. 1945, 16 Apr. 1945.

48. *Ibid.*, 16 Mar. 1945. Flight traffic clerks, enlisted men whose major function was to promote the comfort and safety of passengers, had been placed on ATC transports in 1944. See correspondence between General Arnold and General George in 1109th AAF BU, Early History of the Air Transport Program, Sept. 1942—Oct. 1944, Exhibit XV.

49. See *AAF in WW II*, II, 618–19; History of the European Wing from Early 1943 to D Day 1944, pp. 5–12.

50. Hist. of the European Wing from Early 1943 to D Day 1944, pp. 31–34, 79–84, 189–91; msg., ATU 1198, Burrows for CG, ATC, 24 Sept. 1943.

51. EURD, Historical Record Report, September and October 1944, App. 24. See also pp. 45–55 and documents reprinted in Volume I of the appendixes thereto.

52. EURD, Historical Record Report, September and October 1944, pp. 48–55, and documents appended thereto, esp. ltr., Lt. Col. Kenneth F. Montgomery, Actg. AC/S, Plans, ATC, to DC, ATC, *et al.*, sub.: Current Approved Plans for ATC Operations in Continental Europe, 1 Nov. 1944, and attached report, dated 31 Oct. 1944; ltr., Lt. Gen. Carl Spaatz to Gen. H. H. Arnold, 20 June 1944.

53. EURD, Historical Record Report, September and October 1944, pp. 4–5, 106, and App. 56.

54. EURD, Historical Record Report, September and October 1944, pp. 14–17, 67–73; November and December 1944, pp. 36–50. The St. Mawgan–Naples run was the successor of the earlier shuttle linking the United Kingdom with North Africa.

55. ERUD, Historical Record Report, November and December 1944, pp. 13–14.

56. EURD, Historical Record Report, January to V-E Day 1945, pp. 55–57; ATC Monthly Reports, 16 June 1945; 16 July 1945.

57. EURD, Scandinavian Operations of the European Division, Air Transport Command, 1944 and 1945, pp. 1–3, 13–14, 94, 151–52.

58. *Ibid.*, pp. 12–27, 82–94.

59. *Ibid.*, pp. 25–27, 34–37.

60. *Ibid.*, pp. 53–64.

61. *Ibid.*, pp. 7–9, 13–15, 27–33.

62. *Ibid.*, pp. 4, 113–28.

63. *Ibid.*, pp. 4–5, 129–44.

64. *Ibid.*, pp. 53, 83–94, 153–54; EURD, Historical Record Report, September and October 1944, Apps. 21–29; NAD, History of the North Atlantic Division, ATC, 1 October 1944—1 October 1945, Pt. I, pp. 310–14. This last is based upon a NAD monograph, United States to Sweden Air Transport Service, to which is appended a valuable collection of documents fundamental to the study.

65. ATC Monthly Reports, 16 Aug. 1944—16 June 1945, incl.

NOTES TO CHAPTER 5

1. Msg., Ammisca #226, Magruder to TAG, 28 Jan. 1942, and draft reply; Ltr., Roosevelt to Gen. George C. Marshall, 25 Feb. 1942.

2. The China National Aviation Corporation was owned 45 per cent by Pan American Airways and 55 per cent by the Chinese government.

3. Memo for C/S from Brig. Gen. Robert Olds, sub.: Air Transport Route from India to China, 25 Feb. 1942; ltr., Brig. Gen. Earl L. Naiden to Lt. Gen. H. H. Arnold, 1 Apr. 1942.

4. Memo for AC/S, A-4, from Lt. Col. Robert M. Love, DC/S ATC, sub.: Transport Aircraft Delivered to Karachi, 29 Aug. 1942, in which aircraft are listed by type, plane number, and delivery date; Capt. Larry Peyton, "Report and Survey of the India-China Air Transport Operations," 9 Oct. 1942.

5. Ltr., Brig. Gen. Earl L. Naiden to Arnold, 1 Apr. 1942.

6. 1st AC Ferrying Gp., Pilots Folder, Chabua Area, 1942; ICW, ATC, Special Historical Report #3, "Weather Conditions from Lalmanirhat, India, to Kunming, China, 29 June 1944"; [Frank D. Sinclair], Memorandum, Re: Air Transportation System Dinjan—Kunming, China, (hereinafter cited as Sinclair Report), attached to ltr., Whiting Willauer, Sec., China Defense Supplies, Inc., to Col. Harold R. Harris, ATC, 23 Sept. 1942.

7. Ltr., Alexander to Love, 26 Mar. 1943.

8. Ltr., Alexander to Maj. Gen. H. H. [*sic*] George, 4 Jan. 1943; ltr., Alexander to George, 20 Jan. 1943; Hist. India-China Wg., ATC, June–Dec. 1943, pp. 183-88.

9. Claire L. Chennault, *Way of a Fighter* (New York, 1949), p. 234.

10. History and Sidelights of the Third Ferry Squadron, First A.C.F. Command, in MATS Hist. File.

11. Hist. India-China Div., ATC, 1944, II, 431–32; ICD Wkly. Summary, 10 Dec. 1944.

12. India-China Route Report for July 1942, 4 Sept. 1942, in MATS Hist. File; ltr., Lt. Col. A. G. Todd, Chief Stat. Control, ATC, to Lt. Col. H. M. Moran, Army Industrial College, sub.: Hump Operations of the Air Transport Command, 6 Feb. 1946, and attached tables; Hist. India-China Wg., ATC, June–Dec. 1943, p. 446. Net tons include the total haul to China, less the weight of gasoline retained for the return flight over the Hump.

13. Memo for C/S from Olds, sub.: Air Transport Route from India to China, 25 Feb. 1942; msg., Arnold to Brereton, 18 Mar. 1942.

14. Naiden to Air Marshal, R.A.F., India, sub.: Airdrome Requirements for the American Military Air Ferry Service from India to China, 10 Mar. 1942; msg., Aquila 118, Brereton to AGWAR, 28 Mar. 1942; ltr., Naiden to Arnold, 1 Apr. 1942; ltr., Naiden to CG, Trans-India Ferry Command, sub.: Activation of Trans-India Ferry Command, 6 Apr. 1942; ltr., Naiden to Col. C. V. Haynes, sub.: Constitution of the Assam-Burma-China Ferrying Command, 17 Apr. 1942; msg., Aquila 393, Brereton for Arnold, 18 Apr. 1942.

15. Memo for Maj. R. M. Love from Lt. J. B. Haines, sub.: History and Present Status of the India-China Route, 10 June 1942.

16. Hists. Hq. and Hq. Sq., 3d, 6th, and 13th Ferrying Sqs., 1st Ferrying Gp., for 1942; History and Sidelights of the Third Ferry Squadron, First A.C.F. Command, India, both of above in MATS Hist. File; Hist. Ferrying Command Operations, 7 Dec. 1941—30 June 1942, pp. 117–20.

17. R&R, AFAFC to AF Military Personnel, sub.: Transfer of 1st Ferrying Group, 2 Apr. 1942; Comment 2, George to AC/AS, O.C.&R., 19 June 1943, to R&R, Maj.Gen. Barney M. Giles to ATC, sub.: Extract from a Directive from General Stratemeyer, 14 June 1943; ltr., Naiden to CG, Trans-India Ferry Command, sub.: Activation of Trans-India Ferry Command, 6 Apr. 1942; ltr., Naiden to Haynes, sub.: Constitution of the Assam-Burma-China Ferrying Command, 17 Apr. 1942; memo for Gen. Stilwell from Brereton, sub.: Operations of the India-China Ferrying Service, 20 May 1942; ltr., Brig. Gen. C. V. Haynes to to Lt. Col. Samuel T. Moore, 20 Apr. 1942; Col. S. T. Moore, Tactical Employment in the U.S. Army of Transport Aircraft and Gliders in World War II, VIII, 2–4; Lewis H. Brereton, *The Brereton Diaries* (New York, 1946), pp. 110–11; See *Army Air Forces in World War II*, I, 498, 501–2.

18. ATC Historical Officer, Air Transportation to China under the 10th Air Force, p. 18, and documents there cited; 3d Ferrying Sq., 1st Ferrying Gp., ICW, "History of Station No. 6, ICWATC, APO #629"; 13th Sq., 1st Ferrying Gp., ICW, "History of Thirteenth Squadron, Station #7," in MATS Hist. File; ltr., Lt. Col. Gordon A. Rust to CG, ATC, sub.: Occupations of Assam Bases Prior to 1 Dec. 1942, 9 March 1945.

19. Sinclair Report; ltr., Col. Ray H. Clark, Tenth AF Technical Supervisor, to CG, AAF, sub.: Report of Technical Inspection, 13th Ferrying Squadron Detachment, 1st Ferrying Group, Bar-Hapjan, Upper Assam, India, 20 Oct. 1942.

20. Sinclair Report.

21. *Ibid.* See also Chennault, *Way of a Fighter*, pp. 203–4; cf., Comment 2, 19 June 1943, to R&R, Maj. Gen. Barney M. Giles to ATC, sub.: Extract from a Directive from General Stratemeyer, 14 June 1943.

22. Capt. Larry Peyton, "Report and Survey of the India-China Air Transport Operation," 9 Oct. 1942.

23. Memo for CG, AAF, from Col. C. R. Smith, sub.: India-China Ferry Operations, 13 Oct. 1942.

24. *Ibid.*

25. *Ibid.*

26. Interview with Lt. Gen. H. L. George by Lt. Col. Oliver La Farge, June 1946; Comment 2, George to AC/AS, O.C.&R., 19 June 1943, to R&R Giles to ATC, sub.: Extract from a Directive from General Stratemeyer, 14 June 1943.

27. Msg., CM-OUT 07065, Marshall to CG, USAF China-India, 21 Oct. 1942.

28. ICW, General Orders No. 1, 1 Dec. 1942; Admin. Hist. of the Ferrying Command, pp. 16, 61.

29. ATC Weekly Report to CG, AAF, 13 Nov., 4 Dec., 18 Dec., 24 Dec., 1942; ATC Résumé of Transportation Operations

for the Weeks Ending 2 Jan., 9 Jan., 13 Mar.
1943; memo, Lt. Col. Grant Mason, Jr.,
to Actg. C/S, ATC, sub.: C-47 Cargo
Study India-China Wg., 16 Dec. 1942; ltr.,
Alexander to CG, ATC, sub.: Comparison
of the Performance of C-87's and DC-3's in
Transporting Cargo from India to China for
March 1943, 2 Apr. 1943.

30. H. H. Arnold, *Global Mission* (New
York, 1949), pp. 310–12; Chennault, *Way
of a Fighter*, p. 216.

31. Memo for Alexander, from Mason,
sub.: Air Transportation Plan for the Supply
of Increased Aerial Combat Operations in
China, 5 Feb. 1943; ltr., Alexander to Arnold, sub.: India-China Air Freight Operations, 19 Apr. 1943; ltr., Arnold to CG,
USAF, China-Burma-India, sub.: Air Transport Command Operations India to China,
7 Feb. 1943.

32. Rpt., Alexander to George, 13 Feb.
1943; Rpt., Alex[ander] to [Love], 13 Feb.
[1943].

33. Rpt., Alexander to George, 4 Jan.
1943; Rpt., Alexander to George, 1943 Program for the India-China Wing, 24 Mar.
1943; Rpt., Alexander to Arnold, India-
China Air Freight Operations, 19 Apr. 1943;
Chennault, *Way of a Fighter*, pp. 247–49.

34. Tables attached to ltr., Todd to
Moran, sub.: Hump Operations of the Air
Transport Command, 6 Feb. 1946; History
of the India-China Wing, ATC, June–December 1943, p. 446.

35. Rpt., Alexander to George, 20 Jan.
1943, ATC Plans Div., Rpt. on Air Cargo
Capacity from India into China during 1943,
8 Jan. 1943; Rpt., Arnold to Alexander, 4
Mar. 1943.

36. See extracts from Roosevelt Der
Tatevasion, "Lifeline for China"; TWA
Pilot's Reports (C. D. Brown and W. H.
Butler), 27 May 1943, in MATS Historical
File.

37. Hist. India-China Wg., ATC, June–
Dec., 1943, pp. 231–46; Hist. Hump Operations, 1 Jan.–31 Mar. 1945, pp. 10–11.

38. Chennault, *Way of a Fighter*, p. 217;
Rpt., Alexander to George, 22 Apr. 1943.

39. Chennault, *Way of a Fighter*, pp. 220–
24; draft ltr., [CG, AAF] to C/S, USA,
India-China Air Transport Wing, 23 May
1943.

40. Copies of the documents on which
this paragraph is based are found in a volume
kept in the ATC Plans Division entitled
"ICATC July and September Targets,

'Project 7,' " now in MATS Hist. File. See
esp. paper entitled "ICATC Program To
Meet Transportation Objectives during July
and September, 1943," 23 May 1943; memo,
Brig. Gen. J. E. Hull, Actg., AC/S for CG,
AAF, 28 May 1943; memo, Col. Fred C.
Milner, AAG, for CG, ATC, sub.: India-
China Air Transport Wing, 1 June 1943.

41. See file cited in n. 40.

42. Project No. 7, Final Progress Rpt.,
17 July 1943; ltr., George to CG, SAW, *et
al.*, sub.: Project No. 7, 21 July 1943; Hist.
India-China Wg., ATC, June–Dec. 1943,
esp. pp. 52–53.

43. Hist. India-China Wg., ATC, June–
Dec. 1943, esp. pp. 65–75; ltr., Alexander to
CG, ATC, sub.: Informational Rpt. on the
India-China Wing, 4 July 1943; ltr., Alexander to CG, ATC, sub.: Weekly Informational Report on the India-China Wing,
11 July 1943; ltr., Capt. Jesse M. Gregory
to CG, ATC, sub.: Weekly Informational
Report, 6 August 1943.

44. Reports cited in n. 43; also ltr.,
Gregory to CG, ATC, sub.: Weekly Informational Report, 6 Aug. 1943.

45. Reports cited in n. 43; tables atchd.
to ltr., Todd to Moran, sub.: Hump Operations of the Air Transport Command, 6
Feb. 1946; Rpt., American Airlines Inc.,
sub.: Project 7-A.

46. Hist. India-China Wg., ATC, June–
Dec. 1943, pp. 76–89.

47. *Ibid.*, pp. 81–89, 299–306, 313–16.

48. *Ibid.*, pp. 334–38, 344; ltr., Brig.
Gen. Earl S. Hoag to George, 26 Nov.
1943; ltr., Smith to George, 5 Dec. 1943.

49. Msg., Aquila W2193, George to
Smith, 16 Sept. 1943; ltr., Smith to George,
5 Dec., 12 Dec. 1943; Hist. India-China
Wg., ATC, June–Dec. 1943, pp. 159–64.

50. Msg., W1943, George to Smith, 3
Sept. 1943; ICATC 743, George to Smith,
7 Sept. 1943.

51. Msg., W1943, George to Smith, 3
Sept., 1943; 396 AQ, Smith to George, 2
Dec. 1943; ltr., Smith to George, 5 Dec.
1943; Hist. India-China Wg., ATC, June–
Dec. 1943, pp. 265, 279; Hist. India-China
Div., ATC, 1944, I, 141–43; Hist. Ferrying
Div., ATC, V, 188–99.

52. Ltr., Arnold to CG, USAF, India-
China-Burma, Pipeline Project, 27 Dec.
1943; ATC Plans Div., "Requirements for
Ledo-Kunming Pipe Line Project," 19 Aug.
1943; ltr., Lt. Col. George Richardson,
Actg. AC/S, Plans, ATC, to AC/AS,

Plans, sub.: History of Project 8, 17 Jan. 1944; Hist. India-China Wg., ATC, June–Dec. 1943, pp. 97–122, and documents there cited.

53. Admin. Hist. ATC, Mar. 1943—July 1944, pp. 68–69; ltr., Stratemeyer to CG, ICWATC, and CG, CBI-ASC, sub.: Organization, Control, and Responsibilities of ICW in CBI Theater, 14 Sept. 1943; ltr., George to CG, I-B Sector, CBI Theater, sub.: India-China Wing, Air Transport Command, 16 Sept. 1943.

54. Ltr., Col. J. H. Douglas, DC/S, ATC, to Hoag, 26 Oct. 1943; ltr., Hoag to George, 26 Nov. 1943; ltr., Smith to George, 1 Dec., 5 Dec., 23 Dec. 1943; Hist. India-China Wg., ATC, June–Dec. 1943, p. 36.

55. Msg., ATC 1088, George to Hoag, 26 Dec. 1943; msg., Aquila W3015, Stratemeyer to George, 27 Dec. 1943; msg., CM-OUT-10137-4142, Marshall to Stilwell, 28 Dec. 1943; draft memo, George for Arnold, sub.: Colonel Thomas O. Hardin, 17 Jan. 1944; WD Press Release, sub.: India-China Wing, ATC, Receives Presidential Citation, 29 Jan. 1944; WD Gen. Orders 10, 29 Jan. 1944.

56. Ltr., Chennault to Hoag, quoted in ltr., Brig. Gen. C. R. Smith to ATC Hq. Div., sub.: Results of Increased "Hump" Tonnage, 18 Feb. 1944.

57. Ltr., Smith to George, 1 Dec., 5 Dec. 1943; Hist. India-China Wg., ATC, June–Dec. 1943, pp. 175–76.

58. Ltr., Hoag to George, 30 Dec. 1943; ltr., Smith to George, 1 Dec., 5 Dec. 1943; msg., 580, Hoag to George, 30 Dec. 1943; msg., CM-IN-454, Smith to George, 1 Jan. 1944.

59. Search and Rescue in the India-China Division, ATC, I, 12–30; ltr., Smith to George, 12 Dec. 1943.

60. Memo for CG, I-B Sector, CBI, from Hoag, 29 Dec. 1943; memo, Arnold for President, sub.: Lift over the Hump, 5 Jan. 1944; ltr., Smith to CG, AAF, sub.: Review of Operation—India-China, 11 Feb. 1944; Hist. India-China Div., ATC, 1944, I, 27–31, and documents there cited.

61. Hist. India-China Div., ATC, 1944, I, 29, 44.

62. *Ibid.*, I, 30, 35–37, 57, 66–71, 84–86, 343–44.

63. *Ibid.*, I, 3, 23–24, 208–13; ltr., Hardin to George, 9 May 1944; AAF Evaluation Bd., IB and China Theaters, Rpt. No. 9, 15 June 1945, p. 12; Moore, Tactical Employ-ment . . . of Transport Aircraft . . . , VIII, 28–31, 59–60.

64. Hist. India-China Div., ATC, 1944, I, 213–16; ltr., Hardin to George, 6 Apr., 9 May 1944; series of messages from CBI theater, Sept. 1943—Jan. 1944, breaking down Hump tonnages by consignee; table 13A, "Breakdown of ICD-ATC Deliveries by Consignee, 1 January 1944—31 December 1944," in AAF Evaluation Bd., IB and China Theaters, Rpt. No. 9, 15 June 1945.

65. Hist. India-China Div., ATC, 1944, I, 216–18; memo for CG, I-B Sector, CBI, from Hoag, 29 Dec. 1943; ltr., Hardin to George, 6 Apr., 9 May 1944; Chennault, *Way of a Fighter*, pp. 311–14.

66. AAF Evaluation Bd., IB & China Theaters, Rpt. No. 9, 15 June 1945, pp. 22–24.

67. Hist. India-China Div., ATC, 1944, I, 233–47.

68. *Ibid.*, pp. 93–116; ATC Monthly Rpt. to CG, AAF, 15 Apr. 1944; AAF Evaluation Bd., IB & China Theaters, Rpt. No. 9, 15 June 1945, table 13A and p. 25.

69. Preliminary Report of Inspection Made by General Nowland, Colonel Harris and Colonel Ireland of . . . India-China . . . Wing, ATC, 25 March 1944.

70. Ltr., Bd. of Officers to CG, AAF, I-B Sector, CBI, sub.: Report of Findings of Board Directed To Investigate the Maximum Delivery of Air Cargo to China, 21 June 1944.

71. Msg., E 291-955, Douglas to George, 23 June 1944; memo for Arnold from George, sub.: Increased Air Transport Lift into China, 3 July 1944.

72. Memo for Arnold from George, sub.: Increased Air Transport Lift into China, 3 July 1944; History of the India-China Division, ATC, 1944, I, 66.

73. Hist. of India-China Div., ATC, 1944, I, 36–38, 64–87; Augmentation of Air Transport Operations between India and China, 26 Apr. 1944.

74. AAF Evaluation Bd., IB & China Theaters, Rpt. No. 9, 15 June 1945, tables 26B, 26C, 35A.

75. Memo for Douglas from Lt. Col. J. Paul Barringer, sub.: Establishment of Hastings Air Base at Rishra, India, 24 June 1944; memo for CG, ATC from Douglas, sub.: Hastings Air Base—India-China Division Headquarters, 4 July 1944; Hist. India-China Div., ATC, 1944, I, 8–9.

76. Ltr., Smith to George, 12 Dec. 1943;

msg. 595A, Baker to George, 22 Aug. 1944; Hist. India-China Div., ATC, 1944, I, 3-4, 14-16; 1945, p. 542.

77. Ltr., White to CO's, AAFBU, ICD, sub.: Production Line Maintenance, 11 Dec. 1944; Hist. India-China Div., ATC, 1944, I, 43-54; 1945, p. 325.

78. Col. R. B. White, "Summary of the Development of Production-Line Maintenance in CID," 15 May 1945, in Hist. Hump Operations, 1 Jan.-31 Mar. 1945, pp. 325-36; ltr., Tunner to CG, ATC, sub.: Summary of ICD Activities (Jan.-July 1945) for ATC Annual Rpt. to CG, AAF, 1 Sept. 1945; Hist. India-China Div., ATC, 1945, pp. 324-29.

79. Hist. Hump Operations, 1 Jan.-31 Mar. 1945, p. 36; Hist. India-China Div., ATC, 1944, III, 764-71; 1945, pp. 14-19, 443-46, 537, 543.

80. Hist. India-China Div., ATC, 1945, pp. 443-44, 542; Hist. Hump Operations, 1 Jan.-31 Mar. 1945, pp. 9-15, 74-82.

81. Hist. India-China Div., ATC, 1945, p. 539; msg., ATC 0323, Smith to Tunner, 5 Mar. 1943; ltr., CG, ICD-ATC, to CO's, all AAFBU, ICD-ATC, sub.: Flying Safety —Accident Prevention, 3 Jan. 1945, quoted in Hist. Hump Operations, 1 Jan.-31 Mar. 1945, p. 48. See also pp. 40-72 for a detailed analysis of the problem.

82. Hist. India-China Div., ATC, 1945, pp. 349-51.

83. Msg., CABX 5105 ACG, Stratemeyer for George, 19 April 1945.

84. Msg., ATC 1505, George to Stratemeyer, 21 Apr. 1945; msg., CAVX 5280 ACS, Stratemeyer to George, 24 April 1945; msg., ATC 1803, George to Stratemeyer, 25 Apr. 1945.

85. Hist. India-China Div., ATC, 1945, pp. 351-53, 539, 542.

86. Ltr., Douglas to Tunner, 24 Feb. 1945; ltr., Tunner to Douglas, 10 Mar. 1945; ltr., Tunner to George, 2 May 1945; msg., CABX 5280 ACS, Stratemeyer for George, 24 Apr. 1945.

87. Ltr., Douglas to CG, ICD, sub.: Restudy of India-China Operation, 28 Apr. 1945, and App. A; ltr., Col. Samuel E. Gates, AC/S, Plans, ATC, to CG, ICD, NAFD, NATD, and CO, CRBD, sub.: India-China Division C-54 Augmentation Program, 7 June 1945; CRBD, Study of the C-54 Pipeline Maintenance Project, 1945, pp. 4-35; Hist. India-China Div., ATC, 1945, pp. 69-73.

88. CRBD, Study of the C-54 Pipeline Maintenance Problem, 1945, pp. 36-119.

89. Ltr., Tunner to George, 2 May 1945; ltr., George to Tunner, 21 May 1945; Hist. India-China Div., ATC, 1945, pp. 43-46.

90. Hist. India-China Div., ATC, 1945, pp. 44-52.

91. Ibid., pp. 52-56, 543.

92. Ibid., pp. 64-68, 312-13; memo, Douglas for George, 7 Feb. 1945, inclosing draft of ltr. to Mrs. Miller.

93. Hist. India-China Div., ATC, 1944, I, 123-27, 254-55, 257; 1945, pp. 321, 542, 544; memo, Lt. Col. Laigh C. Parker for Smith, sub.: Transportation of Raw Materials on ATC Aircraft, 27 Aug. 1943; unsigned draft memo, for the record, P.&T. Div., ATC, sub.: Highlights regarding Movements of Strategic Material during 1944, 13 Dec. 1944.

94. Hist. India-China Div., ATC, 1945, pp. 293-99.

95. Ibid., pp. 32-34, 268-69.

96. Hist. India-China Div., ATC, 1944, I, 188-202; 1945, pp. 119-20; AAF Evaluation Bd., IB & China Theaters, Rpt. No. 9, 15 June 1945, pp. 14-17.

97. Hist. India-China Div., ATC, 1945, pp. 119-27.

98. Ibid., pp. 132-40.

99. Ltr., Tunner to CG, ATC, sub.: Summary of ICD Activities (Jan.-July 1945) for ATC Annual Report to CG, AAF, 1 Sept. 1945; Hist. India-China Div., ATC, 1945, pp. 189-96.

100. Ltr., Tunner to CG, ATC, 1 Sept. 1945, cited in n. 99; Hist. India-China Div., ATC, 1945, pp. 194-95.

101. Ltr., Tunner to CG, ATC, 1 Sept. 1945, cited in n. 99; Hist. India-China Div., ATC, 1945, pp. 168-72.

102. Ltr., Tunner to CG, ATC, 1 Sept. 1945, cited in n. 99; Hist. India-China Div., ATC, 1945, pp. 150-68.

103. Hist. India-China Div., ATC, 1945, pp. 199-209.

104. Ibid., pp. 100-102.

105. Ibid., pp. 102-14.

NOTES TO CHAPTER 6

1. Hist. Alaskan Division, ATC, Nov. 1944—Sept. 1945, pp. 1-2.

2. Ltr., Lt. Gen. H. H. Arnold, CG AAF, to Rear Adm. W. H. Standley, 10 March 1942; memo for AC/S OPD from Col. H. A. Craig, AC/AS, Plans, sub.:

Cablegram To Be Dispatched to Admiral Standley, 6 May 1942, in 373.6 A, Ferry Crews, AAF Classified Files; memo for CG AAF from Brig. Gen. H. L. George, CG ATC, sub.: Possibility of Alaskan-Siberian Route, 22 June 1942; msgs., Pres. Roosevelt to Adm. Standley for Stalin, 17 June 1942, 23 June 1942; ltr., Arnold to Maxim Litvinoff, 29 June 1942. As late as the end of 1942 Maj. Robert M. Leylan, ATC headquarters specialist on the ALSIB movement, wrote with assurance, "Inevitably the ATC route will extend into Siberia proper, to the vicinity of Vladivostok and the interior of China. Russian approval is a matter of time" (ltr., Leylan to CG ATC, sub.: Report on Alaskan Route, 28 Dec. 1942).

3. Hist. Northwest Air Route to Alaska, 1942–45, p. 65, and documents cited in n. 1. This study, prepared by Capt. Edwin R. Carr, Hist. Off. of the Alaskan Division, was, with minor changes, submitted as a Ph.D. dissertation to the University of Minnesota, Oct. 1946, under the title "Great Falls to Nome: The Inland Air Route to Alaska, 1940–1945."

4. Northwest Air Route, pp. 11–13, 18–19. For difficulties with CAA in Alaska, see ltr., Col. D. V. Gaffney, CO ALSW to CG ATC, sub.: CAA Operations in Alaska, 16 Aug. 1943.

5. Northwest Air Route, pp. 19–23. For difficulties with the Canadian government and particularly the Department of Transport, see ltr., Maj. Gen. H. L. George to Col. Thomas L. Mosley, CO ALSW, sub.: Complaint of Canadian Government with Respect to Construction of Various United States Facilities on the Northwest Ferry Route, 22 Feb. 1943, and incl.

6. Northwest Air Route, pp. 58–62.

7. R&R, AFADS to AFDMR, 14 Mar. 1942; memo for CG FC from Brewer, sub.: Ferry Routes to Alaska—Report on Field Study, 30 Apr. 1942.

8. Northwest Air Route, pp. 54–55, 64–69.

9. *Ibid.*, pp. 57–59, 61–64; msg. PO-218, [Col. Joseph A.] Michela, U.S. Air Attaché at Moscow to MILID, 16 May 1942.

10. For an analysis of some of ATC's reasons for preferring the Northwest ferrying route, see memo for Col. Crumline from Col. C. R. Smith, C/S ATC, 5 Aug. 1942.

11. Northwest Air Route, pp. 64–69; memo for CG ATC from Brig. Gen. T. J. Hanley, Jr., AC/AS, A-4, sub.: Delivery of

Aircraft to the Soviet Government, 6 Sept. 1942, in MATS Hist. File; mimeographed paper, sub.: Discussions on the Establishment of the Alaska-Siberia Ferry Route (unsigned, n.d.), in 361, ATC Central Files; ltr., Belyaev to Arnold, 19 Sept. 1942.

12. Northwest Air Route, pp. 76–78, 104–18, 142; memo for Col. L. G. Fritz, A-3 ATC from Maj. Emery M. Ellingson, Asst. A-3 ATC, sub.: Inspection of Air Transport Command Facilities on Northwest Ferrying Routes (Alaska), 5 Oct. 1942; memo for All Military Personnel G-3 ATC from Lt. Col. Milton W. Arnold, Exec. Opns. Sec. ATC, sub.: Staff Conference on 28 Aug. 1942, 29 Aug. 1942. For a more favorable view by a Ferrying Division officer who was active from July until November in overseeing cold-weather preparations along the route, see ltr., Maj. Homer F. Kellems to CO FERD ATC, sub.: Official Report, Northwest Air Route, 9 Nov. 1942.

13. Northwest Air Route, pp. 30–35, 37–40, 43–46, 72–73; Hist. ALSD, Nov. 1942—Dec. 1943, pp. 139–41; memo for Fritz from Ellingson, 5 Oct. 1942; interview with Lt. Col. Arthur J. Larsen by Frank H. Heck, 7 Aug. 1952.

14. Memo for Col. C. R. Smith, C/S ATC from Lt. Col. Marlow M. Merrick, C Engr. Sec. ATC, sub.: Ferrying Operations to Alaska and Delivery of Planes to the Russians, 1 Sept. 1942; ltr., Col. T. L. Mosley, CO ALSW ATC to CG ATC, sub.: Unsatisfactory Construction along the Alaskan Route, 29 Dec. 1942; Northwest Air Route, pp. 73–75; Hist. ALSD, Nov. 1942—Dec. 1943, pp. 215–16.

15. Northwest Air Route, pp. 79–80; Admin. Hist. ATC, June 1942—Mar. 1943 p. 51.

16. Northwest Air Route, pp. 82–83, 142–43; memo for Gen. George from Lt. Col. Robert M. Love, DC/S ATC, sub.: Capt. Yaggy's Report on the Alaskan Route, 10 Feb. 1943.

17. Ltr., CG ATC to CO ALSW ATC, sub.: Letter of Instructions, 5 Oct. 1942.

18. *Ibid.*; Northwest Air Route, pp. 142–43; Admin. Hist. ATC, June 1942—Mar. 1943, pp. 96, 180–82; memo for Maj. Gen. H. L. George from Col. L. G. Fritz, AC/S, A-3 ATC, sub.: Alaskan Wing, 17 Jan. 1943.

19. Admin. Hist. ATC, June 1942—Mar. 1943, pp. 93–95, 188–89; Northwest Air Route, p. 79.

20. Ltr., H. Bradford Washburn, Jr., to Gen. George, 9 Feb. 1943.

21. Ltr., Capt. Edward E. Yaggy, Jr., to CG AAF, sub.: Findings and Recommendations regarding Status of Bases on Alaskan Wing of Air Transport Command, 2 Feb. 1943; memo for George from Fritz, sub.: Alaskan Wing, 17 Jan. 1943; interview with Larsen by Heck, 7 Aug. 1952.

22. Ltr., Maj. Robert M. Leylan to CG ATC, sub.: Report on Alaskan Route, 28 Dec. 1942.

23. Memo for George from Fritz, sub.: Alaskan Wing, 17 Jan. 1943.

24. Northwest Air Route, pp. 186–87.

25. Ibid., pp. 143–45; ltr., Leylan to CG ATC, sub.: Report on Alaskan Route, 28 Dec. 1942; ltr., Yaggy to CG AAF, sub.: Findings and Recommendations regarding Status of Bases on Alaskan Wing of Air Transport Command, 2 Feb. 1943.

26. Statistics on Delivery of Aircraft to Russia, Alaskan Route and Southern Route, 13 Feb.–30 June 1943, in MATS Hist. File.

27. Sum. of Ferried Aircraft Deliveries over the Northwest Route, Sept. 1942—Dec. 1943, prepared from ALSD Aircraft Status Rpts. It will be noted that the totals reported by this and the previous source are not in complete agreement.

28. Ibid.

29. Northwest Air Route, pp. 145–46; Hist. ALSD, The Pre-Wing Period, pp. 212–20.

30. Northwest Air Route, pp. 148–50; Hist. ALSD, Pre-Wing Period, pp. 207–11.

31. Hist. ALSD, Nov. 1942—Dec. 1943, pp. 93–96, 122; Rich and Finnie, Canol (San Francisco, 1945), pp. 17–49, 62–185.

32. Northwest Air Route, pp. 120–21, 125–27; Hist. ALSD, Nov. 1942—Dec. 1943, pp. 258–60, 273–74; ltr., Mosley to Maj. R. M. Leylan, sub.: Increased Facilities To Handle Proposed Traffic over the Alaskan Route, 26 Jan. 1943.

33. Msg., unnumbered, [C. R.] Smith to Mosley, 11 Mar. 1943, in Leylan Cable Bk., MATS Hist. File.

34. Msg., unnumbered, Smith to Gaffney, 12 Mar. 1943; msg. 5662, CO Ladd Fld. to Smith, 13 Mar. 1943, both in Leylan Cable Bk.

35. Msg., ATC-3159, Smith to Mosley, 24 Mar. 1943, in ATC General's Log; Northwest Air Route, p. 86; ATC Daily Diary, Office of Program Monitor, 28 Mar. 1946.

36. Hist. ALSD, Nov. 1942—Dec. 1943, App. I, p. 95.

37. Ibid., pp. 47–48.

38. Ibid., pp. 48–50.

39. Northwest Air Route, pp. 119–34. Cf. documents in Hist. ALSD, Nov. 1942—Dec. 1943, App. III, esp. pp. 630–38, 645–46, 707, 766–68, 920–21.

40. Northwest Air Route, p. 133; Hist. ALSD, Nov. 1942—Dec. 1943, pp. 247–314, esp. p. 297, n. 19.

41. Hist. ALSD, Nov. 1942—Dec. 1943, pp. 194–95, 276–78, 295–315.

42. Hists. ALSD, July 1944, pp. 52–55, 76–78; Feb. 1944, p. 16; Mar. 1944, p. 29; Apr. 1944, pp. 39–40; Northwest Air Route, p. 93.

43. Hists. ALSD, July 1944, pp. 13, 18, 39–46, 63, 68, 82–83; Jan. 1944, pp. 5–8; June 1944, pp. 37–41.

44. Northwest Air Route, pp. 179–80.

45. Ibid., pp. 190–99.

46. Ibid.; cf. Hist. ALSD, Nov. 1944—Sept. 1945, pp. 1–2.

47. Northwest Air Route, pp. 177–78, 191–93; Hist. ALSD, Sept. 1944, pp. 4–6; Hist. Ferrying Div., ATC, III, 102–3; V, 277–79; VI, 342–49; Hists. ALSD, May 1944, pp. 2–3; Nov. 1942—Dec. 1943, p. 176.

48. Hists. ALSD, Nov. 1944—Sept. 1945, pp. 7–11; Sept.–Oct. 1944, pp. 6–11.

49. Aircraft Allocation and Flow, June 1942—Aug. 1945, esp. pp. 82–86; Hist. FERD, V, 319; Hist. ALSD, Sept.–Oct. 1944, pp. 15–25.

50. Northwest Air Route, pp. 181, 193; Hists. ALSD, Nov. 1942—Dec. 1943, pp. 172–75, 181–85; Aug. 1944, pp. 3–5; Sept.–Oct. 1944, pp. 4–7, 15–24, 63–65; Nov. 1944—Sept. 1945, pp. 13–14.

51. Hist. FERD, V, 310–19; VI, 441–42.

52. Ibid., III, 197–210; Hists. ALSD, Nov. 1942—Dec. 1943, pp. 175–80; Feb. 1944, p. 2; Mar. 1944, p. 2.

53. Hists. ALSD, Nov. 1942—Dec. 1943, pp. 172–74; Nov. 1944—Sept. 1945, pp. 128–31; Hist. FERD, VIII, 210–15.

54. Northwest Air Route, pp. 197–99.

55. Ibid., pp. 155, 159, 172; Hist. ALSD, Sept.–Oct. 1944, p. 26.

56. Northwest Air Route, pp. 37–41.

57. Hist. ALSD, Nov. 1944—Sept. 1945, pp. 26, 47–49.

58. Northwest Air Route, pp. 171–72; Hists. ALSD, Mar. 1944, p. 2; June 1944, p. 6; Sept.–Oct. 1944, pp. 26–27.

59. Northwest Air Route, pp. 161–63, 165–69, 172; Hist. ALSD, Mar. 1944, p. 4.

60. Northwest Air Route, pp. 156–59; Hists. ALSD, Nov. 1942—Dec. 1943, pp. 85, 102, 114–16, 122–23, 130–33; Nov. 1944—Sept. 1945, pp. 27, 36–37, 42–43.

NOTES TO CHAPTER 7

1. The ATC in the Southwest Pacific, pp. 11, 25–27; The ATC in the Pacific, 1942, pp. 132–49; PACD, Chronology of Transpacific Routes, pp. 1–14; memo for all Div. & Sing. Comdrs. from Col. R. M. Love, sub.: ATC Route Mileage outside the United States, 12 July 1943.

2. Administrative Hist. of the Ferrying Command, pp. 63–67, 70, 76–79; ATC in the Pacific, 1942, pp. 8, 42–45, 100–104; Hist. the West Coast Wg., AAF, ATC (Durno), p. 13.

3. ATC in the Pacific, 1942, esp. graph ff. p. 99, and also pp. 58, 114–20, 158.

4. *Ibid.*, pp. 121–24. Cf. the rather sweeping claims made. See also Hist. of the Caribbean Div., ATC, Part II, pp. 196–97.

5. R&R, ACFC to OCAC, Materiel Div., sub.: Delivery of B-25 Airplanes to Netherlands East Indies, 28 Jan. 1942, esp. Comment 3, ACFC to OCAC, 6 Feb. 1942.

6. *Ibid.*; memo for Gen. Arnold from Brig. Gen. Robert Olds, sub.: Delivery of Dutch B-25's, 25 Feb. 1942; memo for Lt. Col. Orlady from Capt. Robert M. Love, sub.: Return of Ferry Crews from Australia, 19 Mar. 1942; memo for Lt. Gen. Brehon Somervell from W. C. Teagle, Jr., sub.: Freight Ferrying System to Australia, 18 Mar. 1942; R&R, Arnold to George, sub.: Ferry Service between Honolulu and Australia, 29 Mar. 1942.

7. ATC in the Southwest Pacific, pp. 12–16, and documents there cited; ATC in the Pacific, 1942, pp. 172–78.

8. ATC in the Pacific, 1942, pp. 54–62.

9. ATC in the Southwest Pacific, pp. 16–18, 25–28, 34–36; ATC in the Pacific, 1942, pp. 51–53, 62–76.

10. ATC in the Southwest Pacific, pp. 29–34, 47–48; AHS-17, Air Action in the Papuan Campaign, 21 July 1942—23 Jan. 1943, pp. 66–72; Hist. of the D.A.T. and 322d Troop Carrier Wing, pp. 7–8.

11. ATC in the Southwest Pacific, pp. 25–45.

12. Ltr., Millard to Brig. Gen. Wm. O. Ryan, 10 Jan. 1944.

13. ATC in the Southwest Pacific, pp. 50–55.

14. Memo for Brig. Gen. L. S. Kuter from Brig. Gen. H. L. George, sub.: Policy concerning Control of Aircraft Assigned to AFAFC for the Operation of Established Air Transportation Services, 16 June 1942; memo for Col. R. C. Smith and Lt. Col. R. M. Love from Col. L. G. Fritz, sub.: Transportation from San Francisco to Australia, 2 July 1942; msg. #1734, Lt. Gen. Delos C. Emmons to CG, AAF, 24 July 1942; R&R, Arnold to George, sub.: Transportation of Personal Mail between San Francisco and Hawaii, 28 July 1942, esp. Comment 2, George to Arnold, 30 July 1942; ATC in the Pacific, 1942, pp. 196–202, 277 (n. 278); ATC in the Southwest Pacific, pp. 53, 56, 79–80.

15. ATC in the Pacific, 1942, pp. 180–82, 211–25, 229–49; ATC in the Southwest Pacific, p. 72; Pacific Wg. Monthly Activity Rpt. to CG ATC, 20 Nov. 1942.

16. Ltr., Ryan to Smith, 9 Mar. 1943.

17. Admin. Hist. of the ATC, June 1942—Mar. 1943, pp. 56–57; ATC in the Southwest Pacific, pp. 95–99; ATC in the Pacific, 1942, pp. 80–93; Hist., Pacific Div., 1 Jan. 1943—30 June 1944, pp. 22–24, 34–46, esp. Table I and graphs included. See also, ltrs., Ryan to CG ATC, sub.: Proposed Manning Tables, Pacific Wing, 5 May 1943, and attached "Personnel Requirement Analysis, Pacific Wing, ATC, as of 31 December 1943"; ltr., Brig. Gen. Bob E. Nowland, C/S, ATC, to CG AAF, sub.: Reorganization of the Pacific Wing, Air Transport Command, 20 Aug. 1943.

18. Admin. Hist. of ATC, June 1942—Mar. 1943, pp. 54–56; Admin. Hist. of ATC, Mar. 1943—July 1944, pp. 70–72; Hist., Pacific Div., 1 Jan. 1943–30 June 1944, pp. 16–22, 24–28.

19. Ltr., Ryan to Smith, 9 Mar. 1943; memo for Ryan from Lt. Col. S. W. Delany, sub.: Observations and Recommendations Resulting from Inspection Trip to the Pacific Wing, 19 Aug. 1943; memo for Fritz from Delany, sub.: Observation and Recommendations Resulting from Inspection Trip to the Pacific Wing, 30 Aug. 1943; memo for Gen. George from Capt. Richard M. Davis, sub.: The Pacific Route, 18 Dec. 1943; West Coast Wg., Hist. Record Rpt., 1 Jan. 1943—30 June 1944, pp. 102–4.

20. Table PACD Westbound Traffic Movement, prepared by ATC Office of

Stat. Control, 6 Mar. 1946; PACD, Chronology of Transpacific Routes, p. 12; ltr., Col. H. H. Harris to United Air Lines Transport Corp., sub.: Summary of Operations of the Air Transport Command, 1943, [10] Jan. 1944; Consolidated Aircraft Corp., "Australian Route Statistical Summary," Dec. 1944.

21. Msg., A5058, Kenny to [?], 5 June 1943, in ATC General's Log; memo for Capt. La Farge from Davis, 14 July 1943; Notes on Transpacific Flight, June 21 to July 4, 1943, C-54 Airplane #284, in MATS Hist. File.

22. Ltr., Davis to Lt. Col. Rex W. D. Smith, sub.: Activities of the West Coast and Pacific Wings for the Week Ending April 30, 1943, 1 May 1943; memo for George from Davis, sub.: The Pacific Route, 18 Dec. 1943; ATC in the Southwest Pacific, pp. 108–10, 129–34, 148–49.

23. Memo for George from Davis, sub.: The Pacific Route, 18 Dec. 1943; ATC in the Southwest Pacific, pp. 105–8 and map ff. p. 148.

24. Various notes in Pacific Theater Officer's Log File, 1942; mimeographed paper, "The Pacific Ferry Route," dated 20 Jan. 1943; memo for CG ATC from Brig. Gen. T. J. Hanley, Jr., AC/AS, A-4, sub.: Ferrying Fighter Aircraft in the South Pacific, 4 Sept. 1942; ltr., Col. M. S. Lawton, Chief Exec., Pacific Wing, to CG ATC, sub.: Facilities at Present and Proposed Air Transport Command Stations, 31 Aug. 1943, inclosing a report on each, signed by Capt. Robert M. Wagner; Summary of Operations of the Air Transport Command, 1943, p. 15.

25. Ltr., Lytle to Col. R. C. W. Blessley, sub.: Completion of Delivery of P-38's, 13 Jan. 1943; R&R, George to Hanley, sub.: Flight Delivery of P-38 Aircraft over South Pacific, 4 Feb. 1943.

26. PACD, Chronology of Transpacific Route, pp. 7–27; memo for CG ATC from Maj. M. A. MacIntyre, sub.: Attached Minutes of Wing Headquarters Conference on April 18 and Action Taken Thereon, 14 May 1943; memo for George from Davis, sub.: The Pacific Route, 18 Dec. 1943; memo for Ryan from Davis, 12 Feb. 1944; memo for Ryan from Davis, sub.: Report of ATC Headquarters Activities for the Period 12 Feb. to 24 Feb. 1944, 24 Feb. 1944; unsigned note for Col. Bailen, sub.: Possibilities of Eliminating Duplication of ATC and NATS Facilities in the Pacific, 27 June 1944; ltr.,

Smith to CG AAF, sub.: Discontinuance ATC "Milk Run," 20 July 1944, and 1st Ind., Brig. Gen. Patrick W. Timberlake, DC/AS, to CG ATC, 12 Aug. 1944; msg. #7442, George to C/S, ATC, 27 Mar. 1943; msg., PAW 4146A3, Ryan to George, 11 Apr. 1943, in ATC General's Log.

27. ATC in the Southwest Pacific, pp. 103–5, 117; memo for CG ATC from MacIntyre, sub.: Attached Minutes of Wing Headquarters Conference on April 18 and Action Taken Thereon, 14 May 1943; ltr., Lawton to CG ATC, sub.: Facilities at Present and Proposed Air Transport Command Stations, 31 Aug. 1943, and inclosed report on each signed by Capt. Robert M. Wagner.

28. Ltr., Davis to Love, 12 Nov. 1943; ATC in the Southwest Pacific, p. 122; PACD, Chronology of Transpacific Routes, pp. 11–12.

29. Memo for George from Davis, sub.: The Pacific Route, 18 Dec. 1943.

30. Ibid.; ATC in the Southwest Pacific, pp. 183–88.

31. ATC in the Southwest Pacific, pp. 181–90; PACD, Chronology of Transpacific Routes, pp. 13–30.

32. ATC in the Southwest Pacific, pp. 192–93.

33. Ibid., pp. 209–21, 224–26.

34. Ltr., Lt. Col. Bennett H. Griffin to CG ATC, sub.: Report of Administrative, Technical, and Communications Inspection of Station No. 20, Pacific Wg. ATC, A.P.O. #929, 27 Mar. 1944, quoted in ATC in the Southwest Pacific, pp. 222–23.

35. ATC in the Southwest Pacific, pp. 228–29, 231–35, 309–12, 317–19, 322–25, 328–40, 361–62.

36. Hist., PACD, ATC, Feb.–Apr. 1945, pp. 51–65; May–Sept. 1945, pp. 21–27, and esp. App. 11; ltr., Lt. Gen. George C. Kenney to Maj. Gen. Ennis C. Whitehead, 26 June 1944; ltr., Whitehead to Lt. Gen. Walter Krueger, 8 Aug. 1944; ltr., Krueger to Whitehead, 16 Aug. 1944; Air Evacuation of Sick and Wounded by the Pacific Wg. ATC, 5 Jan. 1943—30 June 1944, pp. 1–8, 10–13, 23.

37. ATC in the Southwest Pacific, pp. 231–33, 256–58, 262–63, 271–76.

38. Ibid., pp. 276–87, and documents there quoted at length; George C. Kenney, General Kenney Reports (New York, 1949), p. 339.

39. ATC in the Southwest Pacific, pp. 279–85, and documents there quoted.

40. *Ibid.*, pp. 285–89, and documents there quoted.

41. *Ibid.*, pp. 295–301, 312–17.

42. *Ibid.*, pp. 294–95, 296, 299–302, 319, 346–52.

43. *Ibid.*, pp. 219–38, 346–48.

44. *Ibid.*, pp. 346, 352–56, 359–61, 363–65, 379, and documents cited, esp.: ltr., Alexander to Ryan, 21 July 1944; ltr., Alexander to Ryan, 8 Aug., 1944; and ltr., Alexander to George, 19 Aug. 1944.

45. ATC in the Southwest Pacific, pp. 310, 373–76; Hist., PACW ATC, July 1944, pp. 6–8; Hists., PACD, ATC, Aug. 1944, pp. 10–11; Sept., 1944, pp. 8–10; Oct. 1944, pp. 33–34, 37–38; Jan. 1945, p. 57.

46. Hists., PACD, ATC, Aug. 1944, p. 15; Oct. 1944, p. 3.

47. Hists., PACD, ATC, Sept. 1944, pp. 6–7; Oct. 1944, pp. 3–6, 45, and graph ff. p. 32; ltr., Alexander to Ryan, 25 Nov. 1944; Hist. Rcd., SWPW, ATC, Oct.–Dec. 1944, pp. 1–16; Hist. Southwest Pacific Wg., 1 Aug. 1944—1 June 1945, pp. 51–64.

48. Hist., PACD, ATC, Nov. 1944, pp. 3–4; Jan. 1945, p. 1–2; Feb.–Apr. 1945, pp. 4–5, 46, 157; Hist. Rcd. SWPW, ATC, Oct.–Dec. 1944, pp. 17–30; Hist., Southwest Pacific Wg., 1 Aug. 1944—1 Jan. 1945, pp. 64–83.

49. Hist., PACD, ATC, Nov. 1944, p. 4, and graph ff. p. 16; Hist. Rcd., SWPW, ATC, Oct.–Dec. 1944, pp. 30–37; Wkly. Activity Rpt., SWPW, 30 Jan. 1945.

50. Wkly. Activity Rpt., SWPW, 23 Jan. 1945, and graphic exhibits atchd. thereto, summarizing wing traffic to 31 Dec. 1944; Hist., Southwest Pacific Wg., 1 Aug. 1944—1 June 1945, pp. 6–14, esp. graphs ff. pp. 8, 10; SWPW, Special Mission #75, p. 26.

51. Hists., PACD, ATC, Feb.–Apr. 1945, pp. 37–49; May–Sept. 1945, pp. 20, 56–57; PACD Wkly. Activity Rpt., 18 June 1945—20 July 1945.

52. Air Evacuation of Sick and Wounded by the Pacific Wing, ATC, 5 Jan. 1943—30 June 1944, pp. 16–23; Hist., PACD, ATC, Aug. 1944, pp. 17–24; PACD, Chronology of Transpacific Routes, pp. 11–30.

53. PACD, Chronology of Transpacific Routes, pp. 31–42; Hists., PACD., ATC, Sept. 1944; pp. 9–10; Dec. 1944, pp. 12–13; Feb.–Apr. 1944, pp. 50, 56–57, 82–83; May–Sept., pp. 13–14.

54. Hists., PACD, ATC, Oct. 1944, pp. 1, 6–11; Nov. 1944, p. 1; Dec. 1944, pp. 1–4; Jan. 1945, pp. 2–3.

55. Hist., PACD, ATC, Oct. 1944, pp. 6–22; Nov. 1944, pp. 11, 13–14; Dec. 1944, pp. 37–39; Jan. 1945, p. 70; Feb.–Apr. 1945, pp. 151–52; May–Sept. 1945, pp. 121–22.

56. Table, "Ferried Aircraft Deliveries —Pacific Route," prepared by ATC Office of Stat. Control, 28 Feb. 1946. Cf. Hist., PACD, ATC, May–Sept. 1945, pp. 121–22.

57. Table, "C-54 Aircraft Assigned to Pacific Division, Air Transport Command," in Hist., PACD, ATC, May–Sept. 1945, ff. p. 130; ltr., Harris to United Air Lines Transport Corp., [10] Jan. 1944; Consairway Div., Consolidated Vultee Aircraft Corp., "Australian Route Statistical Summary," Jan. 1944.

58. Table, "C-54 Aircraft Assigned to Pacific Division, Air Transport Command"; Stat. Control Div., ATC, "Assigned Aircraft," 9 Aug. 1945, p. A-4; "Aircraft Utilization," 23 June 1945, p. AU-4.

59. Ltr., Col. S. E. Gates, AC/S, Plans, ATC, to CG AAF, sub.: Air Transport Command Requirements for Pacific Operations, 5 June 1945; Stat. Control Div., ATC, "Assigned Aircraft," 9 Aug. 1945, p. A-4; table prepared by Office of Stat. Control, ATC, "Pacific Division Westbound Traffic Movement, Hamilton-Hickam," 28 Feb. 1946.

60. Ltr., Capt. R. M. Davis to Ryan, 27 July 1943.

61. Hists., PACD, ATC, Oct. 1944, pp. 47–49; Feb.–Apr. 1945, pp. 14–24, and App. 22; May–Sept. 1945, graph preceding p. 21.

62. Memo for DC ATC from Gates, sub.: Means of Increasing Airlift to the Western Pacific, 28 June 1945; "Estimates of Passenger Lift To Be Developed West of Hawaii," 9 July 1945, and atchd. office memo; ATC Staff Mtg. Min., 7 Aug. 1945, 10 Aug. 1945; ATC Monthly Rpt., 16 Aug. 1945; msg., ATC 2050, ATC Plans Div. to CG PACD, 26 June 1945, in ATC General's Log, p. 696.

63. Hists., PACD, ATC, Jan. 1945, pp. 31–32; May–Sept. 1945, pp. 43–52, 128–30, 132–56, and esp. App. 8, "Transpacific Transport Schedules—Effective 1 August 1945."

64. "The Maintenance Jam Is Cleared," extract from Hist. Rcd. Rpt. of 1503d AAF BU, Feb. 1945; Stat. Control Div., ATC, "Aircraft Utilization," 27 July 1945, p. AU-4.

65. Hist., PACD, ATC, May–Sept. 1945, pp. 7–8; SWPW, Special Mission #75, pp. 1–18, and documents appended thereto; GHQ USAFPAC, Staff Study, Operation "BAKER-SIXTY," 12 Aug. 1945.

66. SWPW, Special Mission #75, pp. 17–18; msg., ATC #0691, ATC Hq to CG NOLD *et al.*, 11 Aug. 1945; msg., ATC #1028 and 1102, ATC Hq to CG ICHD & PACD, 17 Aug. 1945; msg., #2646, CG ICHD to CG ATC, 19 Aug. 1945; in ATC General's Log.

67. SWPW, Special Mission #75, pp. 21, 23–55; rpt. of Maj. Gen. L. S. Kuter in ATC Staff Meeting Minutes, 4 Sept. 1945; Hist., Air Cargo Sec. of A-3, 54th Troop Carrier Wing, Aug.–Sept. 1945, pp. 9–13.

68. SWPW, Special Mission #75, pp. 53–59, 62–73; rpt. of Maj. Gen. L. S. Kuter in ATC Staff Mtg. Min., 4 Sept. 1945.

69. Oliver La Farge, *The Eagle in the Egg* (Boston, 1949), p. 296; SWPW, Special Mission #75, p. 81.

NOTES TO CHAPTER 8

1. Hist. Ferrying Div. ATC, III, 198–211.

2. Hist. FERD, VI, 451; FERD Wkly. Sum., 30 Aug. 1944.

3. Stat. Control Div., ATC, ATC SR-2, Ferrying Opns., 22 May 1945, p. F-1; Monthly Rpts., ATC to CG AAF, 16 May, 16 June, 15 July, 16 Aug., 16 Sept. 1944; Stat. Control Div., ATC, Statistics for Monthly Rpts. to CG AAF, 13 Sept., 13 Oct., 13 Nov., 13 Dec. 1944; 12 Jan., 14 Feb., 13 Mar., 13 Apr. 1945.

4. Admin. Hist. ATC, June 1942—Mar. 1943, pp. 150–56; U.S. Civ. Production Admin., *Industrial Mobilization for War, History of the War Production Board and Predecessor Agencies* (Washington, 1947), I, 371–72, 651.

5. Hist. Med. Dept., ATC, May 1941—Dec. 1944, Pt. II, pp. 2–4.

6. WD GO 8, 20 June 1942.

7. Memo for CG ATC from Brig. Gen. T. J. Hanley, Jr., AC/AS A-4, sub.: Evac. of Casualties by Air, 28 Aug. 1942.

8. *Ibid.*

9. Hist. Med. Dept., ATC, May 1941—Dec. 1944, Pt. II, pp. 4–9.

10. *Ibid.*, p. 8.

11. Ltr., Col. Fred C. Milner, AAG to CG's All AF's, All AAF Comds., sub.: Air Evacuated Casualties, 13 Mar. 1943.

12. ATC Off. Stat. Control, Air Evac. Highlights, ATC, Jan. 1943—Aug. 1947.

13. Memo for Col. Ireland from Maj. Howard G. Kurtz, Jr., Chief, Traffic Procedures Div., P&T, sub.: Failure of ATC To Complete an Assigned Mission—Transportation of Wounded, 28 Sept. 1943; Monthly Rpt., ATC to CG AAF, 16 Oct. 1943.

14. Air Evac. Highlights, Jan. 1943—Aug. 1947; Hist. Med. Dept., ATC, May 1941—Dec. 1944, Pt. II, pp. 16, 18–19, 28.

15. AAF Reg. 20-1, 1 Sept. 1943; WD Cir. 316, 6 Dec. 1943; Hist. MATS, May–Nov. 1944, pp. 158–62; ltr., Brig. Gen. Edwin S. Perrin, DC/AS to CG ATC, sub.: Operating Plan for Air Evac. between Overseas Theaters and U.S., 1 Mar. 1944.

16. Air Evac. Highlights, Jan. 1943—Aug. 1947.

17. Hist. Med. Dept., ATC, May 1941—Dec. 1944, Pt. II, p. 32; ltr., Col. Gordon G. Bulla, Surg. NAW to CG ATC, sub.: Rpt. of Inspection, Air Evac. Activities, North Atlantic Route, ATC, 10 June 1944.

18. Ltr., Col. Harold R. Harris, C/S ATC to CF AAF, sub.: Air Evac. by ATC from European and Pacific Theaters to U.S., 8 Sept. 1944; msg., ATC-CM-IN X1741, Hoag to CG ATC, 9 Jan. 1945; interview with Maj. O. F. Goriup by Oliver La Farge, 6 Jan. 1943, notes in MATS Hist. File.

19. Hist. Med. Dept., ATC, May 1941—Dec. 1944, Pt. II, p. 32; Air Evac. Highlights, Jan. 1943—Aug. 1947.

20. Ltr., Col. Paul C. Gilliland, Surg. ATC to CG AAF, sub.: Air Evac., 16 July 1943; memo for DC ATC from Col. Duran H. Summers, Exec. to Surg. ICW, sub.: Air Evac. of Patients, 6 June 1944; Hist. ICD, ATC, 1944, I, 254–58, 260–63.

21. Air Evac. Highlights, Jan. 1943—Aug. 1947.

22. Air Evac. of Sick and Wounded by the Pacific Wing, ATC, 5 Jan. 1943—30 June 1944, pp. 22–24, 38–40; Hist. NAW, ATC, Apr. 1944, pp. 34–36; May 1944, pp. 27–29; June 1944, pp. 20–23.

23. Hist. NAW, June 1944, pp. 23–24; ltr., unsgd., Hq. EW, sub.: Air Evac. of 1st Normandy Invasion Casualties, 23 June 1944.

24. Air Evac. by PACW, Jan. 1943—June 1944, pp. 7–8, 10, 40–41; ATC Reg. 25-6, 31 Aug. 1944; ATC Memo 25-6, 17 Mar. 1945; Hist. Pacific Div., ATC, Feb.–Apr. 1945, pp. 93–94; Hist. Med. Dept., ATC, 1 Jan. 1945—13 Mar. 1946, pp. 94–95;

advance release by OWI for morning papers, 9 Mar. 1945.

25. Air Evac. by PACW, Jan. 1943—June 1944, pp. 33–34; Hist. Med. Dept., ATC, 1 Jan. 1945—13 Mar. 1946, pp. 92–94.

26. Hist. North Atlantic Div., ATC, 1 Oct. 1944—1 Oct. 1945, pp. 393–99.

27. Air Evac. by PACW, Jan. 1943—June 1944, pp. 11–12, 16–17, 20–23; Hist. PACW, July 1944, pp. 12–15; Hist. PACD, Aug. 1944, pp. 18–20; Sept. 1944, pp. 8–10; Nov. 1944, pp. 34–37; Dec. 1944, pp. 16–18, 21–22; Jan. 1945, pp. 48–51; Feb.–Apr. 1945, pp. 87–88, 90–92, 94–98; May–Sept. 1945, pp. 59–65, 72–73.

28. Hist. Med. Dept., ATC, May 1941—Dec. 1944, Pt. II, p. 1; advance release by OWI for morning papers, 9 Mar. 1945.

29. Hist. Rec. Rpt. 1503d AAFBU, Mar. 1945, extract copy, p. 23, in MATS Hist. File.

30. Plans Div. Rpt. for Wk. Ending 29 June 1944, 3 Oct. 1944; Plans Div. Paper, sub.: Planning Functions of ATC, 2 Oct. 1944, esp. Tab A.

31. AAF Hq. OI #20-2, 13 Sept. 1944.

32. Hist. North African Div., ATC, 1 Mar.–30 Sept. 1945, p. 180; cf. Redeployment, the Role of Hq. Continental Air Forces in the Redeployment of the AAF.

33. Ltr., Maj. Gen. H. L. George to CG AAF, sub.: Redeployment—ATC Requirements, 16 June 1944, and incl.; draft 2d ind., ATC to CG AAF, undated, and incls. 4, 5, 6 thereto, MATS Hist. File.

34. Ltr., Col. Harold R. Harris, C/S ATC to CG NAD *et al.*, sub.: ATC Opns. Plan for Redeployment of Flight Echelons from MTO and ETO to U.S., 5 May 1945; Staff Mtg., Opns. Div., ATC Hq., 30 Apr. 1945; Hist. Caribbean Div., ATC, Returning Aircraft, 1945, p. 14; Hist. NAD, 1 Oct. 1944—1 Oct. 1945, pp. 203–4; Hist. NAFD, 1 Mar.–30 Sept. 1945, pp. 173–80.

35. Staff Mtg., Opns. Div., 30 Apr. 1945; Hist. South Atlantic Div., ATC, May–Sept. 1945, p. 15; memo for AC/S Opns. from Lt. Col. O. W. Coyle, sub.: Wkly. Activity Rpt., Ferry and Tac. Div., 10 May–16 May 1945, 17 May 1945.

36. Monthly Rpt., ATC to CG AAF, 16 May 1945; Hist. Rcd. Rpt., European Div., ATC, 1945, pp. 55–57; Hist. NAD, 1 Oct. 1944—1 Oct. 1945, p. 557.

37. Monthly Rpt., ATC to CG AAF, 16 June 1945; Hist. NAFD, 1 Mar.–30 Sept.

1945, p. 193; tab. ATC Off. Stat. Control, sub.: The White Proj., 16 July 1946.

38. Hist. SATD, May–Sept. 1945, pp. 179–80; AAF Hq. OI #20-2, 13 Sept. 1944.

39. Hist. NAD, 1 Oct. 1944—1 Oct. 1945, pp. 210–11, 224; Hist. SATD, May–Sept. 1945, pp. 18–19, 22; Redeployment, the Role of CAF, I, 167.

40. Ltr., Col. Harold R. Harris, C/S ATC to CG NAD *et al.*, sub.: ATC Opns. Plan for Redeployment of Flight Echelons from MTO and ETO to U.S., 5 May 1945; Hist. Rec. Rept. EURD, May–Sept. 1945, pp. 50–53.

41. Ltr., Harris to CG NAD *et al.*, 5 May 1945; ltr., Lt. Gen. J. E. Hull, AC/S OPD WDGS to CG AAF *et al.*, sub.: Return of Certain Aircraft and Crews from the European and Mediterranean Theaters of Operation, WD 370.5 (10 May 1945) OB-S-E-SPMCT, 12 May 1945; ltr., Col. George W. Phillips, Actg. AG, Continental AF to CG's Continental AF and I TCC, sub.: Instructions Governing Aircraft and AAF Combat Crew and/or Personnel Being Returned to the U.S. by Air, 29 May 1945; Hist. FERD, VIII, 144–45, 154–55; Redeployment, Role of CAF, I, 166.

42. Hist. FERD, VIII, 144–45, 149–51, 154–58; Hist. Rcd. Rpt. EURD, May–Sept. 1945, pp. 59–63; Hist. NAD, 1 Oct. 1944—1 Oct. 1945, pp. 215–18; Hist. NAFD, 1 Mar.–30 Sept. 1945, pp. 184–86, 188.

43. Redeployment, Role of CAF, I, 63–64, 166.

44. ATC Off. Stat. Control, sub.: The White Proj., 16 July 1946; Hist. NAFD, 1 Mar.–30 Sept. 1945, p. 198.

45. ATC Off. Stat. Control, sub.: The White Proj., 16 July 1946.

46. Hist. SATD, May–Sept. 1945, pp. 169, 175, 178–79.

47. ATC Off. Stat. Control, sub.: The White Proj., 16 July 1946.

48. ATC Staff Mtg. Min., 10 Apr. 1945; ltr., CG ATC to CG AAF, sub.: Movement of Personnel by Air from Europe to the U.S., 12 Apr. 1945; transcript, telephone conversation, Col. R. W. Ireland, AC/S P&T ATC and Col. Cortlandt S. Johnson, CO CRBD ATC, 10 Apr. 1945, in Hist. CRBD, The Green Proj. 1945, App., p. 1.

49. ATC Staff Mtg. Min., 17 Apr. 1945; ltr., Maj. Gen. J. E. Hull, AC/S OPD to CG AAF, sub.: Return of Casual Military Personnel from Europe, 17 Apr. 1945; ltr., Brig. Gen. Joe L. Loutzenheiser, Actg.

AC/AS, Plans to CG ATC, sub.: Return of Casual Military Personnel from Europe, 20 Apr. 1945; ltr., Col. Harold R. Harris, C/S ATC to All Staff Divs. ATC, sub.: "Atlantic Augmentation" Proj., 16 Apr. 1945.

50. Hist. Rcd. Rpt., EURD, May–Sept. 1945, pp. 36–38; Hist. NAFD, 1 Mar.–30 Sept. 1945, pp. 120–31; Hist. SATD, May–Sept. 1945, pp. 78–83, 86, 90–91; Hist. NAD, 1 Oct. 1944—1 Oct. 1945, pp. 343–44; Hist. CRBD, Green Proj., pp. 49–50.

51. Hist. SATD, May–Sept. 1945, pp. 75–78; Hist. CRBD, Green Proj., pp. 62–65, 69, 126; Hist. NAFD, 1 Mar.–30 Sept. 1945, pp. 138–39.

52. Ltr., Maj. Gen. J. E. Hull, AC/S OPD to CG AAF, sub.: Return of Casual Military Personnel for Europe, 17 Apr. 1945; rpt., ATC to CG AAF, 16 May 1945.

53. Booklet, Stat. Control Div., ATC, The Green Proj., 15 May 1945; "Factors Entering into Choice of Routes in Movement by Air of 50,000 Military Personnel per Month from ETO and MTO to U.S.," n.s., n.d.; incl. to memo for Special Committee Investigating the National Defense Program, U.S. Senate, from Col. Samuel E. Gates, AC/S Plans, ATC, sub.: Request for Additional Information, 20 July 1945; memo for AC/S Plans, ATC from Lt. Col. Thomas M. Murphy, Actg. AC/S Plans, sub.: Utilization of Various Transatlantic Routes in the Green Proj., 2 July 1945; WD Bur. Pub. Rel. Press Release, sub.: Casablanca, the Hub of the ATC's Redeployment Program, 31 May 1945; Hist. NAFD, 1 Mar.–30 Sept. 1945, pp. 133–34.

54. Hist. NAFD, 1 Mar.–30 Sept. 1945, pp. 143–45; Hist. SATD, May–Sept. 1945, pp. 75–78, 108–24; Hist. CRBD, Green Proj., pp. 8, 59–70, 75–77.

55. Hist. NAFD, 1 Mar.–30 Sept. 1945, pp. 145–48.

56. Hist. CRBD, Green Proj., pp. 108–11; Hist. NAFD, 1 Mar.–30 Sept. 1945, pp. 148–49; Hist. SATD, Mar.–Sept. 1945, pp. 99–101.

57. Hist. SATD, May–Sept. 1945, p. 102.

58. Ibid., pp. 139–40, 244; Hist. NAFD, 1 Mar.–30 Sept. 1945, pp. 148–49; Hist. CRBD, Green Proj., pp. 111–13.

59. Hist. NAFD, 1 Mar.–30 Sept. 1945, p. 6; NAFD Wkly. Activity Rpts., 11 May, 16 May 1945; Hist. NAD, 1 Oct. 1944—1 Oct. 1945, pp. 365–66.

60. Ltr., Col. R. W. Ireland, AC/S P&T ATC to CG NAFD et al., sub.: Traffic Flow and Traffic Procedures for "Green Project," 1 June 1945; Hist. NAFD, 1 Mar.–30 Sept. 1945, pp. 112–13; Hist. NAD, 1 Oct. 1944—1 Oct. 1945, pp. 353–55.

61. Memo for I&S from Lt. Col. A. G. Todd, Chief, ATC Off. Stat. Control, sub.: Green Proj., 22 July 1946, and tables incl.

62. Ibid.

63. Hist. NAFD, 1 Mar.–30 Sept. 1945, pp. 109, 134–35, 163; Booklet, Stat. Control Div., ATC, The Green Proj., 15 May 1945; NAFD Wkly. Activity Rpts., 23 May, 16 Aug. 1945; ltr., Maj. Gen. J. S. Stowell to Frank H. Heck, 11 Sept. 1952.

64. Schedules included in SATD SOP for Green Proj., in Hist. SATD, May–Sept. 1945, App.

65. Ltr., Capt. John G. Harvey to Maj. David W. Long, 12 July 1945, and 6 incl., in MATS Hist. File; Hist. NAD, 1 Oct. 1944–1 Oct. 1945, pp. 356–57.

66. Schedules in SATD SOP for Green Proj., in Hist. SATD, May–Sept. 1945, App.; Log of a Round Trip of Caribbean Div. Bases in Waller-based Green Proj. C-47's, pp. 8–13, 15–18; Hist. CRBD, Green Proj., p. 13; Interview with Maj. John F. Leonard, Capt. Roberts, and Capt. John G. Harvey, 28 May 1946, notes in MATS Hist. File.

67. Hist. CRBD, Green Proj., p. 128; Hist. SATD, May–Sept. 1945, pp. 223, 230.

68. Hist. SATD, May–Sept. 1945, p. 46; Hist. NAFD, 1 Mar.–30 Sept. 1945, p. 167; Hist. CRBD, Green Proj., p. 22.

69. Hist. SATD, May–Sept. 1945, pp. 51–52, 149–50; Hist. NAD, 1 Oct. 1944–1 Oct. 1945, pp. 357–60.

70. Hist. SATD, May–Sept. 1945, pp. 92–94, 150–53, 155–56, 160; Hist. CRBD, Green Proj., pp. 122–23; Hist. NAD, 1 Oct. 1944—1 Oct. 1945, pp. 688–89.

71. Hist. SATD, May–Sept. 1945, pp. 151, 154–55, 202; comment by Pfc. A. H. Train, 28 June 1945, and notations thereon, in MATS Hist. File.

72. Hist. SATD, May–Sept. 1945, p. 168; Hist. NAFD, 1 Mar.–30 Sept. 1945, pp. 154–59.

73. ACT Off. Stat. Control, Green Proj. Rpt., 3 July 1945; Hist. CRBD, Green Proj., p. 135.

74. Hist. NAD, 1 Oct. 1944—1 Oct. 1945, pp. 360–61; Hist. CRBD, Green Proj., pp. 114–18.

75. Hist. SATD, May–Sept. 1945, pp. 160–61; Hist. CRBD, Green Proj., pp. 121–22; ltr., Lt. Col. L. S. Howell, Actg. AG CRBD to CG ATC, sub.: Passenger Comments—Green Proj., 16 July 1945.

76. ATC Staff Mtgs. Min., 7 and 10 Aug. 1945; msg. WAR X48679, OPD to USFET *et al.*, 11 Aug. 1945; memo for AC/S Opns., ATC from Lt. Col. Dallas B. Sherman, Plans Div., Opns. ATC, sub.: Résumé of the "Purple Project," 25 Aug. 1945; Hist. CRBD, Misc. Proj., 1945, pp. 1–9.

77. Memo for AC/S Opns. from Sherman, 25 Aug. 1945; msg. ATC 1345, ATC to CG NAFD, 23 Aug. 1945.

78. Memo for CG AAF from George, sub.: Reduction of the Green Proj., 23 Aug. 1945.

79. Memo for CG AAF from Maj. Gen. H. A. Craig, Chief, Theater Gp., OPD, sub.: Orderly Reduction of the ATC, 28 Aug. 1945; ATC Staff Mtg. Min., 28 Aug. 1945; msg. ATC 1752, ATC to CG NAFD *et al.*, 31 Aug. 1945; msg. ATC 0233, ATC to CG NAFD, 7 Sept. 1945.

80. Hist. CRBD, Green Proj., p. 139; Hist. SATD, May–Sept. 1945, pp. 232–33, 236, 238, 247–49; Hist. CRBD, Misc. Proj., pp. 32–41.

81. Hist. CRBD, Misc. Proj., pp. 10–31.

82. Hist. ATC, 1 Oct. 1945—31 Dec. 1946, I, 174–78; Hist. FERD, VIII, 251–65; ltr., J. M. Johnson, Dir., Office of Defense Trans. to Brig. Gen. Milton W. Arnold, Actg. C/S ATC *et al.*, 6 Dec. 1945.

83. Hist. PACD, May–Sept. 1945, pp. 125–27; Hist. PACD, 1 Oct. 1945–31 Dec. 1946, pp. 93–98; Hist. ATC, 1 Oct. 1945—31 Dec. 1946, I, 109–14. To a lesser degree the Pacific Division, by that time almost denuded of necessary personnel, assisted in SUNSET II (Mar.–June 1946) and SUNSET III (Autumn, 1946), in which 235 and 21 B-29's, respectively, were ferried back to the United States (Hist. ATC, 1 Oct. 1945—31 Dec. 1946, I, 114–17).

NOTES TO CHAPTER 9

1. Col. R. E. Smyser, Jr., Draft of Hist. of Aviation Engineers for Historian, IX Engineer Command, 3 Apr. 1944; Hist. Summary of the Aviation Engineers (hereinafter cited as Arnold Hist. Summary) in General Arnold's file; "The Aviation Engineers Are Five Years Old," *Aviation Engineer Notes* (hereinafter cited as *Avn. Engr. Notes*), June 1945; Brig. Gen. Stuart C. Godfrey, "Engineers with the Army Air Forces," a lecture delivered at the Engineer School, Mar. 1943 (hereinafter cited as Godfrey Lecture).

2. Godfrey Lecture.

3. WD TM 5-255, Aviation Engineers (Tentative), 31 Dec. 1943.

4. Quoted in Godfrey Lecture.

5. Rpt. Bd. of Officers on Aviation Engineers, 20 July 1946, Tab B.

6. Arnold Hist. Summary; 1st Lt. W. L. Wannamacher, Hist. of the Air War in the Pacific Ocean Areas, App. II: The Construction and Development of Air Fields in the Central Pacific through June 1941, pp. 46–73.

7. Capt. R. D. Montgomery and others, Account of the Battle of Agoloma, Bataan, P.I., Regarding Co. A, 803d EAB, Compiled after the War; Capt. R. D. Montgomery, Sketch of 803d EAB, Hist. from June 1, 1941; Office of the Chief Engineer, GHQ, Army Forces, Pacific, *Engineers of the Southwest Pacific, 1941–45* (hereinafter cited as *ESWP*) (8 vols.; Washington, 1947–53), Vol. VI, App. I, pp. 487–91.

8. Maj. Gen. William E. Lynd, "Strategical Function of the Aviation Engineers," *Avn. Engr. Notes*, July 1944, pp. 2–6; Arnold Hist. Summary; Hist. 11th AF.

9. Arnold Hist. Summary; Status of Engineer Aviation Units, in Air Engineer's Folder, Dept. of Def. files, Record Group 506.

10. This point is brought out repeatedly, almost unanimously, in the various unit histories and reports of inspections.

11. Col. George Kumpe, Article Circulated to Battalion Commanders by IX Engineer Command, 22 Feb. 1945, and comments thereon, in folder of the Air Engineer, Dept. of Def. files, Record Group 506 (hereinafter cited as Kumpe Folder).

12. Ltr., Col. George Mayo to Brig. Gen. James B. Newman, 24 Mar. 1944.

13. This publication, despite its usefulness and comprehensiveness, was almost condemned to extinction by Management Control early in 1944. It was allowed to continue minus its morale features. Ltr., Mayo to Newman, 24 Mar. 1944.

14. Normal Assignment of Arms and Services with the Army Air Forces, 26 Aug. 1943 (AG 322, 8 Aug. 1943).

15. Such as the letter from Lt. Gen. M. F.

Harmon to Lt. Gen. B. M. Giles, 13 Oct. 1944.

16. Memo for CG AAF from Brig. Gen. S. C. Godfrey, Sub: Control of Aviation Engineer Troops in Theaters of Operation, 13 Oct. 1943.

17. Report of Conference on Airborne Aviation Engineers, 8 June 1942.

18. WD TM 5-255, 15 Apr. 1944; "Notes on Airborne Aviation Engineers," *Avn. Engr. Notes*, Feb.–Mar. 1943, pp. 1–3.

19. Ltr., Brig. Gen. S. C. Godfrey to Lt. Gen. G. C. Kenney, 28 May 1943.

20. Hq., AAF Study, Aviation Engineer Units, Continental U.S. and Overseas, as of 15 Sept. 1943 shows the variety of these units as well as their small numbers. Occasional letters from the Air Engineer's office in 1943 and 1944 indicate efforts to inspire interest in them on the part of overseas air forces headquarters.

21. Rpt. Bd. of Officers on Aviation Engineers, 20 July 1946.

22. Hist. 8th AF, Jan. 1944–July 1945, Special Staff Sections, traces course of the construction program from the earliest days. Brig. Gen. S. C. Godfrey, Rpt. on Airdromes and Aviation Engineers (hereinafter cited as Godfrey Rpt.), 19 Jan. 1943; 4 Oct. 1943. These development reports were based on Gen. Godfrey's extensive inspection tours.

23. See, among others, unit histories of the 814th, 832d, 834th, and 850th EAB's.

24. Hist. 8th AF, Jan. 1944—July 1945, Special Staff Sections; *AAF in WW II*, II, 646; ltr., CG, AAF to CG, SOS, sub: Delays in Shipment of Equipment for Aviation Engineer Units, 12 Sept. 1942; Hist. USAAF Hq., 8th AF, 19 Aug. 1942—1 May 1943, VII AFSC; ltr., Lt. Col. M. J. Goodman to Brig. Gen. James B. Newman, 6 Dec. 1943; ltr., Maj. Gen. W. H. Frank to Brig. Gen. S. C. Godfrey, 2 Sept. 1942; ltr., Lt. Col. R. E. Smyser, Jr., to Brig. Gen. S. C. Godfrey, 10 Aug. 1942.

25. *Thus We Served*, Hist. 834th EAB.

26. Godfrey Rpt., 19 Jan. 1943.

27. Hist. of the Aviation Engineers in the Mediterranean Theater of Operations (hereinafter cited as Avn. Engr. in MTO), pp. 4–5; Policies Affecting Aviation Engineers in the Mediterranean Campaigns (3d ed.) (hereinafter cited as Policies Affecting Avn. Engr. in Medit.), p. 3; Godfrey Rpt., 19 Jan. 1943.

28. *AAF in WW II*, II, 118; Avn. Engr. in MTO, pp. 7–12; Hist. 814th EAB, 15 Jan. 1942—17 Aug. 1943.

29. Brig. Gen. Donald A. Davison, interview, "Aviation Engineers in the Battle of Tunisia," AFFSAT war room, 8 June 1943 (hereinafter cited as Davison Interview); Avn. Engr. in MTO, pp. 12–13.

30. Davison Interview; Avn. Engr. in MTO, pp. 14–15; Hist. 887th Abn. Engr. Avn. Co., Aug. 1944; Godfrey Rpt., 19 Jan. 1943.

31. Avn. Engr. in MTO, p. 15.

32. Hist. 814th EAB, 15 Jan. 1942—17 Aug. 1943.

33. Ltr., Brig. Gen. S. C. Godfrey to Brig. Gen. Donald A. Davison, 28 Sept. 1943.

34. Avn. Engr. in MTO, p. 17.

35. Davison Interview; Hist. 814th EAB, 15 Jan. 1942—17 Aug. 1943.

36. Ltr., Brig. Gen. S. C. Godfrey to Maj. Gen. Ira C. Eaker, 5 June 1943; Davison Interview.

37. Ltr., Brig. Gen. S. C. Godfrey to Lt. Gen. Carl Spaatz, 27 Jan. 1943; Policies Affecting Avn. Engr. in Medit., p. 6; Avn. Engr. in MTO, pp. 27–37 and 50–53; *AAF in WW II*, II, 119.

38. Ltr., CO, 838th EAB to CG, XII AFSC, 23 Sept. 1943; Avn. Engr. in MTO, p. 59.

39. Col. John C. Colonna, Introductory Note in Policies Affecting Avn. Engr. in Medit.

40. Ltr., Lt. Gen. Carl Spaatz to Gen. H. H. Arnold, 6 May 1943.

41. Godfrey Rpt., 4 Oct. 1943; Avn. Engr. in MTO, pp. 105–6.

42. Avn. Engr. in MTO, pp. 106–12.

43. Summary of Rpt., 815th EAB on Sicilian Operation, *Avn. Engr. Notes*, Apr. 1944, pp. 2–6.

44. Avn. Engr. in MTO, pp. 113–19.

45. *Ibid.*, pp. 121–27, 182–83; special account in 809th EAB Hist. for 1943.

46. Avn. Engr. in MTO, pp. 128–31.

47. *Ibid.*, pp. 135–41, 163–65, 183.

48. *Ibid.*, pp. 158–61.

49. *Ibid.*, pp. 75–81; *AAF in WW II*, II, 560; Policies Affecting Avn. Engr. in Medit., p. 7; ltr., Col. R. E. Smyser, Jr., to CG, 8th AF, 10 Sept. 1943; ltr., Maj. Gen. George E. Stratemeyer to Maj. Gen. Eugene Reybold, Chief of Engineers, 26 June 1943; Memo for Historian, IX Engineer Command from Col. R. E. Smyser, Jr., 3 Apr. 1945.

50. Avn. Engr. in MTO, pp. 191-92.

51. *Ibid.*, pp. 193-94.

52. *Ibid.*, pp. 194-95, 199-200.

53. *Ibid.*, pp. 205-6, 208; Airfields in the MTO.

54. *AAF in WW II*, III, 345; Airfields in the MTO; Avn. Engr. in MTO, pp. 209-12.

55. Avn. Engr. in MTO, pp. 336-44; see also *AAF in WW II*, II, 568.

56. Policies Affecting Avn. Engr. in Medit., p. 13; Avn. Engr. in MTO, pp. 335-37, 344.

57. Avn. Engr. in MTO, pp. 215-16.

58. *Ibid.*, pp. 224-40; *AAF in WW II*, III, 393.

59. Avn. Engr. in MTO, pp. 255-61; Policies Affecting Avn. Engr. in Medit., p. 4.

60. Policies Affecting Avn. Engr. in Medit., p. 4; Avn. Engr. in MTO, pp. 250-55.

61. Hist. 812th EAB.

62. *AAF in WW II*, III, 432; Avn. Engr. in MTO, pp. 283-84, 290-91; Airfields in the MTO; Hist. IX Engineer Command (Wiesbaden, 1945) (hereinafter cited as Hist. IX EC), p. 194; "Reconstruction of Airfields in Southern France," *Avn. Engr. Notes*, Feb. 1945, p. 5; Hist. 887th Abn. Engr. Avn. Co., Aug. 1944.

63. "Reconstruction of Airfields in Southern France," *Avn. Engr. Notes*, Feb. 1945; Engr. in MTO, pp. 315-20; Airfields in the MTO.

64. Avn. Engr. in MTO, pp. 243-47.

65. Memo for Historian, IX Engineer Command, from Col. R. E. Smyser, Jr., 3 Apr. 1945; 9th AF and Its Principal Commands in the ETO, Vol. VII, chap. iii; Hist. IX EC, pp. 12-14.

66. Brig. Gen. Stuart C. Godfrey to Col. Karl B. Schilling, 30 Nov. 1943; Hist. IX EC, p. 16; 9th AF and Its Principal Commands, p. 11; *AAF in WW II*, III, 562-63.

67. Hist. IX EC, pp. 16, 33-39, 40-47; 9th AF and Its Principal Commands, p. 17; Hq., IX EC, Folder of Section Histories (hereinafter cited as IX EC Folder), A-2 and A-4; Hist. 832d EAB; Hist. 834th EAB.

68. Hist. IX EC, pp. 62-64; ltr., Brig. Gen. James B. Newman, Jr., to Col. George Mayo, 22 June 1944.

69. Interview with Brig. Gen. Newman by Maj. B. Wobbeking, 1 Nov. 1944; IX EC Folder; Hist. IX EC, pp. 66; Rpt. of WD Observers Bd., 12 Aug. 1944.

70. Ltr., Newman to Mayo, 22 June 1944.

71. Ltr., Lt. Gen. Lewis H. Brereton to Lt. Gen. B. M. Giles, 5 July 1944.

72. Col. X. H. Price, Rpt. on Avn. Engr., WD Observers Bd., 15 Aug. 1944.

73. Hist. IX EC, p. 67.

74. Ltr., Newman to Mayo, 22 June 1944; Hist. IX EC, p. 70; 9th AF and Its Principal Commands, VII, 20; IX EC Folder; Gordon H. Harrison, *Cross-Channel Attack*, U.S. Army in World War II (Washington, 1951), p. 448.

75. Hist. IX EC, pp. 82, 146; 9th AF and Its Principal Commands, VII, 22; IX EC Folder; "Airfields in France," *Avn. Engr. Notes*, Dec. 1944, p. 4.

76. Newman to Mayo, 22 June 1944. This comment prior to the breakout was generally valid for the rest of the campaign.

77. *AAF in WW II*, III, 567-68; Hist. IX EC, p. 87; "Airfields in Europe," *Avn. Engr. Notes*, Dec. 1944, p. 4; IX EC Folder.

78. Hist., IX EC, pp. 88-91.

79. Col. W. J. Ray, paper presented at meeting, Hq., IX EC, Mar. 1945; Hist., IX EC, pp. 89-90, 100, 148; Hist. 8345h EAB.

80. Col. W. J. Ray Paper, Mar. 1945; Hist. IX EC, pp. 101-4; Hist. 832d EAB; Hist. 834th EAB; 9th AF and Its Principal Commands, VII, 12.

81. Hist. IX EC, pp. 104, 160; Kumpe Folder.

82. Memo for General Arnold from Colonel Mayo, 5 Apr. 1945; Memo for Col. Mayo from Maj. Gen. Donald Wilson, 23 Apr. 1945; ltr., Mayo to Godfrey, 2 Nov. 1944; Hist. IX EC, pp. 102, 146; *AAF in WW II*, III, 570-71.

83. Hist. IX EC, p. 105.

84. Col. George Mayo, Rpt. Air Engineer, On Temporary Duty in ETO and MTO, 10 Jan.-3 Mar. 1945, Tab F (hereinafter cited as Mayo Rpt.).

85. Hist. IX EC, pp. 115, 161; ltr., Lt. Gen. L. H. Brereton to 877th EAB, 7 May 1945.

86. Hist. IX EC, pp. 118-30.

87. Mayo Rpt.; Hist. IX EC, p. 169; 9th AF and Its Principal Commands, VII, 146 (Foreword).

88. IX EC Folder.

89. Kumpe Folder; Mayo Rpt.

NOTES TO CHAPTER 10

1. Office of the Chief Engineer, GHQ, Army Forces, Pacific, *Engineers of the Southwest Pacific 1941-45* (8 vols.; Washington, 1947-53), VI, 16-18, 432; VIII, 156-58. This superlatively detailed and illustrated work (hereinafter cited as *ESWP*) often has an unsympathetic attitude toward Air Force points of view. Volume VI, the most useful for this study, is entitled *Airfield and Base Development.*

2. *ESWP*, VI, 98, 422; I, 39, ltr., Maj. Gen. George C. Kenney to CINC SWPA, 4 Feb. 1943; ltr., CINC SWPA to CG, 5th AF, 24 Feb. 1943, reproduced in Vol. II, App. III; Brig. Gen. S. C. Godfrey, Report on Airdromes and Aviation Engineers around the World, 4 Oct. 1943; memo for CG, AAF, from Col. George C. Mayo, Report on Temporary Duty in the Pacific Theaters, 27 Aug. 1945.

3. *ESWP*, VI, 78, 79, 422.

4. *Ibid.*, pp. 422-25, 432-37.

5. *Ibid.*, pp. 119-22; ltr., Kenney to Col. W. R. Ritchie, 14 Apr. 1943.

6. Early Hist. 871st Airborne EAB; Hist. 5th AF Service Command, Sept. 1942—Jan. 1944, chap. xi; R&R, Godfrey to Arnold, 22 Sept. 1943; *Aviation Engineer Notes*, March 1945, pp. 2-6.

7. Ltr., Kenney to Col. W. R. Ritchie, 14 Apr. 1943.

8. *ESWP*, II, 147, and VI, 168, note.

9. Hist. 872d Airborne EAB, Oct. 1942—Dec. 1943.

10. Hist. Summary, 842d EAB; *ESWP*, VI, 168-76; *AAF in WW II*, IV, 191-92.

11. Early Hist. 871st Airborne EAB; Hist. 872d Airborne EAB, Oct. 1942—Dec. 1943; *Aviation Engineer Notes*, Mar. 1945, pp. 2-6; *ESWP*, VI, 171-74; Operation of the 872d Airborne EAB . . . at Gusap, N.G. (special report).

12. *ESWP*, VI, 180-83.

13. *Ibid.*, pp. 193-94.

14. *Ibid.*, pp. 194-200.

15. *Ibid.*, pp. 222-33.

16. *Ibid.*, pp. 216-18; Hist. Narrative for 1944, 836th EAB; ltr., Maj. Gen. Hugh J. Casey to Col. E. R. Heiberg, 25 Apr. 1944. In this letter Gen. Casey praises the aviation engineers, among other things, for being able to start work almost at once, whereas the Seabees took nine days to set up their own camp before commencing full schedule on the airfield.

17. Hist. Narrative for 1944, 836th EAB; *ESWP*, VI, 242-46; Robert R. Smith, *The Approach to the Philippines*, U.S. Army in World War II (Washington, 1953), p. 231 (hereinafter cited as Smith, *Approach to Philippines*); *AAF in WW II*, IV, 628-29.

18. Hist. Rpt., 860th EAB, 28 Aug. 1944; Narrative Rpt. of Biak and Owi Islands Operation, 864th EAB, 31 Aug. 1944; *ESWP*, VI, 247-50; Gen. Walter Krueger, *From Down Under to Nippon* (Washington, 1953), p. 102; *AAF in WW II*, IV, 641-44; ltr., Kenney to Col. M. C. Cooper, 15 July 1944.

19. Br. Hist. Rpt., Biak Operation, 808th EAB, 27 Aug. 1944; Smith, *Approach to Philippines*, p. 314; *ESWP*, VI, 250-54; Narrative Rpt. of Biak and Owi Islands Operation, 864th EAB, 31 Aug. 1944; Supplement to Hist. Rpt., 860th EAB, 27 Sept. 1944.

20. Ltr., Kenney to Whitehead, 1 Aug. 1944; ltr., Kenney to Col. M. C. Cooper, 15 July 1944; Smith, *Approach to Philippines*, p. 423; *ESWP*, VI, 257-62; *AAF in WW II*, IV, 652, 660.

21. Hist. Narrative for 1944, 836th EAB; *ESWP*, VI, 263-70.

22. *ESWP*, VI, 272, editor's note.

23. *AAF in WW II*, V, 312-14; *ESWP*, VI, 270-77; Smith, *Approach to Philippines*, pp. 490-91; Hist. Rpt., Moratai, by 1876th EAB, 9 July 1945; Hist. Narrative for 1944, 836th EAB.

24. Ltr., Lt. Col. Robert H. Paddock, CO, 1876th EAB, to Air Engineer, Hq., AAF, 23 May 1945; Hist. Rpt., Moratai, by 1876th EAB, 9 July 1945; Hist. Narrative for 1944, 836th EAB; Hist. 5th AF, 15 June 1944—2 Sept. 1945, I, 47-48.

25. *ESWP*, VI, 283-87 and 426; II, 159; Interview, Capt. George Thomas with Capt. Lambert, Asst. Air Engineer, FEAF, 9 July 1945.

26. Ltr., Kenney to Arnold, 28 Dec. 1944.

27. Ltr., Gen. Krueger to Gen. War, 13 Aug. 1951, quoted in M. Hamlin Cannon, *Leyte: The Return to the Philippines* (Washington, 1954), p. 188 (hereinafter cited as Cannon, *Leyte*).

28. There is also an excellent account in *ESWP*, VI, 291-98, as well as in Cannon, *Leyte*, pp. 187-88.

29. Hist. Summary, 26 Sept.-25 Nov. 1944, 808th EAB; Monthly Hist. Summary,

25 Sept.–24 Oct. 1944, 842d EAB; *ESWP*, VI, 298–99.

30. *ESWP*, VI, 300–303; Hist. Summary, 865th EAB, 1944; *Aviation Engineer Notes*, March 1945, pp. 8–9; Hist. 821st EAB; Operational Rpt., 866th EAB, 24 Nov. 1944—1 Feb. 1945; Hist. Summary, 839th EAB, 1 Dec.–25 Dec. 1944.

31. Hist. 839th EAB; Col. Mayo's summary of visit to 842d EAB, 5 June 1945; Hist. 857th EAB, 1944; Hist. 872d Airborne EAB, 1944; Hist. 821st EAB; Hist. Summary, 839th EAB, Dec. 1944; Hist. 1871st EAB, Mar. 1945; Hist. 867th EAB, Mar. 1945.

32. Operational Rpt. 866th EAB, 24 Nov. 1944—1 Feb. 1945; *Aviation Engineer Notes*, May 1945, p. 19; *ESWP*, VI, 314–21; Col. Mayo's interview with 1874th EAB, 11 Sept. 1945.

33. *ESWP*, VI, 321–26; *AAF in WW II*, V, 404, 416–18; ltr., Lt. Col. R. H. Paddock to Air Engineer, Hq., AAF, 15 Aug. 1945; Monthly Hist. Summary, 836th EAB, Feb. 1945; Notes on conference with 864th EAB by Col. George Mayo, 17 June 1945; Interview of Capt. George Thomas with Capt. Lambert, Asst. Air Engineer, FEAF, 9 July 1945; Hist. 810th EAB, 17 Feb. 1945.

34. Report on the Functions and Organization . . . of Hq., FEAF, 7 May 1945; *ESWP*, VI, 332.

35. Hist. Summary, 808th EAB, Feb. 1945; Hist. Summary, 31 Dec. 1945, 855th EAB; Hist. of 857th EAB, Mar., Apr., May 1945; Military record, 863d EAB, 1 Nov. 1942—12 June 1945; Hist. Data, 882d Airborne EAB, Dec. 1944; Hist. 5th AF, 15 June 1944—2 Sept. 1945, I, 47–48; Hist. 871st Airborne EAB, Apr.–May 1945; Hist. Summary, 13 Feb.–31 Mar. 1945, 847th EAB. Col. Mayo's notes on conference with 855th EAB, 10 Sept. 1945.

36. Ltr., Col. George Mayo, Air Engineer, AAF, to CG, FEAF, 19 June 1945; memo for CG, AAF, from Col. George Mayo, 27 Aug. 1945.

37. Hist. 807th EAB, Sept. 1942–April 1944.

38. Rpt. on Field Airdrome Construction, Adak, Alaska, 807th EAB, 15 May 1943; Hist. 807th EAB, Sept. 1942–Apr. 1944; *Aviation Engineer Notes*, Aug. 1943, pp. 4–6, and Mar. 1944, pp. 3–6; Hist. 11th AF, pp. 173–75; Hist. Summary of the Aviation Engineers in General Arnold's

file (hereinafter cited as Arnold Historical Summary); Maj. Gen. W. E. Lynd, "Strategical Function of the Aviation Engineers," *Aviation Engineer Notes*, July 1944, pp. 2–6.

39. Ltr., Col. E. S. Davis, 11th AF, to CG, Alaska Defense Command, 5 Sept. 1942; Rpt. of 896th Eng. Avn. Co., June 1942–44.

40. Rpt. on Field Airdrome Construction, Attu, Alaska, 15 Dec. 1943, by 807th EAB; Arnold Historical Summary.

41. Ltr., Maj. Gen. M. F. Harmon to Brig. Gen. St. Clair Streett, 16 Nov. 1942; ltr., Maj. Gen. M. F. Harmon to Vice-Admiral W. F. Halsey, 20 Nov. 1942.

42. Brig. Gen. S. C. Godfrey, Report on Airdromes and Aviation Engineers around the World, 4 Oct. 1943; Hist. 13th AF, I.

43. Hist. 810th EAB, 1 Jan.–29 Feb. 1944; Fletcher Martin, "Aviation Engineers in New Caledonia," in *Philadelphia Courier*, 5 Sept. 1944; *AAFSAT Intelligence Reports*, Oct. 1943, pp. 31–38; Notes on conference of Col. George Mayo and 810th EAB, 12 June 1945.

44. Early Hist. 821st EAB; Godfrey report, 4 Oct. 1943.

45. As in Godfrey report, 4 Oct. 1943.

46. Baker Island Rpt., 804th EAB; Rpt. of mission at Makin, 804th EAB; The Construction and Development of Air Fields in the Central Pacific through June 1944 by 1st Lt. W. L. Wannamacher, in Hist. of the Air War in the Pacific Ocean, pp. 71, 86–88 (hereinafter cited as Wannamacher, The Construction of Air Fields); Arnold Historical Summary.

47. Hist. 854th EAB, 1 Oct. 1943—31 Nov. 1944; Hist. 804th EAB, Feb. 1944; Arnold Historical Summary; Wannamacher, The Construction of Air Fields, pp. 90–93.

48. Godfrey report, 4 Oct. 1943; Arnold Historical Summary; ltr., Brig. Gen. Clayton Bissell to Maj. Gen George Stratemeyer, 9 Jan. 1943; China Air Task Force Hist., 14th AF, April 1944.

49. Hist. 853d EAB, 1943.

50. Hist. 823d EAB, Feb.–Dec. 1942; Hist. 858th EAB, Jan 44—Sept. 45; Hist. 1880th EAB, March 1943—Nov. 1945; Hist. 1883d EAB, 1942–45.

51. Hist. 1880th EAB, March 1943—Nov. 1945; Arnold Historical Summary; ltr., Godfrey to Stratemeyer, 31 Jan. 1945.

52. Ltr., Godfrey to Arnold, 28 Mar. 1944; ltr., Arnold to Godfrey, 25 Apr. 1944;

ltr., Stratemeyer to Arnold, 3 Feb. 1944; ltr., Stratemeyer to Air CINC, Southeast Asia, 5 June 1944; *Aviation Engineer Notes*, June 1944, pp. 5-7; *CBI Dromes*, July 1944, pp. 13-16, and Dec. 1944, pp. 7-11.

53. Ltr., Capt. E. D. Roscoe to Godfrey, 5 June 1944; Diary to Col. M. J. Asensio, *CBI Dromes*, Dec. 1944, pp. 3-6; ltr., Stratemeyer to General Sultan, 31 Aug. 1944; Rpt. 10th AF Engineer, no date; Hist. 1877th EAB, 1944.

54. Ltr., Godfrey to Stratemeyer, 15 Dec. 1943.

55. *Ibid.*, pp. 59-65; ltr., Brig. Gen. K. B. Wolfe to Godfrey, 25 Feb. 1944; ltr., Wolfe to CG, AAF, CBI Sector, 5 May 1944; memo for Brig. Gen. Robert C. Oliver, CG, Air Service Command from Godfrey, 5 May 1944; Hist. XX Bomber Command, Third Phase, pp. 65-67; Final Report, B-29 Bases, India (Col. Seaman report), Nov. 1944, pp. 3-8; ltr., Godfrey to Maj. W. D. Styer, Hq. AAF, 26 July 1944.

56. Col. Seaman report, pp. 7, 23-24; History of 853d EAB, 1944; Hist. XX Bomber Command, Third Phase, pp. 59-65.

57. Ltr., Godfrey to CG, AAF, India-Burma Theater, 13 Apr. 1945; ltr., Godfrey to Brig. Gen. Lauris Norstad, 24 Sept. 1944; ltr., Godfrey to CG, USAAF, India-Burma Theater, 31 Jan. 1945; China Air Task Force Hist., 14th AF, Apr. 1944; Hist. XX Bomber Command, Fourth Phase, pp. 11-16; ltr., Godfrey to Maj. Gen. T. J. Hanley, 21 May 1944; *Aviation Engineer Notes*, Oct. 1944, p. 13; *CBI Dromes*, Dec. 1944, pp. 16-21, and II, No. 1 (1945), 4-8, 21.

58. Hist. of VHB Construction in the Marianas and on Iwo Jima, Monograph IV, prepared by Capt. James H. Hubbell and Sgt. Edward A. Chalfant (hereinafter cited as Hist. of VHB Construction), pp. 4-10; ltr., Col. A. G. Barber to CO, 463d Base Unit, 15 Dec. 1944; Study by Lt. Col. Willard Roper, Air Engineer's Office, Hq. AAF, 1945; Ladd Board Report, 1945.

59. Arnold Historical Summary; Hist. of VHB Construction, pp. 27-29; ltr., Maj. John W. Paxton, CO, 804th EAB, to Hq. AAF, Air Engineer, 22 Oct. 1944; Rpt. on Air Base Construction, Saipan, Marianas Islands, 17 June 1944—1 Feb. 1945, 804th EAB; *Aviation Engineer Notes*, Feb. 1945, pp. 8-9, and Apr. 1945, p. 2.

60. Ltr., Paxton to Air Engineer, 22 Oct. 1944; Report on Air Base Construction, Saipan, 1944-45, by 804th EAB;

History of 806th EAB, July-Dec. 1944; Hist. of VHB Construction, p. 29.

61. Excerpt from ltr., Hansell to Arnold, quoted in ltr., Arnold to Maj. Gen. Eugene C. Reybold, Chief of Engineers, 21 Dec. 1944.

62. Hist. of VHB Construction, pp. 31-51; ltr., Col. George Mayo, Air Engineer, AAF, to CG, AAFPOA, 5 July 1945; Historical summary of the aviation engineers.

63. Hist. of VHB Construction, pp. 56-73, 108-12; ltr., Col. G. E. Linkswiler to CO, 927th Eng. Av. Regiment, undated.

64. Hist. of VHB Construction, pp. 114-29, 143-45; Hist. 854th EAB, Nov. 1944—Feb. 1945.

65. Preliminary history of the Seventh Air Force, 1 April-13 July 1945; *ESWP*, VI, 386-92; Hist. of VHB Construction, pp. 153-59; Hist. 806th EAB, June-August 1945; Hist. 854th EAB, May-Aug. 1945; R&R, Air Engineer to OC&R, 11 Apr. 1945; Hist. 872d EAB, June 1945; Hist. 801st EAB, 1 Feb. 1943—1 Nov. 1945; Hist 807th EAB, Jan.-June 1945; Hist. 873d EAB, June 1945.

NOTES TO CHAPTER 11

1. Cf. Saster, "Importance of Weather in Modern Warfare," *Army-Navy Journal*, 7 Dec. 1943.

2. Hist. AAF Weather Service, 1935-41, pp. 25-26, 45-46, 70; Brief History of the Air Weather Service, AAF WS, n.d.; 12th Ind. (ltr., Office, Chief Signal Officer to AG, 1 July 1935) Office, Chief Signal Officer to AG, 19 May 1936; memo for C/S from J. H. Hughes, AC/S, 15 July 1936; memo for C/AC from Col. R. B. Lincoln, C/Plans Div., 8 Dec. 1936; Hist. Organ. of Wea. Ser. (Draft in AAF Hist. Div. files, Maxwell AFB, chap. i, p. 17 (hereinafter cited as Draft Hist.).

3. AR 95-150, 1 July 1937; Hist. AAF WS, 1935-41, pp. 45-46; Annual Report of the Chief of the Air Corps, 1937, p. 31; Annual Report of the Chief of the Air Corps, 1938, pp. 34-35; Brief Hist., AWS; AG Ltr. (AG 320.6 GHQ AF, 21 Aug. 1936) Misc. C to C/AC, 28 Jan. 1937.

4. Hist. AAF WS., 1935-41, pp. 45-48; press release, WD, 18 June 1937; office memo, 10-10A, OCAC, Nov. 1937.

5. Hist. AAF WS, 1941-43, I, 61-73.

6. See R&R, T&O to Chief, Air Corps, 31 July 1940, App. 57.

7. Hist. AAF WS, 1941–43, I, 77–85.

8. See especially summary chapter on officer training in Hist. AAF WS, III, 282ff.

9. *Ibid.*, pp. 288 ff.

10. *Ibid.*, V, 550–51.

11. *Ibid.*, pp. 551–67. These are the figures given in the official history. The *AAF Statistical Digest* (p. 72) places the grand total of weather officers trained at 5,924, with a breakdown by year as follows: (1941) 112, (1942) 570, (1943) 3,732, (1944) 1,316, and (1945) 194.

12. Hist. AAF WS, 1941–43, I, 7–9, 18–21, 54–56, 86–87.

13. *Ibid.*, p. 96.

14. A copy will be found in Hist. AAF WS, Vol. IV, App. 165.

15. Detailed discussion is found *ibid.*, III, 198–270.

16. *Ibid.*, V, 295.

17. *Ibid.*, III, 123 ff.; V, 377 ff.

18. *Ibid.*, I, 56–57, 88–94.

19. *Ibid.* Volumes II and V carry lengthy discussions.

20. *Ibid.*, III, 56–60; V, 1–14.

21. *Ibid.*, V, 18–23.

22. *Ibid.*, Vol. V. See chap. ii for full discussion.

23. Hist. Data Pertaining to 6th Weather Reg., 1940–44, pp. 1–9; Hist. 6th Weather Reg., 1940–44, pp. 25–27; Hist. AAF WS, III, 221–24; Hist. 9th Weather Reg., 1942, pp. 1–6.

24. Hist. 8th Weather Reg. Recapitulation, 1941–45, pp. 3–4, 14; Hist. NAD ATC, 1941–42, p. 403; Hist. AAF WS, 1941–43, pp. 212–20.

25. *AAF in WW II*, I, 345; Hist. NAD ATC, 1941–42, pp. 404–9; *ibid.*, Jan. 1943—Apr. 1944, pp. 422, 440; Hist. 8th Weather Reg., 1942, p. 22; Hist. 8th Weather Reg. Recapitulation, 1941–45, pp. 3–4.

26. Hist. NAD ATC, 1941–42, pp. 409–10.

27. *Ibid.*, pp. 410–11; Hist. AAF WS, 1941–43, p. 212; Hist. 8th Weather Reg. Recapitulation, 1941–45, p. 4.

28. Hist. 8th Weather Reg. Recapitulation, pp. 22–23; *AAF in WW II*, I, 345; Hist. NAD ATC, 1941–42, pp. 440–45.

29. Hist. AAF WS, 1943–45, p. 313; Hist. 8th Weather Reg., 1941, pp. 22–23, 32–35.

30. Hist. 8th Weather Reg., 1941, pp. 412–29; Hist. 8th Weather Reg. Recapitula-

tion, 1941–45, pp. 21, 26–27; Weather Reconnaissance Orlando, pp. 1, 6–8; Hist. AAF WS, 1943–45, pp. 313–14.

31. Hist. 9th Weather Reg., 1942, pp. 31–32; *ibid.*, 1944, pp. 19–20; Hist. Carib. Wg. ATC, July 1943—June 1944, pp. 16–22.

32. Hist. 9th Weather Reg., 1944, p. 21; Hist. AAF WS, 1941–43, pp. 303–5.

33. Hist. 18th Weather Sq., pp. 215–16; Hist. 8th Weather Reg. Recapitulation, 1941–45, pp. 12–14, 22–23.

34. Hist. AAF WS, 1941–43, pp. 259–61; Hist. 18th Weather Sq., 1942–44, pp. 65, 215–16; *AAF in WW II*, I, 625, 639.

35. Hist. 19th Weather Sq., pp. 1–4; Hist. AAF WS, III, 263.

36. Hist. AAF WS, 1941–43, pp. 225–30; Hist. AAF WS, 1943–45, pp. 317–18.

37. Memo ICD ATC, I&S to CG ICD ATC, "Flying Conditions during 6–7 January 1945," in I&S files Hq. ATC.

38. Hist. ICD ATC, 1945, pp. 371–72J.

39. Hist. 10th Weather Sq. to V-J Day, pp. 27–28, 279–87.

40. See, for example, Capt. L. P. Bachmann, "Where Weather Is Born," *Air Force*, XXVIII, No. 8 (Aug. 1945), 20.

41. Hist. 10th Weather Squadron to V-J Day, pp. 28–29.

42. R&R, Arnold to Kuter, 31 Aug. 1942.

43. See discussions in Hist. AAF WS, III, 85–99; V, 348–76.

44. *Ibid.*, III, 235–42; V, 329–39.

45. Hist. 12th Weather Sq., 14 Sept. 1942—30 Sept. 1945, pp. 14–15; Hist. AAF WS, 1941–43, pp. 265–66.

46. Weather Reconnaissance Orlando, Hist. 19th Weather Reg., pp. 5–8, 18–25; 35; Combat Reconnaissance for the 15th AF, pp. 3–8.

47. Hist. AAF WS, III, 257–62.

48. Hist. 21st Weather Sq., 1 May 1943—5 June 1944, p. 27; Hist. AAF WS, 1943–45, pp. 339–41; Hist. AAF WS, 1941–43, pp. 261–62; Hist. 8th AF, 28 Jan.–17 Aug. 1942, pp. 237–39; *AAF in WW II*, I, 625; Bradley Plan File No. 16, Weather, "AAF Weather Service in ETO," 1943.

49. Hist. AAF WS, V, 341–42.

50. Hist. 7th Weather Sq. to 1 May 1944, pp. 2, 16–17; Hist. 17th Weather Sq., 18 Sept. 1942—10 Feb. 1945, pp. 1, 11; Hist. Weather Service, POA, p. 3.

51. Hist. 7th Weather Sq., p. 2; Hist. Weather Service, POA, p. 4; Hist. AAF WS, 1941–43, pp. 242–44.

52. Hist. AAF WS, III, 242–48.

53. Hist. 17th Weather Sq., 1942–45; Hist. AAF WS, III, 254–57.

54. Hist. 7th Weather Reg. to May 1944, pp. 16–18.

55. Hist. 11th Weather Sq., Jan. 1941–May 1944; Hist. AAF WS, III, 231–35.

56. Hist. 11th Weather Sq., June 1944, pp. 1, 11; *ibid.*, Sept. 1944, p. 6; *ibid.*, Oct. 1944, pp. 4–5; Hist. 16th Weather Reg., 1942–44, pp. 23–43; Hist. 11th Weather Sq., 1941–44, pp. 32–33, 54; Hist. AAF WS, III, 231–35, 248–54.

57. Hist. 17th Weather Sq., 1942–45, p. 11; Hist. Weather Service, POA, pp. 9–13; Hist. AAF WS, 1943–45, pp. 322–28; Hist. 7th Weather Sq. to May 1944, pp. 16–17.

58. Hist. AAF WS, III, 271–79.

59. *Ibid.*, V, 521–24.

60. *Ibid.*, pp. 524–26.

61. Hist. Weather Service in POA, pp. 17–19; Hist. AAF Weather Service, POA, Feb. 1945, p. 3; Weather Service POA, Reg. No. 20-1, 14 Feb. 1945; Hist. 7th Weather Sq., 1–10 Feb. 1945, p. 3; Hist. Weather Service in POA, Sept. 1945, p. 12; Hist. AAF WS, 1943–45, p. 329.

62. Hist. Weather Service POA, pp. 19–28.

63. Hist. AAF WS, V, 468–72; interview by J. A. Jonasson with Brig. Gen. D. N. Yates, Washington, D.C., 31 Aug. 1948.

64. Weather Reconnaissance Orlando, pp. 16–17; Daily Activity Repts., OC&R, 4 Oct. 1944, 7 Nov. 1944, 1 Feb. 1945.

65. Hist. AAF WS, V, 484–85; Daily Activity Rept. OC&R, 11 Jan. 1944, 29 Mar. 1944, 16 Oct. 1944, 2 Dec. 1944; ltr., Col. D. Z. Zimmerman to Dr. D. E. Kerr, 8 Oct. 1942; "Radar vs. Weather," *Radar*, Apr. 1944, p. 26; Hist. AAF Weather Service POA, May 1945, p. 10; Daily Activity Rept., Air Comm. O for Gen. Arnold, 2 June 1944; Daily Activity Rept., OC&R, 30 May 1944.

66. Memo for Hist. Div. AC/AS, Intell., from Col. H. H. Bassett, Chief, Weather Div., 23 Oct. 1944; Hist. AAF WS, V, 483; Weather Equipment, AAFSAT, Apr. 1945, *passim*.

67. Hist. AAF WS, V, chap. x, discusses the problem in some detail.

68. Hist. AAF WS, 1941–43, pp. 139–49, 153–58.

69. AAF Reg. 105-1, 18 Sept. 1943; Daily Diary, Air Comm. Br., 17 Sept. 1943; Daily Diary, Weather Div., 8 Sept. 1943; memo for AC/AS, OC&R from Tech. Ser., 31 July 1943.

70. Hist. AAF WS, 1943–45, pp. 392–99, 423–25; Hist. 8th Weather Reg. Recapitulation, 1941–45, pp. 11–14.

71. Hist. AAF WS, 1943–45, pp. 398, 403, 413, 422–29, 438–39.

NOTES TO CHAPTER 12

1. Laurence F. Schmeckebier, *The Aeronautics Branch, Department of Commerce* (Washington, 1930).

2. Hist. AACS, 2 Nov. 1938—2 Sept. 1945, pp. 29–33 (hereinafter cited as Hist. AACS).

3. *Ibid.*, pp. 46–52.

4. Ltr., TAG to CG's *et al.*, sub.: Establishment of the Army Airways Communications System, 3 Nov. 1938.

5. Hist. AACS, pp. 52 ff.

6. *Ibid.*, p. 91.

7. *Ibid.*, p. 22.

8. *Ibid.*, p. 424.

9. *Ibid.*, pp. 121–29.

10. *Ibid.*, pp. 326–39, 205–6.

11. Interview with Maj. Gen. H. M. McClelland, CG AACS, 12 Aug. 1948.

12. Hist. AAF Tng. Comd., 1 May 1945–V-J Day, II, 266–73; Hist. AACS, pp. 939–41.

13. Hist. Radio and Radar Supply, Maintenance, and Training by the Air Service Command, 1944, pp. 84–115.

14. Ltr., TAG to CG AAF and CG ASF, 21 Oct. 1944; AAF HOI #20-75, Dec. 1944.

15. Hist. AACS, pp. 104, 919–20.

16. Ltr., TAG to CG AAF, CO's 7th, 8th, 9th, 13th, 16th Airways Communications Squadrons, 22 Feb. 1943; Hist. AACS, pp. 159, 237, 383, 453, 560, 922.

17. Hist. AACS, pp. 927–28.

18. For full discussion, see *ibid.*, pp. 919–51; also memo for Gen. H. H. Arnold from E. L. Bowles, O/SW, 16 June 1943; memo for Bowles from G. G. Jones, Expert Consultant, 12 Jan. 1944; ltr., Hq. AAF to CO AAF Weather Wg., Asheville, N.C., 22 Feb. 1944; 1st ind., Hq AAF to Hq 14th AF, 25 Sept. 1944; interview with Maj. Gen. H. M. McClelland, 12 Aug. 1948.

19. Lecture by Maj. Gen. H. M. McClelland, on communications, in the officers' interim training program, Hq. AACS, 1947–48 (copy in Hq. ATC Hist. files); Rpt.

on AACS (in files of PIO, AACS), pp. 16 ff.

20. Hist. 8th AF, 1944-45, Sec. O, p. 3; Hist. AACS, pp. 138-43.

21. Hist. AACS, pp. 144-46.

22. *Ibid.*, pp. 168-85.

23. Hist. AAF Weather Service, III, 392, 399.

24. Hist. AACS, pp. 430, 504-32.

25. *Ibid.*, pp. 532-33.

26. *Ibid.*, pp. 614 ff.

27. *Ibid.*, pp. 371-72.

28. *Ibid.*, pp. 210-11, 241-42.

29. *Ibid.*, pp. 213-15.

30. *Ibid.*, pp. 212, 217-23, 253-55.

31. Air Eval. Bd., SWPA, I, ii, vii, 18, 32.

32. *Ibid.*, pp. 10-18, 26, 75-78, 94-96, 189.

33. Msg., #C-2348, Brisbane to WAR (no signature), 11 May 1943; *AAF in WW II*, IV, 156; Air Eval. Bd., SWPA, 1 May 1946, Air Force Communications, I, 38, 98-106.

34. Air Eval. Bd., SWPA, pp. 36-37.

35. *Ibid.*, pp. 40-41, 111; Hist. AACS, p. 396.

36. Hist. AACS, pp. 346-47, 373-74, 384.

37. *Ibid.*, pp. 387, 389-408.

38. *Ibid.*, p. 874.

39. *Ibid.*, pp. 901-10, which include an interesting contemporary press release.

40. Rpt. of subcommittee on Pacific Air Transport Progress, 15 July 1945, in ATC Hist. files; Hist. of Oceanic Air Traffic Control, 3 Sept. 1943—3 July 1946; see also file on OATC Communications, AAF Archives 4933-13; ltr., Col. Gordon A. Blake to CIC, POA, 21 Oct. 1943.

41. Hist. AACS, pp. 631-32.

42. *Ibid.*, pp. 633, 638, 640.

43. *Ibid.*, p. 671.

44. *Ibid.*, pp. 688-93.

45. *Ibid.*, pp. 660-62, 680, 689-92.

46. Air Eval. Bd. Rpt. No. 9, 15 June 1945, China and India-Burma Theater, pp. 33-34.

47. Hist. AACS, pp. 505-19.

48. *Ibid.*, pp. 522-33.

49. *Ibid.*, p. 560.

50. *AAF in WW II*, II, 127; ltr., Col. H. J. Knerr, Dep. ASC to CG ASC, Patterson Fld., 23 June 1943; memo for Dep. C/S, AAF MTO, from Brig. Gen. A. W. Marriner, Commun. Off.

51. Hist., AACS, pp. 564-65.

52. *Ibid.*, p. 572.

53. *Ibid.*, pp. 592, 596.

54. *Ibid.*, pp. 585, 595, 597, 732-37.

55. Consolidated Rpt. of Activities of Signal Sec., Off. of Dir. of Commun., Hq. 8th AF, 15 July 1945, Sec. 10 (hereinafter cited as Consolidated Rpt. on Signals, 8th AF); Hist. 8th AF, 1944-45, Sec. O, p. 3; Hist. AACS, pp. 156-66.

56. Hist. AACS, pp. 706-8.

57. *Ibid.*, pp. 725-27.

58. *Ibid.*, p. 709.

59. *Ibid.*, pp. 721, 729.

60. *Ibid.*, p. 741.

61. *Ibid.*, p. 770.

NOTES TO CHAPTER 13

1. M. M. Link and H. S. Coleman, *Medical Support of the Army Air Forces in World War II* (Washington, 1954) (hereinafter cited as *Medical Support*). Much of the material in this chapter was excerpted from this official medical history.

2. *Ibid.*, pp. 2, 192 ff.

3. The selection and training of flight surgeons also changed progressively during the early years of the war (see, for details, *ibid.*, pp. 159-96).

4. Duties and responsibilities of flight surgeons are described authoritatively in Harry G. Armstrong, *Principles and Practice of Aviation Medicine* (1st ed.; Baltimore, 1939; 2d ed.; Baltimore, 1952), pp. 2-24. (This classic work is hereinafter cited as Armstrong, *Aviation Medicine*.)

5. "By 1926, in spite of all the work that had been done by aeronautical engineers, the problem [i.e., blind flying] seemed no nearer solution than it had been in the beginning, and finally, the aid of medical science was solicited. In that year Maj. David A. Myers, MC, a flight surgeon . . . began a study of the physiologic factors involved in instrument flying and shortly thereafter demonstrated the fundamental principles which have made possible blind flying as we know it today" (*ibid.* [1st ed.]), p. 220).

6. For further discussion of this, see Douglas D. Bond, *The Love and Fear of Flying* (New York, 1952). The quotation of André Malraux is from *Man's Hope*.

7. *Medical Support*, chap. iv.

8. The designation of the human factor as the "weakest link" was Armstrong's estimate of the situation prior to the development of the wartime research program (cf.

Armstrong, *Aviation Medicine* [2d ed.], p. 47).

9. The historical background of this objective is fascinating. In a letter, dated 1 October 1917, to Commanding General, Air Division, Signal Corps, Lt. Col. Theodore C. Lyster, MC, Chief Surgeon, Air Division, wrote substantially as follows: Good administration requires that all medical matters affecting any unit of the Aviation Section (it became the Air Division about this time) be the province of the chief surgeon, and that the medical service, in the name of the commanding general, be permitted to handle all administrative matters without additional orders from the Medical Department of the Army: in other words, an organic medical service. The first indorsement to this letter, recommending approval, was signed by Col. Henry H. Arnold! (*Medical Support*, pp. 14-15).

10. The wanderings of the medical service in the organizational chart of the air arm deserve attention. The chronology and nomenclature were as follows:

1917—Medical Department, Air Division, Signal Corps

1918—Air Service Division, OSG

1919—Medical Division, Administrative Group, Air Service

1921—Medical Section, Office of Chief of the Air Service

1921-29—"various places in organization chart of air service and air corps"

1929—Medical Division, Office of the Chief of the Air Corps

1936—Medical Section, Personnel Division, OCAC

1939—Medical Division, Training Group, OCAC (April)

1939—Medical Division, OCAC (September)

1941—Office of the Air Surgeon, Hq, AAF (October)

11. The efforts of the flight surgeons to retain direct access to command is justified by what happened to the Office of the Surgeon General in the course of reorganization of the War Department, 1942. Prior to 1940, the SG was the chief medical officer of the Army reporting directly to the General Staff. Formal actions of the Medical Department channeled through The Adjutant General and were thus the concern of AC/S, G-1; other medical affairs involved AC/S, G-3; and hospitalization was the responsibility of AC/S, G-4. Although direct communication was authorized between the SG and the divisions of the General Staff, the impact of the medical adviser was not great and the multiple channels led to a cumbersome organization. When mobilization began, the training organization, GHQ, also had medical problems, so there was another subdividing of the SG's authority. The WD reorganization of 1942 established the Services of Supply, to which the Medical Department was assigned. The SG now became a member of the special staff of CG, SOS, and medical matters of concern to the WD General Staff passed through him. This separation of the SG from the General Staff became even greater when an Operations Division was established in Hq, SOS, and was assigned the responsibility for the Hospitalization and Evacuation Branch. The Office of the Surgeon General (OSG) operated on the same echelon as operations, but the functions were separate. Finally, in the latter part of the war, the situation was somewhat improved by abolishing the branch, whose functions were transferred to OSG, and by authorizing direct communication between the SG and the General Staff and the Secretary of War.

12. For a fuller discussion, see *Medical Support*, chaps. i and ii.

13. *Ibid.*, pp. 51-66.

14. *Ibid.*, pp. 539-40.

15. *Ibid.*, pp. 71-74.

16. *Ibid.*, p. 94.

17. Bond, *Love and Fear of Flying*, p. 125.

18. From instructions concerning physical examination of candidates for aviation duty, published by WD, 2 Feb. 1912, quoted in Armstrong, *Aviation Medicine* (1st ed.), p. 8.

19. *Medical Support*, pp. 180-81.

20. *Ibid.*, p. 8.

21. *Ibid.*, p. 11.

22. WD SGO, Air Service Division Memo No. 79, 3 June 1918.

23. *Medical Support*, pp. 547-48.

24. Supplement, *Journal of Medical Education*, Dec. 1956.

25. AAF Regulation No. 55-7, 30 May 1942.

26. Ltr., Hq., AAF, to All High Altitude Indoctrination and Classification Units, sub.: "High Altitude Indoctrination and Classification Program, 19 Mar. 1942."

27. *Medical Support*, p. 212; see also *ibid*, pp. 210-17.

28. *Ibid.*, pp. 189-91.

29. Morale is discussed exhaustively below, chap. 14. Careful reading of this chapter discloses no evidence that deficiencies in the medical service contributed to low morale. Virtually every other aspect of military life is the object of criticism.

30. *Medical Support*, pp. 647-55.

31. *Ibid.*, pp. 635-47; see also *ibid.*, p. 679.

32. *Ibid.*, pp. 655-60.

33. The relationship between plane losses and grounding for neuropsychiatric (or emotional) reason was studied extensively by Bond and is discussed in *Love and Fear of Flying*, pp. 177-90. Data collected by Bond in England were interpreted to demonstrate a significant correlation $(r = +0.7)$ between emotional casualties and aircraft losses. For a one-year period (May 1943—May 1944), the ratio of emotional casualties to losses was said to be 1:2. Likewise, when the loss rate of planes (per month) exceeded 8 per cent, Bond reported a "sharp increase" of emotional casualties. It is to be noted that many of the "casualties" were returned to flying status after rest leave, appropriate treatment, etc.

34. *Medical Support*, Table 83, p. 703, and Table 85, p. 706; see also *ibid.*, pp. 704-8.

35. *Ibid.*, pp. 617-35.

36. *Ibid.*, pp. 679-80.

37. Quoted from General James H. Doolittle's Introduction in Bond, *Love and Fear of Flying*.

38. *Medical Support, passim.*

39. *Ibid.*, p. 80.

40. *Ibid.*, p. 104; see also *ibid.*, pp. 103-7.

41. *Ibid.*, p. 571.

42. The estimate of "a few per cent" is obtained as follows: During the three-year period (July 1942 through June 1945) 421,-162 individuals from the air forces in Western Europe were hospitalized, losing a total of 3,469,015 man-days from duty. This works out to about 100,000 man-days per month. In a sample month (February 1944) 1,370.22 (the decimals are meaningless) mandays "would have been saved if AAF hospitalization was available." In another sample month, the saving would have been 848.94 man-days. Taking 1,000 man-days as a fair average, and doubling it for aircrewman, gives the "few per cent" estimated. Had data been available from other theaters, it seems probable they would have been similar. This agrees substantially with other figures given in *Medical Support*, p. 708.

43. *Ibid.*, p. 565. This is an astounding statement and demonstrates clearly the wide area of disagreement between the respective medical services. Apparently, General Hawley realized that it was beyond the SG's power to provide the medical supplies that the ground forces required for a modern medical service.

44. *Ibid.*, p. 671.

45. Chap. 9.

46. AAF Regulation No. 35-16, 20 Oct. 1944; and AAF confidential letter 35-18, 7 Dec. 1944.

47. *Medical Support*, p. 498.

48. *Ibid.*, p. 663.

49. *Ibid.*, p. 857.

50. *Ibid.*, p. 856.

51. *Ibid.*, p. 234, Fig. 8.

NOTES TO CHAPTER 14

1. For other definitions, see Hist. 8th AF Special Staff Sections, Jan. 1944—July 1945, chap. c, p. 4; Gen. Sir William Slim, "Morale," *Military Review*, XXVIII (Nov. 1948), 73-75; Hist. 12th AF Medical Section, Aug. 1942—June 1944, p. 60; "'What Is Morale?' What the Soldier Thinks," I (Dec. 1943), 1-7. For an able discussion, see Col. Dale O. Smith, "What Is Morale?" *Air University Quarterly Review*, V (Winter 1951-52), 42-50.

2. USAF Extension Course No. 403, Phase 4, "Military Management" (Montgomery, Ala., 1949), p. 47.

3. See, e.g., Hist. 10th AF, Nov. 1944, p. 28.

4. In some cases historians found it difficult to get material from officers and enlisted men who were afraid to put criticism on paper. See, e.g., Hist AAFORD, Greensboro, N.C., 1 July-30 Sept. 1944, I, vi-vii.

5. For an example of conflict between upper and lower echelons regarding the state of morale, see 100th Ftr. Wg. A-1 Periodic Reports for Dec. 1944, and Hist. 379th Ftr. Sq., Dec. 1944; see also IX Engr. Comd. A-1 Periodic Reports, in AFSHO 544.116, Mar.-July 1944, and lower echelon reports in AFSHO 544.07, 1943-44.

6. See, e.g., Hist. 38th Bomb. Gp., July 1945, p. 14.

7. Hist. XX BC, Aug. 1944, pp. 8-9; Hist. Hq. and Base Services Sq., 86th Sv.

Gp., Sept. 1944; Foster Rhea Dulles, *The American Red Cross: A History* (New York, 1950), p. 496; Marcel Junod, *Warrior without Weapons* (New York, 1951), p. 163.

8. For the effect on AAF morale of transfers, or the threat of transfers, to the AGF, see ltr., Lt. Gen. Ira Eaker to Lt. Gen. Barney Giles, 4 Jan. 1945; Hist. 404th Bomb. Sq., Feb. 1945, p. 1; Hist. Hq. IX FC and Hq. IX TAC, Feb. 1945, "Life in a Headquarters Squadron"; Hist. 77th Bomb. Sq., Dec. 1944, p. 4; Hist. AAFSC/MTO, 1 Jan.–8 May 1945, pp. 507-8.

9. See, e.g., AR 615-275, 16 Feb. 1940, and later revisions; FM 21-5, 16 July 1941; FM 21-50, 15 June 1942; memo, AC/AS Training to Chief of Air Staff, 10 June 1943, in Morale and Welfare Folder, AGO 330.11.

10. FM 21-5, 16 July 1941; FM 21-50, 15 June 1942; Morale Board Report, 15 Nov. 1939, in AAG 384.7.

11. Hist. AAF Training Command, VII, 1299; Monograph on Basic Training, p. 81.

12. Hist. First District, AAFTTC, 10 Mar.–31 Dec. 1942, I, 158-59; Monograph on Basic Training, I, 64; Hist. Jefferson Barracks, 7 Dec. 1941—1 Jan. 1943, I, 151.

13. Monograph on Basic Training, I, 61-62, 65, 67-71, 150-51; USAF Historical Studies, No. 49: Basic Military Training in the AAF, 1939-44, pp. 58, 150-51, 240, 375, 395, 397-401; Hist. of AAFTC, VII, 1314-15.

14. What the Soldier Thinks, Report No. 46, Feb. 1943; *ibid.*, No. 2, Report No. 58, Aug. 1943; Monthly Progress Report, Section 10, Special Services, 30 Sept. 1943; Attitudes toward Job Assignments in the Air Corps, Report No. B-39, 23 June 1943.

15. Monograph on Basic Training, p. 166; ltr., Brig. Gen. L. A. Lawson to CG AAF ETTC, sub.: Eliminated Pre-flight Aviation Cadet Applicants, 20 Jan. 1944, AFSHO 101-49.

16. USAFHS-49, pp. 395-96; Monograph on Basic Training, p. 83; Hist. AAFTC, II, 324-25; VII, 1300-1301; memo for Gen. Arnold from Col. H. W. Shelmire, 14 Oct. 1943, in Morale and Welfare Folder, AGO 330.11A; Hist. AAF Training Center No. 1, 1 Mar.–1 July 1944, p. 144; Hist. Jefferson Barracks, 1 Jan.–7 July 1943, I, 70, 72, 74-75; Hq. 8th AF Narrative History, Mar. 1945.

17. Monograph on Basic Training, pp. 36, 140, 146, 153-54; USAFHS-49, p. 398.

18. Henry L. Stimson and McGeorge Bundy, *On Active Service in Peace and War* (New York, 1948), pp. 379-80.

19. Monograph on Basic Training, pp. 156-57, 159-60; Hist., Hq. 2d AF, Activation to Dec. 6, 1941, pp. 300-305; Hist. AAFTC, I, 162; USAFHS-49, p. 400.

20. USAFHS-49, pp. 85-86, 396-97; Hist. AAFTC, VII, 1322; Hist. BTC #7, 29 June 1942—15 Aug. 1943, II, Sec. XI S, 5, n. 6; Hist. Jefferson Barracks, 1 Jan.–7 July 1943, p. 369.

21. See, e.g., USAF Historical Studies, No. 15: Procurement of Aircrew Trainees, p. 77; memo, Lt. G. B. Ryan to Col. DuBose, 8 Dec. 1942, in AGO 319.1 'C'; Hist. AAFTC, III, 428; V, 1045; VIII, 1681.

22. The same thing had occurred in World War I. See H. H. Arnold, *Global Mission* (New York, 1949), p. 61.

23. USAF Historical Studies, No. 21: Aviation Cadet Ground Duty Program: Policy, Procurement, and Assignment, pp. 54-55; USAFHS-15, pp. 76-77; Hist. AAFTC, II, 300-301, 400; III, 428-44. A more lurid but less typical illustration of the tie between pools and poor morale was the glider-pilot program. See USAF Historical Studies, No. 1: The Glider Pilot Training Program, 1941-43; and Hist. AAFTC, VI.

24. Hist. AAFTC, III, 607, 620; IV, 845; V, 942, 985; VII, 1406; VIII, 1514.

25. USAF Historical Studies, No. 8: Bombsight Maintenance Training in the AAF, p. 64.

26. Hist. AAFTC, I, 25, 70-71; II, 353; IV, 806-7.

27. Occasional visits by instructors to tactical units, where they could watch the alumni of technical schools at work, not only provided an escape from tedium and lifted morale but raised the quality of instruction as well. See Hist. AAFTC, VII, 1376.

28. USAF Historical Studies, No. 48: Preflight Training in the AAF, 1939-44, pp. 31, 35-36, 41, and Tab 10, pp. 3-4, 6-7; Hist. AAFTC, II, 207, 272; III, 476; IV, 479.

29. Hist. AAFTC, V, 1082; VII, 1377; USAF Historical Studies, No. 31: Flexible Gunnery Training in the AAF, p. 22.

30. USAF Historical Studies, No. 60: Individual Training in Aircraft Armament by the AAF, 1939-45, p. 98; USAFHS-31, p. 22; Hist. AAFTC, II, 273; IV, 792; V, 1013-14; VII, 1377-79.

31. Preflight students who had been classified as pilots were in the "eager" category. See USAFHS-48, p. 48.

32. Hist. AAFTC, VII, 1362–63; USAFHS Historical Studies, No. 26: Individual Training in Aircraft Maintenance in the AAF, p. 150.

33. As far as many reluctant trainees were concerned, armament training and clerical training fitted into the drab category. See USAFHS-60, pp. 94–96; and Hist. AAFTC, VIII, 1631–32.

34. A typically non-virulent morale problem was that created by delays in giving cadets back pay and reimbursement for travel. See Monograph on Classification Centers (Aircrew), 1 Jan. 1939—31 Dec. 1944, p. 110.

35. USAFHS-1, p. 57; R&R, AFRAS to AFRIT, 3 Oct. 1942.

36. USAFHS-1, pp. 9, 12, 15, 18, 29, 39, 45, 49, 61; Hist. AAFTC, VI, 1113, 1115, 1117.

37. Hist. Scott Field, 7 July 1943—1 Mar. 1944, IV, 942.

38. USAFHS-60, p. 76.

39. USAFHS-48, pp. 48–49; Hist. AAFTC, III, 482–83; USAFHS-60, p. 97.

40. Hist. AAFTC, II, 289, 311–13; IV, 788; V, 972; Hist. AAF Personnel Distribution Command, V, 163–64.

41. Hist. AAFTC, III, 570.

42. Hist. AAFTC, VIII, 1328, 1358; R&R, AFDAS to AFAAP, 13 July 1942; USAFHS-26, pp. 151, 159; Survey of Soldier Opinion, USAFIME, 4–18 May 1943, Part II, p. 4.

43. Hist. AAFTC, III, 583; IV, 712; USAF Historical Studies, No. 18: Pilot Transition to Combat Aircraft, pp. 75, 160–61.

44. Hist. 500th Bomb. Gp., May 1944, pp. 6–7; Hist. 313th Bomb. Wg., July 1944, p. 36; Hist. 40th Bomb. Gp., Jan. 1944, p. 4; Hist. 25th Bomb. Sq., Feb.–May 1944, p. 2; Hist. Original XII Air Force Service Command, Aug. 1942—Jan. 1944, pp. 251–52; Hist. 34th Air Depot Gp., 21 Jan. 1942, p. 2; Hist. 45th Bomb. Sq., Mar. 1944, p. 1; Hist. 444th Bomb. Gp., Mar.–Aug. 1943, p. 4; Hist. 44th Bomb. Sq., Nov. 1943; Hist. 395th Bomb. Sq., Feb. 1944, p. 3.

45. Hist. 34th Bomb. Gp., Jan.–Aug. 1943, p. 4.

46. Arnold, *Global Mission*, pp. 66–67, 299; Air Room Interview with W/C J. Rankin and S/L A. R. Wright, RAF, 20 Nov. 1942; Hist. 14th Ftr. Gp., 15 Jan. 1941—May 1943, pp. 3–4; AAFHS-18, pp. 90, 112; USAF Historical Studies, No. 9: The AAF in Australia to the Summer of 1942, pp. 121–23; ltr., Capt. Frank A. Moore to CO 320th Bomb. Gp., sub.: Morale of Flying Personnel in the 320th Bomb. Gp., 6 Sept. 1942, in Conduct-Morale Folder, AGO 250.1A; Journal of 340th Bomb. Gp., 1 Jan.–20 June 1943, 3, 13 Jan. 1943; ltr., Maj. Gen. Barney Giles to Maj. Gen. St. Clair Streett, 25 June 1943, in Morals and Conduct Folder, AAG 250.1B.

47. Hist. 2d AF, 1943, pp. 407, 412, 425, 698; and Hist. 2d AF for 1944, II, 313–14.

48. Hist. 34th Bomb. Gp., Jan.–Aug. 1943, pp. 3–4.

49. Hist. 2d AF for 1944, I, 270–71.

50. Journal of 340th Bomb. Gp., 20 Jan. 1943; Hist. 25th Bomb. Sq., Oct. 1943; Hist. 73d Bomb. Wg., Apr. 1944, Part I, p. 8; May–June 1944, Part I, pp. 3, 11; Hist. 500th Bomb. Gp., Feb. 1944, p. 7; Mar. 1944, p. 4.

51. Hist. 73d Bomb. Wg., Apr. 1944, Sec. I, p. 12; Hist. 313th Bomb. Wg., June 1944, p. 25; Hist. 500th Bomb. Gp., July 1944, p. 7; Hist. 395th Bomb. Sq., 20 Aug.–30 Sept. 1943, p. 7.

52. Hist. 313th Bomb. Wg., June 1944, p. 28; Hist. Original XII AF Sv. Comd., Aug. 1942—Jan. 1944, p. 255; Hist. 345th Sv. Sq., 2 Mar. 1942—15 Jan. 1944, p. 6; Hist. 2d AF for 1944, I, 260–61.

53. Hist. AAFORD, Greensboro, N.C., May–June 1944, I, 76, 243–46, 263–64; July–Sept. 1944, I, vi, 229–32; Hist. AAF Personnel Distribution Command, I, 131–32; Hist. AAFORD, Kearns, Utah, Jan.–June 1944, pp. 21–23; Hist. 45th Bomb. Sq., Mar. 1944; Hist. 2d AF for 1944, I, 261–62.

54. Hist. 2d AF, 7 Dec. 1941—31 Dec. 1942, I, 224, 303–4; The Staging Period at Camp Kilmer, in Hist. 332d Sv. Gp., 2 Mar. 1942—Aug. 1943; Journal of 340th Bomb. Gp., 10 Jan. 1943; Hist. 462d Bomb. Gp., Jan. 1944, p. 4; Hist. 40th Bomb. Gp., Jan. 1944, p. 4; Hist. 395th Bomb. Sq., Feb. 1944, p. 3; Narrative History of XXI Bomber Command, July–Aug. 1944, p. 60; Hist. AAF PDC, III, 1010; Hist. 494th Bomb. Gp., Apr. 1944, p. 9; Hist. 444th Bomb. Gp., Feb. 1944, p. 1; Mar. 1944, p. 4; Hist. 73d Bomb. Wg., 17 July–30 Nov. 1944, p. i.

55. The Air Echelon from the U.S.A. to Iceland, in Hist. 310th Bomb. Gp., Mar. 1942—Aug. 1943; Hist. 310th Bomb. Gp., Mar. 1942—Aug. 1943; Hist. 310th Bomb. Gp., Mar. 1942—Aug. 1943, pp. 20–21; Daily Journal, 375th Bomb. Sq., Feb. 1943; Hist. 82d Bomb. Sq., 15 Jan. 1941—1 Sept.

1943; Hist. 73d Bomb. Wg., 17 July—30 Nov. 1944, p. 63.

56. Hist. 27th Bomb. Gp., Jan. 1940—Sept. 1942, p. 5.

57. Air Reference History, No. 1, The AAF in the South Pacific to October 1942, p. 75; Hist. 38th Bomb. Gp., Jan. 1941—Mar. 1944, p. 12; Hist. 3d Air Depot Gp., 1942, p. 9; Hist. 12th Bomb. Gp., 15 Jan.—1 Oct. 1943, p. 3; 57th Ftr. Gp. Narrative; Hist. 84th Bomb. Sq., 15 Jan. 1941—Aug. 1943, pp. 10-11; Journal, 340th Bomb. Gp., 17 Feb.-8 Mar. 1943; Hist. 308th Bomb. Gp., 14 Sept. 1942—31 Dec. 1943, p. 9; Hist. Rpt., 224th Medical Dispensary Aviation, 1943-44, pp. 8-9; Hist. 410th Bomb. Gp., Mar.-Apr. 1944, p. 3; Hist. 444th Bomb. Gp., Mar. 1944, p. 3; Hist. 2d Bomb. Maint. Sc., Feb.-Apr. 1944, p. 1; Hist. 500th Bomb. Gp., 1 Aug.-2 Sept. 1945, I, 190; Hist. 494th Bomb. Gp., June 1944, p. 4; Hist. 73d Bomb. Wg., 17 July-30 Nov. 1944, pp. 12-27; Hq. XXI Bomber Command Diary, 20 Oct.-6 Dec. 1944, pp. 2-3.

58. Historical Summary of 8th AF Activities, Jan. 1942—Oct. 1943, Incl. 8; George C. Kenney, *General Kenney Reports* (New York, 1949), pp. 77-79; Hist. 23d Ftr. Gp., Mar. 1942–Sept. 1943.

59. Hist. 12th Bomb. Gp. 15 Jan. 1941—1 Oct. 1943, p. 3.

60. Hist. XX BC, Third Phase, Feb. 1944, p. 147.

61. Hist. V FC, Nov. 1942—June 1943, pp. 129-30.

62. *Ibid.*, p. 130. See also Hist. 27th Bomb. Gp., Jan. 1940—Sept. 1942, p. 15; Problems of Air Service Command in SW and Western Pacific, p. 9; Hist. 38th Bomb. Gp., Jan. 1941—Mar. 1944, p. 25; Hist. Hq. Sq. 11th AF, 15 Jan. 1942—July 1944, p. 6; Hist. 404th Bomb. Sq., July 1944, p. 1; Hist. XX BC, Third Phase, Feb. 1944, pp. 138, 141; Hist. IX BC, Middle East, 12 Oct. 1942—12 Oct. 1943, pp. 9-10; Hist. 82d Bomb. Sq., 15 Jan. 1941—1 Sept. 1943; Administrative History, 12th AF, Part II, VI, Annex 26, pp. 11, 49; USAF Historical Studies, No. 38: Operational History of the Seventh Air Force, 6 Nov. 1943—31 July 1944, pp. 28-29; Preliminary Org. Hist. VII BC, 1 May 1931—31 July 1944, p. 45; Air Evaluation Board, SWPA, Rpt. No. 32, AAF Morale Factors in SWPA, pp. 3-4 (hereinafter cited as Morale Factors in SWPA); Lt. Gen. M. F. Harmon, The Army in the South Pacific, pp. 40-41; Incl. 59, Medical History of the Seventh Air Force; Medical History of ICW and ICD, ATD, 1942-45, pp. 3-15, 20.

63. USAF Historical Studies, No. 120: The Thirteenth Air Force, Mar.-Oct. 1943, p. 36; Hist. V FC, Nov. 1942—June 1943, p. 8; Air Transportation to China under the 10th AF, Apr.-Nov. 1942, p. 27; ltr., Arnold to Brig. Gen. Clayton L. Bissell, 12 Sept. 1942; AAF Evaluation Board, POA, Rpt. No. 1, p. 54.

64. Hist. 404th Bomb. Sq., July 1944, p. 1.

65. CM-IN-5475, CAIRO to MILID, 1039, 15 May 1942; Hist. of ICW ATC, June-Dec. 1943, pp. 391-95, 438; ltr., Harmon to Arnold, 18 Aug. 1942; Maj. Robert B. Nelson, Jr., Report to Air Surgeon, AAF, sub.: Morale of Flying Personnel, 20 May 1943 (hereinafter cited as Nelson Report), in Morale and Welfare Folder, 23 Nov. 1942—30 Dec. 1943, AGO 330.11A; Hist. Original XII AFSC, Aug. 1942—Jan. 1944, p. 271; Hist. 404th Bomb. Sq., 14 Jan. 1941—1 Jan. 1944, p. 11.

66. USAF Historical Studies, No. 113: The Fifth Air Force in the Huon Peninsula Campaign, Jan.-Oct. 1943, p. 13; Hist. XII AFSC, 1 Jan.-15 July 1945, p. 6[?]; War Diary, 34th Bomb. Sq., 6 Oct. 1943; Hist. 13th AF, Oct.-Dec. 1944, p. 26; Air Intelligence Combat Unit, AFRS #3, Reports C-274, C-449, C-467, and C-852; Hist. AAFSC/MTO, 8 May-30 Nov. 1945, Annex No. 2; Morale Factors in SWPA, pp. 8-9.

67. Hist. AAFSC/MTO, 1 Jan.-8 May 1945, pp. 513-14; 8 May-30 Nov. 1945, Annex No. 2; Historical Summary of 8th AF Activities, Jan. 1942—Oct. 1943, Incl. 8; Hist. 354th Ftr. Gp., June 1944, p. 64; Sept. 1944, p. 86; Hist. XIX TAC, Mar. 1945, Sec. I, p. 10.

68. War Diary, 58th Ftr. Sq., 10 Dec. 1942.

69. *Ibid.*, 14 Nov. 1943.

70. Administrative History, 12th AF, Part II, Vol. VI, Annex 26, pp. 58, 83; Hist. IX BC, Middle East, 12 Oct. 1942—12 Oct. 1943, pp. 8, 10; Medical Hist. 33d Ftr. Gp., p. 12; 12th AF, Inspection of Combat Groups—Interviews, *passim;* War Diary, 1st Ftr. Gp., 31 Dec. 1943; Hist. 437th Bomb. Sq., Mar. 1944, p. 2; War Diary, 307th Ftr. Sq., 29 Oct. 1943; Hist. 71st Ftr. Sq., Feb. 1944, War Diary, 7 st Ftr. Sq., 26 Feb. 1944.

71. Hist. 3d Air Depot, Mar. 1943; Hist. 68th Sv. Gp., Feb. 1944, p. 1; USAFHS-113,

p. 13; Hist. 41st Bomb. Gp., Nov. 1944, p. 2; Hist. Hq. and Hq. Sq., 23d Sv. Gp., July 1944, p. 7; Hist. 77th Bomb. Sq., Sept. 1944; Oct. 1944; Form 34, 449th Ftr. Sq., 3–9 and 10–16 Oct. 1943; Hist. 13th AF, Oct.–Dec. 1944, p. 26; Org. Hist. VII BC, Aug.–Sept. 1944, p. 109.

72. Hist. 11th Bomb. Sq., Jan.–Apr. 1944, pp. 5–6; Form 34, 76th Ftr. Sq., 19–25 Mar. 1944, 7–13 and 14–20 May 1944; Medical Hist. 11th Bomb. Sq., Feb. 1945; Form 34, 373d Bomb. Sq., 11–20 Apr. 1945; Hist. 1760th Ord. S & M Co., Avn., June 1945; Hist. ICD ATC, 1944, II, 413–14, 416–18, 420.

73. Morale Factors in SWPA, pp. 8–9; Hist. V FC, Nov. 1942—June 1943, pp. 131–32; Hist. 13th AF, Oct.–Dec. 1944, pp. 24–26; Jan.–Mar. 1945, Sec. V, p. 24; Org. Hist. VII BC, Aug.–Sept. 1944, pp. 109, 112–15; Apr. 1945, pp. 421, 425; Medical Hist. 7th AF, pp. 4–5; USAFHS-120, pp. 209–10; Hist. 5th AF, Part III, 1 Feb.–15 June 1944, pp. 29–30; 15 June 1944—2 Sept. 1945, I, chap. 1, 85; Kenney, *General Kenney Reports*, pp. 75, 119; ltr., Maj. Gen. Ennis Whitehead to Kenney, 6 Aug. 1944; Hist. V AFSC, Dec. 1944, p. 1; Feb. 1945, p. 43; Hist. 11th Bomb. Gp., Dec. 1944, p. 7.

74. Air Room Interview with Capt. Charles L. Marburg, 6 Oct. 1942; War Diary, 58th Ftr. Sq., 15 Jan. and 4–7 Feb. 1943; Hist. V AFSC, Sept. 1942—Jan. 1944, p. 37; ltr., Whitehead to Kenney, 6 Aug. 1944; Hist. ICD ATC, 1944, III, 898–99.

75. Morale Factors in SWPA, p. 2; USAF Historical Studies: No. 17, Air Action in the Papuan Campaign, 21 July 1942—23 Jan. 1943, p. 101; USAFHS-113, pp. 238–39; Hist. V AFSC, Sept. 1942—Jan. 1944, p. 89; USAF Historical Studies, No. 101: The AAF in the South Pacific to October 1942, pp. 72, 80; USAF Historical Studies: No. 35, Guadalcanal and the Origins of the Thirteenth Air Force, p. 51; Interview with Capt. James Vande Hey, 20–25 Feb.[?] 1944.

76. Form 34, 23d Ftr. Gp., 31 Oct.–6 Nov. 1943. See also Form 34, 76th Ftr. Sq., 10–16 Oct. 1943; Form 34, 23d Ftr. Gp., 17–23 Oct. 1943.

77. Air Room Interview with Col. H. W. Shelmire, 13 Oct. 1942; Col. H. W. Shelmire, Rpt. to Gen. H. H. Arnold on Trip through Alaska and Aleutian Islands, n.d. [probably late Sept. or early Oct.] 1942, Tabs F and J; Hist. XI BC, 19 Mar.

1943—31 Mar. 1944, p. 10; Hist. 79th Ftr. Gp., 9 Feb. 1942—18 Aug. 1943, p. 9; Narrative History of Hq. 8th AF, June 1944, p. 17.

78. Hist. 98th Bomb. Sq., Nov. 1944.

79. Hist. 11th Bomb. Gp., July 1945, p. 8.

80. Hist. 3d Air Depot, Jan.–May 1943.

81. Hist. XII AFSC, Jan. 1944—July 1945, p. 68.

82. Ltr., Capt. Frank H. Albrecht to CG USASTAF (Admin.), sub.: Morale Report, 12 Aug. 1945, p. 4; AICU, AFRS #3, Report C-724; Hist. 11th Bomb. Gp., Dec. 1944, p. 5; Hist. ICD ATC, 1944, III, 736.

83. Hist. 11th Bomb. Gp., Jan. 1945, pp. 1–2; Hist. 41st Bomb. Gp., Sept. 1944, p. 3; Hist. 13th AF, July–Sept. 1944, p. 26; Hist. 494th Bomb. Gp., July 1944, p. 9; Hist. 436th TCG, Feb. 1944, p. 1.

84. Hist. Original XII AFSC, Aug. 1942—Jan. 1944, p. 266.

85. Medical Support of the U.S. Army Air Forces in the MTO, p. 52.

86. Hist. ICW ATC, June–Dec. 1943, p. 394. See also Hist. 72d Airdrome Sq., Feb.–Mar. 1945; Hist. 325th Ftr. Gp., Dec. 1944. Within tactical units, those noncombat men who actually worked on or near aircraft were likely to have higher morale than men involved in clerical activities. See Medical Hist. 310th Bomb. Gp., 1 Jan.–31 Mar. 1945, p. 2; and Hist. 362d Ftr. Gp., Mar. 1944, p. 4.

87. Hist. 13th AF, Oct.–Dec. 1944, Sec. V, p. 27.

88. Hist. 11th Bomb. Maint. Sq., Sept. 1944, p. 3.

89. Hist. 313th Bomb. Wg., Mar. 1945, I, 10.

90. Hist. 98th Bomb. Sq., July 1945, p. 10. See also Hist. 492d Bomb. Sq., Dec. 1944.

91. AICU AFRS #1, Rpt. A-165.

92. Interview with Capt. Hubert C. Huebner, 1 June 1944.

93. Hist. FEAF, I, 41; Hist. AAFSC/MTO, 1 Jan.–30 June 1944, II, 495; Hist. 13th AF, July–Sept. 1944, p. 23; Jan.–Mar. 1945, Sec. V, pp. 25–27; Apr.–June 1945, Sec. V, p. 26.

94. Hist. V AFSC, 15 June–31 Aug. 1944, App. A, p. 27; Hist. AAFSC/MTO, 1 Jan.–8 May 1945, p. 515.

95. Hist. 43d Sv. Gp., Sept. 1944, p. 12.

96. *Ibid.*, p. 13.

97. Hist. V AFSC, 15 June–31 Aug. 1944, App. A, p. 27; Hist. 13th AF, July–Sept. 1944, p. 23.

98. USAFHS-101, p. 98; USAFHS-120, p. 42; USAFHS-35, pp. 165, 187–88; Hist. 12th AF Medical Sec., Aug. 1942—June 1944, p. 10; USAFHS-9, pp. 126, 142–43; USAF Historical Studies: No. 34, Army Air Forces in the War against Japan, 1941–42, p. 146; Morale Factors in SWPA, Annex 9, pp. 19–20; Kenney, *General Kenney Reports*, pp. 42, 46–47; Hist. 73d Bomb. Wg., 17 July–30 Nov. 1944, p. 95.

99. Diary, 91st Ftr. Sq., 24 Feb. 1943. See also Hist. 324th Ftr. Gp., 23 Dec. 1942.

100. Daily Diary, Office of the Radar Officer, 77th Bomb. Sq., 6 Nov. 1944.

101. General Spaatz felt that the loss of more than thirty C-47's in the HUSKY airborne missions had not damaged the spirits of his troop-carrier crews; senior officers of the Eighth Air Force were just as certain that high losses had had little effect on their bomber crews. See, Ltr., Gen. Carl A. Spaatz to Arnold, 14 July 1943; Arnold, *Global Mission*, p. 451; ltr., Eaker to Arnold, 22 Oct. 1943.

102. Hist. 13th AF, Apr.–June 1944, pp. 73–74. See also Hist. 17th Bomb. Gp., 1931–43, pp. 4–5, 7.

103. Air Room Statement by Col. John R. Kane, 14 Dec. 1943.

104. War Diary, 512th Bomb. Sq., 28 Dec. 1943. See later entries and Hist. 512th Bomb. Sq., Apr. 1944.

105. Kenney, *General Kenney Reports*, p. 438.

106. *Ibid.*, pp. 387–88.

107. History of Hump Operations, 1 Jan.–31 Mar. 1945, pp. 74–75.

108. Air Room Statement by Col. John R. Kane, 14 Dec. 1943; Hist. 95th Ftr. Sq., June 1944, pp. 1, 3; Hist. 376th Bomb. Gp., Aug. 1944, p. 2; Hist. 77th Bomb. Sq., 15 Jan. 1941—31 Dec. 1943, pp. 27, 36; Historical Daily Diary, Mess Hall Section, 77th Bomb. Sq., 20 May 1945; ltrs., Eaker to Maj. Gen. George E. Stratemeyer, 2 and 30 Jan. 1943; Interview with Brig. Gen. H. S. Hansell, 9 Aug. 1943; Interview with Crew of 324th Bomb. Sq., 91st Bomb. Gp., [date?]; Air Room Interview with Col. Howard E. Engler, 27 May 1943; Nelson Report, pp. 2, 5, 10; Hist. 17th Bomb. Gp., 1931–43, pp. 4–5, 7–8; War Diary, 1st Ftr. Grp., 31 Dec. 1943.

109. Air Room Interview with Col. Malcolm Grow, 20 Sept. 1943; USAF Historical Studies, No. 103: The Ploesti Mission of 1 August 1943, pp. 76–77; Air Room Inter-

view with Col. J. E. Smart, 14 Dec. 1943; Hist. 313th Bomb. Wg., Mar. 1945, I, 10.

110. Hist 11th AF, Sec. II, Sept. 1942—Sept. 1945, pp. 201, 395.

111. Air Evaluation Board, POA, Rpt. No. 2, p. 25; History of the Air War in POA, Text, III, pp. 12–13; Hist. Air War in POA, Text, Vol. IV, chap. xxxi, pp. 6–7.

112. Nelson Report, p. 4.

113. Hist. IX BC, Middle East, 12 Oct. 1942—12 Oct. 1943, p. 8.

114. Ltr., Col. C. G. Williamson to Col. F. L. Anderson, 10 Oct. 1942, appended to Interview with Col. Williamson on Alaska.

115. Hist. Air War in POA, Text, Vol. iv, chap. xxxi, pp. 7–8; Hist. 7th AF, 14 July–2 Sept. 1945, p. 81; Air Room Interview with Col. L. C. Craigie, M. S. Roth, and J. F. Philips, 12 Jan. 1943; Hist. 38th Bomb. Gp., Mar. 1944, p. 3; Hist. 11th Bomb. Gp., Aug. 1944, pp. 3, 5; ltr., Col. Glenn L. Nyeto, CO, 3d Bomb. Wg., sub.: Future Operations, 10 Oct. 1943; Hist. 514th Bomb. Sq., Dec. 1943.

116. Hist. 41st Bomb. Gp., May 1944.

117. USAF Historical Studies, No. 117: The Tenth Air Force, 1943, p. 110; Hist. 7th Bomb. Gp., Apr. 1945.

118. War Diary, 37th Bomb. Sq., 6 and 7 Oct. 1943, 15 June 1944.

119. Air Room Interview with Maj. A. V. Martini, 9 Sept. 1943.

120. Ltr., Streett to Giles, 6 Nov. 1944.

121. USAFHS-117, pp. 24, 77–78; Hist. Air War in POA, Text, Vol. I, chap. i, p. 6; Kenney, *General Kenney Reports*, pp. 66, 438; Hist. 13th AF, Apr.–June 1944, pp. 73–74; July–Sept. 1944, p. 24; Air Room Interview with Lt. Col. Carl Norcross, 5 Jan. 1943; ltr., Spaatz to Arnold, 17 Feb. 1943; ltr., Eaker to Giles, 29 Feb. 1944; Narrative Hist. Hq. 8th AF, July 1944, p. 4.

122. Hist. 678th Bomb. Sq., May 1945, p. 6.

123. Hist. 8th AF, 17 Aug. 1942—1 May 1943, II, 441–43, 445; Air Room Interview with Col. Malcolm Grow, 20 Sept. 1943; ltr., Giles to Maj. Gen. William O. Butler, 2 July 1943; Hist. 500th Bomb. Gp., Dec. 1944, p. 1. Parachute deficiencies, for example, had the opposite effect. See Air Room Interview with Cols. L. C. Craigie, M. S. Roth, and J. F. Philips, 12 Jan. 1943.

124. Interview with Col. W. K. Skaer, 13 Sept. 1945.

125. History of MAAF, 10 Dec. 1943—15 Oct. 1945, pp. 319–36, 340, 340a; Hist.

1 5th AF, 1 June–30 Sept. 1944, pp. 21–22; USAFHS-35, pp. 103, 105–7; Hist. 13th AF, Oct.–Dec. 1944, pp. 6–11; Jan.–Mar. 1945, pp. 6, 8–11; Hist. of Air War in POA, Text, Vol. IV, chap. xxx, pp. 32–33, 35–37, 58–59; Hist. 5th AF, Feb. 1944, pp. 11, 31; May 1944; Hist. 38th Bomb. Gp., Feb. 1944, p. 6; Air Room Interview with Air Commodore A. H. C. Sharp and Wing Commander J. Roland Robinson, 10 Aug. 1943; Air Room Interview with Col. Malcolm Grow, 20 Sept. 1943.

126. Ltr., Maj. Gen. Willis Hale to Arnold, 29 Dec. 1943. See also, Lt. Col. Frederick J. Freese, Jr., MC, Status Report on Medical Department Officers in Thirteenth Air Force and in Other AAF Units in SPA, as of 9 April 1943; and ltr., Maj. Gen. Howard C. Davidson to Giles, 11 Feb. 1944.

127. Kenney, *General Kenney Reports*, p. 43.

128. Preliminary History 7th AF, Oct.–Nov. 1944, p. 30.

129. Kenney, *General Kenney Reports*, p. 173; Hist. 11th Bomb. Gp., Nov. 1944, p. 6; Hist. 362d Ftr. Gp., Aug. 1944, pp. 58; Hist. 13th AF, July–Sept. 1944, p. 23; FEAF Reg. 35–40, Awards and Decorations, 23 May 1945; ltr., Brig. Gen. E. Moore to CG AAFPOA, sub.: Awards and Decorations, 21 Mar. 1945; Moore to Maj. Gen. Junius W. Jones, 26 June 1945; Morale Factors in SWPA, pp. 25–28; Org. Hist. VII BC, Feb. 1945, p. 358; War Diary, 37th Bomb. Sq., 11 July 1944; The 9th AF and Its Principal Commands in ETO, Vol. I, Part I, chap. viii; Hist. 449th Bomb. Gp., Nov. 1944, pp. 1–2; ltr., Eaker to Kenney, 11 June 1945.

130. Morale Factors in SWPA, pp. 6, 27; FEAF Reg. No. 35–40, Awards and Decorations, 23 May 1945; AAFRH-20, pp. 155–56, 219.

131. Ltr., Davidson to Arnold, 2 June 1944.

132. Ltr., CO 9th Bomb. Gp. to CG XXI BC through CG 313th Bomb. Wg., sub.: Comments and Recommendations concerning Decorations Policies, 7 July 1945.

133. Hist. 73d Bomb. Wg., Feb. 1945, p. 25; Aug. 1945, p. 14; Hist. 25th Air Sv. Gp., Aug. 1945; Hist. 58th Bomb. Wg., July 1945, p. 4; Hist. XX BC, Jan. 1945, pp. 20–21; Feb. 1945, p. 24; War Diary, 324th Air Sv. Sq., 24 Nov. 1944; The 9th AF and Its Principal Commands in ETO, Vol. I, Part I, chap. viii; *ibid.*, Part II, chap. v, p. 405;

Hist. 81st Airdrome Sq. (Sp.), Mar. 1945; ltr., Hq. IX TCC (Fwd.) to Distribution A, sub.: Battle Participation Awards, 24 May 1945; File 124; memo, AC/AS, Personnel, Awards Div. to AC/AS, Personnel, Air Chaplain Div., 23 May 1945.

134. Form 34, 22d Bomb. Sq., 9–15 Apr. 1944; Hist. of Chaplains Section, Hq. XX BC, Dec. 1944; File 124; Medical Support of the U.S. Army Air Forces in the MTO, pp. 48–49, 51; ltr., Spaatz to Stratemeyer, 26 Mar. 1943; ltr., Eaker to Giles, 8 Apr. 1944; Hist. 23d Sv. Gp., Aug. 1944, p. 3; Hist. 80th Ftr. Gp., Jan. 1944; Hist. 73d Bomb. Wg., 17 July–30 Nov. 1944, p. 81; Hist. 500th Bomb. Gp., Dec. 1944, pp. 10–11; Feb. 1945, pp. 11–12; Mar. 1945, pp. 8–9; 1 Apr.–31 May 1945, I, 31; Hist. 77th Bomb. Sq., Dec. 1944; June 1945.

135. Ltr., Lt. Col. John Davies to Hq. Northeast Area, Townsville, Queensland, 15 May 1942, in Hist. 27th Bomb. Gp., Jan. 1940—Sept. 1942.

136. USAFHS-9, p. 144; USAFHS-17, p. 101; Kenney, *General Kenney Reports*, p. 79; Hist. of ICW ATC, June–Dec. 1943, p. 352; War Diary, 307th Ftr. Sq., 23 Oct. 1943; War Diary, 17th Bomb. Gp., 20 Mar. 1944; AICU AFRS #2, Rpt. B-2005.

137. Hist. A-1 Section, Hq. 11th AF, 16 Mar. 1942—31 May 1944, p. 13; ltr., Hq. Alaskan Defense Command to CG 11th AF, sub.: Promotion of Officers, 24 Sept. 1942; Hist. of ICW ATC, June–Dec. 1943, pp. 350, 352–55; Hist. of ICD ATC, 1944, III, 751–52.

138. Ltr., Stratemeyer to Eaker, 7 July 1943.

139. Ltrs., Stratemeyer to Giles, 22 Aug. and 4 Sept. 1943.

140. Hist. 313th Bomb. Wg., Mar. 1945, I, 10; File 124; Brig. Gen. Clayton L. Bissell, Comments on General Arnold's Letter, Sept. 12, 1942, 24 Oct. 1942; Form 34, 22d Bomb. Sq., 5–11 Mar. 1945; Hq. XX BC, Personnel Section Historical Report for Dec. 1944; ltr., Kenney to William L. Ritchie, 14 Apr. 1943; Incl. 3, Re-organization, in ltr., Eaker to Arnold, 21 Mar. 1944; ltr., Kenney to Whitehead, 2 Nov. 1943; USAF Historical Studies, No. 104: The Tenth Air Force, 1 Jan.–10 Mar. 1943, p. 6; Hist. of 12th AF A-1 Section through end of 1943, pp. 9–10; USAF Historical Studies, No. 116: The Fifth Air Force in the Huon Peninsula Campaign, Oct. 1943—Feb. 1944, pp. 182–83; ltr., Stratemeyer to Bissell,

7 July 1943; Hist. of A-1 Section, Hq. 11th AF, 1 Nov.–31 Dec. 1944, p. 17; Hist. AAFSC/MTO, Jan.–June 1944, II, 500; Hist. 13th AF, Oct.–Dec. 1944, p. 27; Hist. FAFSC, Mar. 1945, I, 16; Hist. Hq. and Hq. Sq., 12th Sv. Gp., Mar. 1945, p. 2; CM-IN-11430, AGWAR to AFHQ (Arnold to All Commanding Generals), 13 Dec. 1944; Interview with M/Sgt. Andrew A. Butler, Sgt. Major of Hq. CACW, 19 Mar. 1945; Hist. Hq. and Hq. Sq., 68th Sv. Gp., Sept. 1945, p. 2.

141. Cf., Morale Factors in SWPA, p. 23.

142. Hist. 95th Bomb. Sq., Apr. 1945. See also Hist. 3d Air Depot Gp., 1942, p. 23; Hist. Hq. and Base Services Sq., 86th Air Sv. Gp., Dec. 1944; Hist. 494th Bomb. Gp., July 1944, p. 10; Hist. 303d Air Sv. Gp., Aug. 1945, p. 8.

143. Morale Factors in SWPA, p. 21; Org. Hist. VII BC, Dec. 1944, p. 232; AAFRH-13, pp. 124–25; Hist. 5th AF, 15 June 1944–2 Sept. 1945, I, chap. i, p. 87.

144. CM-OUT-1625, AGWAR to AQUILA, 506, 7 June 1942; USAFHS-104, pp. 8–9; CM-IN-1322, Cairo to AGWAR, AMSME 4405, 2 Feb. 1943; CM-OUT-1568, SPXAT-M (AGO APS), to CG USAF AMSME Cairo, 3219, 4 Feb. 1943; CM-IN-4986, Cairo to AG, 1134 AMSEG, 18 May 1942; Interview with Col. C. G. Williamson on Alaska, 10 Nov. 1942; Hist. Air War in POA, Text, Vol. I, chap. ii, p. 35; Air Room Interview with Capt. Charles L. Marburg, 6 Oct. 1942; Nelson Report, p. 4; AAF-CBI Evaluation Board, Report No. 1, 15 Sept. 1944, par. 89; Hist. XX BC, Dec. 1944, pp. 91–92; Hist. Forward Echelon Det. XX BC Dec. 1944; Hist. 95th Bomb. Sq., Apr. 1945; Hist. 500th Bomb. Gp., 1 Aug.–2 Sept. 1945, I, 34; Hist. 11th Bomb. Sq., Jan.–Apr. 1944, pp. 6–7; Jan. 1945, p. 2; Morale Factors in SWPA, pp. 22–24.

145. USAFHS-120, p. 218.

146. Nelson Report, p. 3; 12th AF Admin. Hist., Part II, Vol. VI, p. 11; The 9th AF and Its Principal Commands in ETO, VII, 55.

147. Hist. 8th AF, Vol. I, 28 Jan.–17 Aug. 1942, p. 272; ltr., Eaker to Air Chief Marshal Sir Charles Portal, 12 Aug. 1943; 12th AF Admin. Hist., Part II, Vol. I, p. 5; War Diary, 58th Ftr. Sq., 24 Dec. 1943; Dulles, *The American Red Cross*, p. 428.

148. The 9th AF and Its Principal Commands in ETO, Vol. I, Part II, chap. v, p.

448; Hist. 17th Bomb. Gp., Nov.–Dec. 1943; Hist. 8th AF, Vol. II, 17 Aug. 1942—1 May 1943, p. 222; Hist. 8th AF Special Staff Sections, Jan. 1944—July 1945, chap. P, pp. 4–15; Rough Draft of Hist. 8th AF, Part I, p. 16; Hist. XII AFSC, Jan. 1944—July 1945, pp. 293–95, 309; Hist. MAAF, 10 Dec. 1943—15 Oct. 1945, pp. 91–92, 277, 512–14; ltr., Maj. Gen. Nathan F. Twining to Eaker, 24 Dec. 1944; War Diary, Hq. Sq. 41st Sv. Gp., 1 Jan. 1945.

149. Hist. of MAAF, 10 Dec. 1943—15 Oct. 1945, pp. 274–75; Hist. of AAFSC/MTO, 1 Jan.–30 June 1944, I, 238–39; 1 Jan.–8 May 1945, p. 167; 12th AF Admin. Hist., Part II, Vol. II, Annex 3; The 9th AF and Its Principal Commands in ETO, Vol. IV, Part I, pp. 71–73; Hist. 8th AF Special Staff Sections, Jan. 1944—July 1945, chap. P, pp. 2–4, 17–22; ltr., Giles to Eaker, 30 Nov. 1944.

150. Dulles, *The American Red Cross*, pp. 424–44; Hist. 8th AF, Vol. I, 28 Jan.–17 Aug. 1942, pp. 201–3; ltr., Eaker to Portal, 12 Aug. 1943; Hist. 8th AF Special Staff Sections, Jan. 1944—July 1945, chap. P, p. 6; Rough Draft of Hist. 8th AF, Part I, p. 16; 12th AF Admin. Hist. Part II, I, 5, 8; Hist. 356th Ftr. Sq., Jan. 1945, pp. 3–4; Hist. 381st Bomb. Sq., Feb. 1945; War Diary, 84th Bomb. Sq., 3 July 1944. See also AAF Operation of Rest Camps in MTO, 19 Dec. 1942—31 Oct. 1945.

151. Admin. Hist. 7th AF, 1916—May 1944, pp. 121–27; Hist. 11th AF, Sec. II, Sept. 1942—Sept. 1945, p. 214; Hist. 3d Air Depot Gp., June 1943; Historical Study 4, Hist. XX BC, 4th Phase, pp. 43–51; Hist. Fwd. Echelon, XX BC, Aug. 1944, pp. 9–10; Morale Factors in SWPA, p. 5; Hist. 5th AF, 15 June 1944—2 Sept. 1945, Vol. I, chap. i, p. 60; USAFHS-17, p. 101; Air Room Interview with Capt. Charles L. Marburg, 6 Oct. 1942; Hist. 13th AF, Jan.–Mar. 1945, Sec. VI; Apr.–June, 1945, Sec. VI; Hist. 51st Ftr. Gp., 1 Jan. 1942—25 Mar. 1943, p. 25; Hist. ICW ATC, June–Dec. 1943, p. 387; Hist. ICD ATC, 1944, III, 742; memo, Brig. Gen. Ernest Moore to Maj. Gen. Junius W. Jones, 26 June 1945; Form 34's, 76th Ftr. Sq., 29 Aug.–4 Sept. 1943, 12–18 Sept. 1943; Form 34, 375th Bomb. Sq., 14–20 Nov. 1943; Form 34, Hq. 23d Ftr. Gp., 14–20 Nov. 1943; Hist. 38th Bomb. Gp., July 1945, p. 55; Administrative Narrative, 5th AF, p. 6.

152. Hist. ICW ATC, June–Dec. 1943,

pp. 389–91; Hist. V FC, chap. i, Nov. 1942—
June 1943, p. 135; Org. Hist., VII BC, Apr.
1945, p. 422; Hist. 28th Bomb. Gp., Oct.
1944, p. 4; Prelim. Org. Hist. VII BC,
1 May 1931–31 July 1944, p. 68; Hist. 28th
Bomb. Gp., May 1944, p. 7; Hist. 400th
Bomb. Gp., Aug. 1945, I, 36; Hist. V FC,
chap. i, Nov. 1942—June 1943, pp. 135–36;
Hist. 5th AF, Mar.–Apr. 1944, p. 44.

153. Morale Factors in SWPA, pp. 29–
31, 35–44; Hist. 7th Bomb. Gp., July 1945;
Hist. ICD ATC, 1944, III, 743; USAFHS-
113, p. 111.

154. Org. Hist. VII BC, Feb. 1945, p.
354; Hist. 13th AF, Jan.–Mar. 1945, Sec. VI;
Hist. Personnel Services Sec., 11th AF, 1
July 1941–1 May 1945, pp. 4–6, 9–10.

155. Hq. XX BC Special Service Histori-
cal Report, Nov. 1944, p. 1; Org. Hist. VII
BC, Jan. 1945, p. 284; Mar. 1945, p. 391;
Hist. 313th Bomb. Wing, June 1945, I, 10;
Hist. 5th AF, 15 June 1944—2 Sept. 1945, I,
chap. i, 63; Morale Factors in SWPA, An-
nex 31; Hist. 13th AF, Apr.–June 1945, Sec.
VI; Historical Report from Information-
Education Officer, VII FC, 5 July 1945.

156. USAF Historical Studies, No. 116:
The Fifth Air Force in the Huon Peninsula
Campaign, Oct. 1943—Feb. 1944, pp. 188–
89; ltr., Whitehead to Mr. Nyles Christian-
son, 17 Jan. 1944; ltr., Whitehead to Kenney,
24 and 28 July 1944; The Tenth Air Force
Chaplaincy, p. 8; Admin. Hist. 5th AF, p. 3;
Hist. 3d Air Depot Gp., Aug. 1943, p. 6;
Jan. 1944; Hist. 13th AF ARC; Prelim.
Org. Hist. VII BC, 1 May 1931—31 July
1944, p. 42; Hist. 7th Bomb. Gp., Feb. 1945;
Hist. ICW ATC, June–Dec. 1943, p. 387.

157. Hist. 8th AF, Vol. II, 17 Aug. 1942
—1 May 1943, pp. 439–41; Historical Data,
Hq. IX TCC, June 1944, p. 9; Hist. XIX
TAC, 1 July 1944—28 Feb. 1945, pp. 190–92;
The 9th AF and Its Principal Commands in
ETO, Vol. II, Part I, pp. 67–68; Hist. Hq.
& Hq. Det. 1586th QM Gp. (Avn.), Mar.
1945; ibid., Apr. 1945; ibid., May 1945; Nel-
son Report, pp. 3, 9; 12th AF Admin. Hist.
Part II, Vol. II, Annex 3; ibid., Annex 26;
ibid., Vol. VI, Annex 26; Med. Hist. 33d
Ftr. Gp., p. 41; AAF Operation of Rest
Camps in MTO, 19 Dec. 1942—31 Oct.
1945; Hist. 439th Bomb. Sq., Dec. 1943;
War Diary, 84th Bomb. Sq., 23 Feb. and
9 Aug. 1944; Hist. 5th Bomb. Wing, July
1945; Hist. AAFSC/MTO, 8 May–30 Nov.
1945, pp. 18–19.

158. Hist. 51st Ftr. Gp., 1 Jan. 1942—

25 Mar. 1943, pp. 10, 12; ltr., Brig. Gen.
C. V. Haynes to Bissell, 31 May 1943; Hist.
80th Ftr. Gp., June 1944; ibid., July 1944;
Hist. 377th Sv. Sq., Nov. 1944; Hist. 51st Sv.
Gp., Jan. 1945; Hist. ICD ATC, 1944, III,
762; Med. Hist. ICW and ICD ATC, 1942–
45, pp. 38–44; Hist. 770th Bomb. Sq., July
1944, p. 2; Hist. 1st Bomb. Maint. Sq., 19–
30 June 1944; Hist. XX BC, Aug. 1944, pp.
8–9; Historical Data, 769th Bomb. Sq. and
10th Bomb. Maint. Sq., Sept. 1944, p. 2;
Hist. 584th Materiel Sq., Dec. 1944; Hist.
Med. Sec. XX BC, Nov. 1944; Hist. XX BC,
Nov. 1944, p. 12; Hist. Hq. XX BC Personnel Sec., Dec. 1944; Form 34, 76th Ftr. Sq.,
2–8 Jan. 1944; Hist. 68th Sv. Gp., Oct.
1944, p. 1; Hist. 11th Bomb. Sq., Nov. 1944,
p. 2; Hist. 23d Ftr. Gp., May 1945, p. C;
Hist. 1088th Sig. Co., Sv. Gp., Aug. 1945,
p. 2.

159. Morale Factors in SWPA, pp. 16–17;
ibid., Annex 17; Hist. V FC, chap. i, Nov.
1942—June 1943, p. 134; USAFHS-116, pp.
192–93; Hist. 43d Bomb. Gp., Feb. 1944, p.
A; Hist. 5th AF, Part III, 1 Feb.–15 June
1944, p. 44 of Mar.–Apr. section; ibid., App.
II, Vol. V, documents 562, 563; General
Kenney Reports, p. 416; ltr., Kenney to
Whitehead, 1 Aug. 1944; ltr., Millard Harmon to Arnold, 2 Nov. 1942; ltr., Twining
to Arnold, 27 Apr. 1943; Lt. Col. Frederick
J. Freese, Jr., MC, Status Report on Medical
Department Officers in Thirteenth Air
Force and in Other AAF Units in SPA, as
of 9 Apr. 1943; Hist. 13th AF, Apr.–June
1944, pp. 72–74; ibid., July–Sept. 1944, pp.
21–22; ibid., Oct.–Dec. 1944, Sec. V, p. 27;
AAF Evaluation Board, POA, Report No. 1,
p. 55; Hist. VII FC, Sept. 1944, p. 6.

160. Extract from Monthly Intelligence
Summary No. 1, Hq. V AFSC, 20 June–20
July 1944.

161. Hist. 5th AF, 15 June 1944—2 Sept.
1945, Vol. I, chap. i, p. 85; Hist. V FC,
chap. iv, July–Dec. 1944, Annex I, Incl. 34;
Hist. V AFSC, Dec. 1944, p. 14; ltr., CG
5th AF to CG FEAF, sub.: Rest Area for
Combat Crew Personnel, 11 June 1945.

162. Hist. 500th Bomb. Gp., Feb. 1945,
p. 11; Hist. 73d Bomb. Wing, Feb.–Mar.
1945, pp. 34, 69, 72; ibid., Apr. 1945, pp. 37,
40; ibid., June 1945, p. 29; ibid., July 1945,
p. 24; Hist. 313th Bomb. Wing, Apr. 1945,
Part I, p. 34; ltr., Col. K. H. Gibson, CO
6th Bomb. Gp., to CG 313th Bomb. Wing,
sub.: Rotation Rest and Recreation Plan, 20
Apr. 1945; ltr., Barney Giles to Eaker, 12

June 1945; ltr., Eaker to Barney Giles, 4 July 1945.

163. Survey of Soldier Opinion in New Guinea, 29 Oct. 1943, Part II, p. 29; Hist. 308th Bomb. Gp., Jan. 1945, p. 1; Hist. 40th Bomb. Gp., May 1945, p. 14; War Diary, 717th Bomb. Sq., 12 Mar. 1944; AAF Evaluation Board, POA, Report No. 2, pp. 29–30; ltr., Eaker to Arnold, 14 Aug. 1944.

164. Morale Factors in SWPA, pp. 12–15; Hist. V FC, chap. iii, Jan.–June 1944, p. 121; Hist. 5th AF, 15 June 1944—2 Sept. 1945, Vol. I, chap. i, p. 83; Monthly Intelligence Summary No. 7, Hq. V AFSC, 20 Dec. 1944—20 Jan. 1945; Hist. 13th AF, Jan.–Mar. 1945, Sec. V, p. 22; Hist. of Air War in POA, Text, Vol. IV, chap. xxxi, p. 18; Org. Hist. VII BC, Apr. 1945, p. 421; Incl. 1: Personnel and Administration, in memo, Maj. Gen. J. W. Jones, The Air Inspector, to CG AAFPOA, sub.: Inspection VII Fighter Command, 29 June 1945; Hist. 404th Bomb. Sq., Sept. 1944, p. 11; AAF-CBI Evaluation Board, Report No. 1, 15 Sept. 1944, par. 88; Hist. 12th AF Med. Sec., Aug. 1942–June 1944.

165. Hist. 8th AF, Vol. I, 28 Jan.–17 Aug. 1942, p. 301; ibid., Vol. II, 17 Aug. 1942—1 May 1943, p. 436; Hist. 12th AF Med. Sec., Aug. 1942—June 1944, p. 74; Hist. 12th AF A-1 Sec. through end of 1943, pp. 5–6, 8; ltr., Eaker to Stratemeyer, 2 Jan. 1943; ltr., Maj. Gen. James H. Doolittle to Maj. Gen. Davenport Johnson, 8 Jan. 1943; ltr., Millard Harmon to Arnold, 16 Dec. 1942; Hist. A-1 Sec., Hq. 11th AF, 16 Mar. 1942—31 May 1944, pp. 18–19; CM-OUT-10824, OPD to CG USAFIME AMSME Cairo 4539, 26 Apr. 1943; WD Circular 127, 29 May 1943; Nelson Report, pp. 7–8; ltr., Barney Giles to Stratemeyer, 9 Oct. 1943.

166. Ltr., Arnold to Brig. Gen. Ralph H. Wooten, 16 Feb. 1944. Similar letters were sent to other overseas air force commanders.

167. Morale Factors in SWPA, pp. 13–14; Happy Warriors Folder; Col. Charles G. Williamson, First Partial Report of Alaskan Inspection, 12 Nov. 1942; Memo, CG USAFISPA for Brig. Gen. Thomas J. Hanley, Jr., 8 Dec. 1942; ltr., Millard Harmon to Arnold, 16 Dec. 1942; ltr., Eaker to Stratemeyer, 2 Jan. 1943; ltr., Doolittle to Johnson, 8 Jan. 1943; AAFHS-35, pp. 167–69, 175–77; Lt. Col. Frederick J. Freese, Jr., MC, Status Report on Medical Department Officers in Thirteenth Air Force and in Other AAF Units in SPA, as of 9 Apr. 1943; ltr., Spaatz to Arnold, 14 July 1943; ltr., Barney Giles to Spaatz, 24 Aug. 1943; ltr., Kenney to Arnold, 28 July 1943; ltr., Arnold to Kenney, 31 Aug. 1943; ltr., Arnold to Eaker, 2 Jan. 1943; ltr., Johnson to Lt. Gen. Frank M. Andrews, 15 Jan. 1943; ltr., Stratemeyer to Whitehead, 29 Jan. 1943; ltr., Stratemeyer to Millard Harmon, 11 Feb. 1943; ltr., Barney Giles to Maj. Gen. Howard C. Davidson, 11 May 1943; ltr., Arnold to Doolittle, 11 Feb. 1944; 8th AF Memo 35-1, 4 Mar. 1944; ltr., Doolittle to Arnold, sub.: Policy on Relief of Combat Crews, 4 Mar. 1944; ltr., Maj. Gen. James M. Bevans to Kenney, 25 Apr. 1944; ltr., Barney Giles to Eaker, 19 June 1944; ltr., Barney Giles to Spaatz, 19 June 1944; Narrative Hist. Hq. 8th AF, Mar. 1944, p. 4; ibid., July 1944, pp. 1–2, 93–94.

168. CM-OUT-2083, SPXPE-A to CG USAF AMSME Cairo, 3724, 5 Mar. 1943; ltr., Arnold to Kenney, 31 Aug. 1943; ltr., Bevans to Twining, 12 Jan. 1944; ltr., Barney Giles to Eaker, 19 June 1944.

169. Morale Factors in SWPA, p. 12. See also ltr., Brig. Gen. Paul B. Wurtsmith to Dep. Comdr. 5th AF, sub.: Replacement Personnel, 19 June 1943; ltr., Kenney to Arnold, 28 July 1943; ltr., Wurtsmith to Dep. Comdr. 5th AF, sub.: Medical Officer's Report, 9 Nov. 1943; ltr., Doolittle to CG AAF, Att.: Bevans, sub.: Personnel, 19 Nov. 1943.

170. Hist. V FC, chap. i, Nov. 1942—June 1943, pp. 134–35.

171. Hist. 12th AF A-1 Sec., through end of 1943, p. 12; ibid., 2d quarter 1944; ibid., 4th quarter, 1944; ibid., 1st quarter 1945; ltr., Hq. 5th AF to All 5th AF Unit Commanders, sub.: Temporary Duty to United States, 6 Apr. 1945; File 124; Morale Factors in SWPA, pp. 6, 14–15; ibid., Annex I, pp. 5–6; ibid., Annex 1-A; Hist. 5th AF, 15 June 1944—2 Sept. 1945, Vol. I, chap. i, p. 83; Extract from Monthly Intelligence Summary No. 1, Hq. V AFSC, 20 June–20 July 1944; Extract from Monthly Intelligence Summary No. 2, Hq. V AFSC, 21 July–20 Aug. 1944; Monthly Intelligence Summary No. 7, Hq. V AFSC, 20 Dec. 1944—20 Jan. 1945; ibid., No. 11, 20 Apr.–20 May 1945; Hist. 13th AF, Jan.–Mar. 1945, p. 22; ibid., Apr.–June 1945, p. 21; Hist. 11th Bomb. Gp., Aug. 1944, p. 5; ibid., Sept. 1944, p. 5; ibid., Oct. 1944, p. 6; ibid., Dec. 1944, pp. 5–6, 8; ibid., Feb. 1945, pp. 5–6; Hist. 26th Bomb.

Sq., July 1945, p. 15; Hist. of Air War in POA, Text, Vol. IV, chap. xxxi, p. 18; Incl. 1, Personnel and Administration, in memo, Maj. Gen. J. W. Jones, The Air Inspector, to CG AAFPOA, sub.: Inspection VII Fighter Command, 29 June 1945; War Diary, 84th Bomb. Sq., 29 Jan. 1944; War Diary, Hq. & Hq. Sq. 306th Sv. Gp., 13 Mar., 20 Apr. 1944; War Diary, 1666th Ord. S & M Co., Avn., 26 Apr., 24 Oct. 1944; Hist. 31st Ftr. Gp., Oct. 1944, pp. 5–6; War Diary, 1068th Sig. Co., Sv. Gp., 19 Nov, 1944; War Diary, 1062d Sig. Co., Sv. Gp., 18 Nov. 1944.

172. Quote from Eaker in memo for CGs 1st, 2d, 3d, 4th, 6th, and 7th Air Forces from Arnold, 22 Apr. 1943. See also ltr., Eaker to Stratemeyer, 2 Jan. 1943; memo for Chief, Research Br., Div. of Morale Services, from Maj. Douglas Waples, sub.: Information Obtained from Returnees at AFRS #1, 22 Nov. 1943; Report on Survey of Aircrew Personnel in the 8th, 9th, 12th and 15th Air Forces, p. 61; Morale Factors in SWPA, p. 6.

173. Ltr., Brig. Gen. Frederick L. Anderson to Stratemeyer, 21 July 1943; Interview with Col. M. A. Preston, 3 July 1945; Report on Survey of Aircrew Personnel in the 8th, 9th, 12th, and 15th Air Forces, pp. 62, 64–65; Nelson Report, p. 7; Morale Factors in SWPA, p. 6.

174. For examples of successful leadership and its morale consequences, see memo for CGs 1st, 2d, 3d, 4th, 6th, and 7th Air Forces from Arnold, 22 Apr. 1943; USAF Historical Studies, No. 109: The Fourteenth Air Force to 1 Oct. 1943, p. 9; *General Kenney Reports*, pp. 64, 382–83; Hist. 404th Bomb. Sq., 14–15 Jan. 1941—1 Jan. 1944, p. 42; Hist. 79th TC Sq., Mar. 1945, p. 6. For examples of poor leadership and its morale consequences, see Hist. of FEAF, I, 23–24; Interview with Capt. Edward M. Woodrop, 12 Apr. 1944; Interview with 1st Lt. Kenneth H. Oppenheimer, 11 Apr. 1944; Interview with 1st Lt. George C. Riggins, 12 Apr. 1944; Interview with Col. Millard L. Haskin, 15 June 1945; AICU No. 5, Reports E-29, E-32; Hist. of ICD ATC, 1944, I, 272–76; Hist. 332d Sv. Gp., 2 Mar. 1944; Hist. of ICD ATC, 1944, I, 272–76; Hist. 332d Sv. Gp., 2 Mar. 1944, pp. 2–3. For many examples of the concern of AAF commanders for the morale and welfare of their men, see Operations Letters, Vols. I and II, in Air Historical Archives, *passim*.

NOTES TO CHAPTER 15

1. Ltr., Hq. USSTAF to CG 8th AF, 30 Aug. 1944.

2. Ltr., Maj. Gen. B. McK. Giles to CG ATC, 30 June 1943; AC/AS OC&R, Req. Div., Daily diary, 22 July 1943, 3 Aug. 1943.

3. AAF Memo No. 20–10, 25 Aug. 1943.

4. JCS Memo for Information No. 58, 1943, App. to encl. B; ltr., C/AS to Sec., JCS, 30 July 1943; memo re: mtg. on sea rescue of aircraft, 15 July 1943, attended by representatives of Navy, OPD WDGS, and AAF (n.d. or addressee indicated).

5. See note above; memo for JAC from JCS Joint Staff Planners, 23 Aug. 1943; ltr. Comdt. USCG to COMINCH and CNO to JCS, 1 Sept. 1943. Rpt. of JAC on air-sea rescue operations, 22 Sept. 1943.

6. 1st ind. (basic ltr., Lt. Col. O. C. Van Haesen, AG to CG AAF, 25 July 1943) Hq. AAF to CG 5th AF, 28 Aug. 1943; AC/AS, OC&R, Daily diary, 27 Aug. 1943; memo for C/AS from Maj. Gen. H. A. Craig, 1 June 1944; memo for Col. C. V. Whitney from Maj. Gen. L. S. Kuter, AC/AS Plans, 5 Aug. 1944.

7. Ltr., Giles to Eaker, 16 May 1945; ltr., Eaker to Giles, 1 June 1945; memo for Ch. Rescue and Survival Br. from Thomas R. Dunn, 3 Oct. 1945.

8. Memo for SECNAV from Adm. Wm. D. Leahy, 15 Feb. 1944; Navy BUMED News Letter, 4 Aug. 1944.

9. Hq. AAF, Air Comm. O, Daily acty. rpt. (to Arnold), 19 Apr. 1944; memo for Arnold from Kuter, 15 Apr. 1944; memo for Col. C. V. Whitney from Kuter, 5 Aug. 1944.

10. Memo for OPD WDGS from Brig. Gen. Patrick W. Timberlake DC/AS, 21 Feb. 1945; AAF Reg. No. 20–54, 3 Feb. 1945; Ltr., Maj. Gen. H. L. George, CG ATC, to Giles, 28 Mar. 1945; memo for Arnold from Kuter, 22 Nov. 1944.

11. USSTAF, Dir. on Air Sea Rescue Training and Equipment Program in 8th and 9th AF's, 30 May 1944 (hereinafter cited as USSTAF, Dir. on ASR); Statistical Summary, 1943, air-sea rescue activities, VIII BC and VIII FC; ltr., Hq. USSTAF to CG 8th AF, 31 May 1944; AC/AS, OC&R, Daily acty. rpt., 18 Sept. 1944, 13 Nov. 1944, 22 May 1945; memo 8th AF to CG's I, II, III, Air Divs., Rpt. Anoxia, Frostbite, Ditching, and Parachuting, 28 Mar. 1945.

12. AC/AS, OC&R, Daily acty. rpt., 14 Mar. 1945, 24 Apr. 1945; AC/AS, OC&R, Wkly. rpt. for General Council Mtg., 15 Mar. 1945; *AAF in WW II*, V, 601–2.

13. USSBS, Strategic Air Operations . . . VHB, p. 24.

14. ETO, Air Tech. Sec., Tech. Rpt. No. 321, 13 July 1943; 8th AF, Rpt. on B-17 and B-24 bail-out and ditching, Feb. 1945; USSTAF, Dir. on ASR, 30 May 1944; 13th AF, Opns. Analysis Sec., "An Analysis of Water Landings by 13th AF Bombers," 5 July 1944.

15. USSTAF, Air Sea Rescue Narrative No. 2, 19 June 1944.

16. Narrative of Ditching of Crew of A/C #282, 8 June 1944.

17. USSTAF, Dir. on ASR, 30 May 1944; ltr., Hq. VIII FC to CO's of Wings *et al.*, 12 Feb. 1944.

18. 8th AF, Rpt. on B-17 and B-24 bail-out and ditching, Feb. 1945; ltr., Hq. 2d Bombard. Div. to CG's Bombard. Wings *et al.*, 26 Aug. 1944.

19. 1st Lt. Harry Schulman and 1st Lt. M. A. Lester, 2d ER Sq., Memo on Army and Navy air-sea rescue, 7 June 1945; 8th AF, Memo. No. 50-10.

20. USSTAF, Dir. on ASR, 30 May 1944; ltr., 8th AFSC to CG USSTAF, 10 Feb. 1944.

21. ATSC, Hist. Development of Survival and Rescue Equipment for the Army Air Forces, pp. 74–76 (hereinafter cited as Search and Rescue Equipment); ltr., Hq. 8th AFSC to CG VIII BC, 26 Oct. 1943.

22. Search and Rescue Equipment, pp. 76, 82–83.

23. *Ibid.*, pp. 84–94; AAF Mat. Center, Memo rpt. on raft, pneumatic life, Type E-2, 20 Mar. 1943; Hq. AAF, Mil. Req. No. 33, 28 Aug. 1944; memo for Col. Hunter (material for Gen. Arnold's Monday mtg.) 23 Oct. 1942.

24. Search and Rescue Equipment, pp. 94 ff.; USSTAF, Dir. on ASR, 30 May 1944; Liaison O's Diary, 2 Aug. 1943, 28 Aug. 1943.

25. AC/AS, OC&R, Daily acty. rpt., 1 Dec. 1943; Search and Rescue Equipment, pp. 97–98; memo for Col. M. R. Wood, Ch. Supply Div., 8th AFSC from Chaffee, 8 June 1943.

26. Search and Rescue Equipment, pp. 108–13.

27. *Ibid.*, p. 121.

28. *Ibid.*, pp. 120–29.

29. *Ibid.*, pp. 130–38; Unsatisfactory rpt. on vest life-preserver, Type B-3, by CO, 56th Ftr. Gp., 12 Feb. 1943; 363d Ftr. Sq. Emergency air-sea rescue rpt., 27 Feb. 1945.

30. Search and Rescue Equipment, pp. 140–50; AC/AS, OC&R, Wkly. Rpt. for General Council Mtg., 23 Mar. 1945; ltr., Hq. II Air Div. to A-2 and S-3 Sec., 15 Mar. 1945.

31. Search and Rescue Equipment, p. 150; AC/AS, OC&R, Daily acty. rpt., 23 Apr. 1945.

32. AC/AS, OC&R, Daily acty. rpt., 17 May 1945

33. Ltr., Hq. VIII BC to CG's Bombard. Wings *et al.*, re RAF Single Point Quick Release Harness (n.d.); ltr., Hq. 92d Bombard. Gp. to C/AS, AAF, 18 Oct. 1942, *and* 4th ind., Hq. AAF to Liaison O, 8th AFSC, 21 Jan. 1943; AAF Mat. Comd., Memo Rpt. on parachute comments from the ETO, July–Sept. 1944.

34. AC/AS, OC&R, Daily acty. rpt., 1 Dec. 1943.

35. Search and Rescue Equipment, pp. 151–65 *passim*; Hist. Search and Rescue in the India-China Div., ATC, Dec. 1942—Dec. 1945, pp. 55–59.

36. Search and Rescue Equipment, pp. 170–79.

37. Search and Rescue Equipment, pp. 8–36 *passim*; ltr., Hq. VIII BC to A-4, Hq. 8th AF, 8 July 1943; ltr., Hq. 8th AF to CG VIII BC, 27 June 1943.

38. USSTAF, Dir. on ASR, 30 May 1944; Search and Rescue Equipment, pp. 8–30.

39. *AAF in WW II*, IV, 79; ltr., Hq. EAC to Hq. 231st Gp., 18 July 1944; memo by Hq. Prov. Med. Fld. Service Sch., 8th AF, 24 June 1943.

40. Memo for Maj. R. R. Brunner from Lt. J. M. Hertzberg, AFTSC, 17 Aug. 1942; Exhibit "A" to min. to mtg. of Sig. Corps Tech. Com. No. 226, 12 Jan. 1942; memo for Controls Div. from Lt. Col. J. R. Cunningham, Ch., Radio Div., AFTSC, 10 July 1942; AC/AS, OC&R, Daily acty. rpt., 29 Mar. 1944.

41. Ltr., Hq. VIII BC to CG 8th AG (n.d., but 1st ind. is dated 6 Mar. 1943, and subject is dinghy transmitter-SCR-578); ltr., Air Ministry to CG 8th AF, 21 Oct. 1943.

42. Ltr., Lt. Col. J. W. Burgard, Ch., Emergency Rescue Br., Req. Div., OC&R, to Air Member, Canadian Joint Staff; JCS

Directive, 659/3 Vol. II, 27 Mar. 1945; AS/AS, OC&R, Daily acty. rpt., 28 Mar. 1945; memo for AC/AS, Oprs. Div., Policy Sec. (Prog. rpt. on communications equip.), 16 Dec. 1944.

43. USSTAF, Dir. on ASR, 30 May 1944; memo for Sig. O, USSTAF, from A-3, 27 Sept. 1943; memo for Col. A. R. Maxwell, Dir. of Opns., Hq., USSTAF from Hq. Advisory Specialist Gp., USSTAF, 29 Mar. 1944.

44. Ltr., Hq. EAC, SEA to Hq. AC, SEA, 24 Nov. 1944; memo for CG AAF from CG XX BC (summary or rpt. on air-sea rescue facilities), Nov. 1944; ltr., Hq. AAF India-Burma Theater to CG XX BC, 16 Mar. 1945.

45. AS/AS, OC&R, Daily acty. rpt., 21 Mar. 1944, 12 May 1944; USSTAF, Dir. on ASR, 30 May 1942; memo for Maxwell from Advisory Specialist Gp., USSTAF, 29 Mar. 1944; ltr., Hq. RAF 222d Gp., to RAF Sta., China Bay, 10 May 1944; 1st Lt. Wayne Z. Schandelmeier, 2d ERS, memo on radar on search missions, 26 May 1945.

46. Msg., Hq. AC, SEA, to CG EAC, SEA, 29 Oct. 1944.

47. RAF, 292d Sq., Monthly prog. rpts., Dec. 1944, Jan. 1945; ltr., Hq. EAC, SEA to Hq. AC, SEA, 22 Jan. 1945; ltrs., Hq. AC, SEA to Hq., EAC, 31 Jan. 1945, 9 Mar. 1945; ltr., Hq. AC, SEA to Hq. RAF, Bengal-Burma, 29 Mar. 1945; postgram, RAF, 231st Gp. to RAF, 222d Gp., 4 Mar. 1945.

48. Ltr., Hq. SAF, to Hq. EAC, SEA, 2 Mar. 1945; *AAF in WW II*, V, 604–5.

49. Memo for CG AAF from Col. H. O. Russell, Dir. ADTIC, 29 Mar. 1944; ltr., Surgeon, Hq. USSTAF to Col. R. W. Chafee, ASC, USSTAF, Liaison O, Wright Fld., 7 June 1944; memo for C/AS (Wkly. Rpt. for General Council Mtg.), 22 June 1945; AC/AS-3, Daily acty. rpt., 3 Dec. 1945.

50. AC/AS, OC&R, Daily acty. rpt., 12–28 Oct. 1943; Daily diary, Req. Div. (to CG AAF), 17 Nov. 1942, 4 Dec. 1942; Daily diary, Req. Div., OC&R, 18 Oct. 1943; ER Br., AC/AS-3, list of emergency rescue equipment.

51. Encl. to ltr., Hq. EAC to Hq. 231st Grp., 18 Jan. 1944; ltr., Hq. EAC, SEA to Hq. AC, SEA, 24 Aug. 1944; 1st Lt. D. N. Perta, subpatrol B-25, South Atlantic, memo on crash boats, 19 June 1944; memo Hq. SAF to Hq. EAC, 13 Oct. 1944; min. of mtg. held in Calcutta on 9 Nov. 1944 to discuss

action to be taken to insure adequate air-sea rescue facilities.

52. Daily diary, Mil. Req. Div., 19 Feb. 1943; AC/AS, OC&R, Daily diary, 6 Jan. 1944.

53. Historical essay on air rescue service by Dr. Charles H. Hildreth, Air Historical Office (hereinafter cited as Hildreth Essay).

54. Memo for Comdt. Prov. Med. Fld. Service Sch., 8th AF from Hq. Prov. Med. Fld. Service Sch., 8th AF, 24 Jan. 1943; ltr., Hq. USSTAF to CG 8th AF, 30 Aug. 1944.

55. USSTAF, Dir. on ASR, 30 May 1944; rpt. by 1st Central Med. Establishment, 8th AF, history and evaluation of 8th AF personal equipment program (n.d.).

56. Memo for Col. M. R. Wood, Ch., Supply Sec., 8th AFSC from Capt. R. W. Chaffee, Req. Sec., 8th AFSC, 21 Nov. 1942; ltr., 8th AFSC to CG ASC (received 27 Apr. 1943); msg., 8th AF to CG AAF, 11 June 1943.

57. Hildreth Essay; ltr., Hq. 8th AF to CG VIII BC, 10 Sept. 1943; ltr., Hq. II Air Div. to A-2 Secs., all Wings *et al.*, 15 Mar. 1945; ltr., Hq. USSTAF to CG 8th AF, 30 Aug. 1944.

58. Hildreth Essay; memo by Maj. Charles H. Williams, 12th Ftr. Gp., 29 Apr. 1944.

59. See discussion in Hildreth Essay.

60. *Ibid.*; see also, account of operations in SWPA in *AAF in WW II*, Vol. IV.

61. Hist. 5th AF, 15 June 1944—2 Sept. 1945.

62. AC/AS, A-3, Daily acty. rpt., 22 Aug. 1945; Hildreth Essay.

NOTES TO CHAPTER 16

1. Henry L. Stimson and McGeorge Bundy, *On Active Service in Peace and War* (New York, 1948), pp. 480–81.

2. Margaret Culkin Banning, *Women for Defense* (New York, 1942), pp. 4–5.

3. Mattie E. Treadwell, *The Women's Army Corps*, U.S. Army in World War II (Washington, 1954), pp. 6–9 (hereinafter cited as Treadwell, *WAC Hist.*).

4. G-1 Staff Study, "Participation of Women in War," G1/8604–1, 21 Sept. 1928.

5. Treadwell, *WAC Hist.*, p. 14.

6. *Ibid.*, p. 15.

7. Despite the warnings, American forces arriving in the British Isles initially used some of the personnel of the British women's auxiliaries. A tendency to abuse this practice

resulted in publication of a War Department policy "of using members of the British Women's services only in cases of emergency." The emergency lasted until sufficient numbers of Wacs could arrive in the ETO. "Study of the Women's Army Corps in the European Theater of Operations," by the General Board, Feb. 1943—May 1945, p. 3 (hereinafter cited "Study of the WAC in the ETO"). The General Board was established by GO 128, Hq ETO, U.S. Army, 17 June 1945, as amended by later orders, to prepare a factual analysis of the strategy, tactics, and administration employed by U.S. forces in the ETO.

8. Memo, Brig. Gen. Wade H. Haislip, G-1, for C/S, 29 Apr. 1941, G-1/15839-10, cited in Treadwell, *WAC Hist.*, p. 17.

9. H.R. 4906, 77th Cong., 1st sess., 28 May 1941.

10. Treadwell, *WAC Hist.*, pp. 20–21.

11. Edith Nourse Rogers, "A Women's Army?" *Independent Woman*, XXI (Jan. 1942), 38.

12. *New York Times*, 23 Jan. 1942; ltr., Gen. George C. Marshall to Hon. John W. McCormack, 6 Feb. 1942.

13. *Cong. Record*, Vol. LXXXVIII, No. 55, 17 Mar. 1942; *New York Times*, 18 Mar. 1942, 13 May 1942.

14. *Ibid.*, 23 Mar. 1942; *Time*, XXXIX (15 June 1942), 39.

15. Col. Frank U. McCoskrie, "I Learned about Women from Them," *American Magazine*, CXXXVI (Nov. 1943), 17.

16. Dwight D. Eisenhower, *Crusade in Europe* (New York, 1950), pp. 132–33. See also "Study of the WAC in the ETO," p. 11; Mark W. Clark, *Calculated Risk* (New York, 1950), p. 339; and Mark W. Clark, "Women May Be Drafted Too," *This Week Magazine*, 9 May 1954, pp. 12 ff.

17. Treadwell, *WAC Hist.*, pp. 169–87; *Public Opinion, 1935–1946* (Princeton, N.J., 1951), pp. 1048–50, 1052.

18. Treadwell, *WAC Hist.*, pp. 173–90, 231–32; "Study of the WAC in the ETO," p. 6; Ruth E. Peters, "Why I Don't Join the WACS," *American Mercury*, LIX (Sept. 1944), 293–97; Dorothy C. Stratton, "Our Greatest Unused Source—Womanpower," *New York Times Magazine*, 1 Oct. 1950, p. 17 (hereinafter cited as Stratton, "Womanpower"); *Newsweek*, XXI (14 June 1943), 34–36; *ibid.* (21 June 1943), p. 46.

19. Col. Oveta Culp Hobby, "Women's Army Corps in 1944," *United States at War,* *Dec. 7, 1943—Dec. 7, 1944, Army and Navy Journal*, LXXXII, 94.

20. Ltr., S/W to Bur. of Budget, 12 Nov. 1942; Exec. Order No. 9274, 19 Nov. 1942. Executive Order No. 9364, 26 July 1943, raised the WAC ceiling to 200,000, the President being authorized by Public Law 110, 78th Cong., to set the limits of the Corps.

21. Treadwell, *WAC Hist.*, p. 92.

22. Memo, Classif. & Repl. Br. AGO for Col. Catron, 21 Oct. 1942; Rpt., Classif. & Repl. Br. AGO for WAAC Hqs, 25 Nov. 1942; Biennial Report of C/S to S/W, 1 July 1943—30 June 1945.

23. Joint Agreement for the Recruiting of Women for the Armed Services, signed by Henry L. Stimson and Frank Knox, 10 June 1943; ltr., James F. Byrnes to Henry L. Stimson, Frank Knox, Paul V. McNutt, and Elmer Davis, 12 Aug. 1943.

24. Rep. Frances P. Bolton, "Women Should Be Drafted," *American Magazine*, CXLVII (June, 1949), 133.

25. Ltr., GHQ AF to C/AC, 27 Dec. 1941, no sub.

26. Memo, "G.C.M." to Gen. Stratemeyer, 27 Nov. 1942, no sub.

27. Treadwell, *WAC Hist.*, pp. 78–79.

28. "The WAC Program in the AAF," p. 14. This study (hereinafter cited as AAF WAC Hist.) was prepared by Lt. Col. Betty Bandel prior to her departure from military service in the fall of 1945.

29. *Ibid.*, p. 17.

30. The original WAC staff directors in the domestic AAF, with their rank at the time of assignment, were as follows:

Capt. Mary Freeman, AAF Training Command Hq.
Capt. Helen Woods, Western Flying Training Command.
Capt. Wilma Hague, Central Flying Training Command.
Lt. Jack Phillips, Eastern Flying Training Command.
Capt. Juanita Stryker, Technical Training Command.
Capt. Geraldine May, Air Transport Command.
Capt. Louise Kennedy, Air Service Command.
Capt. Ruth Kerr, Troop Carrier Command.
Capt. Elizabeth Gilbert, First Air Force.
Capt. Mary Kersey, Second Air Force.

Capt. Virginia McCauley, Third Air Force

Capt. Betty Clague, Fourth Air Force.

Lt. Elenor Sweet, School of Applied Tactics.

Capt. Elizabeth Guild, Proving Ground Command.

Capt. Marjorie Ludwigsen, Independent AAF Activities.

The following were later added:

Capt. Mary Elrod, Materiel Command.

Capt. Jessie Morris, Personnel Distribution Command.

Capt. Grace Barth, Army Airways Communications System.

Capt. Esther Pease, Weather Wing.

Capt. Virginia Hardesty, Western Technical Training Command.

Capt. Katherine Johnson, Central Technical Training Command.

Capt. Jenny Lea, Eastern Technical Training Command.

31. WD Circular 462, Par. 5a, Sec. I, 6 Dec. 1944.

32. An exception to this policy was made in the summer of 1943 when the AAF assigned several hundred WAC cooks to AAF hospitals, assuring the patients of attractive meals and releasing several hundred male cooks for shipment overseas with combat units (AAF WAC Hist., p. 38).

33. Whenever Wacs did carry out military-police duty, it was attempted with no undue publicity, and Wacs were never authorized to carry arms on such duty. One of the successful MP patrols was at the AAF School of Applied Tactics, where authorities felt that Wacs ordinarily could cope with members of their organization better than male MP's. "Historical Data, WAC Staff Director, AAF Tactical Center," Appendix E; AAF WAC Hist., pp. 2, 36-41.

34. AAF WAC Hist., pp. 93-94.

35. Ibid., p. 69; ltr., Maj. Betty Bandel to WAC Staff Directors, 23 Feb. 1944; "Historical Data, WAC Staff Director, AAF Tactical Center, March 1943—March 1944."

36. Ltr., Arnold to CGs, All AFs and Comds, no sub, 25 Feb. 1944.

37. Col. Don C. Faith, who commanded the first WAAC training center at Fort Des Moines, had already noted the need for explaining things to the Waacs. "The American woman is the most co-operative human being on earth if she fully understands an order," he said (New York Times, 2 June 1942).

38. Treadwell, WAC Hist., pp. 282-83.

39. Ibid., pp. 256-58; AAF WAC Hist., pp. 33 ff.

40. Public Law 110, 78th Cong. The law was approved on 1 July 1943, to take effect two months later (actually 30 September).

41. In the spring of 1942 Mrs. Hobby had insisted on an amendment to the Rogers bill which would make the WAAC a part of the Army. But this step only delayed passage of the bill and the amendment was defeated (Treadwell, WAC Hist., pp. 33-34).

42. The AAF had the lowest average loss of the three major commands, perhaps because of General Arnold's personal efforts to convince the Waacs that they were needed in the AAF (ibid., p. 228).

43. Ibid., pp. 214, 228.

44. AAF WAC Hist., pp. 43-48; ltr., Marshall to Hon. Andrew Jackson, May, 1 Mar. 1943; "Study of the WAC in the ETO," pp. 4-5. Tables in this chapter are based on information gathered by the Office of Statistical Control, Headquarters AAF.

45. WDGS Disposition Form, Col. R. W. Berry, Exec., for AC/S G-1, to CG ASF, 21 Aug. 1943; ltr., Brig. Gen. J. M. Bevans, AC/AS Personnel, to CG AAF Training Comd., 9 Sept. 1943; AAF WAC Hist., pp. 49-53.

46. AAF WAC Hist. pp. 53, 59; Charlotte Knight, "Our Air WACS," Air Force, XXVII (Feb. 1944), 42-43.

47. AAF WAC Hist., pp. 65-72.

48. AAF Ltr. 50-8, dated 20 Nov. 1943, sug: "Army Air Forces Training Policy for Wacs."

49. AAF WAC Hist., p. 86.

50. First Report of CG AAF to S/W, 4 Jan. 1944.

51. Knight, "Our Air WACS," pp. 42-43.

52. Maj. Lavinia L. Redd, "History of Military Training, WAAC/WAC Training, Army Service Forces," in WD Hist. Div. files.

53. Treadwell, WAC Hist., pp. 590-91.

54. AAF WAC Hist., p. 40.

55. Ibid., pp. 75-78.

56. Lt. Col. Mattie E. Treadwell, chap. xix, "Military Service in the Women's Army Corps," draft in AFSHO files.

57. AAF Memo 35-38, "Selection and Preparation of WAC Personnel for Overseas Assignments," 6 Mar. 1944.

58. "Study of the WAC in the ETO," p. 28; "WAC Personnel," 29 Sept. 1944, in AFSHO files; AAF WAC Hist., p. 79.

59. AAF WAC Hist., pp. 82–84.

60. "Study of the WAC in the ETO," pp. 49–50, 119, 123–24; Treadwell, *WAC Hist.*, pp. 370–71, 395–96.

61. Treadwell, *WAC Hist.*, p. 372.

62. *Ibid.*, pp. 397, 439–44, 451.

63. *Ibid.*, pp. 372, 399, 477.

64. "Wacs in the European Division, ATC, June 1944—Aug. 1945," in AFSHO files; "Study of the WAC in the ETO," pp. 37–39.

65. Treadwell, *WAC Hist.*, p. 588.

66. "Study of the WAC in the ETO," pp. 38, 48; ltr., Bandel to Staff Directors, 23 Feb. 1944.

67. "Wacs in the European Division, ATC, June 1944—Aug. 1945," pp. 21–28.

68. AAF WAC Hist., pp. 83–84; "Study of the WAC in the ETO," pp. 31–33; ltr., Bandel to Staff Directors, 23 Feb. 1944.

69. "WAC Personnel," 29 Sept. 1944.

70. Ltr., Bandel to Staff Directors, 23 Feb. 1944.

71. "Wacs in the European Division, ATC, June 1944—Aug. 1945," p. 79.

72. "Study of the WAC in the ETO," pp. 92–93, 99–100.

73. George C. Kenney, *General Kenney Reports* (New York, 1949), pp. 423–24.

74. *Ibid.*, pp. 483–84, 542.

75. Treadwell, *WAC Hist.*, p. 434.

76. *Ibid.*, p. 449; AAF WAC Hist., pp. 82–83.

77. AAF WAC Hist., pp. 80–81.

78. "Study of the WAC in the ETO," pp. 6–7.

79. Memo from Air Wac Officer for Plans and Liaison Div., AC/AS Personnel, sub: Place of the WAC in the Post-war Air Force, 29 Mar. 1944.

80. Third Report of CG AAF to S/W, 12 Nov. 1945.

81. AAF WAC Hist., p. 3; USAF Historical Studies, No. 55: "Women Pilots with the AAF, 1941–1944," p. 8.

82. *Ibid.*, pp. 2–3; H. H. Arnold, *Global Mission* (New York, 1949), p. 311.

83. "Women Pilots in the ATC," 1946, p. 31, in AFSHO files.

84. USAFHS-55, p. 17.

85. Designations for the WASP organization varied slightly during its existence. AAF Reg. 40-8, dated 21 Dec. 1943, is titled "Women Air Force Service Pilots"; AAF Reg. 40-8, dated 3 April, and its revision of 30 Dec. 1944 are headed "Women Airforce Service Pilots."

86. USAFHS-55, pp. 24–25.

87. *Ibid.*, pp. 35–36; "Women Pilots in the ATC," pp. 25–27.

88. Since military aircraft were constructed for men, the women sometimes suffered fatigue in instances where inadequate stature or leg length necessitated makeshift aids. In the AT-6, for example, some of the smaller women used as many as six or seven pillows to obtain the proper elevation, but at this height it was difficult for them to reach the gear handle and also to give full rudder in case it was needed (USAFHS-55, p. 33; AAF CFTC WASP Hist., I, 74).

89. AAF Training Comd WASP Hist., p. 36; USAFHS-55, pp. 27–30.

90. CFTC, "History of the WASP Program."

91. "Women Pilots in the ATC," pp. 77–78, 148, 151–57, 160; Arnold, *Global Mission*, p. 358.

92. 4th AF Hist. Study No. V-3, "Women Airforce Service Pilots in the Fourth Air Force," p. 17; EFTC WASP Hist., pp. 16–17; WFTC WASP Hist., pp. 55–56.

93. "Women Pilots in the ATC," p. 125; Capt. Nels O. Monserud, MC, "Medical Consideration of WASPs," in files of Air Surgeon's Office; Charlotte Knight, " 'She Wears a Pair of Silver Wings,' " *Air Force*, XXVII (Jan. 1944), 50.

94. Hist. of CFTC, WASP Program, Vol. I, Appendix; memo, J. Cochran to Col. K. P. McNaughton, C/S, AAFTC, 15 Dec. 1942; Hist. of WASP Program, WFTC.

95. Before the appointment of Miss Cochran as Director of Women Pilots, the AAF had planned in the spring of 1943 to place the women pilots in the WAAC as soon as Congress changed the Corps to the WAC. No objection was raised by WAC authorities, but Miss Cochran's views prevailed, and the AAF reversed its original plans for militarization of the women pilots (Treadwell, *WAC Hist.*, pp. 285, 784–85).

96. Arnold, *Global Mission*, pp. 358–59; "The WASP Training Course at the AAF School of Applied Tactics, 19 Apr. 1944—29 Sept. 1944," in AFSHO files; USAFHS-55, pp. 78–101.

97. UAFHS-55, pp. 76–77, 101–8.

98. *The Official Guide to the AAF* (New York, 1944), pp. 92–94; Dorothy Schaffter,

What Comes of Training Women for War (Washington, 1948), pp. 40, 123 (hereinafter cited as Schaffter, *Training Women*).

99. Betty Peckham, *Women in Aviation* (New York, 1945), p. 21.

100. *Ibid.*, pp. 14–19; *The Official Guide to the AAF*, pp. 94–95.

101. Schaffter, *Training Women*, pp. 134–39; Peckham, *Women in Aviation*, p. 37.

102. USAF Historical Studies, No. 58: "Civilian Personnel Administration in the AAF, 1939–45," p. 29.

103. *Ibid.*, p. 68; Peckham, *Women in Aviation*, pp. 38–41.

104. USAF Historical Studies, No. 19: "Civilian Volunteer Activities in the AAF," p. 3; USAF Historical Studies, No. 16: "Legislation Relating to the AAF Personnel Program, 1939 to May 1944," pp. 25–27; "Special Report of the Civil Air Patrol," April 1943; ltr., Capt. Kendall K. Hoyt, Hq CAP, to Hist. Div., AC/AS Intell., 2 Oct. 1943.

105. *The Official Guide to the AAF*, pp. 97–98.

106. Stratton, "Womanpower," p. 17; Peckham, *Women in Aviation*, p. 81.

NOTES TO CHAPTER 17

1. DA SR 320-5-1, Aug. 1950.

2. WD TM 20-205, 18 Jan. 1944.

3. John G. Sparrow, *History of Personnel Demobilization in the United States Army* (Washington, 1952), pp. 5–7 (hereinafter cited as Sparrow, *Personnel Demobilization*).

4. *Ibid.*, p. 299.

5. Frederic Logan Paxson, *The Great Demobilization and Other Essays* (Madison, 1941), p. 7.

6. James R. Mock and Evangeline Thurber, *Report on Demobilization* (Norman, 1944), pp. 127–28. See also, ltr., Ch. of Opns., WDGS to President, Army War College [Oct. 1918].

7. Mock and Thurber, *Report on Demobilization*, p. 134.

8. *Ibid.*, p. 131; Peyton C. March, *The Nation at War* (Garden City, N.Y., 1932), p. 316.

.9. Sparrow, *Personnel Demobilization*, p. 16.

10. *Ibid.*, p. 300.

11. Mock and Thurber, *Report on Demobilization*, pp. 135–36.

12. Sparrow, *Personnel Demobilization*, p. 25.

13. *Ibid.*, p. 28.

14. Memo for General Arnold from Maj. Gen. George Stratemeyer, C/AS, 13 Mar. 1943; ltr., General Arnold to Special Projects Officer, 2 Apr. 1943.

15. Memo for CG ASF from C/S, 5 Apr. 1943, attached to memo for CG AAF from Maj. Gen. I. H. Edwards, AC/S, G-3, 14 Apr. 1943. Sparrow (*Personnel Demobilization*, p. 348) gives the date of General Marshall's memo as 14 April.

16. Memo for the US/W and C/S, from S/W, 7 July 1943.

17. Memo for US/W and C/S from S/W, 7 July 1943; memo for Dir., SPD from Robert P. Patterson, Acting S/W, 22 July 1943, in AAG 381-A.

18. Kent Roberts Greenfield, Robert R. Palmer, and Bell I. Wiley, *The Organization of Ground Combat Troops*, U.S. Army in World War II (Washington, 1947), p. 442; memo for Chiefs of all Divisions from General Arnold, 22 July 1943.

19. JCS 431, 30 July 1943.

20. Min., mtg. of General Council, 26 July 1943, Copy No. 18, p. 1.

21. Memo for the CG AAF from Col. J. H. McCormick, DAC/AS, Personnel, 30 June 1943.

22. Memos for Dir. SPD from Handy, 13 and 21 Sept. 1943.

23. Memo for C/S from Brig. Gen. W. F. Tompkins (n.d., but prior to 24 July 1943).

24. Hist. AAF PDC, I, 22.

25. Min., mtg. of General Council, 16 Aug. 1943, p. 5; see also, Hist. AAF PDC, Vol. I.

26. Memo for Chiefs of Branches, SPD from Brig. Gen. W. F. Tompkins, Dir. SPD, 24 Aug. 1943. This date was not universally accepted; it appears that CCS, JCS, and JPS were using 1 Oct. 1944, and that the AAF also preferred the later date (memo for DC/S from Brig. Gen. W. F. Tompkins, Dir. SPD, 8 Feb. 1944).

27. Sparrow, *Personnel Demobilization*, p. 41.

28. Ltrs., Maj. Gen. J. A. Ulio, TAG, to CG's all Forces and Commands, 8 Dec. 1943; 29 Aug. and 24 Nov. 1941; WD Cir. 341, 19 Aug. 1944 and WD Cir. 485, 29 Dec. 1944.

29. Memo for Dir. SPD from Col. F. T. Davison, 8 Dec. 1944.

30. Daily diary, D&PR Br., AC/AS, Personnel, 24 Apr. 1945.

31. Memo for the C/S from Gen. H. H. Arnold, 22 Apr. 1944.

32. Ltr., Arnold to Lt. Gen. Ira C. Eaker, 24 June 1944.

33. Ltr., Maj. Gen. B. M. Giles, C/AS to Maj. Gen. Claire Chennault, CG 14th AF, 14 Oct. 1943. The proposed transfer was not carried out; the two groups were in Germany at the end of the war.

34. Hist., 33d Ftr. Gp., Apr.-Oct. 1944 and Hist., 81st Ftr. Gp., June-Oct. 1944.

35. Hist. 33d Ftr. Gp., Sept. and Oct. 1944.

36. Hist., 12th Bombard. Gp. (M), Jan.-May 1944, July 1945.

37. Hist., 64th TC Gp., Apr.-July 1944; Hist., 4th TC Sq., Apr.-June 1944.

38. Memo for DC/S from Brig. Gen. W. F. Tompkins, 1 Feb. 1944.

39. See especially R&R, Brig. Gen. Edwin S. Perrin, DC/AS to Davison, 24 Mar. 1944. R&R, Davison to Perrin, 20 Apr. 1944; SPO's Demobilization Planning Report for the Year 1944. See also, ltr., Brig. Gen. L. S. Kuter to Postwar Plans Division and Logistical Plans Division, AC/AS, Plans, 30 Nov. 1943.

40. AAF Reg. 20-45, 13 Sept. 1944; AAF Hq. office instruction, 13 Sept. 1944.

41. AAF Ltr., 151-53, 3 Jan. 1945, sub: Redeployment Manning Policy.

42. AAF Ltr., 35-248, 18 June 1945, sub: Policies Pertaining to Recommitment of Personnel Completing Only Partial Overseas Tours.

43. By letters to the various commands, such as that addressed to ATSC: ltr., Hq. AAF to Hq. ATSC, 30 Mar. 1945.

44. 1st ind. (ltr., Hq. AAF to Hq. ATSC, 30 Mar. 1945) Hq. ATSC to Hq. AAF, 9 Apr. 1945.

45. AG Ltr., 322 (12 Dec. 1944) OB-I-AFRPG-M, sub: Constitution and Activation of Headquarters, Continental Air Forces.

46. Hist. Andrews Field, 1 Jan.-16 April 1945, p. 2.

47. Redeployment: The Role of Headquarters, Continental Air Forces, Hq. SAC, June 1946, I, 106 (hereinafter cited as Redeployment . . . , Hq. SAC).

48. Dwight D. Eisenhower, *Crusade in Europe* (Garden City, N.Y., 1948), p. 429.

49. Sparrow, *Personnel Demobilization*, p. 172.

50. Narrative Hist. Hq. 8th AF, 8 May-16 July 1945, pp. 7-13.

51. Redeployment Problems in 12th AF, Jan.-Aug. 1945, Hq. 12th AF, 30 Aug. 1945.

52. Memo for CG 12th AF from Lt. Col. A. W. Jensen, AC/S A-1, 12th AF, 6 Aug. 1945.

53. Hist. 2d AF, 1945, I, 57-58.

54. *Ibid.*, p. 63.

55. *Ibid.*, pp. 84-87.

56. Hist. 1st AF, Part III (June, 1946), I, 50; Hist. 3d AF, 1 Jan.-31 Mar. 1945, pp. 140 ff.; Hist. Bradley Field, 1 Nov. 1944-1 Feb. 1945, chaps. i and ii; see also, Hist. 489th Bombard. Gp. (H), 10 Nov. 1944-28 Feb. 1945, p. 8.

57. Hist. 2d AF, 1945, I, 67-69.

58. 1st AF, Monograph I (May 1945), First Redeployment, January to May 1945, p. 15.

59. Hist. 514th Air Serv. Gp., Dec. 1944-June 1945, p. 6.

60. Redeployment . . . , Hq. SAC, I, 43.

61. *Ibid.*

62. 1st AF, Monograph I (May 1945), First Redeployment, January to May 1945, pp. 23, 89.

63. *Ibid.*, p. 36; Redeployment . . . , Hq. SAC, I, 45, 108-9.

64. 1st AF, Monograph I (May 1945), First Redeployment, January to May 1945, p. 40.

65. *Ibid.*, p. 105.

66. Hist. 319th Bombard. Gp., 1 Jan.-1 Aug. 1945, p. 2.

67. 1st AF, Monograph I (May 1945), First Redeployment, January to May 1945, p. 89, 90.

68. "Redeployment . . . , Hq. SAC, I, 47.

69. Hist. 319th Bombard. Gp., 1 Jan.-1 Aug. 1945, p. 4; Hist. 514th Air Serv. Gp., Dec. 1944-June 1945, pp. 7-9.

70. Redeployment . . . , Hq. SAC, I, 91-92.

71. *Ibid.*, pp. 92, 123-24, 127.

72. Narrative Hist., Hq. 8th AF, 8 May-16 July 1945, p. 3.

73. *Ibid.*, p. 4; Admin. Hist. Part I, Sec. 2, pp. 26-91; Hist. 15th AF, 1 May-31 July 1945, p. 8.

74. AAF Stat. Digest, World War II, p. 16 (hereinafter cited as AAF Stat. Digest).

75. USAF Stat. Digest, 1947, p. 16.

76. Memo for CG AAF from Brig. Gen. Charles F. Born, Chief, Separations Sec., CAF, 10 Oct. 1945; Organization and Mis-

sion: Headquarters CAF, Hq. SAC, June 1946, p. 72; Demobilization and Redeployment, PDC, p. 60.

77. Daily diary, D&PR Br., AC/AS-1, 12 Oct. 1945.

78. Daily diary, D&PR Br., AC/AS-1, 10 Oct. 1945.

79. Memo for CG AAF from Brig. Gen. Charles F. Born, 10 Oct. 1945; Daily diary, D&PR Br., AC/AS-1, 17 Oct. 1945.

80. Memo for CG AAF, as cited in preceding note.

81. Daily diary, D&PR Br., AC/AS-1, 1 Nov., 30 Nov., 4 Dec., 19 Dec. 1945.

82. Daily acty. rpt., Office Chief of Personnel, AC/AS-1, 20 Feb. 1946.

83. Ltr., Streett to Arnold, 8 Oct. 1945.

84. Daily diary, AID, 17 Dec. 1945, 14 Jan. 1946.

85. USAFE Scrap and Surplus Property Disposal, 8 May 1945—31 Dec. 1948, p. 104.

86. Ibid.; Outline of the Development of WD Surplus Property Disposal, Feb. 1944—Feb. 1947, p. 2. 170.1-20; Public Laws 181, 584, 79th Cong.

87. USAFE Scrap and Surplus Property Disposal, 8 May 1945—31 Dec. 1948, pp. 127-37, 153.

88. Information Pertaining to the Readjustment and Demobilization and the Reorganization of the Pacific Air Command, USA, Tabs I-1 and I-3.

89. Hist. AMC, 1946, I, 127-29.

90. History of the AF Storage and Withdrawal Program (1945-52).

91. Hist. AMC, 1946, I, 142.

92. Ibid., p. 143.

93. Ibid., pp. 144-46.

94. A Five-Year Summary of USAFE History, 1945-50, p. 37.

95. For USSTAF, GO 115, USAFE, 16 Aug. 1945 pursuant to WD ltr., AG 322 (4 Aug. 1945) OB-1-AFRPG-M, 7 Aug. 1945; for MAAF, GO 22, MAAF, 25 July 1945; for AAF/MTO, ltr., AG 322/030 C-O, MTOUSA, 12 Sept. 1945; for 12th AF, ltr., 322/02, AAF/MTO, 30 Aug. 1945; for 15th AF, ltr., 322/02, AAF/MTO, 1 Sept. 1945.

96. AAF Stat. Digest, 1946, p. 34.

97. A Five-Year Summary of USAFE History, 1945-50, p. 37.

98. Organization Chart, USAFE, 31 Mar. 1946.

99. WD ltr., AGAO-I 322, 6 Dec. 1945.

100. Chart, Disposition of Pacific Air Command, 1 September 1946.

101. Hist. Air Force Activities, China Theater, 1 Jan.–31 Mar. 1946, p. 1.

102. GO 3, 11th AF, 21 Dec. 1945 and GO 240, Alaskan Depart. USA, 21 Dec. 1945; AAF Stat. Digest, 1946, p. 12.

103. WD, ltr., AG 322 (24 July 1946) AO-I-AFCOR (190[e])-M; AAF Stat. Digest, 1946, p. 34.

104. Hist. ATC, 1 Oct. 1945—31 Dec. 1946, I, 1.

105. Hist. SAC, 1946, I, 18-19, 23.

106. Hist. ADC, Mar. 1946—June 1947, p. 3.

107. Hist. TAC, Mar–Dec., 1946, I, 14, 21-22.

108. Ibid., I, 56.

109. Hist. AMC, 1946, passim.

110. Ibid., I, 22.

111. Hist. AAFTC, 1 Jan. 1939—V-J Day, I, 35, 85.

112. Hist. AAFTC, 1 Jan. 1946—30 June 1946, I, 41-42.

113. AAF Stat. Digest, 1946, pp. 28-29.

114. Air Proving Ground Historical Data, 2 Sept. 1945—30 June 1949.

115. WD ltr., AG 322 (15 Nov. 1945) OB-I-AFCOR-M, 19 Nov. 1945, sub.: Assignment and Establishment of Army Air Forces Schools.

116. Comment No. 2 (R&R, Ch. SPO to AC/AS, Plans, 7 Aug. 1943), AC/AS, Plans to Ch. SPO, 23 Aug. 1943.

117. Attach. to R&R, Brig. Gen. L. S. Kuter to Col. F. T. Davison, 28 Sept. 1943. A later statement (Ltr., Brig. Gen. Howard A. Craig, DC/AS to Brig. Gen. E. L. Eubank, AAF Bd., 8 Nov. 1943) appears to deny that planning had reached this stage. General Craig wrote that "no effort has yet been made to deploy the 105 groups, either in the Western Hemisphere or overseas." It seems likely, however, that what General Craig meant was that no attempt had been made to assign specific groups to specific bases.

118. Memo for General Arnold from Brig. Gen. L. S. Kuter, 24 Dec. 1943.

119. Min., mtg. of Committee To Resurvey the Postwar Strength, 27 Dec. 1944.

120. Deployment Chart, in AAG "Initial Post War Air Force," Tab "E," 15 Feb. 1944.

121. Memo for C/AS from Col. F. T. Davison, 23 Oct. 1944.

122. Memo for Advisory Council from Col. F. T. Davison, 13 Dec. 1944.

123. Min., mtg. of Committee To Re-survey Postwar Strength, 27 Nov. 1944.

124. Memo for Members of Committee To Re-survey Postwar Strength, from Col. R. C. Moffat, 30 Nov. 1944.

125. Memo for Members of Committee To Re-survey Postwar Strength from Col. G. E. Textor, Chairman, 1 Dec. 1944.

126. War Department Plan for the Post War Military Establishment, Nov. 1945, p. 26.

127. USAF Stat. Digest, Jan. 1949—June 1950, p. 5.

128. Hist. SAC, Jan.–June 1950, Vol. IV, Tab. 34; Hist. TAC, 1 Jan.–30 June 1950, pp. 34–35.

129. USAF Stat. Digest, Jan. 1949—June 1950, p. 28.

120. USAF Stat. Digest, 1947, p. 16.

GLOSSARY

GLOSSARY

*   *   *   *   *   *   *   *   *   *   *

AACA	Asiatic Airways Communications Area
AACS	Army Airways Communications System
AAFPGC	Army Air Forces Proving Ground Command
AAFPOA	Army Air Forces, Pacific Ocean Area
AAFSC	Army Air Forces Service Command
AAFTC	Army Air Forces Training Command
AAFWS	Army Air Forces Weather Service
AC/AS	Assistant Chief of Air Staff
ADC	Air Defense Command
AGF	Army Ground Forces
ALSIB	Alaska-Siberia
AMC	Air Materiel Command
ASF	Army Service Forces
ASR	Adjusted Service Rating
ATSC	Air Technical Service Command
AWPD	Air War Plans Division
CAA	Civil Aeronautics Authority
CAF	Continental Air Forces
CBI	China-Burma-India
CCS	Combined Chiefs of Staff
CCTS	Combat crew training station
CINCPOA	Commander-in-Chief, Pacific Ocean Area
CNAC	China National Aviation Corporation
CPT	Civilian Pilot Training
DAT	Directorate of Air Transport
EAB	Engineer Aviation Battalion
ERS	Emergency Rescue Squadron

ETO	European Theater of Operations
FEAF	Far East Air Forces
ICD	India-China Division, ATC
JAC	Joint Administrative Committee
JACSPAC	Joint Airways Communications System, Pacific
JANATC	Joint Army-Navy Air Transport Committee
MAAF	Mediterranean Allied Air Forces
MATS	Mediterranean Air Transport Service
MOS	Military Occupational Specialty
MTO	Mediterranean Theater of Operations
NAAF	Northwest African Air Forces
NATOUSA	North African Theater of Operations, U.S. Army
NATS	Naval Air Transport Service
NRPB	National Resources Planning Board
OCAC	Office, Chief of Air Corps
OC&R	Operations, Commitments, and Requirements
OPD	Operations Division, WDGS
OTU	Operational training unit
PAAF	Pan American Air Ferries
PDC	Personnel Distribution Command
PLM	Production line maintenance
POM	Preparation for overseas movement
RAAF	Royal Australian Air Force
RAFTC	Royal Air Force Transport Command
RCAF	Royal Canadian Air Force
RCO	Regional control officer
RTU	Replacement training unit
SAC	Strategic Air Command
SAM	School of Aviation Medicine
SCAT	South Pacific Combat Air Transport
SHAEF	Supreme Headquarters, Allied Expeditionary Force
SOPAC	South Pacific
SOS	Services of Supply
SPD	Special Planning Division

SPO	Special Projects Office
SWPA	Southwest Pacific Area
TAC	Tactical Air Command
TTC	Technical Training Command
USAFE	U.S. Air Forces in Europe
USAFICA	U.S. Army Forces in Central Africa
USAFSA	U.S. Army Forces in South America
USASTAF	U.S. Army Strategic Air Forces in the Pacific
USSTAF	U.S. Strategic Air Forces in Europe
WAA	War Assets Administration
WAAC	Women's Army Auxiliary Corps
WAAF	Women's Auxiliary Air Force
WAC	Women's Army Corps
WAFS	Women's Auxiliary Ferrying Squadron
WASP	Women Airforce Service Pilots
WDGS	War Department General Staff
WRS	Weather Reconnaissance Squadron

INDEX

INDEX

✳ ✳ ✳ ✳ ✳ ✳ ✳ ✳ ✳ ✳ ✳

fanita Lanier